9780837118826

LEADERSHIP AND
POLITICAL INSTITUTIONS
IN INDIA

Leadership and Political Institutions in India

EDITED BY RICHARD L. PARK
AND IRENE TINKER

Seminar on Leadership and Political Institutions in India. University of California, Berkeley, 1956.

PRINCETON, NEW JERSEY
PRINCETON UNIVERSITY PRESS
1959

Copyright © 1959 by Princeton University Press
All Rights Reserved

✧

Publication of this book has been aided by the Ford Foundation program to support publication, through university presses, of works in the humanities and social sciences.

The Library of Congress catalog entry for this book appears at the end of the text.

✧

Printed in the United States of America
By Princeton University Press, Princeton, New Jersey

342.54
S471l
Asia
May 14, 1959.

PREFACE

*T*HE papers appearing in this volume are a selected group, edited and revised, of those originally presented at the seminar on Leadership and Political Institutions in India held at the University of California, Berkeley, August 12 to 17, 1956.* The seminar was cosponsored by the Modern India Project at Berkeley and the Committee on South Asia of the Association for Asian Studies.

It has been assumed by most analysts of modern India that the contemporary urge toward rapid economic development and concomitant social change requires the active and effective leadership of the relatively small group constituting India's ruling elite. The primary responsibility accepted by this select group has been the setting of national goals, under conditions of extensive public consultation, and the placing in motion of the social and economic machinery necessary to raise the levels of life of India's 400 million people. An additional task testing the capacities of these leaders for imaginative guidance has been their attempt to recruit their own replacements and to broaden vastly the base of significant participation in public life. As greater measures of success are achieved in raising the economic status of living in village, town, and city, the demands for a much broader based and more vigorous leadership will arise, since marked success in the meeting of expectations in all probability will result in greater discontent and more insistent demands for betterment rather than less. Further, the changing values involved in economic advance increasingly are being challenged by the more traditional secondary leadership elites. Thus the burdens placed upon India's present-day leadership are very great, indeed; not only for the urgent problems of today, but in establishing the foundations for tomorrow and beyond.

The seminar addressed itself to these problems of leadership in political institutions, concentrating upon the case of India, but comparing experiences in other countries as well. In attempting this task, a number of Indian colleagues participated—both in person and in writing. The seminar members from the United States were invited because of their field experience in India, and on the basis of the variety of academic disciplines that they represented and the range of regional exploration in India that they had undertaken.

* See page viii for a list of participants.

v

PREFACE

In planning the seminar, the directors studied the extensive theoretical literature on "leadership" that has been contributed mainly by sociologists, anthropologists, and social psychologists over the past several decades.† In addition, the directors sought the advice of specialists in this field of academic study concerning the application of their body of knowledge on leadership to our seminar's purposes. Invariably the advice given was to take a fresh look at the Indian scene and not allow the formal literature to stand in the way of insights that might arise, unshackled from hardened terminology, in the course of our endeavor. This advice was followed, and the papers presented in this volume reflect an attempt to explore a few of the critical areas in Indian life where the leaders of the country are playing important roles in changing the habits and traditions of the past to meet the needs of modern times.

It will be noted that emphasis in this book has been given to *political* institutions in relation to more general problems of leadership. Other emphases might have been devised, but the political orientation seemed best calculated to raise many of the most significant questions. The skills and interests of the bulk of the contributors, also, were better utilized in the framework of broadly political analysis. At the same time, the papers published here range over a wide field—from political theory and studies of the more formal institutions in the political order, to the role of influence groups, guidance in rural development, and leadership at the village level. Leadership in India's villages is particularly difficult to comprehend and to assess; but since it constitutes the base upon which all other realms in Indian political life rest, considerable attention has been devoted in this collection to village India.

This symposium was completed in 1956 and, for the most part, the individual studies are based on research and field work carried on at that time or somewhat earlier. In some cases the papers were revised to include new data up to 1957-1958, but in other cases such revision was not possible.

Acknowledgments

All members of the seminar are indebted to the Indian participants for the vigorous and constructive exchange of views that was made possible by their presence. Among other things, the Indian members challenged on a number of occasions the overly facile application to Indian circumstances of social science methodology and analysis that has been

† A bibliographical study was prepared by Mr. William L. Kimball to aid in this inquiry, "The Study of Leadership and Political Leadership," Modern India Project, Berkeley, August 1955 (mimeographed).

PREFACE

developed within the framework of the western tradition. For example, terms such as "westernization" were replaced in the discussion by others, in this case "modernization," in the process of a mutual seeking for understanding that characterized much of the seminar.

Acknowledgment is made of the generous grant from The Rockefeller Foundation that made the seminar possible. Funds available to the Modern India Project, supported by a grant from The Ford Foundation, also were allocated to the budget of the seminar.

Dr. Helen V. Hammarberg of University of California Extension, other members of the University staff, and the staff of the Modern India Project are thanked for their assistance in making the seminar a pleasant as well as fruitful experience for all concerned.

We reserve special appreciation for the expert editorial assistance and advice of Mr. Patrick Wilson, which were invaluable in seeing the papers through to completion. Mrs. Toni Volcani prepared the Index and gave valuable editorial advice, and Miss Donna Divine handled the extensive correspondence and typing supervision connected with the book with her usual dispatch. The editors of the Princeton University Press are thanked for the cordial manner by which they have assisted in publishing this book.

The analysis presented by Gene D. Overstreet in his essay on "Leadership in the Indian Communist Party," pp. 225ff., originally prepared for the Berkeley seminar, has been stated by him in somewhat different form in *Communism in India* by Gene D. Overstreet and Marshall Windmiller, University of California Press, Berkeley, 1959.

The authors and editors speak for themselves. Neither the University of California, nor the Rockefeller and Ford Foundations are to be held responsible for any of the views presented in this book.

RICHARD L. PARK
IRENE TINKER

Center for South Asia Studies
University of California
Berkeley

LIST OF PARTICIPANTS

Seminar
on
Leadership and Political Institutions in India
August 12 to 17, 1956

SATYA P. AGARWAL
RICHARD BACHENHEIMER
ALAN R. BEALS
REINHARD BENDIX
JOAN V. BONDURANT
D. MACKENZIE BROWN
W. NORMAN BROWN
ROBERT I. CRANE
A. R. DESHPANDE
LELAND C. DE VINNEY
SUSHIL K. DEY
CHARLES DREKMEIER
MARGARET W. FISHER
GEORGE M. FOSTER
CONSTANCE A. FREYDIG
DWARKANATH GHOSH
CHADBOURNE GILPATRIC
MERRILL R. GOODALL
A. D. GORWALA
EDWARD B. HARPER
SELIG S. HARRISON
HENRY HART
STEPHEN N. HAY
JOHN T. HITCHCOCK
HAROLD R. ISAACS
HAROLD G. JOSIF
VAN DUSEN KENNEDY
HELEN B. LAMB
RICHARD D. LAMBERT
ALBERT LEPAWSKY
OSCAR LEWIS
DAVID G. MANDELBAUM

STANLEY MARON
WILLIAM MC CORMACK
LAURENCE K. MC LAUGHLIN
WILLIAM S. METZ
MORRIS D. MORRIS
ROBERT C. NORTH
MORRIS E. OPLER
HENRY ORENSTEIN
GENE D. OVERSTREET
NORMAN D. PALMER
RICHARD L. PARK
MAUREEN L. P. PATTERSON
HORACE I. POLEMAN
BIMLA PRASAD
THOMAS A. RUSCH
CHATTAR SINGH SAMRA
BIDYUT SARKAR
MILTON SINGER
BAIJ NATH SINGH
DOROTHY SPENCER
M. S. SUNDARAM
PHILLIPS TALBOT
SHANTI S. TANGRI
CARL TAYLOR
PAUL S. TAYLOR
CLARENCE E. THURBER
IRENE TINKER
MILLIDGE P. WALKER
DOUGLAS WAPLES
MYRON WEINER
MARSHALL WINDMILLER

CONTENTS

PREFACE v

1. **TRADITIONS OF LEADERSHIP** 1
   Traditional Concepts of Indian Leadership 3
   D. MACKENZIE BROWN
   Some Hypotheses on the Politics of Modernization in India 18
   MYRON WEINER

2. **PERSONALITY AND LEADERSHIP** 39
   Nehru: the Hero as Responsible Leader 41
   MARGARET W. FISHER
   Subhas Chandra Bose: an Indian National Hero 66
   CHATTAR SINGH SAMRA
   Sardar Vallabhbhai Patel: the Party Organizer as Political Leader 87
   BALKRISHNA GOVIND GOKHALE

3. **POLITICAL INSTITUTIONS** 101
   The Indian Council of Ministers: a Study of Origins 103
   ROBERT C. NORTH
   Decision Making in the Indian Parliament 115
   NORMAN D. PALMER AND IRENE TINKER
   Factors of Tradition and Change in a Local Election in Rural India 137
   MORRIS EDWARD OPLER
   Leadership and Language Policy in India 151
   SELIG S. HARRISON

4. **POLITICAL PARTIES** 167
   The Leadership of the Congress Party 169
   ROBERT I. CRANE
   Dynamics of Socialist Leadership in India 188
   THOMAS A. RUSCH
   Hindu Communal Groups in Indian Politics 211
   RICHARD D. LAMBERT
   Leadership in the Indian Communist Party 225
   GENE D. OVERSTREET

5. **INFLUENCE GROUPS** 249
   Business Organization and Leadership in India Today 251
   HELEN B. LAMB
   Trade Unions and the State 268
   MORRIS DAVID MORRIS

ix

CONTENTS

The Nonconventional Political Leader in India 279
JOAN V. BONDURANT

6. PUBLIC ADMINISTRATION 299
   Who Does the Planning? 301
   WILFRED MALENBAUM
   Organization of Administrative Leadership in the
   Five Year Plans 314
   MERRILL R. GOODALL
   The Public Services and Democracy 329
   A. D. GORWALA
   District Administration and Local Self-Government 337
   RICHARD L. PARK

7. RURAL DEVELOPMENT AND ADMINISTRATION 345
   Community Projects in Action in India 347
   SUSHIL K. DEY
   The Impact of the Community Development Program on
   Rural Leadership 358
   BAIJ NATH SINGH
   Patterns of Influence within Rural India 372
   EVELYN WOOD

8. LEADERSHIP AND CHANGE IN THE VILLAGES 391
   Leadership in a North Indian Village: Two Case Studies 395
   JOHN T. HITCHCOCK
   Leadership and Caste in a Bombay Village 415
   HENRY ORENSTEIN
   Leadership in a Mysore Village 427
   ALAN BEALS
   Factionalism in a Mysore Village 438
   WILLIAM MC CORMACK
   Elements of Leadership in an Andhra Village 445
   R. BACHENHEIMER
   Political Organization and Leadership in a Karnataka Village 453
   EDWARD B. AND LOUISE G. HARPER

INDEX 471

x

1. TRADITIONS OF LEADERSHIP

CONCEPTS of leadership in Indian political thought have been expressed historically within the frameworks of two opposing traditions, the Brahman and the Kshatriya. During the past three centuries, the basic ideas of liberal thought in the western heritage have become part of the Indian tradition, in concert with the two major strains of the indigenous outlook. From the resultant interaction and reaction of these differing patterns of political belief have arisen most of the contemporary Indian ideas on the nature of leadership in a political society.

D. Mackenzie Brown's paper traces some of the influences of classical thought on the development of modern political leadership in India. The manifold effects of westernization (or modernization) on Indian political ideas and concepts of leadership are examined by Myron Weiner.

TRADITIONAL CONCEPTS OF INDIAN LEADERSHIP

D. MACKENZIE BROWN

Although consideration of traditional Indian concepts of leadership requires a clear definition of the term leadership itself, this is not a simple task. Webster defines a leader variously as a guide, a conductor, a chief, a commander, as the head of a party or sect, and as one who precedes and is followed by others in conduct, opinion, and undertakings. Such definitions indicate the various possibilities of the term but they do not give us much help in establishing a working concept.

Modern social science has, however, given considerable attention to this definition and we find useful analyses in the work of Michels, Merriam, Mosca, and others. Possibly the most incisive attack on the political phases of the problem has been made by the German political scientist, Richard Schmidt.[1] He defines leadership as "the relation between an individual and a group built around some common interest and behaving in a manner directed or determined by him." He insists that true leadership must be distinguished from similar relationships at each extreme of "leadership." On the one hand, an individual holding his position and power by a recognized tradition or established situation is an authority with subordinates, rather than a leader with followers. On the other hand, if he is a mere agitator appealing to the passing emotions of the mob, he is to be considered a demagogue, since his followers are not independent agents, acting of their own free will. True leadership exists only when persons follow an individual from free choice and upon rational grounds rather than by blind hysteria. We must distinguish, therefore, three related phenomena: leadership, authority, and demagogy—recognizing, of course, that these may exist, under given circumstances, not in pure form but in overlapping complexities.

We can further elaborate the concept of leadership by defining two

---

D. Mackenzie Brown is Professor of Political Science and Chairman of the South Asia Studies Program on the Santa Barbara Campus of the University of California.

[1] See Otto Butz, *Modern German Political Theory*, New York, Doubleday, 1955, pp. 29-31. His basic two-volume work, *Allegemeine Staatslehre*, appeared in 1901. In 1907 he was cofounder and first editor of the journal *Zeitschrift für Politik*. These are major sources for his theories. For a concise summary of his concepts of leadership see his article in the *Encyclopaedia of the Social Sciences*, IX, 282-86.

forms: the symbolic and the creative. The "symbolic" is exemplified by such heroic figures as Rama or Wu Sung. "Creative" leadership, or the development and serving of group interests, is, in Schmidt's view, the only concept of leadership deserving to be classed as "genuine" in the context of modern political situations. It is concerned with the determination of factors which enable a leader to appear and recruit a following —factors which stress the personality of the leader or the nature of the circumstances in which he operates. Thus in describing the aptitudes commonly found among contemporary political leaders, Professor Charles E. Merriam lists the following: a high degree of social sensitivity; facility in personal contact; facility in group contacts and group diplomacy; facility of dramatic expression; capacity for the invention of political formulas, ideologies and plans; a high degree of competitive courage.[2] These are the tools of "creative" leadership.

Gaetano Mosca, in his now classic study of the ruling elite, states that one thing is obvious in the organization of all political systems, namely, that "two classes of people appear—a class that rules and a class that is ruled. The first class, always the less numerous, performs all political functions, monopolizes power and enjoys the advantages that power brings, whereas the second, the more numerous class, is directed and controlled by the first, in a manner that is now more or less legal, now more or less arbitrary and violent."[3] We find this so-called elite concept emerging in the work of Pareto, and in Michels, with his "iron law of oligarchy," and continuing in the elaborate studies of Lasswell and other contemporary political scientists.[4] Mosca concludes that "the whole history of civilized mankind comes down to a conflict between the tendency of dominant elements to monopolize political power and transmit possession of it by inheritance, and the tendency toward a dislocation of these old elements with an upsurge of new forces—this conflict producing an unending ferment of endosmosis and exosmosis between the upper classes and certain portions of the lower."[5]

In these ideas we see the recognition of a continual process of political

[2] Charles E. Merriam, *Systematic Politics*, Chicago, University of Chicago Press, 1945, pp. 108-12. See also his "Political Leadership" in Richard C. Snyder and H. Hubert Wilson, *Roots of Political Behavior*, New York, American Book Co., 1949, pp. 141-45.

[3] Gaetano Mosca, *The Ruling Class*, trans. by H. D. Kahn, rev. and ed. by Arthur Livingston, New York, McGraw-Hill, 1939. The original Italian version was first published in 1896.

[4] See Harold D. Lasswell, *Politics—Who Gets What, When, How*, New York, McGraw-Hill, 1936; also Lasswell et al., *A Comparative Study of Elites*, Stanford, Stanford University Press, 1952.

[5] Mosca, op.cit., p. 65.

group formation, each group headed by a leader or potential leader. In particular, the whole phenomenon of leadership in the modern state is intimately associated, in the minds of the theorists, with the operation of political parties.

Indian Concepts of Leadership

Before describing the traditions of Indian leadership in the light of the foregoing definitions, it is essential first to indicate certain premises. We are not so much concerned with the historical development of leadership theory as with those basic ideas which have come down to contemporary India and which may serve as rationalizations in the thinking of present-day Indian leaders. Nor are we concerned with whether or not the traditional Brahmanical interpretation of that theory or of such terms as dharma is or is not reasonable or correct. The orthodox Indian tradition, persisting from early times, has left a legacy which has been and is being used by men like Tilak, Gandhi, Bhave, Radhakrishnan, and others to authorize, justify, and promote programs and theories of political action.

It should be noted here that many contemporary Indian thinkers have criticized and rejected the orthodox traditions. Some of these have attempted to apply a type of Marxian dialectic to the interpretation of Indian history and thought. In this approach, "Brahmans and non-Brahmans" are often substituted for "capitalists and proletariat," and the whole of Indian history viewed as a continual conflict between the two. The great landmarks of Hindu literature such as the *Mahabharata*, are seen as works of propaganda by the Brahmanic side of this controversy in its attempt to retain privileges based on the authority of the Vedas. The Code of Manu is seen as an attempt to preserve the caste system against the ravages of non-Brahmanic Buddhist revolt.

This point of view also rejects the traditional Brahmanical interpretation of such terms as dharma. The latter is not considered to be an ultimate power which transcends man and society and supports both by the establishment of an eternal system of morals and law. Instead, dharma is defined as social conformity, established custom, or specific civic duty in a given polity. The late brilliant Bengali theorist, Dr. Benoy Kumar Sarkar, gives us a western positivist definition of dharma when he says: "Dharma is the creation of the state and the state as such has the sanction of Danda. . . . Dharma is obeyed as Dharma only because of the coercive might of the state."[6] Here he shows his direct affiliation with the nineteenth century British positivist writer Austin, and also shows his rejection of the outlook of such contemporary thinkers as MacIver, who consider basic law as transcending the mechanisms of government and state. While recognizing these positivist interpretations as possible analyses of Indian political development—however accurate historically—we may still present the orthodox Indian tradition as the major element of Indian thought not influenced directly or indirectly by such western theorists as Austin or Rousseau.

As to the foundations of leadership in India, the Rig-Vedic concept was that of the king as a military leader. Indra, king of the gods, was the hero who could defeat Vritra, the gods' enemy, Indra's status being that of first among equals. The Brahmanas provide us with the earliest account of the origins of kingship. Thus the *Aitareya Brahmana* describes how, when the gods and demons were at war and the gods were suffering defeat, they assembled and decided to name a leader to head them in battle. (I, 14). They appointed Indra and won the war. A later account in the *Taittiriya Upanisad* tells, in a different version, how the gods first sacrificed to the supreme god Prajapati who sent them his son Indra as their king. (I, 5). Prajapati is recognized as superior to Indra and the Brahman as superior to the Kshatriya. Thus the priest is established, in theory, as the source of royal power. The *Arthasastra* of Kautilya, often quoted by Sarkar and others as constituting the basis of positive or secular thought in ancient India, gave little attention to religious theory and mysticism, but stressed the value, from a propaganda standpoint, of such legends concerning the basis of leadership. (I, 13).

The *Manusamhita* is, of course, the classic statement of kingly power (Chaps. VII, VIII). It pictures royal leadership not simply as a lordship but as an office with clear responsibilities. The ruler is primarily concerned with the operation of the varna, to see that each individual performs his caste duties. The leader king is himself strictly bound by caste obligations, and by properly performing his own functions he inspires all others to emulate his conduct. When, by example, by supervision, and by punishment (*danda*) he sees all duties done, his is a prosperous state. The king is therefore protector of his country and his people.

"The individual versus the state," the favorite theme of western political thought, is not stressed in Hindu thought. All individual rights

[6] Benoy Kumar Sarkar, *The Political Institutions and Theories of the Hindus*, Leipzig, Markert & Petters, 1922 [Calcutta, 1939], pp. 207-208.

are related to the performance of individual caste function. Therefore, rights tend to be social or caste rights, and it is individual duty to caste which is emphasized—not individual rights against the state administration.

In this connection, we may note various modern claims of an actual democratic leadership tradition for India, such as those put forth by K. P. Jayaswal.[7] The extent to which the power of the king was checked by so-called constitutional controls has been a subject of keen debate. But the actual formal limitations on his power are not very severe. A careful appraisal of the king's position indicates that the real checks upon his absolute sovereignty were more subtle. A ruthless king could, no doubt, flout or disregard sacred law, but Brahmanic disapproval of royal behavior continued as a severe threat since it provided a basis for popular revolt and might undermine the very title to royal office. It remains broadly true that Hindu theories do not provide for legislative systems based on organized competing interests as in modern democratic practice. The royal decrees (*sasana*) were not so much new legislation as executive orders governing special cases. Basic law or tradition was considered inviolable and the royal commands constituted specific applications of the sacred law. The ideal was that of a stable society governed by an established king-leader, ruling under fixed law.[8] Yet, however enduring or

---

[7] Consult his *Hindu Polity—A Constitutional History of India in Hindu Times*, 3rd edn., Bangalore, Bangalore Printing and Publishing Co., 1955, especially Chapters II, III, XI, XII. For a criticism, consult U. N. Ghoshal, "On the Nature and Function of Vedic Assemblies" and "The Origin and Nature of Hindu Kingship" in his *The Beginnings of Indian Historiography and Other Essays*, Calcutta, R. Ghoshal, 1944, pp. 104-57. Jayaswal concluded, "The constitutional progress made by the Hindu has probably not been equalled, much less surpassed by any polity of antiquity.... What a coincidence that the race which evolved the greatest constitutional principles in antiquity should be placed in contact with the greatest constitutional polity of modern times." *Hindu Polity*, pp. 366-67.

Professor Vincent Smith who, according to Jayaswal, was responsible for the latter's detailed study of Hindu republics, commented: "The early tribal constitutions of a republican or, at any rate, oligarchical character . . . all perished without leaving a trace. Autocracy is substantially the only form of government with which the historian of India is concerned. Despotism does not admit of development." V. A. Smith, *The Oxford History of India*, 2nd edn., Oxford, Clarendon Press, 1923, p. xi.

Dr. Beni Prasad stressed no doubt the most characteristic feature of Indian "democratic tradition." "Here," he states, "the democratic element is to be found at the bottom, in village communities and in group organizations on the basis of kinship or function all over the country. But democracy at the centre, either in the Greek or the modern European sense, was, except for small tribal republics, ruled out by the facts of geography and the difficulties of transport." Beni Prasad, "Political Theory and Administrative System" in R. C. Majumdar, ed., *The History and Culture of the Indian People*, Bombay, Bharatiya Vidya Bhavan, 1951, II, 319.

[8] "Strictly speaking, Hindu political theory vests sovereignty in the Dharma, or law

effective, the very existence of the early republics, the Vedic assemblies (*sabha* and *samiti*), and the panchayats of the self-governing villages has provided inspiration to contemporary Indian thinkers such as Radhakrishnan and Nehru.

There are various possible exceptions to this Indian ideal. One is provided by the Hindu cyclical concept of government—a degenerating cycle of rule leading to the seizure of power by the Sudra.[9] But, even here, within this degenerating spiral we still have a concept of relative stability at each stage rather than the western idea of a system of contending political parties struggling for power under rival leaderships.

Buddhist republican theory does not provide us with any real exception to the status type of government for there are specific warnings in the Buddhist literature against factional or divided rule, and the Buddha's advice warned against departing from the tradition of the elders.[10] Nor does Muslim theory conflict too seriously with this Hindu tradition. In the famous Muslim political work, the '*Ain-i-Akbari* we find the same emphasis on stable authoritarian rule.[11]

A fundamental characteristic of orthodox Brahmanic leadership theory was the goal to which it was directed. Political thought was, to use Mukerji's term, always integrated with a "morally valid philosophy of life."[12] Under the classical Hindu scheme of values, the struggle of group against group and individual against individual for the sake of material political advantage was not morally valid—unless it occurred as an aspect of interstate rivalry. Contentious leadership for the seizure and exercise of power within the state was not considered a desirable form of political activity.

In general, we have an orthodox tradition of leadership in India which may be expressed in the term *rajadharma*. Its essential points may be summarized as follows: The king enjoyed divine sanction for his office.[13] He himself was bound by the conditions of that sanction, since

---

in the widest sense of the term. But administration was entrusted to the King." Beni Prasad, *op.cit.*, p. 319.

[9] *Harivamsa*, CLXXXII.   [10] *Maha-parinibbana Sutta*, I, 1-5.

[11] The ideal of the "benevolent despotism" is well illustrated in the following advice: "Just monarchs exact not more than is necessary to effect their purpose, and stain not their hands with avarice." See '*Ain-i-Akbari* of Abul Fazl-i-Allami, trans. by H. S. Jarrett, 2nd ed. corrected and further annotated by Sir Jadu-nath Sarkar, vol. II (Bibliotheca Indica, work no. 271), Calcutta, Asiatic Society of Bengal, 1949, p. 57.

[12] K. P. Mukerji, *The State*, Madras, Theosophical Publishing House, 1952, p. 363.

[13] Such sanction is not, however, to be equated with western "divine right" concepts which featured European political history. See D. R. Bhandarkar, *Some Aspects of Ancient Hindu Polity*, Benares, Hindu University, 1929, pp. 158-62.

he was subject to the dharma. His main duties were protection of his people and the furtherance of caste function. He was theoretically subject to the advice of Brahmans, as interpreters of the dharma—even as he himself represented the royal arm of dharma, wielding the scepter of *danda*, or punishment, to maintain order. His office and power functioned in relation to an integrated society and were not subject to competitive challenge as in modern democratic party struggle. Failure of the king to be established legitimately by official coronation or failure to carry out his duties and enforce the dharma and the functioning of the caste structure might undermine his position; but insofar as he was duly established and proceeded to perform the duties of his office, he was not subject, theoretically, to challenge except, of course, by the ruler of an enemy state. So far as the state is concerned, we find no concept comparable to that of inalienable individual right or freedom as in modern western thought. All is related to proper caste function. Law and duty are not matters to be debated and invented. They are preexisting in the very dharma structure, which is to be accepted rather than created, to be lived by rather than contended for. We have, in other words, a stable society, operating under established symbols, with an accepted myth of authority.

There are other historical systems of thought beside the orthodox, but like the *carvakas*, or materialists, of early India these others appear not to have survived as powerful forces. Specifically, the *arthasastra* literature has been an important element of Indian political tradition, but though admittedly it may yet inspire the policies or actions of some statesmen, it has not provided the basis of contemporary ideologies in India. Instead, western concepts have provided the rival ideologies. They have emphasized the idea of progress, to be achieved by individual and group planning and leadership as against the older Indian acceptance of an established order or deteriorating political system subject to forces beyond man's control.

Of the several aspects of leadership defined by Schmidt, the Indian ideal would correspond to his term "authority" or, under conditions of revolution and warfare, to his definition of "heroic" leadership—to the concepts of leadership by authoritarian status or by individuals incorporating in high degree the already accepted values of a community. But Schmidt's idea of true "creative" leadership in the modern sense—of individuals leading specific followings aimed at separate and distinct competitive goals—is not a characteristic aspect of the Indian tradition.

Where such concepts of leadership are found in India today they generally have western parliamentary or Marxian roots.

In tracing the historical persistence of classic principles we find that the Maurya dynasty left a legacy of the *cakravartin*, or universal ruler, which became an important concept not only of orthodox Hinduism but of Buddhist and Jain thought. The universal emperor was a "divinely ordained" figure and this tradition inspired the diplomacy of many rajas, some even claiming to be themselves universal emperors in the medieval period. Indeed, most of the medieval kings of India claimed to trace their genealogies to Manu through Manu's son or daughter, who established the solar and lunar lines of royalty. Other customs, such as the horse sacrifice and the temple worship of the Chola kings, stressed the high status of Hindu rulers.

The seventeenth century Maratha warrior, Shivaji, had himself installed, after his victories over the Muslims, as *cchattrapati* or "Lord of the Umbrella." In fact, local Hindu rajas had refused to sit below him until he had undergone the ancient purification and coronation ceremonies.[14] Shivaji symbolizes both the heroic type of leadership in his military campaigns and rule by authoritarian status at the height of his success.

A fervid worshipper of Shivaji, Bal Gangadhar Tilak, stands out as the foremost modern proponent of the classic tradition of rule in India. As a onetime key figure in the nationalist movement and as a powerful influence on the ideology of *swaraj*, his views are of major significance in the continuity of ideas. He says: "During Vedic times, India was a self-contained country. It was united as a great nation. That unity has disappeared, bringing on a great degradation and it becomes the duty of leaders to revive that union." He thus stresses another form of leadership which is complementary to that of the established ruler-leader. He holds that when India enjoys social or political union and stability, the leadership function is performed by the raja in his recognized status. But when stability and independence are lost, a different need arises, namely, for one who can free the country from disunion, oppression, and a falling away from the dharma. This is the heroic or charismatic form of leadership. Tilak exclaims, "In the absence of unity India cannot claim its place among the nations of the world. We have the grand and eternal promise Sri Krishna has given in the *Gita* that whenever there is a decay of Dharma, he comes down to restore it. When there is

---

[14] See K. V. Rangaswami Aiyangar, ed., *Krtyakalpataru of Bhatta Laksmidhara*, Vol. XI, Rajadharmakanda, Gaekwad's Oriental Series, no. 100, Baroda, 1943, p. 26.

decay owing to disunion, when good men are persecuted, then Krishna comes down to save us." It must be noted that the protest leadership process ceases when its ends have been achieved and the old concept of leadership by status has been reestablished. Thus under conditions of revolt against foreign rule Tilak approves factional leadership and revolt. But he would emphasize the *rajadharma* concept once national unity and *swaraj* are achieved.[15]

Tilak's ideas have had an enduring effect. He introduced the national objective of *swaraj* and gave new impetus to the tradition of Indian unity based upon a universally accepted myth of authority. Tilak made an important contribution to contemporary Indian thought by his elaborate reinterpretation of the *Bhagavad Gita* in his *Gita Rahasya*. He emphasized the *karma marga*, or path of duty in this world, insisting that political action rather than priestly indifference to worldly matters was essential for Hindus.[16]

Gandhi's ideals of *swaraj*, *ahimsa*, and *satyagraha* have native roots. The general emphasis is on nonviolence, self-control, and renunciation—all Hindu virtues. His *sarvodaya* concept, promoted by Vinoba through the *bhoodan* movement, is of western origin, but in its emphasis on universal welfare it has an integral character, consistent with traditional ideas.

Nehru has not drawn heavily upon the orthodox heritage nor shown much interest in such protagonists of it as Tilak. With a background of liberal western education he stresses the democratic interpretation of Indian political development. Thus in 1946 when asked, during debate, as to why the new government for India was described in the proposed constitutional draft as a "republic" and not as a "democratic republic" he replied, "It is conceivable, of course, that a Republic may not be democratic, but the whole of our past is witness to the fact that we stand for democratic institutions."[17]

Dr. Radhakrishnan also uses the Indian past for liberal goals. He too sees "democracy" in the Hindu tradition—but not the western parliamentary brand.

---

[15] Quotations from a speech at Banaras, January 3, 1906, in *Bal Gangadhar Tilak—His Writings and Speeches*, Madras, Ganesh & Co., 1919, p. 38.

[16] Bal Gangadhar Tilak, *Srimad Bhagavadgita Rahasya*, trans. by B. S. Sukthankar, 2 vols., Poona, Tilak Bros., 1935-36. See especially I, 70-101.

[17] Jawaharlal Nehru, *Independence and After—A Collection of Speeches 1946-1949*, New Delhi, Ministry of Information and Broadcasting, 1949, p. 349: "A Speech moving the Objectives Resolution delivered at the Constituent Assembly, New Delhi, December 13, 1946."

The religious tradition of India justifies democracy and if she has not been faithful to this principle, she has paid for it by her suffering and subjection. Spirit is never more persuasive than when it suffers silently beneath the heel of oppression. Democracy is an achievement forged in the fires which make a nation's soul. When I speak of democracy, I am referring not so much to parliamentary institutions as to the dignity of man, the recognition of the fundamental right of all men to develop the possibilities in them. The common man is not common. He is precious and has in him the power to assert his nature against the iron web of necessity. To tear his texture, to trample him in blood and filth is an unspeakable crime.[18]

A final note on the Indian tradition today is the persistence in the popular mind of such ideals as the "Rule of Rama," referring to a golden age of government when a high sense of public duty prevailed on the part of both ruler and subject. Despite the retention of such ideals, there can be no doubt that the orthodox Brahmanic tradition has receded, in practice, at least, far into the background of modern Indian thinking. More and more, we find material welfare of the state and earthly society viewed as goals to be reached by means of competitive political activity and governmental planning—with the participation of all citizens. And it must not be forgotten that even where traditional ideas and sources are utilized, the eventual ideological product of such influence may bear little resemblance, in its modern version, to the original source.

Leadership Theories in Contemporary Ideology

The modern western leadership tradition dates from Machiavelli, Locke, and other postmedieval theorists, but it reaches its mature expression in the thought of David Hume. He rejected a tacit assumption of eastern thought, namely, that a leader leads and rules by a mandate of heaven, universally recognized and accepted, or by the will of Prajapati, which is not to be challenged. In Hume's view, no new leader receives the adherence or loyalty of all of the people. The ruler's ascendancy is based, in the first place, upon the approval of some limited group with specific interests. Other groups with other interests are then, in time, subdued and governed by force or persuasion. But only after a long period of evolution does wide voluntary acceptance replace force in the political process.[19] The essential concept of a society composed of

---

[18] S. Radhakrishnan, *Education, Politics and War*, Poona, International Book Service, 1944, p. 36.
[19] See Henry D. Aiken, ed., *David Hume's Moral and Political Philosophy*, New York, Hafner Publishing Co., 1948.

different elements with competing interests remains in western thought, in marked contrast to Indian ideas involving noncompetitive castes which recognize a single source of political power and virtue. Modern western thought holds that individuals follow a leader because they discover him to be a protagonist of those particular interests, usually economic, which they value most. "Political leadership implies politics and politics means politicians."

A major exception to these observations on the central tradition of western thought lies in the work of Hegel and the Marxian school. Hegel discards the notion of popular sovereignty in preference to a monarchial or authoritarian system; he stresses the importance of an autocratic leadership principle and the necessity for public submission to the ruling power. In Hegel's view the individual should not enjoy the freedom and personal protection provided by Lockeian principles. In his model state the legislature represents not individuals but classes such as landowners, industrialists, and professional persons. Man's true freedom comes not from the exercise of his individual will and the satisfaction of his own desires but rather from his identification with the ultimate necessity of state and law.

Although the Marxists have rejected the conservative conclusions or implications of Hegel's philosophy and have substituted materialism for the idealism of the latter, Marxism has remained firmly grounded in basic Hegelian doctrines. The individual is subject to sacrifice for the party, for the communist state, or as a pawn in the class struggle. The various classes, "workers, peasants, and soldiers," transcend the individual in communist tactics and strategy. Even more important is the rejection of the role of a "loyal opposition"; instead there is only the party line, the deification of a state that can brook no opposition to its fundamental spirit or power.

The Hegelian-Marxian approach has some elements which find sympathetic response in the East Asian mind. There is an abhorrence of violence in much of the Hindu heritage, but, if the question of means is forgotten, the avowed ends of communism may, at least in part, find acceptance. The traditional Indian social system considered the individual as a caste member and not as a unit divorced from his caste role and caste characteristics. Hegel believed that the individual should be politically articulate only as a member of a social group or class—not as a mere citizen as in liberal democracies. Communist theory has this same group emphasis. It proclaims a social goal—an ideal to be accepted by all persons—in place of a struggling "factional society" searching for "new answers to its newest problems." It emphasizes public duty and discipline. In China, of course, Marxism is official policy. Mao Tse-tung calls the Chinese government a "democratic dictatorship," explaining that it is "democratic" because it is for "the people" and that it is a dictatorship as against those who would oppose it (the people).[20] This is in stark contrast to the liberal emphasis on civil liberties for minority factions. To use MacIver's term, "the myth of authority" is not subject to question by any group whatsoever.[21] Instead, discipline and self-criticism within the communist ruling hierarchy are supposed to provide the correctives normally supplied by the "loyal opposition" of liberal democratic states.

It is risky to generalize by contrasting East and West in rigid categories. There are too many exceptions posed by the panchayat "democratic" tradition, by cycles of caste change and other features of Indian thought. And in the West there are so many examples in the thinking of Plato and Aquinas and others of an essentially "eastern" outlook that we are apt to lose sight of the fact that these categorical distinctions are in no sense clear cut. But perhaps we can safely find enough emphasis on the integral concept in the East and on the group interest concept in the West to suggest reasons for differences in outlook between the western democracies and the East at the present time. That Indian leaders are themselves keenly aware of the contrast between the foregoing traditions is clearly indicated by the comments of Indian visitors to Communist China, as analyzed by Drs. Fisher and Bondurant.[22] One of these recent visitors stated, "The idea of government and people working together appeals to me much more than the practice of the people continuously judging, criticizing and opposing their government." Another comment from another Indian observer adds, "Their whole system is based upon the enthronement of a new conception of social virtue over the decadent western ideal of individual right." The authors of the above analysis have suggested that this subordination of individual to group may have elements in common with the dharma ideal of India.

It may well be true that Marxism, by emphasizing social duty and the entire society as against the individual rights and party policies of European liberalism has an edge in East Asian psychology. In this connection C. P. Fitzgerald's comment on the early stages of the Chinese

---

[20] Mao Tse-tung, "On People's Democratic Dictatorship," June 30, 1949, quoted in H. Arthur Steiner, *Maoism: A Sourcebook*, Los Angeles, 1952, p. 126 (mimeo).

[21] See R. M. MacIver, *The Web of Government*, New York, Macmillan, 1947, pp. 39-60.

[22] Margaret W. Fisher and Joan V. Bondurant, "The Impact of Communist China on Visitors from India," *Far Eastern Quarterly*, XV, February 1956, pp. 261, 263.

Communist regime is of interest: "The Chinese scholar class still rules, and still holds the same sort of basic philosophy of government as its grandfathers of the Empire. . . . The all-embracing doctrine, the universal society, are still dominant."[23]

From the standpoint of leadership theory the question here is, "Does the leader lead factions or does the leader lead society?" The Indian tradition as well as the authoritarian Hegelian-Marxian doctrine answer that it is society that he leads. When one proceeds further and asks, "To whom is the leader responsible?" he may find a key. In traditional Indian theory, he is responsible to the dharma, or law in the highest sense. In communist theory he is responsible to the "people," which means, in practice, to the ruling elite, which by its very existence may claim to have the "mandate of heaven." In western parliamentary theory the leader is responsible to his faction, or estate, or party until he is successful and then he is responsible to the majority in parliament however its composition may fluctuate. In this respect, Manu and Marx may have more in common than Manu and Hume.

There is one particular Hindu tradition which might indicate an acceptance of proletarian rule. The *Harivamsa* (CLXXXXII), describing the political deterioration of the Kali Age predicts that the Kshatriyas will be disinherited of kingdoms and that the Sudras will challenge the Brahmans. Sudras will lead a prosperous life, will be held in honor despite their "ungodly views," and caste distinctions will be abolished. But this is hardly likely to bring much support for proletarian rule since the period is to be noted for its lawlessness, its immorality, its disease, its discontent. In modern times Vivekananda echoes this same theme in his theory of the cycles of caste rule, although he does not give us such an unfavorable picture of living conditions under proletarian or Sudra supremacy.[24] However, even this interpretation of political forces does not provide the modern communist with much support, since Vivekananda views Sudra power as merely another temporary phase in a revolving cycle of caste rule—a phase which will bring some advantages, but which like each of the other caste-rule phases, will have its own fatal and self-liquidating defects. This is quite different from the outlook of the communist who sees the dictatorship of the proletariat as leading to the perfect society.

Moreover, there is not lacking a thoroughgoing criticism of Marxism itself among Indian leaders. Vinoba has said, "Communism with the

[23] C. P. Fitzgerald, *Revolution in China*, New York, F. A. Praeger, 1952, p. 194.
[24] See his *Modern India*, Almora, Advaita Ashrama, 1923.

Communists is not a living thought. They have turned it into a dogma based on a book. Like the Arya Samajists they pin their faith in that book and take leave of both the existing conditions in a given place and their intelligence. Actually there should be a proper synthesis between their book, the conditions and one's own reasoning. But they regard the book as their Veda. . . . The Communists have no knowledge of the ten thousand years of the development of Indian thought. . . . I therefore find that the Communists have two very serious defects: One, they are book worshippers, and two, they are ignorant of Indian thought."[25]

We also encounter the possibility of a reconciliation of Indian tradition, of communism, and of western liberal democracy in the work of the modern theorist K. P. Mukerji. He appears to recognize the values in Mosca's term "juridical defense." Mosca holds that under parliamentary democracy the individual and the faction receive their greatest protection from abuses by the majority or by the corruption of the ruling elite because attacks are permitted upon this elite even while the broad myth of authority is tacitly accepted. This "loyal opposition" makes possible a continual influx of new blood into the ruling class and prevents it from destroying itself by stagnation.[26] Mukerji seems anxious to defend such liberties. He reconciles individual freedom with universal welfare in this manner: "Why do we presume," he asks, "that to follow the law of our nature is the desirable or moral way of living?" He answers: "Because we also presume that immanent in nature (or in the universal order of which the human order is an integral part) there are natural laws whose normal operation can lead the universe and man, through the evolutionary process, to desirable ends and when we act according to the promptings of our inner nature we act in harmony with those universal laws and thereby act in a desirable or moral manner."[27] Thus Mukerji agrees with western thinkers such as Green and Krabbe that there is a necessary harmony and correlation between individual freedom of will, or human nature, on the one side and natural law or public welfare on the other. While recognizing the extreme importance of dharma and the whole moral order, Mukerji would say that dharma is not a fixed dogma and that individual conscience is an essential element in its expression. He would include juridical defense and other western liberal democratic ideas in his ideal or *varnasramic* state even as

[25] Vinoba Bhave, *Bhoodan Yajna; Land Gifts Mission*, Ahmedabad, Navajivan Publishing Ltd., 1953, p. 128.
[26] Mosca, *op.cit.*, pp. 120-153.
[27] Mukerji, *op.cit.*, p. 250.

he recognizes the values of the total welfare concept of the communists.[28]

We may summarize, then, as follows: The Indian tradition of leadership lends itself to authoritarian or status concepts but not readily to the modern western tradition of party struggle. Communist theory, by its emphasis upon leadership of the whole "people" and "duty" as against an emphasis on group interest and individual right has a natural advantage in relation to Asiatic authoritarian traditions in China, Southeast Asia, and India. At least in India there are signs that religious and democratic values which decry the use of violence and decry ruthless authoritarianism will bring a rejection of these features of the communist approach. There are also signs that in the thought of Vinoba, Mukerji, and others there is a possibility of synthesizing the Indian tradition of status, the Hegelian tradition of state unity, and the western liberal tradition of individual freedom and party competition—to establish an ideal which might qualify under Schmidt's definition of true "creative" leadership. Such is the framework in which the present struggle for men's minds in India is taking place, so far as the institutions of political leadership are concerned.

[28] *ibid.*, pp. 75-77.

SOME HYPOTHESES ON THE POLITICS OF MODERNIZATION IN INDIA

MYRON WEINER

WITH the achievement of independence by the colonial countries of South and Southeast Asia at the close of the war, a new phase of western influence began.[1] For a large part of the past 250 years, western influence in these nations came largely through the merchants and bureaucrats of the occupying powers. Not until the middle of the nineteenth century did there develop in India—and in some countries not until much later—a westernized native class to interpret and mediate the new ideas and institutions. With the arrival of independence, this westernized intellectual class emerged into power, dedicated not to the rejection of all things western, but to the contrary, concerned with establishing western parliamentary institutions and a remodeling of Indian society in accordance with its own image of what is modern.

There is some difficulty in referring to this class as westernized or even as western-oriented. In many ways, it makes more sense to speak of a "response to the West" and to describe precisely what that response has been, than to speak of westernization. But even here it becomes difficult to separate from the behavior and attitudes of groups and individuals that part which is a response to western ideas and that part which grows out of an indigenous tradition. There is obviously a danger too in looking upon the tradition as static, western influence as dynamic, and to consider all change, therefore, a result of the new outside stimuli.

For purposes of clarity, however, we had best be arbitrary in our definitions and speak of western-oriented or westernized elites as those who favor a unified national state, large-scale economic development, and

---

MYRON WEINER is an Assistant Professor of Political Science at the University of Chicago. He was in India from July 1953 to December 1954 under a Ford-Fulbright grant. When this paper was presented he was a member of the staff of the Center of International Studies at Princeton University.

[1] I am especially indebted to the following writers whose papers on various aspects of politics in nonwestern areas were highly suggestive: George McT. Kahin, Guy J. Pauker, and Lucian W. Pye, "Comparative Politics of Non-Western Countries," *American Political Science Review*, XLIX, December 1955; Dankwart A. Rustow, *Politics and Westernization in the Near East*, Princeton, Center of International Studies, 1956; and Gabriel A. Almond, "Comparative Political Systems" in H. Eulau, *et al.*, *Political Behavior*, Glencoe, The Free Press, 1956, pp. 34-42.

are concerned with making substantial modifications in the social structure. By this definition both the Communists and the Congress leadership would be considered westernized, although one favors democratic institutions while the other does not.[2] We can speak of the process advocated by these elites as one either of modernization—which side-steps the question of the source of the ideas which make up the process—or westernization—which is frequently the more common expression.[3]

The western-oriented elite now in political power in India is attempting to restructure Indian society on a vast scale: the constitution, especially the Directive Principles of State Policy, is a statement of their intentions; the five year plans are directed toward modifying the Indian economy, and similarly the Hindu Code Bill is directed toward the Hindu social structure; the Community Projects Administration directs its attention toward changing not only the *techniques* of agriculture in India's villages, but *attitudes* toward social change itself.

This restructuring, unlike the prewar Soviet and Japanese efforts, is being attempted through democratic parliamentary institutions. Such institutions are viewed by this elite as more than an instrument for achieving social change, but as part of the desired end product itself. But the long process of development through which democratic institutions went in Great Britain and the United States is telescoped. It is perhaps an oversimplification, but not altogether an inaccurate one, to say that democratic parliamentary institutions as they exist in most of the newly independent areas exist on the sufferance of a small educated minority which could, if it chose, destroy those institutions. This willingness to share its own power and to risk its loss is so much more amazing in the light of this fact. What is surprising is not that restraints on democratic rights exist, but that thus far there have not been even more restraints.

Many of the conflicts in Indian politics are less over questions of group interest—narrowly conceived—than over the process of moderni-

[2] It should be clear both from the definition and the illustration that "western-oriented" or "westernized" in no sense involves one's attitude toward the western powers. If anything, there is a tendency for the most "westernized" or "western-oriented" groups to be antiwestern in foreign policy.
[3] A good case could be made for distinguishing between the concepts "modernization" and "westernization," the one being synonymous with industrialization and those patterns of behavior and values which accompany industrialization; the other involving the acceptance of institutions and values associated with parts of the West, but which are not necessarily part of the industrial process, e.g. democratic values or women's dresses. These distinctions, however, are beyond the scope of this paper and will have to be dealt with elsewhere.

zation, as defined above, and the political structure which has been created to further the process. While the degree of disagreement varies from one group to another, one can for the sake of clarity distinguish among at least three groups: the antiwestern Hindu-minded, who either have strong reservations about the changes taking place or are in outright opposition; the western-minded who in principle accept the goals of modernization—industrialization, programs to change the Hindu social structure, and a unified national state—but who individually or as part of a group have been unsuccessful in achieving economic, social or political status or a combination of these; and finally, the westernized leadership in government itself which works for modernization, as defined above, but which has some reservations about the extent to which the goals of democratic political institutions are compatible with their modernization program.

The Hindu-minded

In newly independent areas where the process of political development along democratic western lines has been telescoped in time, conflicts or tensions between the minority of western-educated men and the traditional rulers and their associates are not uncommon. Traditional authority, as the expression has been used by Max Weber and more recently by Talcott Parsons, emphasizes a system in which the sphere of authority and the individual's private activities are not clearly separated. This type of authority is distinguished from rational-legal authority with which we in the West are so familiar in our daily lives. Here we think of "office" with its clearly defined "spheres of competence," with holders of the office treated as private individuals with no more authority than anyone else when outside this sphere. Here we think of all the accoutrements of office—fixed salaries, promotions and demotions—bureaucracies in which fitness for office is determined by technical competence rather than kinship relationships or caste position.

As sociologists use this framework, these types are "pure" and rarely if ever found in existing societies. But the framework does help us to understand the kind of conflict which can develop in societies, like India, in which a transition is being made from more traditional to more modern forms. There is, needless to say, a certain amount of dragging of feet. Not everyone benefits from the new order. Not everyone supports it. Those who because of their caste or family position wielded authority in the old order are obviously not going to be pleased with the new criteria for authority and status in the society—position in government, university education, fluency in English, etc. There are of course many who would have held status in the old order and now hold status in the new (the Kashmiri Brahman holding the Prime Ministership for example) but there are others who have been less successful.

It would, however, be incorrect to say that the Hindu communal bodies are made up solely of orthodox, high caste Hindus who look forward, or rather backward, to a society in which the new criteria for status are irrelevant and where traditional criteria would be employed. For these groups do not necessarily advocate a return to caste and its strictures, although Ram Rajya Parishad does go so far as to accept not only caste, but untouchability as well, a point on which the more "progressive" Mahasabha and Jan Sangh are in strong disagreement. There is, however, a general feeling within the Hindu parties that those who live and think in more traditional ways—often irrespective of caste position—are entitled to greater status in the society. Then, too, it should be noted although little statistical evidence is available, that much of the supp/ for the Hindu parties comes from middle caste groups. While large tions of the Brahman castes have become economically, politically, educationally successful in the new order, lower caste groups hav/ come increasingly dedicated to Sanskritization.[4] Many of the non-/ man castes resent the movement towards a more secular order and, they too do not necessarily favor a caste society, there is a feelin/ the government leadership is so westernized that it fails to show tive identification with the Hindu faith.

What weakens the Hindu parties in their political efforts is th ure to have a clear-cut political program for returning to the ol theirs is to a large extent a kind of rear-guard action, aiming to the passage of government legislation affecting the Hindu soc ture, to minimize the use of English in the educational sys more positively, to fight for the passage of legislation ban slaughter. (Support for such legislation has increasingly beco bol of one's identification with the Hindu faith.) While Mu a conception of an Islamic state, there is no such popular equivalent notion in Hinduism; nor is there in Hinduism a/ church as in Catholicism which would give the Hindu parti zational base. With neither a readily adaptable political j a church organizational base, the orthodox Hindus enter

[4] See the very stimulating article by M. N. Srinivas, "A Note on Sa Westernization" in *The Far Eastern Quarterly*, XV, August 1956.

arena with serious handicaps. Perhaps in part this is why their recent attempt to move from an anti-Muslim position to an anti-modernization position thus far has been politically unsuccessful.

The "Unsuccessful" Western-minded

Among those who can be called western-minded, but who have also been unsuccessful politically, and frequently economically, since Independence, there exists a second kind of reservation about the new political system. I am thinking here of those who are in the forefront of linguistic and provincial agitation in India, who accept the desirability of large-scale economic development, but at the moment are primarily concerned with the rearrangement of political boundaries; for the most intense agitation for rearrangement has come from those who are *not* in positions of authority: the Maharashtrians in Bombay, the Nagas in Assam, the Sikhs in the Punjab, and the Telugus in Madras. Essentially, these groups feel that they have not shared in the profits of modernization—in terms of government jobs, business and educational opportunities, and so on. It is interesting to note that the leadership in the linguistic agitation has not always come from high-caste groups, but often from lower castes. Many of the members of the high castes have, as we have already noted, been somewhat successful in adjusting to the "new order." They have for the most part a disproportionately high number of positions in government and the professions in comparison with their number. Less successful castes, who for one reason or another are discontent with the new order and their place in it, can in this way focus their anger upon the more westernized—and frequently Brahman—minority. The anti-Brahman sentiment in the old Justice Party and the Peasants and Workers Party can, for example, be viewed in this context.

It should also be noted that the westernized leadership is something less than enthused about linguistic demands. In the Center there has been a certain amount of suspicion regarding the motivation of the leaders of the linguistic agitation—a suspicion not always without foundation; for there is truly an attempt on the provincial level, not only to redistribute boundaries, but to redistribute the political plums of office.

There are, one might add here, considerable differences between those who lead the linguistic agitation and those who lead the Hindu communalists. The former are more frequently eager to assert themselves by winning political power; among the latter there are many, although by no means all, who refuse to participate in the struggle for political office. Until recently, for example, the RSS leadership was intent upon avoiding any involvement in conventional politics. Instead its aim was to "revitalize and rejuvenate Hindu society through cultural work." And likewise, the Ram Rajya Parishad places great emphasis on nonpolitical educational work and cultural activities. One finds in these groups not only a preference for cultural activities, but a positive revulsion against struggling for political office in the new system.

The Western-oriented

A third and different kind of reservation about the political system exists among those who are in positions of political leadership and who have been successful in Indian politics. There can be little doubt that Nehru and those around him are firmly committed to a democratic system. However, Indian leaders are often torn between their commitments to democratic institutions and methods, on the one hand, and their commitment to national unity and economic development, on the other. There is a desire on the part of the Indian leadership to build a strong unified nation based on the values of nationalism, democracy, secularism, and the welfare state. But parties and parliaments and politics often appear divisive. The opposition appears to oppose solely for the sake of winning power; personalities clash and parties split; strikes in the labor front retard industrial development; and peasant *satyagrahas* like trade union agitation are fomented by parties for political purposes. Some would go as far as Mr. P. Kodanda Rao of the Servants of India Society who said that political parties were unnecessary and suggested that they should be banned. "Political parties," he said, "tend to subordinate the people to the interest of the party and deny to their members the democratic freedom of speech and vote in the legislature and are antidemocratic."[5]

But while few would fully agree with Mr. P. Kodanda Rao, many in the government and in the Congress Party share his feeling of annoyance at party politics, especially as exercised by those in opposition. The government, for example, has not hesitated to make use of Section 144 (which prohibits meetings under certain circumstances) and the Preventive Detention Act (which allows imprisonment without bail or trial)

[5] *Statesman* (Calcutta), February 26, 1956. Comparable statements indicating an impatience with the party system have been made not only by M. N. Roy and Jayaprakash Narayan in India, but by the President of Indonesia as well. This feeling that democratic practices often come in conflict with modernization—i.e. the unified state, economic development, and changes in the social structure—is found in a number of newly independent countries.

when, in the opinion of the government, there is a threat or potential threat to the "public welfare." This desire for national unity and national strength tends to lead to the development of a kind of unprincipled authoritarianism where the ideals of a democratic, pluralistic society operate, but where, in reality, government is centralized, leadership tends to be authoritarian, decisions are made by a relative few, and responsibility, except in the sense of a kind of self-imposed responsibility, is weak and remote.

Conceivably, the process of building national strength through economic development contains some built-in authoritarian consequences which grow out of the need to accumulate capital, increase savings, mobilize the population for specific tasks, restrict consumption, and the like.[6] At this point it would be very foolhardy indeed to argue that authoritarianism or totalitarianism cannot evolve in India. We have seen democratic nations with a relatively minimal degree of government participation industrialize and we have seen totalitarian nations almost totally dependent upon government activity and control industrialize, but we have not yet seen the rise of industrial economies which are based upon both government planning *and* democratic institutions.

The very existence of a democratic ideology in the minds of the Indian elite may in itself affect political developments. Nondemocratic practices may at times be pursued, but they are often followed by a sense of guilt and accompanied by a feeling that such practices are only temporary. The termination of the Government of India Press Act reminds us that there is a difference between nondemocratic practices which are accepted reluctantly, subjected to protest, and conceived of as temporary, and those practices which are permanently institutionalized and conform to a nondemocratic ideological framework. The real danger in India, however, is that nondemocratic practices, originally conceived of as temporary, may become institutionalized and a part of an ideological framework. Thus far there is little evidence of such a development, but the possibility of its occurrence cannot be ruled out.

In closing this rather brief discussion of the attitude of various groups toward modernization and the political institutions now being utilized to achieve those objectives, several considerations should be noted. The first is that the organization of political groups does not always coincide with the broad categories described here. The Congress does in fact represent the western-oriented leadership essentially committed to using state

---

[6] Such a position is forcefully argued by Zbigniew Brzezinski in "The Politics of Underdevelopment" in *World Politics*, IX, October 1956.

power for a program of achieving national unity and modernizing the economy and the social structure, but within the Congress Party itself there are groups which are reluctant to use state powers in all cases for such purposes. The Hindu-minded groups, for example, both within and without Congress, oppose attempts by the state to make intrusions into the social system, which would change the Hindu social structure, but many elements of the same Hindu-minded groups are increasingly becoming interested in the use of state power for developmental purposes.

Then, too, our three categories do not so neatly apply to the Gandhian groups. The antimodernization aspects of the Gandhian movement are very different from those of the Hindu communalists. The Gandhians—including the Gandhian elements of both the Socialist and Congress parties—have no special love for the old order as it existed, but do fear the breakup of what they feel is the organic unity of Indian society. They want change (especially "change of heart"), but they "dream of making society an organic whole, instead of a collection of warring atoms, by means of universal cooperation," as Ostrogorsky wrote when describing the Christian Socialists of nineteenth-century England. They accept the need for some kind of economic development, but are fearful of the cultural and social consequences of a large-scale development program.

As for the Communists, a case can probably be made for viewing the young Communists, at least, as a western-oriented group which has not been successful—particularly in the job market—in the new order. Although no statistics are available, it is my impression that the Communists are particularly successful in recruiting members in the large city universities and in attracting unemployed intellectuals, who often find society unable to utilize their training, and who have developed a set of expectations which to them appear unobtainable in the society in which they live.

The point here is that those who are in opposition to the westernized minority in power are attempting to displace them either by some form of religious revivalism, as in the case of the Hindu communal groups, by reasserting the cultural heritage of linguistic, tribal, or religious groups, as in the case of many of the regional parties, or by a political revolution, as in the case of the Communist Party. This is not to argue that communalism, regional agitation, or communism in India are solely the product of this conflict, since obviously a considerable number of other elements are involved; but the struggle between the westernized elites, the tradition-oriented nonwesternized groups, and the less westernized—or at least the politically and economically unsuccessful westernized—groups plays a major part here.

The broad and perhaps overgeneralized categories suggested here call attention to the need for further statistical evidence on the make-up of various political groups. Relatively little is known, for example, on the caste and occupational backgrounds of the leadership, both on the top and on the secondary levels, of linguistic groups in various localities, of the Communist Party (especially on the provincial and district level), the Hindu parties, and so on. Precisely what relationship, if any, exists between caste membership and the historic and contemporary position of one's caste in the community, both in a ritual and secular sense, and one's attitude toward modernization and toward western-type democratic institutions is not yet clear from the data now available.

Some Hypotheses

An American or Briton in India soon senses that while the political institutions he views are not altogether unlike those with which he is familiar, much of the behavior and many of the characteristics of Indian politics appear rather exotic. If he knows something of Indian history, he soon realizes that the patterns he sees or senses are neither characteristically British (or American) nor characteristically traditional (i.e. pre-British Indian). Dankwart Rustow, in his study of Near Eastern politics and westernization,[7] has suggested the term "amalgamate" patterns, although this term unfortunately suggests patterns which are one part traditional, one part western, rather than what is really intended, namely, patterns of behavior which arise out of mixing political cultures but which are found in neither the traditional nor western societies. In the remainder of this paper we want to look briefly at some of these patterns in Indian politics with a view toward offering descriptive hypotheses rather than explanations as to why these patterns exist or how they are related to one another. Many of these patterns can be found in other societies; indeed, almost all these patterns in one degree or another can be found in other colonial areas, and individually some of the patterns can be found in the United States or Great Britain. But in these latter two western countries, the patterns are often of a lesser degree of intensity, nor is the entire syndrome to be found. While it is beyond the scope of this paper to demonstrate in what specific ways each pattern in Indian politics is related to the other, the reader will

[7] Rustow, *op.cit.*, p. 6.

no doubt intuitively if not analytically detect that relationships do exist. Perhaps at this stage of our knowledge of modern Asian politics, students of the area must proceed first, and cautiously, to build up a body of empirical data and middle range hypotheses that will ultimately contribute to the development of higher levels of generalization about political behavior in nonwestern societies.

One of the more striking patterns in Indian politics has been the rise of charismatic political leadership. Recently, in a report to the Committee on Comparative Politics of the Social Science Research Council, a group of Southeast Asian scholars stated:

The process of breaking from a traditional past creates attitudes that are strongly inclined toward accepting charismatic leaders. Native ruling houses and aristocracies are rapidly losing, or have lost already, an authority sanctioned by supernatural beliefs. Withering of the deep emotional roots of respect for traditional authority is taking place which leaves habits of obedience free-floating, in search of new attachments. In the meantime, the slow spreading of education of a rational character and the scarcity of media of mass communication retard the development of a new consensus based primarily on intellectual persuasion. In such periods of transition, charismatic leaders are likely to fill the vacuum.[8]

Charisma is not a set of qualities, but a relationship between leaders and followers, involving a measure of "devotion to the specific and exceptional sanctity, heroism or exemplary character of an individual person, and of the normative patterns or order revealed or ordained by him."[9]

Both Gandhi and, to a lesser extent, Nehru emerged in India as charismatic leaders, along with several other national or regional figures who possessed a measure of charisma. Pant, Prasad, Rajagopalachari, and Patel have had charismatic relationships with some followers; but whether or not one uses the term charisma to describe these men, the fact is that along with Nehru and Gandhi they have revealed or supported new normative patterns. Milton Singer, describing the way in which villagers have come to accept the development program, quotes one village Brahman as saying:

Gandhiji said the village should be improved, and Gandhiji had a disciple, Nehru, who made a five year plan for the villages, and we who are Nehru's disciples will help him carry out the plan in our village.[10]

[8] Kahin, Pauker, and Pye, *op.cit.*, p. 1025.
[9] Max Weber, *The Theory of Social and Economic Organization*, New York, Oxford University Press, 1947, p. 328.
[10] Milton Singer, "Cultural Values in India's Economic Development," *The Annals of the American Academy of Political and Social Science*, May 1956, pp. 89-90.

Perhaps the most important function of this national leadership has been to rally the country around a new set of values and to provide a sense of unity necessary for the new state to function. These men are in fact "national" leaders, less associated with the cause of any one group than they are with nationalist aspirations. We have seen during the past few years how important the issue of national unity has been, when so much of the time and effort of Nehru and the top leadership has been devoted to the linguistic province agitation. For Nehru, the details of administration and in some instances even of policy have been pushed aside by the overwhelming issue of national unity and by the need to destroy the divisive tendencies which operate against unity.

In a sense, the presence of such charismatic leadership lends a note of unreality to Indian politics. Disagreements within the states between provincial Congress organizations and provincial governments tend to be resolved by Nehru's intervention or by his emissaries. In the recent linguistic disputes, local groups have focused their pressure on the Congress Working Committee and especially on the Prime Minister; and where a deadlock has occurred among groups, all eyes have turned toward the Prime Minister. As a result, a sense of latency has developed in Indian politics, a feeling expressed in India by the phrase, "After Nehru, what?" Beneath this question often lies the feeling that basic differences have been submerged and that these differences will burst forth when the Prime Minister has left the political scene. Within the Congress Party there have developed the machinery and some body of experience and precedent for dealing with intraparty disputes, but it is still an open and crucial question as to whether political groups and leaders inside Congress have developed a sense of responsibility for settling differences which can keep the Congress Party together after Nehru is gone.

In contrast with India, the demise of charismatic leadership in Pakistan has forced that nation to cope with its basic disagreements without the benefit of godlike figures who can effectively resolve such differences. Disputes between provinces and between one section of the country and another, differences between traditional and western-oriented groups have been accordingly more difficult to resolve. Constitution making has been delayed. Governments have been unstable. Planning has been retarded. The absence of national unity has become marked.

India, however, has been fortunate in that its nationalist leaders have served throughout the period of constitution making, the initial task of state integration, the first and perhaps most crucial phase of national economic planning, and, more recently, a period in which regional agitation has increased. But in time India's present nationalist leadership will be gone and the problems of national unity, of planning, and of adapting Indian society to democratic political institutions will continue. For some time after the passage of India's present leadership a feeling of void will exist in India, and what Nehru and his associates have done will then meet the greatest test. In that sense, then, the test of India's experiment with western democratic political institutions is to come.

Another striking feature of Indian politics is the substantial gap between ideal and real behavior. The constitution, for example, guarantees basic rights such as prohibition of discrimination on grounds of religion, race, caste, sex, or place of birth, the abolition of untouchability, and the right to practice any profession or carry on any occupation. A set of directive principles calls for free and compulsory education by the state for all children under fourteen by the year 1960, and promises that the state will direct its policy toward security for all citizens, the right to an adequate means of livelihood, and equal pay for equal work for both men and women; and in general pledges "a social order in which justice, social, economic, and political, shall inform all the institutions of the national life."

Only to list these ideals is to call attention to the vast gulf between the ideals of India's political leadership and the realities of Indian society. For while India's democratic constitution is among the most advanced in the world, her government is at this point further from achieving these goals than most western nations. In a sense, the Indian constitution is more than a set of rules guiding behavior; it is a kind of charter for her westernized leadership, a set of goals and expectations. It is almost as if the whole of this lengthy constitution were a body of directives.

But perhaps the most conspicuous gap between ideal and real behavior in India—at least as far as political behavior is concerned—is the role of Parliament as a decision-making body. Ideally, and according to India's constitution, Parliament and the Cabinet are responsible for crucial decisions in the Indian government. Existing evidence, however, suggests that in practice authority rests not with one institution or group of institutions, but rather with a handful of men who, regardless of the formal posts they hold, wield decisive influence. In the two most important issues before Parliament in 1956—the Second Five Year Plan and the States Reorganisation Bill—the basic decisions with regard to them were made outside of Parliament, and only secondarily in the

Cabinet. If any one institution is of greatest importance, it is probably the Working Committee of the Congress Party. Interestingly enough, linguistic pressure groups throughout the country recognized the importance of the Working Committee by submitting their requests for changing the State Reorganisation Commission report to the committee rather than to the Cabinet or members of Parliament. And in fact, modifications of the report were made by the Congress Working Committee rather than by any other body.

But one probably ought not to overstress the importance of the Working Committee either. P. C. Mahalanobis, as economic adviser to the Prime Minister, wrote the draft of the Second Five Year Plan but is not on the Working Committee. Nor is V. K. Krishna Menon, the Prime Minister's adviser in foreign affairs. One gets the impression that a handful of men, some in the Cabinet, others on the Congress Working Committee, others of importance in the provinces, have joined together to make the most important government decisions. Authority often seems to reside more in the personality than in any particular office. In India, the office often tends to assume authority depending upon the personality holding the office. It was in recognition of this that Sardar Patel and Nehru approached the problem of how to decrease the importance of the role of Congress president after Independence by placing in that office men of relatively secondary stature.

This disparity between ideal and real behavior is obviously not peculiar to the Indian political process, or to the politics of other non-western areas. In the United States, for example, there is obviously an enormous gap between our ideals of equality and the reality of our practices. The differences in India, however, are of a degree so great as to be almost one of kind rather than degree. The fact is that India's leadership has a set of ideals far in advance of existing practices, and the problem for India's leaders is not only to narrow the gap between ideals and practices, but to inculcate in the masses of the country a respect for a new set of ideals which are in many ways the antithesis of the old.

The extent to which it has been possible for some men to function rather successfully, in what outsiders would view as two different worlds, with no apparent indication of ambivalence, is another feature of Indian politics. This capacity is illustrated by Morarji Desai, the former chief minister of Bombay, who plays the role of an ascetic but is considered at the same time a modernizer in his economic development program in Bombay State. Gandhi, too, appealed to both the religious- and the secular-minded; Jayaprakash Narayan of the Praja Socialist

Party has some of that same appeal. There is here an element of what Professor von Grunebaum, in his imaginative metaphor, described as an attempt to play to two galleries at once. It is interesting to note that the western identifications of many Hindu political leaders is stressed by their followers. For example, N. B. Khare, former president of the Hindu Mahasabha, is always referred to as *Doctor* Khare; N. C. Chatterjee, another Mahasabha leader, is frequently spoken of as a well-known and capable Supreme Court barrister. This "looseness" of affiliation may be one of the reasons why it was possible for someone like Shyama Prasad Mookerjee to resign from the Mahasabha, function for some time as an independent, and later form the Jan Sangh as a "noncommunal" pro-Hindu party.

Both religious and secular roles have their appeal, and people move back and forth from one to the other, and sometimes operate in both simultaneously—like the M.P. from Ram Rajya Parishad who lives at an orthodox Hindu school in Delhi, but who takes part in the proceedings of Parliament. One way of life tends to be highly ritualized and authoritarian, the other rational and equalitarian. Deferential bows, kissing of feet, reverential titles are all part of one mode; parliamentary rules, discussions of specific issues of state policy, and relatively equalitarian relationships are all part of the other mode. There are others, besides Mahatma Gandhi, who perform what to westerners would appear to be both religious and political roles—Vinoba Bhave, Swami Karapatri and Guru Gowalkar, for example. It is more frequently the westerner than the Indian who tries to distinguish between the roles. One is reminded of the question westerners often ask of Gandhi—was his the political use of religion, or the religious use of politics?

The absence of a basic consensus in India about the forms and purposes of political activities comprises still another characteristic of the political setting in India. Different responses to the western impact have introduced a new cleavage into Indian society which is sometimes described as a conflict between the communal and secular parties, or between the Hindu-minded and the western-oriented. In fact the western model itself has become an ambiguous one, with some political groups looking toward the Anglo-Saxon model and others toward the authoritarian model of the Soviet Union. While those in authority support nationalism, secularism, and democracy, there are many groups in the society which do not accept the same basic framework. Traditional cultural and linguistic feelings, by their very nature, challenge national loyalties.

India is thus fragmented in at least two ways. There is, first of all, the fragmentation of the western-nonwestern groups, about which we have already spoken; and secondly, the fragmentations which involve ethnic, class, religious, and linguistic pluralisms. The Sikhs, the Naga tribesmen, the Maharashtrians, and the Anglo-Indians tend to feel, in different degrees of intensity, a sense of being second class in status. What fortunately mitigates the effects of fragmentation in India is that the western-nonwestern split does not coincide with ethnic divisions as in Malaya, Algeria, and many parts of Africa. The absence of a consensus in India ought to be seen therefore not only in the context of a rapidly changing society in which the traditional basis for consensus has been eroded, but also in the context of a society with considerable fragmentation in the social system.

The need for both minimizing the strains involved in such cleavages and establishing a consensus with regard to political forms and purposes is now seen by the Indian leadership—and rightly so—as a necessary step toward modernization. Without a substantial measure of agreement on the basic values and objectives of Indian life, modernization or westernization as we have defined it here—a unified state, economic development, and modifications in the social structure—is hardly possible.

Many of the differences within Indian society are temporarily obscured by the presence of charismatic leadership; people who disagree on fundamentals may join in a common response to a charismatic personality. In this respect, these early years of Indian political development are extremely important, for they provide a crucial opportunity for a group of leaders to ameliorate feelings of alienation and provide a sense of unity and—perhaps most important of all—to inculcate in the population a sense of commitment to the new political procedures which may provide a continuous basis for compromise and adjustment by social groups.

To students of American or British politics one of the most apparent differences between those countries and India is the relative lack of organized special interest groups in India. Only a small fraction of peasants and workers are yet organized. Kahin, Pauker, and Pye in their report on the politics of nonwestern countries note that many potential political elements are not organized, thus creating an element of latency in the politics of such countries. The result is that unorganized and generally inarticulate segments may suddenly find ways of expressing themselves. Mob violence, sporadic peasant revolts, and unpredictable forms of behavior may result, because in the absence of the formal organization of potential interests there is not a "continuous form of adjustment of relative power" as in the West.[11]

This characterization of nonwestern politics certainly applies to India as well, but anyone spending time in other nonwestern areas is struck by the *relatively* large number of organized groups in India. Under the aegis of the national movement there arose an enormous number of local groups, peasant organizations, welfare bodies, cooperatives, and handicraft bodies which took part in the national struggle but which also developed some interests of their own. Many of the Gandhian organizations, for example, have persisted since Independence and have put pressure on both the government and the Congress Party. There is some reason to believe that since 1947 the number and size of interest organizations throughout the country has increased. Many of these interest groups have entered politics as political parties, thereby blurring the distinction between parties and pressure groups as we know them in the West: the one concerned with winning power, the other with influencing power. A closer examination of many of the smaller political parties on the local level would probably find such groups attempting to perform both functions. Perhaps an obvious example is the dual role which the Akali Dal party has performed recently both by participating in the electoral process and by attempting to exert influence on the central government with regard to the states reorganization plan for the Punjab region.

Relatively little is known about the exact extent to which local political organizations function, how they are organized, what techniques they employ, what the sources of their leadership are, and—of particular importance—what kinds of dislocation led to the growth of local political organizations. But if our impressions are accurate, then the political consequences are enormous. On the one hand, it may mean that the occurrence of erratic and violent outbursts could become less likely, or on the other hand, that violence may be more systematically canalized for political purposes. Mob violence is usually an ineffective device for achieving political change unless such violence is directed and planned by an elite concerned with achieving specific goals. The ominous statements by Sikh leaders in 1956 that violence in the Punjab was likely to accompany the violence in Bombay unless compromises by Congress were made on the linguistic issue were essentially an assertion by the Sikh leaders that they could precipitate violence. As political groups become more effectively organized and as a larger part of the society

[11] Kahin, Pauker, and Pye, *op.cit.*, p. 1026.

becomes politically organized, the danger exists that violence may become an instrument for attempting to achieve political change. As discontented groups become organized and learn to focus their discontent on specific issues, the possibilities of achieving compromise through the political processes are of course enormous. At this point the task of statesmanship is to demonstrate that the existing legal channels provide adequately for bringing about changes in public policy. It is here that the test of democratic institutions is most likely to occur.

Closely related to the growth of interest groups in India has been the growing scope of government, that is, the growing power of the government to influence and shape the lives of the Indian people. In the West the scope of government increased rather gradually with the growth of divergent interest groups which pressed the government to act on their behalf. In the Near East, as Dankwart Rustow has pointed out, "governmental power expanded largely in response to foreign pressure rather than domestic need . . . growth of civic consciousness, social organization and political responsibility has lagged behind." Governments of the Near East, like the government of Japan, expanded, therefore, to cope with the encroachment of the western powers. This lag in the growth of social organization and civic consciousness is, according to Rustow, a major source of political unrest and instability in the Near East. "Political and social power is exercised irresponsibly, since there is no effective representation of interests to support or control the expanded power structure."[12]

In India, where the pattern of western intrusion differed from that of the Near East, the scope of government has grown in recent years not as a means of coping with western intrusion, but in large measure to cope with an enormous rise of mass expectations. Perhaps the single most important consequence of the nationalist agitation was that it aroused mass expectations which forced the newly independent government of India, like its counterparts in Burma, Indonesia, and elsewhere, to cater to these expectations in order to survive. The role which the nationalist movement played in building expectations may be one of the reasons why more organized interest groups have developed in India than one finds in Thailand (even given the difference in size), or Liberia, or Ethiopia, three countries which experienced no period of national struggle for independence. It is striking that among the underdeveloped countries of Asia and Africa, those which lived under alien rule and which struggled for independence appear to have developed a

[12] Rustow, *op.cit.*, p. 16.

larger number of organized interest groups—peasant organizations, trade unions, political parties, etc., than others. If these observations are accurate, and if the existence of intermediary groups between the government and the masses is a prerequisite for responsible government, then in this respect the prospects for responsible government in India are probably greater than in most of the Near East.

The growth of parties and interest groups represents more than a political development; it also involves considerable social changes in Indian society. It has become commonplace to refer to the breakdown of traditional patterns of allegiances in India—especially among the urban intellectuals—but what has taken the place of these traditional patterns or grown alongside these patterns has been less studied. There is some reason to argue that political groups in India assume some of the functions which family and caste groups performed, especially for the large number of displaced intellectuals in India's urban centers. The intensity of devotion of members of political groups, the absence of continuous and ready communication with outside groups, the importance of the group and factional leaders to their members, the development of a *Weltanschauung* in many political parties which provides a new orientation toward life, all indicate the enormous needs which political groups fulfill for so many of their members.[13]

It is also interesting to note how few Indians have several group identifications. Party members, especially those in opposition parties, participate in party work almost to the total exclusion of work in other organizations and groups. Party workers and members of interest groups in Great Britain and the United States are at the same time members of their family, business and church groups, trade unions, veterans organizations, and so on. Indians do not have such multiple group memberships. Party workers in India generally come from urban areas where traditional values have been disrupted and where the traditional social structure for many Indians has been breaking down. Young party workers have often broken from the tight-knit organization of their village, their caste, and even their joint family. Many party workers, for example, are bachelors whose bachelorhood represents a break from the joint family. The party thus provides both an alternative set of values and an alternative social structure. There are few outside loyalties to temper the intensity of party membership. The fact that British and

[13] See Myron Weiner, *Party Politics in India: The Development of a Multi-Party System*, Princeton, Princeton University Press, 1957, for a more detailed discussion of this point.

American parties and pressure groups contain members who frequently belong to a wide variety of groups—political or otherwise—means that such political groups are often forced to make compromises in order to retain the support of their members.[14] One can't help but wonder whether the lack of multiple memberships is not a factor in the unwillingness of many Indian political groups to coalesce.

Conclusion

We have commented on some of the striking features of Indian politics—the telescoping in time of the whole process of parliamentary development, the presence of charisma, the gap between ideal and real behavior, the tendency for power to reside in men rather than in offices, the extent to which it has been possible for men to function in what would appear to outsiders as contradictory roles, the absence of a consensus, the small but growing number of interest groups, the rapid growth of the scope of government, and the integrative functions of political groups. These patterns have to be seen in the context of the basic conflicts within the political system between those who are westernized and those who are not.

During the past two hundred or so years India has been under continuous western influences. These influences affected trade and commerce, education and religion, and more recently, political life. The impact was greatest first on the urban areas and more recently in the rural areas. The West has left India but the western impact continues through the activities of a native intelligentsia. Its aim is to make over society in its own image; its technique, in part, is to use the power of government. At one time one could speak of Indian society with hardly a reference to government. Today that has become virtually impossible. Government and politics have now become major instruments for social change. The present direction of change is that of integrating the masses of Indians into the value scheme of the westernized minority which now dominates the country. One generally thinks of integrating or assimilating a minority into the major community, but in India as in other nonwestern areas, the process is in reverse. The relatively small educated elite which, in general, accepts the democratic, parliamentary, and secular form of government, is seeking to get the mass of voters to accept its value scheme. This group sees a democratic, secular, national welfare state as

[14] See David Truman, *The Governmental Process*, New York, Alfred A. Knopf, 1951, Chapter 6.

desirable, and uses the party and electoral systems as a means of persuading the population to accept that political framework.

Politics in India represents more than a set of conflicts between interest groups but, as we have noted throughout this paper, involves something far deeper: the conflict between the forces for modernization and those against. Here we are dealing with what Gabriel Almond called a conflict betwen two *political cultures*. Almond refers to the pre- or partially industrialized and westernized political systems as mixed political cultures and mixed political systems in which a western system with its parliament, electoral system, bureaucracy, and the like are mixed with more traditional political forms.

Thus there may be a parliament formally based on a set of legal norms and regulations, but operating within it may be a powerful family, a religious sect, a group of tribal chieftains, or some combination of these. These are elements of the traditional role structure operating according to their own traditional norms. The student of these political systems would be greatly misled if he followed western norms and expectations in describing such a decision-making system. What would be corruption in a western parliament would be normatively oriented conduct in a mixed parliament of the kind often found in the regions outside of the Western-European American area.[15]

These political cultures may not only be mixed within the parliamentary arena or *within* political parties, but as we have seen they may be expressed in conflicts *between* political parties. Those who resent the process of modernization are forced to use the political instruments created by the westernized. Orthodox Hindu communalists, whether in Ram Rajya Parishad, the Hindu Mahasabha, the RSS, or Jan Sangh, increasingly use the accoutrements of western democracy—parties, parliaments, elections—to achieve their objectives. The Hindu-minded have lost much of their traditional authority and therefore find it necessary to accept the weapons of the more westernized elites. The more westernized obviously have the advantage of being able to use weapons of their own choosing; being in a position of political power, they also have the opportunity to solidify their position and extend their influence. But the more traditional, on the other hand, have the advantage of being able to appeal to traditional feelings and institutions and may attempt to direct these feelings toward religious fanaticism, antimodernism, tribalism, racialism. But the possibility exists that the Hindu-minded parties will not only be forced to utilize western political forms, but in time may come to accept them. The recent interest among younger members of

---

[15] Almond, *op.cit.*, pp. 38-39.

the Jan Sangh in some of the more secular problems of economic development and their recent attacks against the "undemocratic" Communists may indicate a growing acceptance of the new society with its western-type political institutions. The growing acceptance of democratic institutions and values by sections of the Catholic community in France—as politically expressed in the Mouvement Républicain Populaire—may be analogous.

I have tried in these remarks to unravel some of the complexities of Indian politics. Needless to say, these have been more in the way of hypotheses than statements of undisputed fact, and certainly a great deal remains to be done by way of empirical investigation of these hypotheses. An underlying theme of this paper is that it is in the political sphere that modernization in India is now undergoing its greatest test, and that what happens here will have great impact on all aspects of India's life. Toynbee has written of the "psychology of encounters," and in recent years we have been told a great deal about the sociology of acculturation. What I have tried to suggest here is that there is a politics of acculturation as well. A new political system has been introduced into a setting far different from the one in which it originated. Further research and analysis of both the orientation and political position of various groups supporting and opposing new changes, as well as the political patterns emerging, would not only provide greater understanding of the ways in which Indian politics now functions, but might give us additional insight into the direction of change.

2. PERSONALITY AND LEADERSHIP

POLITICAL leadership in India has long been associated with the personalities of those who have shown the capacity to capture the imagination of the Indian people. But the characteristics of personality that have met the challenge of leadership differ widely. The following three profiles concern well-known leaders in the independence movement: Jawaharlal Nehru, Subhas Chandra Bose, and Vallabhbhai Patel. Each of these men illustrates a different facet of leadership in India. Together with Mahatma Gandhi, whose legacy is considered by Joan V. Bondurant in Section 5, they encompass the more important of the major types of leaders functioning in modern India in its urban setting.

The genius of Vallabhbhai Patel was to be found in his ability to organize. His training and political accomplishments are reviewed by Balkrishna Govind Gokhale, himself a native of Patel's Gujarat. Subhas Bose, at the other extreme, was an activist and revolutionary. His frustrations over the inactivity of the Indian National Congress led him into the unusual role of being a leader of the Indian National Army under the Japanese. Bose's political history is recounted here by Chattar Singh Samra. Jawaharlal Nehru is less easily classified, but he is certainly distinct from the leadership patterns of either Patel or Bose. As the only one of these men still alive, Nehru's personality is of great contemporary interest. In an effort to understand the cumulation of psychological forces that have determined Nehru's actions, Margaret Fisher has presented Nehru largely in his own words.

NEHRU: THE HERO AS RESPONSIBLE LEADER

MARGARET W. FISHER

*T*HERE is perhaps no more controversial or complex figure on the world stage today than Jawaharlal Nehru, Prime Minister of India, and since the death of Mahatma Gandhi, "Idol Number One" of the Indian people. He inspires devotion, envy, adulation, resentment, exasperation—strong emotions all. Few if any remain indifferent to the complex, dynamic "political heir" selected by Mahatma Gandhi. He has at various times been called an autocrat, a communist, a fascist, a convinced democrat and a liberal humanist. He calls himself a socialist; but the brand of socialism he professes tolerates—even "encourages"—private industry in the interests of production, and shuns dogma and doctrine in attempting to industrialize at a humane pace while establishing an egalitarian society through appeals to reason.

What manner of man is Jawaharlal Nehru? Next to the Mahatma himself, there is no one in India more written about than Nehru, nor one who has written more revealingly about himself. A compassionate and conscience-pricked aristocrat whose family wealth went into the independence struggle, his rapport is least with India's "middle class," and from a section of Indian journalism representing political opposition and "middle class" viewpoint Nehru receives virtually constant criticism often barbed with ridicule. Criticism from abroad, however, usually serves to close Indian ranks behind their Prime Minister.[1]

Nehru's hold is greatest upon the cultivated upper class and upon the common man. What image the villager has of Nehru cannot be said, but the highly articulate educated class leaves no doubt as to the source of allegiance or opposition, as the case may be. Nehru is criticized in some quarters as a dangerous innovator bent on destroying Hindu values and in others as a laggard in bringing about social change. He is accused

MARGARET W. FISHER is Editor of the *Indian Press Digests* and a Lecturer in Political Science at the University of California at Berkeley.

[1] It would, of course, be a mistake to take the volume of daily needling too seriously. One Indian journalist who both admired and respected the Prime Minister explained to me that he engaged in constant gibes at Nehru for the following reasons: his mail showed that people would rather read criticism than praise; people had the habit of being suspicious of government, and when things went wrong in any way, they felt less uneasy if they thought someone was constantly on the watch.

at once of behaving like a dictator and of lacking the capacity to take decisive action. Moodiness, impatience, bursts of temper and imperiousness are defects he has acknowledged in his autobiography and elsewhere. These defects have indeed cost him some support, but for the most part his adherents are ready to make allowances. The outbursts are quickly over, they point out, and are never accompanied by malice or rancor;[2] his impatience, if at times excessive, is directed mainly towards that which is stupid, inefficient, ugly, or evil. He has won and held devotion by his breadth of vision, generosity of spirit, sense of honor, dedication to duty, fearlessness, candor, and remarkable vitality, combined with a radiant personal charm. The glamor of the aristocrat who has sacrificed and suffered in the common cause attaches strongly to him, in addition to that bestowed by his unique relationship with Gandhi. The characteristics which led Gandhi in 1929 to select the youthful Jawaharlal as Congress president were unsurpassed bravery and love of country, the "dash and rashness of a warrior" combined with "the prudence of a statesman," and the proven capacity to submit to irksome discipline. Nehru also filled the need for a president who would appeal to the young radicals without alienating their more conservative elders, for although he was "undoubtedly an extremist thinking far ahead of his surroundings," he was also "humble and practical enough not to force the pace to the breaking point." As to his character, Gandhi testified: "He is pure as crystal, he is truthful beyond suspicion. He is a knight *sans peur, sans reproche*. The nation is safe in his hands."[3]

It may be at once imprudent and presumptuous to attempt an evaluation of a leader of Nehru's caliber and complexity at this moment in time when developments both in India and abroad are confronting him simultaneously with critical situations the handling of which must inevitably affect any final evaluation. Nevertheless, these same circumstances lend urgency to the effort to search out significant keys to a comprehension of this exceptional and influential personality, however partial and inconclusive such an effort is doomed to be.

In attempting to arrive at an understanding of the basic elements in

[2] During 1937 when differences within the Congress Working Committee were acute, Gandhi's secretary, Mahadev Desai, in describing an "exceptionally difficult" meeting, wrote of Nehru: "He frets and fumes, he storms, he is often in a rage, but after all he is a sport and so quickly regains his balance, makes rapid amends and sees that there is no unpleasantness left behind." G. D. Birla, *In the Shadow of the Mahatma: A Personal Memoir*, 2nd edn., Bombay, Orient Longmans, 1955, pp. 205-06.

[3] D. G. Tendulkar, *Mahatma: Life of Mohandas Karamchand Gandhi*, Bombay, Jhaveri and Tendulkar, 1952, II, 490.

Nehru's leadership, the most obvious ingredient is, of course, his character as hero. The long hard hours Nehru spends at desk work are interrupted from time to time by quick trips here and there to lay a cornerstone, break ground for a dam, open a school, unveil a statue, inaugurate an industrial plant, or officiate at one or another of the myriad functions clamoring for his presence. On these occasions he is thronged by adoring crowds, and draws sustenance from the experience. As he has put it: "A man who sits cooped up in an office becomes static and a dead-weight. If I may make a personal confession, that is why I occasionally want to run away from New Delhi and rush about from place to place. I want to escape from the deadly static atmosphere of paper and files and ink in which one forgets there are human beings in India.... Well, I get out and I see the faces of my people and your people and derive from them inspiration and what is much more important, something dynamic and growing. I grow with them and to some extent get in tune with them. I hope, I also affect, to some extent, the mood and tune of their minds..."[4]

The adulation Nehru receives, however restorative he may find it, is undoubtedly a factor in the suspicion with which he is regarded in some parts of the western world and, indeed, within India. Can any mortal receive adulation on such a scale and escape deterioration? It is not a question which can hastily be brushed aside. It is a question which was pondered by Nehru himself more than twenty years ago, when during the forced inaction of a long prison term he attempted to resolve inner conflicts by tracing his own mental growth. "Only a saint, perhaps, or an inhuman monster could survive all this [hero worship], unscathed and unaffected," he wrote, and he could place himself in neither category. The adulation had gone to his head, intoxicated him a little, but it had also given him confidence and strength. Probably, also, it had made him "just a little bit autocratic . . . just a shade dictatorial," he hazarded; but his conceit, he thought, had not "increased markedly." He was "by no means humble" about his abilities, he wrote, but neither did he find them at all remarkable; and he was very conscious of his failings. He was inclined to credit a habit of introspection—developed in prison, he tells us—as aiding him in retaining his balance and in taking a detached view of his experiences. Popularity was "not an invariable sign of virtue or intelligence," he mused, but was as often "the hand-

[4] From Nehru's speech at the silver jubilee celebrations of the Central Board of Irrigation and Power, New Delhi, 17 November 1952. *Jawaharlal Nehru's Speeches 1949-1953*, Delhi, Ministry of Information and Broadcasting, 1954, p. 68.

maiden of undesirable persons" in public life. Did he perhaps owe his popularity to his failings rather than to his accomplishments? He pursued the question further. To the question "Why indeed was I popular?" he discarded a number of possible answers. Intellectual attainments would not explain it, he wrote, for they were "not extraordinary, and, in any event, they do not make for popularity." His "so-called sacrifices" he minimized, along with his reputation as a hero, which he characterized as "entirely bogus." He found the "heroic attitude or the dramatic pose in life" merely "silly" and considered himself "the least romantic of individuals." The virtues he allowed himself were "some physical and mental courage" based, he conjectured, upon "pride: personal, group and national, and a reluctance to be coerced into anything."[5]

Nehru then went on to examine the content of the legends which had grown up about his famous father and himself: his supposed friendship with the Prince of Wales (whom he had never met), and the "fantastic and absurd" tales of the family's conspicuous spending. Throughout these legends he found a common strand—"the idea of mixing in high society and living a life of luxury and then renouncing it all"—and renunciation, he knew, "has always appealed to the Indian mind" (p. 205).

Renunciation for renunciation's sake seemed to Nehru "the negation of life, the terrified abstention from its joys and sensations." His preference was for "the active virtues," although he valued renunciation and sacrifice as "mental and spiritual training" analogous to the training required by an athlete. "I have not consciously renounced anything that I really valued," he stated, adding immediately, "but then values change" (pp. 205-06).

Nehru then turned back once more to the question of the effect of the crowd's hero worship upon himself. He analysed his ambivalence skillfully, conscious that, although there were times when he longed to escape from it, "on the whole, the crowd had filled some inner need" of his. On the one hand, his "will to power" was partially satisfied by his ability to sway the crowd; on the other, he was subjected to "a subtle tyranny" by their very confidence and affection, which "moved inner depths" within him. In the last analysis, he found, the shouting crowds and "the dust and tumble of politics" touched him "on the surface only, although sometimes the touch was sharp and pointed." The real conflict

---

[5] Jawaharlal Nehru, *Jawaharlal Nehru: An Autobiography*, new edn., London, John Lane, 1942, pp. 204-05. First published in 1936. Citations to the *Autobiography* from this point on will be indicated in the text by page reference only.

lay deep within himself, in the "conflict of ideas, desires and loyalties." He was conscious of being a battleground, and conscious too that he rushed into action as a means of escaping from this inner conflict: "outer conflict relieved the strain of inner struggle" (pp. 206-08).

Recently Nehru has stated that the three men who had most influenced him were his father, Gandhiji, and to a lesser extent Rabindranath Tagore[6]—a most diverse trio, each in his own way a powerful figure. Gandhi's relationship with Jawaharlal—twenty years his junior—was in many ways virtually that of a second father. It says much for the strength of the younger man's character that he was able to assert himself in opposition to two such overpowering personalities: the leonine Motilal Nehru, "a kind of renaissance prince," a man of "strong feelings, strong passions, tremendous pride and great strength of will" (p. 23), who amassed—and enjoyed—great wealth; and the formidably "meek" Mahatma who, having renounced possessions and the normal enjoyments of living in a relentless quest for truth, was enabled to exert a "psychic coercion ... which reduces many of his intimate followers and colleagues to a state of mental pulp" (p. 539).

Two such men as Pandit Motilal and Mahatma Gandhi, although a mutual respect and warm friendship developed between them, nevertheless represented conflicting value systems for a young man attempting to chart a satisfactory life pattern for himself. Jawaharlal, in contemplating "the strange combination," was reminded of Walter Pater's analysis of how the saint and the epicure, starting from opposed points and travelling different paths, could yet, because of the very stress and earnestness of outlook each possessed, understand each other better than either could understand the mere man of the world (p. 65). Jawaharlal could respond to both appeals. These conflicting values were not new, but had made their claims on him from an early age.

In the remarkable autobiography which was the product of his seventh prison term, Jawaharlal Nehru has described a lonely childhood. He was the first—and for eleven years the only—child of the famous, strong-willed, vibrant Motilal Nehru and a daintily beautiful and doting mother. His family was of high standing in the highest caste—Brahmans of the Kashmiri Pandit community. His father, Jawaharlal once wrote, was "never moderate in anything but his politics, and step by step his nature drove him from even that remnant of moderation." He was also a "modern," with the courage to be the first of his group to re-

[6] In an interview broadcast over All-India Radio on the occasion of the birth anniversary of Pandit Motilal Nehru, *Hindu Weekly Review*, May 14, 1956.

fuse to undergo even a token version of the purification rites required of all Hindus upon return to India from overseas. Motilal Nehru and Jawaharlal's older cousins, who during his boyhood lived in the same household, refused to take religion seriously. This was not true of the women of the family, however (p. 8). Indeed, one frequent member of the household was his mother's elder sister, who had been widowed in her teens and had renounced the world to live a life of service.[7] From his mother and aunts the young Jawaharlal imbibed the age-old values as set forth in the great Hindu epics, although most of all he was drawn to the youthful Prince Siddhartha who, "after many inner struggles and pain and torment, was to develop into the Buddha."[8] He also remembers enjoying participation in the ceremonies observed by the women at the same time that he "tried to imitate to some extent the casual attitude of the grown-up men of the family." His father impressed him greatly as the embodiment of "strength, courage and cleverness," but the child also stood in awe of his father's prodigious temper—"indeed an awful thing and even in after years I do not think I ever came across anything to match it in its own line" (p. 7).

After several years with a private tutor during which he developed a liking for poetry, an interest in the natural sciences, and a transient enthusiasm for theosophy, at age fifteen Jawaharlal Nehru was taken to England and placed at Harrow. Here, he says, he managed to fit in to some extent, but "was never an exact fit." On the whole, he found the English boys dull. The news of uprisings in India in 1906 and 1907 stirred him tremendously. He was given as a prize for good work in school a volume of Garibaldi, which set him daydreaming of leading a similar gallant fight for freedom in India (pp. 18-19).

After two years at Harrow he entered Cambridge, where he took the Natural Sciences Tripos at Trinity College. Here his intellectual horizons widened. He learned to discuss such writers as Nietzsche, G. B. Shaw, and Havelock Ellis; the aesthete in him responded to Oscar Wilde and Walter Pater. At this time he was greatly attracted to "a vague kind of cyrenaicism"—"the idea of going through life worthily, not indulging it in the vulgar way, but still making the most of it and living a full and many-sided life" (p. 20)—a pattern, it would appear, not too unlike that then exemplified by his father. While at Cambridge there was some talk of his embarking upon a career in the Indian Civil Service.

[7] For a tribute to this aunt see Krishna Nehru, *With No Regrets*, New York, John Day, 1945, pp. 125-29 and 152-54.
[8] Jawaharlal Nehru, *The Discovery of India*, New York, John Day, 1946, p. 122.

The idea was eventually given up, largely, he says, because his father and mother wanted him near them and looked with disfavor on the extra year in England which would have been required, as well as the possibility that he would afterwards be posted far from home. Accordingly, Nehru decided upon the law as a career and joined the Inner Temple. After two years, during which his studies were not allowed to interfere with his enjoyment of London life, he passed his examinations and was soon called to the Bar (pp. 24-26).

In the autumn of 1912, after a stay of over seven years in England and on the Continent, broken only by two holidays spent at home, Jawaharlal Nehru returned home to India. He joined the Allahabad High Court, and for a while found life pleasant enough. It was not long, however, before the dull routine gave him feelings of futility. His "mongrel, or at least mixed, education" kept him from fitting into things as he found them, in spite of a "fairly congenial" home atmosphere. There was at this time no political movement which attracted him: the bomb throwers repelled him, and the Congress was too moderate. He felt admiration for the members of the Servants of India Society who gave up their careers in the service of their country, but the type of work they were doing was not such as to tempt him to join them. When Gandhi came forward in 1919 with the proposal to start a Satyagraha Sabha whose members would be pledged to court jail deliberately by disobeying the much-resented Rowlatt Bills, Nehru's enthusiasm was immediately aroused. He felt "tremendous relief," he says, that a way out of the tangle appeared, "a method of action which was straight and open and possibly effective" (p. 41). He would have joined at once but for his father's strong opposition, which was reinforced by a counsel of moderation from Gandhi himself who wanted both Nehrus on his side. The Jallianwala Bagh massacre of April 1919 and the conduct of the subsequent inquiry had a profound effect upon Motilal Nehru who, after considerable inner turmoil, reached the decision to give up his lucrative practice and join Gandhi's noncooperation movement. For the younger Nehru no pangs were involved in rejecting glittering offers from business firms as well as tempting suggestions of a government career to follow Gandhi. For him, turmoil was to come later and to display a vastly different visage.

The relationship between Jawaharlal Nehru and Gandhi was of vital importance to them both and it is impossible to assess Nehru's leadership without at least making an effort to understand the effect the two men had on each other. It is well known that on the intellectual plane Nehru and Gandhi differed greatly—at times fundamentally—but their "heart union" was dear to each of them, and Gandhi particularly was adept in repairing this bond whenever it frayed under strain. Gandhi appears to have understood Jawaharlal very well; but from the beginning there was much about Gandhi that the younger man found it difficult to understand. He disliked the religious phraseology in Gandhi's politics, nor did he ever accept nonviolence as a creed, although it seemed right to him as a policy given the Indian situation and traditional background. What attracted Nehru was the moral and ethical side of the movement, and especially its appeal to courage and manhood.

Nehru, with his lucid and logical mind, wanted to outline a definite program leading to an agreed-upon and clearly stated goal. He was as convinced as Gandhi of the desirability of ethical means; but means to him remained means only, while to Gandhi, he eventually came to realize, means *were* ends. Means, Gandhi argued, were necessarily more important than ends, for ends were beyond human control and it was only the choice of means that was open to mankind. Gandhi's unremitting search for truth led him to the conclusion that nonviolence, providing it was "pure," offered the perfect means, and the more distant ends should not be a matter for concern—"one step enough for me." One step was never enough for Nehru, who chafed under the metaphysical language in which Gandhi expressed his program although his systematic mind was ready to concentrate upon "first things first." Gandhi, whose method of converting others to his views was always to stress areas of agreement, seems to have found it not too difficult to establish important areas of complete agreement which temporarily would still Nehru's lingering doubts. Nevertheless, his ideas of how to use the Gandhian method continued to differ sharply from Gandhi's, and intense conflict was created in him as Gandhi took one step after another which appeared irrational to Nehru at the time, but which later he was usually ready to concede had been brilliantly vindicated in the outcome.

Conflict both in the form of argument with Gandhi and of searching self-analysis appears to have persisted throughout Nehru's long association with Gandhi. During much of this period Gandhi was the "permanent superpresident" of the Congress movement, while Nehru's energy and efficiency soon made him almost equally indispensable. He became for some years the "semipermanent secretary," served several times as president, and was eventually designated by Gandhi—despite the many acknowledged differences in viewpoint—as his political heir.

Those of Gandhi's followers who abjured political work for social welfare activities found no great admirer in Nehru, nor were they ready to acknowledge Nehru as "an older brother," as the late K. G. Mashruwala (who succeeded Gandhi as editor of *Harijan*) has pointed out. Mashruwala once asked what quality Gandhi found in Nehru which led him not only to choose Nehru as his heir and successor, but also "to take pride in the choice?" The answer, he thought, was that Gandhi saw in Nehru a sincerity and dedication to the service of the people as great as was his own. Gandhi was convinced by Nehru's "fine balance of intellect, faith and action," continued Mashruwala, that he could not become "a fanatic of any 'ism' but rather a devotee of Truth alone."[9]

Mashruwala's analysis is undoubtedly correct as far as it goes, although the nature and direction of Nehru's "faith" would be no simple matter to define. None of the world's religions has been able to satisfy his intellect, although some aspects of Buddhism have attracted him, as has also the traditional Chinese concept of the Tao. He has mused aloud on such questions more than once. On one such occasion he conceded that Voltaire might be right concerning the necessity to invent God if he did not exist, but added this "reverse proposition: even if God exists, it may be desirable not to look up to him or to rely upon him. Too much dependence on supernatural factors may lead, and has often led, to a loss of self-reliance in man and to a blunting of his capacity and creative ability." He then went on to acknowledge the impossibility of not believing in *something*, although the closest he has come to defining that elusive something appears to make of it a kind of innate drive toward perfection. "Perfection may be impossible of attainment," he once wrote, "but the demon in us, some vital force, urges us on, and we tread that path from generation to generation."[10] He has more than once stated that his reading of the lessons of history has left him confident of the possibility of an infinite advance for man.

Recently, in January 1956, when it was put to him that these basic assumptions of nineteenth century liberalism were very much on the defensive today, his reply indicated no interest in exploring what he considered an academic question. He readily agreed that faith in the inevitability of human progress had been greatly shaken, but also indicated that although he was prepared to concede that his belief might not be well founded, nevertheless he retained a faith that mankind possessed some strength which made for survival and that as mankind surmounted

---

[9] Nehru Abhinandan Granth Committee, *Nehru Abhinandan Granth: a birthday book presented to Jawaharlal Nehru*, Calcutta, Aryavarta Prakasan Griha, 1949, pp. 136-37.
[10] Nehru, *Discovery of India*, pp. 524-25.

difficulties, each survival also meant the attainment of a relatively higher plane.[11] This "faith" would appear to be the expression of a buoyant optimism of temperament, and of less significance in his make-up than are doubt, self-questioning, and the quest for rationality.

The balance between intellect and action is in Nehru observably delicate and sensitive—a source at once of a certain surface irritability and a fundamental dependability. Nehru's sincerity is of that disquieting sort which appears at virtually all times to force him to observe himself, and sometimes to go further and observe himself in the act of observing himself. His extemporaneous addresses give evidence of the constant self-criticism to which he subjects himself. Many of these addresses may seem diffuse and lacking in the literary quality of his published writings, but they are no less rewarding if read attentively. When he permits himself to think aloud, as he often does, it is possible to observe his critical faculties swiftly reviewing and modifying his statements even as he utters them. In his writings we ordinarily see only the finished product, and not the process, although a published facsimile page in his handwriting gives us a glimpse of this revising process. The neat and orderly page shows few corrections, but those he has made are modifications of too-sweeping statements in the interests of accuracy and sobriety: "which interests nobody" was changed to "which interests few"; "affects nobody" became "affects an even smaller number"; "is entirely based" was modified to read "is in theory at least entirely based."[12] Here we see Nehru's self-discipline at work and can appreciate his sense of responsibility.

In searching out a single word which would most nearly catch the essential quality of Nehru's leadership, the writer was led adjective by adjective to the final choice—"responsible"—in its wide meaning of acceptance of accountability to moral principles. His is the responsibility of the aristocrat who is at once part aesthete and part moralist; it is based upon a high sense of duty, of personal honor, and of loyalty to colleagues, and characterized by a fastidious disdain for unethical methods and unworthy behavior.

It was largely because of these characteristics that the youthful Jawaharlal rose rapidly to a position of influence in the Congress hierarchy, even though he made no secret of holding views considerably to the left

---

[11] Tibor Mende, *Nehru: Conversations on India and World Affairs*, New York, Braziller, 1956, p. 102.

[12] This facsimile page appears between pages 80 and 81 of the *Nehru Abhinandan Granth*.

of the great majority of his colleagues. It was because of these characteristics that although Nehru argued—often passionately—for his viewpoint, when he could not carry the group with him he subordinated smaller issues to the main issue and to the maintenance of unity. The history of Nehru's role in the Congress throughout the 1920's and 1930's is dotted with recurrent crises. He was disturbed by the revivalist aspects of the Khilafat movement, and yet he managed to work well as Congress secretary with Maulana Mohamed Ali as Congress president. He was angry as well as disappointed when Gandhi, early in 1922, called off what appeared to Nehru (then in jail) as a highly successful civil resistance movement because "a mob of villagers had retaliated on some policemen by setting fire to the police station and burning half a dozen policemen in it." The success of the Salt Satyagraha caught him by surprise. He was sensitive to taunts concerning "the timid Hindu" and to criticism from the left that the Congress had ceased to be a political party and had instead become an organization for the saving of souls. He accepted Gandhi's challenge to point out where he had been wrong, and in the end he usually concluded that Gandhi's decisions had been sound, although all too often put into effect in a manner which "left much to be desired." Gandhi often acted "almost by instinct," Nehru commented, and only later "for the benefit of his surprised and resentful colleagues" made an effort "to clothe his decisions with reasons"—a covering which in Nehru's judgment was "often very inadequate" (p. 85). Throughout the recurrent crises which Gandhi's extraordinary conception of nonviolent revolution created within the Congress leadership, Nehru kept the need for group unity very much in the forefront, much as he occasionally suffered in the process.

Perhaps Nehru's faith in the ability of mankind to rise to higher levels through the surmounting of crises has been nurtured at least in part by awareness of the manner in which his own strength developed under conditions approaching maximum strain. One of the most traumatic of these crises, although it occurred more than twenty years ago, is illuminating enough to be considered in some detail. From it Nehru was taught the hardest and most painful of the many hard lessons he had learned. He wrote, ". . . it is not possible in any vital matter to rely on any one. One must journey through life alone; to rely on others is to invite heartbreak" (p. 507).

Let us turn back to April 1934. Nehru was in prison at the time, where he had served somewhat less than two months of a two-year sentence for sedition (his seventh prison term). His last period of freedom, which had lasted less than six months, had been devoted to an attempt to gain support from Gandhi and other Congress leaders for greater emphasis on the economic program (of a mildly socialist nature) which he had succeeded in persuading the Congress to accept at the last previous session (at Karachi, in March 1931). He had also done what he could to discourage the growing sentiment among Congressmen to give up the struggle and enter the legislatures, as he feared that such action would prove premature. However, it was clear to him that the Congress was not to be kept from participating in future elections, and it therefore occasioned disappointment but no great surprise when he learned from the prison superintendent that Gandhi, with his "wonderful knack . . . of sensing the mass mind," had judged that the time had come when Congress leaders could pursue the goal of independence more fruitfully in legislative halls than in prison cells. When some days later Gandhi's statement of explanation reached him, Nehru, "oppressed and frightened" by its implications, was engulfed in emotional turmoil, feeling that the bonds of allegiance that had held him to Gandhi had snapped (p. 506).

Essentially, the issue which divided them was the old unresolved question: could the Gandhian method of civil disobedience be utilized solely as a political weapon or was it inescapably also a form of religious experience? As Gandhi saw it, civil disobedience carried on according to the strict rules which he had laid down, was "a purely spiritual weapon," and although it could be used for seemingly mundane ends through the instrumentality of men and women who did not understand its spiritual nature, it could only be effective if *directed* by one who did understand it. After much soul searching, consequent upon the discovery that even "a valued companion of long standing" had transgressed the rules—he had been "found reluctant to perform the full prison task . . . preferring his private studies to the allotted task"—Gandhi had reached the conclusion that the spiritual weapon upon which he had centered his hopes for Indian freedom must be used by himself alone. All others were to desist from its use except under his own personal supervision, inasmuch as "spiritual instruments suffer in their potency when their use is taught through non-spiritual media." As to what the civil resisters should do in order to prepare themselves for Gandhi's call, he instructed them to "learn the art and the beauty of self-denial and voluntary poverty" and to immerse themselves in nation-building activities: hand-spinning, hand-weaving, the eradication of untouchability, the spread of Hindu-Muslim unity, and the like.

Gandhi was striving less for independence as such than for the India of his dreams, an India with a message for humanity. Nehru, who was anxious to put an ethically attractive weapon to effective and immediate political use, felt utterly frustrated. Gandhi's statement was a tremendous blow to him on more than one count. As a prisoner, he had himself often been guilty of preferring his books to the allotted prison tasks, but he remained "wholly unrepentant." He had endeavored to live up to worthy standards of conduct, high among which he placed "loyalty to a cause and to one's colleagues." It seemed to him both "monstrous" and "immoral" that "a vast national movement involving scores of thousands directly and millions indirectly" should be thrown out of gear for the error of an individual, even had it been a serious error rather than this "very trivial affair." He was oppressed by a moral arrogance that was so sure of having "discovered truth and the whole of it, that it did not take the trouble to search for it; all that concerned it was to tell others of it." There was other violence than that of the sword. "What of the violence," he demanded, "that comes quietly and often in peaceful garb and starves and kills; or worse still, without doing any outward physical injury, outrages the mind and crushes the spirit and breaks the heart?" (p. 508).

But having cried out in anguish he then melted to tenderness as he thought again of him "who was the cause of this commotion" within him. "What a wonderful man was Gandhiji after all, with his almost irresistible charm and subtle power over people . . . And his services to India, how vast they had been. He had instilled courage and manhood in her people, and discipline and endurance, and the power of joyful sacrifice for a cause, and with all his humility, pride. Courage is the one sure foundation of character, he had said, without courage there is no morality, no religion, no love . . ." (p. 508).

The question with which Nehru had to grapple, however, was not Gandhi's greatness, his services to India, nor even the "tremendous" personal debt to Gandhi of which he felt conscious, but the practical matter of the course of action to be pursued. Poverty and suffering were conditions Nehru was eager to abolish. As far as he was concerned, the "simple peasant life," far from promising true happiness, seemed "almost as bad as imprisonment"—something from which he wished "to drag out even the peasantry." He did not have in mind the urbanization of the peasantry, he hastened to add, but "the spread of urban cultural facilities to rural areas." The idealization of peasant simplicity seemed to Nehru a flight from things of the mind.

To Nehru it appeared that socialism offered the answer to the problems besetting the Indian peasant, and he had once assumed that Gandhi would of necessity eventually reach this same conclusion. This assumption, however, now required reexamination. During the previous December Gandhi had sent Nehru press cuttings of an interview he had given "almost apologising" for Nehru's activities on behalf of socialism and expressing faith that Nehru's "rectitude" would keep him from committing the Congress to "novel" socialist ways. Gandhi's own views appeared to offer a "defence of the big zamindari system" (pp. 477-8). Again in January Gandhi had exasperated Nehru by interpreting the Bihar earthquake as punishment for the sin of untouchability. Why Bihar, if such were the case, Nehru asked; if Gandhi had to explain natural events in this way, would not have been more appropriate, in view of the fact that the Maharaja of Darbhanga was one of the major sufferers, to have called it a judgment on the zamindari system? (p. 490). Nehru had begun to wonder whether the gulf existing between his ideas and Gandhi's was not too great to permit him to remain a member of the Congress Working Committee, when his imprisonment made the question irrelevant.

The year 1934 proved to be a year of decision for the Congress as a movement. Following the suspension of civil disobedience, all but a handful of Congress prisoners—those imprisoned for "sedition"[13]—had been released, and preparations for the November elections at once began to take shape, awaiting final Congress decisions. Nehru, however, was not permitted his accustomed role in the formulation of these decisions. Instead he was suffering solitary confinement, dependent for news on the papers allowed him by prison authorities. Little of the current news was welcome to him. The treatment of the socialists within the Congress particularly aroused his indignation. Just prior to the opening of the Congress session at Patna in May (1934) they had formed an organized group within the Congress (the Congress Socialist Party). Whether because of or in spite of their organization, the issues for which they fought were soundly defeated in the Congress meeting. When it was over, the Congress Working Committee adopted a resolution (obviously aimed at this group) which reminded Congressmen—"in view of the loose talk about the confiscation of private property and necessity

---

[13] The belief was often voiced that this distinction had been drawn for the purpose of keeping Nehru behind bars until after the next Congress session and the November elections. Letters published in G. D. Birla's *In the Shadow of the Mahatma* reveal how greatly the British feared Nehru's influence upon Gandhi.

of class war"—that the Karachi Resolution (introduced by Nehru at the last previous Congress session) neither contemplated confiscation of private property "without just cause or compensation" nor advocated class warfare. Confiscation and class war were both "contrary to the Congress creed of non-violence," the resolution further stated (p. 557).

Whether Nehru, had he been free, would either have succeeded in modifying the decisions taken at Patna or would have resigned from the Working Committee is a question not touched upon in his writings. He did, however, state that he would not immediately have joined the Congress Socialist Party—not for lack of sympathy with their major objectives, but because of an "irresponsible element" to be found among them. He was much disturbed, however, that the Congress had not only turned away from the path he thought he had successfully marked out, but had even accepted as their election platform a program "far more cautious and moderate than any the Congress had sponsored during the past fifteen years." Their action, he presumed, was aimed at "gaining the support of men of property in the coming election" (p. 558).

The Congress Socialists made a final effort to bring Gandhi to their side. Gandhi had gone off to Orissa on his Harijan tour, and Minoo R. Masani walked with him, attempting to convert him. Gandhi listened, read the recommended books, but in the end reduced the Socialists to frustration in typically Gandhian fashion: "I too claim to be a socialist," he told Masani.[14]

Nehru, trying to follow events from his isolated prison cell, became a battleground of conflicting ideas and emotions. Noncooperation seemed to him a tremendous force, but Gandhi's insistence upon pure nonviolence introduced a metaphysical aspect which was very difficult for him to accept. On the other hand, he was aware that it was the ethical aspect which most attracted him. There was a dynamic potential to Gandhi's nonviolence, also, so that it was possible at any moment that Gandhi "might again galvanise the country in a forward movement." Nevertheless, many of the persons attached to Gandhi seemed to Nehru to be either out of touch with reality, or opportunists "interested in maintaining the present order," and taking "shelter under non-violence for this purpose." If present trends continued, and Gandhi succeeded in siphoning off the most active and devoted workers into a life of humble service, the scope for the opportunists would become greater than ever. Most of those currently coming to the fore, Nehru noted, "had studi-

[14] M. R. Masani, "Is Gandhi a Socialist?" in *Gandhiji, His Life and Work*, edited by D. G. Tendulkar *et al.*, Bombay, Karnatak Publishing House, 1944, p. 103.

ously kept aloof from the movement so long as it was risky to join it." In an effort to master the conflict raging within him, Nehru (in June) undertook an assessment of the Congress movement from the time he had first been active in it. In the interests of orderly thinking he decided to frame questions and write down his answers, engaging his mind "in a definite task and so diverting it from worry and depression" (pp. 559-60).

Part of this worry and depression centered upon the serious illness of his wife, Kamala. During August 1934 her illness reached a critical stage, and Nehru was suddenly released from prison to be with her. He did not expect to be at liberty long enough for talks with Gandhi, and therefore, after twenty-seven crowded hours of freedom, sat down at midnight to write Gandhi of Kamala's condition, and poured out much else that was troubling him (pp. 564-5). He wrote of his anguish and utter loneliness upon reading Gandhi's explanation for calling off civil disobedience, and gave expression to some of his distress and bitterness over recent Congress developments. He scolded Gandhi for giving a private meaning to the word "socialism," saying: "A person who declares himself to be an engine-driver and then adds that his engine is of wood and is drawn by bullocks is misusing the word engine-driver." He closed his long letter with a further complaint against the Congress leaders for what he considered misuse of trust property (in connection with Anand Bhawan, the palatial home which Motilal Nehru had turned over to the Congress prior to his death), and declared his intention to take upon himself the complete financial responsibility for its proper upkeep.[15]

Gandhi in his reply took full responsibility for the resolutions which had pained Nehru, but tried to convince him that his grief and disappointment were not well founded. Many of the Congress Socialists were worthy colleagues, Gandhi said, but they were "too much in a hurry." In closing he promised to look further into the trust property (he had not thought there was anything wrong), but delivered a rebuke to Nehru's pride: "I would ask you not to take this matter so personally as you have done. It more becomes your generous nature to give the same credit to your co-workers for regard for your father's memory that you would take for yourself. Let the nation be the custodian of father's memory and you only as one of the nation."

At the time of this exchange of letters, Gandhi had barely terminated

[15] The major part of this letter, excluding the references to Kamala, and all of Gandhi's reply were published for the first time in 1952 in Tendulkar's *Mahatma*, III, 379-85.

a week-long fast which had considerably impaired his strength and Nehru was in a highly charged emotional state consequent upon sudden emergence from "six months of absolute seclusion and little exercise." Had they been able to meet and talk, Gandhi's skill in stressing areas of agreement might once again have succeeded in overshadowing those areas of disagreement of which Nehru was so conscious. However, Nehru was rearrested after a bare eleven days of freedom. Gandhi, "considerably pained" by the letter as Nehru subsequently learned (p. 565), soon thereafter severed "all official or physical connection with the Congress."[16]

To what extent Nehru's letter influenced Gandhi's decision is not clear. Space limitations do not permit extensive consideration here of the available evidence. The writer is inclined to believe that although we know Gandhi had considered such a move before receiving Nehru's letter,[17] nevertheless it was a step he took reluctantly and the pressure to reconsider might well have succeeded but for that letter.[18]

Throughout September and October there was intense excitement over the possibility that Gandhi might leave the Congress, and the papers were filled with pleas that Gandhi reconsider. His final decision was put off from day to day and argued daily in the press, only becoming conclusive with the Bombay Congress session, late in October. Nehru, following Congress developments as best he could from the newspapers supplied him, minimized the significance of Gandhi's withdrawal, saying Gandhi could not "rid himself, even if he wanted to, of his dominating position . . . his personality forces itself on one's attention and cannot be ignored" (p. 574). The papers passed on to Nehru may or may not have carried the rumor from Bombay—and its subsequent denial, although not by Gandhi—that a letter of his was the cause of Gandhi's action. In either case it is doubtful that Nehru, the "explosion" over,

[16] From Gandhi's letter to Patel (then Congress president), dated September 1934 and published in Tendulkar, *Mahatma*, III, 386-88.

[17] See his letter to Mirabehn dated August 7, 1934 in *Gandhi's Letters to a Disciple*, London, Gollancz, 1951, pp. 159-60. He was then "conferring with friends" as to the advisability of such a step.

[18] His letter of resignation (dated September 1934 but not made public at that time) expressed his heaviness of heart at leaving the Congress, and indicated that he did so because "the most intellectual Congressmen" were "hampered" by an "unexampled loyalty" to him, and would otherwise take a course opposite to his. He referred to Nehru's failure to share his ideals, and said that whereas Nehru's "great affection" would wish him to remain, his "reason" would endorse his leaving. "And since a great organization cannot be governed by affections, but by cold reason, it is better for me to retire from a field where my presence results in arresting full play of reason." Tendulkar, *Mahatma*, III, 386-88.

would have credited his letter with that much influence over Gandhi, whom he considered "far and away *the* master figure in India" (p. 573).

It was well that he should not have been burdened with the responsibility for Gandhi's retirement at that time, as another more pressing personal responsibility weighed heavily upon him. He had been returned to prison because medical reports indicated that Kamala was no longer in danger. He had feared, however, that her condition might deteriorate with the shock of his rearrest, and word soon reached him that his fears had been justified. Suggestions also reached him "through various intermediaries" that informal assurances that he would keep away from politics for the remainder of his term—approximately a year and a half—would be sufficient to effect his release. It was also put to him that his presence at his wife's side might make the difference between life and death. However, despite the fact that what he had seen of politics during his eleven days of freedom had filled him with disgust, to give such an assurance was for him "an impossible condition." To be "disloyal to my pledges, to the cause, to my colleagues, to myself," he wrote, would have meant "inflicting a mortal injury on the roots of my being, on almost everything I held sacred." Kamala's own pride and courage spared him the dilemma of having to weigh his honor against her life. He was confident that any assurance on his part to abandon politics "would shock and harm her" (p. 567). Nevertheless the pressure on him must have been intense. It was increased—we must presume deliberately[19]—by the local prison authorities who after informing him that he would be allowed brief visits to his wife twice a week and even fixing the times for these visits, left him in solitude without explanation when the promised days arrived. He was at first allowed brief daily reports on her health, and then these too were stopped. We do not know what newspaper was allowed him during this period, but one Indian newspaper with which the writer is familiar—the *Tribune* (Lahore)—carried frequent items concerning Kamala's deteriorating health: her high temperature, recurrent heart attacks, imperative need for an operation to collapse one lung, and weakness so extreme as to prevent her from turning from one side to the other without assistance. It

[19] Nehru was kept in Alipore Prison, in the environs of Calcutta, through the heat of March and April and into May, when public protest induced the authorities to transfer him to Dehra Dun. Before the transfer went into effect, however, the fence facing his new cell was raised an extra four or five feet to cut off any view of the mountains he loved. (*Autobiography*, p. 553.) It had become a matter of family pride; Nehru's niece wrote later, that the authorities at Allahabad had said: " 'Those damned Nehrus! If we could break them, it would be easy to deal with the rest.' " Nayantara Sahgal, *Prison and Chocolate Cake*, New York, Knopf, 1954, p. 118.

is easy to understand why that September was for Nehru "the longest and most damnable thirty days" that he had ever experienced (p. 567). When he was at length taken to see Kamala early in October she was almost dazed with fever but managed to whisper to him that he was not to give an assurance to government. Kamala thus gave powerful reinforcement to her husband's pride at a time when it had just been under attack by Gandhi.

Taking all these circumstances together, it appears that the principal emotional ties in Nehru's life—to father, mother,[20] and wife, as well as to Gandhi—had become deeply involved in the mental conflict then assailing him. One result was that the effort which had begun as an assessment of the Congress Party's course under Gandhi's leadership went broader and deeper, turning into an inquiry into his own mental development. This inquiry, when published after his eventual release from prison, provided a moving autobiography, by turns reticent and revealing, which immediately won acclaim as a notable contribution to English literature.

In the meantime, however, the "pride: personal, group and national" and the "reluctance to be coerced into anything" along with a deeply ingrained code of loyalty to a cause and to colleagues, had kept him in prison although virtually all other Congress prisoners had been freed. Kamala, dangerously ill, had been removed to a sanitorium in the German Schwarzwald. Nehru was not released until September 1935, when his sentence was suddenly "suspended" because of Kamala's critical condition. Nehru hurried to Europe by air to be with her in her final illness, returning the following March with her ashes.

From the pages of this autobiography, written under great stress, emerges a vivid portrait of Nehru in his forties: a man of principle, unyielding under pressure, but warmly responsive to generosity, sensitive but resilient, logical rather than intuitive, forceful but reflective, explosive but magnanimous, proud but aware of his own deficiencies. He strove to cultivate detachment, "and to some extent I succeeded," he has written, adding this disarming confession: "though not much, I fear, as there is too much of a volcano within me for real detachment. Unexpectedly all my defenses are hurled away and all my detachment goes."[21]

---

[20] During this period he was haunted by the remembrance of his mother's face as it had looked when she came running after him, arms outstretched, when he was being carried off to prison once more after those few days of freedom. (*Autobiography*, p. 565.) For all the seclusion and loneliness in store for him, he was aware that "the real burden . . . had to be shouldered, as always, by the womenfolk. . . ."

[21] Nehru, *Discovery of India*, p. 57.

PERSONALITY AND LEADERSHIP

Space considerations do not permit following his subsequent career in any detail. In his later books[22] can be found the record of his achievements and frustrations during the difficult years just preceding and following the outbreak of war, and of the tensions produced within the Congress as its leaders grappled with the problems which the war forced to a decision. Throughout this stormy period Nehru demonstrated concern for the maintenance of unity within the organization. As Congress president during 1936 and 1937 he placed loyalty to the organization and its main goal, independence, ahead of his own ideas of social reform. He exercised his prerogative in appointing the Congress Working Committee in a manner which made it representative of the Congress organization rather than of his own views. In consequence he suffered considerable frustration, but he could also point to positive achievements. The Congress organization was made much more efficient, and in the 1936-1937 election campaign he established himself as an outstandingly effective leader able to command the love and trust of India's village millions. This election campaign was for him a veritable tour of discovery of India to which he responded with excitement; but on the whole these were frustrating years, and he often longed for respite from political affairs. After the Congress took the decision to form ministries in those provinces in which they had won a majority, he became more and more uneasy over the course of developments. The Congress seemed to him to be losing its edge as a tool for the achievement of independence at the same time that the leftist groups, and particularly the leadership of the peasant organizations, were becoming "astonishingly irresponsible."[23]

Nehru, feeling more and more of a "misfit" in India, decided to go to Europe in the summer of 1938, in the hope of being more useful to the Congress cause there. Fast-moving international events claimed most of his attention. He visited Spain and Czechoslovakia, as well as London, Paris, and Geneva. He was stirred by the heroism which he witnessed in Spain, disgusted and disillusioned by the surrender at Munich. He contrasted the failure of the Czechs to resist with the spirit which India had displayed, and returned home in the fall convinced that the capitalist world, which had demonstrated a lack of both courage and morality, was fast crumbling, leaving the people of the world a choice only as between types of socialism.

[22] *Eighteen Months in India: 1936-1937*, Allahabad, Kitabistan, 1938; *The Unity of India*, New York, John Day, 1941, covering the years 1937-1940; and *The Discovery of India*, New York, John Day, 1946, written in prison in 1944.
[23] Nehru, *The Unity of India*, pp. 105-09.

In preparation for the debacle which he foresaw, he made the strengthening of ties with India's neighbors his main concern. He spent several days in Cairo on his return home, one consequence of which was that a Wafd delegation attended the 1939 Congress session. Later he spent some time in Ceylon, and following that paid a visit to Chiang Kai-shek which was cut short by the outbreak of war.

In the meantime, his comprehension of India's problems had been enlarged by service as chairman of a National Planning Commission established by the Congress. This commission undertook to prepare a ten-year plan for India; but while the reports of the various subcommittees were still under consideration, the commission ceased to function. Nehru was for the eighth time lodged in a British jail.

This is not the place for analysis of the complex tangle of cross-purposes in which the Congress, the Muslim League, the rulers of the princely states, and the British government were caught up during these years. The developments which culminated in the partition of India in 1947 can be assumed to be well known, in outline at least. During these years Gandhi and an important group of Congress leaders, of whom Nehru was one, twice came to the parting of the ways: for the first time in June 1940, as a consequence of the fall of France, and again in 1942 at the time of the Cripps mission. Both times the Congress, having failed to win the requisite concessions from the British, returned again to Gandhi's leadership. The breaks occurred because the full implications of Gandhi's conception of how to conduct a revolution had not been accepted by the majority of his colleagues. But if only a tiny minority could follow Gandhi to the transcendent level to which his overriding concern with nonviolence carried him, the others caught enough of his vision to sustain them through further dreary prison terms, courted voluntarily by them. Nehru for one—whose sentences were always many times heavier than those meted out to others for the same offense—spent the years from the beginning of November 1940 until the end of the war, save for an eight-month interval in late 1941-1942, in a British jail, although he clearly would have much preferred to have been organizing a *free* India as a staunch ally on Britain's side of the war. In the course of the Indian struggle for independence Nehru spent in all somewhat more than nine years (between his thirty-second and fifty-sixth birthdays) behind prison walls.

There is no doubt that these years strengthened and toughened Nehru, and they probably also contributed to the self-knowledge which he appears to possess in unusual degree. By the time Nehru became prime minister of free India he had both by virtue of character and of breadth of experience become uniquely qualified for such a post. In addition to his extensive knowledge of Britain and the European continent, he had had unusually varied experience within India. He had played a vital role in Congress politics for more than two decades; he had worked with peasant groups; he had obtained intimate acquaintance with municipal problems during 1923-1924 when he made a notable record as president of Allahabad municipality; he had been closely connected with the attempts to organize the people in the princely states; he had also grappled with Indian problems on a nationwide basis as chairman of the National Planning Commission. His election tour had carried him over the length and breadth of the land. He possessed good health, a tremendous capacity for hard work, a passion for efficiency, a buoyant temperament able to shake off depression, and a zest for life which relishes a touch of danger.

Acceptance of the discipline imposed by Gandhi had also worked ineradicable alterations within him of a broadly spiritual nature.[24] He has himself suggested that his zestfulness might have taken him on a somewhat different course but for Gandhi's influence. It was contrary to his nature to accept anything on authority which he could not himself understand. In his many differences with Gandhi he argued strenuously for his viewpoint, only to have to yield to Gandhi who, he often later concluded, had been right. Was his self-confidence thereby undermined? It would appear that this might be so from a rather touching statement that he made in the course of an address to a Congress youth training camp, held in New Delhi in September 1955. Nehru had been explaining to them that he was not prepared to accept any views of others, whether on religion, communism, or socialism, unless he could understand them himself; he suddenly broke off to say: "My association with Gandhiji was for many years. You know that he was a great personality, a great man. It becomes harmful to live too close to a great man, for one's personality shrinks; it cannot develop fully. You will see that nobody living near a great man can himself become great. He becomes subdued. He cannot develop creativeness. One cannot grow under the shadow of a big tree. . . ."

Gandhi's prediction of 1942—that when he was gone Nehru would speak his language—has not as yet been fulfilled, nor does it seem likely to be in all particulars. Yet it is probably fair to say that Nehru's appreciation of Gandhi has if anything grown deeper with the years. In

---

[24] See his discussion of Gandhi's influence upon him in Mende, *op.cit.*, pp. 19-36.

insisting to the Congress youth training camp that revolution did not mean violence, Nehru referred to Gandhi as "the greatest revolutionary in our country, of the present age, and of the previous age." Nehru continued: "By his own sacrifice he shook India. He not only shook it, he brought about great changes. This is revolution. He has abolished a thing which was deeply rooted in our society, in the Hindu society, and which many great reformers could not do much about. There was untouchability here. There were many great men—Gokhale, Ranade—who were great reformers, and who used to give big lectures. Their influence on Hindu society was, however, small. Gandhiji uprooted untouchability. . . ."[25]

Nehru is deeply convinced of the importance of right means, and insists that both men and movements are to be judged by the means they employ. Nehru's own leadership, notwithstanding occasional lapses, when judged in these terms, must be rated very high. As an election campaigner, he discards most of the usual methods and devices. His first experience with election campaigns was in 1936-1937. He was not himself a candidate, nor did he speak on behalf of individuals. His only promise was of "unceasing struggle till freedom was attained," and he charged the people "not to vote for the Congress if they disagreed with this objective."[26]

The 1951-1952 election campaign, in which he covered India once again, had the character of an attempt to educate and unify the electorate. This time he was himself a candidate, but he did not campaign in his own constituency. Again, he did not beg for votes, nor did he pander to the prejudices of the district where he spoke. On the contrary, he treated the country "like the head of a clan," as one correspondent put it, telling the people what was wrong with them. He asked them to help strengthen the Congress, to stand united, to rise above petty selfishness, and to forget wrongs and hatred. Whether Congress won or lost was less important than the way the elections were conducted, he told them, for the nation would be judged by the people's conduct. To a shouted interruption asking why corrupt people had been allowed to be Congress candidates, he answered: "Don't vote for them. I am not infallible and I may have made mistakes but if you know they are corrupt and dishonest don't vote for them."[27]

[25] Jawaharlal Nehru, *Towards a New Revolution*, Youth Congress Series, No. 2, New Delhi, Indian National Congress, 1956, pp. 5-6, 13-14.
[26] Nehru, *Discovery of India*, pp. 54-55.
[27] Nehru, as a member of the Congress Central Election Committee, had been involved in the choice of Congress candidates all over India. For the full report of this

Nehru's towering preeminence in India today has led to the expression of concern over undue concentration of power in the hands of a single individual. Democracies do well to make the question of power concentration a continuing concern; but democracies, on the other hand, can also suffer from the bane of mediocrity in leadership. The dilemma can be posed in terms of how to give scope to the functioning of an exceptionally gifted leader while protecting both him and the national institutions against the corrupting influence of power. Sidney Hook, in his study *The Hero in History*, has warned the democratic community to be eternally on guard against the hero and has outlined the dynamics of the hero's descent into demagogy through misuse of the instruments of democracy: the process of corruption begins when the hero panders to the crowd to win majority support; his very success then breeds contempt for the electorate, and with contempt the foundations of democracy have been undermined.

Nehru's leadership of India is poles apart from any such process as this. Pandit Nehru partakes of the character of the pedagogue rather than of the demagogue. He consistently couches his appeal in rational terms, and the enthusiasms he seeks to arouse are large, generous and all-inclusive. He himself is thoroughly aware of the danger latent in the exercise of power, and has distinguished between "what might be called a prophet" and a leader. Was he perhaps thinking of Gandhi and himself when he recently stated the dilemma of leadership? Conceding in his characteristically candid fashion "that there are many things I have to do, which I cannot justify by high principles. I cannot take certain risks about my country," he went on to state: "A prophet, as we all know, speaks the highest truth but is usually stoned for it. He is honored afterwards, no doubt. The leader has to adapt the truth as he sees it to circumstances in order to make it acceptable; because a leader, more especially in a democratic country, will only be a leader in so far as he can carry his people with him. . . . Now, therefore, a leader occupies a difficult and dangerous position. I hope that the leader wants to adhere to principle and the truth as he sees it. But, inevitably, he tends to compromise. . . . Now compromise with truth is a dangerous thing. It has to be done. And once you start compromising, you may go on compromising till you are at the bottom of the pit, because no standards are left. Nevertheless, there is no other way for a leader but to

---

correspondent, including details of local prejudices challenged by Nehru, see L. N. M., "The Greatest Adventure," *National Herald* (Lucknow), January 20, 1952.

adapt himself (remembering always the principle) to circumstances to the extent that he must. Therefore, while I lay down high principles, I recognize that countries cannot, as countries or as governments, function purely on the basis of high principles. They have to consider the facts as they are, the difficulties of a situation, the dangers of it, and adapt themselves to it, but remembering the principles all the time. . . ."[28]

[28] From the text of Prime Minister Nehru's speech at the German Association for Foreign Affairs, Bonn, on July 14, 1956, as released by the Information Service of India, Embassy of India, Washington, D. C.

SUBHAS CHANDRA BOSE: AN INDIAN NATIONAL HERO

CHATTAR SINGH SAMRA

*R*EGION, religion, parentage, caste, and class play important parts in the make-up of a man. The political leadership role of Subhas Chandra Bose as a dynamic leader of Indian nationalism becomes more intelligible when viewed in the perspective of his cultural origins and background.

It is significant to note that unlike Gandhi, who belonged to the trading Vaishya caste, and Jawaharlal Nehru, who comes from the learned and priestly Brahman caste, Subhas Bose was a Kayastha—claimant to the martial status of the Kshatriya caste. It is expected that a Kshatriya will be militant, powerful, and dynamic. To meet force with force is his tradition. Resort to the sword is his way to settle a score. Prompt to visualize the utility of armed resistance, he is slow to grasp the virtues of less positive action against an armed foe. At least so the tradition holds.

In addition to a Kshatriya heritage, there was in the Bose family a tradition of devotion to Shakti, "the primal power" which controls and regulates the creative forces of the universe. Subhas' attachment to Shakti multiplied many fold in his school days when he studied the works of Swami Vivekananda, a foremost expounder of this assertive doctrine, so much so that Subhas was known to make obeisance in public to symbolic representations of Shakti—Goddesses Kali and Durga. This setting of the Kshatriya and Shakta (devotee of Shakti) legacies is important for an understanding of this man who spent the latter half of his forty-eight years seeking political power.

Another notable feature which seems to have influenced the course of Subhas' leadership was that he hailed from Bengal, a center of virulent nationalism. Bengal, it may be recalled, was the first province to pass under British rule and one of the first to initiate agitation for its liquidation. London's conquest of this Gangetic region, wrote Thomas B. Macaulay, resulted from the utter weakness of the Bengali, "enervated by the soft climate and accustomed to peaceful employment." Contended

CHATTAR SINGH SAMRA has been a member of the Modern India Project, University of California at Berkeley.

Macaulay: "There never, perhaps, existed a people so thoroughly fitted by nature and by habit for a foreign yoke."[1]

On the eve of the twentieth century, however, Macaulay's countrymen were to discover with bewilderment that the Bengali was made of sterner stuff. Stung by the conqueror's contempt for Bengal's peaceful nature and inspired by the revivalist dispensations of Hinduism by such men as Ramakrishna and Vivekananda the Bengali began to assert himself.[2] To secure redress of his grievances, he took to the cult of the bomb and revolver—the language he thought that Britain understood best. The Bengali became distinguished for self-sacrifice, courage, and valor. It may be noted that no similar transformation occurred either in Gandhi's Gujarat or in Nehru's United Provinces.

Subhas was a product of revolutionary Bengal. A descendant of the Boses of Mahinagar—a village fourteen miles south of Calcutta. He was born on January 23, 1897, in the home of Janakinath and Prabhavati Bose at Cuttack, then in Bengal and until recently the capital of Orissa. He was the sixth son and the ninth child of his parents. Janakinath was a well-to-do lawyer. He had a "cloak of reserve around him and kept his children at a distance," Subhas tells in his autobiography.[3] Mother Prabhavati was "more humane," although she was also held "in awe by most of her children." However, "to be overawed by my parents was not the only tragedy," says Subhas. "The presence of so many elder brothers and sisters seemed to relegate me to utter insignificance." Thus he started life "with a sense of diffidence." "I lacked innate genius," he remarks modestly, "but had no tendency to shirk hard work. I had, I believe, a subconscious feeling that for mediocre men industry and good behavior are the sole passports to success." While the large family environment helped Subhas to become sociable rather than self-centered, broadminded rather than parochial, it failed, he observes, to "rid me of that shy reserve which was to haunt me for years and which I doubt if

---

[1] T. B. Macaulay, *Lord Clive*, New York, Henry Holt, 1911, pp. 54-55. Subhas Bose remarks in his book, *The Indian Struggle, 1920-1934* (London, Wishart, 1935, p. 336) that Macaulay's "calumny" that Bengalis were "a race of cowards" "went deep into the hearts" of the Bengali people.

[2] The Rowlatt Committee, which was appointed in 1917 by the Indian government to investigate the nature and extent of revolutionary movement in India and to suggest measures to cope with it, recorded Ramakrishna and Vivekananda as among "various powerful influences" which gave rise to the revolutionary movement in Bengal. See Sedition Committee, 1918, *Report*, Calcutta, 1919, pp. 16-17.

[3] These and further comments on Bose's early life come from Subhas Chandra Bose, *An Indian Pilgrim; or, Autobiography of Subhas Chandra Bose, 1897-1920*, Calcutta, Thacker, Spink, 1948, pp. 3-5, 24-32, 40-58, 63-75.

I have yet been able to shake off. Perhaps I was and still remain an introvert."

Subhas' first contact with western ways and education came when, at the age of five, he was admitted into the Protestant European School meant primarily for European and Anglo-Indian children, and run by the Baptist Mission along English lines. He was topmost in studies, but did badly in sports which made him cherish "a poor opinion" of himself. Subhas was at this school for seven years, and it was here that he began to discern the gulf dividing the Indian from the English or Anglo-Indian. He noted that Indian students were not permitted to sit for scholarship examinations; that they were not allowed to join the volunteer corps and shoulder the rifle; that they were fed up with the teaching of the Bible; and that in occasional clashes and bouts between Indian and English or Anglo-Indian boys, sympathies split along racial lines.

It is important to note that these feelings of resentment which Subhas imbibed at this non-Indian school remained dormant during his next four years (1909-1913) in the Indian atmosphere of Ravenshaw Collegiate School. This could have been due partly to his lack of immediate contact with the ruling race and partly to his inner struggle in search of "a central principle, which I could use as a peg to hang my whole life on."

In Quest of the Ideal

"It was a period of acute mental conflict," writes Subhas of the several years he spent in search of a goal of life. Then one day "by sheer accident," he recalls, "I stumbled upon what turned out to be my greatest help in this crisis." The help came from the works of Swami Vivekananda, Ramakrishna's versatile Bengali disciple who was the first Indian to win renown and recognition in the West as an orator and learned interpreter of Hindu religion and culture—a fact which, in Jawaharlal Nehru's words, acted "as a tonic to the depressed and demoralized Hindu mind and gave it self-reliance and some roots in the past."[4]

The Swami's personality and teachings left a lasting imprint on Subhas' sensitive mind. Only fifteen years old, Bose was deeply touched by Vivekananda's crusading call to his countrymen, especially the youth, for service to the motherland, for the regeneration of the Indian masses, and for the elimination of the social evils of caste, bigotry, priestcraft, inaction, and superstition.

[4] Jawaharlal Nehru, *The Discovery of India*, New York, John Day, 1946, p. 338.

Coming from a Kshatriya family with a tradition of Shakti worship, Subhas was particularly impressed by Vivekananda's statements on the acquisition of moral and physical power. "Strength, strength is what the Upanishads speak to me from every page," the Swami exhorted his compatriots. "And the more I read the Upanishads, my friends, my countrymen, the more I weep for you. . . . What we need is strength." If there was any sin in the world it was weakness, asserted Vivekananda. He urged Indian youth to become strong. "You will be nearer to Heaven through football than through the study of [the] Gita . . . You will understand [the] Gita better with biceps, your muscles, a little stronger."[5]

In Vivekananda's precept that the way to salvation lay in service of humanity—*Atmano Mokshartham Jagaddhitya*—Subhas found the goal of his life. The service of humanity presupposed the service of India, and a perfect performance of this service, Subhas learned from Vivekananda's master, Ramakrishna, required self-abnegation and the renunciation of lust and gold. Thus he resolved to serve the motherland and mankind, and to abandon, as a means to this end, worldly pleasures of the senses.

Dedication to this ideal, which was not to assume concrete form for several years, brought radical changes in Subhas' life. It meant, first of all, laxness in studies, although thanks to his brilliant mind he managed to stand second in the matriculation examination of Calcutta University. Renunciation further involved breaking away from parental restraints. "I no longer recited Sanskrit verses inculcating obedience to one's parents; on the contrary, I took to verses which preached defiance." And defiance, it should be noted, was to be the keynote of Subhas' political career. In order to overcome sexual lust, he, like Vivekananda, took the important step of abstaining from marriage—a step which is highly commended in Indian society and culture. To attain spiritual stamina and to transcend sex-consciousness, Subhas took to meditation and yogic disciplines. But when no tangible success attended his initial efforts in these realms, he ran away from home and spent two months at religious places in an unfruitful quest for a living guru for guidance, just as Vivekananda had found such a source in Ramakrishna. However, none of Subhas' self-imposed rigors at renunciation of sensual desires and material cravings troubled him so much as the attempts to sublimate the

[5] Swami Vivekananda, *Complete Works*, 6th edn., Almora, Advaita Ashram, 1948, III, 237-42.

sex instinct. This, in his words, was "the most bitter struggle"—a struggle which he was to lose in the closing years of his life.

Imbued with these ideas of renunciation and service, Subhas joined Presidency College, Calcutta University's premier institution, in June 1913. Here, he gathered around himself a group of like-minded students who were inspired by Vivekananda's gospel. The object of this group was "to bring about a synthesis between religion and nationalism, not merely in the theoretical sphere but in practical life as well." This concept of synthesis later became an important premise in his thinking after he studied Hegel's dialectic. Subhas was impressed by Aurobindo Ghose's "synthesis of Yoga" which showed the way to scale the highest truths by following different yogas. However, it was not Aurobindo's mysticism (which he later criticized), but his call for national renaissance which deeply moved Subhas. He was fired by Aurobindo's passionate summons which urged: "I should like to see some of you becoming great; great not for your own sake, but to make India great, so that she may stand up with head erect amongst the free nations of the world . . . Work that she may prosper, suffer that she might rejoice."

This emerging national consciousness in Subhas was intensified by his contact with Europeans in Calcutta's political atmosphere. Two things, he wrote later, compelled him to develop politically: the offensive behavior of Englishmen in public places, and the national implications of the first World War. What particularly influenced his career in a political direction was the "Oaten affair" which made him a hero in Calcutta. In February 1916 an English professor, E. F. Oaten, was "beaten black and blue" by Indian students for manhandling a student. As one who had organized the student action, Subhas was rusticated for being "the most troublesome man in College." Commenting on the significance of this episode in his life, Subhas writes:

> Little did I then realize the inner significance of the tragic events of 1916. My Principal had expelled me, but he had made my future career. I had established a precedent for myself from which I could not easily depart in future. I had stood up with courage and composure in a crisis and fulfilled my duty. I had developed self-confidence as well as initiative, which was to stand me in good stead in future. I had a foretaste of leadership—though in a very restricted sphere—and of the martyrdom that it involves. In short, I had acquired character and could face the future with equanimity.[6]

[6] Bose, *Indian Pilgrim*, pp. 84, 90-93. For a detailed account of this incident and its implications see Hamendranath Das Gupta, *Subhas Chandra*, Calcutta, Jyoti Prokasalaya, 1946, pp. 14-32.

The university prevented Subhas from joining any other institution for a year, and he spent this period doing social service in villages for victims of cholera and smallpox epidemics. In July 1917 he was permitted to join the Scottish Church College and he took to his studies in earnest. An enterprise which filled him with a feeling of "positive pleasure" and a sense of self-reliance and strength was the soldier's training—a vocation usually denied to "unwarlike" Bengalis in peacetime—that he got in the University unit of the Indian armed force. In 1919 he received his B.A. with first-class honors in philosophy. He was disappointed in his study of western philosophy, for it provided him not with wisdom, as he had hoped, but rather an "intellectual discipline and critical frame of mind."

Soon after receiving his bachelor's degree, Subhas was prevailed upon by his parents to go to England to study for the Indian Civil Service. In October 1919 he joined Cambridge University. He was impressed to note in the new atmosphere a spirit of freedom and initiative, a sense of time and organization, and an *esprit de corps*. In regard to the last term, Dilip Kumar Roy, an intimate classfellow of Bose in India and England, remarks that Subhas often used to "cull his phrases from the military dictionary"—a fact which becomes significant in the light of the last phase in Subhas' career as commander in chief of the Indian National Army. Some of the favorite maxims of Subhas in England were: "India, too, like England, expects every man to do his duty . . . And never court the company of women—no playing with fire if you please." No wonder that austere Bose, unlike the worldly Gandhi of school days in England, kept away from taking dancing lessons. Subhas' racial ego received satisfaction at being served by members of India's master race. "What gives me the greatest joy," he remarked revealingly in a letter, "is to watch the white skin serving me and cleaning my shoes."[7]

In July 1920, after eight months of study, Subhas passed the stiff civil service examinations, ranking fourth in order of merit. Not long afterwards he added to his laurels the Mental and Moral Sciences Tripos from Cambridge. No sooner did he pass the civil service tests than a momentous question agitated his mind: should he join the service which assured a life of ease and comfort, or should he resign and join the nationalist movement, an enterprise which, although in keeping with his ideals of self-abnegation and service, promised nothing but a life of struggle, suffering, and toil? Reflecting on the hazards of the latter

[7] Dilip Kumar Roy, *The Subhash I Knew*, Bombay, Nalanda Publications, 1946, pp. 50-53, 126.

course, he wrote to his brother Sarat Chandra that "for a man of my temperament who has been feeding on ideas which might be called eccentric—the line of least resistance is not the best line to follow. Life loses half its interest if there is no struggle—if there are no risks to be taken. The uncertainties of life are not appalling to one who has not, at heart, worldly ambitions."[8] He did not think he could serve his country and the British government both at the same time. Thus after months of soul-searching, Subhas took an unprecedented step and resigned from the coveted civil service in May 1921 in order to take an active part in the Indian freedom struggle.

Not one Indian in history, Subhas wrote to Sarat, had voluntarily given up the civil service with a patriotic motive, and he wanted to set the example. "The best way to end a Government is to withdraw from it. I say this not because that was Tolstoy's doctrine nor because Gandhi preaches it—but because I have come to believe in it," observed Subhas. Sarat wanted his rebel brother to delay his resignation for a few more months, but the politician in Subhas astutely noted the psychological value of resigning in May when the noncooperation movement was gathering momentum. "If I resign now, I may return by July," he wrote. "In six months' time much water will have flowed through the Ganges. In the absence of adequate response at the right moment, the whole movement might tend to flag, and if response comes too late it may not have any effect." Subhas added prophetically: "I believe it will take years to initiate another such movement and hence I think that the tide in the present movement must be availed of." He contended that the delay in resigning might have "some untoward effect on the movement. I know full well that I can do but little to help the movement—but it will be a great thing if I have the satisfaction of having done my bit."

Thus at midpoint in his forty-eight years of life, Subhas' long-nurtured objective of serving the country took a definite form. The goal had been set, and now began the battle to secure its fulfillment. The restless Bengali had developed, acquired, and exhibited in his boyhood and school days such distinct traits and characteristics as an impatience with half-hearted measures, a lure for a life of adventure, a propensity to fight to the finish; and these qualities had to come into full play on the Indian national scene.

[8] Bose, *Indian Pilgrim*, pp. 126, 132-34.

Achieving the Ideal

Subhas came back from Britain in July 1921, and from then until his death in August 1945 he was in the thick of the struggle for Indian independence, staking his all and summoning his countrymen to greater measures of resistance to the foe. It was with sincerity and selflessness, valor and dynamism, sacrifices and ordeals that he forced his way to national eminence and esteem. His uncompromising hostility toward British rule made him the terror of Britain.[9] On no top-rank nationalist leader, Gandhi and Nehru not excepting, did the wrath of British oppression fall so frequently and relentlessly as on Subhas. He was incarcerated eleven times to serve long terms totaling about seven years. In addition, he spent almost eight years abroad either as an exile or for medical treatment. The more he suffered, the more defiant he grew. He became, in the words of *Newsweek*, "the most implacable British-hater of all Hindu radicals."[10] His long record of suffering greatly endeared him to his countrymen. Gandhi once criticized the government for burying Subhas "alive" in a Mandalay prison.[11] Jawaharlal Nehru, on other occasions, spoke of him as "this brave comrade . . . a dear and valued comrade" who had "suffered enough at the cost of his health." Nehru added ruefully: "Helplessly we watch this crushing of our men and women, but this helplessness in the present steels our resolve to end this intolerable condition of our people."[12]

Strange as it may seem, the patriotic drives and attitudes which had led Subhas to undertake the fight against British rule and thus had paved his way to national prominence brought him into frequent conflict with the Gandhian leadership of the Indian National Congress because of its occasional relapses into inaction, constitutionalism, vacillation, and moderation. As a matter of fact, Subhas entered into Indian politics with marked doubts about the Gandhist program for *swaraj*. After his first hour-long interview with the Mahatma in July 1921, the novice came out "depressed and disappointed," for he sensed "a deplorable lack of clarity" in Gandhi's plan of action. His disenchantment with Gandhi,

---

[9] As early as 1930 Bose's extremist position repelled historian Edward Thompson, an Englishman otherwise sympathetic to Indian nationalism. "I honestly cannot see," remarked Thompson, "how an Independent India would find a use for him. His value is when in opposition." See Thompson, *The Reconstruction of India*, London, Faber and Faber, 1930, p. 173.
[10] *Newsweek*, March 16, 1942, p. 34.
[11] D. G. Tendulkar, *Mahatma*, Bombay, 1951, II, 407.
[12] Jawaharlal Nehru, *Toward Freedom*, New York, John Day, 1942, pp. 396, 416-17.

"the virtual dictator" of the Congress, increased further when eight months later the Mahatma called off the civil disobedience movement due to an outbreak of violence. "To sound the order of retreat just when public enthusiasm was reaching the boiling-point," commented Subhas, "was nothing short of a national calamity."[13]

Quite the opposite was the effect on Bose of his first meeting with Deshbandhu ("Friend of the Nation") C. R. Das, the Congress leader from Bengal, who, in Subhas' words, was "a man who knew what he was about ... to whom youthfulness was not a shortcoming but a virtue." Subhas felt that "I had found a leader and I meant to follow him." He found that Deshbandhu, unlike the Mahatma, was clear-headed, fully conscious of his exact role, with the sound political instincts of a practical politician. Das, in Bose's words, "knew more than anyone else that situations favorable for wresting political power from the enemy do not come often and when they do come they do not last long."[14]

Bose followed his acknowledged political guru with such zeal and devotion that Deshbandhu once lauded him as "the best of my jewels." It was under Das's tutelage that Subhas played an active role as organizer, editor, and agitator in the Swaraj Party which was formed in 1923 by Deshbandhu and Pandit Motilal Nehru due to dissatisfaction with the Gandhian program. Deshbandhu's death in June 1925 was a great setback to Subhas. He lost a mentor who could guide him and could exercise restraint over his impulsive actions—the kind of mentor whom Jawaharlal Nehru found in Gandhi.

As early as 1915 Subhas had written that in pursuit of his life's goal "I am not to drift in the current of popular opinion." And he seldom did. He had the audacity to act as he felt even if it meant incurring the wrath of government authorities or of a popular national leader. In 1928, much to the chagrin of some of his friends and followers, he attacked both the Sabarmati and Pondicherry schools of thought, respectively of Gandhi and Aurobindo Ghose: the former for its deprecation of modernism, and its glorification of a bullock-cart economy, its advocacy of soul development at the expense of physical culture and military training; and the latter for its emphasis on yoga and mysticism. The net effect of these preachments, he asserted, was the inculcation not of philosophic but actual passivism. In the vein of his spiritual guru, Vivekananda, he called for a philosophy of activism "inspired by robust optimism."[15]

---

[13] Bose, *Indian Struggle*, pp. 37, 68, 90.   [14] *ibid.*, pp. 69, 130-31.
[15] Jagat S. Bright, ed., *Important Speeches and Writings of Subhas Bose*, Lahore, Indian Printing Works, 1946, pp. 57-58.

This is not to suggest, however, that Subhas as Congressman was reluctant to follow Gandhi's creed of *satyagraha* and its concomitants such as fasts, hartals, boycotts, and imprisonments. In many respects, Subhas followed the Mahatma zealously. However, what caused friction between him and the Mahatma was that with Gandhi nonviolence was an indispensable article of faith, but with Subhas it was an expedient weapon. There were many Gandhian leaders, including Jawaharlal Nehru, who agreed with Subhas on this point, but none of them challenged the Mahatma as did the Bengali firebrand. The attainment of *swaraj* was a constant, consuming passion with Bose and he was prepared to adopt, as he later did, violent means to achieve that end. This prompted Gandhian Pattabhi Sitaramayya to declare: "With Gandhi means are ends. With Subhas ends are means."[16]

Further, the Mahatma was ever ready to negotiate and bargain with Britain. His nonviolent noncooperation movements were, in effect, strategies to wrest more and more concessions from the rulers by exercising an *orderly* mass pressure without precipitating a mass upheaval destructive of social order. He always avoided extreme measures if he could. He was essentially a reformist who at times took revolutionary measures under the compulsion of domestic and international events. Subhas, on the other hand, was essentially a revolutionary who often followed passive programs because of the force of internal and external circumstances. He had little faith in compromise and conciliation, and thus advocated a more radical—a more vigorous—course of action to liberate India. He wanted noncooperation and civil disobedience campaigns to proceed in successive stages culminating in complete surrender on the part of the foe.

An important illustration of this emphasis came in 1929 when the Congress declared itself in favor of complete independence rather than dominion status and authorized Gandhi to launch the civil disobedience campaign to that end. Subhas, seeing the absence of any definite plan to achieve the goal, proposed a resolution that the Congress should aim at establishing a parallel government to paralyze the British regime and should mobilize the forces of youth, the peasantry, and the proletariat. Not only was the resolution roundly defeated, but also its proponent was excluded from the Gandhi-picked Working Committee of the Congress of which Subhas, along with Jawaharlal Nehru, had been a general secretary for two years. Nehru proceeded from his post as general secretary to become, with Mahatma's blessings, the youngest president of the

[16] B. Pattabhi Sitaramayya, *The History of the Indian National Congress*, Bombay, Padma, 1947, II, 679.

PERSONALITY AND LEADERSHIP

Congress. Disillusioned with Congress leadership, Bose announced the formation of a Congress Democratic Party. But before long he was behind bars.

The Gandhi-Bose disagreement came to focus in 1933 when the Mahatma unconditionally suspended the civil disobedience movement. Subhas, along with the venerable Vithalbhai Patel, issued a statement from Vienna where both were undergoing treatment, assailing Gandhi's decision as "a confession of failure." Asserting that the Mahatma had failed as a political leader, they declared: "Time has, therefore, come for a radical reorganization of the Congress on a new principle and with a new method. For bringing about this reorganization a change of leadership is necessary ... If the Congress as a whole can undergo this transformation it would be the best course; failing that, a new party will have to be formed within the Congress, composed of all the radical elements." As for the credo of noncooperation, they asserted that the form of noncooperation, "will have to be changed into a more militant one and the fight for freedom will have to be waged on all fronts."[17]

The failure of Gandhi to free India, wrote Subhas Bose in 1934, was the result of his lack of understanding of the character of his adversary, his neglect of the weapons of diplomacy and international propaganda, his effort to reconcile inherently incompatible social interests, and his attempt to play the dual role of a nationalist leader and a world teacher.[18]

Subhas' repeated criticism of Gandhi cost him dearly. Had he followed the Mahatma reverently, he might have challenged Nehru's position as Gandhi's successor, and he might have been alive today leading India. But had this happened, he would not have been the same Bose who chose to tread the unbeaten path and live a life of adventure. It was Gandhi's apprehension about Subhas' dynamic ways which prompted the former twice to prevent the latter from becoming the Congress president. Finally, in 1938, the Mahatma allowed the virile Bengali to succeed to the presidency, apparently in the hope of converting Bose to his (Gandhi's) way of thinking. However, the hope proved futile. In 1939 Subhas, despite Gandhi's opposition, stood for the presidency and won it after a bitter contest with Gandhian Sitaramayya. The Mahatma and his followers struck back with the same weapon they had used to confound John Bull: noncooperation. This worked, and Subhas, hesitant to shoulder the responsibility of a wide-open split in Congress at that

[17] Gordhanbhai I. Patel, *Vithalbhai Patel, Life and Times*, Bombay, R. A. Moramkar, 1930, II, 1219.
[18] Bose, *Indian Struggle*, pp. 229-30.

critical juncture, resigned. A few months later Bose was virtually expelled from the Congress for challenging its policies. The resolution disqualifying Subhas for holding any elective office for three years was drafted by Gandhi, although the Mahatma had not been a Congress member for several years. Nevertheless, the Mahatma continued to regard Subhas as "a leader born" with "a record of great sacrifice to his credit."[19]

Aside from political basis, the conflict between Bose and Gandhi had cultural dimensions. Subhas represented the militant traditions of the Kshatriya and the Shakta. The Mahatma, on the other hand, represented the nonmilitant tradition of the Vaishya. Subhas symbolized the spirit of warriors like Arjuna and Maharana Pratap. Gandhi symbolized, on the contrary, the spirit of Buddha, the apostle of love and nonviolence. Since both leaders tapped and typified the potent ancient currents in Indian culture, both were, and are, honored and idolized by the people with somewhat equal passion.

Like his mentor Deshbandhu Das, who after a disagreement with Gandhian leadership had resigned his position as Congress president to found the Swaraj Party, Subhas after his feud with Gandhi resigned from Congress to form the Forward Bloc, the kind of organization he had been considering for several years, "to serve as a common platform for all the Left elements inside the Congress." The program of the Forward Bloc stated, as an indirect rebuke to Gandhism, that the new body would seek to eliminate mysticism from politics. Using Hegelian dialectic to show the perennial conflict between progress and reaction, Subhas argued that the Forward Bloc was a "historical necessity," in effect an "antithesis" of action and advance against the "thesis" of Gandhian inaction and stagnation. He confidently predicted that the new organization would grow from strength to strength.[20]

However, subsequent events proved otherwise. The causes for the failure of the Forward Bloc were manifold. Unlike Deshbandhu who in forming the Swaraj Party had the support of such national stalwarts as Motilal Nehru, Lala Lajpat Rai, and Vithalbhai Patel, Subhas had little backing from prominent Congressmen. Besides, it was relatively easy in Das's time to defy Gandhian leadership, whereas in the thirties Gandhi had become strongly entrenched. Subhas' following was volatile, heterogeneous, and fragmentary. It consisted of such diverse elements as radical Congressmen, students, Congress Socialists, Royists (M. N. Roy's

---

[19] Tendulkar, *op.cit.*, I, 189-92, 374.
[20] *Forward Bloc*, August 5, 1939, pp. 3-4, 13, 15.

adherents), and Communists; the last three groups deserted ranks within a year. Geographically, most of Bose's followers were centered in areas with traditions of violent nationalism—Bengal, Maharashtra, and the Punjab. In contrast, Gandhi's following was all-Indian, stable, strong, and persuasive. Bose had spent most of his political life either in prison or in exile, thus leaving him little time to build up a personal following like Gandhi's. Lastly, the Forward Bloc's failure to develop into a mass organization was due to the fact that a year after its formation the founder and his leading followers were put in prison, and this action was followed by a ban on the party.

The Forward Bloc was accused of fascist leanings by the British. Some Congressmen, including Jawaharlal Nehru, made similar charges by implication. It was quite possible, said Nehru, that fascist and communal elements might enter the Forward Bloc ranks "to exploit it to further their animus against the Congress and its anti-Fascist policy."[21] Bose angrily replied that if by the term fascist was meant Hitlers, super-Hitlers or budding Hitlers, "then one may say that these specimens of humanity are to be found in the Rightist camp."[22]

In this connection it is important to note that the Bose-Nehru disagreement on fascism went back to the early thirties. In a statement to the press in December 1933 Nehru asserted that "fundamentally the choice before the world today is one between some form of Communism and some form of Fascism, and I am all for the former, that is Communism." Nehru's choice was certainly narrow, and so was Bose's. Subhas argued that both communism and fascism had, despite wide differences in some respects, certain common traits: the supremacy of the state over the individual, one-party dictatorship, planned industrial reorganization, and ruthless suppression of dissenting minorities. Following Hegelian terminology, Subhas regarded the two ideologies as thesis and antithesis and asserted that "the next phase in world-history will produce a synthesis between Communism and Fascism. And will it be a surprise if that synthesis is produced in India?" Subhas wanted India to work out that synthesis, which would consist of the common traits of the two doctrines. He believed in "government by a strong party bound together by military discipline, as the only means of holding India together and preventing a chaos" when India became free.[23] Subhas con-

---

[21] Jawaharlal Nehru, *The Unity of India*, London, Lindsay Drummond, 1941, p. 164.
[22] "Our Critics," *Forward Bloc*, August 19, 1939, p. 3.
[23] Bose, *Indian Struggle*, pp. 345-47.

tinued to hold that belief for the rest of his life. According to him, the solution of Indian problems required economic reforms on a socialistic basis. Since these reforms could not be put through under a democratic form of government, India "must have a political system—a State—of an authoritarian character."[24]

Talking to American correspondent Alfred Tyrnauer in 1933, Subhas had predicted that fascism would inevitably lead to a new world war and that this would offer India "a unique opportunity to emancipate herself from the British yoke."[25] Six years later the war came and Subhas looked upon it as a god-sent opportunity for India to free herself. However, in his efforts to prepare the country for a decisive assault, he found himself excommunicated from the Congress on the one hand, and shut behind bars by the government on the other. The war was on, but Bose was in prison lying idle. In desperation he undertook a fast unto death or release. Fearful of a grave reaction in case of death, the government released Subhas on the ninth day of the fast in December 1940, but placed him under house arrest guarded by sixty-two policemen. However, the government was startled to learn on January 27, 1941, that the Bengali firebrand had escaped from the house despite strict supervision. In February the escapee arrived in Kabul en route to Moscow, but he failed to contact the Soviet embassy.[26] As a last resort, he contacted the German legation which managed to send him to Berlin by air in March. The news of his arrival in Germany was kept secret for a year.

Subhas was in Europe for two years. During this period, his most important activities were the propaganda broadcasts he beamed from Berlin calling upon his countrymen to overthrow British rule. The broadcasts began on February 27, 1942, twelve days after the fall of Singapore, and created a sensation in Britain. "A wireless campaign of unprecedented vehemence," wired the London *Times* correspondent from the German frontier.[27] "The Indian revolution is on," warned the *London Weekly Tribune*. "There is only one possible chance to make up a little of the lost time still to spike the guns of the Bose opposition. Nehru must be asked to become Prime Minister and Minister of Defence . . . Make no mistake. This is not opportunity knocking at our door—it is history battering it down."[28] Goebbels noted with satisfaction

[24] Bright, *op.cit.*, p. 378.
[25] Alfred Tyrnauer, "India's Would-be Fuhrer," *Saturday Evening Post*, March 11, 1944, p. 22.
[26] Uttam Chand, *When Bose Was Ziauddin*, Delhi, Rajkamal, 1946, pp. 14-16, 49-50.
[27] *Times* (London), March 3, 1942.
[28] *Newsweek*, March 16, 1942, p. 35.

that Bose's broadcasts were "gradually getting on the nerves of the British."[29]

In India the reaction to Subhas' campaign was one of hopeful excitement. With British prestige and morale at low ebb, Indians hoped that the Bose factor would put further pressure on London to grant India independence. The prestige of the Bengali firebrand soared high. This was abundantly shown by the profound grief which was expressed by the people at the report of his death in an air crash in March 1942. Anti-Axis Gandhi wired to Subhas' mother: "The whole nation mourns with you the death of your and her brave son. I share your sorrow to the full. May God give you the courage to bear the unexpected loss."[30] After the death report proved false, Mahatma Gandhi and Maulana Azad led the public rejoicing by sending a telegram to Subhas' mother: "Thank God what purported to be authentic has proved to be wrong. We congratulate you and the nation."[31] When asked later by Louis Fischer as to why the anti-fascist Mahatma had shown such heartfelt concern over the life and death of a man who had joined the fascist ranks, Gandhi replied that Bose was "a patriot of patriots," though he was "misguided."[32] Indians loved Bose the patriot, the fighter, the implacable enemy of British imperialism. The impact of his broadcasts was probably the decisive factor which prompted the anti-Axis Congress to launch the "Quit India" movement in August 1942 for fear that if London did not free India the people might welcome the Japanese invaders as liberators.

While in Europe Subhas had interviews with Hitler and Mussolini which were widely published in the press. The talks with Il Duce were more cordial and encouraging than those with the Führer. This distressed cautious Count Ciano who thought that "the value of this youngster [Bose] is not clear" and that "he is trying to turn the water to his mill."[33] Other activities of the Indian exile included the publication of a monthly magazine, *Azad Hind* (Free India), and the organization of a Legion Freies Indien of about a thousand men from among Indian war prisoners. In 1942, after forty-five years of celibacy, Subhas married Fräulein Emilie Schenkl, a Viennese, and his close acquaintance for the past nine years.

[29] Louis B. Lochner, ed., *The Goebbels Diaries, 1942-1943*, New York, Doubleday, 1948, p. 161.
[30] *Tribune* (Lahore), March 30, 1942.
[31] *ibid.*, March 31, 1942.   [32] Tendulkar, *op.cit.*, VI, 122.
[33] Hugh Gibson, ed., *The Ciano Diaries, 1939-1943*, New York, Doubleday, 1946, pp. 363, 481.

In June 1943 Subhas arrived in Tokyo after a perilous submarine voyage from Germany. His mission was to build up an army of liberation and a provisional government from among nearly three million Indians in East Asia. "Only an armed struggle can bring about the freedom of India," declared Subhas over Radio Tokyo. "Nonviolent *satyagraha* alone is not enough to overthrow British rule which is maintained by the sword."[34] His object in leaving India, he explained in a radio broadcast, was "to supplement from the outside the struggle going on at home."[35]

At a gathering of Indians in Singapore on July 4, 1943, Subhas was hailed as Netaji ("Venerable Leader") of the liberation crusade. The following day he declared the formation of the Indian National Army (INA) of 60,000 Indian war prisoners and volunteers. "Comrades! My Soldiers!" Subhas thundered, "Let your battle-cry be: 'To Delhi, to Delhi' . . . You are today the custodians of India's national honour and the embodiment of India's hopes and aspirations . . . For the present, I can offer you nothing except hunger, thirst, suffering, forced marches and death."[36] *Jaya Hind* became the stirring salute of the INA. The army units were named after national leaders: Gandhi, Nehru, Azad, and Bose. A women's regiment was given the name of the heroine of the 1857 uprising—the Rani of Jhansi.

On October 21, 1943, Netaji announced the creation of the Provisional Government of Free India. He became the head of state, prime minister, minister of war, foreign minister, and the supreme commander of the INA. The government was recognized by the Axis powers. Four days after its birth it proclaimed war on Britain and the United States, but not on Soviet Russia, with whom Japan was at peace. It was not until February 1944 that the INA went into action. The following month, after severe fighting, the INA entered Indian territory and raised the tricolor flag on captured British outposts. However, the INA failed to advance any further. The coming of the monsoons, a shortage of food supplies and war materials, the withdrawal of air support by Tokyo for home defense, and Allied reinforcements, all combined to force the INA to fall farther and farther back. In April 1945 the provisional government moved its headquarters to Bangkok. The disintegration of the INA followed in May.

Contemplating the approaching collapse of Japan, Netaji looked, as

---
[34] Arun, ed., *Testament of Subhas Bose*, Delhi, Rajkamal, 1946, p. 143.
[35] Bright, *op.cit.*, p. 327.
[36] *ibid.*, p. 326.

he had in 1941, to the Soviet Union as a power which might become the champion of Indian freedom. "The whole world knows," he declared on May 25, 1945, "that the war aims of Soviet Russia are quite different from those of the Anglo-Americans." In a broadcast on June 19 he urged Indian leaders to reject the British offer of a provisional government because the acceptance of the offer would make India a domestic problem within the British Empire, a fact which would make it impossible for foreign powers such as Soviet Russia "to intervene on behalf of Indian independence." Since the defeat of Germany, he noted, the Soviet Union "has been taking an increasing interest in the affairs of Asia."[37]

However, Netaji was not destined to lead any more struggles. On August 18, 1945, en route to Tokyo, he died after his plane crashed in Formosa. Nevertheless, rumors still abound that he is alive somewhere behind the bamboo curtain waiting for an opportue moment to return. To put an end to these rumors, the Nehru government, although convinced of Netaji's death, appointed a three-member commission in 1956 to investigate the circumstances of the death eleven years after its occurrence. The commission has concluded (with one dissenting vote cast by Subhas' brother Suresh Bose) that Netaji died as a result of the injuries suffered in the reported plane crash.[38]

For his alliance with the Axis, Subhas was condemned by Allied observers by such epithets as "the notorious would-be Quisling," "this Indo-Fascist adventurer," "Goebbels' voice," a "prospective puppet," "the greatest and most sinister figure of the war in Asia," "an agent of Hitler and a tool of the Japanese," "a prized specimen in Hitler's covey of Quislings," a "traitor," "a stooge of Doctor Goebbels," "a criminal type."[39] Likewise, the Communist Party of India, in its fanatic fervor for the "People's War," denounced Subhas as the "arch-traitor to In-

---

[37] Arun, *op.cit.*, pp. 79, 90-91.

[38] The latest rumor about Netaji was set in motion by M. L. Thevar, deputy chairman of the All India Forward Bloc, who declared in Calcutta on February 22, 1956 that he had been in contact with Bose for the last seven years. Bose, he said, was now in Sikiang in China on the Assam border with the full authority of the Chinese government. Netaji, said Thevar, had been leading a section of the "Asian Liberation Army" which was now preparing to "liberate" India from the Anglo-American influences. *Poona Daily News*, February 23, 1956. For the findings of the government inquiry committee see *Netaji Enquiry Committee Report*, New Delhi, 1956.

[39] M. Zaslavsky in *Pravda*, January 7, 1946, quoted in Arun, *op.cit.*, pp. ii-iii; *Times* (London), April 4, 1942; Frederick L. Schuman, *International Politics*, 4th edn., New York, McGraw-Hill, 1948, p. 565; Tyrnauer, *op.cit.*, p. 22; *Newsweek*, March 16, 1942, p. 34; *Times* (London), April 17, 1944; G. C., "The Guilty," *Collier's*, September 30, 1944, p. 52.

dia's freedom," "the henchman of Japanese Imperialism," and the "running dog of Japanese Fascism."[40]

However, the Indian people, excepting the Communists, looked differently at Subhas' concert with the Axis. Gandhi expressed the popular sentiment when on the eve of the Quit India campaign he told Stuart Emeny of the *News Chronicle* that Subhas was "a man of great self-sacrifice, who might have had a distinguished career in the Indian Civil Service, but who is now an exile because he cannot possibly tolerate this helpless condition and feels that he must seek the help of Germany and Japan."[41] The Mahatma's view that Subhas was "a patriot of patriots" was shared by the general public, but Gandhi's belief that the patriot was "misguided" was that of only a small minority. Indians, on the whole, viewed the Subhas-Axis phenomenon in simple national, racial, and psychological terms. They knew and idolized Subhas the dedicated patriot. Their foremost concern being national liberty, they saw eye to eye with the patriot that their enemy's enemy was a friend. They knew a lot about British imperialism, but little or nothing about Axis designs. They rejoiced at the overthrow of the white man's rule in East Asia by an Asian power under the battlecry of "Asia for the Asians." They were thrilled to learn that, with the assistance of that Asian power, their revolutionary leader Subhas had set up an Indian National Army to challenge the mighty British Empire in the field of battle for the emancipation of the motherland. The very idea of an Indian army founded and commanded by an Indian of unquestionable loyalty and patriotism was enough to evoke enthusiasm and applause from an unarmed people long used to watching the displays of Britain's military might. The people's vision on the complex issues of the war was conventional, and was conditioned by feelings of national pride, racial revenge, and repeated frustrations in the freedom struggle.

These feelings were amply manifested during the government's trial of the INA leaders on charges of treason. The Indian people, led by Jawaharlal Nehru, rose to the defense of the INA. Legal defense measures, reinforced by nation-wide demonstrations compelled the government to release the INA leaders and the rank and file members. The agitation touched off by the trial spread the saga of Subhas and his INA throughout India. The members of the INA were welcomed as heroes and *Jaya Hind* became India's popular salute.

[40] Sita Ram Goel, *Netaji and the CPI*, Calcutta, Society for the Defence of Freedom in Asia, 1955, pp. 47-49, 57.
[41] Tendulkar, *op.cit.*, VI, 161.

PERSONALITY AND LEADERSHIP

When in 1940 Subhas urged Gandhi to adopt a drastic course of action against the British, the Mahatma had told him that "if success attended his [Subhas'] effort and India gains her freedom, it will justify his rebellion, and the Congress will not only not condemn his rebellion but welcome him as a saviour."[42] Subhas did organize the rebellion on an unprecedented scale. The rebellion failed, but it generated volcanic forces after the war which brought the dream of freedom remarkably close to realization. Thus Gandhi and the Congress, while disagreeing with Subhas' methods, rushed to hail him as a national hero. The Mahatma admired the spirit of unity which Netaji had infused among his men of various castes and creeds. He significantly noted that Subhas' "most notable" achievements were his activities outside India.[43] Erstwhile adversary Pattabhi Sitaramayya declared that Subhas had proved to the world that India was still "a land of valour and prowess." The name of immortal Subhas, Pattabhi lavishly contended, would endure in history in common with such historic figures as Alexander, Darius, Caesar, Ghenghiz Khan, Timur, Cromwell, and Hitler.[44] Netaji's followers hailed him as India's "saviour" and "patriot saint."[45] Philosopher Sarvapalli Radhakrishnan observed that future generations would read the amazing story of Subhas' life "with pride and reverence, and salute him as one of the great heroes who heralded India's dawn."[46]

It is important to bear in mind that these glowing tributes to Subhas were tributes to the sincerity of his motives and the selflessness of his dashing patriotism. They were tributes not to his concert with the fascist powers, but to the purposes he planned to accomplish through that ill-fated alliance. They were tributes to the patriotic spirit and solidarity which Netaji instilled into the minds of the INA. On the part of the antifascist Congress leaders the praise of Netaji might have been prompted to a degree by guilt feelings, since their excommunication of Subhas was an important factor in forcing the Bengali leader to leave India.

What could have happened if the INA had succeeded in overthrowing the British rule in India? This was the question which Indian leaders conspicuously avoided raising while extolling Netaji and his army. During the war Gandhi and Nehru had expressed strong opposition to Sub-

---

[42] *ibid.*, V, 375.
[43] "Netaji's Unique Achievement," in Shri Ram Sharma, ed., *Netaji: His Life and Work*, Agra, Shiva Lal Agarwala, 1948, p. iii.
[44] "Subhas the Immortal," in Sharma, *op.cit.*, pp. 143-44.
[45] See S. A. Ayer, *Unto Him a Witness*, Bombay, Thacker, 1951, p. xxii, and Suniti Kumar Chatterji, "Subhas Chandra Bose: Personal Reminiscences," in Sharma, *op.cit.*, p. 138.
[46] "Netaji Subhas Chandra Bose," in Sharma, *op.cit.*, p. iv.

has' plans for the liberation of India with Axis aid. They were convinced, even from a purely national standpoint, of the dire consequences which could flow from such a course. This was pointed out even by a Subhas admirer, Dilip Kumar Roy. If Subhas had succeeded in his "rash project," stated Roy, "Nippon would then have kept India safe and groaning under its octopus tentacles aided and perhaps shared by Germany and then, for decades to come, we would be exploited and enslaved in a way compared with which our present enslavement would feel like a nursery mimicry of cheerful servitude."[47] When viewed against this background, it would seem that the INA's failure was a necessary part of the enshrining of Subhas as a national hero.

The Leader and his Legacy

The chief legacy of Subhas Chandra Bose is his story of selfless dedication to the cause he lived and died for—the attainment of Indian independence. He did not live to see his dream become a reality, but the forces engendered by his crusading actions were a powerful factor in obtaining the ideal's fulfillment.

Although a brilliant scholar and facile writer, Subhas was no man of thought in a true sense of the term. Fundamentally, he was a man of action, a *karma yogi*, in the tradition of Shivaji. He was happiest and at his best when in action. A skillful organizer and administrator, he had a supreme contempt for halfhearted measures. Unlike most men of action, he was not an extrovert, but an introvert. He was revolutionary without being ruthless. He was an agitator without being an orator. It was the earnestness and directness of his appeals, rather than eloquence or fluency, that inspired his listeners. His tall stature gave dignity to his fiery summons, while the melancholy seriousness of his imposing face impressed the urgency and grimness of the task ahead.

Ideologically, the Bengali leader tended to be pragmatic and eclectic. However, he had come to believe that a synthesis of communism and fascism, modified in terms of the national interest, would serve the needs of underdeveloped India better than some form of democratic government. He believed that for many years following Independence India would need a strong totalitarian form of government in order to strengthen the bonds of nationhood and to build up a socialistic structure of society. Western democracy, in Bose's view, was ill suited for such gigantic tasks.

[47] Roy, *op.cit.*, p. 187.

First and last, Subhas was a nationalist, a fact that accounted for both his political strength and weakness. His staunch patriotism enabled him to visualize better than his internationalist colleagues the realities of power relations in domestic politics, but it also made him lose sight of the true nature and meaning of international trends and their impact on India. His outlook on national and international politics was largely conventional. While understandable in the traditional framework of imperialist rivalry, such an attitude was outmoded by World War II. In his bitter hatred of British imperialism, intensified by personal sufferings, Subhas Bose sought to banish British evil by enlisting the assistance of an evil far more ominous and ruthless—Axis imperialism.

Whatever its hazards and implications, Bose's nationalistic outlook was shared by India's millions whose deep-seated hostility to Britain made them look upon British enemies as virtual friends. From the national viewpoint, Subhas symbolized India's incessant frustrations and failures in the struggle for freedom. His endeavor to defeat one tyranny with the aid of a bigger tyranny was, therefore, more a counsel of desperation than of statesmanship.

As it often happens in the affairs of men and movements, leaders are remembered or forgotten on the basis of their performance in major enterprises of life. So seems to be the case with Subhas Bose. His concert with the Axis powers was the principal and final act of his life, and it is chiefly in terms of this enterprise that he is deified in India and damned in the West.

SARDAR VALLABHBHAI PATEL:
THE PARTY ORGANIZER AS POLITICAL LEADER

BALKRISHNA GOVIND GOKHALE

*F*OR over a quarter of a century Vallabhbhai Jhaverbhai Patel played a dominant role in the history of Indian politics. Along with M. K. Gandhi and Jawaharlal Nehru, he held a position of top leadership in the Indian National Congress. As a leader of the several Gandhian campaigns at Kheda, Borsad, Nagpur, and Bardoli, he displayed remarkable qualities of organizational ability and skill. As a member of the Working Committee of the Congress, he occupied a controlling position over mass activities launched by the Congress. As a leading member of its parliamentary subcommittee, he controlled parliamentary activities with unvarying efficiency. After the transfer of power in 1947 he took over the States Ministry and showed outstanding tact and skill in bringing about the integration of some 500 princely states into the fabric of the evolving Indian Union. His rugged exterior and taciturnity in times of trouble expressed his iron will. Standing in sharp contrast to both Gandhi and Nehru, Patel typified the rise of a new kind of leadership in Indian politics—that of a party organizer controlling the levers of action in a vast, efficient, militant party machine.

Vallabhbhai Patel, one of the five children of Jhaverbhai Patel, was born on October 31, 1875, in the village of Karamsad in the Nadiad District of Gujarat. His ancestors came of sturdy peasant stock: industrious, intelligent, and proud. His father, Jhaverbhai, is reported to have participated in the Great Revolt of 1857; though in later life he was more interested in religious affairs, he seems to have bequeathed some of his militancy to his two sons, Vithalbhai and Vallabhbhai. Vallabhbhai spent his childhood under the watchful eye of his mother and her brother and was educated at a village school. Later he went to the English school at Nadiad where he became better known for his agitational activities and his "captaincy of mischief" than for his scholastic achievements. After his graduation from high school, Vallabhbhai passed the district pleaders' (lawyers') examination. Then, in cooperation with his brother, Vithalbhai, he began to practice law in Borsad and Godhra where he be-

BALKRISHNA GOVIND GOKHALE is Professor and Head of the Department of History, Siddharth College, Bombay, India.

came well known for his expert handling of some complicated criminal cases. His rise as a successful lawyer brought him money, and he began to make plans for going to England to qualify as a barrister-at-law. He had to defer his visit for some time in preference to his elder brother, but eventually he went to England where he created a good impression by his studious habits and intelligence. He returned to India in 1913.

On his return Vallabhbhai decided to shift to Ahmedabad, the great textile center, as it offered him better opportunities for the display of his professional talents. The late G. V. Mavlankar, a contemporary of Patel's who later became speaker of the Indian Parliament, described the impression created by the young barrister-at-law in those days in the following words:

> A smart young man dressed in a well-cut suit, with a felt hat worn slightly at an angle, piercing and bright eyes, not given to many words, receiving visitors with just a smile but not entering into any conversation, maintaining firm and pensive looks, appearing to look upon the world with an air of confidence and superiority. Whenever he opened his lips, carrying an impression of sternness and reserve. Such was the new barrister who had come to Ahmedabad for practice. There were in Ahmedabad, at that time, about six barristers, only a couple of whom had busy practices. The new barrister was naturally a centre of attraction for the Junior Bar. His personality, demeanour, etc., had their own attractions—mixed feelings of attraction, respect, awe, and, perhaps, a feeling of subdued resentment at the way in which he seemed to look at others.[1]

Patel was soon a great professional success. He spent his leisure hours at the Gujarat Club, then the rendezvous of the professional and social elite in Ahmedabad. He loved a game of bridge. When Gandhi was speaking at the club one evening Patel sat in a corner and continued his game rather than pay any particular attention to the speaker. But Patel was becoming interested in municipal affairs. He was also interested in the work of the Gujarat Sabha, which later became the Gujarat Provincial Congress Committee. In 1917 he was elected a secretary of the Gujarat Sabha. When Gandhi became its president, there commenced a close association between Patel and Gandhi, an association which was soon to ripen into a lifelong friendship and was to influence profoundly Patel's own life.

The Gujarat Sabha, though not overtly political in its aims and activities, could not but be drawn into the politics of the day. In 1917 the Kheda District in Gujarat had insufficient rainfall and suffered condi-

---

[1] Quoted in P. D. Saggi, ed., *A Nation's Homage*, Bombay, Overseas Publishing House, 1949, pp. 8-9.

tions of scarcity. The farmers had requested the government to reduce revenue dues but the government refused to accede to the request. The Gujarat Sabha leaders interested themselves in the grievances of the peasants and presented petitions to the government on their behalf. When this action failed to move the government, Gandhi decided on "direct" action. As Gandhi was busy elsewhere at that time, Vallabhbhai was nominated as the leader of the campaign. Gandhi could not have made a better choice. Beneath his recently acquired western veneer Patel had preserved the deep peasant influences of his youthful days. He shed his western dress and wore with ease the homespun prescribed by Gandhi. He could speak the peasant's patois with natural felicity and knew the area well. With single-minded devotion he applied himself to the tasks of the new leadership entrusted to him and prepared the peasants for a struggle involving nonpayment of rents. The campaign was successful, and Patel had begun his political career. As Gandhi himself stated: "The Kheda *Satyagraha* marks the beginning of an awakening among the peasants of Gujarat, the beginning of their true political education . . . it was the Kheda campaign that compelled the educated public workers to establish contact with the actual life of the peasants. They learnt to identify with the latter. They found their proper sphere of work, their capacity for sacrifice increased. That Vallabhbhai found himself during this campaign is no small achievement."[2]

Patel had arrived on the Gujarat political scene, and responsibilities of leadership came his way. In 1921 he again showed his flair for organizational work as the chairman of the reception committee of the annual session of the Congress, then held in Ahmedabad. This work involved the collection of funds to defray the expenses of the session, and the drafting of workers to look after the arrangements of the session; in these duties Patel showed remarkable ability. Shortly afterwards he was elected president of the Gujarat Provincial Congress Committee, which established his leadership in Gujarat.

The next event which brought Patel to the forefront as an organizational leader was the Borsad campaign. This event came about as a consequence of a punitive tax imposed by the government on the residents of the Borsad area. The area suffered from the depredations of a notorious dacoit named Babar Deva. The police blamed the failure of their attempts to apprehend this dacoit on the reluctance of the people to cooperate with authority, while the people charged the police with

[2] M. K. Gandhi, *An Autobiography; or, The Story of My Experiments with Truth*, trans. by Mahadev Desai, Ahmedabad, Navajivan, 1945, p. 538.

collusion with the bandit. When the government quartered a special police force in the area and called upon the people to pay a special tax to defray its expenses, the people resented it. Patel took the lead in preparing the people to resist the payment of the extra tax and asked them to stand firm in their resolve. The campaign was a success.

Then came the Nagpur Flag *Satyagraha*. Nagpur authorities had banned the flying of the Congress flag or its being carried in processions in certain areas of the city. The Congress decided to defy the ban and Patel was put in charge of the campaign. Patel successfully drafted recruits to volunteer for a systematic defiance of the ban and soon the jails were filled. Obviously the government could not carry on long in the face of such a movement of passive resistance conducted with vigor and discipline, and so a settlement was made.

But it was the Bardoli campaign that established Patel's position as the undisputed organizational leader of Congress. Bardoli is the easternmost taluk of the Surat District in Gujarat. In its 222 square miles of area it has 137 villages inhabited by as many as six different communities. These are the Patidars—to which community Patel himself belonged—Banias, Anavlas, Muslims, Parsis, and the Raniparaj, a backward tribal group. Its farming population numbered 87,000. In 1928 the government had raised the rate of assessment of agricultural revenue by twenty-five per cent on the assumption that the condition of the peasantry was prosperous. The peasants, on their part, knew that they were far from prosperous and protested against the imposition of the enhanced rates. The government refused to give in to these protests and a campaign of resistance was in the offing. The natural choice of leadership fell on Patel who had already led such campaigns in the past with remarkable skill. Patel organized the peasant masses for determined and disciplined action. He spoke to the peasants calling upon them not to pay the taxes and to take the consequences of their action as disciplined fighters in the cause of justice. The government struck back with forfeitures of the property of the defaulting peasants; during the course of the campaign as many as 5,000 forfeiture notices were served and property running into thousands of rupees in value was put up for auction. But Patel had prepared the people so well that the auctioning program of the government was a failure as very few people were prepared to come forward to buy the goods and chattels of the peasants who were carrying on a struggle against such unjust demands. In the end Bardoli was a great victory for the peasants and won for Patel the title of *sardar* or leader.

An examination of the planning and strategy of this campaign by Patel throws light on the organizational processes that were evolving at this time. The campaign at Bardoli was no haphazard movement. Patel realized that it meant much to the success or failure of the nationalist movement not only in Gujarat but over the country as a whole. He examined the campaign plan carefully. His first task was to create an organization that would galvanize the peasant masses into action and then would provide leadership for the peasants at the different levels of operation during the whole course of the struggle. For this purpose he divided the Bardoli area into four major centers at Bardoli, Sarbhon, Madhi, and Vedcchi, with operational headquarters at Bardoli. Additional centers were opened at Valod, Buhari, Vankaner, Varad, Bamni, Balda, and Kamalcchod. At these eleven centers he appointed his divisional leaders under whose orders the campaign in the area was to be conducted. An efficient courier system relayed information at regular intervals from the various centers to headquarters, and conveyed orders from the supreme leader to the centers. With great care Patel selected his lieutenants, among whom were most of his old trusted workers. He appointed Swami Anand as his personal secretary; Mohanlal Pandya, Ravishankar Maharaj (today an outstanding leader in the *bhoodan* movement), and Darbar Gopaldas were nominated for second-echelon leadership. Under these men worked twelve local commanders. A publicity department was also set up to distribute mimeographed bulletins and pamphlets containing speeches of Patel. In addition to this, the weekly *Navajivan* and the nationalist press were also drafted to disseminate information to the people on the developments in the movement.[3] Each community was led by people in whom the community placed implicit trust. Special attention was paid to the training of women to face the hard tasks of the movement. Patel was on the move constantly, keeping in touch with the centers, holding conferences, and speaking to the peasants—rousing their spirits against the iniquitous demands of the government. The organizational pattern set up during the campaign became a standard pattern for succeeding movements. The main features of this pattern were: a centralized command; a secondary command; an army of field workers trained and disciplined to work uninterrupted through varying conditions; a publicity department insuring the dissemination of information, countering government propaganda and occasionally providing advanced information on the moves of the

---

[3] For details of the campaign see Mahadev M. Desai, *The Story of Bardoli*, Ahmedabad, Navajivan, 1929, pp. 54-60.

opponents; provision of funds, either collected from the area itself before the start of the campaign, or by donations and collections from large centers like Bombay, Surat, or Ahmedabad.

The movement involved, as has been pointed out earlier, some 80,000 people belonging to six different groups. An intense propaganda campaign preparatory to the movement was essential, and this was conducted by Patel and his immediate subordinates, Darbar Gopaldas, Mohanlal Pandya, and Ravishankar Maharaj. Patel kept himself in touch with the secondary and tertiary leadership through frequent conferences and spot visits. A centralized command could work successfully only on the assumption of iron discipline throughout the ranks from the leaders to the field workers. It was during this campaign that Patel developed most of the organizational ideas which he later tried out in mass movements like Dandi and in parliamentary activities. The Bardoli campaign transformed the Congress into a fighting political machine. The principle of a hierarchical leadership with a narrow circle at the top became the set pattern of Congress organization during its period of militant activity.

It was during this campaign that some of the ideological and moral elements in Patel's leadership crystallized. He had come to love the peasant proprietors of Gujarat from whose rustic philosophy he had assimilated his deep religious sense and his faith in individualism. He had assimilated the social and economic ideas of Gandhi as well, and had an unbounded faith in the philosophy of passive resistance propounded by the Mahatma. Through his work in the Textile Labour Association of Ahmedabad he had come to know something of the mind of the Indian industrial worker, although the peasantry always remained his first love. The ruggedness of his peasant sense led him to regard with suspicion all theorizing, particularly Marxist theorizing. His religious attitude and peasant background made him look with distrust, if not horror, on the expropriation theories of Marxism. Later his personal experience with the Communists in the ranks of the Congress created in him a sense of bitter opposition to communism which he openly expressed until the last days of his life.

The Bardoli campaign established Patel as a national leader almost equal in rank to Gandhi. Gandhi's political philosophy and Patel's organizational skill transformed the Congress into a mass party geared for militant action. Before Gandhi and Patel, Indian politics was mainly the concern of the urban middle classes nurtured in the tradition of the nineteenth-century British liberalism and constitutionalism. Tilak, it is true, had led mass movements in 1905, but the scope of the movements of the thirties was more extended and complex. If Gandhi had moralized politics, Patel had "mechanized" political activity designed for mass participation.

Increasingly, as the Congress movement began to acquire a mass basis, the problems of leadership and of finance gained in importance. The new leadership for mass action had to be "professional" in the sense that it was asked to undertake full-time political work. In the old leadership, perhaps with the exception of Tilak, politics had been regarded as a part-time interest. But such part-time leadership clearly was not equipped to lead mass struggles. Again the participation of masses of men in such movements required the existence of an apparatus of leadership, which had to be financed on a massive scale. Such financing required the support of a wealthy middle class whose interests, political and economic, were served by the new movements.

In Gujarat a wealthy entrepreneurial class willing to support political movements, and a leadership which could lead the masses with organizational skill were available. In addition, the homogeneous social composition of the people of Gujarat precluded a split in the mass of followers and thus aided the transformation of the Congress into a militant organization. The social composition of Gujarat was far more homogeneous than that of, say, Maharashtra or Tamilnad. In the latter areas the Brahman—non-Brahman controversy had created obvious splits. Compared to these areas, there was no cleavage between Brahmans and non-Brahmans in Gujarat. Moreover, Gujarat possessed a wealthy mercantile class which was conspicuous by its absence in Maharashtra. In the twenties and thirties the mercantile classes of Gujarat had the capacity to collect and disburse large amounts of money needed to finance political activity. Patel had won the confidence of these classes in Gujarat, Bombay, and other areas of India, and thus was in a position to influence the Congress financially.

In Indian politics, as in the politics of other countries, the personal element exerted a deep and pervasive influence. In the early thirties Gandhi had emerged as the undisputed leader of Indian nationalism and with him Patel was regularly associated. Patel had shown by his leadership of the various campaigns in Gujarat and in Nagpur that he possessed an ability and an efficiency which could scarcely be equaled. As the tempo of the nationalist movement quickened, Gandhi came to rely on Patel for organizational leadership in increasing measure. The Mahatma once said that he and Patel were as one; "we work alike and think alike."[4] Patel was always Gandhi's right-hand man, his operational commander in whom he had implicit trust. If Patel gave Gandhi his unswerving devotion and loyalty, the Mahatma, on his part, relied on Patel to run the party machine efficiently and well.

The growth of the Congress itself as a mass organization had profoundly altered its old structure. At the base there was the ordinary member paying four annas as his annual subscription. Such primary members were organized into taluk committees, which in their turn were controlled by the district committees. Then came the provincial Congress committees which formed, through their delegates, the All India Congress Committee. As this AICC was a numerous body with hundreds of members, executive powers were delegated by it to the Congress president and his Working Committee. Patel was once elected president of the Congress, and was a member of almost every Working Committee and of many of its subcommittees. When the phase of mass movement temporarily ended and that of parliamentary activity began, Patel revealed that his organizational powers could be effective as much in parliamentary activities as in mass action. He had gained valuable experience of municipal affairs in Ahmedabad, and had not a little to do with politicalizing and radicalizing that civic body. This experience helped him understand the problems of parliamentary government when he functioned as a member of the all important parliamentary subcommittee of the Congress Working Committee. This subcommittee controlled the activities of the Congress members in the various provincial legislatures, as well as the Congress Party ministries in the seven provinces in which Congress held a majority of the legislative seats. The subcommittee divided itself into three zones of which the western, comprising the key provinces of Bombay, Madras, and the Central Provinces, was placed in Patel's charge. He was directly responsible for the work of the Congress governments in these provinces and as such wielded tremendous power.

But this power wielded by Patel did not stem from his position in the Working Committee or in its parliamentary subcommittee alone. His membership on these committees was a recognition of his influence in the Congress. In the years after Bardoli, Patel had established cordial relations with a number of provincial leaders. Among them may be mentioned Gangadharrao Deshpande of Karnatak, Patwardhan of Poo-

---

[4] D. G. Tendulkar, *Mahatma*, Bombay, Times of India Press, 1951, IV, 264.

na, Shankarrao Deo of Maharashtra, K. M. Munshi and B. G. Kher of Bombay, C. Rajagopalachari of Madras, Ravi Shankar Shukla and D. P. Mishra of the Central Provinces, and B. C. Roy of Bengal. To these may be added Pattabhi Sitaramayya of Andhra and S. K. Patil of Bombay, who assumed leadership of the Bombay Congress in the forties. Through these contacts Patel could influence Bombay, Karnatak, Maharashtra, Tamilnad, Andhra, the Central Provinces, and Bengal. And in Gujarat his leadership was unquestioned. Thus Patel was in a unique position to influence the thinking and decisions of provincial Congress committees in major areas of the country. These provincial leaders constituted the second echelon under his leadership. Many of them had their first lessons in organizational work under Patel's inspiration and guidance. The creation of this secondary leadership, ready to step into positions of responsibility when called upon to do so, was a major achievement of Sardar Patel in his work during the thirties and forties.

Patel's work as a member of the parliamentary subcommittee deserves notice here. The function of this committee was to be "in close and constant touch with the work of Congress parties in all the legislatures in the provinces, to advise them in all their activities, and to take necessary action in any case of emergency." Patel was intimately connected with the task of winning the elections held under the Government of India Act of 1935. After the elections he also played a controlling role in the selection of leaders for the legislature parties in the various Congress provinces.

This aspect of his work in Bombay involved him in a controversy in 1937. At that time the late K. F. Nariman was selected for the leadership of the Bombay legislature party and, in consequence, would have been named the first chief minister of Bombay under the constitution. Contrary to expectations, B. G. Kher was elected as leader in the place of Nariman. Nariman complained of interference in this provincial Congress election by Sardar Patel. As K. M. Munshi, a close associate of Sardar Patel states, the Sardar "selected Mr. Kher and commissioned some of us to get the latter's consent. He piloted the activities which ended in Shri Kher's choice as leader. This choice was Sardar's stroke of generalship."[5] Nariman's failure raised bitter controversy, although an investigating committee, consisting of Mahatma Gandhi and Bahadurji, exonerated the Sardar from all accusations and placed blame on

[5] Quoted in Abdul Majid Khan, ed., *Leader by Merit*, Lahore, Indian Printing Works, 1946, p. 83.

Nariman instead. The net result was that Nariman was eliminated from the Congress politics of the province.[6]

It must be appreciated, when considering this controversy, that the circumstances of the times were delicate. The Congress was forming ministries for the first time and the selection of governmental leaders involved great responsibility. Patel was actuated by considerations involving the welfare and the good name of the Congress organization. He had to exercise disciplinary control over Congress members in public office and in the legislatures, the slightest relaxation of which might have resulted in grave damage to the party and to its machine. If the punishment meted out to Mr. Nariman appeared harsh, the circumstances leading to it were also extraordinary.

The Khare episode came about in 1938. Dr. N. B. Khare was elected chief minister of the Central Provinces which had a Congress ministry. There were splits in the team of ministers working with Dr. Khare. In spite of the efforts made by the Congress High Command to arrive at a workable understanding, the differences persisted. Finally Dr. Khare tendered the resignation of his ministry to the governor of the province in an attempt to prepare for a reconstitution of his ministry. The Congress High Command took prompt and drastic action, and declared Dr. Khare unworthy of holding office. As in the Nariman controversy, this episode generated great heat, and charges and countercharges were made frequently.[7] Patel was involved directly in this case since the Central Provinces was one of the provinces for which he was responsible to the parliamentary subcommittee.[8] The Congress Working Committee, in its resolution of July 26, 1938, charged Dr. Khare with "grave errors of judgement" which "exposed the Congress in the C. P. to ridicule and brought down its prestige." Like Nariman, Dr. Khare was pronounced as being unworthy of holding office, or of a position of responsibility in the Congress.

These two cases reveal the nature of the organizational grip which Sardar Patel had over the Congress Party. His actions in both cases must be viewed in the light of Patel's primary interest, which was to maintain the integrity and discipline of the party. The Congress was a

---

[6] The late Mr. K. F. Nariman's case in this controversy is put forth with great vigor by Khurshed D. Anklesaria in his *Conspiracy Unveiled, the Nariman-Patel Controversy*, Bombay, 1938.

[7] Dr. N. B. Khare presented his case in the pamphlet, *To My Countrymen: My Defence*, Nagpur, 1938.

[8] The *Hitavada* of Nagpur described Patel as the "Zone Dictator" in its dispatch of July 10, 1938.

fighting machine and thus had to centralize control and direct the activities of Congressmen at all important points. The Congress had secured victory at the polls; Patel did not want the fruits of this victory to be frittered away by factional disputes and personal rivalries in the provinces. Even during this parliamentary phase, Patel was intent on preserving the character of the Congress as a party machine ready to plunge into mass struggle, if need be, at short notice. The demands of party discipline necessitated ruthlessness in enforcing its norms. A Socialist leader, the late Yusuf Meherally, evaluated Patel's role: "either one agrees with him and is incorporated in his machine or one disagrees with him and is sent to the wall. He has ruthlessly but tactfully eliminated opponents out of his path."[9] Parenthetically, it must be stated, however, that the opponents so "purged" were not his personal rivals, for neither Mr. Nariman nor Dr. N. B. Khare could be described as rivals of Patel in national leadership. Nor was there any question of a struggle for power, for this power was evenly distributed within the national triumvirate comprising Gandhi, Nehru, and Patel. Patel's motives were impersonal and were influenced by considerations of organization and discipline, and in the larger national context.

How effective Patel's opposition could be is exemplified in some other cases. In 1938-1939 the late Subhas Chandra Bose had defeated Dr. Pattabhi Sitaramayya in the election for the presidentship of the Congress in spite of the active support given to the latter by Mahatma Gandhi. Later Bose discovered that he could not constitute his Working Committee without the inclusion of the majority of the Mahatma's trusted and loyal followers, including Patel, Maulana Abul Kalam Azad, and Dr. Rajendra Prasad, and that he could scarcely expect their full, ready, and willing cooperation when he had successfully opposed the Mahatma's wishes. Ultimately Bose's second presidentship broke on the rock of this contradiction and this in turn led to his exit from Congress leadership.

In 1947 Acharya J. B. Kripalani resigned from the presidentship of the Congress. The name of the late Acharya Narendra Deva, a leading Socialist, was suggested as his successor by several prominent Congressmen and was reported to have had the support of Jawaharlal Nehru also. But Patel opposed Narendra Deva, and consequently Dr. Rajendra Prasad was elected President. Patel was stoutly opposed to the Socialists and resisted any attempt on their part to occupy positions of power within the Congress. The last evidence of his influence in the Congress came

---

[9] Quoted in Abdul Majid Khan, *op.cit.*, p. 83.

in 1950, the year of his passing away. At that time Babu Purshottamdas Tandon was nominated for the office of Congress president. Jawaharlal Nehru opposed Tandon and supported Kripalani. Tandon won. The winner enjoyed Patel's support, and Patel's backing counted.

In ideological matters Patel was a conservative. He was suspicious of Marxist ideas and was an unrelenting opponent of Indian Communists. He had always suspected their patriotism, and when they rose in armed insurrection in Telengana in 1948-1949, he suppressed their rebellion with vigorous and stern measures. He implicitly believed that class war was not only unnecessary but also undesirable; he preached cooperation and copartnership between capital and labor. In his religious views he was traditional, although he rarely missed any opportunity of denouncing the obscurantism of the religious fanatics. He was great in his patriotism and in his personal virtues of simplicity and generosity. Nehru, honoring Patel's seventy-fifth birthday, said that Patel was "strong of will and purpose, a great organizer" who "inevitably roused powerful reactions." He was no visionary, but was a realist with the mind and conscience of a peasant. Much of his work after 1935 was done behind the scenes, in committee rooms and small caucus meetings. He selected his men well, and posted them in positions of authority and control in almost all the provinces of India. His contacts with industrialists and commercial magnates enabled him to provide the necessary resources for the Congress in its years of struggle. The party machine, over which he exercised unrelaxing control, was primarily his creation. Effective as a speaker in his own blunt way, he rarely displayed Nehru's flair for abstractions. He rarely spoke on international events; all his attention was riveted on the Congress and on its role in the country. His strength lay in organization, and it was he who was mainly responsible for building his party into a powerful political machine capable of waging mass struggles and also of functioning efficiently as a parliamentary unit. His career was symbolic of the growth of a new phenomenon in Indian politics, namely that the new politics involving masses of men in action had to have a new type of leadership skilled in disciplined organization of secondary leaders, field workers, and a host of helpers engaged in "professional" political activity. That the machine to which he gave form and impetus has preserved its integrity and its efficiency so long after his death is proof of his organizational genius. Most of the provincial Congress chiefs responsible for running the organization today were trained by him.

If the British bequeathed to India its administrative stability in the form of the Indian Civil Service, it was Patel who gave to India after 1947 its political stability through the party organizational framework which he so ably built over several decades. If Gandhi was the prophet of Indian nationalism and Nehru was its philosopher, Patel was the creator of its organizational instrument, through which alone both the ideas of Gandhi and the idealism of Nehru could find adequate and effective expression.

3. POLITICAL INSTITUTIONS

THE formal institutions of politics are the channels through which democracy is exercised, in India as elsewhere. The following selection of papers gives an introduction to Indian political institutions from the Center to the village, and adds a discussion of the thorny issue of language policy that has all-India ramifications.

Robert North opens with an analysis of the members of a central cabinet, followed by Norman Palmer and Irene Tinker discussing the role of the Parliament in the making of political decisions in India. Finally, Morris Opler analyzes elections at the village level and the meaning of village self-government. Readers may wish to reread Professor Opler's paper in conjunction with the papers on "Leadership and Change in the Villages" presented in Section 8.

Selig S. Harrison reviews language policy in India, a subject of considerable controversy within India's formal political institutions, and within and between her political parties. Contrasting the separatist tendencies inherent in the use of regional languages in state legislatures with the pressing need for a unifying linguistic force in India, Harrison examines the possible future of this perplexing question.

THE INDIAN COUNCIL OF MINISTERS: A STUDY OF ORIGINS

ROBERT C. NORTH

Our intention in this paper is to examine the Indian Council of Ministers in terms of individual backgrounds and the chief career characteristics of the various members in their climb to positions of governmental decision-making and authority. From a comparative analysis of the biographical data collected we shall attempt to formulate a number of broad conclusions about the kinds of people who were serving as the executive committee of the Indian Union in 1956, drawing what inferences we can about the social strata from which they have emerged. From time to time we shall compare certain of our findings with parallel characteristics of recent British Cabinets.

Before proceeding with this analysis we should remind ourselves of the council's position within the Indian governmental framework and of the main functions which it serves. The Constitution of the Republic of India, which derives directly from the Government of India Act of 1935, was adopted November 26, 1949, by the Constituent Assembly. Members of this body had been raised to office by elections held during July 1946. Each province had been allocated a number of seats at the ratio of approximately one seat for every million inhabitants. The number of seats was divided among Sikhs, Muslims, "general," and others in proportion to their population in the province. The representatives allocated to each community were elected by members of that community in the provincial legislative assembly.

After Partition and until 1951 the Indian legislature consisted almost entirely of supporters of the Indian National Congress. In the 1951-1952 elections the Congress obtained 74.43 per cent of the seats in the Lok Sabha, or House of the People, on a 45.1 per cent total vote, a record which they repeated in the 1957 elections.

The executive power of the Indian Union, according to constitutional specification, is vested in the President and is to be exercised by him either directly or through appropriate subordinate officers within the government (Article 53). Elected through a process of proportional representation by members of an electoral college consisting of the

ROBERT C. NORTH is a Research Associate at the Hoover Institution on War, Revolution, and Peace; and an Associate Professor of Political Science at Stanford University.

elected members of both houses of Parliament and the elected members of the legislative assemblies of the states (Article 54), the President holds office for a term of five years (Article 56) and is eligible for re-election (Article 57). All executive action of the Government of India is taken in the name of the President (Article 77).

To "aid and advise the President in the exercise of his functions," the Constitution of India provides for a Council of Ministers with the Prime Minister at its head (Article 74). The President appoints the Prime Minister and—with the advice of the latter—the other ministers. Individual ministers hold office during the pleasure of the President, but the Council is held collectively responsible to the House of the People. A minister who for any period of six consecutive months is not a member of either house of the Parliament shall cease to be a minister at the expiration of that period (Article 75).

It is a duty of the President to make rules for the convenient transaction of the business of the Government of India and for the allocation of this business among the ministers (Article 78). The Prime Minister, in turn, must communicate to the President all decisions of the Council of Ministers relating to the administration of the Union and proposals for legislation; furnish such information relating to the administration of Union affairs and proposals for legislation as the President may call for; and submit for the consideration of the Council of Ministers, if the President so requires, any matter on which a decision has been taken by a minister but which has not been considered by the council (Article 78).

These various constitutional provisions establish a parliamentary government generally after the British model. It is characterized, theoretically at least, by responsible government, collective responsibility, and the leadership of the Prime Minister. In practice, moreover, the President—despite his designation as repository of all executive power—leaves the functions of government to the Cabinet in a fashion paralleling that of the British Crown. The Cabinet, in turn, formulates policy, conducts the administration of the Union government, determines its legislative program, and exercises initiative in the introduction and passage of all government legislation.

In its functioning, the government proceeds quite as much on the basis of certain conventions—again largely derived from British practice—as upon the formal provisions of its constitution. The President's choice of Prime Minister, for example, is limited to the leader of the party or group commanding a majority in the House of the People. So, too, while the Prime Minister in selecting his colleagues enjoys considerable latitude, it is assumed, nevertheless, that he cannot ignore the more important men of his own party.

Theoretically, as noted above, the ministers are collectively responsible for the policy and acts of the Cabinet. Moreover, no minister is expected publicly to dissent from Cabinet policy; if his disagreement proves to be fundamental, he resigns. The Cabinet itself is responsible to the legislature and resigns if it is defeated on a major issue in the legislature.

In India it has frequently been difficult to adhere strictly to the principle of collective ministerial responsibility. Before the achievement of responsible government Indian Cabinets were, in fact, coalitions which obtained solidarity through their opposition to British rule.[1] Immediately after Independence, moreover, Cabinet portfolios, especially in the more technical fields, often were assigned on the basis of individual knowledge and practical experience rather than party loyalty or affiliation.

As constituted in 1956, the Union Council of Ministers consisted of the Prime Minister and fifteen other members of the Cabinet, twelve ministers of Cabinet rank, and fourteen deputy ministers. In this study we shall confine ourselves to a consideration of Cabinet members and ministers of Cabinet rank at that time.[2]

COUNCIL OF MINISTERS, 1956

CABINET

Jawaharlal Nehru	Prime Minister; External Affairs
Maulana Abul Kalam Azad	Education; Natural Resources and Scientific Research
Jagjivan Ram	Communications
Rajkumari Amrit Kaur	Health
C. D. Deshmukh	Finance
Gulzarilal Nanda	Planning, Irrigation, and Power
Dr. Kailas Nath Katju	Defense
Govind Ballabh Pant	Home Affairs
T. T. Krishnamachari	Commerce and Industry; Iron and Steel
C. C. Biswas	Law and Minority Affairs
Lal Bahadur Shastri	Transport and Railroads
Sardar Swaran Singh	Works, Housing, and Supply
Khandubhai Desai	Labor
K. C. Reddy	Production

[1] Sidney D. Bailey, *Parliamentary Government in Southern Asia*, New York, International Secretariat, Institute of Pacific Relations, 1953, pp. 66-67.

[2] The Cabinet formed in May 1957 following the general elections had only twelve Cabinet members besides the Prime Minister, fourteen ministers of Cabinet rank and twelve deputy ministers.

Ajit Prasad Jain	Food and Agriculture; Rehabilitation
V. K. Krishna Menon	Minister without Portfolio

MINISTERS OF STATE

Satya Narayan Sinha	Parliamentary Affairs
Mahavir Tyagi	Defense Organization
Dr. B. V. Keskar	Information and Broadcasting
D. P. Karmarkar	Commerce
Dr. Panjabrao S. Deshmukh	Agriculture and Food
H. V. Pataskar	Law
Dr. Syed Mahmud	External Affairs
Keshav Dev Malaviya	Natural Resources and Scientific Research
Manilal Chaturbhai Shah	Revenue and Civil Expenditure
Arun Chandra Guha	Revenue, Defense Expenditure
Meher Chand Khanna	Rehabilitation
Nityanand Kanungo	Industry

The questions now arise, who were these ministers? From what social and educational strata did they emerge? From what parts of India did they come? What language groups did they represent? From what religious communities did they spring? What were their interests and what was the nature of their careers?

To obtain biographical material we first consulted various readily available sources of the "Who's Who" and yearbook variety.[3] Beyond this, we sent questionnaires to a number of governmental agencies and private institutions and also to individual observers,[4] our purpose being to check information yielded by standard references, and also to fill certain gaps—particularly pertaining to caste. In comparing our various yields, we found ourselves confronted—almost inevitably—by occasional conflicts among the data supplied by separate sources. Wherever possible, we achieved some kind of resolution through further search; failing

[3] These sources include: *The Times of India Directory and Year Book Including Who's Who, 1955-1956*, ed. by Frank Moraes, Bombay, Bennett, Coleman, and Co., 1956; G. D. Binani and T. V. Rama Rao, *India at a Glance*, Bombay, Orient Longmans, 1953; *Hindustan Year-Book 1954, 1956*, Calcutta, Sarkar and Sons; Parliament of India, Council of States, *Who's Who, 1952*, New Delhi, 1953; Parliament of India, House of the People, *Who's Who, 1952*, New Delhi, 1952.

[4] In this regard we are especially indebted to the American Embassy, New Delhi; the Democratic Research Service, Bombay; Mrs. Margaret W. Fisher, Indian Press Digests Project, University of California, Berkeley; the Information Services of India, Embassy of India, Washington, D. C.; Girja Kumar, Librarian, Indian Council of World Affairs, New Delhi; Bidyut K. Sarkar, Dr. Laxmi Singhvi, and Ravi S. Sharma, University of California, Berkeley; *The Times of India*, Bombay.

this, we fell back upon our own judgment, or assigned the uncertain item to a "don't know" column.

Members of the 1956 Council of Ministers originated from both the Council of States and the House of the People, eight (28.5 per cent) having been drawn from the former and twenty (71.4 per cent) from the latter. The Cabinet proper consisted of six members (37.5 per cent) belonging to the upper house and ten (62.5 per cent) belonging to the lower house. Among ministers of Cabinet rank, on the other hand, only two (16.6 per cent) were from the Council of States, while the other ten (83.3 per cent) belonged to the House of the People.

All members of the Cabinet and all ministers of Cabinet rank were members of the Congress Party during their tenure in office, though at least five had been active in other parties or organized movements in the past: Arun Chandra Guha, in the Jugantar Party before World War I; M. C. Khanna in the Hindu Mahasabha; Pandit G. B. Pant in the Swaraj Party; Dr. Syed Mahmud in the Khilafat Movement; and Sardar Swaran Singh in the Panthic Panth and Akali Dal groups.

In planning this paper we made tentative—and probably brash—gestures toward an analysis of the political inclinations of individual members of the Council of Ministers. To bolster our own insecure judgments, we tapped a number of independent sources both in the United States and in India, and then looked hopefully for concordance. In this we were over-optimistic. On a few well-known figures there was almost universal agreement, but judgments about many of the others were anything but congruous. In the interests of objectivity, therefore, we abandoned the venture for the time being at least and devoted our attention to somewhat more verifiable data.

It has been stated that the Prime Minister, by convention, must find representation among his advisers from the major states and, indeed, from the various geographical sectors of the country.[5] An examination of the 1956 Council of Ministers reveals, however, that certain states provided a remarkably large proportion both in the Cabinet and among ministers of Cabinet rank, whereas other parts of the country were noticeably under-represented.[6]

[5] M. P. Sharma, *The Government of the Indian Republic*, Allahabad, Kitab Mahal, 1951, p. 125.
[6] States not represented among members of the Council of Ministers were: Assam (population 9,043,707), Manipur (577,635), Tripura (639,029) and Sikkim (137,725) in East India; Travancore-Cochin (9,280,425) and Coorg (229,405) in South India; Saurashtra (4,137,359) and Kutch (567,606) in West India; Hyderabad (18,655,108), Bhopal (836,474) and Vindhya Pradesh (3,574,690) in Central India;

Uttar Pradesh claimed eight members of the council (28.5 per cent), Bombay six (21.4 per cent), and Bihar three (10.7 per cent). West Bengal and Madras provided two (6.2 per cent) apiece, and Delhi, Himachal Pradesh, Punjab, Madhya Pradesh, Madhya Bharat, Orissa, and Mysore one each (3.5 per cent).[7] The under-representation of South India—in view of that region's cultural and linguistic individuality—was particularly notable.

Most members of the Council of Ministers were born in or near the parts of India they represented. Thus, a total of twenty (71 per cent) were native to the Gangean watershed and the Bombay region, while only three—T. T. Krishnamachari, K. C. Reddy, and V. K. Krishna Menon—were born in South India. Mecca was the birthplace of one (Azad), and three were born in what is now Pakistan: one on the Northwest Frontier, one in the Punjab, and one in East Bengal. In view of the strong Brahman influence in South India, it is worth noting that only one council member of that caste came from south of the Vindhyas.

Cabinet members tended to have been born in cities and ministers of Cabinet rank in towns or villages. Three of the former listed Calcutta, Bombay, and Madras as their places of birth;[8] four came from cities with populations between 100,001 and 500,000; three from cities between 20,001 and 100,000; and three from towns and villages of less than 20,000 population. This distribution is not remarkably different from that of British Cabinets for the years 1886-1950.[9] Among ministers of

---

Rajasthan (15,290,797), PEPSU (3,495,685), Jammu and Kashmir (populations unrecorded in 1951 census), Ajmer (693,372) and Bilaspur (129,099) in Northwest India. These population figures are from *Census of India Paper No. 1 of 1952, Final Population Totals—1951 Census*, Delhi, 1952, p. 2.

[7] Population figures for states represented in the council are: Uttar Pradesh 63,215,742; Bombay 35,956,150; Bihar 40,225,947; West Bengal 24,810,308; Madras 57,016,002; Delhi State 1,744,072; Himachal Pradesh 983 367; Punjab 12,641,205; Madhya Pradesh 21, 247,533; Madhya Bharat 7,954,154; Orissa 14,645,946; Mysore 9,074,972. (*ibid.*)

[8] Population of Calcutta is 2,548,677, for Bombay 2,839,270, for Madras 1,416,056; *ibid.*, pp. 24-25.

[9] The distribution of British Cabinet members according to place of birth for the years 1886-1950, according to Thomas E. Summers and Richard B. Fisher, "The British Cabinet," draft memorandum of the RADIR Project, Hoover Institute and Library, Stanford University, California (no date), p. 26, is as follows:

Rural and towns to 2,500	11.0 per cent
Towns 2,501-20,000	7.8
Small cities 20,001-100,000	10.4
Medium cities 100,001-500,000	11.4
Large cities: over 500,001 (except London)	8.1
London	17.6
Unknown	33.7

The unknowns for the Indian Cabinet are 18.7 per cent.

Cabinet rank, one was born in a city belonging to the 100,001-500,000 range; two from cities in the 50,001-100,000 group; one from a city falling between 20,001 and 50,000; and six from towns and villages of less than 20,000 population.[10] A cluster of five Brahmans claimed towns and villages for their places of birth. For the others, as for the non-Brahmans and non-Hindus, there was no distinctive pattern.

Most members of the Council of Ministers spoke Sanskrit-derived languages as their mother tongues. Of these, ten claimed Hindi, four Marathi, three Punjabi, two Urdu, two Bengali, and two Gujarati. Four spoke Oriya, Tamil, Telugu, and Malayalam respectively.[11]

In most cases precise information about paternal professions was not ascertained. Among the 1956 Cabinet members we know that Prime Minister Nehru's father, Motilal Nehru, was a successful lawyer and onetime leader of the opposition in the Central Legislative Assembly; C. D. Deshmukh was another lawyer's son; the father of the one woman in the Council of Ministers, Rajkumari Amrit Kaur, was Raja Sir Harnam Singh of Kapurthala, a small Sikh state in Punjab; the father of Gulzarilal Nanda was the headmaster of a school; and the father of Sardar Swaran Singh was a provincial leader among the Sikhs. Among ministers of Cabinet rank we have found that H. V. Pataskar was the son of a civil judge; the father of Nityanand Kanungo was a district magistrate; S. N. Sinha came from a zamindar family; the father of Dr. Syed Mahmud was also an important landholder. Data about the caste, education, and travel backgrounds of other members of the Council of Ministers will suggest that many, if not most of them, have come from families of stature in their communities.

In forming his Cabinet the Prime Minister, it has been asserted, must bear in mind that as far as possible all the more important communities should be represented among its members. "A Cabinet in which there was no Muslim," according to Professor M. P. Sharma, "or Sikh, or a representative of the Scheduled Castes ... would hardly be a satisfactory one."[12] As constituted in 1956 the Council of Ministers precisely observed this convention: in addition to twelve Hindu members—of whom one belongs to the Scheduled Castes (Jagjivan Ram)—the Cabinet included a Muslim (Azad), a Protestant Christian (Kaur), a Sikh (Singh), and a Jain (Ajit Prasad Jain); ministers of Cabinet rank include eleven Hindus and a Muslim (Mahmud).

[10] The birthplaces of two ministers of Cabinet rank were not ascertained.
[11] The mother tongue of one minister of Cabinet was not ascertained.
[12] Sharma, *op.cit.*, p. 125.

Of the twenty-three Hindus in the 1956 Council of Ministers at least thirteen (46.4 per cent of the Council membership) were Brahmans,[13] seven serving in the Cabinet and six being ministers of Cabinet rank. Among the non-Brahmans, two belong to the Kayastha caste,[14] one (Ram) to the Scheduled Castes, and one to the Kapu.[15]

It is not surprising, perhaps, that members of the Council of Ministers turned out to be a highly educated group. All but two, who describe themselves as privately educated, graduated from colleges or universities in India or abroad. Of the Cabinet members, 93.7 per cent attended institutions of higher education as compared with 76.6 per cent of the British Cabinet members for the period 1886-1950.[16] Twenty-two, including ten Brahmans and eight non-Brahmans, list Indian colleges; eight, three Brahmans and five non-Brahmans, most of them already college graduates, list degrees from Indian universities; five, all but one of them Brahmans, have degrees from British universities including Oxford, Cambridge, Edinburgh, and London; one (Kesker), also a Brahman, received his doctorate in Paris and one, a Muslim (Mahmud), in Germany; another Muslim (Azad) is a graduate of Al Azhar University in Cairo.

The list of degrees held by these men is impressive: ten B.A.'s, three B.Sc.'s (including Ram), ten M.A.'s, three M.S.'s, eight LL.B.'s, two B.L.'s, two Ph.D.'s, two D.Litt.'s, and four LL.D.'s. Nine men held two degrees, five men held three degrees, and one holds five. Two, Lal Bahadur Shastri and Dr. B. V. Keskar, list themselves as Kashi Vidyapeeth. Of those holding two degrees, three are Brahmans, three non-Brahmans, one a Jain, one a Sikh, and one a Muslim. Three Brahmans and one non-Brahman hold three degrees. Krishna Menon with five degrees, one of them honorary, is a non-Brahman.

C. C. Biswas topped the examination lists at Calcutta University. Before studying law, Sardar Swaran Singh took his M.Sc. degree in physics. Pandit K. D. Malaviya has a diploma in oil technology in addition to an M.Sc. The academic career of Khandubhai Desai has been described as "brilliant." Prime Minister Nehru took a Tripos in natural sciences at Cambridge and was later called to the bar from the Inner Temple. C. D. Deshmukh, who also took a Tripos in natural sciences

---

[13] The caste of two ministers of Cabinet rank was not ascertained.
[14] A caste of writers.
[15] A numerous caste of South India, primarily cultivators. In some districts, according to J. H. Hutton (*Caste in India*, 2nd edn., Bombay, Oxford Univ. Press, 1951, p. 282), they rank next to the Brahmans and claim a Rajput origin. They use the title "Reddi."
[16] Summers and Fisher, *op.cit.*, p. 48.

from Cambridge, has the unique distinction of standing first in all his principal examinations leading to the Indian Civil Service; he is also the holder of the Frank Smart Prize in Botany, which he won in 1917. B. V. Keskar took his doctorate, with highest honors, in sociology at the Sorbonne.

A total of eleven members of the Council of Ministers listed the law as their profession. Of Cabinet members, 37.5 per cent are lawyers as compared with 37 per cent of British Cabinet members for the period 1886-1919 and 28.5 per cent for the period 1919-1950.[17] Six of the eleven lawyers in the Indian Council of Ministers are Brahmans. Two council members have been teachers; one (Nanda) is a professor of economics. C. D. Deshmukh had a career in the Indian Civil Service, and Rajkumari Amrit Kaur served eighteen years as Gandhi's secretary. Other professions represented included one member each as businessman, editor, trade union organizer, and judge.

It appeared, however, that only six members of the Council of Ministers could be said to have devoted the weight of their time and energy to nonparty, nongovernment careers. In specific cases, one sometimes finds difficulty in separating the party career from the government career, but eight members of the Council of Ministers appeared to have risen largely through the Congress hierarchy, while the biographies of fourteen showed a concentration of government positions. Of those with predominately government careers, twelve had held primarily legislative posts, one rose through the Indian Civil Service, and one, Krishna Menon, occupied a series of appointive posts including alternate delegate to the United Nations General Assembly, high commissioner for India in London, ambassador for India to Ireland, and delegate to the United Nations General Assembly.

In addition to Krishna Menon, several other members of the Council of Ministers have held important posts in international organizations and conferences. C. C. Biswas was alternate delegate to the General Assembly of the League of Nations in 1936. K. C. Reddy visited the United Kingdom and the Continent in 1945-1946 as representative of the All-India States People's Conference and to attend the International Miners' Conference. B. V. Keskar served as delegate to the United Nations General Assembly in 1950. D. P. Karmarkar was a delegate to the International Conferences on Trade in Geneva and Havana in 1947 and to the United Nations General Assembly in 1949; he was also leader of the Indian delegation to the Economic Committee for Asia and the

[17] *ibid.*, p. 58.

Far East conferences at Lahore (1951) and in Rangoon (1952); during 1952-1953 he was vice-chairman of ECAFE.

Jagjivan Ram was leader of the Indian delegation to the ILO Conference in Geneva in 1947. Rajkumari Amrit Kaur served as deputy leader of the Indian delegation to UNESCO in London in 1945 and Paris in 1946, as leader of the Indian delegation to the World Health Organization for four consecutive years, and was elected president of the WHO Assembly in 1950. C. D. Deshmukh has been a member of the International Bank for Reconstruction and Finance and also chairman of the International Monetary Fund.

Nearly all members of the Council of Ministers have held important posts in various organizations which stand quite apart from their party, government, or professional careers. These include the editorship of an Urdu journal (Azad); the editorship of a law journal (Katju); service on the Executive Council of the Hindu Banaras University (Katju); chancellor of Santiniketan University (Nehru); chairman of the Indian Red Cross (Kaur); president of the Indian Council for Child Welfare (Kaur); president of the Delhi Music Society (Kaur); secretary of the Textile Labor Association (Nanda); presidency of various trade unions (Ram); president of the All-India Depressed Classes League (Ram); and Boy Scout commissioner in Madras (Menon). Dr. P. S. Deshmukh, a Brahman, has served as president of the All-India Federation of Backward Classes.

The biographies of at least nineteen members of the 1956 Council of Ministers record jail terms. Twelve members reported a total of seventy years imprisonment, which yields an average of just under six years apiece. The woman Cabinet member, Rajkumari Amrit Kaur, was imprisoned for two and one-half years. Pandit Keshav Deva Malaviya spent a total of eleven years in various prisons; Arun Chandra Guha spent twenty-three years. The biographies of seven members did not specify the length of prison terms, but record only the number of incarcerations: two were imprisoned once; one was imprisoned three times; three were imprisoned four times; one (Nehru) was imprisoned nine times; and another (Tyagi) was imprisoned eleven times.

The average age of members of the Council of Ministers in 1956 was 57.7 years, there being no significant age difference between Cabinet members and ministers of Cabinet rank. By comparison, the average age in British Cabinets was fifty-five years for the period 1886-1919 and fifty-six years for the period 1919-1950. For the Indians the average age of entering the Council of Ministers was 52.6 years. For British Ministers the average age of entering the Cabinet was forty-six years for the

1886-1919 period and fifty-four years for the 1919-1950 period, or fifty-one years for the 1886-1950 span.[18]

The age of the youngest member of the Council of Ministers in 1956 was forty-six years; the two oldest were sixty-nine. Of the council as it was constituted in 1956, the youngest member at the time of appointment was thirty-nine years, the oldest sixty-eight. Members of the Council of Ministers first reached parliamentary status (that is, membership in the Indian Legislative Assembly, the Constituent Assembly, or the Parliament proper) at an average age of 51.3 years. This contrasts with average ages of thirty-three years and thirty-seven years for the first election to Parliament of British Cabinet ministers for the periods 1886-1919 and 1919-1950 respectively.[19]

Eleven members of the Council of Ministers listed publications in their biographical sketches. Five have written articles on a variety of subjects including history, economics, politics, international relations, law, religion, and agrarian problems. At least five have published book-length nonfiction and one has written novels and short stories. Book titles include: *The Origin and Development of Religion in Vedic Literature* (P. S. Deshmukh); *A History of Wage Adjustment in the Ahmedabad Textile Industry* (Nanda); *A Commentary on the Code of Civil and Criminal Procedures*; *Reminiscences and Experiments in Advocacy*; and *My Parents* (Katju). Krishna Menon once served as a first editor for Pelican Books and editor for the Twentieth Century Library. Prime Minister Nehru's books—his *Autobiography, Glimpses of World History, Soviet Russia, Discovery of India* and others—are known throughout the world.

At least twenty-one members of the 1956 Council of Ministers had been married. Of the remaining seven Rajkumari Amrit Kaur and B. V. Keskar were unmarried; the status of five was not ascertained. Three had lost their wives through death. One of these, C. D. Deshmukh, first married an English woman who died in 1949 leaving one daughter. In 1953 he married Shrimati Durgabai, a member of Parliament from Andhra State.

Members of the Council of Ministers waited longer to marry than is the custom among most of their countrymen. The average age (in the cases of the ten for whom marriage dates were ascertained) was 26.6 years. Of these, the youngest at marriage was eighteen, the oldest forty-two.

[18] *ibid.*, p. 19.
[19] *loc.cit.*

It could not be said that members of the 1956 Council of Ministers were unprolific. The nineteen men who listed children have produced a total of seventy-seven—an average of 4.05 each. Four fathers reported one child; one father reported two children; three fathers reported three children; four fathers reported four children; two fathers reported five children; and six fathers reported six children. Of these seventy-seven offspring, thirty-seven were sons and forty were daughters. C. C. Biswas achieved distinction in a very special way by producing six of these forty daughters.

Fourteen members of the Council of Ministers have listed their hobbies and special interests in published biographical sketches. Gardening, reading, walking, swimming, and mountain climbing appear to be favorite pastimes, but other hobbies include chess, bridge, tennis, badminton, rowing, billiards, photography, philosophy, Sanskrit, civil welfare, beekeeping, "playing with small children," and "helping lepers and other helpless and poor people."

From the data which we have collected it seems clear that there was no typical member of the Council of Ministers in 1956. The group, on the contrary, consisted of individuals with a wide variety of backgrounds and personal characteristics. Yet there are a number of broad generalities which can be formulated about the council as a whole.

A preponderance of its members originated from and represented constituencies in the Bombay area and the Gangean watershed. Cabinet members tended to have been born in cities and ministers of Cabinet rank in towns or villages. Most members of the 1956 Council of Ministers spoke Sanskrit-derived languages as their mother tongues. As a group they appeared to have emerged from relatively well-to-do families. Nearly fifty per cent were Brahmans. Members of the Council of Ministers tended to be highly educated; they held, among them, an impressive number of advanced degrees.

A considerable proportion of the ministers were trained in law. Several had had teaching experience. Most had risen to eminence through careers in the Congress Party or in government. Several had had experience as delegates to the United Nations and other international bodies. At least nineteen had been imprisoned under the British for their political activities.

By and large, then, members of the Council of Ministers were intellectuals; they were strong family men; they had broad and varied interests; and most of them had devoted years of their lives, first to the achievement of independence for India, and now, to its governing.

DECISION MAKING IN THE INDIAN PARLIAMENT

NORMAN D. PALMER AND IRENE TINKER

*T*HE decision-making approach to the study of the Indian Parliament is particularly appropriate if the distinctiveness of Indian political phenomena is to be made clear. Because of its organization, functioning, and place in the political system, the Parliament in India is so much a replica of the "mother of Parliaments" that a strictly institutional survey might suggest a similarity in political process that would be more apparent than real. Such an impression might be strengthened by the observation that many members of Parliament seem to be more familiar with western political thought and institutions than they are with their own heritage. Further, Indians themselves are prone to measure the effectiveness of their own Parliament with that of Great Britain. The first speaker of the Parliament, who himself wielded great influence in the development of Indian parliamentary practice, the late G. V. Mavalankar, referred to British practice as the "ideal" which could only be "reached in the course of time." He reported that Indians "observe all the outward forms of parliamentary government. But it must be admitted so far as the substance is concerned, in India there is much headway to make."[1]

This tendency to judge the Indian Parliament by the British model is encouraged by the preference of many Indian commentators to write in formalistic terms. In a recent book entitled *The Indian Parliament*, many of the thirteen contributions suffer from this tendency.[2] Several others suggest that the major difference between the British and the Indian systems lies with India's written constitution. This "legal" approach leads to intriguing conjectures, but in reality has little to do with the actual functioning of the Indian Parliament. Both of these formal approaches must be avoided if any insight is to be gained into the way the Indian Parliament operates and how decisions in it are actually made. It is particularly important to remember that the Indian Parliament does operate in a unique political environment.

NORMAN D. PALMER is Professor of Political Science at the University of Pennsylvania. Irene Tinker was associated with the Modern India Project at the University of California at Berkeley from 1954 to 1957.

[1] "Parliamentary Life in India," *Parliamentary Affairs*, 1950, IV, 114.
[2] A. B. Lal, ed., *The Indian Parliament*, Allahabad, Chaitanya Publishing Co., 1956.

Underscoring the distinctiveness of the Indian environment Professor William Morris-Jones, in his study of the Indian Parliament as it had developed up to 1954, calls attention to "the degree of strangeness manifested by the various aspects of Indian life" and suggests that in approaching the study of Indian politics the western student of politics "is well advised to be on his guard. He should not assume, for instance, that institutions with familiar names are necessarily performing wholly familiar functions. He should be ready to detect political trends and forces in what he will be tempted to set aside as non-political movements." Morris-Jones warns against assuming that there is only one pattern of Indian political behavior, which is essentially the western pattern with certain special modifications imposed by peculiar features of history and social life, for there exists in India another "level of politics" which "draws its inspiration from religious teachings and represents a development of an aspect of Gandhian politics. It leads its own life, alongside and not wholly unconnected with the world of 'normal' politics, but largely independent of it. It is possible to say that it is not politics at all. . . . But it seems more in keeping with the facts to allow that it is politics, even if it is of a kind quite distinct from that of modern Europe."[3]

Many Indians would seem to prefer politics to exist on this level alone and thus find themselves out of sympathy with the political trends in their country since independence. To them the present government of India is not their idea of the kind of government their country should have; it is a feeble imitation of the western—particularly the British—system; it is moving in the wrong direction; it is not meeting the real needs of India; it has departed from the principles for which they want India to stand. Some of these critics would be happier if the government of India were centered in a kind of glorified ashram at Sevagram instead of in the sham magnificence of the British-built piles in New Delhi, which, they maintain, are quite out of place in the Indian environment and which are objectionable from a symbolic as well as from an architectural point of view. Some, indeed, would seem to prefer no real government at all, but a kind of state of nature or decentralized anarchy which would turn the clock back to earlier or even to nonexistent eras.

More realistically, there are many who realize that India must have a modern government for the modern world, but who nevertheless have a deep distrust of government and authority, and who have particular

[3] W. H. Morris-Jones, *Parliament in India*, Philadelphia, University of Pennsylvania Press, 1957, pp. 2, 37.

misgivings about parliamentary democracy or indeed almost any form of "democracy." Many Indians who believe in parliamentary democracy, moreover, would encumber it with responsibilities and procedures that would greatly hamper its successful operation. Many take a dim view of political parties, elections, constitutional limitations, and other arrangements that are accepted as a matter of course in more mature democracies. The operation of parliamentary democracy in India would be difficult under the best of circumstances; it is further jeopardized by the lack of a substantial democratic tradition in India. Other factors complicating the successful functioning of parliamentary government in India are fissiparous tendencies of many kinds, caste and class and regional, linguistic and religious divisions, and widespread illiteracy and poverty which effectively remove the great majority of the people of India from positive participation in political life, at least on the national level.

It is well to bear in mind these serious handicaps of mind and of environment; but it would be quite unwise to conclude that parliamentary government in India cannot possibly operate because of these handicaps. As a matter of fact, it is operating now and seems to be operating with growing effectiveness, in spite of a multitude of problems and obstacles. There is a danger that real progress may be discounted because such progress runs counter to theoretical preconvictions predicting failure. For to assert a priori that parliamentary democracy because of its roots in western culture lacks the transmissibility that would allow it to function in India is as fallacious as to assume that the Indian Parliament would not be complete until it resembles some imagined British ideal.

Members of Parliament

Thus far we have been mainly concerned with the broad political environment in which the Indian Parliament must operate. Before considering the extent to which the decision-making processes lie within the Union Parliament, it is important to review its membership procedure and committee structure as it existed during the first elected Parliament from 1952 to 1957. Attention will be focused upon the House of the People (Lok Sabha), since, as in most bicameral legislatures, it is the more influential house. Further, the actual status and future of the Council of States (Rajya Sabha) are indeterminant. The Council members themselves are lobbying for equality with the Lok Sabha; in the first session of its existence the Council resisted attempts by the government to limit the question hour to two days, and succeeded in increasing these question periods to four days a week as compared to five in the House.[4] The peculiar habit of ministers introducing or speaking to bills in the upper house while being members of the lower also tends to lend prestige and a semblance of equality to the Council of States. Any possible trend toward increased regional autonomy would further strengthen the upper house. But at present its position as the lesser chamber and its lack of a distinctly states' point of view make it merely a shadow of the lower house.

There were 499 members of the first House of the People of whom ten were nominated; in 1957 the total number of members was increased to 504. Nomination of members is a strictly temporary measure; in both Parliaments the six members from Jammu and Kashmir were nominated, though they should be elected as soon as the political future of that state is settled. The provision for two nominated Anglo-Indians is limited in the constitution to ten years, and is most unlikely to be extended. The special tribal representative from Assam and the member representing the Andaman and Nicobar Islands will eventually be elected. In 1952 the Amindive and Minicoy Islands were granted one nominated representative.

It is perhaps not surprising that over one fifth, 21.6 per cent, of the members of the first Lok Sabha who filled out the official biographical form listed themselves as lawyers. The next largest group in the House was formed by the agriculturists, 9.2 per cent, a term which undoubtedly covered a multitude of landowners. Businessmen and industrialists made up 7.4 per cent of the membership, while another 6.4 per cent considered themselves to be authors or journalists; and 4.4 per cent listed education as their profession. Medical doctors of all persuasions—allopathic, homeopathic, ayurvedic—totaled 3.8 per cent of the House. Using the results of a different questionnaire, Morris-Jones raises the percentage of members occupied on "land" to 19 per cent, those in business to 10 per cent. By adding to these figures those members in other occupations who nonetheless have interests in land or business, he gives these percentages: 24 per cent with land interests; 14 per cent with business interests.[5] Under landed interests are presumably included the four ex-ruling princes and one princess who were elected to the House. In view of the furor raised during the election campaign by Nehru and others who inveighed against princes daring to contest the elections, this low percentage is noteworthy, particularly since it represents exactly half of

[4] *Gazette of India*, May 16, 1952 and July 11, 1952.
[5] Morris-Jones, *op.cit.*, p. 120.

those princes and princesses who contested parliamentary seats.[6] Of the total membership only nineteen, or 3.8 per cent, were women; their party affiliations were: Congress–14; independent–2; Communist–1; Kisan Mazdoor Praja Party–1; Hindu Mahasabha–1.

Statistics on the age of members given by Morris-Jones reveal that the 1952 Parliament was a slightly younger body than the Provisional Parliament, although in both bodies the 40-49 year age group predominated. By parties, the Congress not surprisingly had the largest number of members in the 50-59 year age group while only 27 per cent of its members were below 40 years, as compared with 38 per cent of the Socialist members and 58 per cent of the members of the CPI group. This party differentiation is not carried over into education, for all parties clearly draw upon the educated elite for their members. Over half the members have university degrees, 9 per cent holding degrees from abroad. Only some 15 per cent of the members received no education above high school; however in legislative assemblies perhaps one third of the membership would fall into this category.[7] This elite character of the Parliament is increased by the language problem, for the better educated Indians tend to debate, discuss, and write in English.[8] In Parliament, business is transacted in both English and Hindi although, according to Article 120 of the constitution, any member "who cannot adequately express himself in Hindi or in English" is permitted to address the House in his mother tongue. In retribution for an English-speaking member's speech in Hindi, a Tamil member, who also speaks English well, rose to speak in his mother tongue; it was difficult in the ensuing commotion to hear the member at all. No matter in what language the member speaks there will be many other members who do not understand him for there is no language qualification required of members of Parliament either before or after they are elected, as there is, for instance, in Malaya.

Indeed there is not even a literacy requirement. While it is quite possible for an illiterate voter to exercise his franchise, it would seem an

[6] Princely candidates for seats in assemblies and electoral colleges were more successful with only two of the twenty-three princes and one of the three princesses losing their elections. In addition, over twenty members of important ruling families stood for assembly seats. Three princes and one princess were elected to the Council of States, two of them after being defeated in the popular election.

[7] See tables in Morris-Jones, *op.cit.*, pp. 215-21. For comparable statistics on Britain's elite Parliament see J. F. S. Ross, *Parliamentary Representation*, 2nd edn., London, Eyre and Spottiswoode, 1948, esp. Part IV.

[8] For an elaboration of this problem see Selig S. Harrison's paper in this volume, p. 151ff.

obvious disadvantage for a member of any legislature not to be literate in the language used in the house. Not to be literate in any language at all reduces the member's effectiveness almost to zero. The tragic case of Muchaki Kosa, Scheduled Tribes Member from Bastar in Madhya Pradesh, illustrates this point too well. Kosa is the head of his Maria community and, by local standards, a wealthy and influential man. When he stood against the Congress candidate he won so completely that the Congressman lost his deposit. Aware that Kosa spoke only the little-known language of Mari, the Maharaja of Bastar sent a secretary to accompany Kosa to Delhi. During the first session Kosa faithfully attended the House but spoke to no one for the simple reason that besides his secretary there was no person in Delhi who spoke Mari. The day Parliament prorogued Kosa was seen crying in the lobby and finally, with the help of other tribal members who spoke languages similar to Mari, his story came out.

Kosa had only the foggiest idea what Parliament was; indeed he had never seen a train until he began his trip to Delhi. His secretary put him into the servants' compartment and travelled by first class himself. The secretary had also appropriated Kosa's rooms in New Delhi and forced Kosa to sleep on the terrace; later he had even rented one room to a stranger. Finally, the day before the end of Parliament the secretary had absconded with most of Kosa's salary and his ticket home. The M.P.'s took up a collection to send the distraught member home; the House promised him an official interpreter for the next session—if he ever did return.

It could be argued that if the Maria community is to be represented in Parliament neither a language nor a literacy qualification could possibly be introduced at present, since possibly half a dozen tribals of this group know another language and Mari is not a written language. Kosa could have studied Hindi, for free lessons were offered to all M.P.'s. But until he mastered it his constituency would have in fact been deprived of active representation. Surely every candidate for any elective office should be required to have a reading knowledge of one of the languages recognized by the constitution and to learn to speak the language, or one of the languages, in which proceedings in the legislature are conducted. Without knowing what is happening in Parliament it is patently impossible for members to participate in any sort of decision-making process at all.

Procedures and Committees

Essentially, procedure in Parliament remains close to the British pattern although significant changes have been made, primarily on the initiative of the speaker or his secretariat.[9] The same devices for assuring adequate airing of controversial points are employed. Question hour is an important and lively affair in both houses. M. N. Kaul, Secretary to Parliament, has spent much time abroad studying the techniques used elsewhere, in order to speed Indian replies. There are provisions for short-notice questions relating to matters of great public importance; in such cases the ten-day period for reply is shortened as much as possible. Twice a week, half an hour (from 5:00 to 5:30 P.M.) is allotted for raising discussions on matters of public importance which have been the subject of questions.[10] Adjournment motions are possible, but the speaker has been frugal about granting permission for such debates. Nonetheless there would seem to be sufficient opportunity for any member to obtain answers to his questions and to debate the matter briefly if need be.

In addition, members may ballot for the privilege of introducing private bills, though less time was afforded to such bills in the first session than is normal in the House of Commons. Members may also influence bills as members of the various select committees or joint committees set up by a motion on the more important bills. Members of the important financial committees, the Committee on Public Accounts and the Committee on Estimates, are elected from the houses on the system of proportional representation by means of the single transferable vote. There are also appointive committees such as the Rules Committee, Business Advisory Committee, Committee on Petitions, Committee on Privileges, Committee on Subordinate (delegated) Legislation, and Committee on Government Assurances.

Of all the eleven committees which functioned during the first Parliament, the two finance committees were undoubtedly the most important and influential. Both the Public Accounts Committee and the Estimates Committee were set up in their present forms in 1950. Under the rules of procedure of the Lok Sabha, both committees are charged with examining the financial accounts of the government, the one prior to, the other after expenditure. Enlarging their functions, both committees have concerned themselves with problems of efficiency, waste, and extravagance. They serve, as does Parliament itself, as a channel for grievances; their reports perform a valuable educative service both within Parlia-

---

[9] See Morris-Jones, *op.cit.*, pp. 205 ff.
[10] *Rules of Procedure*, House of the People, C. B. No. 8 and C. B. No. 4.

POLITICAL INSTITUTIONS

ment and without; the committee members themselves receive excellent training in the economics of government. These indirect influences of the committees seem to Morris-Jones to be more important than their direct influence on the government. He comments:

> To a very real extent, this type of committee, inspired as it is by the idea not simply of economy nor even of efficiency alone but also of acting as a check against an oppressive or arbitrary excutive, achieves a special political significance as a substitute for a real Opposition. Indeed, it may well be that in an underdeveloped country—in which there is a wide measure of agreement not only on goals but also on methods—this kind of arrangement may be more suitable.[11]

The Committee on Government Assurances, established in December 1953, deserves special mention as an Indian innovation, and had in the first Parliament the added distinction of being the only committee presided over by a leading member of the opposition, Mrs. Sucheta Kripalani. The rationale of this unique committee is thus explained by Professor N. Srinivasan:

> It is common experience that when criticised Governments are profuse in their assurances that mistakes pointed out will not be repeated, that reparation would be made for any injuries or wrongs complained of and that steps would be taken to implement some particular policy. But no means or machinery exist in democratic countries to enforce the fulfilment of such assurances other than the continued interest of private members. The Committee on Government Assurances set up by the new rules of the House is an attempt to provide such machinery.[12]

These various committees function more as watchdogs than as decision-makers. Advisory standing committees, first introduced into the Central Legislative Assembly in 1922, are no longer part of the Indian Parliament. These committees had at first been selected by the government from an elected panel of names and paralleled departments. At first only four committees were formed due to the reluctance of the government. From 1931 the members of the committees were directly elected and the number of committees gradually increased. In 1947 such committees as then existed were dissolved automatically with the dissolution of Parliament on August 15, 1947. After careful consideration these committees were continued during the life of the Constituent Assembly and of the Provisional Parliament on the ground that there was no opposition group in either legislature.[13]

[11] Morris-Jones, *op.cit.*, pp. 307-08.
[12] N. Srinivasan, *Democratic Government in India*, Calcutta, World Press, 1954, pp. 260-61.
[13] It was of course the same body under different names.

DECISION MAKING IN PARLIAMENT

The tenure of these committees expired on the 31st of March 1952; they were not reconstituted. Four members of the opposition representing various groups demanded on the 4th of July 1952 that the standing committees be revived, but to no avail. The official position is that such committees are inconsistent with true representative government since historically they were consulted before bills were introduced. This procedure would be untenable under fully conceived parliamentary government, so it was felt that the whole system should be abolished.

Presumably the real reason for Congress' refusal to continue standing committees is the fear of having to give information to Communists. Some members, however, insist that the standing committees are invaluable for educating new members as well as being helpful to the minister concerned. N. V. Gadgil said he found his standing committee useful when he was minister of communications and insisted that members could and did influence details of bills.[14] It would seem that some form of standing committees which functioned after the bill was introduced but which had a wider and continuing membership would be a useful institution in promoting the decision-making process in Parliament. Meanwhile the Congress Parliamentary Party committees do substitute for standing committees as far as a majority of the members of the house are concerned.

PARLIAMENTARY PARTIES

India's first Parliament was an overwhelmingly Congress house, with 364 out of the total of 489 elected members contesting the elections as Congressmen.[15] In various by-elections up to November 30, 1953, Congress had lost four seats, bringing down its total to 360 members. However, eight of the ten nominated members sit with the Congress and tend to vote accordingly; only the Anglo-Indian members are identified with the opposition. Nineteen other parties elected representatives to the Parliament, as Table 1 shows. Changes in party strength due to by-elections up to November 30, 1953, gave the Praja Socialists four more members, bringing that combined party (before the Lohia split) up to 26 members in Parliament. The Communists also picked up one seat at the expense of the Jan Sangh when the Jan Sangh leader, Shyama Prasad Mookerjee, died.[16]

---

[14] Interview by Irene Tinker, New Delhi, 1952.
[15] Seven of these Congressmen were declared elected in uncontested constituencies.
[16] By-election statistics are from the *Indian Press Digests*, II, January 1955. For full statistics see *Report on the First General Elections in India, 1951-1952*, 2 vols., Delhi, Election Commission, 1955.

POLITICAL INSTITUTIONS

TABLE 1
Seats won in the House of the People in the
1951-1952 Elections, shown by Party

PARTY	TOTAL SEATS
Indian National Congress	364
Communists and Allies	26[a]
Socialist Party	12
Kisan Mazdoor Praja Party	10
Ganatantra Parishad	5
Hindu Mahasabha	4
Akali Dal	4
Tamilnad Toilers' Party	4
Jan Sangh	3
Ram Rajya Parishad	3
Jharkhand Party	3
Commonweal	3
Scheduled Castes Federation	2
Peasants and Workers Party	2
Revolutionary Socialist Party	2
Lok Sevak Sangh	2
Krishikar Lok Party	1
Forward Bloc (Marxist)	1
Madras Muslim League	1
Travancore Tamilnad Congress	1
Independents	36

[a] Includes seven People's Democratic Front members from Hyderabad and three independents from Travancore who were actually United Front or leftists' candidates.

Opposition Groups

With such a one-sided House, the organization of any form of opposition was difficult. To be recognized as an official party in opposition such a party must have 10% of the total membership in the House of the People, all of them elected on the party ticket. Such parties would be accorded certain privileges accruing to the opposition including the provision of rooms in the Parliament building, regular consultation, presence of its leader at official functions, etc. But no party in either the first or second Parliament had the fifty members required to be so recognized.[17]

After the 1952 elections there was some hope among opposition members that if a conglomerate group could be formed they might become the official opposition by default. There were several attempts, principally by Shyama Prasad Mookerjee and Jaipal Singh, to form a

[17] There is an Opposition Room for the use of all non-Congress members.

group of all the opposition members except the Communists. The situation was fluid for some months. Meanwhile in the Bihar legislature the Jharkhand Party and the Socialists formed an alliance; in Madras the KMP Party went into a united front with the Communists. At the same time the leaders of the Socialists and KMP Party were discussing merger. The election alliance between the Jharkhand Party and the Ganatantra Parishad suggested cooperation in Parliament.

The Socialists balked at joining with communal parties in Parliament and refused to meet with them, but most other noncommunist opposition members tried to form a united opposition group. As the KMP Party–Socialist merger became imminent the KMP Party withdrew from this group. The communalists and caste parties separated from the mere Tribal and Scheduled Castes; Ganatantra Parishad went along with S. P. Mookerjee, while several princes joined with Jaipal Singh. Eventually three major "groups" appeared, but their memberships were in constant flux.[18]

S. P. Mookerjee's group called itself the Democratic Nationalist Party, drew up a group program, and attempted some sort of party discipline.[19] Members of the House who belonged to this group during the 1952 Budget Session included the three members belonging to the Jan Sangh, the five of the Ganatantra Parishad, the four of the Hindu Mahasabha, the four of the Akali Dal, the four of the Tamilnad Toilers' Party, and the three of the Commonweal. Significantly it did not include any members of the Ram Rajya Parishad. Also in the group were seven independents of whom two had had Justice Party support, while another was connected with the Dravidian Federation. One of the independents was Annie Mascarene who had the unasked-for support of the Communists during her campaign in Travancore.[20] Unaccountably the

[18] These groups are primarily House groups though members of the Council frequently join their relevant group. In the Council itself the only group confined to that chamber which was formed in the first session was Professor N. G. Ranga's, consisting of himself and four others. Much of the information concerning these groups came from extensive interviews of persons concerned by Irene Tinker. Lanka Sundaram, in his chapter on "The Role of an Independent Member" in A. B. Lal's *The Indian Parliament*, stresses the fluidity of these groups. Hari Sharan Chhabra's book on *Opposition in the Parliament* (Delhi, New Publishers, 1953) is incomplete and not too reliable.

[19] The program was a mixture of all policies, sounding deceptively progressive and much like the Jan Sangh election manifesto. It included decontrol, an early settlement of the Kashmir dispute "treating this territory as a part of the Indian Union," and carrying on a policy of firmness and reciprocity towards Pakistan. Foreign policy, it believed, should be guided by an enlightened self-interest; education and government should become more efficient; the Preventive Detention Bill should be abolished.

[20] She and a fellow Indian Christian, also in the group, are the only Indian Christian independents in the house; there are Christian members of Parliament in Congress and the Communist Party.

one member of the Forward Bloc (Marxist) in the House also belonged to this group, bringing the temporary total to 31. S. P. Mookerjee functioned as party leader and was by far its most outstanding member, his interventions receiving almost as much press attention as those of Nehru. A Justice-Independent acted as deputy leader, while the Maharaja of Patna (Ganatantra Parishad) was general secretary. The group attempted to debate important issues among its own members and to decide upon a party "line" for debate in the house, imposing a whip except when the member pleaded conscience. The group also selected the speakers from its ranks to debate different bills. While the lists for debating worked rather well during the first session, no party discipline was in fact enforced, only encouraged, for the group was not cohesive enough to establish a real party policy. The Akali flirtation with the Communists in PEPSU upset, but did not destroy, the group.

Even more diffuse was Jaipal Singh's Independent Group of some 14 members. The Jharkhand Party's three members were joined by three rajas, one rajmata, three jagirdars, a cotton magnate, and an ex-president of the Federation of Indian Chambers of Commerce; the pathetic tribal Kosa was listed as a member of the group, due presumably to Jaipal Singh's preeminence as a tribal leader. The group entertained no hopes for party discipline though they occasionally discussed policy informally; their only advantage in grouping themselves was possibly some preference in debates.

After their national merger all members of the House belonging to KMP Party or to the Socialists joined together in the Praja Socialist Party under the leadership of Sucheta Kripalani, and later under Acharya J. B. Kripalani. Socialist Sarangdhar Das acted as deputy leader until Asoka Mehta won a seat in the house. At the time of formation the membership totaled 22, but the maverick Babu Ram Narayan Singh, who stood as a member of the Janata Party of Bihar in alliance with the KMP Party, decided to dissociate himself from the group. The group obeyed a whip and was fairly stable.

The Communists had the most cohesive group in Parliament, consisting of the sixteen official Communist members, plus generally at least six of the seven members of the People's Democratic Front and seven or eight independents who received Communist support. Occasional support from other left wing parties has brought the total of this group to 35.[21] A. K. Gopalan was originally the party leader, while Renu Chakravarti and her fellow Bengali, Hiren Mookerjee, the Communists'

---

[21] See Sundaram in Lal, *op.cit.*, p. 64.

most brilliant and accomplished debaters, have both acted as deputy leaders. The other Communists frequently resorted to shouting and disturbances in order to press their points. On more than one occasion the party staged a walkout both in Parliament and in the state legislatures, a procedure which emphasizes the lack of consensus within the party on parliamentary techniques.[22] Congress is officially patient with them on the theory that their relation to Congress is similar to Congress' old relationship with the British government; both in their time used extraparliamentary means to press their view. On the other hand the Indian press today is unsympathetic to such tactics and gives them poor reporting. Indeed there are many observers who feel the Communists have been discredited both by their techniques and their ineffectiveness within the various legislatures; they claim that it does not suit a revolutionary party to participate in a "bourgeois capitalist Parliament."[23]

A miscellaneous collection of 29 opposition members belonged to no group at all. These included the five members representing the various Marxist parties: the Peasants and Workers, the Revolutionary Socialist Party, and the United Socialist Organization. The two members of the Scheduled Castes Federation in the House remained apart from other members of the House but evidently canvassed Congress Scheduled Castes members whenever any legislation in which they were interested was under discussion. Ram Rayja Parishad's contingent of three members walked about in a world of their own. The two members of the Lok Sevak Sangh, the one Muslim Leaguer, the one member of the Krishikar Lok Party, and the one member of the Travancore Tamilnad Congress maintained a hopeful isolation in which they were joined by a group of 14 independents.

Probably the only independent with any influence was Lanka Sundaram who espoused his own position in his chapter on "The Role of an Independent Member" in A. B. Lal's book on *The Indian Parliament*. "Independents," he claimed, "have a place in the country's political life to an extent unheard of anywhere in the world today." While it is undoubtedly true that Sundaram as well as certain outstanding opposition

[22] On March 23, 1952, the opposition in Hyderabad walked out on the Nizam; the Rajpramukh of PEPSU was confronted with a similar demonstration. In Punjab some of the opposition members refused to hear the governor's address, while in Madras the united group under Prakasam first delivered a tirade against the governor and then walked out. In Parliament the Communists walked out during the first session over the arrest of the Communist member from Tripura. The entire opposition walked out over the arrest of the Parliamentary leader of the Hindu Mahasabha.

[23] The tenure in office of the CPI in Kerala will provide new fuel for this controversy.

party members influence the government out of proportion to their numbers, this phenomenon is not likely to continue once opposition parties achieve greater strength in Parliament. It is interesting to note that Sundaram himself was defeated in the 1957 elections.

These, then, are the groups in opposition. But totaling as they do only one-fourth of the House and being internally split into so many factions it may well be asked how much influence they can possibly have upon decision making. Yet how much influence has any opposition in other parliamentary systems now that party whips are so strong? That there is some influence is admitted; how much can never be measured. It is a question of feeling the pulse of the nation. Despite the fact that Congress overtowers its opposition, it cannot afford to ignore their contribution to the interpretation of public opinion, particularly since so many of the opposition were once within the Congress fold and have admirers who are still in Congress. If Congress was a homogeneous party, its strength in numbers in the house might allow it summarily to dismiss the opposition; the fact that Congress still shows signs of disintegration and that the leader and the party do not always see eye to eye gives an added weight to opposition arguments. Nehru has been known to acquiesce to opposition demands against protests within his own party.

This influence of the opposition was underscored when the highly controversial Preventive Detention Bill was on the floor of the House during July 1952. After an uneven four-day debate, the various opposition members performing brilliantly, Congress putting up second- and third-string spokesmen, "Vedette" commented scathingly: "Given a good speaker the case for preventive detention would not be so feeble as it appeared during the debate. . . . So far the debate . . . has shown a regrettable lack of appreciation that public opinion must be wooed, if necessary by strong words, not merely conquered by votes."[24] The opposition demanded that the bill be referred to a select committee empowered to consider the parent act as well. The Home Minister, Dr. K. N. Katju, intimated that only minor points could be discussed. Then Nehru rose to contradict the Home Minister and say that in the select committee the government was prepared to go into any section of the act—even those not covered by the present bill. As a result of this concession the bill was in fact liberalized in committee.[25]

A more recent example of opposition influence came toward the end of the explosive debate on the States Reorganization Bill in August

[24] "Vedette," in the *Statesman*, July 26, 1952.
[25] *New York Times*, August 3, 1952.

1956. Finance Minister C. D. Deshmukh resigned on July 25 over the "cavalier and unconstitutional manner" in which the decision was reached to make Bombay City a Union territory. During the subsequent debates it became clear that this decision was reached in the Congress Working Committee rather than in the Cabinet. N. V. Gadgil, in the debate on July 27, said that such action caused the sovereignty of Parliament to become virtually meaningless. At this discouraging moment, a return to the bilingual solution of the Maharashtra-Gujarat problem was proposed by Asoka Mehta. This proposal gained momentum in the House so quickly that the government acquiesced.[26]

In addition to these relatively rare occasions in which opposition debates actually alter governmental decisions, the opposition continually forces Congress to argue its cases clearly and to consider not only public opinion but also any reaction within Congress itself which might produce further splintering. Yet there is no doubt that opposition influence in the Indian Parliament is of a very different character than that exercised in the British Parliament.

The Congress Parliamentary Party

The great decisions in India are usually made within the Congress Party, and the members of the Congress in Parliament probably do more to shape these decisions as party members than as members of the central legislature. Almost all of the leading Congress M.P.'s hold some important post or posts in the party hierarchy, including membership in the All India Congress Committee and perhaps on the Congress Working Committee as well, the highest executive authority of the Congress. All Congress members of Parliament are associate members of the pradesh and district Congress committees in their constituencies, assuming that they have been primary members of the party for at least two years and are now active members. M.P.'s who are on the executive committee of the Congress Parliamentary Party are also associate members of the AICC, unless they are regular members. The Working Committee has also set up a Parliamentary Board, but this board devotes far more time to liaison with and between Congress members of state assemblies than to affairs in the Parliament.

There is clearly a great deal of interlocking and close liaison between the leaders and main organs of the Congress party and the Congress Parliamentary Party. Indeed the question of parliamentary decision

[26] A summary account of this debate is given in Ajoy Kumar Gupta, "The Indian Parliament and States Reorganization," *Parliamentary Affairs*, X, 104-15.

making is greatly complicated by the lack of clear lines of division between the party organization within and without Parliament. While this phenomenon is true of all the Indian parties—many leaders of opposition parties did not even contest the elections—it is crucial within the Congress party. This problem has been of concern to Congress party leaders, as was evidenced at the first post-election meeting of the All India Congress Committee which met at Indore in September 1952 where the question of the relationship between the pradesh Congress committees and the various Parliamentary committees arose. Some party members felt that Congress was taking a back seat to the ministries,[27] but the newspapers seemed more concerned over the need for the party in Parliament to be responsible to Parliament and not to the party. The *Hindustan Times* asked how Congress would "relish a situation in which the Government will take its orders not from the sovereign Parliament of the country but a party clique who may dictate to the Government what it should or should not do?"[28] The *Times of India* suggested alternative interests for the party:

Once party governments are formed in a democracy, inevitably there is an overshadowing of the party as such by the Government and the only way the former can rehabilitate itself is not by trying to define its relations with the latter too closely but by the constructive service it can still render to the people. The opportunities for such service are still vast in a country like India and there is no reason why Pradesh Congress Committees should not take the fullest advantage of it.[29]

Such levelheadedness typified the Indore meeting; the crisis passed almost unnoticed. Arrangements were made to include more state ministers in the pradesh committees; at least fifty per cent of the Working Committee would in the future be central ministers. But despite this attempt at a solution the problem continues.

Nehru's subsequent resignation was seen by many as a further effort to clarify the distinction between the parliamentary and the national party and to lend prestige to the parliamentary party by his premier position within the elective party group. Yet decisions with regard to the States Reorganisation Bill, which were made within the Working Committee rather than in the Cabinet, once more brought the problem to the fore. It would seem obvious that until the parliamentary party leadership is identical with or takes precedence over the Working Committee, and

[27] N. R. Malkani, "The Challenge of India," *Hindustan Times*, Sept. 18, 1952.
[28] *Hindustan Times*, Sept. 2, 1952.
[29] *Times of India*, Aug. 19, 1952.

legislative parties precede pradesh committees in importance, the real decision making in India's Congress-dominated legislatures will be severely limited.

Yet Congress has avoided converting itself from an all-inclusive nationalist movement into a political party, a move which would inevitably weight the parliamentary wing of the party. The *Hindu* blames the confusion among the opposition on this refusal of Congress to set up a "distinctive and homogeneous programme" and nominate "candidates who fully share the political convictions of the top leaders."[30] Further, as one political scientist points out:

The average Congressman is slow, hesitant, and even reluctant to accept the new position in which the Congress has become a mere party. Being used to opposing the government for a long period in his life, the average Congressman has not been able to shake off his old enmity toward administration.[31]

Thus besides attempting to influence decisions within the party and within Parliament, the Parliamentary Congress Party is faced with the added burden of schooling its members in the role of the responsible legislator and of educating the less accomplished members in the whole scope of government. For although Congress had the largest proportion of members in the 1952 Parliament with previous legislative experience, still 49 per cent of the M.P.'s entirely lacked such experience.[32] In addition there is need for the party to keep its large membership interested and aware of the proceedings of Parliament and to prevent them from feeling neglected. During the first session of Parliament the Congress speakers were drawn from perhaps 15 per cent of the party's parliamentary membership.

The Parliamentary Party, which is charged with these tasks, includes both M.P.'s and M.C.'s and has eleven office-bearers, headed by the leader, the deputy leader, and the chief whip. The leaders are elected by the Parliamentary Party for the life of the Parliament; but the chief whip is nominated by the leader. General meetings of the Congress Party in Parliament are held at least once a month during sessions. A General Council, established in 1952, is composed of 20 per cent of the total membership elected proportionately by Congress M.P.'s sitting in state groups; it supposedly meets nearly every Friday, but in practice has not.[33] The eleven office-bearers plus twenty-one elected

[30] *Hindu Weekly Review*, Jan. 7, 1957, editorial.
[31] A. Avasti, "Political Parties in India," *Indian Journal of Political Science*, XII, January-March 1951, p. 9.
[32] Morris-Jones, *op.cit.*, p. 122.
[33] During the first session, twelve full party meetings but only four General Council meetings took place.

members (fifteen chosen by Congress M.P.'s in the House of the People and six by those in the Council of States) form the Executive Committee, an important body which meets very frequently. Its relationship to the Council of Ministers is nebulous but tends to reflect the non-ministerial point of view. Most of the thirty-three ministers, deputy ministers, and parliamentary secretaries appeared much too engrossed in their ministerial problems to stand for the committee, though they attend meetings whenever legislation affecting their ministry is under consideration. "The constitution of the Party in Parliament lays down that, so far as possible, all important Government motions, bills and resolutions should be placed before the Executive Committee in advance of their consideration by Parliament. There is even a Sub-Committee which considers the amendments which have been suggested and advises the Executive Committee."[34]

Of particular interest and importance are the twenty-seven party standing committees.[35] As mentioned, these committees do in a sense provide a substitute for the all-party standing advisory committees which were abolished in 1952; but they are not, of course, an integral part of the parliamentary machinery. Instead, they are party study groups, and they provide an opportunity for party members in Parliament to gain insights and information on both procedural and substantive issues. They are vehicles less for influencing decisions of party leaders than for educating party M.P.'s; but their total impact on policy as well as on procedure is considerable.

A useful channel for the presentation of state attitudes and problems to top party leaders and to appropriate departments of the government is the state group. Congress M.P.'s in a state group often consult with opposition members from the same state before making representations on particular issues to their party leaders or to the government in the form of resolutions.[36] This is a device which has been popular with the

[34] Morris-Jones, *op.cit.*, p. 263.

[35] These committees cover all the ministries but add certain special problems which were felt to require special attention such as river valleys, tribal affairs, small-scale industries and members' amenities. Railways is a separate committee from transport. Other groups are: communications, food, agriculture, health, home affairs, states, defence, education, planning, natural resources, commerce and industry, information and broadcasting, external affairs, labour, production, rehabilitation, housing, law, finance, works, supply. The largest group during the first session was agriculture with 35 members; transport attracted only 12 members.

[36] Even the Manipur "committee" of one, with utmost earnestness, sent in the following report for June 17, 1952: "The State committee discussed matters relating to war compensation in Manipur. It viewed with great concern the report of the arrest and imprisonment of the 84 peasants of Kakching Basti. It further sounded a note of warn-

Congress M.P.'s, and which seems to meet a real need for communication.

The office of the Congress Party in Parliament serves the members in many ways. It helps them to keep in touch with their constituencies, and acts as a liaison with the party machinery at the Center and in the state assemblies. The office is of particular assistance to the chief whip, who is an important official in the government and the party, as well as in the Parliament. He is a member of the AICC, he is minister for parliamentary affairs and chairman of the Cabinet's Parliamentary Affairs Committee, and he is a member of the Business Advisory Committee of the House of the People. He is never very far from the people and agencies who make the major decisions of policy and of procedure, and his own role in decision making is by no means minor. He and his deputies keep in close touch with the members of the Congress in Parliament and relay their opinions and frustrations to the party leaders. In an address at a conference of Congress party whips in 1952 the Chief Whip of Parliament, Satya Narayan Sinha, said: "The Whips are not only shock-absorbers, but also indicators of the Party; they are not only barometers of the different regions and opinions, but also the Counsellors of members."[37]

On the floor of the House few of the Congress members take an active part in debates, and those who speak almost never express opinions at variance with official government policy. A striking exception to party discipline occurred during the debate on the bill to ban cow-slaughter. Despite the application of the whip after Nehru made the question one of confidence, some Congressmen—notably Purshottamdas Tandon—voted against the government. Nehru, in a subsequent letter to Tandon, admitted the difficulty of maintaining party discipline on matters of conscience. But on equally delicate but political issues, such as the linguistic states controversy, Congress M.P.'s who entertained different viewpoints from those of their party leaders seldom expressed these differences in public unless they had resigned from the party, as C. D. Deshmukh had. His indictments of party dictatorship are echoed by Lanka Sundaram who feels that "the tyranny of the ruling Party vis-à-vis the Opposition is one thing, and the bigger tyranny of the governing oligarchy of the ruling Party is another."[38] Party leaders insist that Congress

---

ing that unless these peasants were released before the cultivation season was over, the rural economy in that area would be disturbed." (Parliamentary Congress Party Report, Budget Session, 1952.)

[37] As quoted in Morris-Jones, *op.cit.*, p. 196.
[38] Sundaram in Lal, *op.cit.*, p. 68.

M.P.'s have ample opportunity to express themselves freely within the parliamentary party machinery, a view shared by Morris-Jones. Yet some of the more vocal members of Congress nonetheless frequently by-passed the Parliamentary Party preferring to approach the ministers, or even Nehru, directly, relying upon personal prestige to gain them a hearing. They justified this action on the grounds that the party committees had little power and were in any case conducted like schools. These men and women gained a hearing as members of the governing elite, much the way that opposition leaders gained access to Congress leaders. The continued influence of this now splintered elite is perhaps not unusual in an underdeveloped country where most leaders display agreement on major goals; but the possible alteration of this pattern in India in favor of regional elites suggests that no firm conclusions should be based upon this fairly free access of certain Congress and opposition members to governmental leaders.

Decisions To Be Made

Various political processes in the 1952 Parliament having been reviewed, the question must now be asked just how much of a part can Parliament play in decision making. In theory Parliament is clearly the central institution in any system of parliamentary democracy and, subject to ultimate popular control, is the major agency for decision making. The Prime Minister and the Cabinet make the day-to-day decisions and chart broad lines of policy, and if they have enough support in the Parliament they can in effect make most of the great decisions of policy; but they must have the effective backing of the majority in the Parliament, and Parliament can hold them responsible for decisions and actions which they have taken and for those which they intend to take. Parliament, in short, can control the executive and in the last analysis is the great decision-making agency of the government.

It is quite clear that the Parliament of India does not yet function in this way. The most caustic critics would say that the Parliament is "no more than Pandit Nehru's *durbar*," while A. B. Lal refers to a Cabinet "dictatorship."[39] Even the most optimistic devotees of the system of parliamentary democracy would argue only that Parliament is exercising a growing role of leadership and that it is performing a variety of useful functions which in time will give greater life and strength to Indian democracy. Few observers would argue that Parliament in India is the main decision-making agency, except perhaps in a theoretical sense.

[39] Lal, *op.cit.*, p. xi.

The consensus on this subject, supported by the Deshmukh incident, would probably be that Jawaharlal Nehru, aided by a handful of confidants, really makes policy; or that the major decisions are made in the Working Committee of the Congress Party or elsewhere in the apparatus of the dominant political party, often on the initiative of the Prime Minister and in his presence and seldom without major consideration of his wishes. To the extent that Parliament plays a role in these decisions, according to this approach, it does so largely as a rubber stamp; or, said another way, those members of Parliament who have a real hand in making the decisions do so as members of the dominant party and more likely through the party than through the Parliamentary machinery. Yet this condition would not be too much unlike the role of members of Parliament in western countries if the Indian Parliament really played a dominant role in the political life of the country or if a really effective opposition party existed, one that could provide an alternative government.

In many other respects the Parliament in India is subject to serious handicaps. It is, after all, a relatively new phenomenon in Indian political life. There were, to be sure, legislative bodies of various types in India during much of the period of British rule, and a kind of central parliament in one form or another existed for some years prior to Independence. But there is a vast difference between a legislative body with limited functions, subject to the paramountcy of a foreign power, and the parliament of an independent state which has adopted the parliamentary system of government. In the one case the position in the political structure is peripheral whereas in the other it is central. The Indian Parliament has in fact been in existence only since 1952, and it is still an underdeveloped body. It is hardly surprising that it has not yet realized its full potentialities.

If the Parliament itself is inexperienced, many of the members of that body are much more so. Parliamentarians of vast experience still sit in it, but most of the present M.P.'s have had only limited previous experience and are learning only slowly how to function as the lawmakers of a great new nation. They are not only inexperienced; they are also poorly educated, poorly paid, and usually are in straitened circumstances. They lack adequate staff assistance, and they receive little help in research and preparation of speeches and reports. Moreover many M.P.'s do not even make good use of the limited facilities at their disposal. It is difficult for them to find the time or the opportunity for serious reflection or study; their ways of life as well as their living arrangements make them very easy prey for hordes of people who may flock about them at all hours. Often they are out of touch with their constituents, who in any event, if they have any interest in politics at all, are probably more interested in their representatives to local bodies and the state assemblies than in their representative in far-off New Delhi. Most of the subjects in which the Indian people are most interested are state subjects and are not on the Union or concurrent lists. This relative lack of contact with constituents has certain advantages, as any member of the American Congress would fervently attest, but it poses serious problems of political education and of the future of democracy in a vast country like India where illiteracy and prejudice and regional loyalties may seriously hamper the development of true national unity.

It is apparent, therefore, that because of the nature of the Indian environment and traditions, the limited experience with modern political institutions and practice, the dominant position, at least at the Center, of a single political party and the close identification of party and government, the practice of making decisions within the party rather than elsewhere—usually by a handful of top leaders—and many other internal factors relating to its own character and operations, the Parliament of India plays only a limited role in decision making as far as basic policies are concerned. It is, however, the major lawmaking body, and it serves a useful role in the ventilation of grievances and as a public forum. If it does not effectively control the executive, nonetheless it can hardly be ignored even by a person with the stature and influence of the present Prime Minister, who fortunately does not aspire to rule by unparliamentary means. Unless a major reversal occurs in Indian politics, Parliament will almost certainly gain in influence and prestige.

FACTORS OF TRADITION AND CHANGE IN A LOCAL ELECTION IN RURAL INDIA

MORRIS EDWARD OPLER

On December 16, 1955, an important local election was held in the villages of Senapur and Daudpur in the Jaunpur District of Uttar Pradesh. Senapur is a village of about 2,100 people; Daudpur, which adjoins Senapur, is credited with a population of less than 250 and therefore, by state law, had to be linked for election purposes with a more populous center. At stake in the election were the twenty-seven seats of the government Village Panchayat and the selection of an executive officer of that panchayat. Three of the successful candidates for the panchayat were later to be appointed to a local court dealing with minor cases of a circle of some ten villages of the vicinity. Of the twenty-seven panchayat members, twenty were to come from Senapur and seven from Daudpur. The two villages were divided into seven election districts and each district was to have representation roughly according to its population. Candidates for the panchayat had to be residents of the districts which they aspired to represent and could only receive the votes of fellow residents of their own district. All the voters of the two villages were entitled to cast a ballot for their choice for executive officer of the panchayat, however.

This particular election was overdue. The five-year term of the former Village Panchayat and executive officer had ended in February. But legislation modifying the rules pertaining to the election and conduct of the Village Panchayats delayed the drawing up of the voting rolls. When these rolls were completed, a total of 1,068 eligible voters was listed for the two villages. Of these, 974 actually voted for one or the other of the two candidates for executive officer.

To say merely that the election was a spirited and exciting event is an understatement. It was in fact a most tense and turbulent affair. The attempt to garner votes was so energetic and the means employed often so questionable that tempers flared and violence and reprisals were threatened. Both sides appealed to the authorities to protect their supporters against intimidation at the polls and against outbreaks of violence on the part of the opposition. Armed police arrived the day before the

Morris Edward Opler is Professor of Anthropology at Cornell University and Director of the Cornell University India Program.

election and remained until the balloting was concluded. The two contenders for executive officer had to post high bonds which would be forfeited if they or their followers precipitated violence. As the polling was concluded in one district, crowds rushed to the next booth to announce the news and learn the latest results. When it became apparent who the new executive officer was to be, he was cheered and garlanded by his supporters and an elephant was brought from a nearby village so that he might ride around the village in triumph.

Adult suffrage has existed for Indians only since Independence and this was but the second election of village officials in which the new electorate has participated. It may be difficult for westerners who have been bored by many an apathetic local election to believe that so vigorous a campaign could take place in India on the village level after so brief a span of political experience and participation. Consequently, it may be helpful to point to some of the factors, traditional and emergent, which gave this election and elections in thousands of other Indian villages such a meaningful and dramatic quality. An analysis of these factors and the trends they suggest should, moreover, tell us something of the dynamics of present-day Indian political life on the local level.

Factors of Personal Prestige and Power

If there is any Gandhian ideal which the present Indian government has persistently pressed, it is the strengthening of village government and the attempt to advance village economy and social welfare through its operations. Consequently government orders and requests are channeled through the Village Panchayat, and its executive becomes the link with government. Requests of the village for grants and aids and projects from the government must pass through the Village Panchayat, and in these days of development plans this is an important consideration for any community. The Village Panchayat can levy taxes of various kinds, receives a share of the income of the local courts, and falls heir to unclaimed land, trees, and other property within its boundaries. Officials, when they visit the village, first contact the executive officer of the Village Panchayat. It is obvious that the executive officer of the Village Panchayat will have a good many favors to bestow and will automatically have a good deal of prestige and influence. If he is already the leading man of the village his position will be augmented and consolidated. If he is not, but is a forceful person, he can soon rival whoever formerly outstripped him in prestige.

The growing and potential importance of the Village Panchayat was understood or sensed by a relatively young man of Senapur who has sought ceaselessly for the last decade to improve his social and economic status. In the election of 1949 he was elected a member of the local court. Later he approached the head of the local court when he was very ill and induced him to turn over his official duties to him. As head of the court he then engaged in activities calculated to call himself to public attention, and as far back as two years ago he began to voice his interest in becoming the next executive officer of the Village Panchayat.

The story of this man, whom we shall call A, illustrates the fluctuating fortunes of individuals and families which mark Indian village life. It also pictures the new sources of wealth and power which have lately altered conditions in the village. Following a separation of a joint family, the branch to which A belongs fell upon hard days. The family fortunes were somewhat restored when the present generation of young men grew up. While A managed the family lands, his older brother left the village to become manager of an estate. He lost this promising job when the landlord abolition law was passed and implemented. He quickly recouped his fortunes by getting into the highly profitable business of selling mechanical chaff cutters. Earnings from the business made it possible for the family to improve the family landholdings, to acquire additional land in the village, and to lend to villagers at an advantage. Marriages of the young men to girls of prominent families of the area further improved the standing and connections of the family. A younger brother did well in his studies, has earned scholarships, and has excellent future prospects.

Thus, outside employment, business, and education have been important in the recent elevation of this family. The elder brother has been outside of the village quite constantly on business and the younger one has been away in connection with his studies. It is A who has remained in the village and who has translated his ambitions into local political terms. In this he has the backing of the elder brother, who has given financial support unstintingly and who came back to the village to campaign for him in the recent election crisis.

A's efforts to gain recognition and prominence brought him into conflict with B, a respected member of the same lineage. These men are descended from different branches of the joint family which, to the detriment of A's family, separated some decades ago. B affords a contrast to A in many ways. He is well to do, but his wealth is in land and stored grain. He is one of the largest landowners of the village and, while he is one of the most progressive farmers of the area and will experiment with crops, fertilizers, and implements, he is land-centered and village-centered. Neither he nor members of his household look outward for income. His father was a prominent leader of the village who was noted for his shrewd farm management, and this son has followed the same path. Under the older conditions B would be assured of a place of power and honor in the village and could expect to be called upon to arbitrate many disputes. B, too, had political ambitions and hoped to be the new executive officer of the Village Panchayat. But, being a man who had risen high, he did not want to risk a fall. He did not care to campaign actively for office but preferred to be nominated without opposition. However, with A engaging in an active campaign, there was no possibility of this.

Meanwhile the rivalry and opposition between A and B was steadily growing. The fathers of A and B had not been on good terms and the two younger men had a heritage of interfamily rancor. When a joint family separates, the division of property that takes place is often a continuing bone of contention, and so it was in this case. During their lean years, A and his family felt that they were being treated like poor relations by B, and since A was so much younger, he was treated with scant respect by B and was conscious of this. As he grew in years, wealth, following, and political office, he began to challenge B at every opportunity. These thrusts and challenges were at first not direct and open. If B would advocate some measure or give some village event his blessing, A would find some reason to oppose it. If B interested himself in some dispute or court case, A would give aid or advice to the opposition. Any setback of a cause with which B was associated began to be recognized as a victory for A. Before long B was employing the same tactics against his rival, and soon the two men and their close associates were on opposite sides of almost every village issue that arose. Moreover, each increasingly called upon his tenants, closest relatives, friends, and those dependent upon him for favors of different kinds to assist him. The lines were drawn and there was growing talk of the two "parties" or factions. It was not long before events took an even more ominous turn. During September and October of 1955 the standing crops in the fields of prominent members of the two "parties" were cut at night. In spite of their prominence and threats of vengeance the two leaders of the parties suffered the same kind of loss. Large groups of men stayed out in the fields guarding crops all night. Crop cutters were threatened with severe beatings. Villagers were shaking their heads and prophesying that it would all end in the death of someone. With this contest and rivalry existing between them on every level, B could hardly allow A to gain the important and focal position of executive officer of the Village Panchayat without challenge. During the early part of November, B decided to run in the election. The final date for filing nomination papers was November 21.

Although the emphasis of the state government was on the formation of a democratically elected Village Panchayat of civic-minded villagers, and although any registered voter was entitled to pay his five rupee fee for filing nomination papers and to offer himself as a candidate in his constituency, the activities of the two powerful rivals made any independent candidacy impossible. The leaders of the two factions recruited candidates for each constituency from among their followers. They paid the required fees for the men of their slates. Since the village taxes of any candidate had to be paid up to date before his papers were accepted, they made up any arrears of this kind for their men, too. It was soon apparent that any person who lacked the backing of one of the political machines would not have the slightest chance of accomplishing anything but getting into trouble; consequently, no one not affiliated with one or the other of the "parties" offered himself as a candidate. What was intended to be a contest for twenty-eight seats ended essentially as a struggle between two men.

The elected village assembly is a new organ of government and the process of openly running for office is a new experience for the villager. Leadership has hitherto been an inheritance to which the proper person succeeded at the right time. The spectacle of prominent villagers taking the initiative in their own behalf and actively campaigning and pleading for votes must raise questions concerning the traditional concepts of status and pave the way for an aggressive and more self-assertive leadership.

Caste

The ideal in village self-government is to elect an assembly which will represent the interests of the village as a whole without regard to caste lines but in which each caste, nevertheless, will have adequate and proportional representation in case its interests require defense.

Actually, in this campaign and election, caste was a very important and perhaps crucial factor. Long before the election the members of low-caste groups of the village were assuring one another that, since they outnumber the high castes of the villages so decisively, the new executive officer should come from their ranks. In 1949, at the time of the first election, the low castes, stimulated by talk of the abolition of untouchability, abolition of landlordism, and the general atmosphere of reform, created a People's Party. They nominated an impecunious and undistinguished high-caste man whom they felt they could control, and ran him for executive officer. Most of the prominent high-caste villagers refrained from participating in the election either as candidates or as voters. Many refused to allow family members to involve themselves in any way. As a result the candidates of the low castes swept the election. Their high-caste figurehead proved a great disappointment to the low castes. At the first real crisis he abandoned them in favor of his caste fellows. This man was eager to run again, but the high castes never forgave him for running on the ticket of the low castes and the low castes never trusted him after his defection.

Consequently, the low castes resolved to have their candidate a member of their own group this time. Yet it was not easy to find low-caste persons who could run for the leading office. The executive officer of the assembly receives a good many written messages and directives from the government and has to send reports and inquiries in turn. Literacy is therefore a requirement. Also a certain amount of wealth is needed; outsiders and officials who stop in the village are directed to this official's home and have to be offered hospitality. Few low-caste villagers have had much education, and most of those who can read and write are quite young. But the younger men ordinarily do not have much means for entertaining visitors. It was asked, also, whether the representative of the village, if he were of low caste, could command the required respect and would be taken seriously by outside officials, most of whom are of the higher castes. Moreover, members of low castes, trained in diffidence to the higher castes, find it hard to feel at ease in the company of high-caste officials. For these and other reasons all low-caste aspirants except one relinquished the notion of running for the post of executive officer.

The high castes, however, were determined that no low-caste person would occupy the main position. The one undaunted low-caste man, who claimed to be thirty-two years of age, was told that his school records had been altered to prove that he was less than the thirty years of age required of a candidate for executive officer. He was warned that if he entered the contest he could be prosecuted for acting illegally. This prospect of getting into legal difficulties with the government frightened him and caused him to withdraw his name. Consequently the low-caste section of the community was left with the task of deciding which of the two contending high-caste leaders would be more favorably disposed toward them.

But even though the two leading contenders were of the same high caste, the importance of caste in the situation could not be ignored. Each faction sought to attract the votes of caste blocs by inducing caste leaders and spokesmen to run for panchayat membership on its side. Moreover, a number of the districts or constituencies of the villages were really hamlets of the village wholly or mainly populated by single castes. Campaigning in those quarters became a matter of appealing to the resident caste and its leaders. Elaborate arguments were devised by A and B to prove their regard and consideration for the low castes and the particular caste being addressed. When one of the two leading candidates was out of favor in a hamlet or caste residential area, he sought nevertheless to split the vote and to secure as much backing as possible. Every imaginable means was used. If a low-caste man had been a tenant of A or B or of one of their high-caste followers, or if his family had hereditary work relations with a high-caste member of one of the "parties," appeal was made to the sentiments surrounding this institution. Cajolery, bribery, and threats of reprisal were freely employed. As a result of the changes in land laws the ownership of a good many small parcels of land is in dispute. Heads of low-caste families who hope to acquire title to some of this land were promised aid in proving their rights. Or, if they proved politically obstinate, they were told that their claims would be opposed. Such promises of help or hindrance are most effective, for the low castes, mostly illiterate and fearful of officialdom, depend on the backing and help of literate and experienced high-caste persons in these matters. Moreover, threats of reprisal are received fearfully, for most low-caste individuals depend on high-caste sources for timely loans of money and seed and for other aid. Indeed, for many dependent low-caste members the problem became one of giving no offense or the least offense. Some low-caste family heads carefully split the vote, ordering wives, sons, and daughters-in-law to vote so that their ballots were evenly divided between the main contenders.

Pressure was exerted on the low-caste population until the very last minute. They were constantly harangued by A, B, or their lieutenants and called to political meetings. The day before the election strong-armed men of one faction came to stay at the quarters of a vacillating group of low-caste people and made it impossible for the opposition to reach them and plead its cause. The night before the election the tenants and hereditary workmen of one of the contestants were asked to sleep in his compound, from where they were herded to the polls the next day. This policing of voters, extraction of promises to vote one way or the other, and threats of reprisal were quite effective, for the voting was carried on by a raising of hands in an open place and not by secret ballot; anyone could see how a particular individual voted when a candidate's name was called.

Though the lives of the low-caste population were made miserable by the incessant electioneering focused on them, and though they were subject to rather ugly pressures and threats when flattery and bribery did not suffice, it would not be true to say that the low castes did not gain a point or two as a result of the campaigning. The shrewd among them were able to gain concessions and aids of various kinds in return for their support. While the high castes succeeded in preventing another people's party from forming and frustrated the plans to nominate a low-caste candidate for the highest office, they did have to display an unparalleled friendly concern for the low castes during the campaign. High-caste individuals who had never before visited low-caste quarters did so now. Symbols of deference which high-caste individuals usually demand of the low castes were genially waved aside. The change in attitude and the display of intercaste comradeship was so marked that it became a source of amusement and cynical comment for the low castes. But even though it was generally accepted that so great a relaxation of caste barriers could not be expected to continue beyond the election, the former conditions can probably never be entirely restored either.

Caste entered the election in still another way. In its efforts to better the lot of the untouchables, the government is making sure that they receive reasonable political representation. For the present this is being achieved by reserving seats for them in political bodies. Thus eight seats were reserved in the Village Panchayat for the untouchables or scheduled castes and could be contested for only by candidates from these groups.

Actually it was caste solidarity and the action of a particular caste which went far to decide the election. In one of the hamlets and election districts of Senapur live the Nonia, the third-largest caste group of the village. This hamlet is further from the main settlement than any other, and the Nonia, who own more land than any other low-caste group, are the most independent of the low castes in their attitude toward the high castes. Irritated by the incessant pressures to which they were being subjected by the two parties and by the attempts to split their group, the brotherhood met to decide what course of action to take. They decided to vote as a unit and selected B as the candidate to support. Frantic efforts were made by A to regain lost ground. But in the main the group held firm and while the vote was quite close in every other district, it was overwhelmingly for B in this constituency. B was elected executive officer of the Village Panchayat by a comfortable figure; but had the same margin of votes by which B won in this hamlet gone to A, he would have been elected to the post which he coveted.

Family

In theory every adult was entitled to cast his vote for the candidates of his choice. In practice the villagers, with few exceptions, were bound by family decisions. Usually these represented the views of the male heads of nuclear or joint families. The dominating position of the family head was well understood by the candidates. Ordinarily it was the family head alone who was invited to a political meeting. Heads of large and important families were the special targets of the candidates and their agents. In a counting of the potential strength of one side or the other reference was constantly made to the number of votes that a family head could "give." Once a family head voiced his support of a candidate or faction he might be requested by that side to bring his wife back to the village from a visit to her parents' village in time for the election or to delay the departure of his son from the village for outside employment until after the balloting, etc. In other words, it was assumed that he controlled the votes of his family and household members. Where the family vote was divided, it was ordinarily by design and by order of the family head. Some of the petty tradesmen, for instance, who hope for business from all villagers, directed half of their family members to side with A and the others to vote for B. Some persons who favored one candidate, but whose home is built on the land of the other or on that of one of his friends, sought to avoid persecution and eviction by splitting the family vote also.

Sex

In theory adult residents of the village of either sex were entitled to vote. Approximately as many women as men cast ballots. It has been mentioned that daughters and wives were brought from visits outside the village to participate in the election and that those who had intended to make trips during this period were kept in the village until they had performed their civic duty. Yet for all this formal participation of women it was a male-dominated election. Of the forty-nine candidates who ran for office, not one was a woman. In interview after interview the women voiced surprise at the notion of voting in any other way than the husband or family head or in a way contrary to his wishes or directions. The women were prevailingly aware of the rivalry of A and B and of the stand of their families in respect to these two office seekers. But they were usually uninformed about the contests for panchayat membership in the districts and confused about the identities of the candidates. When they were asked for whom they would vote, a common answer was that they would be told what to do by the senior males of the family when the time came. Actually, when the time came many were confused and nervous, and some caused amusement and despair by voting, despite instructions, for the wrong man, or by attempting to cast two votes for the same office.

Compromise

When A and B, who had sought ascendancy over each other through the use of many issues and devices, including court cases and crop cutting, began to use the political arena as a further test of strength, a feeling of foreboding grew in the village. In many responsible quarters it began to be asserted that things had gone too far, were getting out of hand, and that a compromise of some sort had to be arranged. A respected elder of the village, whom we shall call C, announced a meeting for November 12 and invited representatives of the various castes and sections of the village to attend. C, a man seventy-two years old, had been *sarpanch* or head of the appointed Village Panchayat which had ruled until Independence and the passage of the state laws setting up the new forms of village self-government. He is a high-caste man. Because the first local elections following Independence took place here in an upsurge of low-caste animus against high-caste rule and domination, C refused to run for office at that time and boycotted the whole political scene. Despite his exit from formal office, C remained a powerful figure behind the scenes. People could not forget that his father and elder brother had been important village leaders before him and that he had been not only a leader in Senapur but also the representative of the village to regional conferences which used to be held. His age, caste, large family, reputation for shrewdness and wisdom, and extensive landholdings guaranteed him respect. When the first elected executive officer lost his following among the disillusioned low castes and was simply tolerated for the remainder of his term of office, C was more and more consulted about village affairs and became extremely active in hearing and settling disputes. It became plain from remarks that he and his close associates made that he still harbored political ambitions. He wanted to become executive officer of the village—but on his own terms; he wanted to secure the office by draft or acclamation and without opposition. He was too proud to beg for votes and he dared not risk the crushing blow to his prestige that a defeat would entail.

It was no secret that at the meeting of the twelfth C hoped A and B could be induced to withdraw their candidacy for the sake of the peace of the village and that the way would be open to ask him to run unopposed. In fact, B had entered the lists only after he had been requested by C to do so, and C had made no commitments of support since. Many saw in C's maneuverings a strategy which had brought A and B into opposition and was forcing a solution which would eliminate both and propel C to the fore as the benign compromise candidate who would restore harmony to the village.

There were, however, some considerations which militated against the selection of C as a compromise candidate. One was that C was reputed to be a hard taskmaster to the low castes, one who still exacted *begar* or unpaid labor from them and who insisted upon deference to his high-caste status. Also he had a reputation for being grasping and not too scrupulous about money entrusted to him. It was said that he had gone to great lengths to nullify the claims of his tenants to the tiny parcels of land they might have acquired under the new land laws, and that money which had been collected for public purposes in the village and put in his care had not been properly accounted for. Consequently, there were mixed feelings about this elder, and while the meeting of leaders did request the two embattled candidates to step aside in favor of someone who would be nominated by the whole village and run unopposed, the man they settled on was not C.

When the two rival candidates were asked if they would withdraw in favor of the person named at the meeting, B agreed to do so if A would also withdraw. A would only say that he would consult his supporters. Eventually he refused to drop his candidacy; the person named by the meeting declined to become involved and the political tussle between the two main candidates continued.

It may be that B knew that A was too deeply involved financially and emotionally to withdraw at this point and counted on this. At any rate he benefited handsomely by his stand and A lost correspondingly. The mechanism of compromise, of providing some means whereby both parties to a quarrel can retreat with honor, is a cherished and important means of mitigating conflict in village India. A person who does not respond to such an opportunity to emerge with dignity from an intolerable situation is considered a hothead and a troublemaker. After this it was possible, when objections were made to the difficulties raised by the election, for B to point out that he had been willing to drop his candidacy entirely and that A must accept responsibility for the bitterness of the continued effort.

In the course of the next weeks a number of other attempts at compromise were made by elders of neighboring villages and even by outside officials. One suggestion was that one of the two men should become executive officer of the assembly by common consent, the other should become the head of the local court, and that the panchayat seats should be divided between the supporters of the two. All such efforts at compromise failed. Actually the principals were quite favorably disposed toward one of these plans and, left to their own devices, might have come to some agreement. By this time, too, they were somewhat overawed and frightened by the storm they had aroused. But by now so many promises had been made, so much money was involved, and so many subsidiary feuds had flared that supporters of each man stood in the way of any retreat.

Age

Another factor which had considerable influence upon the result was that of age. It was bad enough that men of the same line were thus opposing one another; it was more serious still that a much younger relative was confronting his elder so unyieldingly. When C was sure that he was out of the running, he did throw his considerable influence behind B. He explained that the prestige of A, who was so much younger a man, would survive a defeat; but that B, if he lost to his younger competitor, could never again hold his head up in the village. When A heard that a Brahman who serves as family priest for both his family and B's was openly advocating the election of B, he remonstrated with the man, reminding him that his clients should all be the same for him. The Brahman gently reminded him that it was his duty, in a family crisis, to cooperate with the family head and not with the junior members of the family. A also sought the support of a villager who was once his schoolteacher, recalling to him that he had been his good and obedient pupil. The older man remarked that this was just his dilemma, that A had been a pupil in the lower grades when B was a grown man. An official who came to the village during the campaign and was told of the bitterness of the contest and that distant relatives were seeking the same office, at once demanded to know which was the elder and advised the younger of the two to withdraw from the race. This respect and consideration for age and the feeling that a markedly younger man, and especially a younger relative, should not openly challenge his elder, was a handicap which A could overcome only with the greatest difficulty.

The Outcome and Analysis

In the election which took place on December 16, B became the executive officer of the Village Panchayat. He won by 164 votes, receiving 569 votes to his opponent's 405. What is more, B's supporters won in all of the seven voting districts of the two villages. In all but one of the districts the vote was close, and a handful of votes in the other direction would have turned the tide. In Daudpur the margin of victory was only one vote. The decisive victory was in the hamlet where the caste panchayat had ruled for B and ordered its membership to vote accordingly. The victory of B's slate was just as pronounced. Since the contest was one between factions or "parties" rather than for individual seats it could be expected that a victory for B in a district would be paralleled by the triumph of a candidate for the panchayat backed by him. Of the twenty-seven panchayat seats at stake, all but two went to followers of B.

Thus the election was really a translation into political terms of a struggle between two village stalwarts and the rival factions they headed. The existence of factions of this type has been noted in most of the studies of Indian villages that have been issued recently. Indian social organization emphasizes hierarchy and notions of prestige, and infringements in these areas lead to retaliation, dispute, and division. In an atmosphere of friction and tension, an election is simply a means of giving a new turn to an old quarrel.

The man who was selected reflects traditional values in a number of ways. His father was a leader of the village. He is the elder and leader of his family. His source of wealth and prestige is the land. His opponent, on the other hand, represents ambitious youth and new wealth brought into the village by business enterprise. Villagers admire him and his family and yet are troubled by the forces, represented in him, which are disturbing the smooth flow of the village prestige and status system.

Moreover, the younger man is not even the head of his own joint family; that position is reserved for his older brother, who is out of the village most of the time in connection with his business interests. We have indicated above how traditional caste and sex attitudes entered the contest.

Yet despite the echoes of traditional usage in this election a number of new notes were sounded. Whatever the motives, the results depended upon a counting of votes. Some sections of the low-caste electorate were harassed and intimidated, but others were flattered, bribed, and persuaded. In either case they were impressed with the importance and power of the vote and have learned a lesson that will doubtless stand them in good stead in future political bouts. The manner in which a single resolute caste was able to deliver the vote must certainly have its effect too.

But the most important innovation of this election campaign, perhaps, is the realization that from this point on title and office in the village will have to be actively and openly sought. The old hereditary leadership is passing from the scene. Six years ago B and C and most other accepted village leaders disdained to sully their hands with new-style politics, and preferred to stand aside and watch developments. The highest office went to a weak and vacillating man who accomplished little and discredited himself. This time C tried to manipulate things in such a way that he might gain office without actively campaigning. He failed dismally. B hoped against hope for this same kind of a miracle; when it did not occur he entered the lists and waged a vigorous campaign—and won. There are those who criticize him for taking the risk of losing ignominiously to a younger relative. During the actual electioneering it was many times charged that he was foolhardy and had been drawn into the fray by his enemies rather than by his friends. But for the first time in the history of the village a respected village elder has gone out to seek office and honor rather than to assume that it would accrue to him in due course. This is a temper that will introduce new blood into local self-government and will help effect a transition from the old village administrative structure to the new.

LEADERSHIP AND LANGUAGE POLICY IN INDIA

SELIG S. HARRISON

I closed my eyes and it could have been Anthony Eden!" exclaimed Adlai Stevenson. "The very same words, the very same way of approaching the problem!" In New Delhi on his 1953 world tour, Stevenson had just conversed with the late Sir Girja Shankar Bajpai, Secretary-General of the External Affairs Ministry. Now the archetypal Sir Girja is gone; his passing reflects the demise of an elect fraternity in Indian political leadership. Whatever the new archetype ten or twenty years hence, the western visitor will in all likelihood not turn to thoughts of Anthony Eden. Perhaps little more than this can safely be said. For Indian leadership is in the process of linguistic sea change which could conceivably yield no single archetype at all, but instead a series side by side in uneasy company.

Even in pre-Independence years there was no clearly preeminent archetype: was it Sir Girja any more than Gandhi? For the most part, however, Indian leadership did share a common linguistic heritage. The colonial educational regime which produced a nationwide bureaucratic "steel frame" also brought forth the unified pan-Indian Congress challenge. British educational policy was in essence a language policy—English as the medium in the universities and as the prerequisite for government employment. Macaulay's Education Minute of March 7, 1835, signaled this historic policy. Lord Hardinge's resolution of 1844 placed a premium on English for government jobs, and by 1857 the B.A. degree became mandatory for higher government employment to establish finally English dominance. It is relatively unimportant whether this man or that did become, as Macaulay's minute envisioned, "Indian in blood and color, but English in taste, in opinion, in morals and in intellect." The enduring fact is simply that so extensive a governing elite could communicate in a language which "acquired a wider currency

SELIG S. HARRISON spent three years in India (1951-1954) as a correspondent for the Associated Press. On his return he studied Indian language policy as a Nieman Fellow at Harvard University; during this period he was associated with the Modern India Project, University of California, Berkeley, and with the Language and Communication Research Center at Columbia University. He is now Associate Editor of *The New Republic*.

simultaneously all over the country than any other language in the history of India."[1]

This heritage of English could be dismissed more blithely during the freedom movement than the realities of nation-building now permit. As early as 1908 Gandhi argued in *Hind Swaraj* that "it is the English-knowing men that have enslaved India."[2] It was a major article of the Gandhian faith that English should give way to the regional languages in education and administration. Gandhi pleaded that Indian leadership could not in fact lead a profound national regeneration unless able, quite literally, to speak to the people in their own language. In his basic education plan Gandhi emphasized the mother tongue, as did Tagore when he lamented that,

> We pass examinations, and shrivel up into clerks, lawyers and police inspectors, and we die young. Man's intellect has a natural pride in its own aristocracy, which is the pride of its culture. When this pride succumbs to some compulsion of necessity or lure of material advantage, it brings humiliation to the intellectual man. Modern India, through her English education, has been made to suffer this humiliation. . . .
>
> A language is not like an umbrella or an overcoat, that can be borrowed by unconscious or deliberate mistake; it is like the living skin itself. If the body of a draft horse enters into the skin of a race horse, it would be safe to wager that such an anomaly will never win a race, and will fail even to drag a cart.[3]

Initial pressure to replace English with the mother tongue was limited to secondary education. With the increasing use of the mother tongue in secondary schools, however, Indian universities soon came under increasing attack for their use of English in instruction, and most of all in the entrance examination. In 1937 Punjab and Calcutta universities became the first Indian universities to permit the use of the regional language in entrance examinations in all subjects except English itself. Sir Philip Hartog, chairman of the Simon Commission's education committee, warned at the time that as the entrance examination goes, so would go all language policy in Indian education.[4]

The shift to the regional languages in secondary education immediately affected Indian leadership. Even in the thirties, Pattabhi Sitara-

---

[1] M. Mujeeb, "Indian Education–Retrospect and Prospect," *Pacific Affairs*, XXVI, September 1953, p. 213.

[2] Cited in "Secondary Education Through the Medium of the Vernaculars," *The Speeches and Writings of Annie Besant*, Madras, G. A. Natesan, 1921, p. 249.

[3] Rabindranath Tagore, *Creative Unity*, London, Macmillan, 1922, pp. 180, 191. In his Bengali essay *Siksar Vahan* (The Medium of Instruction) Tagore conceded the desirability of English for those pursuing university postgraduate studies.

[4] Sir Philip Hartog, *Some Aspects of Indian Education, Past and Present*, London, Oxford University Press, 1939, p. 44.

mayya recalls, more than one hundred members of the Madras legislature did not know English.[5] Moreover, the regional languages gained at the expense of standards of English instruction. Those who did learn English could not use it well enough to make the most of a university education conducted entirely in this medium. The Punjab University Inquiry Committee reported in 1929:

> A large proportion of the pupils are unable to think or write clearly in any language and cannot follow lectures delivered in English. Yet hundreds of thousands of them, who cannot write five lines of correct English, who often do not know when to say yes and when to say no in answer to a question, are made to read en masse Shelley's 'Skylark,' Milton's 'Ode On The Morning of Christ's Nativity,' and Shakespeare's plays. They have never seen a skylark; they do not know why a highborn maiden sits in her tower. . . .[6]

By 1953, the decline of English had reached alarming proportions. The Secondary Education Commission reported then a serious dearth of "well qualified and experienced teachers who can handle English classes in schools and colleges," declaring this shortage to be "one of the important reasons for the rapid deterioration in the standards of English at the university stage."[7]

Indian educators have long been divided on the university medium of instruction and examination. But the post-Independence nationalist *élan* throughout India aggravated this controversy, arousing as it did intense pressure for a rapid shift to the regional languages. Defenders of English pointed to the shortages of textbooks and adequately trained teachers in many Indian languages. Hindi enthusiasts advocated the Union language as the medium of instruction. Both of these foes of the regional-language medium warned that without a uniform medium throughout the country India's intellectual unity—and ultimately political unity as well—would be gravely jeopardized.

For the English-speaking educational elite, a vested interest in administrative and teaching posts was at stake. But there were regional intellectuals with their own vested interests. It became apparent from January 1948, when independent India's first National Education Conference assembled in New Delhi, that the regional language advocates had gained the offensive.

A conference subcommittee's own better judgment cried between the lines of its recommendation that,

---

[5] B. Pattabhi Sitaramayya, *The History of the Indian National Congress*, Bombay, Padma Publications, 1947, II, 93.
[6] Cited in S. N. Chib, *Language, Universities and Nationalism in India*, London, Oxford University Press, 1936, p. 3.
[7] *Report of the Secondary Education Commission*, Ministry of Education, Publication No. 165, New Delhi, 1953, p. 69.

... it would be necessary to reconcile ourselves to the idea of having the regional languages as the media of instruction and examination at the university stage when English ceases to hold the position enjoyed during years of British rule.[8]

The committee recommended that English should be replaced by Indian languages within five years. A year later, the University Education Commission declared with unabashed inconsistency that English

... has become so much a part of our national habit that a plunge into an altogether different system seems attended with unusual risks. It appears to us, however, that the plunge is inevitable.[9]

It was one thing, however, to order English banished in five years and quite another to conjure up the necessary textbooks and teachers to install the regional languages. Nor were the English-speaking powers-that-be in Indian education possessed of the will necessary even to begin to find a way. The provincial exasperation arising from this impasse was reflected in two successive meetings of the Congress Working Committee in 1954. In April the committee reminded the nation that normally university teaching should be conducted in the regional language, with an option to use Hindi or English only in special cases. Again in July, the committee reiterated this position.[10]

The final outcome of the controversy must remain in doubt, but the regional languages are for the present clearly in the ascendancy as the media of instruction and examination in Indian universities. While a clear policy remains to be decided in sixteen Indian universities, ten have already formally proclaimed that instruction is to be in an Indian language, and even now, at least sixteen[11] are actually teaching some nonscientific undergraduate courses in Indian languages (only two of these, Vallabh Vidyanagar in Gujarat, and Osmania in Andhra, are Hindi- or Hindustani-medium institutions outside Hindi territory, and the future of Osmania is uncertain in the new Andhra State):

[8] *Report of the Committee on the Medium of Instruction at the University Stage—1948*, Bureau of Education, Ministry of Education, Pamphlet 57, New Delhi, 1948, pp. 11, 36.

[9] *Report of the University Education Commission, 1948-49*, Delhi, 1950, I, 478.

[10] *Times of India*, April 7, 1954; *Hindu Weekly Review*, July 5, 1954.

[11] This collation is based on "Hindi and the Regional Languages as Optional Media of Instruction in Universities in India," a statement prepared for the author by the Education Ministry, Government of India, November 1955, a revised version prepared in January 1957, and extensive correspondence with registrars of all universities on the Education Ministry register.

Agra	Calcutta	Nagpur	Saugor
Allahabad	Gujarat	Osmania	Thackersey
Banaras	Karnataka	Poona	Vallabh Vidyanagar
Bihar	Lucknow	Roorkee	Visvabharati

The pioneer in this field has been Nagpur University, which has permitted the use of Hindi and Marathi as examination media since 1950, and has made it nominally compulsory since 1954 that students select either Hindi or Marathi as their medium for undergraduate arts and science courses. Even here, as a result of the textbook-teacher dilemma, the university has reported that "provision is made for special permission in certain cases to offer the English medium, and at present such permission is granted on a liberal scale."

A breakdown of the undergraduate examinations at Nagpur in 1954 showed that 14 per cent of the 2,036 students in nonscience courses chose the English medium, while 88 per cent of 1,032 science students used English.[12] The undisputed place of English in science education is further illustrated by the use of English as the medium of instruction for undergraduate science courses leading to the degree.

Wherever the attempt to switch to the regional languages is made, it is the shortage of textbooks that proves the greatest frustration. The confusion that results is typified in Calcutta University, where the medium is now "English, or a mixture of English and Bengali, or Bengali," S. K. Chatterji writes. Students may answer examinations in the mother tongue in all subjects except English language instruction itself.[13]

Where the authorities have not yielded to the regional languages, as in Bombay University, a first-class political furor has resulted. The advocates of the regional languages in multilingual Bombay raised a loud cry when the Committee on the Medium of Instruction appointed by the university syndicate recommended that ultimately the medium "should be Hindi alone." The committee set a period of ten years, ending in 1970, however, during which English should continue to be the over-all medium while Hindi was gradually being introduced. This was understandably viewed on the one hand as a blow to the regional languages, and on the other as a veiled victory for English.

Students entering the university after June 1955 would face special difficulties, the committee conceded, "since the majority of them had

---

[12] Computed from statistics provided by the registrar, Nagpur University.
[13] S. K. Chatterji, "The Language Problem in Indian Education," a lecture delivered at the Ramakrishna Mission Institute of Culture on June 6, 1953, reprinted from the *Bulletin* of the Ramakrishna Mission Institute of Culture, January 1954, p. 9.

been taught through regional languages, and their defective knowledge of English would not have enabled them to follow the lectures delivered in English in the college classes."

Discussing the "short-term problem" presented by this decline of secondary school English, the committee reported that,

> ... in order to enable students to follow lectures in English with ease, teachers had been instructed to use simple language, to dictate summaries of lectures at the end of the period, and to hold special classes of small groups of students where the students were given lessons in composition. On the whole, their experiences showed that the difficulties created by the situation were not insuperable, although some of them doubted whether the students would be able to answer their examination papers satisfactorily in the English language.[14]

A significant barometer which will indicate whether the regional languages are actually proving to be usable media of higher education is the extent to which they are used for theses and postgraduate dissertations. To date, the only formal attempt to force the pace in this respect has been at Lucknow, where the university court passed a resolution in May that students should either write their thesis in Hindi or attach a Hindi translation in the event that it is written in English. This has not yet been put into practice.[15]

Even more important to watch will be the entrance examination, as Sir Philip Hartog has forewarned. The prestige of English will depend first upon whether it remains as the examination medium, and should that go, whether it is a compulsory examination subject. Pointing out that English is still a mandatory subject on most entrance examinations, the *Times of India* deplored the Punjab University Senate's decision in September 1955 that English would be optional on the examination and that Hindi and Punjabi would henceforth be the compulsory language subjects.[16] As yet this by no means typifies the national pattern, for even Gujarat University, outspoken in its advocacy of the regional language medium, has decided that English must be a compulsory requirement for entrance.[17]

---

[14] *Report of the Committee on the Medium of Instruction*, Bombay University, 1955. Two dissenters from the committee report, G. D. Parikh and G. M. Kurulkar, have stressed the narrow majority which decided the committee's Hindi recommendation. Out of the 23 members of the committee, only 12 favored the designation of Hindi as the sole medium; of 31 constituent colleges in Bombay University, 25 replied to the committee questionnaire, out of which only 11 favored Hindi.
[15] "Language for Theses," *Times of India*, May 7, 1956.
[16] *Times of India*, September 11, 1955.
[17] Letter from M. P. Desai in *Times of India*, May 19, 1956.

Surveying the general prospect in Indian education, Dr. Horace I. Poleman has understandably prophesied that "the transition from English to other languages will inaugurate a period of intellectual pandemonium." With the would-be national leader required to learn first his mother tongue, then Hindi, then English, Poleman foresees that "a few intellectual giants may survive this ordeal; the rest of the students may well be of a very inferior grade."[18]

The outcome of the controversy over the university medium of instruction must inevitably carry grave implications for the future of Indian political leadership. Representative leadership such as the Parliament may in fact become less and less representative. For the politician competent solely in the regional language may be compelled by the very nature of the situation to remain in his local sphere; and, barring a new lease on life for the beleaguered Hindi cause, one competent in Hindi or English who does go to New Delhi is likely to typify increasingly an elite apart from the mainstream of cultural and political life in the constituencies. But university policy will leave its mark on representative leadership only over a period of many years. It is in the realm of administrative leadership that language policy decisions can most decisively alter the immediate course of events, independent of university policies and perhaps even in competition with them. Indeed, possibilities of cleavage here, between university policies determined largely by local political pressures and central policies decided on the basis of national considerations, pose an increasingly serious dilemma.

Alongside the demand for the use of the regional languages in the universities has come the corollary demand for the option to write civil service examinations in the mother tongue rather than in English as now required.

The report of the 1948 Committee on the Medium of Instruction declared that federal civil service examinations "may be conducted through the language of the region, but candidates who are accepted by the government should be required to pass a test in the federal language and to take further training in that language."[19]

The University Education Commission, while urging that English "continue as the medium for federal business . . . until the provincial educational institutions have spread the federal language adequately," clearly appeared impressed by the fears of the non-Hindi regions.

---

[18] Horace I. Poleman, "The Problem of Language," unpublished paper read at the American Oriental Society annual meeting, Washington, 1954.
[19] *Report of the Committee on the Medium of Instruction at the University Stage*, p. 5.

Granted that Hindi will be the federal language of India, the report asks:

> How will it affect the participation in the affairs of the federation of those whose mother-tongue is different? Members of the federal legislature will be required to speak in the federal language; members of the central government, officials of the secretariat, judges of the federal court will employ it. How will all this affect the personnel of the legislature, the executive and the judiciary? Will it give to those whose mother-tongue is Hindi an undue advantage and a disproportionate influence in the affairs of the state? Will this arrangement deprive the central government of the valuable services of the intellectual elite of India irrespective of the regional and linguistic provenance?[20]

The crucial importance of the examination medium as a determinant of all language policy is apparent in the Madras University Syndicate's recommendation, in September 1955, that English should be retained for official purposes for at least thirty years, by constitutional amendment if necessary. This stand followed a Union Home Ministry circular to the Inter-University Board on the introduction of Hindi in the all-India competitive examinations for the civil services.[21]

Similarly, Bombay University's Hindi policy has the recruitment examination in mind. Ultimately, the public service examinations should be held in Hindi alone, the committee recommended, with a period of ten years elapsing before this decision is put into effect and with English and Hindi permitted to continue meanwhile as alternative media. But even in Bombay, "some members were of the opinion that candidates for public service examinations held by the center should be permitted to answer questions in their regional languages."[22]

Poona University, weighing its relations with other universities in the Indian Union, reported in 1951 that "the direction and pace of future progress [in resolving the medium of instruction issue] depends on the policy adopted by the governments of the union and the states, especially regarding the language of administration, the mode of recruit-

---

[20] *Report of the University Education Commission*, I, 320.

[21] *Times of India*, September 19, 1955.

[22] Pointing to the absence of a "uniform standard by which merit could be assessed" if the regional languages were permitted, the committee suggested preliminary screening examinations in the regions to be taken through the regional language medium, with winning candidates then appearing for federal examinations in which candidates would necessarily "answer their papers in a few subjects, such as public administration, in Hindi. They should also be required to write an essay in Hindi, because a good knowledge of Hindi will be essential for them if they are to discharge their official duties satisfactorily. They should, however, be at liberty to write their answers to the other papers in their own mother-tongue."

ment to the services and the policies of the other Indian universities."[23]

It was the consequences in the national civil service that disturbed the Bombay Congress Committee in its opposition to linguistic demarcation of political boundaries in 1954. In its memorandum to the States Reorganization Commission, the committee warned that linguistic states would reduce Indian universities to "tenth rate institutions. There will be unequal competition between students of one state and another in all competitive examinations conducted for central recruitment. In our view, general educational policy and particularly university education should have been the subjects in the union list and not in the state list as at present. . . . One simply shudders at the thought of what will happen to our education if the language knights succeed in their mission. This is bound to lower our educational standards and make administration loose and inefficient."[24]

At present, examinations for the 1,539 regular posts in the Indian Administrative Service and the 937 posts in the Indian Police Service must be written in English. Nor can "beggars be choosers," as Asoka Mehta put it in discussing the educated unemployment which brought 40,000 applicants flocking in 1956, when 300 I.A.S. vacancies were announced. For the long haul, however, the place of English as the *de facto* administrative language in India does not jibe with declared nationalist intentions. Official Congress policy would permit the recruitment examination to be in the regional language to assure a fair chance for non-Hindi candidates. The Congress Working Committee said in April 1954 that examinations for the all-India services should be in Hindi, English, or the regional languages, with the choice of the medium left to the candidates themselves.[25]

Whatever it is, the language of the civil service examinations will have decisive prestige in a society where government employment itself enjoys so high a station. S. N. Agarwal, Congress Party General Secretary, recognized this when he argued that Hindi be given at least optional status as an examination medium. Otherwise, he feared that the lure to use English as the medium of instruction in higher education would persist.[26]

The power of economic incentive which government language policy

[23] *Report of the Committee on the Medium of Instruction at the University Stage*, p. 36.
[24] "Hands Off Bombay, A Plea for National Unity and First Things First," Memorandum submitted by the Bombay Pradesh Congress Committee to the States Reorganisation Commission, Bombay, 1954, p. 25.
[25] *Times of India*, April 7, 1954.
[26] *ibid.*, October 6, 1954.

can exercise is illustrated in the case of the Marathi minority in the former state of Madhya Bharat. The *Times of India* reported in 1955 that Marathi was only an optional subject in the high school examination in predominately Hindi-speaking Madhya Bharat and that the tendency to study languages other than Marathi was gaining ground even among pupils whose mother tongue is Marathi. The secretary of the local Marathi Sahitya Sammelan attributes this to "the existing economic stresses and strains," meaning, explained the reporter, "that the better prospect of official jobs which education in Hindi would offer tomorrow was weaning away Maharashtrian boys from Marathi to Hindi. If this tendency was allowed to grow, the Sammelan was afraid there would soon be a generation of Maharashtrians unlettered in Marathi."[27]

Much of the general opposition to Hindi in the non-Hindi regions is linked to the civil service examinations. Aspirants to the bureaucracy in the non-Hindi regions fear that sooner or later Hindi enthusiasts will foist the union language upon them as a mandatory medium, inevitably favoring those whose mother tongue is Hindi. Even a nationalist Tamil leader such as Chakravarti Rajagopalachari raised a thundering protest when talk of the use of Hindi as the medium for the civil service examinations mounted in early 1954. Rajagopalachari wrote:

There is justice in asking our children to learn Hindi. It is also right if we tempt children that they will get high offices if only they learn Hindi. . . .

But, at the same time, if it were to be said that all examinations for the recruitment to high and responsible posts in government would be conducted in a foreign medium—it is foreign in so far as Tamils are concerned—then, legitimately, there is reason to be angry over it. I am myself angry.

Tamil children can learn and master Hindi. In fact, they can learn any language. Have they not learned even English to a degree that they get quite a large number of government jobs? When they have learned English, is it difficult to learn Hindi? There is no doubt about it. But all my doubts center around the Hindi language itself, for it is still in its infancy. It is in an undeveloped stage. It is not surprising, therefore, that Hindi is not equal to English. It is not equal to Tamil, Bengali, or Marathi. In these circumstances, what ought to be done? Surely, it should not be to threaten Tamil children.

In Delhi parliament, members from Jawaharlal Nehru down to anyone who is educated to some extent express themselves briefly and clearly whenever they speak in English. They leave no room for doubt in what they say. But when they use the Hindi medium, they repeat themselves quite often and still find it difficult to express their ideas precisely, correctly and fully.

[27] *ibid.*, February 1, 1955.

This difficulty arises because of the poverty of the Hindi language and of its want of growth. Hindi vocabulary lacks in precision. So our first act should be to put Hindi at school, rather than to ask the Tamil people to learn Hindi. It is not the Tamil children that have to pass the examination, rather it is Hindi itself that should pass the test.[28]

In his testimony before the Official Language Commission at Cuttack, Orissa, C. M. Acharya, former vice-chancellor of Utkal University, pleaded in November 1955 for the retention of English for at least fifty years and warned that the all-India administrative services would fall into the hands of the Hindi-speaking states if Hindi replaced English at the present time.[29] The Mysore Pradesh Congress Committee said in its memorandum to the commission that English and the regional languages should both be recognized as media for the Union Public Service examinations. The Mysore government did not suggest the regional language but argued against Hindi as the mandatory medium.[30]

Reassuring the non-Hindi regions, President Rajendra Prasad has said that while Hindi would become the medium, exceptions would be made to permit question papers in English or in the regional languages —yielding to the opposition while trying to make it appear otherwise. His qualification was that after their entrance into the civil service, the non-Hindi speaking candidates would have to pass a test in Hindi.[31]

Home Minister G. B. Pant wrote to Rajagopalachari, agreeing that candidates from non-Hindi speaking areas should not be handicapped or placed at a disadvantage in competing with their counterparts from Hindi-speaking areas:

The question of the adoption of Hindi as the official language of the union need not be inextricably bound up with the language or languages that may be adopted for conducting the All-India examinations. We should stick to the time table prescribed by the constituent assembly for the replacement of English by Hindi in the central offices; but nothing should be done that would tend to deprive the country of the services of the best qualified youths on account of any avoidable difficulty in the matter of examinations.[32]

[28] C. Rajagopalachari, "The Language Problem," *Kalki* (Tamil weekly, Madras), April 19, 1955.
[29] *Amrita Bazar Patrika*, December 1, 1955.   [30] *Times of India*, January 14, 1956.
[31] In its 1954 resolution on the progressive introduction of Hindi in the examinations for all-India civil service posts, the Congress Working Committee had recommended that candidates using Hindi or a regional language in the examinations should also pass a separate test in English, with successful regional-language candidates required to pass a test in Hindi at an early date. Those using Hindi were to take a compulsory test in English and a regional language other than Hindi. Candidates passing the examination in English were to take a compulsory test in Hindi, and for all non-English examinees, English was to be a compulsory subject.
[32] *Indian Express*, June 4, 1955.

The *Times of India*, commenting on Pant's assurance, declared that even after 1965, students appearing for all-India civil service examinations "can be allowed the option of answering their papers in English or a regional language. Not much will be lost if Hindi does not become the language of examinations until 1970 or even 1975."[33]

These are the possible linguistic patterns of tomorrow's Indian leadership:

First, English may complete a triumphant comeback. The initiative for retaining English comes not only from educational leaders who see the long generations of development ahead before many Indian languages can be effectively used in education. Even stronger support for the English cause comes from leaders in non-Hindi regions who see in English a vehicle of national unity which offers at the same time a way to forestall the acceptance of Hindi. English also gains greatly from the link between English and the increasingly vocational and technological orientation of Indian education. The ambitious technician-administrator who wishes to go outside his region will realize far more sharply than the political administrator the inescapable necessity of English as a window to world progress in his field.

Secondly, the regional languages may maintain their present momentum, and the various mother tongues may become optional media of the recruitment examination for the central government services. It would seem, in fact, that once university education has clearly passed into the regional languages, irresistible pressure to permit use of the regional languages in the civil service examinations is bound to follow. If this does happen, then it seems inevitable that the central civil services will lose their cosmopolitan character and become subject to the same regional stresses as the larger Indian body politic—although this is not to say, of course, that central civil servants will be altogether ignorant of Hindi.

Or, there is the possibility that Hindi may in time acquire sufficient emphasis in the educational system and sufficient prestige as a prerequisite for Indian leadership to secure its position. This seems to be the least likely of all the three alternatives, however, if only because Hindi is so clearly less developed as a language than such rivals as Tamil, Bengali, and Marathi, which cannot be expected to yield to Hindi without the most ruthlessly determined pressure—pressure of a degree that only a single-minded, revivalist central regime is likely to risk.

[33] *Times of India*, June 9, 1955.

There is, of course, a fourth possible alternative which may be more likely than either of these three clear possibilities: a middle way in which the incentives to learn English and Hindi produce substantial national leadership competent in one of these languages, while men competent primarily in the regional languages are propelled willy-nilly to New Delhi by their own unrivalled strength in their regions. Speaking with a measure of authority itself eloquent enough to compensate for their linguistic rough edges, these regional leaders might somehow manage to function at the national level. Whatever the ultimate resolution of the issue, for the next generation some such pattern as this appears likely.

The writer sees equally great disadvantages in each of the clear-cut possibilities. Total Hindi dominance, achieved at the expense of other languages, would evoke festering resentment in the non-Hindi regions and would thus be self-defeating; total triumph of the regional languages would minimize India's intellectual and political communion; total decline of English would sever India from meaningful contact with western technology. Perhaps most dangerous of all, since it is so lively a possibility, the continued exclusive use of English as the *de facto* Union language of India can only perpetuate the division between the central leadership and the swelling millions of new literates in the regional languages. Even when he was pleading in 1955 for a continued place for English, Nehru reiterated the nationalist view that "to carry on the administration in English would create a gap between the government and the people. We must carry on the administration in an Indian language. But all the same, we must not ignore English."[34]

Is India settling into its age-old linguistic pattern of past autocracy in which government has been largely a political overlay speaking a court language unknown to the masses of the people? Taken together with the decline in party politics on the national level, the tactical retreat to English on the part of non-Hindi regions points to precisely this possibility. Vital as English may be to the cause of Indian unity, it is important to recognize that the cause of unity in many respects makes claims antithetical to the cause of representative political institutions.

Indeed, the most readily apparent escape device from India's language policy impasse would seem to presuppose totalitarian central authority. It was only the strident nationalism of Subhas Chandra Bose, albeit mingled with a Bengali bias against Hindi, that could envisage the introduction of the Roman script to harmonize the regional lan-

[34] *The Statesman*, December 9, 1955.

guages, English, and Hindi in a strong central administration. To establish the Roman script and the "common educational policy" which Bose championed at the 1938 Haripura Congress might well necessitate totalitarian controls. In any case, Bose himself quite frankly looked to the iron-handed leadership that Ataturk had exercised:

> Special efforts will be needed to keep our people together when the load of foreign domination is removed, because alien rule had demoralized and disorganized us to a degree. To promote national unity we shall have to develop our lingua franca and a common script. Further, with the help of such modern scientific contrivances as airplanes, telephone, radio, films, television, we shall have to bring the different parts of India closer to one another and through a common educational policy shall have to foster a common spirit among the entire population. There is nothing sacrosanct in a script. The choice of a uniform script for the whole of India should be made in a thoroughly scientific and impartial spirit, free from bias of every kind. I confess there was a time when I felt that it would be anti-national to adopt a foreign script. But my visit to Turkey in 1934 was responsible for converting me. So far as our masses are concerned, since more than ninety percent are illiterate and not familiar with any script, it will not matter to them which script we introduce when they are educated.[35]

As a merely mechanical problem, it will grow increasingly difficult to carry on a parliamentary democracy with competence in English on the downgrade and Hindi unable to win acceptance at a corresponding pace. The States Reorganisation Commission has pointed to the increasing use of the regional languages in political life, declaring that "already in some of the states a large percentage of members in the Legislature know only one language and this trend is likely to become more and more emphasized. In some states, even ministers know only one regional language. Discussions in legislatures would become difficult, if not impossible, if a considerable number of members are unable to follow the proceedings."[36]

In states constituted on a linguistic basis, it will be all to the good for lawmakers to use the popular medium at the provincial level. The difficulty will develop at the central level. There is at hand the great danger, as the University Education Commission prophesied, that the central government will be "deprived of the valuable services of the intellectual elite of India irrespective of the regional and linguistic provenance."

[35] *Famous Speeches and Letters of Subhas Chandra Bose*, Lahore, Lion Press, 1946, p. 27.
[36] *Report of the States Reorganisation Commission*, Delhi, 1955, p. 36.

For the present the momentum is on the side of the regional languages, leaving the English-speaking intelligentsia stranded as cultural DP's. As a reaction to the sense of isolation and hopelessness in which they find themselves, many are becoming more and more uprooted from their intellectual environment and are seeking spiritual nourishment entirely from the West. Still others are turning to an exaggerated revivalism and cultural chauvinism, rejecting completely their English heritage. The trend to the regional languages, K. K. Sinha writes, is promoting "an atmosphere and a cultural climate which is a sudden drop from the past. The older educated generation must live in the midst of this climate, in their homes, their working places, and their clubs. Either they get slowly eaten up by this overwhelming climate or they isolate themselves from the general current."[37] Some English-educated Indian educators are developing a "peculiarly superior mystique that is India and the ancient past, as against the modern Western attitude or scientific approach, while still others are preoccupied with provincial superiority—regional chauvinism with an odd mixture of Hindu religious and mystical appeal."

With increasing mass political participation Sinha sees "a peculiar kind of distrust toward the English educated." Asoka Mehta, too, has observed that,

> ... a new group prejudice is slowly emerging in political parties. It is the group strength of persons inadequately educated. The prevalence of a foreign language, English in the case of India, as the official language of the country, has created a special type of monopoly. Only a handful of men who know English are able to operate effectively in political and administrative matters. As a strong opposition grew up against Latin in Europe in the Middle Ages, so in India against the English-knowing 'neo Brahmins' an opposition is growing up.[38]

This then, is India's dilemma: with English, a widening chasm between the leaders and the led; without it, the danger, as S. K. Chatterji has warned, that "we shall become what is called in Sanskrit *kupa mandukas*, or Frogs in the Well, thinking too much of our little world and cutting ourselves off from the rest of India and the world outside."[39]

---

[37] K. K. Sinha, editor of the *Indian Journal of Power and River Valley Development*; analysis prepared for the author, Calcutta, January 11, 1956, p. 9.
[38] Asoka Mehta, in *Group Prejudices in India*, ed. by M. B. Nanavati and C. N. Vakil, Bombay, Popular Book Depot, 1953, p. 43.
[39] Chatterji, *op.cit.*, p. 4.

4. POLITICAL PARTIES

A STUDY of the major political parties of India is essential in any review of political leadership in India. The "umbrella" function of the Indian National Congress during its dominance in the nationalist movement is examined by Robert I. Crane in his historical account of the changing demands of the nationalist movement and of the changing types of leaders that led that movement. The problems encountered in newly independent countries in developing opposition parties are reviewed in Thomas Rusch's study of Indian socialism. Richard Lambert emphasizes the difficulties that traditional religious groups have had in counteracting the dominance of western institutions. The unique role played by the Communist Party in India is discussed by Gene Overstreet.

THE LEADERSHIP OF THE CONGRESS PARTY

ROBERT I. CRANE

*T*HIS essay is designed to study the nature of the leadership of the Congress Party through time. Special attention will be paid to origins, matters of motivation, issues of organization, and to the special problems which the leadership had to face in the achievement of their goals as nationalists and as leaders of a political movement.

It must be stressed at the outset that the state of knowledge regarding Congress leadership is far from satisfactory. Certain gaps regarding salient features of the matter exist. Some of the kinds of data that would be required for precise judgments have not been collected, while the pertinent questions may not yet have been formulated. Thus some of the statements made herein should be viewed as little more than hypotheses.

The underlying assumption on which the essay rests may be put as follows. The nationalist movement in India developed as a response to European contact and domination. This is true in the sense that European education helped to create many of the core ideas of nationalism and in the sense that European rule served to create a number of the preconditions necessary for the growth of national sentiment. Moreover, alien domination produced a reaction amongst Indians regarding those aspects of foreign control which were felt to be intolerable. From this it may be argued that the nationalist leadership—serving as a kind of epitome of Indian response to Europeanization—sought to express or to represent the Indian reaction in such a way as to unite Indian opinion, mobilize public sentiment, formulate popular demands, and state nationalist goals and objectives. This also involved the channeling of public opinion in an organized fashion so as to bring pressure to bear upon the government.

Though this remained the central problem facing the leadership throughout the period until Independence, it is quite apparent that the dimensions of the problem and the nature of the methods used by the leaders varied from time to time. Such variations may be said, at least as a first approximation, to reflect different stages in the growth of nationalism in India. By closer study of each stage in the growth of the nationalist movement we may hope to illuminate the peculiar problems

ROBERT I. CRANE *is an Associate Professor of History at the University of Michigan. Formerly he was on the staff at the University of Chicago.*

faced during that stage of growth as well as the kinds of solutions adopted by the leadership for the problems of that stage.

The device of closer analysis of the problems faced by leadership in the successive stages of development of the movement is useful for another reason. It can be argued that each stage "produced" a somewhat different kind of leadership, or different kinds of leaderships, in the nationalist arena. Seen in this light the concept of stages of development should make it possible to sharpen our insights into the basic issue of the kinds of leadership that developed in the Congress movement. Furthermore, analysis of the problems of each stage avoids generalizations over the whole period of the Congress movement. Such generalizations could, of course, conceal more than they reveal.

We may cite as an example of the need for this kind of analysis the following problem. Throughout the history of the Congress the leadership had to attempt to represent, accurately and effectively, the feelings and aspirations of the inarticulate public. This problem was not always handled in the same way, but it may be argued that as the Congress developed it was able, by increasingly effective means, to meet the issue. While the leadership of one period may not have been able to achieve so effective a response, the leadership of the next stage may have been able to devise new solutions or to take advantage of new developments in public consciousness so as to solve the problem.

In its inception Congress leadership was quite homogeneous.[1] This homogeneity included levels of socio-economic origin, occupational status, common viewpoint, and a characteristic approach to political issues. The homogeneity of the early leadership was, as one might expect, reflected in the tenor of the resolutions passed by the Congress as well as in the kinds of problems that were taken up.[2] This was the period of Moderate domination and has been discussed sufficiently in the literature so that only a few points need be made here.

One of the characteristic features of the early Congress leadership was its uniform recruitment from the ranks of the western-educated. A concomitant characteristic was that the bulk of the Moderate leaders were men of the professions. These professions—such as the law—were, of

---

[1] See B. Pattabhi Sitaramayya, *The History of the Indian National Congress*, Bombay, Padma Publications, 1946, Vol. I; E. Thompson and G. T. Garratt, *Rise and Fulfillment of British Rule in India*, London, Macmillan, 1934, pp. 543ff.; M. A. Buch, *Rise and Growth of Indian Militant Nationalism*, Baroda, Atmaram Press, 1940, pp. 71ff.

[2] See the discussion of homogeneity of viewpoint in Bimla Prasad, "The Indian Nationalist Movement and Economic Policy, 1802-92," *Current Studies*, Patna College, 1954.

course, based upon the fact of European contact. It was the introduction of European legal systems and other practices that provided scope and demand for trained professional men.

The point to be noted is that, especially in the early period of nationalism, European education was available only to those whose families were numbered among the upper-income groups of Indian society. This fact carries certain implications for origins as well as for the matter of motivations. In origin the leadership of the Moderate period was generally upper-income; in education it was relatively completely assimilated to the prevailing European outlook and value system; in interest it found many points in common with the prevailing system of government, administration, and control.

As is well known, the orientation of the Moderates was twofold. In the realm of politics theirs was a demand, couched in parliamentary and constitutional terms, for greater association of the Indian educated classes with the administration of India. This did not include a demand for self-government or for breaking the imperial ties with Britain. This demand was not centered upon economic grievances although reference was made to economic matters that were of concern to the nascent middle class. In connection with this demand some effort was made to point to the economic condition of the masses in order to argue that British rule could fulfil its promise if Indian statesmen were associated with the councils of government and were thus in a position to press for ameliorative measures on behalf of the masses. But these references to common economic problems often exhibited the bias of origin of the Moderate leaders.

The Moderates also had an important orientation toward social reform. By this was meant the reform of traditional social practices of Hinduism which the new value system imported from Europe could not condone. It also meant the reform of traditional systems of thought in light of principles of scientific and rational method learned in the West. It is interesting to note in this connection that one of the arguments advanced by the Moderates was that they should be associated with the government so as to be able to facilitate social and intellectual reform in India.

The nature of Moderate interests, objectives, and point of view was such as to separate them from the bulk of Indian society. Their very parliamentarianism was, of course, sufficient guarantee of this fact. This situation, by the way, made it possible for the government to discount the Congress as being but a "microscopic minority."[3] These facts posed an important and difficult organizational and strategic problem for the Moderate leadership. In what ways could the Congress program and the organization of the Congress be modified so as to secure wider public support or even a mass following?

As time passed it became increasingly apparent that Moderate agitation was ineffectual, even in terms of its limited objectives. The Moderates were too few in number and too parliamentarian in their approach to move the government *or* to excite the public.[4] Even within the Congress itself, there developed elements that deprecated the procedures used by the Moderate leadership. The following quotation from the *Bengalee* serves to illustrate the situation:

> We have come to the conclusion and even sceptics have been converted to the view that the principles of Liberalism are not meant for India. . . . There is but one party which governs India . . . the party of reaction . . . which will not hesitate to set at naught the elementary principles of justice. . . . The disillusionment has come.[5]

The failure of the Moderate program and tactic brought organizational and programmatic problems to the fore. If the Congress were to command enough strength to influence the government it was going to have to expand its ranks, attract greater and wider public support, and devise new techniques for applying pressure. This meant extending the influence and the organization of the Congress down from the top through varied layers of Indian society. In effect, a political party had to be created, and that party had to reach the masses and give an organizational lead to mass pressures.

The majority of the Moderates were not, however, equipped to create or to lead a mass movement, nor was there at hand the basis for creation of a mass organization. For that matter, it is probably fair to say that the typical Moderate was so far separated from the intellectual and emotional world of the Indian masses that he could not communicate effectively with them. Moreover, as has been indicated, the typical Moderate was unable to think in terms of what we might call "grass roots" organizational techniques. This was true in part because India had no tradition of popular political parties based on a vocal following among

[3] Quoted in R. C. Majumdar, H. C. Raychaudhuri, K. Datta, *An Advanced History of India*, 2nd edn., London, Macmillan, 1950, p. 894.

[4] V. P. S. Raghuvanshi, *Indian Nationalist Movement and Thought*, Agra, L. N. Agarwal, 1951, pp. 3ff. Also, Sir Henry Cotton, *New India: or, India in Transition*, London, K. Paul, Trench, Trubner, 1909, pp. 2-4.

[5] Quoted in Buch, *op.cit.*, p. 39. See also his comments on pp. 71ff.

the peasantry or town craftsmen and because the goals and objectives of western-educated leaders were not readily translatable into the traditional Indian idiom.

This being the case, the affairs of Congress in its efforts to gain redress of elite grievances had reached something of an impasse by the turn of the century. Meanwhile, however, other developments in India had begun to create conditions from which new kinds of impetus could be given to the nationalist movement. New kinds of leadership were arising and new pressures in support of nationalist objectives, as well as new objectives, appeared.

Of importance in this respect was the spread of European education among larger circles of the Indian population during the last two decades of the nineteenth century, a trend which was intensified during the twentieth century.[6] Whereas the Moderate leadership, which had taken its European education at an earlier date, had generally come from the upper-income segments of the Indian population or had found employment in professions which were not yet overcrowded, it is apparent that the ranks from which the educated young men were drawn, as the century wore to its close, were of a different level. Moreover, as larger numbers of Indians secured the prized degree, the fields of respectable employment into which they might pass tended to fill. All the evidence we have indicates that the newer generation of western-educated Indians came largely from lower-income levels of society and found it harder to secure gainful and respectable employment after completing their education.[7]

Unlike the Moderate leadership, therefore, the rising voice of educated India represented acute grievances that resulted from personal economic frustration as well as from the social frustration implicit in certain aspects of the normal relationship between Indians and their European rulers. Perhaps of greater significance is the fact that so many of the newly educated group came from a more humble socio-economic status, for it can be hypothesized that they were, as a group, closer to the basic population at least in thought, in idiom, and in motivation.[8]

Moreover, careful examination of the available evidence seems to

---

[6] B. T. McCully, *English Education and the Origins of Indian Nationalism*, New York, Columbia University Press, 1940, p. 177.

[7] Sedition Committee, 1918, *Report*, Calcutta, Superintendent Government Printing, 1919, p. 111. See also the comment on page 16 of the *Report*.

[8] While direct evidence on this point is difficult to find, there are a number of oblique references which would seem to establish the fact. See, for instance, C. Y. Chintamani, *Indian Politics Since the Mutiny*, London, Allen & Unwin, 1940, pp. 85-86.

indicate that many of the newly educated were but imperfectly assimilated to European ideas by their education while numbers of them responded to European values in a negative fashion.[9] In the first place, many of the newly educated secured less western education than had the older generation. Many of the young men of the extremist wing and of the terrorist groups that were spawned after 1905 had little more than a high school education and at best an imperfect understanding of western values. Furthermore, it seems apparent that the bulk of the newly educated came from classes of Indian society that were, by birth and by tradition, the carriers of orthodox Hinduism. For these folk contact with the European value system was a threat to the indigenous and orthodox values which they carried and it may be assumed that this threat was reinforced by the dislocative effects of European control upon the older status system.[10] When these people, alarmed by the implications of European ideas and disturbed by the loss of status implicit in the European-inspired social revolution that was in the making as India was modernized, ran into personal frustration over jobs and status, a radicalism was engendered that fed the extremism of the new phase in nationalist development.

These people, by virtue of their origins and their incomplete or negative assimilation to western ideas continued to be able to speak in the authentic idiom of India, in an idiom that could reach directly to the masses because it contained so much of an assertion of the older, pre-European value system. By contrast the Moderates, being pioneers in westernization, may have had to come from groups in India that were less firmly wedded to traditional values or that had to revolt against the traditional background in order to take advantage of the new opportunities opened to them by European contact and educational facilities. Whatever the reasons, it seems clear that the bulk of the Moderates were rather effectively wedded to the values of the West, while it is equally clear that this was by no means the case among the extremists who arose from the newly educated classes.

In this connection another aspect of change in India may be mentioned.

[9] This is spelled out in some detail in "Origins and Characteristics of the Extremists in Indian Nationalism," a paper read by R. I. Crane at the Far Eastern Association meeting, Philadelphia, April, 1956.

[10] As indicated by W. Norman Brown in his *The United States and India and Pakistan*, Cambridge, Harvard University Press, 1953, p. 51: "Another aspect of secularization appears in the weakening of Brahman prestige. . . . All over India the Brahman has to face competition from every caste down to the untouchables in seeking posts that a century ago would have seemed his by rightful monopoly."

After the opening of the Suez Canal the process of Europeanization went on more briskly and effectively than it had before. Put simply, the extent, scope, and vigor of contact with European ways and practices increased toward the end of the nineteenth century. It seems apparent that this process called into question, in a more persistent fashion than at any previous time, a number of the basic values and institutions of traditional India, while at the same time it caused larger segments of the population to experience direct and sometimes unpleasant effects flowing from such contact. The enhanced contact implied, among other things, the opening of Indian society to wide relationships with the market-oriented commercial economy of Europe and this in turn brought new levels of Indian society into a situation characterized by dislocation and social trauma. Near the turn of the century specific incidents such as great famines and serious visitations of the plague only served to sharpen the impact of change upon the Indian masses. This mass unsettlement, it is here argued, served to create a new basis for nationalist agitation but the new situation was one with which the Moderates could hardly cope.

Since many of the newly educated were drawn from those elements of Indian society which were most orthodox—the *bhadralog*—and since they could compare their present depressed condition with their superior status in an earlier era, it was but natural for them to connect their personal frustrations with the growth of general dislocation implicit in the spread of European contact and control. More important, it would seem to be logical for them to couch their protest in traditional terms, as a defense of traditional values from alien debasement. These classes sensed or saw that Europeanization threatened their own position or prospects in society. These classes stood close to the orthodoxy of the traditional system that was perceived to be "under attack" and these classes could speak in an idiom that the non-Europeanized masses could understand and support.

When the last years of the century witnessed the hardships mentioned above, a new leadership—attuned to mass sentiments—could emerge to propose new goals and new techniques for the Congress. In the midst of famine and plague, in an era of growing dissatisfaction with Moderate parliamentary agitation, in a situation marked by the appearance of ever larger numbers of western-educated young men bitter over their position and prospects, it was perhaps but natural that cultural and religious revivalism came to be significant elements of the new, extremist politics, and that these values enrolled substantial numbers of the new kind of leaders in the Congress. It seems also but natural that these new voices on the scene should move to transform the nationalist movement, reshaping it along new lines. The significant fact is, of course, that the voice of the new generation was much more closely in tune with the sentiments of the Indian masses, so that a link with mass support could now be secured.

It was shortly after the turn of the century that this new leadership developed in the ranks of Indian nationalism and, increasingly, in the Congress itself. Bal Tilak was the herald of the new extremist view in Indian politics, but his followers were many. Among them were the editors of new vernacular papers which sprang up to spread the message of extremism in politics and of Hindu revivalism. It should be noted in this connection that a large proportion of extremist leadership, as of the membership in terrorist bands, was recruited from Brahman and Kayastha families.

This was also the period of the use of Hindu festivals, Hindu societies, and Hindu religious forms for whipping up support for political objectives.[11] Indeed, as the report of the Sedition Committee so clearly indicates, extremist politics were a mixture of political, social, and religious grievances and themes, with religious revivalism buttressing and reinforcing political or social protest.

In 1905 the significance of the new link between political agitation and traditional values was for the first time convincingly demonstrated. The agitation over the partition of Bengal, though its history has never been written in any satisfactory fashion, was not commenced by the older Moderate leadership nor was it inspired by the older formulas of constitutional reform. Actually it seems that the Moderates were rather surprised by the popular demonstrations involving large numbers of people and that the Moderates joined the agitation rather than led it.

The campaign of 1905 was of special significance because new techniques of mass participation were used. Boycott, hartal, and demonstrations for Swadeshi proved to be valuable instruments in creation of a

[11] Apart from his role as a thinker and speaker, Tilak was of major importance in the development of a new phase in Indian nationalism because he moved toward the use of new mechanisms for mobilizing the masses and channeling their political energy. The Ganpati festivals that he organized, attended by the growth of exercise and drill groups among Hindu boys, were embryonic manifestations of the search for organizational methods that would link the program to its necessary mass support. M. A. Buch gives great importance to this phase in the development of the Congress; see *op.cit.*, pp. 92-93, 116ff., and 125-26, where Buch says, "Tilak was thus able to effect the union of the new political spirit with the tradition and sentiment of the historic past and of both with the ineradicable religious temperament of the people, of which these festivals were the symbol."

popular upsurge that mobilized the rank and file in nationalist activity. At the same time a fillip was given to the organization of secret societies, such as the Anushilan Samiti, which spawned terrorism in the name of Hindu patriotism. The antipartition agitation moved large numbers of people into action and facilitated the growth of secret societies but did not, of itself, contribute in a direct fashion to the creation of mass organizational bodies within the Congress.

The campaign did, however, draw the attention of the Congress to popular agitational methods and strengthened the hand of those in the Congress who desired direct action. As a result Congress for the first time accepted several of Tilak's slogans as official goals in 1907, and the 1908 constitution of the Congress provided for creation of distinct and functioning provincial Congress committees. The 1905 campaign was important for another reason. The Swadeshi demonstrations showed the rising Indian business class that organized nationalism could help them gain their own objectives and caused an increasing number of businessmen to lend support to the Congress. At a somewhat later date the financial support derived from business gave the Congress the means by which party organization could be extended to the local level.

The Congress was not, as yet, fully committed to the implications of extremism. Many of the older Moderates remained uncomfortable in the face of the new trend, and divided leadership was the result. After several years of internal strife the staunch Moderates withdrew from Congress. This left the field to the extremists. Such a solution was not, however, satisfactory for the nationalist movement for one important reason.

If the Congress were to represent India in the face of European control it had to try to speak for *all* of the major elements of the Indian population. Just as the Moderates had proved ineffective because they spoke for such a limited section of India, so the extremists—with their emphasis on Hindu revivalism—spoke only for segments of the population. Congress had to stand as a national front, and this meant a leadership that could bridge the differences in Congress ranks and secure support from all levels of the nation.

With the first World War it can be said that the basis was laid for a new stage in the growth of Indian nationalism. This was true for several reasons. In the first place, the war gave considerable impetus to the growth of modern industry in India. This meant the growth of urbanization, of a factory working class that could be mobilized for political action, and of the Indian business community which could be drawn into support of the Congress. The war also caused considerable dislocation of the Indian economy with resultant hardships that spread a feeling of discontent among large sectors of the population. The spreading discontent arising from wartime dislocation and shortage could be used to mobilize support for Congress.[12]

Then too, the war disturbed the Indian Muslims and propelled them into antigovernment activity. The result was a *rapprochement* between Congress and the Muslims that was quite marked even though rather temporary. Thus, for the time being, the nationalist program could be brought to large circles of Indians including Indian Muslims. The war also affected nationalism in another way. Indian cooperation in the war effort combined with the widespread enunciation of democratic postwar goals by the Allies led the British government to promise self-governing institutions to India. Though no specification was made as to when such institutions might actually be granted, nationalism received a needed lift from talk of what was to come.

All of these factors implied the spread of conditions among broad sections of the Indian population that were favorable to the nationalist cause. This, as has been said, implied the need for a leadership that could unite various elements and create a single mass movement which could mobilize the energies and loyalty of a heterogeneous following.

Fortunately the kind of leader needed was found. Mahatma Gandhi appeared on the scene during the war and soon demonstrated that he was, by origin, by temperament, by experience, and by training, almost ideally suited to bring unity to nationalist ranks. Only in two respects did Gandhi fail to provide the ideal leadership for the needs of Indian nationalism after World War I. Gandhi apparently could not function successfully as a leader of Hindu nationalism and at the same time satisfy the needs of the Muslim community. Despite his efforts the Muslim community drifted away from the Congress and its united front. Gandhi also failed to eradicate—though he certainly did succeed in inhibiting—the radical wing. Actually, with the passage of time, the radical wing grew in effectiveness and in organizational skill.

Gandhi came from a Hindu family of modest but decent status in the caste system. He was a Vaishya. Situationally he was, therefore, in a position to speak to all elements of Hinduism.[13] More important, of

---

[12] The significance of the first World War in the development of Indian nationalism has been examined carefully in the second chapter of R. I. Crane, *The Indian National Congress and the Indian Agrarian Problem, 1919-1939, An Historical Analysis* (Ph.D. dissertation, Yale University, 1951).

[13] Thompson and Garratt point to this fact (*op.cit.*, pp. 606-07).

course, was his loyalty to and inspired use for political purposes of major strands in traditional Hinduism. Drawing upon orthodox values but interpreting and using them in a nonrevivalist fashion, Gandhi was able to speak as the champion of tradition but also as a champion of conciliation and mutual adjustment among the various segments of nationalist support. Gandhi spoke—indeed he lived—in an idiom to which all elements of Indian society could immediately respond, while he emphasized a toleration of other points of view that was both traditional and important to a bifurcated following.

In addition, Gandhi had received European education and had lived in Europe. He could thus talk to the westernized elites in their own terms. Moreover, by being more Hindu than most of them were, Gandhi could command their respect because they felt intuitively that he retained values which were crucial to the Indian scene, but which they themselves had lost the power to evoke.

Gandhi had another important characteristic. Unlike the disorganized lower middle class which spawned terrorism because it could not think in terms of mass organization, Gandhi saw the importance of mass organization and operated in such a fashion as to create a genuine mass movement. It is of significance that Gandhi chose peasant grievances for his initial campaigns in India—and this at a time when intellectuals in the Congress were writing books to demonstrate to other intellectuals the need for getting an awareness of peasant problems.[14] The Champaran and Khaira peasant nonviolence campaigns launched Gandhi as a prominent leader of Indian nationalism, gave him an effective protest weapon which could be used to link the peasantry with the Congress, and brought important new leaders into the Congress. Sardar Patel, Acharya Kripalani, Rajendra Prasad, and others joined Congress ranks in connection with these early struggles.[15]

The Champaran and Khaira campaigns were of great importance in another respect. Up until this time the Congress had primarily represented the interests of the middle classes. The bulk of the Indian population was peasant, and Congress had had little to say to the peasantry. By leading organized campaigns on behalf of the depressed peasants of Champaran and Khaira districts Gandhi gave the Congress a method and an entree to the bulk of the population. After Champaran and

[14] This is quite apparent in such books as N. N. Gangulee, *Problems of Rural India*, Calcutta, Calcutta University Press, 1928.
[15] Discussed at some length in R. I. Crane, "Modern India: A background," *University of Chicago Magazine*, November 1956, pp. 10-11.

Khaira no Congress mass movement of record was without its active peasant *satyagraha*. Congress could now function as a truly national organization. In addition, Gandhi emphasized a village constructive program that forged important mass organizational links.

This stage of Indian nationalism created new problems while it gave nationalism new strength. One of the new problems was organizational. Prior to mass civil disobedience, Congress had not been pressed to think in terms of systematic organization of the rank and file. Now such organization was required. This meant that Congress party units had to be established at the village level, at the level of the tahsil, at the district level, and at the provincial level.[16] A whole superstructure of authority had to be created, along with the appropriate chain of command and lines of communications. Under Gandhi's influence the Congress was reorganized by the Nagpur constitution of 1920 so as to give it the basis for this kind of organized structure with clear links from the local level up through the top. The 1920 Nagpur session made several significant changes under the influence of Gandhi. Not only were the provincial Congress committees reorganized on the basis of the creation of twenty-one linguistic provinces, but also the provincial Congress committees were authorized to form district Congress committees and taluk (tahsil) Congress committees.[17] At the same time the Congress was given a new body—the all-important Congress Working Committee. Perhaps most important of all, with the 1920 reorganization the provincial committees were to be elected annually by the district and lower-level Congress committees.

The system, though it varied in degree of implementation in different parts of India and at different times, was rather simple. The lowest-level Congress committee elected members to the next larger territorial Congress committee and this committee, in turn, elected members to the next larger territorial committee. By this means, at least on paper, a clear link was erected between the four-anna member of a local unit up through various committees to the provincial committee.

As is known, this structure was capped by the national organization with its annual meeting, its All India Congress Committee and the Working Committee as the supreme executive organ of the party. The rank and file and the provincial organizations were tied to the national

---

[16] N. V. Rajkumar, *Development of the Congress Constitution*, Delhi, AICC, 1948.
[17] Discussed in Susanne H. Rudolph, *The Action Arm of the Indian National Congress: The Pradesh Congress Committee*, Cambridge, Massachusetts Institute of Technology, Center for International Studies, 1955 (mimeographed).

body both by means of the annual sessions, to which the provincial committees normally went as delegates, and by means of provincial representation on the All India Congress Committee (AICC). As this structure developed it gave the High Command the means whereby its instructions could be sent down through the various levels of the Congress to the four-anna member at the base of the pyramid. This structure was born of the needs of the movement that Gandhi created.

The creation of a new organizational structure did not, however, solve all of the problems facing Congress. The various sectors of the Indian population which supported Congress had their own special interests, peculiar grievances, differing objectives, and unique ideologies. With peasants, zamindars, businessmen, factory workers, westernized intellectuals and devotees of traditional Hinduism in its ranks it was quite apparent that internal disagreements over strategy, tactics, and long-term goals would remain an ever present factor. From the time of the first civil disobedience campaign the internal history of the Congress was the reconciliation of a multitude of special interests and different points of view. This complicated play of interests within the Congress had a major effect on the formulation of over-all Congress policy in the struggle against British domination. Document after document produced by the Congress in the years that were to follow clearly exhibited the nature of the balance that had to be maintained if the Congress were to be held together for the larger fight against government.[18] The well-known emergence of the so-called right wing leadership and of the left wing group was an expression of the tendency toward bifurcation that was inherent in the composition and role of the Congress as a mass national organization.

Many instances could be given of the organizational problem faced by the leadership in terms of this situation. One may be mentioned briefly to indicate the course of events. When the Government of India Act of 1935 gave provincial autonomy in respect of a number of the functions of government, Congress decided to contest the elections and form ministries wherever possible. As is known, Congress was able to form ministries in six provinces in 1937. The election campaign had been conducted vigorously by the Congress and had involved important statements of programmatic goals, as in the so-called Agrarian Programme.[19]

[18] See, for instance, Indian National Congress, United Provinces Congress Committee, *Agrarian Distress in the United Provinces*, Allahabad, 1931.
[19] The text of the Agrarian Programme is given in *The Indian National Congress, 1936-37, Being the Resolutions Passed* . . . , Allahabad, AICC, 1938, pp. 96 ff.

With the Congress ministries installed in office the question of fulfilling the Agrarian Programme came quickly to the fore. At the provincial level the Congress ministerial group was frequently put under overt pressure from the rank and file for a rapid fulfillment of the promises made in the Programme. The provincial ministries were not, however, responsible solely to the elected majority in the legislatures or to the electorate. There was also the All India Congress Parliamentary Board which claimed directive powers over the ministries. While popular elements put pressure on the ministries from below in behalf of land reform, elimination of rural debt, and the disestablishment of the landlords, the Congress Parliamentary Board exercised considerable restrictive control over the ministries from above, in behalf of moderation and protection of zamindar interests.

If the voice of the membership, or even of the Congress members in the legislatures had been followed, the result in several provinces would undoubtedly have been a radical program of land tenure, rent, and agrarian reform. But this would have alienated influential segments of the population with whom Congress could ill afford to break. During this period the Congress had repeatedly to remind its following that due respect for private property was an important element of the Congress program and that loose talk of confiscation was to be deprecated. The Parliamentary Board, meanwhile, sat on the situation and prevented the ministries from giving in to many of the popular demands.

This situation, however, carried its own frustrations for Congress. Mass support was essential, but mass support had to be won by championing mass demands. If Congress failed by too wide a margin in satisfying the people it risked loss of popular esteem and gravely enhanced internal bickering. Furthermore, disillusionment with Congress vacillation provided the raw material upon which the radical movement could play. What might have been the outcome if the second World War had not intervened is hard to say, but surely as time passed the delicate balance that the High Command was trying to maintain would have satisfied smaller numbers of people.

As it was, this was a period of real growth for the Congress Socialists. Formed in 1934, the Socialists had experienced a relatively rapid growth in effectiveness and in numbers. Untrammeled by the conservative instincts of the existing leadership, the Socialists put pressure on the High Command to proceed with a more vigorous and popular program. Moreover, the Socialists thought in terms of strengthening mass organizations that represented distinct segments of the public. This too provided a problem for the Congress leadership. The basic philosophy of the Congress had been that *it* should represent all sections of nationalist opinion and that *it* was the spokesman for the united front of nationalism. But the pressures for separate organizations representing different interest groups, generated or supported by the Socialists, grew apace. This led to severe strains within the Congress Party.

The case of the peasants may be taken as an example of this trend. Kisan Sabhas had been organized at about the same time as the Congress Socialist Party, and generally by Congress Socialist leaders. The Kisan Sabhas agitated for their own program of agrarian reforms, a program that was more radical than the Congress Agrarian Programme. Difficulties arose between the two organizations even before the formation of Congress ministries,[20] and these differences grew while the ministries were in office. From the viewpoint of the kisan leaders and of the Congress Socialists, the Kisan Sabhas had the right to agitate for their own program through their own organization. This differed sharply from the Congress belief that such groupings as the Kisan Sabhas should be no more than parts of the Congress front for independence. Congress therefore took steps in 1936 and 1937 to reprimand and coerce those Congressmen who, in the judgment of the High Command, were supporting "independent" organizations in a manner designed to damage the effectiveness of the Congress as the leading organization speaking for Indian nationalism and on behalf of all popular grievances.[21] This was one of the issues that continued to trouble the Congress and played its part in the departure of the Congress Socialists from the ranks of the Congress Party after the end of the second World War.

These difficulties were but indicative of the sharpened bifurcation of the Congress into so-called right wing and left wing blocs. This matter came to a rather dramatic head in 1939 when Subhas Bose was reelected as Congress president despite the opposition of Gandhi. Thereupon thirteen of the fifteen members of the Working Committee resigned, causing Bose to resign as president at the Calcutta AICC meeting in April of 1939. Shortly thereafter, of course, Bose started a new political

[20] Information contained in a letter from Smt. Kamaladevi Chattopadhyaya, New Delhi, India, September 2, 1950, to the author. See also *The Indian Annual Register, 1936*, Calcutta, Annual Register Office, II, 282, 293ff.

[21] *Indian Annual Register, 1936*, II, 284-86. Information contained in a letter from Ram Nandan Misra, General Secretary, Hind Kisan Panchayat, Patna, India, dated September 27, 1950, to the author. See also Indian National Congress, *Report of the General Secretary, January 1937-February 1938*, Allahabad, All India Congress Committee, 1938, pp. 31ff.

party, the Forward Bloc, to press for his own point of view in the national struggle. It should be noted in this connection that the resignation of Bose involved a series of issues that stood between the left wing and the High Command, and not just the matter of Congress' opposition to the federal scheme provided for by the Government of India Act of 1935.[22]

The coming of World War II did little to resolve the differences in Congress ranks. One element was prepared to support the war effort, at least in a limited fashion, others stood by the official Congress position as exemplified in Gandhi's plan for individual *satyagraha*, while others—notably those of the Congress Socialist group led by Jayaprakash Narayan—went into an underground that sought more or less actively to hinder the war effort. Furthermore, while the bulk of the Congress leadership was in jail, there was a revival of Mahasabhite elements within the Congress. These folk attacked left wing Congressmen more or less indiscriminately along with Muslims.[23]

These bifurcations were, basically, manifestations of the ambiguous situation in which Congress found itself. A multi-interest party has always to face the problem of satisfying its constituent elements. In view of this it seems surprising that Congress was able to contain within its ranks so many divergent interests and still preserve a substantial measure of united-front thinking and action over a period of years. Three major factors seem to explain the degree of success achieved.

In the first place, so long as India remained dependent, the various interests could submerge their differences in the over-all struggle for freedom. By its skill in linking all sorts of grievances with the central issue of gaining political independence the Congress could appropriately ask Indian interest groups to work with it and under its guidance on the premise that the winning of independence was the critical factor in solving all other problems.

In the second place, Gandhi gave the Congress the kind of leadership that could best secure wide popular support, even from interest groups that felt their own problems to be unique. The Gandhian ideology, if it may be called that, stressed factors of accommodation and cooperation among Indians—in terms of elements of the Indian tradition—that operated to minimize differences. Perhaps more important, Gandhi spoke

---

[22] Ram Nandan Misra, Secretary General of the Hind Kisan Panchayat, has, for instance, argued that it was as much the matter of meeting kisan demands as any other single factor that led to the Bose resignation. Information contained in letter to author, dated September 27, 1950.

[23] W. C. Smith, *The Muslim League, 1942-45*, Lahore, Minerva Book Shop, 1945, pp. 290 ff.

in an idiom that was so authentically Indian that it tended to command respect even from political opponents. With this Gandhi exhibited sound appreciation of organizational techniques that would fit the Indian scene and his leadership represented the use of such techniques effectively. Thus his leadership could be but disadvantageously dispensed with and could not be challenged effectively by any rival. If anyone could claim to speak for a majority of Indians it was Gandhi, and the mantle of his authority covered the Congress.

Finally, under the pressure of two great civil disobedience movements, of Gandhian thinking, and of the experience in office of 1937-1939, the Congress had improved and developed its organizational tools. At the time of the first World War, Congress was really a floating but vocal elite with few real ties to its followers. When the second World War broke out Congress had an effective organizational structure reaching from the Working Committee down through several levels of territorial organization to the villages. Funds derived from nationalist businessmen had facilitated this development, and operations such as the Mass Contacts Programme of the mid-thirties had strengthened contact with the public. In addition, the Village Constructive Programme, on which Gandhi had put so much emphasis through the years, had borne its fruit in organizational groupings that linked Congress structurally with the masses. This was true also of the Congress youth program. Though the four-anna membership of the Congress fluctuated noticeably during the Gandhian era, membership figures were always higher than in any previous period of Congress history.

Membership and contact with the masses doubtless also benefited from the ability of Congress to dominate local elections to organizations such as municipal boards. Local politicians, aspiring to elected office, associated themselves with Congress—even if not from purely patriotic motives—because such association could materially improve their chances of election. Normally such local leaders brought a loyal constituency with them.

In all of these ways Congress built a mass following that was linked organizationally with the higher echelons. This process in turn gave Congress the structural and directive ability to mobilize its members and followers for specific issues, both at the local level and on all-India issues. In this sense the Gandhian era may also be seen as a stage in the development of Indian nationalism, for if the fact of European domination had not, by the interwar period, given rise to situations that affected the lives and welfare of Indians at all levels, Gandhian leadership by itself could not have created a mass nationalist agitation.

The Congress also benefited from one other growing source of strength. After the first World War the number and quality of vernacular papers pledged to the nationalist cause appears to have increased. Each such paper, with its local following, was in a position to publicize Congress goals and educate the public on important developments. Apart from the few papers which Congress published or controlled, it could benefit from the support of a number of these vernacular papers. Moreover, the vernacular press could expose local grievances to which Congress needed to be attuned, thus bringing a variety of issues effectively before the eyes of the High Command.

Thus, though there was no tradition of political parties and of party action, as such, in India, during the Gandhian era the Congress Party moved rather effectively in the direction of creating a framework for and structure of political party existence such as we know in the West. This would seem to be true despite the existence of special features that may be said to be distinctive to the Indian milieu. Among such special features one may count the continuing importance of charismatic leadership in holding the movement together and in making its significant decisions as well as the continued importance of regional-cultural factors in deciding political loyalties.[24]

If the Congress had failed to create the basis for political party behavior in modern India by the time Independence came, it would have been difficult indeed for it to have continued as the major political force in the Republic of India. For, although there have been differences within the Congress since Independence—as exemplified by the clash in 1951 between Purshottamdas Tandon and Pandit Nehru—and despite the fact that a number of the earlier conflicts have not been resolved, it is noteworthy that Congress is making the difficult transition from a nationalist agitation and action movement to that of a political party, seeking to represent the electors through a legislative program, with apparent success.

However, it seems obvious that the transition to the status of a political party competing for electoral support marks a new stage in the development of the Congress. During the period of officeholding in 1937-1939, Congress could blame its lack of success on the continued control

---

[24] Reference is here made to instances such as the recent rioting in Bombay over the linguistic states issue. Though it is quite clear that factors other than the cultural and linguistic play a role in such affairs, it is also clear that regional-cultural nationalism remains important, at least by European standards.

of an alien power. That argument is no longer useful. The question is therefore raised as to the kinds of leadership which will have to emerge in Congress ranks if the party is to continue effective under the new conditions. Though it is difficult to elicit trends in a situation so fluid and so very current, some of the emerging parameters may be noted.

As of today it would seem that the issue between the politically westernized and the adherents of traditional attitudes has not been resolved. While the former have certain distinct advantages at their command—such as their ability in the technical sense to staff a modern administration or to manipulate propaganda symbols for political purposes—it is also apparent that their skills continue to separate them from the bulk of the electorate who respond to traditional motifs. While the Congress as a party continues to pin its political hopes on its ability to promote programs for improvement of the conditions of life of the Indian masses, and expects to accomplish this objective through means that are essentially modeled upon what may be called a western design, such hopes face two concrete difficulties.

If the program for dramatic improvement of living conditions falters for any one of a number of good reasons or if the improvements are not sufficiently dramatic, the action program of the Congress may stand condemned, or at least be called seriously into question. On the other hand, it is argued with increasing fervor that there are other models for rapid economic development that are better suited to the Indian milieu. If the bias in favor of such methods which are more characteristic of the Indian way were to grow considerably, the Congress would have either to shift ground expertly or to stand firmly in favor of the present approaches. There is, indeed, evidence of such shifting of ground even now within Congress ranks.

It can be argued, however, that Congress as presently constituted would find it difficult to shift its ground with sufficient grace and expedition; if this be the case, granted the premises, the traditionally oriented kinds of leadership would seem in a position to gain favor. In the event of the emergence of that trend it would seem likely that the party would have to come under the control of traditionalists or lose much of its popular appeal. That this could happen so long as Pandit Nehru remains active seems highly unlikely. But the next generation of leadership may find it necessary to revamp the party in order to give it operational links with the traditional social, intellectual, and emotional milieu. That Congress could remain a national political party under those circumstances seems uncertain.

DYNAMICS OF SOCIALIST LEADERSHIP IN INDIA

THOMAS A. RUSCH

*S*OCIALIST leadership in India, as defined here, means the leaders of the present Praja Socialist Party, its recent offshoot, the Socialist Party of India, and their immediate common predecessors, the Socialist Party (1947-1952) and the Congress Socialist Party (1934-1947). Each of these party names indicates an important lineal phase in the leadership's development. By reviewing these phases, examining the social characteristics, the self-defined concepts of socialist leadership, and the traits and basic assumptions of its political behavior, certain tentative generalizations regarding the character and direction of socialist leadership in India may be drawn.

Congress Socialist Party: The Loyal Opposition

Socialist leadership arose within the Indian National Congress in response to what the socialists felt were three leadership "failures" associated with the second and third civil disobedience movements of 1930-1934. First there was the failure of the Gandhian and moderate nationalist leaders to achieve the goal of independence, or at least to propose a sufficiently radical, secular economic program plus militant, uncompromising methods, to take the edge off defeat. Secondly there was the inability of left wing nationalists (led by Subhas Chandra Bose, Jawaharlal Nehru, and others)[1] to organize a united leadership able and willing to challenge the Gandhians and Moderates for control of the Congress. Finally there was the alienation of the Communist Party leaders from the nationalist movement.[2] Faced with the absence of a leadership for revolt, the disillusioned Congressmen of socialist per-

THOMAS A. RUSCH was associated with the Modern India Project, University of California at Berkeley, from 1954 to 1956; at present he is with the Center for South Asia Studies at the University of California.

[1] Leaders of underground terrorist groups, trade unions, peasant organizations, and Congressmen opposed to ending civil disobedience under the Gandhi–Irwin compromise of 1931.

[2] From 1928 to 1935, the Communist Party followed the international policy of attacking the Congress as "bourgeois" and "reactionary." Being declared illegal in 1934, the CPI could not function openly even when its policy changed in 1935.

suasion organized groups, first in the province of Bihar (1931), later in the Nasik Central Prison (1932-1933), then in the provinces of Bombay and the United Provinces (1933-1934). These groups collectively constituted the initiating, loyal, hard core of the Congress Socialist Party. Ten of these persons constituted the heart of leadership in the socialist leadership through most of its phases. These ten central socialist leaders were highly educated, young (average age of thirty in the nineteen-thirties), north Indian Congressmen, predominantly of the urban, middle-class professions, many of whom gave up families or marriage in favor of professional politics.[3]

Ideologically, the ten were divided by three amorphous and overlapping tendencies: Marxism, social democracy of the British Labor Party type, and a democratic socialism tempered by Gandhian concepts of decentralization and the use of nonviolent civil disobedience techniques for nationalist and class struggle. The outstanding exponents of the first persuasion were Jayaprakash Narayan and Acharya Narendra Deva; of the second, Minoo R. Masani and Asoka Mehta; and of the third, Achyut Patwardhan and Rammanohar Lohia. Among them there was no clearly defined ideology, but an uneasy compromise between the Marxists and the non-Marxists.[4] As a result, the party's theses, programs, and resolutions were allowed to reflect Marxian terminology, the party was described as Marxist, and Marxists from other radical parties were admitted into membership on a restricted basis. But it was not permitted to be called a Marxist-Leninist party dedicated to the dictatorship of the proletariat, nor to be affiliated with either the Second or Third Internationals. Though a majority of these ten leaders were non-Marxists, the most influential were the Marxists, whose views were shared by a wide majority of the entire leadership cadre and of the party membership.

Doctrinal differences were compromised in the interests of unity, but organizational and tactical questions proved a source of disruption. Some of these crucial problems were: whether to admit, and later to expel, the communists from the party before 1940; the extent of participation in parliamentary activity, including the Constituent Assembly; how far

[3] The ten leaders were: Jayaprakash Narayan, Rammanohar Lohia, Asoka Mehta, Acharya Narendra Deva, Achyut Patwardhan, M. R. Masani, Kamaladevi, Purshottam Tricumdas, Yusuf Meherally, and Ganga Sharan Sinha. For biographies see G. S. Barghava, *Leaders of the Left*, Bombay, Meherally Book Club, 1951; and Yusuf Meherally, *Leaders of India*, 2 vols., Bombay, Padma Publications, 1946.

[4] Madhu Limaye, *Evolution of Socialist Policy*, Hyderabad, Chetana Prakashan Ltd., 1952, p. 1.

to support left wing leader Subhas Chandra Bose against the right wing in 1939; how to revive the party in 1946-1947—under what name and organizational structure; and whether to become—eventually—the leadership of the Congress or of an opposition party.

Some cohesion was found among these leaders based on the fact that they shared a common loyalty to nationalism and an organizational fealty to the Indian National Congress. All of them possessed high moral values and a personal code of ethics which one leader described as "instinctive abhorrence of Communist amoralism, deceit and doubletalk; respect for the values of truth and decency . . . peaceful methods, decentralization,"[5] and which another described as "honesty and purity of means."[6] In addition they all agreed on the central issues facing the nationalist movement. Perhaps the most important cohesive factor among them was intense personal friendship.

These ten leaders were the center of a wider circle of socialist leaders who shared, in most respects, the same general social characteristics, doctrinal and policy differences, and unifying elements. Together this broader frame of socialist leaders constituted the loyal hard core of party leadership. A peripheral group of leaders had been recruited in the prewar period under a "socialist unity" policy which presumed the creation of a single party of Marxian socialism. In the struggle for control of the party, all these peripheral elements were expelled or withdrew by the middle of 1940. This action destroyed party leadership and organization in southern and eastern India, a blow that created a permanent socialist weakness in these areas which has been only partially corrected by recent recruitment and mergers.

The core leadership tried to create left wing unity among such disparate anti-right-wing elements as Jawaharlal Nehru, Subhas Chandra Bose and his followers (later called the Forward Bloc), the Communist Party of India, the dissident communist sect of "Royists" (later called the "League of Radical Congressmen"), and others. Initially this alliance was successful in influencing Congress resolutions which promised some radical land reforms, nationalization of selected industries, progressive labor legislation, the reorganization of Congress for greater mass contact, and proportionate representation of the left wing. Their combined efforts succeeded in 1939 in electing Subhas Chandra Bose as Congress president against right wing opposition. However, this left wing unity

---

[5] Limaye, *op.cit.*, p. 3.
[6] M. R. Masani, *A Short History of the Communist Party of India*, New York, Macmillan, 1954, p. 4.

failed to create the programmatic or organizational cohesion necessary to achieve the socialists' objectives. These objectives were: to influence Congress policies in the direction of creating a united front of peasants, labor, and the middle class dedicated to achieving independence through the merging of class struggles with the nationalist effort; promising radical agrarian and socio-political changes; and waging uncompromising, mass direct action, initially nonviolent, but destined eventually to lead to armed overthrow of British colonial authority. In addition the core leadership hoped gradually to gain control of the Congress under a "composite leadership" theory which presumed gradual displacement of retiring right wing leaders by the left wing; or, failing that, to split the Congress, preferably after the achievement of independence, confident they could "carry the whole body of Congressmen" with them after waging a "systematic campaign" on an issue of "political and economic importance."[7]

An analysis of the socialist leadership's political behavior until 1947 reveals certain outstanding characteristics, some of which persist to the present time. Most importantly, there were demonstrated errors concerning certain basic assumptions and expectations which underlay the socialists' political action. Their theory of "socialist unity" was based on the false assumption that a common interpretation of Marxism and nationalism and loyalty to party leaders could be created among the disparate groups which had entered the party, and that such understandings were sufficient to create unity. Similarly, an unforeseen but inherent lack of agreement on leadership, tactics, organization, and policies made the larger left wing unity unworkable. The "composite leadership" theory did not lead either to a united left wing gradually replacing the right wing leaders, or to their splitting the Congress, because they failed to build up the required cohesive and numerical strength to force the issue successfully in their favor. Nor had socialist leaders anticipated that the postwar transference of power to a Congress interim government would give Congress' parliamentary leaders permanent dominance over the Congress organization itself, and thus check Nehru's intervention on the socialists' behalf. Further, they did not foresee that as a consequence of resigning their seats in the Constituent Assembly and the Congress Working Committee, coupled with their refusal to accept seats in Nehru's cabinet, they would destroy whatever possibilities of success existed for a "composite leadership." Most important, the fundamental assumptions underlying all others and therefore the base of their entire strategy

[7] Jayaprakash Narayan, *Why I Joined the Working Committee*, manuscript, n.d.

—namely, that Britain would never grant independence except through defeat by an armed revolt, and that Congress would never agree to the creation of Pakistan—were belied by events.

A second characteristic of the political behavior of the socialist leadership was its mixture of authoritarian and democratic biases. A selective, restricted party was created whose mass membership base resided not in the organization itself, but in the Congress, trade unions, peasant organizations, and youth movements, within which party members worked as disciplined socialist caucuses. Party recruitment was confined consciously, though not always consistently, to the active elements (or leaders) in these organizations. Members were required to join the Congress, were assigned specific work in other organizations, were placed on probation before acceptance into the party, and were divided by work quotas into classes. During the war and again in 1946, the leadership functioned through illegal underground cells. Within the party, constitutional control of policy-making bodies rested with the "active members," full-time functionaries who never constituted more than one sixteenth of the party's membership.[8]

In practice, central policy making and control, as distinct from provincial, rested primarily with the ten previously mentioned leaders who constituted the center of the leadership. Though usually represented on the party's National Executive, some of these members occasionally acted unofficially to reverse official policies or to make crucial decisions on their own. Though there were compromises and differences within this group, deference was usually given to the views of the acknowledged central leader, Jayaprakash Narayan, whose influence over the party's emergence in 1931 and 1934, and reemergence in 1947, was very great. There were crucial occasions when he acted for the party against the majority views of the National Executive itself, or made unilateral decisions without its prior approval.[9] The leadership as a whole sometimes discouraged discussion of controversial issues, such as criticism of the Soviet Union in the prewar period; the "habit of invoking authority" was used occasionally to explain unorthodox decisions by justifying them

[8] At the height of the party's growth in 1938-1939, it had an estimated eight to ten thousand members of whom only five hundred were "active members." Exact published figures are not available. This estimate was obtained from interviews with Dr. Rammanohar Lohia, Jayaprakash Narayan, and Ramnandan Mishra.

[9] Information in this paragraph is based on: Jayaprakash Narayan, *Towards Struggle*, Bombay, Padma Publications, 1947, pp. 177-81; private notes of Jayaprakash Narayan; and an interview with Mohanlal Gautam.

as consistent with selected quotations from Marx and Lenin.[10] Various elements combined to produce this authoritarian pattern: the leadership's communist and revolutionary organizational predilections, the competitive struggle for power within the Congress and mass organizations with both right wing and left wing elements, the party's wartime status of illegality, and the influence of India's strong cultural tradition of deference to established leadership.

But endemic indiscipline modified this authoritarian characteristic. In the prewar period, the struggle between the loyal hard core and the various peripheral leaderships for control of the party fostered national and provincial factions based on loyalty to particular leaders, groups, or organizations. Some of these, like M. N. Roy, Subhas Chandra Bose, and the Communist Party, were outside the Congress Socialist Party. A tradition of attacking leaders and policies in press statements and engineering "mass resignations" was established. Some leaders worked against selected party candidates for Congress committees or for seats in the provincial assemblies. Provincial leaders were accused by the national leadership of failing adequately to support the national party organ, the *Congress Socialist*. Many were known to ignore financial appeals from the central office, and some even sent false membership figures to the national office. But even in the postwar period, when left wing peripheral leaders were no longer in the party, loose leadership groups or factions continued to function. At this time, however, they tried to revolve around the personality or policies of individual leaders who had gained prominence in the 1942 civil disobedience resistance, or around those who commanded loyalties by their linguistic-regional identification.

Inconsistency on certain crucial matters of strategy, tactics, and policy implementation encouraged indiscipline. Though exhibiting a high degree of consistency concerning their basic assumptions and program for the Congress, they failed to maintain it for the strategy, tactics, and organizational decisions necessary to implement their own party's policies. When left unity reached a point in 1939 where a bid for capturing or splitting the Congress through Subhas Chandra Bose's election might logically and successfully have been made, they withdrew support, remained neutral in the open Congress session, and sought to mediate a compromise.

Similarly, "composite leadership" theories were undermined by intermittent resignations from, and refusals to serve on, the Congress Work-

[10] Limaye, *op.cit.*, p. 20.

ing Committee, by reversal in 1946 of a previous decision to serve in the Constituent Assembly, and by prohibiting socialists from serving in Congress ministries in 1937-1939, and again in 1946-1947. Furthermore, though branding the British Cabinet Mission proposals of 1946 as "dangerous" and "futile" and voting against them the first time, they later remained neutral when the All India Congress Committee voted approval.

Decisions on internal party matters exhibited the same tendency. Theoretically, the party organization was tightly disciplined, but in practice it functioned loosely. Party ideology was couched in Marxist terms, yet the majority of the aforementioned ten central leaders were not Marxists. Communists were to be admitted only under strict National Executive surveillance and approval, while in practice they were admitted indiscriminately.

These inconsistencies were the result of chronic indecisiveness. The leadership hesitated for three years before expelling the communists, although the latter's captious plans and intentions were fully known as early as 1937. They remained neutral concerning restrictions on Subhas Chandra Bose at Tripuri (1939). They hesitated over whether and how the party should reorganize, and later over the question of leaving Congress. This temporizing was caused in the prewar period by the loyal leaders' attempt to reconcile the strong cross pressures exerted on them from outside the party by the Congress and left wing elements, and from within the party by various peripheral leaders. Indecision among the loyal cadre arose from their attempt to maintain unity simultaneously with the Congress, the left wing, the peripheral Marxists within the party, and among themselves. When confronted with the consequences of their false assumptions about the course of political events, they sometimes found either no decision at all or a reversal of position the only ways to preserve both party unity and their position within the Congress. The socialists' dilemma, in part, was the clash between adherence to doctrinaire assumptions and theories, and some regard for political realism. When crises came, they knew and publicly stated that only Gandhi and the Congress could rally mass support sufficient to resist the British and represent the Indian nation, however much they might disapprove Congress policies.

It was a unique characteristic, therefore, that the socialists' delays, neutrality, and reversals usually favored Congress on the crucial issues facing the nationalist movement. Unlike all other left wing parties and groups, their primary loyalty lay in Congress unity and policy even as against that of their own party. Their real role was not indicated in socialist leadership theories, but in their actual behavior—which was that of a loyal opposition attempting to correct Congress policies in the interests of the Congress itself.

A primary reason for the socialists' erroneous assumptions was a doctrinaire ideological and intellectual approach to politics, more so in the prewar than the postwar period. They tended to examine political problems primarily on the basis of uncritical dogmas, rather than with the aid of empirical data. Thus, unity with the communists was presumed to be possible because of an allegedly common adherence to Marxism; parliamentarianism was condemned as futile, reformist "constitutionalism"; Congress leaders were either "bourgeois" or under bourgeois influence; "capitalist-imperialist" Britain was believed inherently incapable of granting independence peacefully, etc. New policies and tactics were justified in the form of long, Marxian-phrased "theses."

In the organizational realm, the emphasis was given to agitation and propaganda rather than to solid organizational activity. There was a tendency to confine party leaders' influence to top committees of the Congress, or to labor, youth, and peasant movements that were "not rooted in solid labour and *kisan* organization."[11] Continual condemnation of parliamentary activity and a refusal to participate in the Congress governments and the Constituent Assembly deprived the leaders of administrative experience as well as the opportunity to win public and Congress confidence in their ability to govern. Moreover, their behavior strengthened certain Congress leaders' efforts to exclude them from, or reduce their influence in, those positions which became strategic for control of both the Congress and the central and provincial governments when the British finally transferred power in 1947.

Socialist Party Phase: Disinherited Leadership

At the Kanpur Congress Socialist Party Conference early in 1947, decisions were made to drop the word "Congress" from the party's title, to recruit non-Congressmen as members, and to emerge from underground, illegal status as an independent Socialist Party. This was to be in exchange for the withdrawal of a Congress Constitution Committee's proposal to outlaw political parties within Congress ranks. The negotiated compromise, made with the help of Gandhi's mediation, temporarily prevented socialist leaders both from being forced out of the

[11] Limaye, *op.cit.*, p. 8.

Congress and from splitting up among themselves. In the postwar turbulence, when the destiny of India and the Congress was unclear and established political relationships were undergoing rapid change, there was indecision and division among both Congress and socialist leaders as to the place of the latter group in Indian politics. Moreover, experiences of the previous decade and of the war and postwar periods had fundamentally altered the power relationships in both organizations.

Congress had moved towards the socialist political program in its "Quit India" resolution of 1942, and towards socialist economic goals in its 1946 election manifesto, and in the draft "Economic and Social Programme" in early 1948, though these objectives fell considerably short of a full socialist program. Organizationally, Congress sought to accommodate socialist leaders by adopting some of their ideas for Congress reorganization and by offering them minority status on the all-important Working Committee, the Constituent Assembly, and on Nehru's provisional cabinet. Informal talks had taken place at the annual Congress session at Meerut (1946) for naming a socialist as general secretary of the Congress, a key organizational position, and for increasing socialist representation on the Working Committee.

These trends indicated that the former right wing was no longer united in hostility to the socialists. Gandhi, as the single greatest individual political force within Congress and India, had successively changed from prewar positions of hostility to a position favoring personal and political *rapprochement*. On political and economic questions, Gandhi found himself in increasingly greater agreement with the socialists, even going so far as to accept socialization of the economy, to share socialist opposition to the Congress endorsement of the grouping scheme for organization of the Constituent Assembly, and to oppose the final partition plan which created Pakistan. Organizationally, Gandhi suggested the names of socialist leaders Acharya Narendra Deva and Jayaprakash Narayan as possible candidates for the Congress presidency in 1947; he prevented the possible expulsion or withdrawal of the socialists from Congress in the same year; and he mediated the 1947 negotiations with the Congress leadership for high positions in the Congress organization and government ministries by urging inclusion of socialists as the men most likely to support Nehru's social and economic policies. Gandhi also proposed the conversion of Congress from a political party to a *lok sevak sangh* (people's welfare organization), a suggestion which had been made earlier by the socialists themselves, and which would have given the Socialist Party great political advantage if it had been adopted.

Gandhi was one of many Congressmen who wanted to accommodate socialist leaders through their inclusion in the highest Congress and government positions and through acceptance of many of their suggested organizational and program proposals. Others who urged accommodation were leaders like Jawaharlal Nehru and Gulzarilal Nanda.

It was these new trends towards accommodation which led socialist leaders like Jayaprakash Narayan and Acharya Narendra Deva to compromise and negotiate, delaying socialist withdrawal from Congress in the hope of achieving acceptance of their program and an effective position in Congress leadership. Opposed to this development were a majority of powerful Congress leaders like Sardar Vallabhbhai Patel, S. K. Patil of Bombay, Pandit Pant of the United Provinces (U. P.), Rajendra Prasad of Bihar, and Harekrushna Mahtab of Orissa. These men controlled the majorities in the national and provincial Congress committees and in parliamentary parties. They had agreed to the 1947 Socialist Party compromise largely for the strategic reason that Congress unity was essential until independence and political stability were gained. Socialist leaders were expected to remain prominent only in a minority status, though some of these opposing Congressmen desired the expulsion from Congress of the socialists. It was the Patel group which blocked the selection of a socialist as general secretary of the Congress as well as the election of more socialists to the AICC, the Working Committee, or the Constituent Assembly in 1946. And it was also this group which forced the Kanpur compromise, stalemated negotiations with Gandhi, urged organization of a rival Indian National Trade Union Congress, and vetoed Gandhi's proposal of a socialist as Congress president in 1947. In 1948, following Gandhi's death, this opposition piloted through the AICC a resolution outlawing political parties within Congress, a move which impelled the socialists to withdraw from the Congress.

Divisions within the socialist leadership were exacerbated by these events, but the Kanpur compromise forestalled temporarily an internal break between the three schools of thought within the party: advocates of a tightly organized socialist caucus within the Congress in place of a formal party organization, adherents of a separatist policy, and those urging revival of a reorganized Congress Socialist Party.

The first viewpoint was held by such socialists as Mohanlal Gautam, Hariharnath Shastri, and Nabhas Choudhary, who were primarily loyal to the Congress and optimistic concerning socialist ascendancy to Congress leadership. In large part, this group came from the provinces of U.P., Delhi, and Orissa, where socialists had a preeminent position in the Congress provincial organizations. Jayaprakash Narayan had held this view in 1946, but he had changed his mind when Congress leaders accepted the British Cabinet Mission proposals for negotiation, and took steps to prevent socialist ascendancy within the Congress. This group was closely integrated with Congress and had the most to lose by withdrawal; therefore they urged party dissolution regardless of the terms offered by Congress leaders.

Leaders of the second approach were generally new wartime resistance recruits, like Aruna Asaf Ali, who had no previous loyalty to the Congress Socialist Party, or to the Congress. These new socialists were joined by certain of the old hard core leaders who favored this course because of disillusionment with Nehru and the Congress (like Rammanohar Lohia), or because of an overly-optimistic assessment of Socialist Party strength (like Asoka Mehta). In general, party leaders from Bombay, Bihar, Gujarat, and South India, where they had been effectively excluded from provincial Congress leadership and had the least to lose by withdrawal, were the most eager to leave Congress. It was no accident that the Bombay socialists anticipated the party's complete exit from Congress by more than two months. In this case, they were expelled from the Congress for successfully presenting socialist candidates against the Congress slate in the 1948 Bombay municipal elections.

The third outlook was characteristic of the old Congress Socialist Party hard core, like Jayaprakash and Acharya Narendra Deva. These men held dual loyalty to the Congress and the Socialist Party, but urged reorganization as necessary both to influence Congress policies and to allow for socialist emergence as an opposition party should that become necessary. In this group were also those who had a status to protect within the old organization and who therefore were apprehensive of dissolution (as advanced by the first group) or the inundation by new members in a new party (as advocated by the second). In struggling for Congress leadership before final acceptance by the Congress of the grouping scheme and partition, most socialist leaders shared the false assumption that a new civil disobedience movement was inevitable, with Congress leaders again going to jail and socialist leaders this time leading their organized underground followers to victory against the British.[12] Even after these Congress decisions they hoped that recognition of socialist services to the nationalist struggle, the advanced age of many

---

[12] Socialists maintained an underground organization, including armed guerrillas, with hidden arms stocks, numbering some 10,000. They claimed the allegiance of 100,000 followers. Information from the author's interview with Jayaprakash Narayan.

Congress leaders, and support from Nehru and Gandhi, would force the Sardar Patel group to give them an effective voice in all key Congress Party and government positions. When negotiations produced concessions considerably below socialist expectations, they continued to hope that Gandhi's plan to dissolve Congress as a political party and convert it into a *lok sevak sangh* might be approved, thereby depriving conservative Congress leaders of their advantage and giving the Socialist Party a political field in which to operate.

As a consequence of these divisions, the party leadership behaved inconsistently and indecisively by leading an independent political party while at the same time striving for Congress Party leadership. In the former role they refused to allow trade unions under their control to join the Congress-sponsored Indian National Trade Union Congress; they resigned positions in the Congress Working Committee and Constituent Assembly; they led labor strikes that were opposed by Congress; and they ran candidates against Congress nominees in the Bombay municipal elections. But simultaneously, they neglected Socialist Party organization, negotiated with Congress leaders on terms for integration, served on key Congress committees, submitted politico-economic programs and reorganization plans for Congress approval, and tried to regain seats in the Constituent Assembly.

Following Gandhi's assassination, socialist leaders charged Home Minister Vallabhbhai Patel with neglect of duty, due to age and overwork, and of friendliness to communal forces. They called for his removal from his Cabinet post and for the resignation of Nehru's cabinet as penance for neglect in not protecting Gandhi. By these tactics they hoped to break Patel's power and to make their own advancement to power possible. To this end, they offered to serve in both the cabinet and Congress Working Committee. But public opinion, the Congress, and Nehru rallied to Patel's defense. It was the socialists who were discredited. When Congress moved to ban all political groupings within the Congress, socialist leaders were faced with the alternative of remaining within the Congress as an unorganized minority waging a continuous struggle for their socialist policies, or leaving. They chose the latter course at the Nasik convention in March 1948, and their unofficial organ *Janata* complained that the "second string" leaders and "the youngest branch of the Congress family had been disinherited . . . by hole and corner methods."[13]

[13] *Janata*, March 21, 1948, pp. 3-4.

Procrastination for a full year caused loss of some younger leaders from the 1942 movement to the Communist Party. The decision to leave Congress lost others from the old hard core like Hariharnath Shastri, President of Indian National Trade Union Congress, Mohanlal Gautam, later a minister in U.P., and Nabhas Choudhary, who became chief minister for Orissa. The majority quietly resigned their Congress membership and government positions, including assembly seats in the states, with a minimum of friction and publicity.

In the post-Congress period of 1948 to 1952, the party leadership experienced some fundamental changes. It created new objectives based on new assumptions, experienced new failures, and revealed some new behavioral characteristics. Most importantly, the central leadership showed signs of declining in numbers and influence by losing four of its ten members.[14] Further, there was a loss to the Communists of Aruna Asaf Ali and her adherents.

But new leadership, primarily in the secondary, provincial, and local levels, was recruited into the party from the 1942 movement and through the merger of small radical parties in eastern and southern India. Of further significance was a growing hiatus between the nationally recognized leadership on the one side, and the secondary provincial leaders and members on the other. This development was directly related to the former's new political direction.

Beginning in 1946, leaders like Asoka Mehta, Jayaprakash Narayan, and Rammanohar Lohia—the articulate triumvirate of the newly emerging party—resolved to eschew doctrinaire political thinking in favor of pragmatic and empirical analyses of India's problems as a necessary first step in evolving a new "democratic socialism" related to Indian realities. In reexamining their former basic assumptions, they created new objectives. Their ideological goal was a "democratic socialist" society as a synthesis of realism, Gandhism, and Marxism. It was to be achieved and maintained nonviolently, to be decentralized and democratic in political and economic structure, and to emphasize the importance of peasant and voluntary group action. The organizational goal was to fashion a democratically structured, mass membership party controlled and financed by its members. Collective affiliation of trade unions and peasant organizations, and organizational mergers or electoral alliances with kindred left wing opposition parties believing in "nationalism, socialism, and democracy" was to insure a mass base. Political action would mean challenging the Congress through methods of Gandhian-type "construc-

[14] M. R. Masani, Yusuf Meherally, Achyut Patwardhan, and Kamaladevi.

tive work," intensive parliamentary activity, and leadership of nonviolent, direct action struggles against "injustice"—"the spade, the vote, and prison." This required a shift in methods from the urban, trade union, revolutionary and agitational, to the constructive, rural, nonviolent, and parliamentary. Such an organization was expected to emerge as the strongest opposition party to Congress, within striking distance of power, during the 1951 general elections. Several new assumptions underlay these objectives: that the wider party leadership and membership would understand and could effectively implement the objectives; that the Congress was becoming increasingly unpopular and weakened by numerous splits, and that this would inevitably redound to the socialists' advantage; and that Congress was an inflexible, conservative party of "famine, corruption, and disguised capitalism," unable to advance and implement the progressive and socialist measures needed to meet popular demand and the needs of the time. In each instance, failure of expectations led to new crises of leadership.

An important section of the leadership and membership—perhaps a majority—either failed to comprehend the changes, or resisted them, for they had been adopted through the sheer weight of the central leaders' personal influence, brilliance of articulation, and continued authoritarian control of organization and finances. Though a democratic constitution was finally adopted, against strenuous opposition, by 1949, the party continued to be controlled by the hard core full-time "active members." These members resisted integration of new leaders and members at the provincial level and admittedly developed "bureaucratic tendencies" and an attitude of "possession" about this threat to their positions. Beyond this, the National Executive was still composed of a carefully self-selected slate presented for unanimous approval at annual party conferences; the ideology, program, and finances continued to be controlled by not more than three leaders, and frequently by only Jayaprakash himself.

This continued authoritarian behavior of the central leadership led to widespread indiscipline. Annual conferences debated the party's fundamentals of ideology, organization, and tactics, impelling national leaders to complain that adopted programs had an air of "tentativeness" because members had "no living faith" in them. The "work clause" imposed on active members was not honored by more than a fourth; initiative remained centralized and discipline decentralized; "groupism" and "factionalism" persisted. Central leaders charged the secondary and local cadres with ignorance of policies, financial irresponsibility, lack of initiative, a tendency to "shirk steady work" and to "live from excitement to excitement," failure to understand local people and problems, preoccupation with theory over action, and disregard of national organizational directives in favor of individual preferences. In turn, national leaders admitted to charges against them of failure to cooperate as a "team" by confusing members through advocacy of differing policies.[15]

The 1951 general election gave a shock to socialist leaders because it challenged the remaining assumptions on which their expectations rested. It was apparent that they had grossly overestimated their own popularity, misjudged that of the Congress and the Communists, failed to foresee dispersal of opposition strength through the rise of independents and numerous small parties, and had wrongly pursued extensive rather than intensive campaigning and organization. In place of the expected second-rank status in India's legislative bodies, the socialists achieved only third place in terms of seats won, though they were second in terms of popular votes. They were forced to accept the defeat of all their national leaders and the election of only one fourth of the seats anticipated. Furthermore, they had underestimated the ability of the Congress under Nehru to compete with the socialists in promising the electorate the same general measures of economic and social reform for which the socialists stood.

Their nonelectoral programs of mass action, such as "On the Move" and "For a National Revival," had failed to win mass support and enthusiasm. Though increasing its parliamentary stature and experience from previous low levels, the party leadership was still largely agitational and intellectual in its behavior. In the postelection period, leaders undertook a reappraisal and admitted that full-time leaders were tending to withdraw from activity for economic reasons, frustrations, and loss of inspiration, and were not being replaced. Though party membership had increased thirty times its original strength from 1948, the number of new active leaders thrown up was "not appreciable."[16] Socialist leadership was losing its numerical strength, its influence politically, and its élan psychologically. Under these circumstances, the socialists negotiated a merger with the similarly disillusioned leaders of the Kisan Mazdoor Praja Party in 1952 as a means of increasing their

[15] See the following convention reports: *Report of the Sixth Annual Conference*, Nasik, 1948; *Report of the Seventh Annual Conference*, Patna, 1949; *Report of the Eighth National Conference*, Madras, 1950; and *Report of the Special Convention*, Pachmarhi, 1952.
[16] *Report of the Special Convention*, Pachmarhi, 1952, p. 120.

parliamentary and geographic strength, thus allowing them to challenge the Communists as the second largest party.

Praja Socialist Party Phase: Disintegrating Leadership

The merger of the Socialist Party with the Kisan Mazdoor Praja Party to form the Praja Socialist Party in 1952 was made possible through an agreement to deal with "principles" and to keep ideology out of the merger talks. Through merger, they hoped to create a party whose combined strength could achieve that opposition status which neither could satisfactorily attain alone. The KMPP leaders, under Acharya J. B. Kripalani, former Congress general secretary and president, were Gandhian ex-Congressmen and dissatisfied Congress parliamentarians who split from the Congress just prior to the 1951 general election after Kripalani had been defeated for Congress president by the Patel group. Placing fourth in the general elections in terms of votes polled, the KMPP's legislative strength lay mainly in the eastern and southern states where the number of socialist legislators was lowest. Their merger thus complemented socialist representation which was concentrated in western and northern states. The KMPP was interested in practical parliamentary activity and Gandhian village constructive work, thereby complementing the Socialist Party leadership's interest in urban trade union, intellectual, and agitational activities. Significantly, KMPP members were given most of the chairmanships and honorary presiding offices in the new party, while former Socialist Party leaders retained control of the provincial party secretaryships. National and provincial executive committee positions were shared equitably, as were the joint national secretarial positions.

In directing the merger, socialist leaders made assumptions which again were either disproved later or at best only partially borne out by events. They correctly assessed this and subsequent mergers (with the Forward Bloc [Subhasist] and others) as moves towards political consolidation which might end the political fragmentation that had dissipated opposition votes against the Congress. But they had felt that progressive elements in all other political parties, whether Congress, Communist, or communal, would eventually merge with the Praja Socialist Party, while all conservative elements would gravitate to Congress. According to this postulate, India would then have a two-party system: a conservative Congress versus a progressive Socialist Party. Secondly, they inconsistently surmised that a party like theirs could be formed without any ideology, and that it could merge Marxism and Gandhism to achieve ideological cohesion and clarity. Both assumptions, as might be expected, have created continuing ideological controversy.

Furthermore, the Jayaprakash-Nehru talks of 1953 concerning possible cooperation, coalition, or merger of the PSP and Congress, undermined the assumed differences between the two parties. Subsequent Congress dedication to a "socialistic pattern of society," at Avadi (1954), followed by government steps towards nationalization of banking and insurance, state trading, and other socialist measures advanced in Jayaprakash's fourteen-point program presented to Nehru, destroyed the supposition that Congress was an inflexible, conservative force unable to adopt socialist policies. The experience of the Praja Socialist ministry in Travancore-Cochin also dispelled the popular belief that there were drastic differences between the parties. These unanticipated moves effectively reduced the party's appeal as an opposition.

Inconsistencies and indecisiveness are still apparent among the leaders over certain matters of ideology, parliamentary strategy, and program. They are unable to agree on whether or not the party needs an ideology, what constitutes an ideology, and whether it should be Marxian, Gandhian, some synthesis of both, or a pragmatic search for a new doctrine of democratic socialism relevant to India.

Parliamentary strategy concerning relationships with the Congress and the Communist Party is the main source of present conflicts and uncertainty. The Jayaprakash-Nehru talks for rapprochement with Congress were later repudiated by a majority of the leadership at the Betul conference. A compromise between the "responsivist-cooperationists" led by Jayaprakash and Asoka Mehta and the "anti-responsivists" of Lohia was reached in the Allahabad thesis (1953),[17] whereby coalitions and united fronts were prohibited in campaigns or ministries, though "electoral adjustments" on seats to prevent three-cornered campaigns were permitted with opposition parties but not with the Congress. Yet the practical political effect of such adjustments in Travancore-Cochin was to identify the party mistakenly with the Communists and other left wing parties in the 1954 state election campaign, just as though it were part of a united front. After the elections, the Praja Socialist Party was unpopularly identified with Congress during the one-year tenure of the minority socialist ministry because it depended on their larger legislative bloc to hold office. Socialists suffered from both types of associations.

[17] *Statement of Policy*, Bombay, Praja Socialist Party, 1954, pp. 19-27.

By the Gaya policy (1955),[18] the remaining PSP leadership went beyond the Allahabad thesis and unconditionally opposed any "alliance, entanglement or adjustment" with the Congress, communal, or Communist parties. But a year later at Bangalore (1956), while reiterating this inflexible posture, the party allowed the National Executive in "exceptional and extraordinary cases," and at the request of a party's state executive committee, to permit electoral adjustments with "different opposition parties."[19] In the 1957 general elections, such exceptional arrangements were allowed in all but four states, while the West Bengal party disregarded the policy by forming an alliance with left parties. This policy was adopted by a sharply divided National Conference, with important national leaders like Jayaprakash Narayan and a majority favoring it, and Asoka Mehta and others opposing it in preference to adjustments with like-minded parties, i.e., Congress and others believing in nationalism, socialism, and democracy.

The inability to agree on a settled parliamentary strategy threatens the remaining vestiges of the socialist leadership's unity. Jayaprakash, and those who support the new policy, some of whom are leaders in states which will most benefit from it, emphasize the "totalitarian" trends of Congress' monopoly of power in India. Electoral adjustments are therefore justified as necessary in order to preserve democracy in India and to maintain the very existence of the party itself. Important leaders of the majority like H. V. Kamath have indicated that they would rather leave the party than strengthen the Congress; others like Asoka Mehta have threatened the same course if this policy strengthens the Communist Party, and predict that new issues will split the party in the post-election period in those states where adjustments were made.[20] The leadership therefore entered the 1957 general elections divided over parliamentary strategy and with the prospect of serious continuing conflict in the post-election period.

General unity exists more on program than on ideology or parliamentary strategy, with the exception of the issue of reorganization of states on a linguistic basis. Though the party agreed to allow every state organization to adopt its own position on the linguistic issue in order to prevent conflict, the championship of regional claims by national and state party leaders in conflict with one another further divided the lead-

---

[18] *Policy Statement*, New Delhi, Praja Socialist Party, 1956.
[19] *Socialist International Information*, V-VI, No. 51-52, December 22, 1956, pp. 888-889.
[20] In particular, Bombay, Kerala, West Bengal, Madras, and Andhra, *New York Times*, December 26, 1956; *ibid.*, January 23, 1957.

ership and has led to resignations and withdrawals of even some important founding leaders, such as Purshottam Tricumdas in Bombay. While important national leaders like Jayaprakash have urged the formation of a unilingual Samyukta Maharashtra, including Bombay City, others like Acharya Kripalani and Asoka Mehta, who reversed himself in Parliament, spoke for the Congress solution of a multilingual state.

Indiscipline also persists. National and local leaders have issued press statements against one another over such problems as the conduct of the socialist ministry in Travancore-Cochin, and this in defiance of the party's own "code of conduct." Informal factions or groups based on regional, ideological, personal, or power considerations continue to function within the leadership cadre.

An authoritarian tendency continues to assert itself at crucial moments. Though Jayaprakash withdrew publicly from active participation and membership in socialist executive bodies and conferences, his advice is sought and is given on important matters facing the party. Despite his ideological trend towards Gandhian *sarvodaya* and nonparty politics, Jayaprakash Narayan continues to influence the party, whether it involves approval of socialist participation in delegations to Communist China, membership in the Indian delegation to the UN, cooperation with the Planning Commission, or the formation and conduct of a state socialist ministry. Publicly, he is still the symbol of the party and speaks for it, whether in an official capacity or not. He has expressed himself on questions of police firings in Bihar, linguistic states reorganization, Soviet intervention in Hungary, and on the new policy permitting electoral adjustments with the Communist Party or communal parties. His influence continues to be great and his access to Nehru important, though he is removed from formal party responsibilities. Indeed, his position is not unlike that of Gandhi after his retirement from the Congress in 1934.

Among most party leaders, the intellectual approach to party politics remains. Ideology, strategy, and tactics are discussed and adopted in perennial theses which analyze the nature of man and society as necessary prerequisites for theoretical clarity. Not the art of the possible, but a science of ideological clarity is presumed to be the necessary first step towards successful political action.

Yet the emergence of countertrends of behavior are discernible. There is a growing scepticism of the importance of ideology. Doctrinaire political concepts are paid formal homage, but decisions are being made more and more on practical political grounds. This was seen in the creation of the Praja Socialist Party primarily out of "practical and pragmatic considerations," as well as in willingness of some central leaders to consider the possibility of cooperation with Congress, even including coalition and eventual merger. Further evidence is seen in the electoral adjustments with the left wing parties in Travancore-Cochin, the use of Congress support to achieve control of a ministry, and the refusal of the Praja Socialist ministry to resign in the face of demands within the party. The best example, however, is the recent general election in which electoral adjustments were admittedly allowed even with communal parties and the Communist Party on grounds of expediency.[21] Though the leadership is divided on whether cooperation with Congress or with the Communists and left parties will most advance party interests and programs, the approach involves the same concern for practical means to achieve power rather than doctrinal clarification. The offshoot Socialist Party of India, formed by Rammanohar Lohia in 1955, refused to engage in alliances or adjustments and followed a lone course of unilateral opposition.

Another marked trend is an impatience with indiscipline. Whereas in previous phases it was regretted but tolerated to a dangerous degree, now indiscipline is carefully circumscribed by a published "Code of Conduct" which has been enforced in a relatively vigorous and speedy manner even against important leaders like Rammanohar Lohia, Madhu Limaye, and others who now head the Socialist Party of India.

Even more striking is the trend towards collective, democratic decision making by state and local leaders and the members nationally as a check on the authoritarian tradition. The national leaders, even Jayaprakash Narayan, have been defeated on some issues by the secondary cadres, as when cooperation and coalition with the Congress, embodied in principle in the general secretary's report, was rejected by the Betul convention, and the Gaya thesis was adopted in the face of opposition by some important leaders. Significantly, the Gaya conference initiated the democratic nomination and contested election of the National Executive from the convention floor; indeed the convention's resolutions and policies were largely the product of the secondary leaders' and members' initiation and discussion.

These new trends are partly the fruition of the central leadership's striving towards the achievement of a practical, responsible, democratic mass party. But they are also the by-products of the dissolution of the old core party leadership. The cohesion once maintained among this group

[21] *Janata*, XII, No. 1, January 27, 1957, pp. 8-9.

which previously gave direction to the party, particularly that among Asoka Mehta, Jayaprakash, and Rammanohar Lohia, is now gone.

Through this disintegration, a shift in leadership has taken place. Secondary leaders on the national and state level, in both party positions and legislative posts, have filled the widening chasm in the national leadership. The initial hiatus between the national and secondary leaders in the Socialist Party phase was replaced by the disagreements between the national leaders in the Praja Socialist Party phase, resulting in the decline of power of the national leaders and the ascendancy of the secondary and state leaders. The party's crises have been those of the national leadership: the party's inability to communicate effectively with the secondary echelons and the membership concerning the changes desired in ideology, organization, and strategy; its failure to assess correctly and adhere consistently to a given role in Indian politics; and its failure to maintain its own cohesion in the face of public adversity and party rebellion.

Party leadership is shifting its focus of action away from the nonparliamentary, agitational, and intellectual leaders of previous phases in favor of a growing group of practical, parliamentary men who are beginning to wield more influence. The Kisan Mazdoor-Praja Party merger increased PSP leadership in the Indian parliament eighty-three per cent and gave it representation from two other states from which it had had no previous representatives. In the state assemblies it gave the party parliamentary leadership in three states, significantly increased existing representation in three others, and added to that in five additional states, for an over-all sixty per cent increase in state legislative leadership.[22] Though by-elections increased parliamentary representation, the Lohia split in 1955 and its aftermath lost one third of the national representation and one fourth of the state legislative representation to the Socialist Party of India, the Congress, and independents. But the PSP was still the major opposition in five states before the general elections of 1957. The recent elections helped the PSP to recoup its losses generally—losing out in some places, gaining in others, and with an over-all balance of a slight loss.

The histories of western socialist parties, as well as that of the Congress Party, have repeatedly shown the moderating influences exercised by a growing parliamentary leadership over these parties' agitational and intellectual elites. The influence of parliamentary leaders is likely to

[22] Asoka Mehta, *The Political Mind of India*, Bombay, Praja Socialist Party, pp. 78, 80.

be exercised in the direction of greater party discipline, coupled with increasing local and state initiative. Within the limits of an opposition status, a trend has developed towards more specific, moderate, realizable programs and pragmatically flexible parliamentary strategy. The experience of the Travancore-Cochin ministry revealed a victory of parliamentary leadership over the party leaders' opposition. Furthermore the Bangalore parliamentary policy (1956) not only indicates the continued influence of Jayaprakash Narayan, but also of the parliamentary leadership of four state parties which had the most to gain from electoral adjustments with other parties.

In brief, with the exception of Jayaprakash's peculiar advisory leadership, the active direction of the PSP is being assumed by the former secondary leaders and an increasing number of parliamentary representatives, plus the leaders of state organizations. The new countercharacteristics among the leadership suggest that although serious divisions remain, the national leadership now is closer to the views of the party membership than previously. They also suggest that some alteration of past characteristics is under way through the impact of experience which may lead to a greater over-all effectiveness.

But even if the leadership had not possessed its peculiar handicap of retarding behavioral traits, or had corrected them for maximum cohesion and effectiveness, there continue to be factors beyond the leadership's control which block its drive for political power. Socialist leadership throughout its existence has exhibited traits of personal ability, honesty, patriotism, selflessness, and keen intellectual powers, but the leadership has also been limited by its own shortcomings. It has suffered by comparison with the superior organization, heritage, and national leadership of the Congress and the latter's flexibility in adopting a socialist goal. Moreover, the fractionalization of Indian politics among numerous small political parties has divided the large total opposition sentiment to the advantage of Congress. A competing Communist Party, possessing superior financial and organizational resources in certain key states, particularly in the south, exacerbates this tendency. Being sensitive to India's unprecedented cultural upheaval, socialist leaders have felt a special responsibility to understand changing political patterns in order better to adapt traditional socialist ideals and methods to India's peculiar local conditions.

In the present fluid state of Indian politics, it is hazardous to predict the future of the Praja Socialist Party. But three possible courses of action suggest themselves. The leadership may continue to disintegrate through desertion to Congress, to Lohia's Socialist Party of India, or to political retirement; thus the party may degenerate into a small sect. Second, the leadership may correct its own mistakes and benefit from any misfortunes which may befall the Congress or the Communist Party, such as a split in either or both of those two parties, to build an increasingly powerful Praja Socialist Party. In this case, a return of former socialist leaders from retirement cannot be ruled out. Third, a return to the Congress by most or all of the leadership would be possible, through favorable circumstances which give socialists a share in the direction of the government and the Congress Party.

HINDU COMMUNAL GROUPS IN INDIAN POLITICS

RICHARD D. LAMBERT

*T*HE term "community," as used in India, is one of those conveniently vague words so helpful in the designation of heterogeneous social units. Today, as a noun, the word usually refers to a host of different geographic areas which are in the midst of an all-points development program. This usage goes at least as far back as Baden-Powell and has a neutral, perhaps pleasant connotation. The adjectival form, "communal" is one of the most negatively weighted terms in the Indian political vocabulary. It is used to describe an organization that seeks to promote the interests of a section of the population presumably to the detriment of the society as a whole, or in the name of religion or tradition opposes a social change which the speakers believe to be a progressive one. It is thus an epithet, implying antisocial greed and reactionary social outlook. Although the implications of the term "communal" are clear, the "communities" represented are anything but homogeneous. They have included the major religious divisions—Muslims, Hindus, Christians, Sikhs, Parsis; ethnic groups—Marwaris, Santals, Sindhis; racial groups—Anglo-Indians, Europeans; linguistic groups—Tamils, Oriyas, Telugus; caste and subcaste groups—Jats, Harijans, Chitpavan Brahmans. For all of these subdivisions the term community has been used; and they are very different kinds of social units.

Communal organizations, then, represent homogeneous political units only in the sense that each is concerned with the prerogatives of a single segment of Indian society—they are pressure groups seeking to secure for the cultural unit they represent a larger measure of prestige, power, wealth, and predominance of cultural patterns. This paper will confine itself to the Hindu communalist parties inasmuch as we are dealing with present-day Indian leadership and there is no Muslim communal group which currently has an important voice in politics in India. In terms of the whole picture of communalism in India, the isolation of the Hindu communalist parties, both from their Muslim counterparts and from British policy, is somewhat like describing the actions of one con-

RICHARD D. LAMBERT *is an Associate Professor in the Sociology of South Asia at the University of Pennsylvania. He was last in India in 1956-1957 as a Fulbright and Guggenheim scholar.*

testant in a boxing match and ignoring his opponent and an erratic referee. However, if the fact that Hindu communalism was matched, perhaps even outdone by Muslim communal organizations is kept in mind, no harm need be done.

In the pre-Partition decades, the conflict of the communities was many-sided, although the main arena was the competition for control of the elective and executive machinery of government. The long nationalist struggle tended to focus attention upon politics as the primary and paramount source of power. Political control presumably carried with it the ultimate control over the economic, educational, religious, and other cultural forms of the society. The struggle for political control was heightened by the fact that the government was the major consumer of the talents of the new western-educated middle class, and government control meant jobs. In the twentieth century the Hindu community was handicapped by their past successes in this struggle. Since, in most provinces and in the nation as a whole, they were the majority community, they would hold power under any proportional representational system. Moreover, the early start of the Hindus in English education and the half-century lag in Muslim participation in western training heavily weighted the civil service with Hindus even in provinces with large Muslim populations. In the competition for political power and jobs, therefore, almost every compromise was a surrender of existing advantages for Hindus and a gain for Muslims. The extremist Hindu communalists spoke of blackmail, of abject surrender of Hindu rights, of an increasingly voracious Muslim appetite encouraged by divisive British policy and Congress appeasement. The extremist Muslim communalists argued that the concessions were trivial in the face of overwhelming Hindu dominance.

During the nineteenth century a series of sectarian movements within the Hindu intelligentsia arose which dramatized the eclectic absorption into Hinduism of many aspects of western culture. In Bengal, the Brahmo Samaj under Ram Mohan Roy developed a new philosophy which discarded many of those social practices then current among Hindus which were under assault by Christian moralists, and sought to reinterpret Hindu tradition to make it more acceptable to the growing class of urban intellectuals. The drift toward disaffection with the British and the West which characterized the latter decades of the nineteenth century gave rise to a number of organizations such as the Arya Samaj, the Theosophists, and the Ramakrishna Mission which reasserted the supremacy of Hindu doctrines as they interpreted them. Many of the leaders and members of these organizations joined in the early nationalist movement, frequently in the ranks of those pressing for strong and, if necessary, violent agitation against the British.

At the same time the groups posed themselves as the defenders of Hindu ideals. Sometimes they took stands against the introduction of social changes which appeared to threaten traditional ways. More commonly, their exaltation of Hindu ideals was more of a rallying cry than a championing of concrete causes. In their concern with the status of Hindu ideals in the abstract, they sought to encourage instruction in sacred learning, emphasize religious rituals on ceremonial occasions, and in general to support those symbolic practices most closely identified with Hindu orthodoxy.

The communalist groups have, in fact, been highly selective in the aspects of Hindu tradition they have chosen to support. For instance, with the exception of the Tilakites each group has been opposed to the practice of untouchability and the social discriminations of caste. The Brahmo Samaj splintered on this issue. Much of the appeal of the Arya Samaj in the Punjab came from its anticaste stand. Ironically, many Hindus were entered as Aryas in the census tabulations of castes. The Theosophists, Ramakrishna Mission, and Rashtriya Swayamsevak Sangh have all taken official positions against caste.

While the Hindu ideals sponsored by communal organizations have been somewhat diffuse, the integration and strengthening of the Hindu community has been a clear and single purpose. A number of enemies of the "Hindu nation" have been perceived: the British, the Muslims, the Congress, the Communists, and the Socialists. The early blending of Hindu nationalism and Indian nationalism is reflected in B. G. Tilak's revival of Shivaji as a national hero and in V. D. Savarkar's rewriting of history in his *The First Indian War of Independence of 1857*. This blend was most strongly expressed in Maharashtra, particularly among the Chitpavan Brahmans settled around Poona and Nasik, who provided some of the most notable moderate leaders, such as G. K. Gokhale, as well as the most inflammatory, such as Tilak and Savarkar.

The drive for unification of the Hindu community was both anti-British and anti-Muslim, but as more and more Muslims followed Sir Syed Ahmed Khan's advice to boycott the Congress and nationalist politics, the anti-Muslim character was emphasized. The choice of Shivaji as a hero glorified a Hindu military leader who had vanquished Muslim armies. In the popular Bengali novel *Anandamath*, Hindu sannyasins defeated the Muslim rulers in Bengal to save the motherland. Hindu-

Muslim riots, although not as common as those of the twentieth century, did occur in the latter part of the nineteenth century in the cities of northern India. In Keer's biography of Savarkar he relates an interesting example of the early mixture of anti-British and anti-Muslim sentiments, cast against the background of Hindu-Muslim riots.

In June 1893, serious riots broke out between Hindus and Muslims in the Azamgarh District of the United Provinces and in August of the same year in Bombay. The news of the atrocities then perpetrated on the Hindus in the United Provinces and Bombay fired his [Savarkar's] blood and he resolved to avenge the woes and deaths of his co-religionists. The boy Savarkar ten years old led a batch of selected schoolmates in a march upon the village mosque. The battalion of boys showered stones upon it, shattered its windows and tiles and returned victorious. This incident gives the first hint of the heroic mettle Vinayak was made of and the key to his future daring life and leadership. The victory, however, was not allowed to go unchallenged. The Muslim schoolboys gave battle to Vinayak, the Hindu Generalissimo. Although the number of his soldiers decreased at the time of joining the battle, Vinayak routed the enemy with missiles like pins, penknives, and thorns with which he had equipped his army. The battle had its lesson. The boy leader fell to training and organizing his group. For the military training the group was divided into two detachments—one Hindu and the other a British or a Muslim—to defend a field or a compound. Always the Hindus won and the Muslims or British lost in the mock fights and warfare.[1]

The victory of the Moderates in the Congress, the entente with the Muslims dramatized by the Lucknow Pact, and the Khilafat agitation alienated many of the Hindu extremists. The period 1924-1928 in many ways marks a watershed in communal relations in India and, during this period, the communal organizations sought to strengthen Hindu society against the Muslims and the Congress moderates. At the same time the deterioration of the Khilafat organization and Muslim attempts to conduct widespread proselytization among the Hindus made the organization of the Hindu community more imperative. The Hindu Mahasabha, although founded the same year as the Muslim League, only emerged as a party of all-India importance in these years. The Rashtriya Swayamsevak Sangh was formed in Nagpur to fight for Hindu interests in the riots that swept that city in 1924. Dr. B. S. Moonje founded the Nagpur Provincial Rifle Association to fight the Muslims. The Maharashtrian Militarization Board was set up in Poona, the Bhonsle Military School in Nasik.

The strength of the Hindu communalist organizations has fluctuated

---

[1] Dhananjay Keer, *Savarkar and His Times*, Bombay, A. V. Keer, 1950.

over the decades in direct proportion to the prevalence of Hindu-Muslim violence. Not, as B. R. Ambedkar and others have implied, that the communal organizations created the conflict, although they frequently provided the *casus-belli*, but that in times of communal violence the communal organizations played several highly functional roles for the Hindu community. They were first of all a striking arm, ranging from the disorganized gangs available for small street brawls to the disciplined troops of the Hindustan National Guard, the Rashtriya Swayamsevak Sangh, the Hindu Rashtra Dal. A millennium of Muslim conquest and rule had established a stereotype of a warlike Muslim minority sometimes allied with but always dominating the more passive Hindus. The militaristic display of the Hindu communal organizations partly offset this stereotype. Moreover, in the breakdown of law and order during riots, members of communal organizations served as defense forces for Hindu enclaves and borderline areas in the cities, and organized rescue and relief parties for victims. It is not surprising, therefore, that memberships and general public support soared in times of communal trouble.

The Hindu communal organization which most clearly embodied the growing Hindu militarism was the Rashtriya Swayamasevak Sangh.[2]

The RSS has never directly committed itself to electoral competition. It is not a communal party in the same sense as the Jan Sangh, the Hindu Mahasabha, or the Ram Rajya Parishad, although it has on occasion operated on the political scene through the Mahasabha and latterly the Jan Sangh. It is a communal force as yet uncommitted as to the means by which it will seek political power. The RSS is a tightly knit, disciplined, hierarchical organization seeking to incorporate larger and larger segments of the public within its ranks. Its primary aim is to establish within its own group a model of a revitalized Hindu society and eventually to secure the adoption of this cultural form in the whole country. The communal parties, on the other hand, are loosely knit unions of diverse elements sharing a common set of attitudes only on matters concerning Hindu-Muslim or Indo-Pakistan affairs. These parties are structured and operate much like other parliamentary parties in seeking political power by electoral means. Organizationally, the RSS is akin to the Communist Party which it unceasingly opposes; the com-

[2] An excellent account of the RSS is contained in a monograph submitted by J. A. Curran, Jr., as a thesis for an M.A. degree at the University of Pennsylvania and published by the Institute of Pacific Relations in 1951 under the title *Militant Hinduism in Indian Politics: A Study of the RSS*. The following account draws heavily upon this source, on the RSS constitution of 1949, and on the author's interviews with Sangh leaders and visits to Sangh camps.

munal parties resemble more the Congress from which they invariably sprang. In program, the RSS promotes an integrated way of life and ideology to which its members are trained and rigidly held. The communal parties take a series of stands on specific communal issues and depend upon supporting opinion from a public otherwise uncommitted to the party. The RSS is an organized social movement; the communal parties, spokesmen for a section of public opinion. It must be added immediately that while in general this characterization holds, there is some overlap in organizational styles. The RSS maintains a series of periodicals which promote its point of view with the general public as well as its own members. The communal parties on occasion have developed militaristic groups, armed and uniformed. In both cases, however, these are peripheral to the primary aims.

The RSS is highly organized and promotes obedience and uniformity of opinion within its ranks. Each member belongs to a cell of about fifty individuals and he must attend the daily exercise sessions held in the early morning and evening. During these sessions calisthenics, lathi drill, group games, and Sangh ceremonies provide a constant sense of active participation and group membership. The military discipline and precise rituals of these sessions are impressive, and the twilight salute to the Sangh saffron-colored flag is the emotional climax to the strenuous exercise. Uniformity of ideology is maintained throughout the organization by means of weekly group discussions, the keeping of identical libraries at the various cell headquarters, and biweekly lectures by itinerant higher officials. Promising members are sent to one of the dozen or so officers' training camps, and the best of these go to a camp in Nagpur where an elite cadre is built up for the Sangh.

The structure of the Sangh is frankly hierarchical and autocratic. The communications network is one-way, from top to bottom. Although the 1949 constitution provided for elections to various posts in the executive hierarchy and deliberative bodies, in practice these elections are formalities; from current evidence, neither the leaders nor the members of the Sangh have any intention or desire to democratize the organization. The formal structure of the Sangh is a mixture of a parliamentary system grafted on an appointed executive hierarchy. Deliberative councils at the central and state levels are composed of a mixture of elected and appointed officials. But the core of the organization is an executive hierarchy known as the Organizers who are appointed independently of the elective bodies and are controlled in a separate chain of command. Unlike the general membership and the elected officials, the Organizers are full-time workers. Each Organizer must take the brahmacharya vow and devote his entire life to the Sangh. At the top of the organization is the Sar Sanghchalak. This office, held for life, is passed down from one leader to his chosen successor. So far it has been held by the founder, Dr. Keshav Hedgewar, and the incumbent, Madhav Rao Golwalkar. The Sar Sanghchalak plays a variety of roles, some of them traditionally Indian, some drawn from other organizational forms. He is called guru, and he does in fact fill some of the roles of this traditional leader-figure in Indian history. Golwalkar's bearded countenance, religious learning, ascetic habits, magnetic personality, oratorical skill, and aura of mysticism place him in the category of charismatic leader. But unlike the traditional guru, he is not a leader of a band of followers who are united only in their personal devotion to him. Major decisions are deferred to a level at least as low as the Central Working Committee, although the opinion of Sar Sanghchalak Golwalkar carries special weight. He is therefore not quite the typical lone guru figure surrounded by disciples who are seeking his special knowledge. At the same time his guru status is used by the organization in many ways. The major fund raising device is an annual contribution by the membership on Guru Purnima. In Hindu tradition, this is the day on which the disciples or students of a guru collect donations for his sustenance throughout the coming year. In the RSS this custom is the major fund raising device. Sometime after Golwalkar's sixtieth year (1956) it is hoped to give him a purse of Rupees 60 lakhs, and about half of this amount has already been raised. The guru status of the leader also serves to insure him and the organization extensive and friendly audiences when he tours the country on membership drives.

By placing the leadership core in a hierarchy of offices which have the power of a military hierarchy and the prestige of devoted ascetic brahmacharis, the system is virtually inviolate to serious internal strains. The most effective power structures are those in which the personal criteria by which prestige and power are allocated are not subject to objective test. In the case of the Sangh, so long as the Organizer does not violate the taboos of ascetic Hinduism, there are few ways of comparing the relative piety or spiritual accomplishments of individual Organizers. As with the Puritan system of predestination, those who are rewarded are *ipso facto* those who deserve to be rewarded. There are no objective measures outside of the system itself which enable the members to judge whether the hierarchy does in fact correspond to gradations in spiritual superiority. As a result the means of upward mobility is to achieve the closest possible conformity to ideal Sangh behavior and ideology.

While the hierarchy of the Sangh is geared to the promotion of Sangh aims, the appeal to potential members lies only partly in ideological conviction. The comradeship in cell membership is a strong appeal, giving a sense of belonging which, unlike the family membership, is one into which the individual seeks membership and is formally admitted. Since he must meet rigid requirements, he feels himself to be a member of a select fraternity. He is presented with a complete ideology and is supported in his desire to dedicate himself by constant association with others who share his need for a cause. Sangh dialectics occupy his mind and the discussion sessions give him a sense of doing something, of continually preparing for a coming victory. He can feel himself to be the true nationalist in that his ideal image of India is unsullied by alien influences. Paradoxically, he can feel superior to his lethargic countrymen by condemning many of those aspects of Hindu custom which have come to be regarded as antagonistic to national growth—aversion to manual labor, strict caste divisions, pacifism, and fatalism. The psychological appeal is apparent particularly for the displaced urban middle class, and the cells are full of college students, heads of small businesses, clerks, schoolteachers, pleaders, and merchants' sons.

The communal organizations reached their peak in the years surrounding partition. In the years following the incarceration of the Congress leaders in 1942, the communalist parties almost alone occupied the national scene. Dr. Shyama Prasad Mookerjee succeeded Savarkar as President of the Hindu Mahasabha at the December 1943 session. Shri Guruji Madhav Sadashiv Golwalkar succeeded Hedgewar as head of the Rashtriya Swayamsevak Sangh in 1940. Under the leadership of these two powerful speakers and skillful organizers the Mahasabha and the RSS flourished. As Muslims rallied more and more behind the Muslim League and its demand for Pakistan and as the increasing tempo of communal riots nurtured uneasy anger in the Hindu community, the communal organizations grew in size and took over leadership functions which the Congress could not or would not perform. Volunteer militias somewhat on the RSS model arose to combat Muslim counterparts: in Bengal the Hindu Shakti Sangh and the Hindustan National Guard; in Bihar the Seva Dal; in the Punjab the Vir Dal which joined with the Sikh's Akali Fauj to establish private armies based in the princely states of southeast Punjab. In at least one case (Alwar where Dr. N. B. Khare, later president of the Mahasabha, was Premier), state troops were used for communal warfare. In the Punjab many Hindus were initiated into the more militant Sikh religion while many Sikhs moved into the extremist sects of their community. Running through all of the volunteer militias was a common core of ex-INA men and demobilized soldiers who trained and officered the communal private armies.

In summary, then, we find the Hindu communalist political and cultural organizations playing a number of roles on the political scene in the decades that led up to Independence:

They elevated Hinduism to a high status position after a millennium of Muslim rule and more than a century of indictment by western critics.

They were one source of violent nationalistic sentiments.

They pressed for the abolition of untouchability and other social disabilities of caste.

They opposed efforts by the government to alter the traditional way of life.

They were a brake upon the speed with which concessions were given to Muslims.

They fostered group cohesion among the many fragments of the Hindu social order in the face of a unified Muslim community.

They precipitated and participated in riots between Hindus and Muslims.

They fostered a martial tradition to combat the stereotype that Muslims were superior in combat.

The coming of independence radically shifted the position and role of the Hindu communal parties in India. Now both as political parties and organized conspiracies they clamored for punitive action against Pakistan, for retribution against the Muslims who remained in India, and for the allotment of more and more of the budget to refugee rehabilitation. While their role had always been one of urging the moderate Congress to stiffen its resistance against Muslim demands, such pressures had been directed against another political party, not against the government. After Partition, the Indian government sought to reassure the minorities within its borders and to protect them not only against violence but against all the more subtle by-products of hostility. This was no easy task. The bitterness of the preceding year lay heavily upon the nation. Refugees overflowed from East Punjab and camped on the main thoroughfares of New Delhi, Bombay, and the towns of the United Provinces. The restoration of law and order in East Punjab and the protection of Muslims from the anger of distraught refugees and their sympathizers were most difficult battles. During the critical months of the fall and winter of 1947 the communal organizations grew stronger and stronger; only the persuasive voice of Gandhi kept India to the letter if not the spirit of tolerance.

The communalist parties had been openly opposed to Gandhi for many years, insisting that his compromises with Muslims constituted betrayal of the Hindu cause. One widely circulated pamphlet spoke of the Gandhi-Muslim conspiracy.[3] When Gandhi was assassinated by two Maharashtrian Brahmans who had past affiliations with the RSS and the Mahasabha, it was assumed that the communal parties were responsible. In Bombay Province a wave of retaliatory mob assaults was directed against the communal groups and in Maharashtra they quickly degenerated into a series of attacks upon Brahmans. Nehru in public speeches accused the Mahasabha of Gandhi's murder. Dr. Khare, Alwar's delegate to the Constituent Assembly and later president of the Mahasabha, was detained for complicity in the affair. Although the hearings found no evidence of direct participation of either the Mahasabha or the RSS in Gandhi's murder, popular sentiment and unofficial government opinion held them responsible and their prestige fell drastically. The Mahasabha, under Mookerjee's leadership, resolved to suspend political activity. Golwalkar and other leaders of the RSS had been imprisoned a few days after Gandhi's assassination; on February 4, 1948, the RSS was officially banned with the announcement of a series of objections to the organization: It had no written constitution; it was a secret organization; it was communalist; it did not recognize the supremacy of the Indian flag.

As the year dragged on, the furor over Gandhi's death died down and relations with Pakistan deteriorated in the wake of the Kashmir war. Communal voices were once again heard. On November 7, 1948, a Mahasabha resolution questioned the mandate of the Congress in agreeing to Partition. The resolution argued that the Congress had been elected in 1946 while it was still committed to opposition to Partition, thus, in later agreeing to a division of the country, it had acted illegally. The Mahasabha held, therefore, that Partition was a party, not a national, commitment and that *Akhand* (United) *Hindustan* should be reestablished. On November 24, 1948, Mookerjee resigned from the Mahasabha Working Committee and on December 29 the Mahasabha voted to resume political activity.

[3] *Gandhi-Muslim Conspiracy*, by a Hindu nationalist, Poona, R. D. Ghanekar, 1941.

The RSS, suffering under the loss of its top leadership, on December 9, 1948 announced a civil disobedience campaign to force the government to reinstate the organization. By the time the campaign had been called off on January 24, 1949, some 40,000 members of the RSS had been jailed. The ban on the RSS was not lifted until July 12, 1949, when an RSS constitution was released which met most of the government's objections and promised that the RSS would remain a nonpolitical, cultural organization.

In the fall of 1949 the trade deadlock resulting from differences with Pakistan over devaluation policy added economic animus to already strained relations between the two countries. As communal sentiments now international instead of domestic flourished, the communal parties took on a new vigor. Northwestern India and Pakistan had been virtually swept clean of minorities, and attention now focused on the Bengal border where refugee columns moved spasmodically across the border each time a saber rattled. At Christmas time in 1949 the Mahasabha gathered in Calcutta for its first national convention since Gandhi's death.

On the day of the arrival of Savarkar in Calcutta, the West Bengal government imposed a ban on assemblies and processions in nearby Howrah where Savarkar was to detrain. In spite of the order, a procession which lasted for two hours escorted him from the station to his quarters; the following day an assembly of about 40,000 people met to hear him speak under a huge pandal in north Calcutta. At this session and at its Working Committee meetings the Mahasabha toyed with many planks for a platform in an attempt to make a strong reentrance into the political scene—planks which varied from accusations of corruption in the Congress and a vote of friendship for the Hindu ruler of Nepal, to opposition to the Hindu Code Bill. The press, by editorials and reporting, was almost unanimous in the opinion that the meetings had been weak and unsuccessful. But there was one plank which was destined to gain notoriety: in addition to the eventual realization of *Akhand Hindustan*, the Mahasabha supported the demand of the Council for the Protection of Minorities for two or three border districts to be taken immediately from East Bengal. The East Bengal premier picked this up, charging that it was encouraged by the Indian government. The Mahasabha pushed its other concerns into the background and swung its complete attention to the Bengal border.

Throughout the course of the Bengal disturbances of February-March 1950, the Mahasabha pressed the Indian government to take sterner measures with Pakistan. After the signing of the Delhi Pact in April

1950 the two Bengali members of the Indian cabinet, K. C. Neogy and S. P. Mookerjee, resigned in protest. Mookerjee's return to Bengal and to outright opposition to the Congress was both a source of strength and of embarrassment to the communalist parties. Personal rivalries and the feeling that he had deserted communal politics when he was needed most made him *persona non grata* among the leaders of the Mahasabha, and yet with Savarkar's retirement there were no leaders of national stature in the Mahasabha's ranks. From Mookerjee's viewpoint, the Mahasabha's name was still tarnished from the Gandhi murder, and it would be difficult for him to gain all-India backing were he again to join this organization. In 1951 he formed a separate party, Bharatiya Jana Sangh, generally called Jan Sangh, which drew its support from refugees, remnants of former princely power, others favoring a stronger policy toward Pakistan, and various groups with conservative economic interests. The Jan Sangh also served as a political voice for the Rashtriya Swayamsevak Sangh.

The elections of 1951-1952 found the Mahasabha suffering its usual rout at the polls. Throughout the history of communal parties they have scored few electoral successes. Even in the 1945-1946 elections, when for several years they had crowded the political arena, the Hindu Mahasabha was badly defeated. It won only three seats out of 1585 in provincial assemblies and none at all in the new central legislative assembly. In the 1952 elections the fate of the Hindu communal parties was not much better. Only one party, the Jan Sangh, gained the necessary three per cent of the popular vote to enable it to remain officially a national party. In the state assemblies and electoral colleges it won only thirty-four out of the 717 seats it contested, nine of which came from West Bengal and eight from Rajasthan. The Hindu Mahasabha won twenty out of the 211 seats it contested and the Ram Rajya Parishad thirty-two of the 342 it contested. In the Lok Sabha the representation was even less. Only three seats went to the Jan Sangh, four to the Mahasabha and three to the Ram Rajya Parishad. Only in Rajasthan where a coalition of former jagirdars, princes, independents, and communalist parties won sixty-two seats did the Hindu communalists command any legislative strength.

For a while the communal parties exercised some influence in the Lok Sabha through the oratorical skill and personal prestige of S. P. Mookerjee, president of the Jan Sangh. Since the death of Mookerjee on June 23, 1953, the legislative influence of the communal parties has been slight. Bizarre parliamentary coalitions did little to strengthen their hand. In the Lok Sabha a parliamentary group was formed of members of the Jan Sangh, Hindu Mahasabha, Ganatantra Parishad, Commonweal Party, Akali Dal, and the Tamilnad Toilers Party. In the Council of States, the Akalis, Ganatantra Parishad, Hindu Mahasabha, Jharkhand Party, Kerala Socialists, Peasant and Workers Party, Tamilnad Toilers Party, and the Communist-dominated Peoples Democratic Front from Hyderabad joined under the leadership of Kalidas Nag. These ephemeral parliamentary groups were more for the purpose of securing blocks of time during debate than for genuine party collaboration. Congress strength and discipline has prevented the exercise of any major opposition. Even on issues so crucial to the Hindu communalist as the Hindu Marriages Act, where demonstrations were staged and Congress members spoke against the various clauses of the Bill, at roll call Congress voting strength remained firm and the communalists made little headway.

After the 1951-1952 elections the one major campaign of the communal parties was the drive to induce a greater integration of Kashmir with India and to liberate Hindu segments of the state from rule by a Muslim government. Mookerjee entered Jammu in defiance of an order requiring a government permit for entry and was arrested. On June 23, 1953, he died in prison and on July 7 the agitation was "unconditionally withdrawn."

In approaching the elections of 1957 the communal parties, like the other opposition parties, had little hope of unseating the Congress. Again like the other opposition parties, the communal parties were reluctant to make outright electoral alliances with other parties but agreed to localized "electoral arrangements" under which their candidates would not splinter the opposition vote in constituencies where their chance of defeating Congress candidates was small. In theory, at least, constituencies were allocated to the opposition party which had the greatest strength. By this means the opposition hoped to cut down the Congress majority, but there is little expectation that such agreements will survive into post-election years.

The Jan Sangh, the only communal party recognized by the Electoral Commission as an all-India party, made no attempt to contest seats in the four states of Andhra, Kerala, Madras, or Orissa. Nevertheless the party increased its representation both in the Center—from three to four seats, and in the state assemblies—from thirty-four to forty-six seats. Jan Sangh's most notable gains were in Uttar Pradesh, while in West Bengal it failed to win a single seat.

On the other hand both the Hindu Mahasabha and the Ram Rajya Parishad did poorly in the 1957 elections. In the Lok Sabha the Mahasabha's representation was cut from four to two; the Ram Rajya Parishad failed to obtain even one seat. In state assemblies the Mahasabha managed to win only eight seats, mainly in Madhya Pradesh where its three top leaders, Dr. N. B. Khare, V. G. Deshpande, and N. C. Chatterjee were all defeated in their attempts to obtain parliamentary seats. The Ram Rajya Parishad retained some strength in Madhya Pradesh and Rajasthan but won a total of only twenty-two assembly seats, ten less than in 1951.

The only new issues in the 1957 campaign manifestos of communal parties were the Mahasabha's support for the remnants of linguistic state dissidence in Gujarat and Maharashtra, although heavy Communist influence in the Mahagujerat Parishad and the Samyukta Maharashtra Samiti has made the Mahasabha somewhat less than wholehearted in this position; the Jan Sangh's bid for a unitary form of government combined with a decentralization of power; and the Jan Sangh's urging the strengthening of India's military might while adhering to nonalignment in foreign policy.

None of these issues succeeded in catapulting the communal parties into power. In addition to the lack of clear-cut issues there are a number of severe handicaps under which the communal parties now operate. There is no leadership of national stature, or for that matter, with the death of Mookerjee, with strong regional appeal. The communal parties have become identified with reaction, revivalism, and that most terrible of political attributes in India, nonprogressiveness. It is interesting to note that this is the same brush with which Jawaharlal Nehru is now proceeding to tar the Communist and Socialist parties. Communal leaders seeking office must also combat an ill-defined but nevertheless strong tradition in India that the religious pundits may advise on policy but the ruling should be done by others. The strength of the Hindu communalist organizations, however, lies outside of the elective assemblies. As before Partition, their primary influence has been as spokesmen for anti-Muslim sentiments and as defenders of the status and forms of traditional ideals. Their importance comes from the catalytic function that they play in exacerbating tensions and divisive forces already present in the society. While past elections would seem to indicate that there is little likelihood that communal parties will man the government in the near future, they do represent a section of public opinion which the government and the Congress must propitiate. It is somewhat ironic that much of their future destiny depends upon Pakistan.

LEADERSHIP IN
THE INDIAN COMMUNIST PARTY

GENE D. OVERSTREET

*T*HE decisive role of leadership is inherent in Marxist-Leninist doctrine. A Communist Party defines itself as the vanguard or leading element of the proletariat, which is in turn the leading class in the next major stage of human history. The party claims an exclusive right to lead by virtue of the revolutionary destiny of the class it represents. It also has an obligation to lead by virtue of the inability of that class to fulfill its destiny spontaneously. In this doctrine, the idea of leadership is given an exalted importance. As summed up in the "Principles of Party Organization" of the Comintern, "Leadership is a necessary condition for any common action, but most of all it is indispensable in the greatest fight in the world's history. The organization of the Communist Party is the organization of Communist leadership in the proletarian revolution."[1]

Internal Organization and Operation

A Communist Party's purpose justifies and indeed demands that it be an efficient instrument of political action, and this is the aim of "democratic centralism" in internal organization. The principles of "democratic centralism" are summarized as follows: all leading bodies of the party are elected and must report periodically to the organization; and decisions of higher bodies are absolutely binding on all below, on the basis of strict discipline ensuring the subordination of the minority to the majority.[2] In theory, power is built upward and exercised downward. Centralization must be genuine, not formal; that is, the leading organs have "the obligation of constantly directing and exercising a

GENE D. OVERSTREET has been a member of the Modern India Project, University of California at Berkeley; at present he is in the Department of Political Science at Swarthmore College. His paper is based upon research done in India from 1952 to 1954 under a fellowship from the Ford Foundation.

[1] Communist International, *Principles of Party Organisation*, Bombay, People's Publishing House, n.d., p. 2.
[2] The classic statement of "democratic centralism" is in the Rules of the Communist Party of the Soviet Union; see James H. Meisel and Edward S. Kozera, *Materials for the Study of the Soviet System*, Ann Arbor, George Wahr Publishing Co., 1953, p. xlix.

systematic influence over the party work." But at the same time, the "democratic" basis of this centralization must be genuine; that is, power must be founded not on mere formal election, but on a "living association" between leaders and led in which the members recognize the legitimacy of inner-party authority. This "democracy" may include the expression of differences of opinion, prior to the actual making of a decision; but differences are regarded as "abnormalities" and above all may not assume the form of factions. Factionalism, or a "contest for supremacy within the party," is absolutely impermissible.[3]

As concretely realized in the formal organization of the Communist Party of India (CPI), "democratic centralism" means a hierarchy of units based on the primary cell—a group of members in factory, village, or urban neighborhood. All the cells in a given locality participate in the basic directing unit of the party, the town or local conference. The town or local conference elects representatives to a district conference, the district conference elects representatives to a provincial conference, and the provincial conference elects delegates to the national Communist Party Congress. Each of the conferences elects its executive committee, which chooses a secretary. The Party Congress, at the top, elects the Central Committee, which in turn chooses the Politburo and the general secretary. The executive committees, from top to bottom, are empowered to act in the name of their respective conferences between sessions and thus become the effective centers of power at each level. Further, the secretaries tend to become the effective wielders of power.

The elective principle in party organization is critically qualified by certain structural features provided in the Indian Communist Party constitution.[4] For example, the secretaries at the lower levels must be approved by the next higher level. The higher units have the power to censure, suspend, or expel any individual member and, moreover, to dissolve or even to reconstitute lower committees. The higher units may postpone conferences at lower levels. The Central Committee is empowered to reconstitute itself, and committees at all levels possess the right of co-optation. In short, the elective principle may be suspended altogether.

The principle of inner-party discussion or debate, formally guaranteed to the rank and file membership, is similarly qualified. The CPI constitution defines "free and business-like discussion of party policy" an "in-

---

[3] *Principles of Party Organisation*, pp. 2, 7.
[4] Communist Party of India, *The Constitution of the Communist Party of India*, Delhi, 1954. The following references to the constitution are from this source.

defeasible right" of every member. But it declares that "interminable" discussion or the attempt to form factional groups is an abuse of this right. Accordingly, it concludes that "wide inner-party discussion" is permissible only under the following circumstances: if it is demanded by one or more provincial organizations, or if it is authorized by the Central Committee itself. In short, only the leading agencies of the party, and primarily the Central Committee, can initiate inner-party debate. Moreover, the CPI constitution provides that when such debate does occur it must be conducted "under the strong leadership of the Central Committee and of the lower committees." Discussion must proceed on the basis of a draft resolution furnished by the Central Committee, and must as far as possible be guided by representatives sent from the top units for this specific purpose.

In sum, the formal structure and rules of operation of the Communist Party of India attach the highest importance to creating and sustaining a strong leadership. Indeed, the Indian party rules formally provide greater centralization than do those of the Russian party which abolished the right of co-optation in 1939 and the right of higher committees to dissolve the lower ones in 1952.[5]

On the other hand, the Indian party also provides unusual channels for the expression of rank and file opinion. Unlike the Russian party rules, the CPI constitution asserts the right of every member or unit of the party to communicate its "wishes, suggestions, remarks or complaints" directly to the Central Committee at any time. Another unusual provision states that members disagreeing with a decision of any unit of the party may appeal to the Central Committee (CC) or to the Party Congress. Finally, the CPI constitution provides for a court of appeal, in the form of the Control Commission, elected by the Party Congress. This agency is empowered to review decisions of all units in matters relating to party discipline. It is formally subordinate to the Central Committee, which must endorse its decisions, but it has a certain claim to autonomy by virtue of being elected by the Party Congress rather than by the Central Committee. It may hear complaints from individual members and units as well as take up cases referred to it by the Central Committee. The Russian party rules create a Committee of Party Control (formerly called the Control Commission), but this body is an enforcement agency of the Central Committee rather than a court of appeal; it is selected by the CC, not by the Party Congress, and

---

[5] Meisel and Kozera, *op.cit.*, pp. 314, 344, xliii-lxi.

is empowered merely to review the activity of lower units on behalf of the Central Committee.

The CPI constitution thus suggests a combination of authoritarian leadership and articulate membership—that is, a paradoxical mixture of centralization and indiscipline. This is in fact the picture that presents itself upon examination of the actual operation of the CPI.

It is clear, first, that circumstances have combined with structural features to produce a very narrow leading group in the party. All-India party congresses, which should according to the constitution meet every two years, have actually occurred only in 1943, 1948, 1953, and 1956— or four times in the twenty-two years since the formal creation of the party. Provincial conferences ordinarily meet only in preparation for an all-India congress, and sometimes not even then. In the long intervals between congresses, the Central Committee is formally vested with full power. The CPI constitution requires that the Central Committee meet every three months, but it does not appear normally to do so. A party report in 1954 stated that the Central Committee had met six times in the past fifteen months but described this as a great improvement; it declared that just prior to that, the committee had not met for six months. In other periods, its meetings have been as much as a year apart. In day-to-day functioning, therefore, leadership falls to the general secretary and a few members of the Politburo who happen to be present at central headquarters. The above-mentioned report implied that the number of Politburo members permanently attached to headquarters was only about two, the others being at their respective provincial offices; it indicated that this handful of leaders at the center made "vital" decisions on behalf of the party as a whole.[6]

This situation is evidently duplicated at the provincial and other levels of the party, with the secretary and a few members of each committee exercising practical authority in long intervals between meetings of the full committee, or of the appropriate conference which is supposedly the source of that authority. Such a concentration of authority is considered a weakness by the party itself, under the label "bureaucratism." But it persists despite all the self-criticism directed against it in pursuit of genuinely "collective" leadership.

Among the apparent circumstances that produce this situation are a

[6] *Communist Conspiracy at Madurai*, Bombay, Popular Book Depot, 1954, pp. 131-32. The authenticity of the documents published by the Democratic Research Service in this volume is not absolutely certain but is generally accepted and has not been denied in detail by the CPI.

lack of the necessary funds to enable a larger number of the officers to serve full time at headquarters and, on occasion, the actual illegality of the party which forces it to operate underground. But, in addition to these, one of the principal problems of the party is the unwillingness of a large part of the leadership to serve in staff capacities either at the center or in the lower levels of organization. Official party reports on organization frequently complain that the committees, from top to bottom, cannot function properly because most of their members are too absorbed in front-line action—that is, in actual on-the-spot engagement in trade union work or other spheres of activity. At best, each committee tends to become a federation of department heads rather than a collectively functioning unit.

This problem is evidently worst at the center; members of the Central Committee and the Politburo are reported to prefer to remain in their respective provincial or local bailiwicks rather than participate in the general work of the Central Committee or the Politburo. A party account of this state of affairs complained that members of the Politburo could not be assigned to work permanently at the New Delhi headquarters because either they or their provincial organizations refused to agree to it.[7] This apparently reflects not only a predilection for engagement in concrete activity, but also a concentration on building provincial or local political machines as a basis of power, both inside and outside the party. Here, then, is an indication that the main locus of CPI activity and strength is not on the national scene but rather at lower levels of the political process.

As a result, the control of general policy falls to a rather narrow bureaucracy. Moreover, the structural devices available to this bureaucracy enable it, in crisis situations or when dominated by more determined personalities, to remake the party itself in policy and personnel. In the period 1948-1950, when the crisis and the personality coincided, the leadership of the party amounted in practice to the General Secretary, B. T. Ranadive, and one or two supporters in the Politburo. With the aid of scattered adherents in other levels of the organization, this group dissolved at least one provincial committee (the Bengal committee) and reconstituted a majority of the rest. It expelled or suspended hundreds, including three dissident members of the Central Committee and even one member of the Politburo. Some of the leading figures in the party

---

[7] *ibid.*, p. 132. The existence of this problem was confirmed in a Central Committee resolution in 1954: Communist Party of India, *Resolution on Party Organisation*, Delhi, 1954, pp. 9-10.

were purged, among them the preceding General Secretary, P. C. Joshi, and the present General Secretary, A. K. Ghosh.[8]

Ranadive pursued a policy which departed increasingly from the mandate of the Party Congress and soon encountered opposition from both the rank and file and the international Communist authorities. But by the use of structural controls, among other devices, he retained formal authority over the party organization for more than two years.

In this and other crisis situations, the Control Commission of the party does not appear to have served as an active check upon the central leadership. In 1950, when P. C. Joshi sought to appeal his expulsion to the Control Commission, the case was decided by the Central Committee itself, on the grounds that the commission could not function since two of its members were in jail and a third had himself been purged from the party. A new Control Commission of five members was elected in 1951 and in the next year and a half it met four times. Its report at the end of this period indicated that it had dealt only with cases of local or provincial importance, although it had reversed a number of disciplinary decisions at these levels.[9] It appears now to serve as an arbiter of minor inner-party disputes, not as a court of appeal against the central leadership.

The rank and file has, however, availed itself amply of the opportunity provided in the CPI constitution for expression of its views directly to the central units of the party. Both individual members and units have voiced their dissent against prevailing policy. One of the most dramatic examples of this process was the so-called "Andhra Letter"—one of a number of statements addressed to the Central Committee by the Andhra provincial organization, quarreling with existing policy in the period 1948-1949.[10] Many other similar documents have come to light, in which members and units speak up against the prevailing line. On occasion prominent leaders may even express public dissent against the prevailing party line. S. A. Dange, a member of the Central Committee, in 1951 made a statement to the press which clearly implied a challenge to official policy; his views were immediately disavowed by the Central Committee but no disciplinary action was taken

[8] For an account of this period, see P. C. Joshi, *Views to Comrades Abroad and B. T. Ranadive*, Howrah, 1950, and his "Documents for Discussion" series, *For a Mass Policy* and *Problems of the Mass Movement*, Allahabad, 1951.

[9] Communist Party of India, *Party Letter*, No. 3, March 12, 1953.

[10] The "Andhra Letter" is summarized in a later document of the Andhra Provincial Committee: Andhra Committee, Communist Party of India, "Self-Critical Report of the Andhra Communist Committee," 1952. A typewritten copy of this document was loaned to the writer by Selig Harrison.

against him. P. C. Joshi, professing to be loyal to the party, aired his protest against the current line in 1949-1951 through a series of pamphlets and a periodical which he published independently. In 1953 B. T. Ranadive wrote a dissenting statement concerning the party's view on economic problems; it was published by the CPI press with a foreword specifying that it did not represent official policy.

In short, the expression of dissident opinion by the rank and file and by rebellious leaders has never been effectively repressed, no matter how strong and determined the official leadership may have been. In fact the Communist Party of India appears to be characterized by a higher degree of indiscipline, as reflected in this form of vocal dissent, than any other Communist party of which we have detailed knowledge.

The Role of the Party Communications System

Thus far the operation of certain structural features of the Communist Party of India has been considered. Another factor which markedly affects the internal leadership process is the communications system.

Perhaps the most important media of communication within the party are its openly published organs. These include a weekly newspaper and a monthly theoretical journal, both in English, published by the center; newspapers and journals published in the provinces in the various regional languages; and a great quantity of published books and pamphlets, most of them in English.

Though the central organs of the party are published openly, they appear to be designed mainly for members and sympathizers rather than for the general public. The weekly newspaper, *New Age*, several years ago had a circulation of only about 8,000. Its contents are in the nature of indoctrination rather than campaign materials, and news of internal party affairs occupies a large amount of space. The monthly theoretical magazine, also called *New Age*, contains more general and authoritative pronouncements on policy questions along with frequent expositions on various aspects of Marxist-Leninist philosophy. Both of these periodicals are directly controlled by the highest units of the party, the newspaper being edited by a member of the Politburo and the theoretical journal by the general secretary himself.

Of about equal importance with the periodical organs are the book and pamphlet publications of the central party press, the People's Publishing House. A recent catalogue of the People's Publishing House listed twenty books and pamphlets on India, twelve on China, six on the Soviet Union, eight on world affairs, four on general history and economics, eight on art and literature, and seventeen on general Communist theory—a total of seventy-five.[11] This is of course, a listing of only those materials which are appropriate to the existing policy-phase of the party; superseded items are withdrawn from circulation. It may be noted that about two thirds of the items listed were by foreign authors.

The party literature published in India is supplemented by a great volume of Communist materials published abroad—primarily in Russia, China, and England. This literature is sent to the CPI by foreign Communist parties or governments, and sold alongside its own publications. Certain periodicals from abroad—notably *For a Lasting Peace, For a People's Democracy!* and the Soviet *New Times*—have served as required reading on a par with indigenous literature. A Central Committee resolution of 1954 stated that all members of the committee must read these two periodicals regularly, in addition to the central and provincial Indian party organs. These international periodicals evidently do not enjoy a large audience, however; before it ceased publication, *For a Lasting Peace* . . . had a circulation of less than 2,000 in India.[12]

Apart from these open publications, there is of course a system of confidential inner-party communications, concerning which some knowledge exists. The so-called *Party Letter* is a periodical intended for the entire membership; it is issued from party headquarters, and contains more detailed reports and instructions on party affairs.

In addition to *Party Letter*, there are media designed for distribution only among provincial and district committees, not the rank and file; an example is an irregular series called "Central Committee Information Document." This secret medium contains very detailed reports of and instructions on party activity, judging by the few available issues.

There are other irregular types of communications, such as circulars and memoranda. And in addition to communications downward, there is in theory a regular system of reports upward. The constitution of the CPI provides that each unit will submit regular reports to the next higher unit, to be officially confirmed by it.

In the transmission of private inner-party media, it is highly doubtful that the CPI entrusts important communications to the Indian postal service. It is known that in the past, the so-called "technical apparatus"

---

[11] *Catalogue of Books, 1954*, Bombay, People's Publishing House, 1954.
[12] E. M. S. Namboodiripad, *On Organization*, Delhi, Communist Party of India, 1954, pp. 68, 73-74.

or secret organization provided for a monthly courier service between the center and the provincial units and similar relays between provincial and district units.[13] In times when the party was illegal, the police have disrupted this service with great effect on the efficiency of the party.

But when functioning properly, the CPI's communication system as a whole clearly provides a great source of power for the central units which control it. The center constitutes the only point at which all information from lower units converges. Apart from sporadic personal contact, the lower units learn of party affairs only through communications from the center. Only the center can claim to have a proper basis for evaluating the over-all position of the party, and by its control over the distribution of information it can stack the cards in support of a given policy.

Moreover, the central leadership has at least a partial monopoly of information concerning the international Communist line for India, and it can exercise some control over knowledge of that line within the party. There have been several occasions when the prevailing Indian Communist leadership has temporarily resisted changes in policy proposed by the international authorities, and has refused to disseminate the relevant international pronouncements to the rank and file. This is not possible in the case of articles in English-language journals such as the Cominform publication, *For a Lasting Peace* . . . ; such articles have been the cause of wholesale debate within the party and the ultimate overthrow of the leadership. But the central leadership may succeed temporarily in withholding knowledge of articles appearing in the Russian-language Soviet journals, which usually contain the first expression of a change in policy and are said by the Indian Communists themselves to be regarded as authoritative.[14] Suppression is also possible when the international statement is communicated confidentially to the central headquarters of the CPI. In one instance, the central leadership attempted to suppress a letter from the British Communist authorities which urged a change of policy for the CPI. The attempt was successful for a number of months and was conclusively exposed only when several members of the party made a trip to London and on their return reported the situation.[15]

[13] Joshi, *For a Mass Policy*, p. 40.
[14] P. C. Joshi on one occasion referred to an article on India in the Soviet Party journal *Bol'shevik* (now *Kommunist*) in the following words: "The leadership of the Communist Party of the Soviet Union spoke on our Party Congress through Alexeyev's article." *For a Mass Policy*, p. 40.
[15] "Talks With Comrade R. Palme Dutt and Other Impressions Gained Abroad by

In this connection it is interesting to note that dissent within the party often finds a rallying point in the so-called party headquarters unit—an organization made up of members of the staff at headquarters. Probably in part because it is at the center of the communications system and thus has access to relevant information and to the mechanics of the system, this unit has on a number of occasions furnished a channel for expression of opposition to the leadership. To provide a platform for dissident views, it has at times printed the so-called "PHQ (Party Headquarters) Open Forum" and called special party meetings. It was largely responsible, for example, for exposing the suppression of the letter from the British party.

The communications system provides great power to those who control it at the top, but this power is reduced somewhat by the relative inefficiency of the system. In the first place, there is the obstacle of illiteracy; some party members are outside the reach of the printed media because they cannot read English or perhaps even the regional language. A recent party source declared that a "large number" of members were illiterate.[16] Moreover, many members and even leaders do not read the media when they can. The low circulation of the open periodicals is one index to this. Party sources themselves complain that there is an attitude of "indifference" within the organization to official party publications; they attribute this to the fact that the leaders do not take an interest in improving the content of the journals or in writing for them, and in some cases do not even read them regularly.[17] The Central Committee resolution mentioned earlier, requiring all committee members to read certain journals, was admittedly a response to the fact that some did not read even the Central Committee organ.

Finally, the communication system may simply fail to produce a response on the part of the lower units of the party. One official source reported that of the dozens of circulars sent out by the Central Committee in a given year, only two received answers from all or nearly all of the provincial committees. It may be added that this source also com-

---

Deven and Bal Krishna," issued by PHQ Unit, January 6, 1951, 6 pp. The letter from the British CP appears in: "Letter of the Political Committee of the CPGB to the Communist Party of India," issued by the PHQ Unit, December 6, 1950, 6 pp. These and certain other documents were loaned by Marshall Windmiller. The writer is especially indebted to Mr. Windmiller, with whom he is collaborating on a forthcoming study of the Communist movement in India, for the use of these materials.

[16] Ajoy Ghosh, *Proletarian Leadership and the Democratic Movement*, Delhi, Communist Party of India, 1954, p. 22.

[17] Namboodiripad, *op.cit.*, p. 74.

plained that many of the reports which were received from lower units were in the regional languages and "for obvious reasons are thus remaining in the files."[18]

The language problem apparently plagues the CPI as well as the rest of Indian politics. It would seem, then, that printed media of communications provide a powerful though by no means perfected instrument of leadership within the CPI.

Another medium which needs to be examined is the system of party schools. There is little available knowledge of this aspect of inner-party activity, but occasional references to schools in official literature give some indication of their nature and purpose. The apparent intention of the party is to build a hierarchical system of schools providing periodic instruction to members at all levels; this would include elementary education to abolish illiteracy, as well as theoretical indoctrination and organizational training. Such a system has evidently not yet been realized in practice, but there have been occasional *ad hoc* central schools, as well as efforts by provincial organizations to create local school systems.

An example of local attempts in this direction is provided in a recent account of this work in Bengal.[19] The Bengal Provincial Committee formed an Education Subcommittee which assumed the responsibility of providing syllabi and teachers for the schools. Both members and "activists" (potential recruits) were enrolled, and eventually there were 55 regular schools attended by 550 students. The introductory lectures took up elementary information on the role of the Communist Party and its program; subsequent classes dealt with the history of the party and the national movement, basic Marxism-Leninism, and the Communist view of various issues such as the agrarian problem. The provincial committee was eventually forced to plan a teachers' training school to meet the demand for instructors; in addition, it arranged for a special textbook series, which consisted of the works of Stalin, Mao, Togliatti, Sobolev, Klugmann, Rostovsky, and other international authorities. Public lectures and film showings were also inaugurated. This ambitious program withered away, however, largely because the lower party units lost their initial enthusiasm and did not assume responsibility for maintaining the schools. This difficulty would appear to be a natural consequence of excessive centralization. Nevertheless, centralization of party education remains a firm principle; in the words of the present general

---

[18] *Communist Conspiracy at Madurai*, p. 133.
[19] Chinmohan Sehanobis, "Some Problems of Party Education in West Bengal," *New Age*, I, December 1952, pp. 76-83.

secretary, "education has to be organised directly by the leading Committees. It has to be conducted and guided by the party leaders. . . ."[20]

It should be apparent from a description of the Communist Party's internal communication structure that one of its chief aims is basic ideological indoctrination. There is abundant evidence that the party leadership regards the inculcation of basic theory as one of the principal instruments for unifying and activizing the organization. A recent Central Committee resolution stated that ideological work was of "decisive importance" and that one of the principal weaknesses of the party was the failure to transform the "elementary anti-capitalist, anti-landlord hatred" of party sympathizers into the "Socialist consciousness" which would make them cadres of the party. Dealing, for example, with the role of pamphlets, the resolution stated that they "activize the party ranks, sharpen their understanding of party policy and unify them politically, thus playing a most important part in *strengthening the organisation of the party*. They make it possible to swing the entire party into action in a disciplined and organised way. . . ."[21] Theoretical indoctrination is thus regarded as a prerequisite of effective leadership.

The content of Communist Party communications suggests several other informal devices of leadership. One is the creation of a spirit of military discipline within the party. It has frequently been observed that Communist parties everywhere make intensive use of military terminology in political analysis and exhortation. This is true of the Indian Communist Party which habitually employs such terms as "defense" and "attack," "front-line" and "rear-guard," "battle" and "truce," "armies" and "troops," and so on. This vocabulary arises naturally out of basic Communist theoretical assumptions concerning the class struggle, but it may be utilized consciously to reinforce discipline within the organization.

Another such device is the creation of a family spirit. There is an unusual recourse to the symbols of family relationships in the CPI vocabulary. This is particularly apparent in the prose style of P. C. Joshi who has a strong penchant for such terminology. For example, Joshi defined the relation of the Congress and the CPI as that between elder and younger brother. He once declared that CPI members regard the Indian people as a whole as "our real parents." On another occasion he gave a very interesting description of the party headquarters staff as "one big joint family"; this staff, which grew in his time from 8 to 120, was

[20] Ghosh, *op.cit.*, p. 22.
[21] *Resolution on Party Organisation*, pp. 6, 21.

organized communally and was presided over by "one single Mai" (old mother).[22] These and many other similar remarks suggest that the CPI leadership may seek to reinforce the unity of the party by emotional bonds analogous to those of the joint family—a device which might have special potency among the many members who have renounced their real families.

It may be added here that Communist Party discipline embraces the personal as well as the public lives of its members. While he was general secretary, Joshi once remarked to Gandhi that "we seek to guide, criticise and mould the entire life, both personal and political, of our members."[23] Announcements of expulsions from the party occasionally describe the reason as "moral lapses," rather than political error. Since the party endeavors to shape the total life of each member, it tends to organize his social, recreational, and cultural activities. Many party units form recreational groups, such as drama clubs, and in addition members are encouraged or even required to join front organizations like the Progressive Writers' Association. The front organizations in general serve a useful function in reinforcing the bonds of party membership, in addition to their utility as propaganda and recruiting agencies.

Party Finances and Internal Leadership

Another factor which influences the leadership process within the CPI is the matter of finances, or the power of the purse. Very little is known by way of quantitative information concerning CPI finances; needless to say, the party does not publish an annual balance sheet. On one occasion, in 1945, when it was especially eager to disprove the charge that it had financial support from the British, P. C. Joshi offered to let Gandhi or his authorized representative inspect the party's accounts and even agreed to reveal the names of contributors listed anonymously.[24] The offer was not accepted then, and has not since been repeated.

There have of course been persistent rumors of Moscow gold, but no convincing proof has been adduced of direct financial subsidies to the CPI from abroad in recent times, though they were common in the 1920's. However, an indirect subsidy of unknown amount is provided by profits on the sale of books and pamphlets shipped free to the CPI by foreign

---

[22] *People's Age*, IV, December 30, 1945, p. 6.
[23] P. C. Joshi, *Correspondence Between Mahatma Gandhi and P. C. Joshi*, Bombay, People's Publishing House, 1945, p. 33.
[24] Joshi, *Correspondence*, p. 9.

Communist governments. The Indian government evidently has not interfered with this practice, except insofar as it prohibits the sale of Communist or other party literature on government property (such as railway stations).

Another major source of funds for the CPI is individual contributions. These are frequently sizable amounts, for the party has succeeded in recruiting a number of wealthy members who have turned over all or a large part of their income to it. E. M. S. Namboodiripad, for example, donated the entire proceeds of his property, Rs. 70,000, to the party. Contributions come also from non-Communist and perhaps even from some business sources. But it appears, on the whole, that the party is not richly endowed with financial backing. In the past it has evidently operated close to the margin. Although it has recently shown signs of greater affluence, its resources do not appear to approach those of the Congress.

The CPI constitution provides for a regular monthly membership fee, but states that these dues are for the use of committees at the district level or below. The provincial and central committees are authorized to make levies on incomes of members for their funds. It is known that party members with larger incomes, including M.P.'s and M.L.A.'s, are required to turn over a fixed proportion of their salaries to the cause; party documents report that they occasionally object to this. In any event, it would appear that the funds at the disposal of the higher units have not in the past been such as to provide them with the power of the purse over the lower units. Indeed, the center has apparently at times been dependent on the lower units for financial support. One party source relates that in a recent period of financial embarrassment the Central Committee appealed to the provincial committees to undertake a special fund drive. The provincial units were to set the quotas for the drive and also to fix the amount to be passed on to the Central Committee. The Central Committee stated that it needed Rs. 100,000 for expenses in the immediate future, but in the end it received only Rs. 5,000.[25]

In such a situation, the provincial or local units with larger financial resources may possess a lever for greater influence at the center. At the least, they may be able to exercise greater autonomy against the central leadership. This would appear to apply to the Andhra party organization, which can draw on the wealth of many landlord members.

[25] Namboodiripad, *op.cit.*, p. 72.

LEADERSHIP IN THE COMMUNIST PARTY

The Legitimization of Communist Leadership

The structure of the Communist Party of India and the structure and content of its internal communications system provide powerful instruments of leadership to those who ascend the hierarchy to its commanding heights. But what are the criteria by which those leaders are selected? What are the values which legitimize leadership within the CPI?

The principal prerequisite of leadership in the CPI is plainly ideological. An entrant to the party must subscribe to its theoretical basis; a leader must maintain the appearance of orthodoxy and, beyond that, must possess a certain facility in manipulating the theory. Whatever the actual origins of Communist policy—whether it be doctrinaire or expediential—that policy is invariably presented as an integral part of a world view based on Marxist-Leninist theory. A good leader must therefore first be able to command the theory.

The theoretical flavor of discourse so apparent in open Communist propaganda evidently prevails in private debate within the party, too. The argument for a given policy may include franker discussion of its expediency, but it always rests upon a theoretical rationale. An official party source has given this description of inner-party debate:

Comrades have been furiously discussing grave political problems and in proportion to their capacity, trying to relate them to the fundamental teachings of Marxism-Leninism. Dusty volumes of Marxist classics have been re-opened to buttress one's viewpoint in the almost interminable discussion going on all round.[26]

As with Communist parties the world over, quotations from Marx, Engels, Lenin, and (formerly) Stalin are an essential part of the argument for any point of view. A somewhat more unflattering description of this state of affairs appears in another party document:

It has become a practice to enter into hair-splitting arguments during discussions even on small issues by the party committees, and to refer to fundamental principles. It has become a disease to call differences in opinion as reformism, sectarianism and deviationism. Consequently it has become common that even on issues wherein there was agreement, no work is done.[27]

The end result of this tendency to scholasticism is, as one party source puts it, "the defect of not patiently analyzing the distinctive features of the Indian situation," which was termed the "dominant defect" in the

[26] Sehanobis, *op.cit.*, p. 76.
[27] Andhra Committee, *op.cit.*, Part III, p. 13.

entire history of the party.[28] The CPI seems, indeed, to exceed nearly all other Communist parties in its tendency to dwell in an ideal world of ideological formulae.

But to assert that "orthodoxy" is the first element in legitimization of leadership in the CPI leaves unanswered the question, "What kind of orthodoxy?" The theoretical framework is sufficiently flexible to permit of a variety of orthodoxies, in different times and circumstances. The answer—up to the present time, at least—is that the orthodoxy of the moment is defined by the international Communist authorities. Leadership within the Indian Communist Party is legitimized above all by the sanction of the international line.

An example of the appeal to international sanction was provided by the reconstituted Central Committee led by Rajeshwar Rao. Defending a new policy line in 1950, this leadership admitted that the tradition of the CPI "has been to swing like a pendulum from one extreme to the other," and that members were therefore "perfectly justified in feeling sceptical this time"; it therefore expressly posed the question, "What is the guarantee that this time the Central Committee has chalked out a correct path?" In answer to this question, it listed three "guarantees," of which the first was, "The direct political guidance of the Cominform Bureau and political assistance of the brother Parties. . . ."[29]

But while doctrinal orthodoxy is essential, other factors play a substantial role in legitimizing the CPI leadership. As in any political party, leaders require certain types of experience, special skills, and personal qualities. What these are in the case of the CPI may best be approached by examining the attributes of the inner-party leaders who have held the post of general secretary since the party's formal inauguration in 1934. All of these persons are at present members of the Central Committee and continue to exercise leadership within the party. They are: Dr. G. Adhikari, P. C. Joshi, B. T. Ranadive, Rajeshwar Rao, and A. K. Ghosh. Biographical data about them is very sparse, but some of their characteristics may be identified. Considering first the general secretaries who served in the period up to 1950—Adhikari, Joshi, Ranadive—certain uniformities may be noted. First, all these individuals have long experience in the party, with a period of membership ranging between twenty-

[28] Bhayyaji Kulkarni *et al., Struggle Against Sectarian Legacy and for a New Perspective*, Poona, 1950. Notes on this document were loaned to the writer by Selig Harrison.

[29] Central Committee, Communist Party of India, *Letter of the New Central Committee (Reconstituted by the Central Committee elected at the Second Party Congress) to All Party Members and Sympathizers*, June 1, 1950, pp. 15-16.

five and thirty years each. They are all college-educated, with degrees including an M.A., LL.B., and D.Sc. They all joined the party while in college or immediately after leaving it; that is, their experience of politics is limited to their participation as Communists. Their most notable skill has been that of ideological manipulation or propaganda; they have been strongly identified with particular "lines" and are all very prolific writers. None of them has a mass following of any consequence nor does any possess marked skill in certain of the arts of mass leadership such as public speaking. They are all North Indian, two of the three being Maharashtrian. These three leaders seem on the whole to be representative of the "Old Bolsheviks" of the CPI. The main qualities which they possess in common are long experience, outstanding intellectual attainments, and skill in doctrine and propaganda. About their social backgrounds the available information is too vague for generalizations.

The present General Secretary, A. K. Ghosh, differs from the above three in having somewhat less party experience, about twenty years, and in possessing considerable political experience outside of the Communist movement. Prior to joining the CPI, he had been active in the Punjab terrorist movement, the Congress, and the Royist movement. He is different, also, in being primarily an organizer rather than a propagandist; though he is required by his position to write authoritatively on doctrinal questions, he does not show an unusual flair for the role. He may represent in these qualities—possessing a broader political background and being less "doctrinaire"— a more "modern" type of inner-party leader.

Rajeshwar Rao, who served as general secretary from 1950 to 1951, is the only South Indian who has occupied that post. He appears to be typical of the leaders from that area, having evidently joined the CPI in the late 1930's, being of wealthy peasant rather than urban background, and representing a doctrinal line giving greater stress to the role of the peasantry on the model of the Chinese Communist experience. The South Indian component of the CPI has been under-represented in the central leadership relative to its apparent proportion of the party membership and of the party's electoral strength. More than fifty per cent of the announced delegates to the recent Party Congress were from South India, delegation strength being based on membership. About seventy per cent of the successful Communist candidates in the first general election were in that area. Yet only forty-one per cent of the Central Committee is South Indian.

The predominance of the North India section is largely accounted for by historical circumstances in the early development of the Communist movement in India. It had its origins in the 1920's almost exclusively in the urban industrial centers of the north, primarily because the emissaries from abroad who were instrumental in organizing it—agents of M. N. Roy and of the British Communist Party—concentrated on those centers as the best recruiting grounds. The Communist Party scarcely existed in South India until the 1930's, and that area has therefore not produced inner-party leaders of such long experience as the "Old Bolsheviks" from the north.

It should be noted, finally, that there are no women in the present Central Committee and that the number of women members of the party is, according to a recent party document, "insignificant."[30]

The Process of Leadership Formation

The dynamic process by which leadership is created within the Communist Party of India is characterized by unstable factional struggle of an intensity unusual among Communist parties. Most Communist parties in the West, and many of those in Asia, have enjoyed relatively stable leadership for many years past—leadership which could survive changes in policy required by the international line, and in the course of time create a more mature and efficient political organization. The Indian Communist Party has not "matured" in the same degree; it continues to be plagued by the type of factionalism which existed in other Communist parties in the 1920's and 1930's. A change in policy means a change of leadership in the CPI; more precisely, it means a change in the balance of power among the various factions which exist within the party.

As in other political parties, factions tend to arise in the CPI to espouse the special interests of various sections of the organization. Although factional alignments are constantly in flux, they appear to be based in part on class distinctions, such as those between trade unionists, peasant representatives, and middle-class spokesmen. They may also be based on function, as in the case of disagreement between the bureaucratic leaders and the parliamentary members of the party. The special attitudes of students and artists in various creative fields may also provide a basis for factions.

Another factor which clearly contributes to factionalism is regional interest. The demands of national party policy may well conflict with the special interests of particular provincial organizations. This has apparently been true in certain cases connected with states' reorganization,

[30] *Resolution on Party Organisation*, p. 27.

such as the issue of Bombay. However, the evidence seems to indicate that the CPI has by and large succeeded in reducing regional antagonisms within the party to a level below that prevailing in the country as a whole, although they have undoubtedly not been eliminated altogether. The same would appear to be true with respect to certain other traditional divisive factors in Indian society, such as caste and communal differences; but further research is needed on this problem, particularly in the form of local case studies.[31]

Personal leadership has had a prominent role in the interplay of factions in the CPI. However, no individual has yet arisen who could submerge special interests and unify the entire party on the basis of an abiding personal authority. On the whole, the primary leaders have been representatives of particular elements of the organization and carriers of particular political lines.

The competition among factions proceeds peaceably enough within the confines of the party when no particular interest is drastically neglected and a reasonable balance is achieved in the party's policy and activity. But when a radical line gives undue emphasis to one set of interests at the expense of another (as in 1948-1950, when peasant interests were slighted, or in 1950-1951, when those interests were unduly emphasized) it becomes so intense as to break into the open, and warring factions virtually take the public platform against one another.

As has been suggested above, the ultimate criterion for the settlement of the factional balance of power is the nature of the international line. The faction prevailing in the CPI will be that representing the policy line which is presumed to be sanctioned by the international authorities. It is necessary to use the term "presumed" because international guidance is not always so clear as to eliminate any possibility of unwitting or deliberate misinterpretation. International Communist pronouncements on India have at critical times been inconsistent and/or vague, and were evidently not immediately supplemented by more conclusive private communications. The result has been that an eager faction within the CPI has at times been able to misread them and claim a sanction from above which was in fact at least doubtful.

In any event, the final recourse in factional competition within the CPI is to international Communist support. The crowning act of P. C. Joshi's opposition to the Ranadive and Rao leaderships was a series of "Letters to Foreign Comrades." In these published pamphlets he de-

[31] For example, see Selig Harrison, "Caste and the Andhra Communists," *American Political Science Review*, L, June 1956, pp. 378-405.

clared that change could not come from within the CPI, and appealed to Communist parties abroad: "Therefore, brothers, it is you abroad who have to act and act quick." He continued, ". . . since we are sincere and loyal communists we will accept our mistakes when they are authoritatively pointed out to us and struggle our hardest to correct them and get in step with International Communism."[32]

Another opposition document of the same period, printed under a pseudonym but evidently written by A. K. Ghosh, declared:

> Today the reality is that nobody in the Indian Party can solve this crisis. It was the international comrades who pointed out our mistakes. Since we are not agreed on the interpretation, only they can help us. We must, therefore, contact the international leaders.[33]

It should be stressed, in connection with factional competition within the CPI, that although it is unusually intense it does not normally extend to action which would split the party itself. The typical reaction of a dissident individual or faction is to oppose the prevailing leadership vocally but to submit in action or merely to assume a posture of inaction. Although the party has at times been reduced to almost total anarchy, it has not been seriously fragmented during at least the past two decades. It has thus shown remarkable cohesiveness relative to other Indian political parties.

Organization and Operation of Party Fractions

In addition to the internal organizational system, a Communist party consists of another distinct operational structure: a horizontal system of party teams or "fractions" radiating from all levels of the vertical organization into the various institutions of the body politic. This system provides the main channel for the party's political action.

The constitution of the CPI states explicitly that all members unless individually exempted must participate in some functional organization, such as a trade union, peasant union, youth group, women's organization, cooperative society, cultural group, etc. Party members in any unit of such an organization constitute a "fraction," which is controlled as a disciplined body by the party unit at that level. In short, a party fraction in a local trade union organization is directed by the local cell; a fraction

---

[32] Joshi, *Views*, pp. 29-30.
[33] "Prabodh Chandra," "On 'A Note on the Present Situation in Our Party,'" *P.H.Q. Open Forum*, No. 12, October 1949, p. 9.

in the provincial committee of the trade union is directed by the provincial committee of the party; a fraction in the national executive committee of a trade union is controlled by the Central Committee of the party.

The basic chain of command for work in functional groups thus lies within the party, and fractions "must carry out, strictly and without violation, the decisions of the party organizations which lead them." The CPI constitution also provides for appropriate specialization of function within the party itself, with individuals or subcommittees being designated at all levels for continuous supervision over particular activities.

However, the constitution provides an added chain of command within the hierarchy of fractions in a given organization. It states that fractions of higher units in organizations may, with the approval of the corresponding party unit, send directives to lower fractions. In short, the higher party units can bypass lower ones in dealing with fractions in a given sphere. In actual practice this seems to be increasingly common; there have recently been a number of all-India conferences of party workers in specific fields, such as trade unions, by means of which the CPI central leadership can make direct contact with the fraction hierarchy in those fields.

The device of the fraction may also be utilized vis-à-vis other political parties during a "united front" period when Communists openly or secretly join other parties. Within these parties they are required to act as organized fractions directed by the appropriate unit of the CPI. Perhaps most important, the fraction system also includes legislative bodies. M.P.'s and M.L.A.'s belonging to the party must act as disciplined fractions in their respective legislatures. Such a principle of party discipline is of course normal in parliamentary systems, but the superior effectiveness of CPI discipline gives it a considerable advantage in parliamentary activity.

The above pattern of organization for political action, based on the systematic operation of party fractions in functional groups, is of course supplemented by direct activity—that is, by direct contact with the population at large. However, it is evident that the emphasis of the CPI, both in organization and in practice, is not upon direct contact with an amorphous public but rather upon indirect contact through penetration of selected functional groups.

This is consistent with Communist theory, since a fundamental attribute of that theory is the identification of *classes* as the active agents of history; a Communist does not conceive of the nation as an amorphous collection of individuals but as an order of classes, each assigned a certain role by the iron laws of dialectical materialism. A Communist party, therefore, regards itself not as a mass party but as a class party. Theory decrees that while a party may at certain stages secure the support (or at least the neutrality) of other classes, the proletariat is the only reliably progressive class, the only class which it should, or indeed can, lead. Thus to a Communist the mass of citizens in a particular geographic area is an unnatural object of political activity and the problem is rather to make contact with the proletariat in its trade unions, or during particular stages with the peasantry or bourgeoisie, through peasant organizations or political parties.

As a result of the systematic use of this technique of political action, the CPI's influence in the Indian scene is pervasive but largely covert and therefore very difficult to estimate. Quantitative measures such as the size of the party or its vote in elections obviously constitute poor indices to the extent of that influence.

But primary reliance on this technique produces certain disadvantages for the party. Perhaps the most important is the fact that it facilitates an emphasis upon specialist leadership rather than popular leadership. It has commonly been noted that the main weakness of the CPI is its failure to raise a popular leader of genuinely wide appeal. In a country in which charismatic leadership counts so heavily, the CPI has not produced mass heroes of national stature. By its nature, it has attracted and valued efficient operators in limited fields such as trade union organizers. This was of course appropriate in the conspiratorial periods of its development, but it is a penalty at present with the party's apparent emphasis upon constitutional action.

However, the CPI has recently developed a type of "mass" leader, in the persons of its parliamentary members. An examination of the attributes of some of the prominent Communist M.P.'s may provide clues to the nature of the "mass" appeal of the Indian party. For this purpose the following may be considered: A. K. Gopalan, K. C. George, Ravi Narayan Reddy, Yella Reddy, D. D. Barman, Hiren Mukherji, and Renu Chakravarty. This list includes all those Communist M.P.'s who are in the Central Committee, plus the two prominent Bengali M.P.'s.

Relevant biographical data is, again, very sparse, but certain generalizations may be hazarded. It should be noted, first, that these leaders were attracted to the party during a time of moderate "united-front" policy—in the periods 1934-1940, or 1945-1947. In nearly all cases they had extensive political experience in the Congress and Congress Socialist parties before joining the CPI. Most of them possess college degrees and active professions such as teaching and law. While information on their social origins is not detailed, most of them appear to have come from prominent social strata in their communities. Finally, most of them come from predominantly peasant constituencies.

In contrast to the inner-party leaders of the CPI, these individuals possess broad political experience and demonstrated competence in popular leadership. They would seem to be, in much greater degree than the "Old Bolsheviks" of the party, "natural" leaders. Their backgrounds, along with the fact that they joined the party during periods of "loyal opposition," indicate that they possess closer bonds with their own society. The future prospects of the Communist Party of India may well depend fundamentally upon its ability to draw such "natural" leaders into its ranks. Since the party has recently entered a new period of moderation in its policy, those prospects may be radically improved.

POSTSCRIPT

At an Extraordinary Congress in March-April, 1958, the CPI adopted a revised constitution which incorporated drastic changes in the party's rules of organization and operation. One important change was an expansion of executive agencies at all levels. At the top, the size of the Central Committee (now called the National Council) was increased by about 250 per cent to 101 members, and the size of the Politburo (now called the Central Executive Committee) was increased proportionately to 25 members. Moreover, there was created a new "Secretariat," composed of five to seven secretaries along with the existing general secretary. Corresponding changes were provided at lower levels of the organization.

A more important change was a devolution of authority from the central to the state agencies. Certain specific aspects of authority within the party were transferred, in whole or in part, to lower levels. For example, the authority to supervise inner-party debate, formerly monopolized by the Central Committee, was transferred to the state committees in cases involving state or local issues. The over-all impression created by the constitution is one of partial decentralization—indeed, the creation of a rudimentary federalism—in the party.

It is clear from statements of party leaders at the Congress that these formal changes were designed primarily to render the CPI more attractive to potential recruits or to voters. Apart from this tactical purpose, however, the changes may represent a realistic adjustment to the heterogeneity of the party's composition and to the indiscipline of its operation. And, inasmuch as form influences function, these changes may have important consequences in the future.

5. INFLUENCE GROUPS

INFLUENCE groups are organizations seeking to affect the nature of governmental decisions through channels of influence rather than through formal political machinery. There are three distinct types of groups in India that may be classified as influence groups. Special interest groups such as those of business, trade unions, or cooperatives, represent modern developments, and have been patterned largely on western models. Their actual functioning does not necessarily mirror the activities of their models, a point emphasized both by Helen B. Lamb in her paper on Indian business, and by Morris David Morris in his discussion of Indian trade unions and their relation to politics.

A second type of influence group is the communal organization which is based on traditional caste or religious grounds. Most of the important communal organizations have contested elections since Independence as political parties, or have been so identified with a party as to cease to be real pressure groups. The orthodox Hindu communal parties are discussed by Richard D. Lambert in Section 4 on political parties.

Unique to India are the influence groups centered around the *sarvodaya* movement which draws its inspiration from Gandhian philosophy. Leaders of these movements exert great political influence, but do so almost entirely outside formal governmental machinery. Because these leaders are not responsible to an electorate, they represent a fundamental challenge to parliamentary democracy in India. Joan V. Bondurant has explored these groups and has traced the implications of their work on the present form of government in India.

BUSINESS ORGANIZATION AND LEADERSHIP IN INDIA TODAY

HELEN B. LAMB

*T*HERE has been little sociological research on the development and motivation of Indian business. Even quantitative analysis of its structure and organization has been neglected, let alone a serious attempt to define its political, economic, and social roles. Thus these findings are somewhat impressionistic. I intend first to describe briefly the nature and extent of business organization in India, and then to attempt an appraisal of Indian business in the larger context of India's political economy. Here the focus will be on the interactions between business and other leadership groups with respect to the paramount issue of India's planned economic development.

The Family

Any analysis of the structure of Indian business organization should start with the family[1]—the basic unit not only in small enterprises but in large ones as well. Eventually, size can lead to a dilution of familial operation and control, and substitution of a more impersonal corporate organization on lines of functional expertise, as it has in the case of India's most outstanding industrial family—the Tatas. This process, however, has not yet gone very far. To be sure, many enterprises have assumed the corporate form; but real control is usually retained within the family through the medium of the so-called managing agency firm, a kind of top holding company. Along with some stock ownership, contracts between the managing agency firm and individual companies allow the family to control what are known as "public" corporations, that is, corporations financed by shares sold on Indian stock exchanges to the investing public.

HELEN B. LAMB has been a member of the India Project of the Economic Development Program at the Center for International Studies, Massachusetts Institute of Technology.

[1] The Indian family has historically been an extended "joint" family with many relatives of different generations and degrees of relatedness all living in the same compound or at least owning business property in common. While the use of the legal form of joint property ownership has declined under the impact of modern life and the new graduated income tax, much of the spirit of the joint family system lives on and provides jobs and security for relatives beyond the immediate family circle.

251

It is true, of course, that some Indian managing agency firms are not family affairs, but consortia of either families or other groups. Cement Agencies Ltd., the managing agency which dominates the Indian cement industry, is just such a mixed group, being composed of Britons, Gujaratis, and Parsis. And there are some corporations run by a board of directors rather than by a managing agency firm. Business is less exclusively family-oriented than formerly. Yet of all those public companies permitted by the law to operate under managing agencies only fifteen per cent are without them.[2] Even where the managing agency is excluded, as in banking, several of India's most important firms are closely identified with prominent business families, for instance, the Central Bank of India with the Tatas and the United Commercial Bank with the Birlas. Certainly the kind of activity usually encountered at the apex of India's business pyramid is that of an Indian family simultaneously engaging in trade, real estate, and banking, and managing industrial corporations through the device of one or more managing agency firms.

Much of India's modern industry is in the hands of a few influential business families whose operations extend over several areas. The Tatas, long important in Indian textiles, have concentrated even more in electric power and heavy industry, especially steel and locomotives. The Birlas, important in cotton textiles and jute, manufacture textile machinery and produce consumer goods such as bicycles and cars. The Walchands, originally identified with construction works and shipping, now have important engineering and sugar interests. Other leading business families like the Dalmias, the Jalans, Singhanias, the Sir Badridas Goenkas, the A. V. Thomases, and the Thapars likewise run a miscellany of enterprises. The degree to which these families rely on funds raised from the general public varies considerably. Tata enterprises are public corporations. At the other extreme, of the forty-three companies run by the Singhania family only twenty-four are industrial companies, and of these only four are listed in Kothari's *Investors' Encyclopaedia* of public companies.[3]

In several consumer goods industries, like cotton textiles and sugar, there is considerable competition from small Indian enterprises not con-

---

[2] Andrew F. Brimmer, "Setting of Entrepreneurship in India," *Quarterly Journal of Economics*, LXIX, November 1955, p. 564.

[3] M. M. Mehta, *Combination Movement in Indian Industry*, Allahabad, Friends Book Depot, 1952, pp. 74-76; Kothari and Sons, *Investors' Encyclopaedia 1951-1952*, Madras, 1952, pp. 357, 399, 1147, 1327.

nected with the dominant families. But in some of the newer industries —rayon, aluminum, steel, auto assembly, and cement—the position of these families often borders on monopoly, with only two, three, or four principal suppliers. Sometimes the underlying corporations are quite substantial in size (as in the case of textile mills run by the Sarabhai, Wadia, and Shri Ram families), but more frequently one finds a string of small units in one industry run by the same managing agency. The Thapars run seven coal mines, the Birlas five sugar companies, and the Lalbhais seven textile companies. Perhaps because of the managing agency type of control there has not been much consolidation. Concentration takes the form of acquiring control of managing agency firms as well as of additional operating companies. Recently Indians have bought up several British managing agency houses. The degree of concentration reflects not only the established pattern of family and managing agency financial control over industry, but also the fact that it is more difficult to do business in India than in the West—especially in the less developed areas within India and in industries which are highly technical or make producers' goods. It is harder to line up a well-trained labor force, assure a flow of raw materials and parts, obtain electric power and adequate capital, and develop new markets.

Yet there is a familiar pattern in this Indian development. Most of the big business families are relatively new to industry, only a few Bombay and Ahmedabad families having been in modern industry for several generations. The development of these families resembles that of leading American business families like the Mellons, the DuPonts, and the Rockefellers who emerged from small beginnings in a combination of trade, banking, and real estate or some one service, and fanned out from there into the management and control of public utilities, mines, and a variety of industries. Concentration of economic power among Indian families, while not nearly so broad as that of their counterparts in the heyday of American capitalism, probably looms as large relative to India's less developed economy. Some of India's leading business families, like our own, have made substantial contributions through their educational foundations to the advancement of education at all levels, including institutes of technology, and to research in the social and physical sciences, thus moving beyond the traditional forms of largesse—assistance to poor members of one's own community, and the building of temples and hostels for religious pilgrims.

~§ The Business Community

A second important unit of business organization is the "community," which means the group within which intermarriage takes place.[4] The leading business communities to enter modern industry thus far have been the Marwaris, with their various subdivisions originating in Rajasthan in the interior, and the Gujarati-speaking Hindu, Jain, and Parsi businessmen dwelling along the coast of western India. The Parsis were the pioneer Indian business community to set up modern industrial corporations; then came several Gujarati-speaking Hindu and Jain business communities, and more recently the Marwaris. There are many other business communities of lesser industrial significance, such as the Punjabis, Sindhis, Muslims, and Bengalis. Some of the newer entrepreneurs are members of trading and moneylending castes going back into early Indian history, like the Chettiars of South India; others, like certain Maharashtrian and Madrasi Brahman industrialists, have quite a different background.

What does the community structure mean for the operation of business, and how does it affect public attitudes toward business? The significance of the business community is sometimes given formal expression, as in the case of commercial associations open only to members of a given community. But it is more apt to be an informal affair—at least so far as its economic operations go—without any real organization except when it comes to dispensing charity, in particular training and educational scholarships, to the poorer members of the group. However informal it may be, it appears to exercise an important influence on the choice of business personnel. It exerts great social pressure to provide opportunities for the less fortunate members of the group. The Indian business community also plays a part in the consolidation of family empires by marital ties. Strong group loyalty and nepotism are not by any means confined to the business communities but pervade much of Indian society and in fact many other societies characterized by a shortage of job opportunities.

[4] For a more detailed discussion of the Indian business community, see D. R. Gadgil et al., *Notes on the Rise of Business Communities in India*, Preliminary Memorandum, New York, Institute of Pacific Relations, 1951; Helen B. Lamb, "The Development of Modern Business Communities in India," in R. L. Aronson and J. P. Windmuller, eds., *Labor, Management, and Economic Growth; Proceedings of a Conference on Human Resources and Labor Relations in Underdeveloped Countries*, Ithaca, Cornell University, Institute of International Industrial and Labour Relations, 1954; idem, "The Indian Business Communities and the Evolution of an Industrialist Class," *Pacific Affairs*, XXVIII, June 1955, pp. 101-16.

The core of business control is the family. The next circle embraces members of the same business community. Beginning to erupt on both of these traditional forms of organization is the concept of the professionally trained man who is hired for his talents irrespective of his community. He exists in engineering, accounting, and management, and has made considerable headway in some fields such as banking. In others the professional man often complains that he has little status or prospect for advancement and that the ultimate decision making is still the preserve of relatives of the head family or of the family's close community associates. Thus the family and community orientation of business contributes to a feeling of alienation from business on the part of many professionals.

The Trade Association

A third unit of business organization is the trade association. Industrial associations, employer associations, and all-purpose chambers of commerce have been growing steadily in India during the last fifty-five years.[5] Sometimes these associations are purely functional, such as the Employers Federation of India, located in Bombay House (Tata headquarters), and the even older Bombay Mill Owners' Association; both of these organizations are composed of important British and Indian industrialists. Sometimes these groupings are organized on religious or individual business community lines; for example, there are Muslim and Marwari chambers of commerce in various cities. With the exception of racial divisions, which were once very strong and still persist to some extent, the trade associations on the whole are moving away from community emphasis. Like similar associations elsewhere, they are interested in creating business solidarity, raising business standards, settling disputes among businessmen, handling industrial relations, and in some instances regulating output as in the case of the powerful Indian Jute Mills Association, until recently an all-British body. They endeavor to present to society a unified business point of view on issues relating to business and industry.

The Voice of Business

India's trade and industrial associations have been integrated into a coordinated network whose top organization is the Federation of Indian

---

[5] Indian Merchants' Chamber, *Directory of Chambers of Commerce and Associations*, Bombay, 1953.

Chambers of Commerce and Industry. It was launched in 1926 with 24 member associations, and has grown enormously. By 1951 it had 132 member associations and 79 associate members, the associates being the leading industrial companies run by Indians. The federation has a broad base and claims to represent 40,000 firms.[6] Members of India's leading Gujarati and Marwari business families with industrial as well as trading interests are heavily represented on the federation's Working Committee and among its past presidents. It is hard to tell how effective this movement has been in integrating the interests of big and little business and in fusing the different business communities into one over-all Indian business community. Certainly the federation's special publications dealing with important questions of economic policy and its many representatives on boards and commissions give Indian business a united voice.

Indian business has other means of communicating its point of view. The All India Manufacturers Organization, which regards itself as the equivalent of our National Association of Manufacturers but is really far more liberal, was started in 1941 and publishes a monthly, *Industrial India*. There is also the All India Organization of Industrial Employers established in 1933 and closely tied to the Federation of Indian Chambers of Commerce and Industry. It has a membership of 26 associations—these are either industrial or employer associations—and 146 individual companies. This organization has representatives on many bodies and committees dealing with questions of employment, industrial relations, technical training, housing, etc.

Indian business controls a substantial part of the press. Leading business families have bought up papers, both in English and the vernacular, and established widespread newspaper chains, e.g. those associated with the Dalmia, Birla, and Ramnath Goenka families. Then there are influential business publications such as *Commerce, Capital* (primarily British), *Indian Finance, The Eastern Economist* (owned by Birla and modeled after the English *Economist*), and the *Tata Quarterly*. In addition there are magazines catering to special industries and their needs. Some of the more important chambers of commerce publish their own journals.

Indian business has an important voice in Parliament. Of six hundred and ninety-nine members elected in 1951-1952 to the two houses, eighty-

---

[6] The Federation of Indian Chambers of Commerce and Industry, "Silver Jubilee; A Statesman Supplement," *Statesman* (Calcutta), March 29, 1952, and *Silver Jubilee Souvenir 1927-51*, New Delhi, 1952

three came under the classification of business.[7] This did not include those members of Parliament engaged in the legal and other professions, some of whom have close business connections or hope to acquire them. Of the eighty-three businessmen in this first Parliament, thirty were designated as industrialists. As one would expect, many of them were Gujaratis and Marwaris. Only a few of India's important industrial families were represented directly in that Parliament. Mr. Bansal, secretary of the Indian Federation of Chambers of Commerce and Industry, was a member of that Parliament.

Indian Business in the Larger Context of Indian Society

So far this paper has read like the success story of Indian business with steady and impressive growth in power and organization. But when one asks the question, how much real influence can Indian business exert on the Congress and on the formulation of development policy?, the answer is not at all clear. Indian business gave valuable help in financing the independence movement, it has presumably filled Congress coffers for local campaigns against the Communist Party, and it can exercise considerable pressure at the local level. But business really has no place to go other than to the omnipresent Congress, and in this organization it is only one of many powerful elements, all seeking to prevail. The Congress Working Committee, the party's highest executive authority, has not been recruited from the ranks of business, though one finds an occasional businessman on it; but rather from highly educated intelligentsia groups with experience in law, journalism, politics, and government service and very little background in business or industry.

Business has the power of money, in India as elsewhere, but it does not have the prestige and general acceptance accorded business in the West. Some people attribute this to the widespread black marketeering and tax evasion by business during the wartime inflation and since. Recently India has produced some financial tycoons on the model of America's "robber barons," and they have not yet been transformed by public relations experts into industrial statesmen.

But the low esteem in which Indian business is held is much more deep-seated. The goals and value system of business enterprise do not permeate Indian society as for instance they permeate our own. Indian

[7] Trilochan Singh, ed., *Indian Parliament 1952-57*, New Delhi, Arunam and Sheel, [1954?].

business has had to operate in a cultural milieu which traditionally holds an organic view of society somewhat like that of feudal Europe. Individuals are members of a group to which they are subordinate, and relations between groups are harmonious and stable with each component performing its due function. This view of society rules out liquidation of any group and reserves for Indian business, along with other elements, its due niche, but it is a subordinate one. Such an attitude is antithetic to those attributes of business enterprise which are equated with virtue in the West—competition, self-assertiveness, and the survival of the fittest, unremitting innovation and the consequent revolution in methods of production and thereby in relationships among people—all set in motion by the profit motive. Modern Indian life has somewhat undermined the ancient view, always more of an ideal than a reality, but old conceptions linger on. The lofty disdain held by highly trained professional bureaucrats toward the humble moneylender origins of many of India's business families still persists and reflects the combined British-Indian cultural tradition in which government service constituted the greatest attraction. The conspicuous consumption of India's merchant princes seems to arouse more disapproval than that of her titular princes among the many Indians by whom simplicity and austerity are valued for their own sake. Though there are notable exceptions, Indian business has not been very aggressive and venturesome in pioneering new industries for India. This may be in part because the spirit of enterprise has not been glorified.[8]

Before Independence Indian business was a minor partner in a united front of many groups organized to oust the British. In this struggle business gave more behind-the-scenes support than outright leadership, though at least one Indian businessman, Jamnalal Bajaj, held high office

[8] But is this not merely a transition phase; and will not Indian business come to assert itself and its values even as the rise of commercial and industrial interests in Western Europe eventually broke the bonds of the old order? This question has been raised, but it seems to me unlikely that the European experience will be repeated in India today when the world setting is so different. Not only does India share the prevalent urge toward a welfare state with all that that implies, but also the models for effective industrial organization throughout the world no longer reflect the social composition of individualistic early capitalism. India faces on the one hand the developed capitalism of America and Western Europe, which has exhibited a marked trend away from individual enterprise and toward giant corporations, with an ever diminishing proportion of the total population playing genuine entrepreneurial roles, and on the other hand the socialist division of the world where industrial production is confined to a handful of state trusts. As the Indian sociologist I. P. Desai intimates, why should India adopt the ideology of a competitive, individualistic society when "it has lost the vigor of its youth and the world looks at it with growing suspicion." I. P. Desai, "Caste and Family," *The Economic Weekly*, February 27, 1954, p. 230.

in the Congress.[9] With Independence, however, there has been a shift from political to economic issues: what are the best means of developing India's resources and of raising the living standards of her people? Here Indians are not united. The viewpoint of business is only one among many and it does not have much support beyond its own ranks.

There are three main approaches to the question of economic development—that of the businessman, of intellectuals who have been influenced more or less by Fabian socialism, and of the followers of Gandhi. Many intellectuals, whether in the Congress or outside it, have long favored a gradual movement toward socialism with increasing public ownership of the means of production in order to speed development, prevent undue concentration of economic power, and bring about an economically more egalitarian society. Those in the Gandhian tradition want a more modest development program centered on the village and on village industry. They are opposed to factory-made consumer goods, especially textiles, because they deprive the village of an important means of livelihood and lead to concentration of economic power by city millowners. Both of these approaches emphasize social welfare and the evils of private concentration of wealth. Their bias against private enterprise, however, has somewhat different roots. Advocates of socialist economic measures charge Indian business with being unenterprising, lacking the dynamism to spur rapid economic growth. The Gandhians, on the other hand, dislike the very efficiency of Indian business in the mass-produced consumer goods industries, especially textiles, which have undercut handicraft production. Indian business thus takes a beating on both sides.

The approach to economic development of Indian business—or rather, of the articulate wing of big business—is somewhat as follows. It favors rapid development and government aid in planning and financing overall industrialization. One of the repeated charges against the British administration of India was that it failed to do precisely this. Perhaps the most positive and imaginative expression of business planning thus far has been the so-called Bombay Plan, proposed immediately before Independence by a small group from some of India's leading business houses. This plan accorded government a crucial role in accelerating industrialization and setting the stage for the eventual achievement of an Indian variant on the private enterprise and social welfare economy

---

[9] Kaka Kalelkar, ed., *To a Gandhian Capitalist, Correspondence Between Mahatma Gandhi and Jamnalal Bajaj and Members of His Family*, Bangalore, Power Press, 1951.
For an account of Mr. G. D. Birla's political activities in behalf of independence, see his book, *In the Shadow of the Mahatma*, Calcutta, Orient Longmans, 1953.

found today in developed capitalist democracies. In brief, business would like a maximum of government aid and protection of industry with a minimum of outright government operation and control.

The three divergent conceptions have led to an uneasy compromise— the so-called socialistic pattern of society. This policy, unlike outright socialism, presupposes a continuing mixed economy—part private and part public enterprise with considerable flexibility of operation and emphasis on the goals of the welfare state rather than on a given ideology for ideology's sake. It raises difficult and as yet unresolved problems as to the functions of and dividing line between the two sectors, their coordination, and the relation between private industry and the government. During this postwar period, when new institutions are being forged and new concepts emerging to bring the socialistic pattern into being through a series of five year plans and other measures, there has been considerable confusion among businessmen. The pattern seems to shift from year to year (it is now the *socialist* rather than the *socialistic* pattern) and to be susceptible of many interpretations. Is it rhetoric, a political appeal to India's masses to make them proof against the blandishments of communism? Or is it real, that is, the entering wedge of socialism? Business is not sure. The government alternately admonishes business for its shortcomings and reassures it as to its future.

Respects in which India's Planning Effort Has Strengthened Business

Despite the alarm raised by new government acts and regulations reflecting a socialist pattern, it is important to note that many steps have been taken to promote and assist Indian business. Protective tariffs against foreign goods have been extended to a number of industries. Financial aid, tax concessions, and depreciation policies favoring new industrial investment in lines where expansion is desired have been instituted. Government has assured India and Indian business a well-integrated industrial complex of many industries by assuming responsibility for tackling any bottlenecks which emerge either because private enterprise is reluctant to enter certain technically difficult or risky fields, or has entered them in insufficient quantity. The government is developing transportation facilities and electric power, thus providing the essential base for industrialization. Above all, it is committed to a rate of spending on public utilities and works in agriculture, industry, and the social services which provides business with a constantly expanding home market and hence virtually guarantees profitable operations. The whole planning effort in India will almost inevitably bolster business organizations since the attempt to plan and to push economic performance necessitates the drawing up of schedules of capabilities and priorities, the licensing of new capital issues and imports, and the allocation of goods in short supply—whether transport facilities or raw materials. All these activities presuppose some form of business organization. Planning can effectively exclude new competitors as it has in industries such as jute where no expansion in capacity is envisaged.

Business Apprehension

Yet business is up in arms over many new government regulations and measures which have been promulgated over business protest. The recent Company Law, for instance, attempts to prevent undue concentration of economic power by regulating and curtailing the managing agency type of control over industry. While it may suffer the familiar fate of trust-busting efforts elsewhere, the bill goes much too far according to Indian business opinion. The Industries Development and Regulation Act of 1951, and in particular the 1953 amendment, grants government extensive powers to participate in the orderly development of industry, to regulate industry, and even on occasion to take over the operation of firms. The nationalization of the Imperial Bank, of India's private airlines, and of the life insurance business caused dismay. The amendment to the constitution declaring nonjusticiable the question of compensation in cases of nationalization poses a question mark for the future. The new industrial policy statement enlarges the sphere for which the government has responsibility. The Second Five Year Plan allocates projected industrial investment in accordance with this shift in emphasis, government undertakings absorbing a far higher proportion of total industrial investment than during the First Five Year Plan. Then too, the proposed financing of the plan moves away from reliance on voluntary saving and investment as determinants of the pace of development and emphasizes increasingly taxation and deficit finance.

An additional cause for business anxiety is the deliberate restriction of new capacity in certain consumer goods industries, especially cotton textiles, and the promotion of cooperative handicraft production subsidized by the government to provide the planned increases. As indicated, this program has the enthusiastic support of the Gandhians to whom handicraft production is a way of life. To India's planners it is a valuable expedient which not only yields the necessary increases in consumer goods but also greatly increases employment opportunities and at the same time releases the maximum of investment resources for heavy industries like steel and machinery, since additional handicraft production requires less capital outlay than would the expansion of capacity for factory-made consumer goods. Established textile manufacturers are vigorously resisting these limitations as they would like to expand to meet the expected increase in textile demand.

In the field of industrial relations many segments of business feel that the government's role has been detrimental to them, that the arbitration awards usually favor the workers. And it is probably true that, with unemployment so prevalent, the workers would tend to receive less without this government intervention—an integral part of the socialist pattern. But even here, the government's strong stand against the strike as a weapon may hamper the development of a vigorous trade union movement and hence relieve business on this score. In any event, it is interesting to note that even though government regulations have multiplied, private investment has increased substantially since 1954 in response to the new expansive forces which stimulate business and release the economy from the shackles of its colonial past.

It is extremely difficult to prepare any kind of balance sheet as to the ability of business to shape India's politico-economic future. One possible measure of its effectiveness might be the substantial differences between the Second Five Year Plan (1956) and the Draft Plan Frame (March 17, 1955), generally considered the high point of socialist planning. On several counts the plan frame was modified on lines favoring private business. For instance, the Second Five Year Plan provides for a higher ratio of consumer goods to producers' goods and for a higher proportion of private to public enterprise than was envisaged in the plan frame. But even in this instance it is possible that the planners were sufficiently politically minded to ask for more than they expected—or even needed—in order to get approximately what they wanted.

Though the Indian government has taken steps that are far more socialistic than any New Deal measures in the United States, business criticism of government in India is by no means so rampant or uniform as it was here. It ranges all the way from Mr. G. D. Birla's enthusiastic acceptance of the socialist pattern as the only way to preserve capitalism to the federation's respectful and cautious suggestion that the Planning Commission should give "further thought" to the relative roles of the public and private sectors.[10] Why this diversity of business response and why the muted character of business criticism? A few hypotheses suggest themselves. Indian business may feel isolated, especially since the death of its powerful friend, Sardar Vallabhbhai Patel. Though there is no precise definition of the socialist pattern, it has received widespread acceptance in India. Criticism by businessmen is therefore usually confined to taking exception to details—especially timing and methods—rather than to the content of the socialist pattern itself. Mr. Birla in particular attempts in his public utterances to convey to the rank and file of Indian business that the social and intellectual climate in India has changed and that they face a new situation to which they must adjust.[11] Businessmen, or at least their more sophisticated spokesmen, realize that in accelerating India's economic development far more government assistance and direction will be required than during the more leisurely course of western economic development. Then too, Indian business is perhaps not as united as the streamlined Federation of Indian Chambers of Commerce and Industry would suggest. Underlying all business efforts to work together are the different business communities. There tends to be a good deal of rivalry between representatives of local business communities newly engaged in modern industrial operations and those members of the more powerful business communities who operate all over India and are felt to have established valuable government contacts.

Business Leadership

An even sharper division within Indian business is, of course, that which separates the big, successful entrepreneur from the little businessmen. The socialist pattern may wear quite a different aspect to different businessmen depending on their economic power and ability, their social status, and their access to government, as well as on their previous industrial experience. Not all Indian business is equally hit by the limitations on expansion of consumer goods industries. As we have already seen, India's most important industrial families have entered new fields, even some producers' goods industries. In fact, the industrial operations of some important families like the Kirloskars and Mahindras with

---

[10] *Hindu Weekly Review* (Madras), May 7, 1956, p. 2; *ibid.*, p. 3. For a convenient summary of the federation's position on a wide range of political and economic issues, see article by G. L. Bansal, "Leaders of Commerce and Industry in Conference," *Indian Affairs Record*, March 1956, pp. 1-4.

[11] See "G. D. Birla's Call to Businessmen" delivered at the annual meeting of the federation and reported in the *Hindustan Times Weekly* (Delhi), March 8, 1954.

engineering, machinery, and aluminum interests appear to be exclusively in this sphere.

At the other end of the spectrum the innumerable small traders and moneylenders may feel that their role has dwindled in the new India where cooperative organization among small producers in industry and agriculture is increasingly stressed. The few modern business enterprisers who have organizing experience and capacity can be used and will play an important part, according to C. Rajagopalachari.

> The days of big business may be thought to be over, on account of the Congress resolution as to the pattern of society that Congress wants to build up. But in reality it is not the case. Big organizations are still wanted and will continue. High taxation and low net profits are no doubt deterrent elements for private enterprise. But though profits do not any longer accrue on the war-period scale, and though taxation is growing heavier and heavier with each budget, big business has its attractions still. As long as talent exists, there is a vocational call for big business to which men cannot say nay, profit or no profit, taxation or no taxation. Big business in that sense has an undying future .... Big men will continue doing big things because they cannot help it.[12]

Government contacts, of value to business in any society, are particularly useful in India where the government is attempting minute regulation of industry. It has become necessary to obtain the permission of some government board for a new capital issue, plant expansion, opening a branch office, and so on. In such an economy the opportunities for wrangling and dissension multiply, but so do the opportunities for discreet negotiation and the winning of special privileges. In a setup of this kind there are likely to be charges of corruption by disappointed applicants whether with or without foundation. As government and semigovernmental institutions play an increasing role in the financing of private enterprise, the value of government contacts will increase. This premium on access to government is accentuated, furthermore, by a significant trend away from the conception of the mixed economy as one of sharply defined exclusive fields of operation for private and public enterprise (embodied in the Industry Policy Resolution of 1948) and toward a new conception of coexistence, that is, private and public enterprise existing side by side in the same industry where government feels this to be in the public interest (Industrial Policy Statement, 1956).[13] The rationale for public enterprise seems to be shifting somewhat from an

---

[12] Quoted in an editorial in *Capital* (Calcutta), August 18, 1955, p. 213.

[13] For an interesting analysis of these two industrial policy statements, see Harry Robinson, *Industrial Development Policy in India*, Menlo Park, Calif., Stanford Research Institute, 1956.

ideological emphasis to one of expediency, with the government operating plants in those industries where private enterprise has not thought it profitable to enter—or has entered but to an insufficient degree. This change in emphasis may even raise the hopes of some of India's most efficient and strategically placed businessmen that Indian development may follow the pattern of the Japanese, where many enterprises started by the government were subsequently sold to private interests once they had proved profitable.

Through regulation and financial aid India is attempting to merge the goals, methods, and even the personnel of public and private enterprise. The new financial institutions bring together representatives of big business and the government. Business representatives are sitting with technical experts and government officials on development councils which have been set up to plan expansion in certain key industries. Prominent businessmen are also members of such tripartite boards as the Labor Panel to the Planning Commission and the Central Advisory Council of Industries, designed to implement and to obtain acceptance for the mixed-economy type of planning.[14] Outstanding business leaders along with civil servants serve on the boards of the new State Bank of India (formerly the Imperial Bank with twenty-two per cent of the nation's banking assets), the now nationalized Reserve Bank of India, the Industrial Finance Corporation, the National Industrial Development Corporation, and the Industrial Credit and Investment Corporation to which the government as well as private industry and foreign capital have contributed. Businessmen and civil servants are directors of the new nationalized industrial corporations such as National Air Services, Sindri Fertilizer, Hindustan Cables, government shipyards, steel mills, and so on. Private businessmen are a distinct minority on these boards but they are there.

In line with the traditional Indian pattern of the fourfold stages of a man's life, the Planning Minister, G. L. Nanda, has appealed to the most successful businessmen to give up their own enterprises after a certain age and to help in the conduct of the public sector. He states that his appeal has received an enthusiastic response. The well-known business journalist, Mr. S. H. Batlivala, writing in the *Times of India* on "The Role of Industrialists" comments on this appeal as follows:

Private industrialists' frequent pilgrimages to the ministerial gods of Delhi have resulted in many of their prayers being granted. The greater is the

[14] A study of the minutes of the meetings of these bodies would throw valuable light on the extent to which they have become two-way means of communication.

reason that some of them should be helpful in the conduct of the public sector.[15]

Of great help in the transition from competition to cooperation between government and industry which India's planning effort calls for is the small group of distinguished businessmen who have already achieved a high status and position. Since Independence there have been several instances of such businessmen sharing in the expanded opportunities for government and public service. John Matthai and T. T. Krishnamachari have served as cabinet members, Sir Homi Mody as governor of Uttar Pradesh, C. H. Bhabha, A. D. Shroff, and Sir Purshotamdas Thakurdas as heads of important government commissions, and G. L. Mehta as ambassador to the United States. There is also a reverse flow of business leaders coming from a background of governmental or professional experience. Sir Arcot Mudaliar, a man of long government service, has recently gone into industry and is chairman of the T. I. Cycle Co. He is also chairman of the Indo-Commercial Bank and the new Industrial Credit and Investment Corporation. Shri V. Ramakrishnan, a most dynamic organizer of new industrial ventures in South India, was formerly an ICS man. Dr. B. C. Roy has had at least three careers—in medicine, in politics (as a member of the Congress Working Committee and chief minister of West Bengal), and in industry. John Matthai has been chairman of the State Bank of India and was previously director of Tata and Sons; he began as a professor of economics. He has alternately served private enterprise and the Government of India in important capacities.

Outstanding business leaders such as these are by no means numerous, but their example is significant in that their own experience is a composite of different viewpoints and they thereby reduce the barriers, real and imagined, between business and other leadership groups in society. This interaction and commingling between different leadership elements may produce the profound modification in private enterprise goals that Rajagopalachari had in mind, and may also have some impact on the elite mentality of the ICS. The Indian business stereotype—that is, a person dedicated exclusively to making money—is being weakened from two directions. Increasingly, people are entering business from a nonbusiness background, from communities with different values and different social status. Concomitantly one sees the sons and grandsons of successful businessmen turning to national service or the more honored

[15] *Times of India*, November 10, 1955.

professions. Those businessmen who become recognized leaders in the cooperative effort may respond increasingly to the traditional concept of an Indian leader as one who is disinterested and dedicated. Given the strong political and economic pressures which are pushing in this direction, it is certainly not beyond the realm of possibility that more business leaders will forswear profits for power and prestige.

Does the socialist pattern mean that large-scale industry will be in effect socialized or that government will take on some of the features of the corporate state? To paraphrase the comments made during conference discussion—will this mystical union of business and government be consummated on a high plane of social service to India with businessmen becoming more and more like government servants, or will it merely legitimize the special privileges of the fortunate few? With India's extraordinary ability for absorbing the new without discarding the old, the end product may be a little of both, an amalgam of many elements, fused into something quite novel and labeled "made in India."

TRADE UNIONS AND THE STATE

MORRIS DAVID MORRIS

*I*NDIAN trade unions have not developed along the lines familiar in the United States or in Western Europe; therefore their role in the political process is not similar to that generally played by trade unions in other parliamentary democracies. Trade unions in India act neither as pressure groups nor as political parties as such. Rather they have been organized by the middle class leadership of the various political parties as arms of those parties. This political use of the trade union movement has led the Congress governments increasingly to use state powers to discipline labor and to regulate its welfare. This role of the state has in turn altered the character and power of trade unions in India.

The creation of a disciplined labor force is a necessary requirement of an industrializing society. There are two aspects to this problem: one is the need to recruit labor from the rural sector into the factories, and the other is the need to discipline that labor force to industrial requirements. In India, the first aspect, obtaining a mobile labor force willing to work in the factory sector, has not been difficult. From the earliest stage of modern factory development, in the mid-nineteenth century, there has been no general shortage of raw, unskilled labor to man the machines.[1]

The other aspect of the problem, labor discipline in the factories, is more difficult. It involves the transformation of a nonindustrial labor force, unaccustomed to collective work, into the equivalent of a human machine responding to regulations of a restrictive sort. This concept of labor discipline, as described here, is a difficult one to measure. But the extremes of indiscipline and discipline seem quite obvious. An undisciplined labor force is one where workers consistently refuse (or are unable) to perform their work and thus frustrate the effective functioning of the industrial complex.[2] A disciplined labor force is one where workers

MORRIS DAVID MORRIS is an Associate Professor of Economics at the University of Washington.

[1] Morris David Morris, "Some Comments on the Supply of Labor to the Bombay Cotton Textile Industry, 1854-1951," *Indian Economic Journal*, I, October 1953, pp. 138-52.
[2] This excludes a situation where labor is unavailable, the problem then being the absence of a labor force, not the degree of its discipline. Nor does a strike necessarily represent a case of indiscipline. In its most organized form, the strike is the expression of successful disciplining of workers to the industrial system.

perform their functions exactly according to the rules laid down by their employers, thus permitting the effective functioning of the industrial process. A perfectly disciplined work force would not only meet this test, but would permit the employer freely to modify, rationalize, or transform discipline along lines demanded by changing technology or the demands of the pricing mechanism.

In a society largely oriented to private decision making, the problem of disciplining the labor force is in the first instance a responsibility left to the private employer. It is he who faces the task of transforming the continual flow of raw recruits into a group capable of making the new operations function effectively. As a region develops a sizeable work force employed in many enterprises the disciplinary experience is generalized throughout that labor market. The working traditions become institutionalized, and the labor force becomes structured in accord with this situation. As long as the labor force is growing rapidly the discipline can be modified if modification is necessary. New recruits to the factory system and to the total employment relationship can be used to swamp any existing tradition. But once the labor force has become large enough so that accretions to it are relatively small, that is, when the rate of labor force growth slows up, the changing of rules and traditions becomes much more difficult. The growth of informal relations among workers in the factory system renders the situation less flexible, and employers find it more difficult to proceed unilaterally.[3]

During more mature stages of industrial development in western countries, unions develop as the overt expression of already existent informal links among workers. As their power expands they intervene to participate in shaping and enforcing the patterns of discipline required by the system. Their intervention frequently has provoked sharp conflicts with employers. While in western experience these issues have been gradually resolved by the contestants, it is possible to suggest that the conflict over the shaping of the disciplinary requirements of modern industry—both in terms of productivity and ideology—sometimes affects the stability of the state. When this occurs, the coercive apparatus of the society may then be brought into play to support efforts at creating and maintaining that level of discipline required for its survival. Under these circumstances the role of the state may cause working-class forms to assume different dimensions than those to which we have been ac-

[3] One of the few studies of the institutionalization of work discipline traditions among unorganized workers is Stanley B. Mathewson's *Restriction of Output Among Unorganized Workers*, New York, Viking Press, 1931.

customed. What has occurred in India is a case in point. Because the cotton textile industry of Bombay City has been the focus around which the labor policy of Bombay State has been developed, and because Bombay State has acted as the bellwether for national labor policy, the cotton industry of Bombay City will be used as the objective evidence of this theme.

Viewed as an institution of an industrial society, the trade union plays two crucial roles—as the agent expressing the wage-welfare ambitions of the labor force and as an organ helping to maintain discipline in the labor force. In the various societies the two functions are blended in different proportions, but for the survival of an industrial society they must both be present. If we can view unions as falling within a spectrum of variations, depending on whether they historically stress the wage-welfare or the disciplinary function, U.S. trade unions would stand at one end of the range, being primarily preoccupied with maintaining and improving the wage-welfare aspects of membership life. Historically, they have been only incidentally concerned with the problem of discipline. At the other end of the range would be unions of the Soviet type where the state determines the wage-welfare aspects of working-class life while the union acts primarily as a device to enforce disciplined response to the needs of the state.

This distinction does not mean that American unions are unconcerned with the problems of labor discipline, but it does suggest that in the United States the disciplinary relationships are established by voluntary negotiations between these organizations and the employers. The discipline established in the collective bargain is merely an aspect of the union's exercise of its wage-welfare function. It is this wage-welfare feature that the unions conceive as their *raison d'être*; it is only through the struggle for economic and social improvement that the unions maintain a disciplinary influence over the work force. Because these voluntary associations have developed to arrange these matters, the role of the state in the United States (and in the West generally) has been kept sharply restricted.

In terms of the crude typology I have suggested, it is my conclusion that trade unions in India have since 1934 developed along lines which place them closer to the Soviet than to the American end of the range, and that they will probably continue to develop in this way. These unions are evolving to the point where they will serve mainly as disciplinary agents, the wage-welfare function being increasingly appropriated by the state. This development has little to do with whether India develops along capitalist or socialist lines, nor does it seem to have anything to do with conscious intent. In fact, this situation seems to run counter to the wishes and effort of Indian policy makers whose experience and political traditions lead them to prefer unions and collective bargaining of the western variety. Yet all efforts to reverse the trend have proved abortive. The fact that unions are increasingly tending to serve as disciplinary institutions is being determined by the larger and more fundamental necessities at work, the need to maintain stable political conditions in the society, and the need to have rapid industrial development.

In the seventy years between 1856 and 1926 the generally prosperous Bombay millowners were able to create a labor force possessing the characteristics necessary for the effective functioning of their operations.[4] However, the end of the first World War brought into a sagging market increasing competition from Japanese and newer Indian mills. The long golden period of Bombay prosperity faded after 1922, and the millowners were forced to consider increasingly desperate action to restore the vitality of their industry. Much of the solution seemed to hinge on the ability to transform the working patterns in the mills, sharply intensifying discipline in such a way as to obtain massive increases in per capita productivity. But the efforts to reorder the traditional labor discipline ran into great difficulty. By this time the labor force was no longer growing; in fact, unemployment was appearing on a large scale. Established patterns of work could no longer be swamped by the addition of new recruits. At the same time, the growing experience with urban employment and the tradition of strikes which ran back to the earliest days of the industry culminated in the appearance of small, unstable trade unions during the mid-twenties.[5] The efforts of employers

[4] By U.S. or British standards of the period one would say that the Bombay mills did not have a disciplined labor force. But viewed in terms of the technical and economic relationships confronting the Bombay industry, the discipline imposed was all that the industry required or could in fact use. Certainly, the impoverished and generally landless rural population that poured into the mills had few if any resources with which to evade the imposition of a more rigorous mill discipline.

The analysis in this entire section draws substantially from my "Labor Discipline, Trade-Unions, and the State in India," *Journal of Political Economy*, LXIII, August 1955, pp. 293-308. However, the analysis of discipline has been significantly modified by later thoughts on the subject. I have here been helped by the opportunity to use an unpublished manuscript by Ann H. F. King entitled "Rural Stagnation and Urban Discipline."

[5] Records indicate that groups of workers in individual departments and mills had struck in protest over various issues in the earliest period of the industry. By the end of the first World War we have the first cases of general, albeit unorganized, strikes in the Bombay mills. There were other general strikes of this sort in 1924 and 1925.

unilaterally to transform the labor discipline of the industry provoked in 1928 and 1929 nearly continuous strike and chaos. In one sense, this employer effort to transform working relationships came too late; the rise of working-class consciousness and the appearance of trade unions made unilateral action virtually impossible. In another sense, the long-run crisis that made it necessary to seek to transform the industry's disciplinary structure had come too early. It revealed itself just at the time that the mill hands were showing a new-found militancy, but before any independent trade unions could give to that militancy any strong sense of direction and discipline. Some employers in 1928 and 1929 publicly recognized that under the changed conditions no reorganization of the mill work system could be accomplished without the aid of strong trade unions.[6] However, these young organizations did not have enough time to develop the requisite authority. They could not create a large membership accustomed to working within the constitutional framework of western-style unions on which they modelled themselves.

The chaotic period between 1926 and 1934 clearly revealed the inability of the employers independently to impose the new and more intense labor discipline on which their survival depended. Similarly, the period illustrated the failure of unions to become strong enough to share responsibility in this matter. In the tumultuous, fear-ridden, and violent atmosphere of these years, the irresponsibly revolutionary demands of the Communist union played directly on worker hostility to the employers. The 1934 general strike, when viewed in connection with the general strikes of 1928 and 1929, showed one thing more: the ease with which the operatives could fall under Communist influence and be turned into a revolutionary political force threatening the very fabric of the social order.

Under these circumstances, the problem of labor discipline ceased to be a matter affecting the industrial vitality of a single industry in a single district. It became a matter seemingly threatening the state itself. It became obvious that in periods of tension the relatively new labor force responded to the agitation of any dynamic group or individual. But though they have been organizationally undisciplined, the cotton textile workers of Bombay are potentially the most effective political force in Western India and perhaps in the whole country. They are the largest single cohesive block of industrial laborers, representing something close

[6] Royal Commission on Labour in India, *Evidence*, Vol. I, Part 1, London, 1931, p. 482; Indian Tariff Board, *Cotton Textile Industry, 1934*, I, Delhi, 1934, p. 87.

to ten per cent of the country's total industrial labor force, and they are concentrated in a small geographical area where communications are excellent. As a result they have developed a sense of collective action perhaps not equalled by any other group in the land. The Indian National Congress recognized this; but in the general strikes of 1928, 1929, and 1934, the Communists were the first to exploit its implications. During the years before Independence both the Communists and the Congress sought to mine this quarry of potential political power in the service of their own objectives. The ideal vehicle for such a scheme being the trade union, the Congress and Communist activists sought to create effective unions the leadership of which would be under their control. This explains the early and continuous involvement of the unions in the political struggles for independence. It also offers partial explanation for the violent indiscipline of the labor force in the years after 1926. The Communists and the Congress, seeking mill-hand support, bargained irresponsibly and propagandized immoderately, trading on the hostility of the workers against their employers to create the forceful political weapon which each of them sought.

The situation did not change with the achievement of independence. The only difference was the addition of the Socialists as important contenders for support from the labor force. The cotton textile workers continued to be a political prize beyond all others. The groups out of power sought their favor in order to get power; the governing party sought their favor in order to keep power. Much of the financing of these cotton textile unions in Bombay came directly and indirectly from the political parties. Partly because of this political jockeying, unions failed to develop any stable power in their dealings with employers; but stable collective bargaining relationships were not, after all, the main objective of the leadership groups involved.

It was this struggle for control of so potentially powerful a group that led the British-dominated government of Bombay Province in 1934 to create a system of labor officers acting in lieu of trade unions, weakening the need for an institution so capable of being subverted to political ends. This is not to imply that the government of the day was antiunion. On the contrary, it was the purpose of the 1934 Bombay Trade Disputes Conciliation Act to ease working-class discontent by pressuring employers into minimum concessions to employee grievances, thus giving time for "responsible" unions of the western variety to emerge. However, this intervention has become steadily more insistent over the years, and it has given rise to a line of development relatively strange to western conceptions. 1934 marked the beginning of state direction of a sphere of activity which in the United States and Great Britain has traditionally been reserved to employers and voluntary associations of workers. For reasons in the first instance associated with social order and subsequently of increasing concern with the process of industrialization, the state in India has undertaken increasing responsibility for the character of the employer-employee relationship. As a result, the trade union role there seems increasingly to differ from that historically played by unions in our country.

Since the general strike of 1934 one of the major objectives of whatever government has been in power has been to create in the minds of the workers a sense of loyalty to the state. The policy of the Congress governments moved in search of the same object, a disciplined and loyal labor force, with techniques that differed only to the extent that they were more elaborate. Step by step, beginning in 1937, the Congress policy has been to impose on employers a uniform system of industrial law and to open for workers formal channels of protest as a means of reducing dissatisfaction and easing the violence of its manifestation.[7]

But the formal structure in itself was not enough. Unions were still too weak to take advantage of the new dispensation and develop independently the framework of collective bargaining from which a jointly determined labor discipline could emerge. No political advantage could accrue to the Congress government without stronger steps being taken. Consequently, the policy of Congress ministries since 1937 has also been to provide to the mill hands the substantive wage-welfare concessions which in western countries have traditionally been obtained through unions bargaining collectively with employers. Since that time every arrangement for keeping step with the rising cost of living, every significant wage increase, every annual bonus, every major standardization of work relations, has been granted through the agency of the state and as a result of the intervention of the state.[8] No genuine collective bargaining developed before the war; none developed after Indepen-

[7] The relevant legislation includes the Bombay Trade Disputes Act, 1934; Indian Payment of Wages Act, 1936 (including the appended Bombay Province regulations); Bombay Trade Disputes Act, 1938; and the Bombay Industrial Relations Act, 1946.

[8] Some of the relevant contributions of the state can be listed: wage increase recommended by the Textile Labour Inquiry Committee, 1938; the annual bonus and cost-of-living allowances informally imposed during the war and formalized through the Industrial Court after the war; the wage standardization scheme of 1947; the "decasualization scheme" of 1949, etc.

dence. The role of the state in shaping the wage-welfare status of mill hands has been strengthened and made more formal.

Where the state is preoccupied with retaining the loyalty of workers by periodical concessions to them, the function of the union as the prime mover of wage-welfare concessions vanishes or never appears. But the state cannot do without the trade union. The law of diminishing administrative returns (as well as ideological preconceptions) requires some such form. Having preempted the wage-welfare function, the state proposed to use the union as the device through which the labor force would be disciplined. In Bombay it has created a situation where only one union, closely linked to it politically, has the power of representing all cotton mill workers even though that "representative union" has not at any time been able to claim more than twenty-five per cent of the work force in its membership. This chosen instrument, supported by the Industrial Court, has become the organ through which the labor force is induced to accept official awards with a minimum of dissatisfaction and disruption. That this has only imperfectly been achieved is irrelevant. Controlling as it does access to the employers and to the official agencies which have ultimate power to dispose of grievances, the union has become the main channel through which all protest can flow. The authority of the union is reinforced by the power of the state to declare strikes illegal (in the case of illegal strikes, striking workers can be deprived of accumulated wages and benefits). And the state has shown its willingness to break strikes that threaten to undermine the fabric of discipline established by judicial fiat, as incidents in 1947 and 1950 specifically show.

There are other factors at work which have forced the state to seek to minimize the rough-and-tumble of independent collective bargaining between unions and employers. The governing party is committed, as are all the major parties, to a program of planned industrial development. It is unable to permit the luxury of sharp and extended conflicts between workers and employers, for to permit this might prove disruptive of all hopes for rapid economic development. Thus the state has been forced to regulate the settlement of almost all industrial disputes, determining by the fiat of its agencies the proportion of social resources to be transferred from industry to the operatives. In this regard, torn by conflicts between the requirements of economic development and social harmony, the state in India has perhaps conceded more to the labor force than is desirable in the interests of rapid economic development.

In considering this problem, one must realize that a backward economy undergoing rapid industrialization faces different conditions than do advanced countries. In the United Kingdom for example, the emphasis on labor welfare and social security measures came more or less at the close of the Industrial Revolution. In a country such as India, on the other hand, unless government provides for transfer of resources from capital to labor for welfare purposes, it is likely to lose the political support of a large section of the population.[9]

In part, the price has been paid in order to strengthen the long-run disciplinary capacities of the unions. It has been done to support the sort of claim made by the Bombay State minister of labor that "in Bombay [City] labor has always gained through methods of adjudication and there has hardly been a strike which has resulted in any substantial benefit to labor."[10] At the same time, the state in the guise of the Congress government has not attempted to force all workers into Congress-dominated unions. Other unions have achieved representative status in other industries, but the state in every case has retained firm control over the unions, viewing them as forces potentially disruptive of economic life. No union can achieve representative status unless it eschews use of the strike weapon and agrees to accept government intervention in all matters of importance.

The pattern I have described for Bombay has, for the same reasons, also manifested itself on an India-wide basis. Although few in number compared to the total working population, the industrial workers tend by virtue of concentration of force to be potentially the country's most powerful political group. Further, they occupy an absolutely critical position in a country dedicated to industrial development. Since 1946 an increasingly formal and officially determined pattern of labor discipline has been established on a national scale; at the same time the national government has become the arbiter of the wage-welfare benefits which flow to the labor force. Following the Bombay experience in the main, the Indian government is also trying to use the trade union as the handmaiden of national development objectives. The general philosophy is clearly articulated in the First Five Year Plan.

The working class performs functions vital to the maintenance of the community's economic life. . . . Labor will be serving itself best by the observation of greater regularity, discipline and meticulous care in the discharge of its duties. To ensure this, much greater attention must be paid to . . . a healthy

[9] C. N. Vakil and P. R. Brahmananda, "Reflections on India's Five Year Plan," *Pacific Affairs*, XXV, September 1953, pp. 254-55.
[10] Speech of S. H. Shah, reported in *Labour Gazette* (Bombay), XXXIII, July 1954, p. 1188.

development of trade unions so that workers are not exposed to exploitation and can act with a growing sense of responsibility. . . . In a system functioning on the basis of competition, private monopoly, or private profit the workers' right to have recourse to peaceful direct action . . . should not be unduly curtailed. . . . In an economy which . . . is organized for planned production and distribution, aiming at the realization of social justice and welfare of the masses, strikes and lockouts have no place. India is moving in this direction.[11]

There are those who have strongly opposed this line of development, favoring instead the creation of unions in the western image. Not least of these has been V. V. Giri, Indian Minister of Labor between 1952 and 1954.[12] Shortly after his appointment to office he stated his determination to revert to a system of independent bargaining between unions and employers. He proposed a revamped system of industrial relations in which he was opposed to "any courts at all." He argued that "undue spoon-feeding by the State cannot but retard" union growth.[13] But the momentum of the complex system created over two decades could not be halted and reversed. By the end of 1953 Giri admitted failure.

I have . . . come to the conclusion . . . much to my disappointment, that compulsory adjudication must continue to remain an important feature of labor-management relations for some time more. . . . We should avoid radical experiments for the present.[14]

And early in 1954 Giri's transformation seems to have been complete. He wrote at that time:

Trade unions should not merely pamper to the workers' demands, but must insist on their discipline inside and outside the walls of the industry and impart to them a sense of responsibility to do a satisfactory work for a satisfactory wage, especially today when the cry is for production and more production. The unions must make every worker understand fully his duties and responsibilities before rights and privileges.[15]

The "Giri approach" vanished virtually without a murmur from the country. When he resigned in September 1954, the *Economic Weekly* commented:

[11] "Draft Outline of the First Five Year Plan," *Labour Gazette*, XXX, August 1951, pp. 1280-82. For evidence that this view continues to dominate official thinking, see statement by the Indian Labor Minister, K. Desai, quoted in *Indiagram*, No. 702, May 19, 1955, p. 4; and the statement by Mr. Nehru, quoted in *Indiagram*, No. 87, May 8, 1956, p. 3.
[12] An outspoken statement from the nonofficial front can be found in R. P. Aiyer, "Future of Compulsory Arbitration," *Economic Weekly*, June 18, 1955, p. 756.
[13] *Labour Gazette*, XXXII, October 1952, p. 124; *ibid.*, April 1953, pp. 811-12.
[14] *Commerce and Industry*, XLI, January 13, 1954, p. 3.
[15] V. V. Giri, "Indian Trade Union Movement; Its Significance in World Problems," in Jagjivan Ram Abhinandan Granth Committee, *The Working Man*, Patna, 1954, p. 49.

What he had been fighting for was a lost cause, which had no active champions. This may be regretted, but it would be unrealistic to ignore the lines of development which have actually been pursued in the last few years . . . [Voluntary collective bargaining devices] have been duly incorporated in the corpus of labor laws, but they have been reduced to mere rituals and have ceased to be effective or alive. . . .[16]

Trade union developments in India move steadily in a direction away from the western tradition as we have known it historically. The state increasingly assumes the burden of distributing the social product and depends to a growing extent on the ability of the trade union to enforce the state's will. There are those who will deny that the lines of development in India are as I have sketched them. They will point to what seems a different line of development in Ahmedabad, one that has the quality of familiarity to western observers. However, the developments in Ahmedabad have been exceptional. Labor relations there have been profoundly influenced by the personal intercessions of Gandhi.

I wish I could be optimistic, but realists as we all are, it must be admitted that to reproduce Ahmedabad in other parts of the country, we must have the Ahmedabad inspiration flowing from that Great Soul, Gandhiji, who has worked up things so successfully. From beginning to end, it is all a question of personality.[17]

There is no other place where his influence was so strong nor where his memory has been so influential. Ahmedabad has been an aberrant development and there is evidence that its special characteristics are now disappearing.

[16] *Economic Weekly*, VI, September 11, 1954, pp. 1001-02. There is need for a careful exploration of policy statements on the subject of collective bargaining and its relation to democracy in India. It is my impression that there is, in fact, a substantial underlying difference between the voluntarist tradition of the West and the philosophic underpinnings that motivate Indian policy. If I am correct, there is less difference between the objective direction of Indian policy and Indian philosophy than I have suggested.
[17] Speech by G. D. Birla, April 8, 1937, reproduced in *The Path to Prosperity: A Collection of the Speeches and Writings of G. D. Birla*, ed. by Parasnath Sinha, Allahabad, Leader Press, 1950, pp. 396-97.

THE NONCONVENTIONAL
POLITICAL LEADER IN INDIA

JOAN V. BONDURANT

*I*N India there is a leadership element, political in intent and effect, which neither holds office nor manipulates machinery, which neither contests elections nor organizes a following. This is a leadership outside party circles, outside government. The tradition which characterizes it follows that of the greatest leader India has had—Gandhi, the Mahatma. The force of this extraparty leadership is not at once apparent to those accustomed to discover leaders in positions of established authority or in places of organizational control. But extraparty leadership has become in India a force to command attention in political analysis, and the emerging nonconventional leaders have become persons to be reckoned with in political calculations.

Acharya Vinoba Bhave and Jayaprakash Narayan are today the outstanding examples of nonconventional leadership in India. They have come from widely divergent backgrounds and each represents a special emphasis. Both are operating within the Gandhian tradition and both are fully aware of the Gandhian pattern. An understanding of the leadership complex which they represent requires an exploration of the characteristics which distinguish the leadership of Gandhi from that of other notable leaders of India. What, then, was the character of the appeal which established Gandhi as the unchallenged leader in a field rich with conventional leaders of great stature? In what way do these distinctive characteristics enter into the leadership of Vinoba on the one hand, and of Jayaprakash Narayan on the other? In exploring possible answers to these questions there emerges a suggestion for the role which nonconventional leadership may play not only in the dynamics of political processes but also in the structuring of political forms.

Several aspects of the leadership complex at once present themselves. In an initial exploration, attention is drawn to the type of personality traditionally characteristic of leadership in India; the social, economic, and political circumstance which gives rise to leadership; the ideational

JOAN V. BONDURANT is Associate Editor of the *Indian Press Digests* and a Lecturer in Political Science at the University of California, Berkeley. She was in residence in India during the years 1944-1946, 1947-1948, and also 1952-1953, at which time she held a Fellowship from the Social Science Research Council.

capacity of the following and the ideal apprehended by them; and the skills involved in communication, especially as they involve the successful manipulation of traditional symbols. I suggest that there is yet a further category required to account for the dramatic success which distinguished Gandhi as a leader and which characterizes the present nonconventional, extraparty leadership in India. It is upon this further component that the question of preeminence in leadership may well turn. But let us first examine the more readily analyzed elements in the Gandhi leadership pattern.

The test of a nation's "cultural background and its conscious or subconscious objective," Jawaharlal Nehru has said, may be found in the answer to the question, "to what kind of a leader does it give its allegiance?" In India, Nehru has told us, "the ideal has continued to be of a man full of learning and charity, essentially good, self-disciplined, and capable of sacrificing himself for the sake of others."[1] These qualities are, without question, taken to be characteristic of the nonconventional leaders of India—of Gandhi, the Great Soul; of Acharya Vinoba Bhave, often called Sant (Saint) and, to a lesser extent, of Jayaprakash Narayan, who has more recently chosen the path of extraparty leadership. It is widely held in India that the saint, who through a rigorous discipline resulting in non-attachment exercises full control of himself, is capable of commanding the universe. The human individual, it is believed, is part and parcel of a cosmic unity; and individuation—divisiveness—accounts for suffering and evil. The human being who realizes his identity with the universal being becomes all-powerful.[2] That the great soul and the saint should be recognized as persons worthy of following is, then, in the tradition.[3] Whether one regards Gandhi's reliance upon the "inner voice" as a tuning in, so to speak, upon the cosmic consciousness, or, in terms more familiar to the West, as a feeling of what the masses expected of him, Gandhi was called a mahatma and was regarded by many to be capable of great knowledge and great power.[4] He was, in

---

[1] Jawaharlal Nehru, *The Discovery of India*, New York, John Day, 1946, p. 62.
[2] Truths which such an accomplished one discovers and holds are achieved through individual effort, for within the reach of every human being is his realization of the fundamental unity. One of the difficulties in applying the Weberian concept of charisma in an effort to understand leadership within the Indian cultural matrix arises out of that part of Weber's concept which suggests that such a leader has powers of divine origin "not accessible to the ordinary person."
[3] For a note on characteristics of the creative role of the great leader in history, see V. P. Verma, "Critique of Marxian Sociology," *Calcutta Review*, June 1955, pp. 299-308.
[4] Louis Renou explains the "inner voice" in western terms in his stimulating article,

the Nehru definition, a leader whom India would follow not only because he was self-disciplined, full of learning and charity, and essentially good, but also because he was capable of sacrificing himself for the sake of others. Gandhi repeatedly endeavored to demonstrate this capacity through fasting and other forms of self-sacrifice; but, it is important to note, he used these traditional forms in nontraditional application to social and political problems.

What, then, of this Mahatma who entered upon the twentieth-century political scene in India? How did he differ from others in an expanse of saints? India has had a wealth of men full of learning and charity—the great *acharyas*, and the rishis of old, distinguished sadhus and men of philosophy. Can it, then, be said that Gandhi was to be distinguished from these others fashioned after the ideal-type, because he alone concerned himself with the social circumstance, with the economic distress of his fellow man, and with politics?

Of the several paths through which the devout Hindu may successfully attain self-realization, *karma-yoga*—the way of good action—has not been the most favored. However, in the process of impact and response to the virile social and political philosophy of nineteenth-century European liberalism, the value of looking outward as well as inward settled into the awareness of a sensitive elite. Social reform, political reform, and finally social and political revolution stimulated the thinking of a potential Indian leadership. The result was, to be sure, not uniform. As the external factors began to form in a manner which was to welcome if not to plead for leadership, there developed in India movements different in emphasis but similar in their embodiment of a response to the impact from alien forces. The Brahmo Samaj, the Arya Samaj, the Ramakrishna Missions not only undertook to reform Hinduism, but also advocated conscious effort in the realm of social service. Gandhi was not set apart through his concern for social welfare. For these essentially religious reform movements had their effect upon the social life of the country, and they had, as well, political implications.

That Gandhi combined religion with politics, that he introduced traditional, spiritual values into the social context, is not enough therefore to explain his dramatic success as a leader. The religious appeal of a Dayanand Saraswati—systematic, rigorous, meaningful—was clearly a more substantial appeal than the ever-changing spiritual offering of Gandhi.

"Gandhi and Indian Civilization," *Gandhi Memorial Peace Number*, ed. by Kshitis Roy, *Visva Bharati Quarterly*, 1949, p. 231.

Both the vigorous lead of the great Tilak, drawing upon religious classics, and the militant mystical appeal of the Bengali nationalists—whose political objectives were firmly based upon the spiritual appeal of Vivekananda, following Ramakrishna—had all the earmarks of charismatic leadership; and both did, indeed, succeed in establishing substantial followings. Yet, under circumstances ripe for the emerging of a national leader and in a field rich in potential leaders, it was Gandhi who captured the whole of India. Was it, then, the degree to which Gandhi introduced a service component into politics—a component which remains today an essential part of successful political programming—that distinguished Gandhi's leadership? Or, again, did the difference perhaps lie in the delicate articulation of the several components in his religio-political approach?

Gandhi's leadership did, without doubt, assume a significant interrelationship between religion and politics. The interrelationship itself became the essence of a concept. With Gandhi there was a quality essentially different from the cleric or the saint doing his bit in the political life of the times. The refinement approached a crystallization of both politics and religion. For, on the one hand, theology played no role, and on the other, manipulation of power was conceived in a strictly unconventional manner. Gandhi approached politics as a total consideration affecting the conduct of the citizen within his immediate group, the group within the larger group, and that larger group within the nation. Politics, for Gandhi, touched upon the entire fabric of an individual's external relations. So also did religion. For religion was conceived in the sense of a moral, ethical system with an inner meaning significant for the individual in terms of needs and predispositions: God, he said, is the atheism of the atheist. Gandhi's politics and his religion both turned upon social conduct. Religiously speaking Gandhi was the *Karma-yogin* par excellence. And into political considerations Gandhi introduced an ethical component which transcended and directed all other components. In this effort he differed at once from the conventional religious leader and the conventional political leader. Gandhi's creative leadership dealt with the whole of human relationships—it had a strictly humanistic emphasis. Humanism characterized the Gandhian approach but humanism—in many respects an alien philosophy—did not account for Gandhi's mass following. Indeed, the essence of Gandhi's humanism encountered as many negative resistances in the traditional culture as his leadership evoked positive responses in the field of practical politics.

The creative character of Gandhi's leadership appears the more remarkable as one explores further the rational humanism of his philosophy. The Gandhian approach is replete with departures from traditional interpretations. In an unending series of transformations Gandhi took traditional precepts, adapted them to the modern circumstance, and used them in the social and political struggle for objectives only recently established and, for the populace, poorly understood. The manner in which he did so bears upon the factor of communication in leadership. To be sure, few have understood the practical use of the symbol as well as did Gandhi. Gandhi spoke to the man in the village in terms he understood. He achieved this in a manner not strictly typical of charisma. For Gandhi identified himself with the lowliest and, through constant contact with village India in the mode of service and with the drama of symbol, he established his appeal. He went on to transform—and to create—values, objectives, programs, and in doing so carried with him a following greater than that of any other historical leader.

So Gandhi measured up to every test for leadership devised by analysts who establish classifications and assign labels: the personality was ideal, the circumstances were ripe, the objectives were fashioned from felt needs, the manipulation of symbols was skilled. And yet, can we be satisfied that we have now adequately accounted for his spectacular leadership? I suggest that there is yet another factor in the Gandhian leadership with which we should reckon. It becomes especially compelling placed alongside the success of contemporary leaders following in the Gandhian tradition—leaders less highly endowed than was Gandhi with other aspects of leadership, and leaders who operate within a situation less fertile for the establishing of a dramatic movement. To no inconsiderable extent this factor has determined why certain Gandhian leaders—and not others—have recently emerged into national prominence. The one most distinguishing characteristic of the entire Gandhian development is not the personality type, nor the dramatic use of symbols; it is not the transformation of values nor the designing of programs. What sets the Gandhian experiment off from all others is the philosophy of action which has infused it.

The key to the Gandhian leadership complex is the technique of action which Gandhi called *satyagraha*.[5] The peculiarly dynamic nature of Gandhian *satyagraha*—and I speak here of the total *satyagraha* concept—lies in its end-creating effect. *Satyagraha*, a technique for conducting

[5] I have tried to show that *satyagraha* is also the key to Gandhian political philosophy in my *Conquest of Violence: the Gandhian Philosophy of Conflict*, Princeton, Princeton University Press, 1958.

conflict, was presented as the tool whereby a revolution might be fashioned. The appeal to his countrymen Gandhi made in terms of action, and they followed him in the manner a people are wont to follow the commander of a popular revolution. Gandhi had everything for the making of a leader under the especial circumstances of his times. But he had something more. For implied in everything he did was a basic philosophy of action and this was to distinguish his leadership. Gandhi led a mass following to accept an over-all political objective (independence), an intermediary program of social welfare (the constructive program), and a new pattern of values. Each of these factors in its turn was conditioned by the operation of *satyagraha*.

Gandhi was a man of action, not a theorist. We can discern only the outline of a philosophy not fully formulated. Certain principles are apparent: nonviolence, relative truth, self-suffering. Certain criteria based upon a pragmatic humanism were in operation: "man the measure," the fulfillment of felt human needs. The mode of behavior was service and the proper embodiment in leadership, the *sevak* (servant). To what extent this further category—a philosophy of action—will necessarily be added to an adequate description of political leadership especially in the extra-institutional, nonconventional sphere, may depend upon analyses of future leadership roles. Yet when we turn to other nonconventional leaders in India, we already find this a useful, perhaps an essential, category in accounting for their emergence into leadership. For who could have predicted in 1948 that it would be Vinoba Bhave who was to share at least a corner of Gandhi's mantle, placed so firmly upon the worthy shoulders of Jawaharlal? Certainly, a "man full of learning and charity, essentially good, self-disciplined, and capable of sacrificing himself for the sake of others," but why, of many such potential candidates—so many Gandhians—Vinoba?

Gandhi had taken two objectives as his major goals. The first was *swaraj*—political independence—and this he worked towards with the technique of *satyagraha*. The second was *sarvodaya*, an ideal social order based upon nonviolence and envisaged in terms of harmonious, casteless, classless society with equal opportunity for all. With the objective of *swaraj* attained, the character of political action necessarily changed. Conventional modes were adopted and conventional institutions were further developed for the democratic governing of a people. The pressures were transformed and so, too, were the channels for dealing with them. The time for revolution appeared to have passed. There remained, in the Gandhian view, the second goal to be attained—the establishment of a *sarvodaya* order of society. The devoted band of constructive workers who, after Gandhi's death, chose to work outside the organized political life of the country, quietly promoted the Gandhian *sarvodaya* program in relative isolation.

But three years after the assassination, a movement emerged with a leadership which had the nonconventional characteristic which had marked Gandhi's leadership. A Maharashtrian constructive worker, Gandhian in orientation and experience, ascetic in inclination and achievement, fulfilling the requisite characteristics of a man Indians might follow, set out upon a mission which he clearly believed was his to fill following Gandhi's death.[6] Circumstances, he wrote, compelled him to "come out and be audacious enough to be an initiator" and this he would not have done had Gandhi been alive.[7] He had been trying, Vinoba said, "to find some field for experiments with non-violence since Gandhiji's death," and felt the need "to go out among the people and to wander about and see the country." He was "under the impression that in thus moving about I would be able to do some service." But the question "haunted" him:

What should be done to implement the fundamental programme of Bapu; how are we to achieve the social revolution, he envisaged, through Ahimsa? And finally I came upon the *chintamani* [talisman], which is now before you in the form of Bhoodan Yajna and Sampattidan Yajna.[8]

The *bhoodan yajna* (land-gift sacrifice) was inaugurated in April 1951. This movement of persuasion carried on by appeals to landowners to deed away portions of land for distribution to the landless has now extended through a series of corollary *dan* (gift) movements to include almost every class of possession. Land-gifts have been supplemented by gifts of wells and gifts of bullocks. *Sampattidan* (gift of wealth) has taken the movement into urban areas where donors are asked to make declarations of their income and to undertake pledges to use a percentage of this income as Vinoba requires. The ultimate gift, *jivandan*, is a life dedicated to the service of India's poor and devoted to the achievement

---

[6] Vinoba had won distinction during the 1940 "individual *satyagraha*" campaign when he was chosen by Gandhi to be the first to offer *satyagraha* and to court arrest. Jawaharlal Nehru was chosen to be the second such *satyagrahi*. "We were symbols," Nehru wrote in describing the campaign, "who spoke the mind of India in the name of India, or, at any rate, of a vast number of people in India. As individuals we may have counted for little, but as such symbols and representatives of the Indian people we counted for a great deal." Nehru, *The Unity of India: Collected Writings, 1937-1940*, New York, John Day, 1948, p. 396.

[7] Vinoba Bhave, *Bhoodan Yajna*, Ahmedabad, Navajivan, 1953, pp. vii-ix.

[8] *Harijan*, February 28, 1953, p. 445.

of *sarvodaya*. Of greatest political significance is *gramdan*—gift of entire villages. For it is in these villages whose lands are deeded over to *bhoodan* committees that the over-all *sarvodaya* order of society is being established under the direction of Gandhian constructive workers. It is here that the revolutionary character centers. Vinoba and his workers aim at the establishment of a stateless society.[9] They have inaugurated the decentralist village-rule which they conceive as a step in the direction of eliminating centralized state power. In so doing they have set themselves in conscious opposition to established aspects of their society: Vinoba, as the leader of this movement, fulfills this requisite of the Weberian charismatic leader.

The significance of the movements led by Vinoba Bhave extends beyond the five million acres of land which he has collected, the two thousand villages, and the wealth and equipment. The recognition of the political potential in this movement is everywhere in evidence. Political parties are vying with one another to become identified with the movement. The anarchist elements in *sarvodaya*, the challenge which the movement poses to the state both in theoretical implication and in the actual course of administration, are areas for political consideration. Most of the principal states have given legal support to Vinoba through *bhoodan yajna* legislation and several have endowed him with extraordinary powers.[10]

Upon examination of the character of Vinoba's leadership one finds that, in the Gandhian tradition, he has captured a following through establishing a technique of action. Just as Gandhi struggled to achieve *swaraj* through *satyagraha* and in applying his technique also conditioned the content of his ends, so Vinoba works towards *sarvodaya* through *bhoodan* and allied *dan* movements. Gandhian *sarvodaya* objectives have been approached through conventional means—through constructive work in village centers and, in some areas (notably Bombay State) through government programs—yet the objective and devotion to it were not enough to establish a national leadership. The distinguishing characteristic of Vinoba's success is the technique devised to press a movement. To what extent Vinoba's technique may alter his objectives remains to be seen. Certainly, as with Gandhi, the technique allows not

---

[9] For a detailed description and analysis of the *sarvodaya* ideal society, see Margaret W. Fisher and Joan V. Bondurant, *Indian Approaches to a Socialist Society*, Indian Press Digests monograph No. 2, Berkeley, University of California, 1956.

[10] For the text of the Vindhya Pradesh Bhoodan Yajna Act, see Fisher and Bondurant, *op.cit.*, Appendix VIII.

only for the revitalization of traditional values, but also for their transformation.

Vinoba, like Gandhi, creates new values for his followers in the course of reinterpreting classical stories by couching a new social ethic in terms reminiscent of the Vedas and by employing aphorisms drawn from the body of Sanskritic culture. "Brahmins, Rishis and Maharajas, used to keep themselves aloof and above the people," Vinoba told an audience in Hyderabad, "but Bapu's teachings have brought them all at par with their countrymen."[11] Like Gandhi, Vinoba attempts to refashion the traditional and to create from a traditional matrix values with social and economic implications. It was traditional, he pointed out, to make gifts, including donations of land, to religious institutions. But it is now, in the changed social circumstance, appropriate to give land as a gift to the landless.[12] Again, he explained, "we have to lay new norms of the duty of kshatriya," for the "duty of a kshatriya does not consist in making war but in preventing war."[13] Repeatedly, Vinoba calls upon traditional stories to illustrate—however strained the interpretation—a new approach with a social objective. The service-centered activity is placed within a religious framework. "The people are God," Vinoba wrote, and explaining where the religious duty lay, he added: "Those who wish to serve this God must give up their cosy hearth and home and go out and serve the millions scattered in our villages."[14]

The significance of *bhoodan* for dramatic mass action may be seen not only by contrasting it with conventional means for effecting social change—that is, means undertaken through established channels of government action or through constructive work institutions—but also by contrasting the homely philosophy in which the *bhoodan* appeal is couched with the systematic and erudite philosophy of such an inviting school of thought as that following Shri Aurobindo. Shri Aurobindo is an excellent example of a leader who early attempted to combine the spiritual and the political. Aurobindo Ghose withdrew from the action programming of the Bengali terrorist movement to establish an institution and a following based upon a philosophy aimed at realizing the life divine. Among the many striking contrasts between the Gandhian leadership and the Aurobindite leadership, perhaps the most fundamental is

---

[11] At Pochampalli on January 30, 1956, reported in *Sarvodaya*, March 1956, p. 299.
[12] In an address to constructive workers at Mathura (UP) on January 11, 1951, reported in *Harijan*, January 5, 1952.
[13] Reported by Dhirendra Mazumdar in *Harijan*, April 26, 1952, p. 80.
[14] In a preface to Narayan Desai's *Ma Dharatine Khole*, Baroda, Yadna Prakashan, n.d., reported in *Bhoodan*, April 18, 1956, p. 8.

in the approach to social change. Shri Aurobindo, in an admirable effort to reconcile modern science and technological development with the Vedantic tradition, presented an approach to philosophy which evokes "a spirit of evolutionary progress and calls upon the individual as well as the society to seek the higher consciousness of the spirit." One of the distinguished members of the Pondicherry ashram, Indra Sen, has decried the elevation of humanism over spiritualism which settled in upon the Indian approach during the past century. "The emphasis has shifted from Reality to man and, therefore, the significance of the contact of Reality to man has grown less." Dr. Indra Sen calls for a reassessment:

> Leaders of thought and life in India have during the last century uniformly represented a life-and-world-affirming outlook in place of the older life-and-world-denying one. But while in action we have adopted the affirming attitude, in inner feeling the denying attitude persists with a considerable force. This makes us divided within ourselves and weakens our acceptance of science, technology and the spirit of social progress of modern life. This calls for a proper philosophy to aid the necessary inner reintegration.[15]

The Aurobindites are critical of taking man as the measure.[16] They would substitute for mass social and political action as the testing ground of truth a reaffirmation and reemphasis of the absolutes of the inner life. Their reinterpretation of the traditional in India follows channels outside considerations of political leadership.

The manner in which Vinoba and the *bhoodan* movement reinterpret the traditional proceeds from assumptions grounded in humanism familiar to the West. Referring to the doctrine of Advaita, Vinoba remarked that "non-duality and service of humanity are complementary"; the power of Advaita, he said, "can become manifest through social service." *Bhoodan* is viewed as an instrument of social change and a challenge to other means for effecting social change. Not only is it a

---

[15] Indra Sen, "The New Lead in Philosophy," *The Philosophical Quarterly*, July 1954, pp. 98, 101.
[16] For a striking contrast to the Aurobindite position, see the stimulating article by P. T. Raju, "Activistic Tendency in Indian Thought," *The Vedanta Kesari*, October 1955. Professor Raju argues that there is a "need for a philosophy of man and of action, properly woven into the great philosophies which our ancient philosophers handed down to us." He finds a humanistic and activistic trend in the Mimamsa school of Indian philosophy. He concludes: "There can be no humanism without activism . . . man cannot act and think as matter only or as the Absolute only; he is the meeting point of both and acts and thinks with his bearing to both. And humanism must include both in its philosophy. There is a real need for this kind of humanistic philosophy of man, who has to live it and test it by life and action." (I am indebted to Professor William F. Goodwin for calling my attention to this article.)

challenge to Marxists, Vinoba recently explained, but *bhoodan* is also "a challenge to the Vedantists and men of God."

Change from within, it [*bhoodan*] says, is an illusion and an escape if it is unable to express itself in actual social relationships. It breaks the duality between Action and Thought, neither can exist separately.[17]

The dynamic quality of Vinoba's reinterpretations is realized in the course of prosecuting the *dan* movements. *Bhoodan* is a technique of action applied to the immediate problem of land redistribution and, together with the movements ancillary to it, is a means for approaching the end objective of *sarvodaya*. *Satyagraha*, precisely speaking, is a technique of action applicable in a conflict situation. *Bhoodan* does not in itself embody the range of Gandhian philosophy as does *satyagraha*. When Vinoba says, as he has on occasion, that *bhoodan* IS *satyagraha*, he suggests the wider reference of *satyagraha*. *Bhoodan* does not, of course, preclude the use of *satyagraha* as direct action in a conflict situation. Indeed, Vinoba has said on several occasions that he is prepared to resort to *satyagraha* as a technique if the *dan* movements do not succeed in promoting the establishment of *sarvodaya*. Action is, throughout, the keynote.

Vinoba's leadership is, then, similar to Gandhi's in the use and the transformation of tradition-reflecting processes of social and economic change. With Vinoba, as with Gandhi, the appeal has been direct to a mass following to whom is offered a technique of action. Conventional organization plays an even slighter role in Vinoba's movements than in Gandhi's. Gandhi used as his instrument the Indian National Congress. But his leadership was primarily that of a movement rather than leadership of an organization. Gandhi was not even a "four-anna" member of the Congress, as he enjoyed reminding his countrymen. Even when he was outside the Congress official hierarchy Gandhi was still looked upon as the party's "permanent super-President."[18] "It makes little difference," Jawaharlal Nehru wrote, "whether he is formally connected with the Congress or not":

The Congress of today is of his making, and he is essentially of it. In any event, the commanding position he has in the country has nothing to do with any office, and he will retain that dominating place in the hearts of the people so long as he lives, and afterwards. In any policy that might be framed he cannot be ignored. In any national struggle his full association and guidance are essential. India cannot do without him.[19]

[17] *Bhoodan*, June 13, 1956, pp. 1, 6.
[18] T. A. Raman, *Report on India*, London, Oxford University Press, 1943, p. 174.
[19] Nehru, *The Unity of India*, p. 122. At the critical Tripuri Congress in 1939 a

When the Congress acceded to power upon the advent of independence, Gandhi remained out of office, apart from and, Indians mostly agreed, above both party and government. After *swaraj* had been attained Gandhi urged that the Congress as a political party be disbanded. He wished to establish a new channel of influence—one which would eschew political power but would be in politics to guide and direct the government. "Under adult suffrage," he declared, "if we are worth our salt, we should have such a hold on the people that whomsoever we choose would be returned."[20]

Like Gandhi, Vinoba has built a movement. Even more than Gandhi, he has expressed a profound mistrust of organization. "I do not deny that a disciplined organization using authority to enforce its will has some power," he has commented; "it certainly has power, but not the power to produce good."[21]

However, as Vinoba extended *bhoodan* to include other aspects of constructive work and as the movement spread throughout India he found it essential to have some administrative body. The Sarvodaya Samaj, a society of those interested in promoting Gandhian ideology, was virtually without an organizational structure. The Samaj Vinoba described as "a free association of individuals whose guiding force in life is the Sarvodaya concept,"[22] and with this sort of association he has felt relatively at ease. But it was essential that the *bhoodan* movement have some operative organization. He began to make use of the services of the Sarva Seva Sangh. Whereas the Sarvodaya Samaj was conceived as an advisory body without discipline and without power, the Sarva Seva Sangh was a "well-knit" body with committee structures and officers.[23] Nevertheless, Vinoba's misgivings about organization extended even to the Sarva Seva Sangh. Early in 1956 he brought before *bhoodan* workers the need to make *bhoodan* "the people's own movement" and called

---

resolution was adopted recognizing the indispensability of Gandhi: ". . . the Congress regards it as imperative that its executive should command his implicit confidence and requests the President to appoint the Working Committee in accordance with the wishes of Gandhiji." *Report of the General Secretary, March 1939 to February 1940*, Allahabad, Indian National Congress, p. 2. The events of this session led to the resignation of Subhas Chandra Bose from the presidency of the Congress, and to his break with the party.

[20] Quoted by Louis Fischer, *The Life of Mahatma Gandhi*, London, Jonathan Cape, 1951, p. 525.

[21] Bhave, *Bhoodan Yajna*, p. 92.

[22] In his opening speech at the Chandil Sarvodaya Sammelan, March 7, 1953, as reported in *Sarvodaya*, June 1953, p. 269.

[23] The Sarva Seva Sangh with headquarters at Sevagram (Wardha), is the successor to the Gandhi Seva Sangh.

upon the Sangh to "decentralise the Bhoodan movement by divesting itself from the organisational responsibility of directing and financing the work all over the country."[24]

Vinoba himself is neither a member of the Sarva Seva Sangh nor does his name appear on the register of the Sarvodaya Samaj.[25] His extra-institutional leadership relies upon the direct appeal, the creating of *jana-shakti*—power of the people. He appears not to concern himself with responsibility, the accepted concomitant of power. He may use the services of the Sarva Seva Sangh, but he is prepared to supersede that organization. This characteristic of direct appeal, of standing outside the daily routine of control, is in the Weberian sense typical of the charismatic leader. "I am not going to take charge" of *sampattidan* collections, announced Vinoba, "nor will I shoulder the responsibility of managing and spending it and keeping the accounts," for, he continued, "I will remain free as always."[26] Again, true to the nonattachment ideal, Vinoba explained that he made "no egoistic claim" that he could solve anyone's problems.

That is why no worries disturb me at night and I go to sleep as soon as I lie down on my bed. I do my work throughout the day. Whether a day brings me four thousand, or four hundred, or only four acres, I am neither elated nor depressed. I sleep and work as king Janaka, and that is the reason for my being able to work day after day.[27]

Contrasting his own leadership with that of the conventional leaders in government, Vinoba again expressed the freedom which his own approach allowed:

I am sure were we to occupy the position and shoulder the responsibility which they do, we would act much in the same manner as they. Whoever occupies office and wields governmental authority must needs think in a narrow, cramped and a set circle. There can be no freedom of thinking for him. He finds himself, as it were, under an obligation to think and act as the world seems to be doing.[28]

How, we may ask, does the established authority in India view this leadership without responsibility? When considered together with its avowed objective of extinguishing present forms of government and reducing the state to a drastically limited role, such a development ap-

---

[24] *Sarvodaya*, January 1956, p. 253.
[25] Suresh Ramabhai, *Vinoba and His Mission*, Sevagram, Sarva Seva Sangh, 1954, p. 156.
[26] *Harijan*, November 29, 1952.
[27] Bhave, *Bhoodan Yajna*, p. 50.
[28] *Harijan*, May 2, 1953, p. 66.

pears replete with dangers. Subversion has perhaps nowhere been more baldly stated, nowhere more eloquently acted upon. Yet, is it possible to imagine Sant Vinoba being brought to book for un-Indian activities? Indeed, not only has established authority in India supported Vinoba by legislation facilitating his land collections, it has also allowed his movement quietly to collect a substantial proportion of all the villages in at least one district (notably in Koraput, Orissa). Pointing to the reconstruction of those areas by *sarvodaya* workers, Vinoba has challenged the Planning Commission to come down from New Delhi and to establish itself in village Orissa. The occasional alarm which is raised that Vinoba is being looked upon as a "superminister" is drowned by the supporting voices of the President and other high officials of state, including even that of the Prime Minister. The argument that Vinoba should not be specified by name as an agency recognized in legislation (as he has been in the *bhoodan yajna* statutes) is eclipsed by such statements as that made by Congress president U. N. Dhebar that:

. . . under the guidance of the two great disciples of Gandhiji, we shall march hand in hand and come closer to that picture of New India which Gandhiji dreamt and which Vinobaji and Panditji are working for in their own ways.[29]

In the exploration of this extraparty, extra-institutional political influence, attention is drawn to the Socialist leader Jayaprakash Narayan. Here is a man, schooled in party politics, experienced in organizational leadership, and devoted to the achievement of certain political goals. Following a gradual evolution in his political thinking which took him from a Marxist to a Gandhian socialist position, he entered into the *bhoodan* movement and, in 1954, offered himself as the country's premier *jivan-dani*—that is to say, he devoted his life to work toward the achievement of Gandhian *sarvodaya*.[30]

Whatever the other elements in the complex of motivation for this decision to leave party politics for a political life outside established channels, Jayaprakash was surely not unaware of its leadership potential. ". . . We must not forget," Jayaprakash has reminded us, "that on the advent of Swaraj, Gandhiji did not accept any power himself." He asked "Why?" and replied: "Simply because he knew that legal authority would not help him to establish such society as promised the good of all people, the Sarvodaya pattern of society."

[29] AICC *Economic Review*, March 1, 1956, p. 4.
[30] For a discussion of Jayaprakash Narayan's association with sarvodaya movements, see Fisher and Bondurant, *op.cit.*

Gandhiji was the greatest statesman India has ever known. Our politicians of to-day all learnt politics at his feet. But Gandhiji did not touch the ruling machinery even with a pair of tongs. If law could bring grist to the mill of the people he would have certainly accepted office. Law cannot be instrumental in changing socio-economic values or outlook towards life. That is impossible without a basic change—change at the root.[31]

When Jayaprakash likens the *dan* movements to Gandhi's breaking of the salt laws, he is suggesting a resemblance in technique and also a resemblance in the creating of leadership. Jayaprakash is clearly out to discover, as he has put it, "the new dynamics of social action which is not a by-product of Government policy." Indeed, at the time Jayaprakash dedicated his life to *bhoodan* he suggested that working together where "no partisan differences exist" might help, "in the context of the direct revolutionary and creative movement, to evolve a new political system."[32]

The revolutionary character of the Gandhian approach clearly appeals to Jayaprakash. As he moved away from the class struggle concept he moved toward Gandhian techniques including both *satyagraha* and *bhoodan*. "The creation of the stateless society begins here and now, and is not relegated to a remote and imaginary period in the future," he commented. "It is therefore a more revolutionary process that is more likely to reach the goal than the other processes."[33] Shortly after Jayaprakash dedicated his life to the realization of *sarvodaya* he established an institute patterned on Gandhian ashram lines to train workers in rural reconstruction. "I felt great need," he explained later, "of organizing intensive reconstruction work in some selected villages that may act as an example to other villages."[34] In this Gram-Nirman-Mandal (village reconstruction. "I felt great need," he explained later, "of organizing order of society are being trained. The potential influence which Jayaprakash may have upon the *bhoodan* movement cannot be overestimated. For Jayaprakash, a man with demonstrated appeal, established himself as a revolutionary leader during the independence struggle. The dynamic quality of *bhoodan* as constructive direct action, together with the eminence of *satyagraha* as a technique for conducting conflict were, it may be speculated, as appealing to Jayaprakash as was the *sarvodaya* objective.

[31] Suresh Ramabhai, "Jayaprakash–Bhoodan & Politics," *Sarvodaya*, April 1956, p. 337.
[32] *Sarvodaya*, July 1954, p. 8.
[33] *Janata*, December 27, 1953, pp. 3-4.
[34] *Bhūdān Yajna* (in Hindi) August 19, 1955 (translated from the Hindi).

Jayaprakash repeatedly says that he has not left politics but that he has left *power* politics. The question of leadership is not least among the many questions which arise when one considers the implications of a movement working towards a *sarvodaya* order of society. Where indeed will rest the locus of power in the villages whose lands are entirely vested in the *bhoodan* committees? The respective roles of *bhoodan* committee, the Village Panchayat, the local administrative officer will require defining and delimiting.

Congress President Dhebar, writing on the need for establishing new leadership in the village, suggests that it cannot "be created in a minute." "The old leadership in the village, ignorant of the fundamental change that is taking place in the relationship between man and man in India today, will linger on for some time." It would be necessary, Dhebar suggested, "to deal with the existing leadership in the village psychologically." This could be done, he said,

... only by a qualified body of persons who understand villagers who could with sympathy bring about the transformation. It means supplementing the leadership of the village. To expect this role from the District Boards of today would be assuming too much.[35]

The question of leadership, Dhebar explained further, was one of "assistance and guidance to the Panchayats with a view not to control but to convert." He then made this suggestive statement:

There must be a sort of non-official-cum-official agency whereby the resources of the State and of the village, as also the experience of all, can be pooled together in the service of the people.

The concept of guide has become a familiar theme both for those who look from government and party positions to Vinoba for assistance and for those who, reassessing the Gandhian leadership, are themselves part of the growing nonconventional leadership. Asked why he remains outside the government and why he does not take up administrative responsibility, Vinoba replied:

Those who are in the Government do not want us to do things which they are doing, but look to us for filling in if we can what is wanting in their work. We have to understand all this and bear it in our minds and devote ourselves to the kind of work which may create what I call *swatantra lok shakti* or the self-reliant power of the people. Then only shall we be able to render real help to the Government and real service to our country.[36]

[35] U.N. Dhebar, "On Village Panchayats," *Economic Review*, January 15, 1956.
[36] Bhave, *Bhoodan Yajna*, p. 86.

Again, Vinoba has recognized that "political power can be an instrument of service."

> That was why we sought it and accepted it and so long as the society needs it, we are not going to give it up. It is certainly an instrument of service, but not the kind of service which may be conducive to creating the conditions which will do away with the use of this particular sanction.[37]

The *sarvodaya* objective is a stateless society. But before the state does wither away—while society is yet being prepared to do without institutions of government—Vinoba is prepared to supplement the work of the government to achieve certain welfare goals. Were the leaders of *sarvodaya* to decide that government objectives no longer merited support but ought rather to be resisted, a conflict would be in the making. Vinoba has made it clear that he would not, under some circumstances, shun the use of direct nonviolent action. The government, he has insisted, will have to change as *sarvodaya* is approached through *janashakti*—power of the people. "I am sure that if Bhoodan develops in the direction of Gramdan, we would be able to transform the Government early," Vinoba has said. But, he continued, "suppose this were not the case and a clash does come, I worry little," for, he added, "I am not afraid of it because my method is of non-violence."[38]

Should *bhoodan* be supplanted by *satyagraha* in a situation of conflict the emergent leadership would be revolutionary in character. But in speculating upon future developments in nonconventional leadership, there is an even more suggestive possibility. If current trends should continue—with the government giving its blessings to the *dan* movements, with a new leadership developing in the *gramdan* villages, and with politically active workers entering into the several efforts to promote *sarvodaya*—could we perhaps witness the development of a new convention in leadership?

The idea of a class of leaders trained to live a simple, nonattached life is not new in the annals of speculation upon an ideal state. The suggestion that, ideally, society would be best governed by a class that does not want to rule but agrees to do so for the good of society has been advanced more than once in the course of centuries of man's reflection upon political processes and institutions. But a system of extraparty, extrainstitutional leadership, established through demonstration of sincerity, service, effectiveness, and direct appeal, and functioning as political con-

---

[37] *Harijan*, May 2, 1953, p. 67.
[38] Suresh Ramabhai, "An Interview with Vinoba," *Sarvodaya*, March 1956, p. 304.

science within a system of representative, democratic government, has not yet been formulated. Such a possibility lies implicit in the recommendations of Gandhi and the suggestions of those who currently reexamine the Gandhian experiment. "Banish the idea of the capture of power," said Gandhi, "and you will be able to guide power and keep it on the right path . . ."[39] Vinoba, advocating the setting up of a group which would keep strictly away from conventional power, suggested that such a group would be "composed of workers totally detached from power, devoted to ceaseless service, with unfailing adherence to the principles of right conduct and morality."

> They will serve the people and keep in touch with them through the service and disseminate among them the right kind of knowledge. The existence of a party of this type only will purify the administration.[40]

Shankarrao Deo, onetime general secretary of the Congress Party, writing in 1949, held that "sacrifice undergone for the realisation of an ideal" and "service rendered out of love that can alone inspire men," provide an ideological basis for leadership, but, he added, "there is a natural limit to men in power leading such a life":

> therefore, they must associate with or belong to an organisation, the members of which are required to lead such a life.[41]

At the time Shankarrao Deo wrote this he believed that the Congress could provide "the golden mean between the two principles of power and service," but four years later he resigned from the Congress and devoted himself to the *sarvodaya* movement.

One can only speculate upon the essentials which might enter into an extraparty, extragovernmental political leadership were it to become a convention in the political life of the country. Such leadership would, of course, remain strictly outside the realm of authority in the legal sense; it would be without limitations of office but also without the power which is based upon the ultimate sanction of the state's instruments of force. The person who could establish himself in the role of "guide" to government could do so only through demonstrating what is spoken of as "moral force." The type of personality that can successfully achieve this force is that of the nonattached man capable of self-sacrifice. Such a leader, I have suggested, cannot assure his success in capturing a mass

---

[39] Quoted by Louis Fischer, *op.cit.*, p. 525.
[40] Bhave, *Bhoodan Yajna*, p. 37.
[41] Shankarrao Deo, *The New Congress*, New Delhi, All India Congress Committee, 1949, pp. 47-48.

following without an adequate philosophy of action and a direct action technique. He would certainly understand the proper manipulation of symbols in communicating with his potential following. Such leadership would necessarily be creative. The personality, the philosophy, the technique, the skills of communication—these would be among the essential characteristics. The atmosphere is receptive in India for making conventional what I have called here nonconventional leadership. Whether or not this is a likely development, the concept itself may stimulate a range of suggestive questions. What, it should at once be asked, would this mean for the established power concept in political thinking? What dangers might not arise from continued reliance upon a leader-guide uncontrolled by positive law? What further meaning might it carry in terms of a sociology of law? And, perhaps most pressing among questions which arise, does such a possibility contradict the virtues of democracy?

That there are dangers in the use of force—whether moral or physical, legal or extralegal—is readily evident. Lord Acton's pronouncement on the corrupting nature of power warned of the "heresy" that the "office sanctifies the holder of it." In extra-institutional leadership corruption by authority is obviated. But what of the further point Acton so eloquently made: "Great men are almost always bad men, even when they exercise influence and not authority."[42] Were it possible to make conventional the type of leadership exemplified by Gandhi and by Vinoba, there would operate within it at least one built-in safeguard. For this influence necessarily derives from moral stature arising from the demonstration of nonattachment and capacity for sacrifice. A purificatory fast is no small undertaking. A fast to the death in sacrifice for a cause is substantial evidence of heroic quality.[43] Out of such experience, attachment to status, to power, even to righteousness becomes reduced to safe and containing limits. There is yet another safeguard in such a leader-

[42] In his correspondence with Bishop Creighton. John Emerich Edward Dalberg-Acton, *Essays on Freedom and Power*, Selected and with an Introduction by Gertrude Himmelfarb, Boston, Beacon, 1948, p. 364.

[43] In a stimulating discussion of the role of tragedy as it operates from the Greek drama to the social and political myth, Naomi Mitchison has suggested that a process of catharsis might supply "a solution to our problem about the tendency of political parties to become immoral." Continuing, she says that perhaps "no leader should be tolerable to the led unless he or she has made the act of acceptance, has experienced the change of focus . . . and is prepared if necessary to be the sacrifice . . . [the led] should insist on their leaders' personal preparedness for all risks, and should also insist on their being in a fairly constant state of catharsis—that is to say, of thinking and acting in the external field, because of moral reasons . . . this would be a very efficient way of stopping oligarchical tendencies in political parties, and, in general, of keeping them alive." Mitchison, *The Moral Basis of Politics*, London, Constable, 1938, p. 288.

ship ideal, a safeguard which lies in the very aspect which distinguishes it—the Gandhian philosophy of action. For the Gandhian leader places in the hands of his followers a technique not only for dramatizing and promoting his objectives, but also for resisting encroachment upon their own rights.

If a technique of direct action supplies the key to success in establishing extra-institutional leadership, it also functions to preserve the integrity of such leadership. For, in the ultimate instance, should the principle of nonattachment fail to effect an abdication of power, a following led by such a leader would have at its command the technique with which they could dethrone him.

6. PUBLIC ADMINISTRATION

DEMOCRACY and planning came to India together. The adaptations required in the leadership of administrative organs at all levels of government are discussed from a variety of points of view. An economist, Wilfred Malenbaum, examines the two five year plans along with their elaborate machinery for carrying out the plans in the states. Observing this same economic development process from the angle of the administrator, Merrill Goodall discusses the dependence of the Center on the states, and stresses the limited number of crucial decision-makers.

The effect of planning and community development upon the administrative structure of India is widespread. A. D. Gorwala, a former member of the Indian Civil Service, examines the dangers that may result from the growth of suspicion between administrative and elective officers. Focusing on the vital figure of the district officer, Richard Park surveys the changes that community development is bringing to district administration.

WHO DOES THE PLANNING?

WILFRED MALENBAUM

*I*NDIA has embarked upon her Second Five Year Plan. The new program builds upon the first: both five year plans are consistently and consciously related to the six year plan originally presented to the Consultative Committee of the Colombo Plan at its London meeting in September 1950. Indeed, the Indian chapter of that early program was the first major responsibility of the Planning Commission, created in March 1950. Key members and key officials of the commission at that time are still with it today. In some ways, the present Indian plans have also built upon a whole series of plans prepared in India over almost the two preceding decades under private, governmental, or mixed sponsorship. Both the reality of planning in India and the consistency of interest and effort over these decades are without parallel in the free world. In particular, the Indian performance stands in marked contrast to that of her Asian neighbours—notably Pakistan, Ceylon, and Burma—countries which one would think would have essentially the same inducements to plan.

The Indian five year plans are domestic products. There are today, as there have long been, literally hundreds of foreign experts in India—all to help the plan in one way or another. These are from the U N and its affiliated agencies; from foreign governments, like the U.S.A., Canada, U.K., U.S.S.R., Czechoslovakia, etc.; from foreign foundations and universities; from private business groups all over the world, etc. Some are official advisors to government or to near-official agencies. Some simply have close personal ties with key Indian political or governmental people. Some come for a few weeks or months; some have virtually become natives of Delhi. Many, if not most, of these foreigners have their say on India's problems, and perhaps to responsible government officials, at some stage of the plan preparation. But it is a safe generalization that every one of the foreign experts has been surprised with the official product. The plans have been prepared by Indians. Again, there are few parallels, at least in the free world. There are clear contrasts with the role of the U N particularly in Latin American countries, and

WILFRED MALENBAUM *is the Director of the India Project at the Center for International Studies, and Visiting Professor in the Department of Economics, at Massachusetts Institute of Technology.*

with the activities of more or less private foreign groups in such Asian countries as Burma and Pakistan.

The Indian plans clearly reveal the hand of professional economists and, I dare say, of other social scientists. This is revealed in their structure as well as in their language. Indeed, I doubt that there is any conceptual device, statistical tool, or theoretical argument known to economists anywhere which has not in some way been used, or mentioned, in the two five year plans. I do not mean to imply in the least that all or many economists would agree with the specific assumptions or estimates that play a role in the Indian program. But the Indian formulations clearly show that these people have given consideration to the very same elements that would any of the "best economists" in any land. Indeed, in *Sankhyā*, India's outstanding journal of statistics, Professor P. C. Mahalanobis has published what is perhaps as skillful an econometric underpinning for planning in India as exists anywhere.[1]

Hierarchy of Planning

Yet, are India's "professional's plans," or are they "people's plans"?

The Plan which is now presented to government for submission to Parliament is a result of the labours of large numbers of persons in the Central Government, in the States at various levels and leaders of thought and opinion in every part of the country. In its preparation, men and women in all walks of life have given generously of their time and experience. . . .[2]

This is a true statement. For the first plan, the time schedule made it necessary that the roots go down, in general, no farther than the state level. Work on the second plan, however, was formally initiated two years in advance. In April 1954, the Planning Commission requested the state governments to arrange for the preparation of district and even village plans, particularly with respect to agricultural production and rural industries, and cooperation where the commission felt that local initiative in formulating plans should be stimulated to the maximum extent. Apparently, this pattern was generally adhered to, and in all the states; village plans and district plans were prepared and formed some basis for the draft plans presented by state governments. Even if the contribution from these lower levels was small, the entire procedure provided opportunity for some public participation. In any event here

---

[1] "The Approach of Operational Research to Planning in India," *Sankhyā*, XVI, December 1955.

[2] Planning Commission, *The Second Five Year Plan*, New Delhi, 1956, p. 4.

was valuable training for both the rural people and the rural officials associated with development.

Simultaneously, preparation for the second plan was undertaken at state and central levels with the chief ministers and development commissioners appraising what needed to be done and, with the aid of the technical ministries, what could be done and what resources and procedures this would require. There were the inevitable and apparently endless rounds of discussion for reconciliation of district-state and particularly state-central differences. Such reconciliation is seldom straightforward: mute testimony of it in this case is given in a single table included as an annex in perhaps the first comprehensive draft of the second plan. Here appears a comparison of the recommended allocation to each state (as of the end of 1955) and the "up-from-the-bottom" estimate submitted by the state.[3] Less mute, I am sure, were the meetings held during the last six months of 1955 by the Planning Commission with the central ministers and with the chief ministers of the state governments. These meetings were paralleled by detailed discussions among senior technicians of the ministries and governments and, of course, the staff of the Planning Commission. The press provided a constant forum for the unhappiness of individual states with the recommendations of the commission. (Many of the states had published in book form their own original plans.) Nor did agreement need to be achieved only between the sum of state "needs" and what the Center could accept as a total; key functional reconciliations were also necessary. Thus, the same memorandum makes clear that the Planning Commission and the Ministry of Food and Agriculture had not yet achieved a common view on the increase in food output that could be obtained from the resource allocation to be made.[4] A comparable situation prevailed in other sectors, notably transport.

The merger of planning which starts from both ends is never easy,

[3] This was in the so-called "*Draft Memorandum,*" December 27, 1955, prepared to obtain the views of the National Development Council and the Consultative Committee of Members of Parliament. In this table, outlay "as proposed by the States," aggregated Rs. 5,741.2 crores; "as tentatively agreed in discussions with the States," Rs. 2,344.3 crores; "as included in the Plan," Rs. 2,214.0 crores.

[4] "*Draft Memorandum,*" VI, 5. The Planning Commission visualized an expanded capacity for foodgrains of 10 million tons; the Ministry of Food and Agriculture claimed that 1.5 million of these were double-counted, that the various development programs could only be expected to yield an increase of 8.5 million. The difference was not resolved; today targets for food output in the published plan are in such an uncertain state that a decision, "it is gathered, is one of the main questions awaiting the Prime Minister when he returns to Delhi in the third week of this month." *Hindustan Times*, (New Delhi), July 13, 1956.

no matter how carefully general principles and objectives are laid down to start. The reconciliation gives full play to technical argument: how much can the economy allocate to investment? how can it best be deployed? what will it yield? But at least as important is the interplay of various groups in the administrative chain of command, from village to district to state to the Center, and in the various levels of the Congress Party, the political organization of the present government.

Moreover, into each of these channels and at various levels there is injected a large number of suggestions of outside groups: the plans of the smaller political parties, of religious and professional groups. For the second plan, these ranged from proposals for motivation by the organization of sadhus to the detailed programs carefully prepared by large business groups and their representatives. Thus, the proposals made through the *Eastern Economist* and by the Federation of Indian Chambers of Commerce impinge upon the official planners at all levels, but particularly at the state and Center, and through all channels—the technical, governmental, and political—to which these groups have special access, given their wide and influential membership.

This entire panoply of popular planning was well revealed in India over the past year or so. Issues were publicly aired and debated in public meetings as well as in the full breadth of published materials. "Draft Recommendations," "Basic Considerations," "Comments," and "Draft Outlines" followed one another and were subjected to review by the full hierarchy of political groups and governmental administrations. Estimates were changed (e.g., the plan's size, as well as its components and output targets); policies varied (e.g., income ceilings, the role of heavy industry, emphasis on the small-scale sector). Eventually, there appeared in May 1956 the *Second Five Year Plan,* presumably the product on the one hand of these broad interchanges of a "people's plan" and on the other of the efforts of Indian economists, social scientists, and technicians, the essential contributors to a "professional's plan."

Staff responsibility for all these drafts is vested in the secretariat of the Planning Commission, and specifically with one Joint Secretary, Tarlok Singh. He ensures that reconciliations occur at staff levels, between state and Center, and among ministries; that such agreements are consistent with the policy from above; that drafts reflect these agreements, and so forth. Indeed, he does a good deal of the actual drafting and even more of the final writing. Outstanding in a service (ICS) of outstanding people, Tarlok Singh is most nearly "the author" of the second plan, as he was of the first.

Perhaps a procedure which somehow combines the votes of the specially skilled and of the people will yield some "best plan." Whether or not it will, the process in India is more apparent than real (and I imagine the same would be true if there were other countries planning over-all in this way). Tremendous credit is due India for retaining the semblance of this multiple interchange, and doing so in the candid hope that its educational benefit will bear fruit for future plans. At the moment, planning is at the top for the bottom. It must nonetheless be granted that there is a sincere interest in critical comment. Strong counter-opinions or counter-proposals which do make themselves heard are examined carefully and may influence actions taken—whether these proposals be from administrative or political leaders in the state, district, or village, or whether these be the views of private persons, businessmen, scholars, the press, and the like.

On the whole, a flow from the bottom can scarcely exist on any significant scale in a land where more than eighty per cent of the population is illiterate, where an even larger number may be only remotely concerned with the need for a development plan or program—to say nothing of a land where higher authority is traditionally accepted. The power of the Center is so great that at the planning stage (perhaps less so at the implementing stage) agreement will be reached reasonably close to the Center's position. Similarly, the roots of party organization in the Congress are still in the top of that organization! Nor, on the other hand, does India yet possess a large cadre of professionals with enough self-confidence to adhere to their technical positions in the face of strong popular or political opposition.

In these circumstances, Indian plans can only be the product of a group very near the top of political and administrative life. The group is small; it constitutes the governmental core of the Planning Commission. The chairman of the commission, the Prime Minister, is of course the key figure. His deputy chairman and his minister for planning constitute one part of the team; the finance minister and the statistical adviser are responsible for the economic and technical problems. While V. T. Krishnamachari and G. L. Nanda are two very different kinds of people, as are C. D. Deshmukh[5] and P. C. Mahalanobis, the individual

[5] T. T. Krishnamachari (not to be confused with V. T. Krishnamachari) now fills the two posts held by C. D. Deshmukh. Deshmukh's resignation as finance minister and member of the Planning Commission took place just after this paper was completed. He resigned not because of any issue arising in the conduct of his ministry, but because he could not go along with the government's decision to keep Bombay City out of the new state of Maharashtra. The "mechanics" of his resignation, perhaps among other things,

differences in each team tend to merge in the distinct roles that each pair plays. Nor can there be any question that the Prime Minister not only arbitrates the alternatives which flow from the two sides, but that his overriding person can make "agreement" where the issues have not actually been resolved.

Planning Leadership

Despite other preoccupations, the Prime Minister keeps his hand in at the commission; he did so particularly during the years when the second plan was being formulated. Perhaps no other head of state has identified his national activities so fully with an economic objective. However removed he personally has been from want,[6] Nehru appears to appreciate the human importance of injecting some upward movement into India's static economy. It is also true that since 1952, if not earlier, planning has been central to Indian political life, perhaps more so than to her economic life. Nehru is clearly India's top politician. Progress on the plan—nationally, regionally, functionally—is an excellent political point of contact with the people. The plan thus plays a key role in the Congress Party and in elections. Nehru is well aware that the maintenance of his key international role requires progress on India's economic front, and he is conscious of time's importance in this regard, given Chinese developments. At the same time, Nehru increasingly reveals a grasp of the economic problems of the plan—better indeed than the plan itself reflects—as can be seen from his comments on the role of agriculture in an industrializing India in his presentation of the first plan to Parliament in December 1952, and his analysis of the employment multiplier in an overpopulated economy in his presentation to Parliament of the second plan in May 1956. His realism on Indian development is well illustrated by his statements on the possibilities for atomic power in a country like India which is in the "cow-dung stage." It is the efficiency of use of this animal by-product that can measure India's near future economic prospects.

---

actually precluded his remaining in a position close to Nehru. Deshmukh is at present the chairman of the University Grants Commission. Pending more knowledge of T. T. Krishnamachari's performance in his new roles, the present paper should be considered as "Who *Did* the Planning?"

[6] And however oblivious he sometimes seems of the poverty about him: he was quite surprised to discover the slums of Delhi, and immediately took action to begin to improve their housing and sanitary conditions. It seemed: "Why didn't someone tell me of these things?" His immediate reaction was "Burn them down." *Times of India* (New Delhi), April 2, 1956.

WHO DOES THE PLANNING

Intimate though the Prime Minister may be with the political and economic facets of India's planning, major responsibility for operations in both these fields must be in other hands. Nanda, the Minister of Planning, Irrigation, and Power perhaps comes closest to supplying the continuity for the political aspects of the plans; Deshmukh, when he was minister of finance, had the comparable role on the economic side. Both men had been on the Planning Commission from its creation in March 1950, with Nanda initially the deputy chairman. V. T. Krishnamachari now holds this position. His background differs greatly from his predecessor's. Nanda was associated with the labor movement in the Ahmedabad textile industry. He had worked with Gandhi in the independence movement from 1921 and is invited to the Congress Working Committee meetings. I am not certain that "Sir V. T." is even a party member: he does not hold a seat in the Parliament. Long the prime minister of the princely state of Baroda, he became recognized as a distinguished administrator. These talents are much needed in a commission responsible for preparing a plan when the functional specialists of government are in the various ministries. Krishnamachari is said to be a skillful chairman and "integrator" of groups in which key figures hold very different views. However unlike these two men are—apparently in temperament as well as experience—I think it is appropriate to consider them together as the prime members of Nehru's team. Krishnamachari has administrative responsibility for getting a "cleared" plan out; one of Nanda's major tasks is to assure the political acceptability and attractiveness of the program. Deshmukh, in his joint capacity as member of the Planning Commission and minister of the key department of government,[7] was responsible for a tremendous store of information which is basic to planning in India; he also had the best economic staff in the government—undoubtedly the most capable group in the country. In J. J. Anjaria, who served him both as the chief of the Resources, Economic Survey and Finance Division of the Planning Commission and as economic adviser to the Ministry of Finance, Deshmukh had an outstanding technician capable both of effective direction of a research staff and of masterly presentation of their product to top government and to the public.

As honorary statistical adviser to the Cabinet Secretariat and as direc-

---

[7] In India, the Finance Ministry has also the budget function. This operation penetrates so deeply into all other ministries that in some countries, like the U.S., the function becomes one of the key activities of the office of the head of government. Under Deshmukh, the ministry fully exercised this over-all function.

tor of the expanding Indian Statistical Institute, Professor Mahalanobis has played an increasingly important role in Indian planning. In November 1954, his institute—a private organization working almost entirely on government contracts—was given responsibility by the Cabinet and the Planning Commission for the preparation of some comprehensive studies of technical and statistical problems relating to national planning. His institute is in charge of the National Sample Survey—probably the most comprehensive collector of statistics on a sample basis in the world. With measurement of developments in unknown India so intimately his responsibility and with some of his outstanding younger men in key positions in government (Pitambar Pant as private secretary to Nehru in his Planning Commission post, and Mani Mukherjee as chief of the National Income Unit), Mahalanobis is in an excellent position to serve as the other member of Nehru's economic and technical team, which is responsible for the arithmetic of the plan.

Both Mahalanobis and Deshmukh were originally trained in the natural and physical sciences. However, Deshmukh had his advanced education in England, joined the ICS, and after a distinguished civil service career became governor of the Reserve Bank of India. Western-oriented, his international reputation is that of a "sound banker." In tone and in substance, his addresses at annual meetings of the International Bank, for example, might have been those of his U.S. opposite number or of any other minister of finance in a well-developed capitalist country. His capable (some would add "conservative") policies restored and subsequently maintained financial stability from the very beginning of the first plan. This same type of policy may also have helped achieve in India a lower over-all total of investment over the five years than resources available to her would have permitted.

Mahalanobis attained an international reputation (FRS, chairman of various U N committees, etc.) as a physicist, mathematician, and statistician primarily on the basis of his professional work in India.[8] Indeed, it was this eminence, and not any record of government service in India, which preceded his designation to high posts in the newly independent nation. Although some of his early statistical work did concern the parameters of the Indian economy, it was probably not until the late 1940's

---

[8] There is little evidence that he had much personal interest in the achievements of the West. In the artistic field, for example, he was closely associated with Rabindranath Tagore over a long period of years, and is said to know more than anyone else of Tagore's writings, music, and paintings.

that he became absorbed in the statistics of India. He served then as chairman of the National Income Committee, and from then on, the ISI, which he has directed since its establishment in 1931, has become increasingly concerned with data pertinent to econometric analysis of the national economy.

It is generally recognized that both men are primarily concerned with technical and scientific aspects of the planning problem. Thus prohibition to Nanda may be the fulfillment of a Hindu and Gandhian tenet; to Deshmukh and Mahalanobis it is the possible annual loss of a number of crores of revenue needed for public investment. Yet, they are frequently contrasted as men whose instincts and convictions pull them in opposite directions of the present cold war. The professor is said to be an advocate of "physical" planning, while the minister advocates a "financial" emphasis. It is certainly true that some of the apparently abundant resources of the ISI have been used to bring to India outstanding economists of the "planned economy" countries, or others from the West with similar orientations. Deshmukh, on the other hand, has had most of his few foreign advisors by courtesy of the U.S. Technical Cooperation Mission.

To this observer, these contrasts seem exaggerated. The Mahalanobis pen sometimes does write as though his "planned economies" are almost by definition more efficient in the use of resources; he does not consider fully the "loss" that might occur if the plans were implemented in the relatively free Indian way. The finance minister did go along with policies on private taxation which appear overly *generous* to the investment that takes place in that sector, given India's factor endowments. If these observations are true, there is also good evidence that Deshmukh moved somewhat the other way on nationalization, for example, and that Mahalanobis has discovered that the performance of his recent western advisers seems to be more useful for Indian planning (to say nothing of being more scholarly?). An appropriate relationship between the physical and financial approaches is well set out in the Second Five Year Plan. And there is every reason to believe that the famous Mahalanobis "Plan Frame," so helpfully injected into India's planning scene in March 1955, was fundamentally a joint effort: his plus that of Deshmukh's economic groups. There is little evidence, substantively or administratively, that the ISI staff, the NSS results, or the work of his "eastern" foreign advisers, played any substantial role.

ECONOMISTS AND THE PLANS

Is this team—with people of such exemplary qualifications and under the leadership of the Prime Minister himself—apt to develop a plan in which the political requirements and objectives are realistically moderated by the technical and economic potentials? I think the answer is negative, and that this is borne out by the experience of the last few years, the period of preparation of the second plan. Political and administrative considerations were dominant, economic realities notwithstanding. This situation may stem from the strength of one part of Nehru's team; it certainly reflects a serious weakness on the technical side.

Not that the political objectives were so clear and consistent. Indeed, the plan is filled with attractive combinations, although many of these could be consistent only under special circumstances. One illustration is income equality plus a wide spread of cooperative organization on the one hand and rapid economic progress on the other. Another is a modern and growing industrial sector—perhaps taxed to assure the maintenance and expansion of more or less self-sufficient villages. The plan speaks of individual sacrifice and extra effort, but the tax burden remains relatively low and the program does not organize non-money contributions. Finally, the plan seems to be a bargain: there is an increase in income which is large relative to the extent to which people are expected to invest their income rather than consume it.

These problems, one would think, lie precisely in the area where the economist can inject realism and can indicate the conditions under which certain objectives might be achieved. On such basic problems as capital/output ratios, employment effects of investment, interdependence of the sectors of the economy, the sources of domestic savings for investment, and more, the plan is casual, to say the least. And this despite the extensive technical structures which head up to the finance minister and to the statistical adviser. Despite the vast apparatus of the sample survey, there is little significant analysis of Indian performance during the First Five Year Plan.[9] Rather, the argument on most of these points proceeds

---

[9] Anjaria's staffs are primarily operational, not research. Indeed, there appears to be a dearth of research personnel in the Ministry of Finance—to say nothing of the Planning Commission, which presumably "coordinates." With respect to the sample survey, there is a wide interval between data collection and availability—with analysis very much later, if at all. Thus, the tenth or eleventh sampling round is now in the field, (July 1956) but the data of the *fourth*, collected April-September 1952, are not yet available. A survey of unemployment in middle-sized cities was conducted in the fall of 1953; results were published in June 1956. The comparable survey of Calcutta for large cities, made at about the same time, is not yet released. Preliminary tabulations of

from a broad, unpointed drawing from experience elsewhere—Europe, Russia, the U.S., etc.—with too little attention to the basic differences in these situations.[10]

The true story on the reconciliation process within Nehru's team is, of course, not available.[11] But a careful observer, although outside, must conclude that the adjustments in the long planning process were primarily in one direction. Thus, the "conclusion" on the last page of the Second Five Year Plan refers to the doubts on some of the above matters just injected by K. C. Neogy, another member of the Planning Commission. But the plan is presented despite these key doubts. Or consider the deputy chairman's observation, when the plan document was already printed, that the same investment in agriculture, India's basic and largest industry, could and should yield an increase in output more than twice that projected in the plan. This from the top of the Planning Commission—after two years of preparation, study and reconciliation of views!

One also wonders why Indian economists not in government service have failed to protest vigorously to this course of developments. The "Panel of Economists," officially constituted by the Planning Commission to advise with respect to the preparation of the plan, contains the leading economic figures of India. They have had an opportunity to present policy proposals and to give their views on the general lines being considered by government. They have been invited to make research contributions for the plan.[12] Indeed, through the Research Programmes Committee of the Planning Commission, university economists are given ample research resources by government with the pre-

---

both surveys were given to key officials in late 1955. But these surveys contain information of basic importance to one of India's key problems. My own observations suggest this is less a staff than an organization problem.

[10] Admittedly, these are not black or white matters. Views on them are bound to differ. Somewhere, therefore, the plan needs to state realistically and convincingly the basis for its conclusions on these key problems.

[11] It would be interesting to know how Nehru himself stands on these issues. The political considerations are always current and perhaps therefore of first importance to him. On the other hand, the Prime Minister's public statements frequently suggest a clearer appreciation of the economic limitations of planning in India than is reflected in the Second Five Year Plan.

[12] Much of this work was released by the Planning Commission in October 1955. See Panel of Economists, *Papers Relating to the Formulation of the Second Five Year Plan* (Delhi, Planning Commission, 1955). It should be mentioned that two Indian economists have in fact reflected some disagreement with the plan formulations at an early stage. See in particular, the "Note of Dissent" written by Professor B. R. Shenoy of Gujarat University in April 1955 (published in *The Second Five Year Plan: the Framework*, New Delhi, Ministry of Information and Broadcasting, 1955), and the article by B. K. Madan, "Some Aspects of the Draft of the Draft Plan-Frame," *Reserve Bank of India Bulletin*, September 9, 1955, pp. 964-72.

cise objective of their pursuing studies that would help in this advisory function. Almost overnight the classic problem of the university economists—shortage of research funds—was replaced by a plethora of funds. University professors protested against the pressures to take on more research; the faculties were becoming business administrators.

All this notwithstanding, some basic economic problems of the plan have yet to be assayed by the professionals—despite the resources already allocated to the ISI, government departments, and the universities. This fact (or this hypothesis) warrants more discussion. It can only be touched upon very briefly and generally here, but it is due to the following factors:

India's leading economists are very busy. Top university men, because of their heavy academic and public advisory responsibilities, have schedules which do not permit their own devotion to study and research on India's current problems.

There is among Indian economists relatively little knowledge about the economy of India. Many have been trained abroad or have, by and large, been educated in India by professors and in a discipline which stresses, apart from theory, the economic experience of the more developed parts of the world. It is from these areas that new advances in the subject seem to come and where extensive documentation can be found. Only within very recent date—and partly with funds from the Planning Commission—have eyes been turned toward the structure and relationships of the Indian economy. The number of these research undertakings completed has been relatively small. There is some evidence that extensive surveys are not yielding meaningful results—partly because the hypotheses being investigated are apparently inappropriate to the Indian situation.

The Indian economist is a great admirer of the more developed countries. Despite their insistence that they are to do things "their own way," it is hard to admit that an Indian way may in fact be different from the admired ways of the richer countries.

Leading Indian economists are held in high public esteem. There may be an unwillingness to admit how limited is the basis of their understanding of India's basic economic structure.

In these conditions, the panel of economists prefers to contribute to "basic considerations" rather than basic facts or basic relationships. About one year ago, when I mentioned to one of India's outstanding economists that my investigations suggested that the Plan Frame was based on a rather low capital coefficient, he made it clear that to him this was not an area for investigation by university economists. This is quite a different view from that which we hold in America, despite the fact that the relevance of this ratio to our economic situation is much smaller.

This situation—the apparent default of these professionals—must be looked at in perspective. It is not likely that intellectual elites of any land could be expected to have greater self-confidence, given the background of colonialism crowned by a decade of independence during which theirs was one of the backward, poor, underdeveloped areas of the world. The striking thing is that so much is happening on the planning front in India—again in such sharp contrast to developments elsewhere.

Moreover, there are signs of a birth of interest in the study of Indian developments. This was the keynote of Professor Ganguli's presidential address to the Indian Economic Association in December 1955. He particularly stressed the barriers between economic classes which impede mobility and growth. His theme will be carried further in the papers prepared for the next annual meeting. Increasingly, too, the subjects which are being pursued under the Research Programmes Committee have greater relevance in this regard. Particular mention might be made of urban-rural relationships, and of capital coefficients for enterprises of different size and over time. India's economic press has also been placing increasing stress upon the need for more empirical analysis and upon a greater role for the expert in the planning process.[13]

In a real sense, time itself must yield a corrective. India is in its second plan. It is in process of testing the results of the first. Over the next few years, actual developments in the economy will make clear the technical requirements for such a program. One can also expect this experience to make possible a more complete assessment of the process of initiating economic growth in the mid-twentieth century. And one can hope that Indian economists will be the interpreters of that process to the rest of the world.

[13] See, for example, the various publications of the *Eastern Economist* (New Delhi), and of the Indian Institute of Public Opinion, which is associated with it. One can raise serious questions about the validity of some of their analyses, but the objective is a good one. See also, "Who Does the Planning?" *Economic Weekly*, June 23, 1956.

ORGANIZATION OF ADMINISTRATIVE LEADERSHIP IN THE FIVE YEAR PLANS

MERRILL R. GOODALL

*P*LANNING for economic development goals has a strong hold on the imagination of people and government in India. The economic plans which were so highly publicized in the years just preceding Independence were expressive of rising popular expectations, of the revolution of demand for rapid economic development. Before the transfer of power in 1947, however, Indian interest in planning was inevitably confined largely to the recommending of basic policy decisions, to statements of broad objective, and only incidentally with the administrative needs or consequences of policy.

That Indian interest up to Independence was concentrated on matters involving fundamental value judgments and not the means of implementing them is understandable. Proposals for development encountered impressive political and constitutional hindrances. By the early 1940's, to cite but one illustration, Indian publicists—on the force of TVA's example, among others—had made a number of proposals for the development of land and water resources on a regional scale. These proposals treated the river valley as a unit and sought to explore the fullest and interrelated uses of such natural regions, irrespective of the political-administrative boundaries which cut across them. Ministries of the central government, organized under the Government of India Act of 1935 and predecessor legislation, lacked the constitutional authority that regional planning and development of this type required. Irrigation and canals, water storage, and water power fell within the jurisdiction of the provincial governments, and none of the provincial governments possessed the needed technical or personnel resources, much less the capacity to plan cooperatively with a neighboring province or state.[1]

MERRILL R. GOODALL is Associate Professor of Asian Studies and Government at Claremont Graduate School. He was Visiting Professor at Delhi University while in India from 1951 to 1953 on a Fulbright Fellowship and as a Fellow of the Social Science Research Council. In 1954-1955 he directed the Cornell-Lucknow Research Center and was Visiting Professor at Lucknow University.

[1] For developments up to 1945, see Merrill R. Goodall, "River Valley Planning in India: The Damodar," *Journal of Land and Public Utility Economics*, XXI, November 1945, pp. 371-75.

While the theory and practice of administration for country-wide development goals were but little advanced in the years up to Independence, certain beginnings were made toward some of the basic research such planning must necessarily draw upon. Private associations and educational institutions contributed more prominently to the flow of administrative and development-minded information than did government itself. Publications of the Gokhale Institute of Politics and Economics supplied a number of down-to-earth but academic-level studies in Indian economics. A few universities, notably the University of Bombay, published doctoral theses of unusual competence in economics; indeed, several of their authors now occupy strategic teaching and governmental positions. But the administrative implications of these studies were not spelled out and there is no evidence of substantial interchange, government to research institutions. The few persons professionally engaged in the study of administration were little disposed to investigate the administrative relations of development planning, particularly so when they doubted that a development program was actually in sight. No collegiate instruction in either public or business administration was offered anywhere in pre-Independence India. The descriptive spadework was taken on almost singlehandedly by one Bombay organization, the Local Self-Government Institute, which was established in 1927. The voluminous published directories and manuals of the institute covered such subjects as municipal finance, accounts, auditing, and law, and were designed to assist the officer of the municipality or district local board.[2] Subject matter for these studies, however, stopped short of development issues.

Administrative planning, of course, was carried on throughout the country's governmental structure. But the goals of governmental planning were not convincingly development goals to majority Indian opinion. Where research for planning was conducted (as in the Central Board of Irrigation and the Board of Scientific and Industrial Research from 1940) it was of an exclusively engineering nature and of a type consistent with traditional or normal classes of governmental operation. In this respect, governmental engineering organizations followed a pattern of interest strikingly comparable to that of the Army Corps of Engineers in the United States. In any case, few of the administrative reflections of government were available publicly; and not until the post-Independence years did such distinguished administrators as, for exam-

[2] See the *Quarterly Journal of the Local Self-Government Institute*, which began publication in 1930.

ple, A. D. Gorwala, produce interpretative materials on the administrative process they knew and served. And only recently has government itself been moved to exchange administrative thinking with persons and groups outside the secretariat.

Administrative traditions change slowly and today's decision is often an outgrowth of yesterday's. The themes already briefly identified—the political demand for development; the extent of provincial autonomy where development choices were to be made; and the absence of a sound descriptive basis for development programming—appear prominently in postwar administration of economic affairs.

In response to the first of these—the political demand—a Planning and Development Department was established by the central government in 1944. This department was terminated in 1946, but during its brief existence, it had invited the provinces to submit plans of development and, moreover, had promised central financial assistance in support of the plans. Various separately conceived provincial plans were soon inaugurated—the greatest expenditure being in agriculture and irrigation—and these were financed mainly by central grants and loans. From 1946-1947 to 1949-1950, in illustration of the extent of this central commitment, well over half of the funds spent in support of provincial development programs were supplied from the Center. In a few provinces, the programs were almost wholly underwritten by central loans and grants; 84.2 per cent of Assam's development finance and 99.4 per cent of the Punjab's came from the Center.[3] There were Center-initiated projects, as well, in the postwar years before 1950, in which year the Planning Commission of the Government of India was established and a general assessment of the divergent plans first became possible. By 1950 major irrigation and power projects alone had incurred since 1947 expenditure of about Rs. 153 crores; probable cost on completion was estimated at Rs. 765 crores. The First Five Year Plan, as it finally emerged, indicated an expenditure of Rs. 518 crores on irrigation and power projects already under construction; new projects were allotted but Rs. 40 crores.[4]

If the activity of the first few postwar years had the effect of committing present and future central funds, it also led to the creation of new administrative forms for the conduct of the new programs. In 1948,

[3] From Table 14, "Finance of the State Development Programmes, 1946-47–1949-50," in Ursula Hicks, *The Public Finances of India*, New Delhi, 1950, (mimeographed).
[4] Government of India Planning Commission, *The First Five Year Plan–A Summary*, New Delhi, 1952, pp. 74-75.

the central legislature established a public corporation, the Damodar Valley Corporation, which was charged with region-wide development responsibilities in the two states of Bihar and West Bengal, both of the states being represented in the corporation. The DVC Act bears resemblance to the TVA Act of 1933. Another river valley project, the Bhakra-Nangal, was financed and undertaken by central ministries in association with the Bhakra Control Board, an agency representative of the Punjab, Rajasthan, and PEPSU (Patiala and East Punjab States Union), Himachal Pradesh, and the Center. The third of the great river valley projects, the Hirakud, in Orissa, was undertaken by the Central Waterpower, Irrigation, and Navigation Commission in 1949.[5]

Other complications were given the growing financial and administrative pattern by the events of partition and the continuance of strong inflationary currents. Partition led to new financial burdens, put new strain on existing administrative resources. Rising price levels forced new estimates of construction cost on the projects already begun.

In these circumstances the Government of India, in March 1950, appointed a National Planning Commission to assess the available resources, formulate a plan for their utilization, determine priorities in respect to programs of development, appraise the progress achieved in each stage, and determine the nature of the machinery of implementation.[6] The 1950 declaration of government which created the Planning Commission is worth noting:

The need for comprehensive planning based on careful appraisal of resources and on an objective analysis of all relevant economic factors has become imperative. These purposes can best be achieved through an organization free from the burden of the day-to-day administration, but in constant touch with the Government at the highest policy level.[7]

As set up in 1950, the commission had no action or executive responsibilities; its role was to be advisory only. Presided over by the Prime

[5] See A. D. Gorwala, *Report on the Efficient Conduct of State Enterprises*, New Delhi, Planning Commission, 1951; V. K. N. Menon, "Government and Corporation in India" in B. B. Majumdar, ed., *Problems of Public Administration in India*, Patna, Bharati Bhawan, 1951; and a brief description in Central Board of Irrigation, *New Projects for Irrigation and Power in India*, Simla, 1950; and Central Waterpower, Irrigation, and Navigation Commission, *Hirakud Dam Project*, New Delhi, 1951.
[6] For a review of these events, see Merrill R. Goodall, "Planning and Operations Machinery in India," in Donald C. Stone, ed., *National Organization for the Conduct of Economic Development Programs*, Brussels, International Institute of Administrative Sciences, 1954.
[7] The government's declaration is quoted and discussed fully by Tarlok Singh in "Administrative Relations in Planning," *Indian Journal of Public Administration*, April-June 1955, pp. 137-51.

Minister, the Planning Commission consists mainly of senior cabinet ministers. The commission and its staff produced a *Draft Outline Five Year Plan* in July 1951; in December 1952 the revised draft was laid before Parliament. The first plan was essentially an estimate of government expenditures for the years 1951-1956.

The Planning Commission found its range of choice limited by two factors, among others: first, by the sizable investment sanctioned in previous years, years in which there were many plans and projects, but no single plan; and second, by the limited factual-statistical basis from which it had to work.

The Organization of Research Leadership

If the Planning Commission could not escape the past, and no decision ever can, it was able to lay in the 1951-1956 period the foundations for a surer informational basis for subsequent planning and decision. A vigorous attempt was made to record and assimilate the administrative lessons of the postwar years and to adapt social science methods and techniques to the evolving needs of Indian administration. It is probable that no other contemporary administrative system has sought as deliberately to sponsor social science research and to relate research results to administrative purpose as did the Indian during the first plan period. A few of the major landmarks in the developing role and organization of social science deserve notice:

The Research Programmes Committee. Under the leadership of the Planning Commission, and the advisory counsel of distinguished scholars and senior public officials, the Research Programmes Committee was organized in 1953. Universities and other research institutions have been accorded government grants for projects in research of direct interest to the Planning Commission. Topics for study include the following: a case study of the office of district collector; land tenure studies, in various of the states; "social surveys" of many of the larger urban-industrial centers; studies of the receptivity to technical change in a number of village areas; studies of *shramdan* and people's cooperation.[8] The majority of these projects are still in progress. Nearly all are being directed by the ranking professor of a university department (most frequently economics, but also anthropology and law, among others). One problem confronting most contractors of the Research Programmes Commit-

---

[8] Research Programmes Committee, "Research in Progress," New Delhi, 1955 (mimeo.).

tee research, almost inevitably, is how to delegate responsibility to academic subordinates, how to supervise group research activities. These problems are not exclusively Indian, of course; they seem to be intensified, however, by the pyramidal structuring of the Indian university and the nature of the gradations which separate academic colleagues.

Programme Evaluation Organization. The Government of India launched, simultaneously with the initiation in 1952 of community development projects, an evaluation study of their administration and impact. An independent evaluation of the action program was sought, and the agency charged with assessment, the Programme Evaluation Organization, was made responsible formally to the Planning Commission and not the Community Projects Administration. Funds to finance the first three years' operation of this governmental unit were supplied by the Ford Foundation. The reports of the Programme Evaluation Organization are today indispensable to anyone interested in Indian development.[9] The degree to which operating officials will benefit from the organization's activity is still unknown. There is evidence, however, that the agency's case method of study has already influenced the teaching of administration in India.

Central Committee for Land Reforms. This committee, established by the Planning Commission, considers and reports upon the progress of land reform measures throughout India.

Indian Statistical Institute; the Panel of Economists. The institute, at the request of the Planning Commission, undertook to prepare for the second plan period, 1956-1961, a "draft of a draft plan-frame."[10] About twenty foreign social scientists, including economists from the U.S.A., the U.K., and the U.S.S.R., with Indian colleagues, and all employed under the direction of Professor P. C. Mahalanobis, contributed to the draft study. The findings of the institute were shared

[9] See Planning Commission, Programme Evaluation Organization, *Evaluation Report on First Year's Working of Community Projects*, New Delhi, 1954, particularly Appendix I, "Note on Organization of the Programme Evaluation Organization"; and its *Evaluation Report on Second Year's Working of Community Projects*, 2 vols., New Delhi, 1955. In an effort to add guidance to the methodology of evaluation, Cornell and Lucknow Universities undertook intensive study in several selected sites. For brief description of the relationship of the universities' project to the work of the Programme Evaluation Organization, see Merrill R. Goodall, "The Cornell-Lucknow Evaluation Studies of the Community Development Programme," *Eastern Anthropologist*, VIII, March-August 1955, pp. 243-45.

[10] See the product of their work in P. C. Mahalanobis, *Draft Recommendations for the Formulation of the Second Five Year Plan, 1956-1961*, Delhi, 1955.

with the economic divisions of the Ministry of Finance and the Planning Commission[11] and a specially constituted Panel of Economists.[12]

Planning Research and Action Institute (Uttar Pradesh). Guidance from social science in the making of decisions for development goals has been sought by state governments, as well. Particularly notable leadership has been taken by the Planning Research and Action Institute of Uttar Pradesh. The order which established this institute gave it the following functions:

> (i) to observe, analyze and evaluate the policies and actual work of the Development Departments in the field, their relations to the people and their own inter-relations, to see whether maximum results are being attained, or whether and how this work and these relations and policies may be adjusted and improved;
>
> (ii) to devise and test out through spot work or pilot experimentation in selected areas, under controlled conditions, individually or in groups, new ideas and methods which, if successful, can be pushed out into general field operations;
>
> (iii) to study, test and adapt, for application in the State, ideas and methods coming up elsewhere in India or in the world;
>
> (iv) to undertake quantitative evaluation and comparison of results of the working of specific projects;
>
> (v) to conduct intensive seminars, short conferences and short-term training courses for specialized workers;
>
> (vi) to disseminate the results of observation, experimentation and evaluation. . . .[13]

The government's note has been quoted rather fully for several reasons. It is indicative of the reliance some officials in this state have begun to place on the social sciences. Secondly, the institute combines action programs and studies in evaluation.[14] Finally, it has conducted a number of intensively investigated case studies in the administrative process.[15]

Institutes and Centers for the Study of Public Administration. By 1951, the start of the First Five Year Plan period, a number of proposals

---

[11] The working paper prepared jointly by these divisions bears the title, *The Second Five Year Plan—A Tentative Framework* (Delhi, 1955).

[12] See its report, "Basic Considerations Relating to the Plan Frame," and the "Note of Dissent" prepared by Professor B. R. Shenoy (both issued in *The Second Five-Year Plan: the Framework*, New Delhi, Ministry of Information and Broadcasting, 1955).

[13] Note of May 10, 1954, No. 3088-R/XXXV/10P/54, Lucknow, 1954. The institute has had a subvention from the Rockefeller Foundation and has employed Americans and other foreigners.

[14] See its *Pilot Project: Tanning*, Lucknow, 1954, a study of its initial effort to promote industrial technique and organization in rural areas.

[15] See its *Reorganization of the District Planning Office*, Lucknow, 1954; *Review of the Existing Structure of Rural Cooperatives and Its Limitations*, Lucknow, 1954; and *The Development Set-up in Uttar Pradesh*, Lucknow, 1954.

were in the air for the organization of clearing houses or university centers for teaching and research of public administration. The first postwar proposal for such an institute was made in 1950 by a committee appointed by Bihar government. The conclusions it reached set the tone for proposals made elsewhere.[16] Today institutes or centers function in Patna, Lucknow, Nagpur, Bombay, and New Delhi. Guidance for the program in Patna comes from a political scientist. The Institute of Public Administration in Lucknow is affiliated with the University of Lucknow and directed by the Law Faculty dean in close association with the university's Department of Political Science.[17] The Nagpur program is organized within Nagpur University as a Department of Public Administration and Local Self-Government.[18] The Indian Institute of Public Administration, formally established in 1954 in New Delhi, is presided over by the Prime Minister. A branch of this institute now functions in Bombay; others are planned for Patna and Calcutta.[19]

The interest in public administration, first developed in the early years of the first plan period, has already produced considerable descriptive material. Though slow in beginning, there is increasing evidence of interchange of fact, impression, and opinion among administrators, the many administrators who are primarily subject-matter specialists—foresters, engineers, public health specialists and the like, and academicians. Between 1945 and 1951 the published materials on public administration in India consisted almost exclusively of the two reports by A. D. Gorwala.[20] Materials presently available include academic studies and monographs,[21] the publications and issuances of government,[22] the reports of

[16] See the report of the committee appointed by the government of Bihar, December 1950, on the establishment of an Institute or Department of Public and Business Administration under the Patna University, Patna, 1951, typescript, p. 4. This committee had the able leadership of Professor V. K. N. Menon of Patna University.
[17] This institute has had financial assistance from the Foreign Operations Administration (U.S.) and receives a recurring grant from the Uttar Pradesh Government.
[18] See its *Prospectus*, No. 29, Parts III and XV, Nagpur, 1952.
[19] See its *Annual Report*, New Delhi, 1955 and 1956.
[20] *Report on the Efficient Conduct of State Enterprises*, New Delhi, Planning Commission, 1951; and *Report on Public Administration*, New Delhi, Planning Commission, 1951.
[21] In addition to the papers edited by B. B. Majumdar, see A. D. Gorwala, *The Role of the Administrator, Past, Present and Future*, Poona, Gokhale Institute of Politics and Economics, 1952; Merrill R. Goodall, *Administration and Planning for Economic Development*, Delhi, Ranjit, 1952; Paul H. Appleby, *Public Administration in India*, Delhi, Manager of Publications, 1953; W. R. Natu, *Public Administration and Economic Development*, Poona, Gokhale Institute of Politics and Economics, 1954.
[22] These include: the reports of the Programme Evaluation Organization; Planning Commission documents, a notable example being the chapters on "Administration and Public Cooperation" in the *First Five Year Plan*, New Delhi, 1952, and 1953; the

the newly established Organization and Methods Division in the Cabinet Secretariat,[23] and the materials appearing in the *Indian Journal of Public Administration*, the official organ of the Indian Institute of Public Administration.

ADMINISTRATIVE ORGANIZATION AND THE SEQUENCE OF DECISION

The Planning Commission shared the process of planning the Second Five Year Plan with a number of other specialized planning units. Plans for specific projects for the second plan period, 1956-1961, were solicited from the states by the Planning Commission in 1954. On November 8 of that year, planning secretaries and development secretaries from the states met with commission officers and made an initial presentation of state, district, and village development proposals for inclusion in the new plan.[24] Subsequent consultation between most of these state government secretaries and Planning Commission representatives was arranged during the six 1955 meetings of the Standing Committee of the National Development Council.[25] Suggestions aimed at achieving a more "integrated" approach in the preparation of state, district, and village plans were contained in numerous letters sent by the Planning Commission to the state governments.[26]

Draft recommendations for the 1955-1961 plan were prepared first by the Indian Statistical Institute. These were considered and reported

---

Syllabus of the Indian Administrative Service Training School, described by S. B. Bapat in the *Indian Journal of Public Administration*, April-June 1955; the *Manual on Administrative Intelligence*, New Delhi, 1955, issued by the Community Projects Administration; and at the state level, the important study by the government of Uttar Pradesh, *Administrative Organization of the State Government*, Lucknow, 1954.

[23] See its *First Annual Report, 1954-1955*, New Delhi, 1955 (mimeo.).

[24] See the report in the *Pioneer* (Lucknow), November 13, 1954.

[25] The National Development Council, presided over by the Prime Minister, consists also of the Chief Ministers of all the states. It meets twice yearly, was organized in 1952. The Standing Committee, comprised originally of the Prime Minister (chairman) and the chief ministers of Bombay, Hyderabad, Madras, Mysore, Punjab, Rajasthan, Travancore-Cochin, Uttar Pradesh, and West Bengal, meets six times yearly. It was formed first in November 1954.

[26] See *Hindustan Times* (New Delhi), April 11, 1955, for a significant illustration of the suggestions given the state government by the Planning Commission. See also the volume, *Important Letters Issued by the Community Projects Administration*, New Delhi, 1955; these circular letters, addressed mainly by the Planning Commission (in its capacity as Central Committee responsible for the Community Projects Administration) to development commissioners and directors of community projects relate primarily to the working of the projects. They are also indicative of the organization of the formal communication system linking the Center and the states, and the limits of that system.

on jointly by the economic divisions of the Ministry of Finance and the Planning Commission. The research memoranda and recommendations of the Statistical Institute and the economic divisions were made available to the Panel of Economists, an official body convened by the Planning Commission. The studies of each of these agencies were published and given fairly wide public distribution, even though their recommendations on goals and means of implementation were far from uniform. Throughout, these published working papers reflect the influence of data presented by the Programme Evaluation Organization and the records of the development commissioners' conferences.[27] The findings of the "Karve report" had an important role in subsequent consideration and review of these data.[28] Draft plan memoranda were reviewed critically by both the National Development Council and its Standing Committee, the central Cabinet, and the Consultative Committee of Parliament on Planning.[29] A final Planning Commission revision was submitted to Parliament on May 16, 1956.

Despite the seeming multiplicity of clearance, the Planning Commission retained responsibility for the completed plan and held its status as the government's central planning agency. Fewer persons were actually involved in the process of decision than is suggested by the number of participating agencies. The Prime Minister is chairman of the Planning Commission; and he heads the National Development Commission and its Standing Committee. Key cabinet ministers serve on the Planning Commission; the Prime Minister, of course, directs the Cabinet. And when the Planning Commission acts as Central Committee for the guidance of the Community Projects Administration, it is again led by the Prime Minister.

Such concentration of decision making is perhaps not unusual at the topmost level of government. The Indian Prime Minister, unlike some other chief executive officers, is not a nominal or titular officeholder. Equally important, however, is the appearance at the next level of a relatively small group of officials in directing roles: Cabinet members double as Planning Commissioners; the Planning Commission reappears as Central Committee for the Community Projects Administration; the

[27] Particularly the *Summary Record* of the Third Development Commissioners Conference, issued by the Planning Commission, New Delhi, 1955.
[28] Committee on Village and Small-Scale Industries, *Report*, New Delhi, 1955, popularly known as the Karve Committee, after its Chairman, Prof. D. G. Karve, the Director of the Programme Evaluation Organization.
[29] Reports on each of these reviews are in the *Statesman* (Delhi), November 11, 1955; January 7, 8, 21; February 10; May 2, 10, 1956.

director of the Indian Statistical Institute serves on the Planning Commission; the evaluating agency—the Programme Evaluation Organization—[30] is affiliated with the Planning Commission; and so on.

Administrative Relations in Development Operations

The First Five Year Plan accentuated the Center's reliance upon the states for the actual programming and administration of development activities and, on the other hand, the states' dependence upon the Center for the financing of these activities. Statistics of actual development expenditure, 1951-1952–1953-1954, show the central outlay for development to have been Rs. 445 crores, that of the states Rs. 440 crores, approximately one third of these sums consisting of central financial assistance to the states.[31]

The Center, of course, is not dependent upon the states' administrative structures for the performance of numerous essential central functions. In such fields as customs, central excises, income tax, railways, and posts and telegraphs, among others, the Union Government maintains and staffs its own field or regional offices. An additional stream of central influence stems from the placement in state administration of personnel drawn from the three principal all-India services: the Indian Administrative Service (IAS), the Indian Police Service (IPS), and the Indian Audits and Accounts Service (IAAS). These services are recruited, examined, and appointed by the Union Public Service Commission. Probably more than half of all secretaries to state government, a majority of district collectors and divisional commissioners are selected from the IAS cadre.

The number of IAS officers deputed to the central ministries, however, is remarkably small. The Planning Commission estimates that the "second five year plan would necessitate the increasing of Indian administrative officers on central deputation from 1,188 to 1,513."[32]

In other words, only about 325 administrative officers will be recruited for central service over the five year period; the additions will come from members of the IAS presently employed in the states, from new recruits secured through the normal procedures of the Union Public

[30] And its distinguished Director, Professor D. G. Karve, among other duties, served the Indian Institute of Public Administration (New Delhi) as its first director.

[31] The figures are drawn from Tables I-IV, in Planning Commission, *Five Year Plan Progress Report for 1953-1954*, New Delhi, 1954, pp. 19-48.

[32] Reply to Parliamentary question, *Statesman* (Delhi) September 4, 1955.

Service Commission, and through various forms of emergency recruitment. Personnel resources of this type were augmented but slowly during the 1951-1956 plan period. New recruits were added to the IAS and given training in the IAS Training School (Metcalfe Hutments, Delhi) at the rate of only about 25-40 per year. And since the IAS cadre is a personnel organization common to both the Center and the states, the officers recruited during this period were not exclusively employed by central agencies. Although records are not available, it is fair to assume that a majority entered administration at the district level. The training syllabi during this period, moreover, reflected the needs of those government agencies not directly concerned with the development program. And the young men recruited during the period, if the writer may rely on personal impressions,[33] were motivated mainly by interest in employment opportunities then prevailing in revenue and regulatory services. The newer job titles then just coming to the fore—such as district planning officer—lacked the appeal of the older, traditional, more solidly entrenched positions. Data on the educational background and social composition of the training classes are not generally available. Seven of thirty-five members of one year's training group, known to the writer, were graduates of a single college. This college offers an excellent instructional program to a student body drawn, by and large, from the upper-income, higher social echelons.[34] Several thousand applications, it should be added, are processed annually for IAS examination.

Most governmental functions of a development nature—agriculture, land tenure, forests, public health, education, to name but a few—fall within the scope of state activity. In practice, major responsibilities for these activities are assumed by officers in the service of state government. The Center lacks the action agencies or personnel to man them. Heavy assignments in these areas of activity, both before 1951 and after, have been thrust upon the district officer (usually known as the district collector), an officer whose main obligation has been thought always to lie in the revenue and regulatory fields. In name, if not in fact, the collec-

---

[33] Impressions gained during 1951-1953 and 1954-1955. The writer had the privilege of lecturing occasionally to the trainees.

[34] The principal of this fine school once remarked to me that his students were "sons of VIPs." A secretary to government, in the dinner group, added: "Yes, and for his college, VIP means 'Very Important Personage.'" A few of the implications of class recruitment to the public services are briefly identified in Merrill R. Goodall, "Democratic Administration," *Dharwar College Bulletin*, 1953.

tor is today the principal development officer of his district.[35] More recently, proposals have been made that would extend further the association of regulatory and developmental functions below the level of the district collector's office. These contrasting governmental roles would be combined so that the tahsildar (known also as the mamlatdar and circle officer) becomes, as well, the block development officer; at the village level such officers as cooperative inspectors and revenue inspectors become the gram sevak, the "multi-purpose village level worker," and the patwari, the village accountant, becomes the assistant village level worker.[36]

The role of the district officer, and that of his subordinates, is laid in a highly stratified rural society. The evidence of the last few years suggests that the discretionary powers of the collector's office in developmental works are likely to be strengthened. This is not to say that this Indian administrator proceeds in the absence of advice. It is not to say, furthermore, that he is free of remarkably detailed financial supervision.[37] Yet, this multiplicity of advice and review does not produce for the Center a clear picture of what the district office is actually doing, or of the extent to which this office can be counted on in the areas of development policy and administration. In practice, guidance on development issues is more likely to reach the district office from either the state ministries or unofficial and nongovernmental sources than from the Center. An important unofficial linkage on policy issues of all kinds between New Delhi and the states is supplied by the Indian National Congress. The close association of the Congress Party and government, at all levels of activity, is perhaps the single most striking characteristic of contemporary Indian politics. The influence of this relationship is inescapable to even the most casual observer. The existence of more than one political party in power, over any considerable period of time, would affect significantly the planning and administrative relations between the Center and the states, including the role of the National Development

---

[35] In support of this conclusion, see *Evaluation Report on Second Year's Working of Community Projects*, New Delhi, Planning Commission, 1955, I, 4.

[36] See the discussion by "Satyakam," in *Kurukshetra*, January 1955, pp. 7-11; and the parallel treatment by U. L. Goswami, "The Structure of Development Administration," *The Indian Journal of Public Administration*, April-June 1955, pp. 110-18.

[37] Central Accounts and Audits function not only for the Union government but are responsible also for supervising and auditing all state accounts. This duty does not extend to municipal and local finances which are supervised by the states. See the point of view expressed in "Audit Runs Amuck," *Eastern Economist*, January 7, 1955, p. 4.

Council and its Standing Committee and of any "zonal councils" which might be organized.[38]

The dependence of government leadership upon party organization as the essential channel of policy communication, New Delhi to the district, has been stressed repeatedly in the last year. Measures designed to associate the activities of the Congress organization and the administration are studied constantly.[39] Party conferences reach elaborate decisions regarding the coordination of Congress work with official agencies like the Community Projects Administration and the National Extension Services and nonofficial organizations like the Bharat Sevak Samaj.[40]

The Congress Party, however, failed to win an absolute majority in four legislative assemblies in the 1951-1952 elections; in the 1957 elections it lacked an absolute majority in two states. On the other hand, after the earlier elections Congress was able to form ministries in all states, but following the latest elections the Communist Party has formed the government in Kerala. An important feature of both elections was the number of parties and independent candidates both contesting and winning seats. Congress easily won a majority in the Center and in most states, but according to the results of the 1957 elections there has been an increase in opposition strength in nine of the thirteen states. These results indicate in some degree the element of fluidity, the low index of assembly-wide cohesion found in certain of the Indian state legislative assemblies. Such an impression would appear to be confirmed by the few pilot arithmetic studies of party cohesion undertaken to date.[41] The looseness of legislative alliance, the changefulness of voting alignment, are perhaps the most surprising features of Cabinet government in several of the states, a parliamentary system which elsewhere contrives to

[38] Discussing the States Reorganisation Commission's report, the Prime Minister said that "in drawing up the second Plan, there has been an attempt made to have the district the unit, so that when a district changed over to another State it would not generally affect its development." Transitional problems arising from states' reorganization, he added, "might be handled by zonal councils, that is, a group of three, four, or five States, as the case may be, having a common council. To begin with, I would say that it should be an advisory council. Let us see how it develops. Let it be advisory; let the Centre also be associated with it in dealing with economic problems as well as the broader problems and other problems that might arise."—*Statesman* (Delhi), December 22, 1955.

[39] See "Co-ordinating Work of P.C.C.s and Ministries," *Statesman* (New Delhi), September 3, 1955; and "Association of D.C.C.s in District Planning," *National Herald* (Lucknow), March 11, 1955.

[40] *Statesman* (New Delhi), May 5, 1956.

[41] For an overview of these studies, see Merrill R. Goodall, "Soviet policy and India: some postwar trends," *Journal of International Affairs*, VIII, 1954, pp. 43-51.

discipline its parties and to produce highly cohesive, solidly united voting units. Voting behavior in the state assemblies is likely to be of import to the administrator as well as the politician. Development programming and operations are, preponderantly, in the hands of the states. Party organization has so far provided a relatively steady link, Center to the states. That link may not be counted upon permanently.

Summary

The popular demand for planning and economic development is a persisting theme in Indian politics. The range of choice and decision open to the Planning Commission is narrowly limited. Well over half of the funds spent in support of provincial development programs from 1946 to 1951 were supplied from the Center. A major share of development funds for the First Five Year Plan period was committed *before* the Planning Commission was established. The First Five Year Plan was prepared on a slim informational basis. Beginning in 1951, government in India sponsored social science research on a large and systematic scale and sought to relate research findings to administrative purpose. The First Five Year Plan brought to Indian administration an interest in applied social science, a quality of interest perhaps without precedent among modern administrative systems. Patterns of consultation and decision making have been established through the experience of the five year plans. The Second Five Year Plan builds on the first, but must yet fully resolve the essential administrative relations of country-wide planning.

Although important problems have yet to be faced, the practices of democratic administration are likely to supply continuing themes to Indian planning. Operations have been based consistently on procedures of law and public consent; development has been sought but without intimidation.

THE PUBLIC SERVICES AND DEMOCRACY

A. D. GORWALA

*T*HE term "democracy" conveys in India a great deal more than its usual connotation. Its intention is not only government by the people through representatives selected by the people at free, lawfully held elections. Several other ideas also enter into it. To these, one point is common: change. The need for change, the urgency in bringing change about, are probably the overtones of the term "democracy" that have the most powerful impact on the Indian mind. The nature of the desired change, too, forms part of the meaning. There must be significant economic progress. This progress must be accomplished not through making the rich richer and providing opportunities for the further growth of concentrations of economic power, but through improving conditions for the underprivileged—the bulk of the population—reducing glaring economic inequalities among citizens, and appropriately mobilizing national resources for the benefit of the whole people. There must be significant social progress toward bringing about, in fact as in law, true social equality among all citizens. Continuous effort towards economic betterment, social improvement, and justice is thus for the Indian implicit in democracy. In its absence, much of the content of the term would for him be lost. In some countries, where the majority of the inhabitants have made great social and economic gains, or where despite considerable discontent on this score the system has become a habit of mind, *status quo* government in social and economic matters over several years may still be seriously considered democracy. In India, it is very doubtful if it would.

Thus is set the framework in which the public services of India have to operate. The public services are in all countries some of the most important instruments through which the policies of government are converted into fact. Their senior members often help by their advice in the making of these policies. The less advanced the country, socially and economically, the less the likelihood of the nonofficial playing a leading part in the carrying out of policy and the more significant the role of the public services. The good public servant then becomes not merely the

A. D. GORWALA, independent columnist and writer, was for twenty-three years a government servant. Since his resignation, he has written reports for the Government of India on a variety of administrative and economic subjects.

implementor; he is even more the encourager of implementation by his fellow citizens in private life. He may not appear to be, but is in reality, the leader. The credit may go, understandably and desirably, to others, but the work is his. In that are contained both his duty and his satisfaction.

With a very large and extremely poor population, with sections of the people still adhering to a social system based on hereditary status distinctions, with illiteracy widely spread and superstition a potent factor in the life of many, India, an amalgam of all the centuries from the thirteenth to the twentieth, must telescope into the next twenty years the essential stages of the economic and social progress that it has taken more fortunate and more developed countries far longer periods to pass through. This process of telescoping is bound to impose strains of a character and nature that were unknown to the developed nations of today at a time when they were perhaps at a stage somewhat comparable to India's. Of such strains, few are likely to cause justifiably greater anxiety than the signs of impatience that appear even among some of those who seem in certain respects to be in the thirteenth century. What is the good of this voting, ask such individuals, if things with us remain just as they were? It is fine that this country is free, say others, but is it not time I got two meals a day? What merit is there in X, the rich mill-owner, a third wishes to know, that he is able to send his son to America to study while in my village there is only a primary school and my son, however clever, can never hope to go to college? If democracy in India is to survive, the answer to these questions must be given in and with such deeds that hope at least is not destroyed. Hence the resort to planning, the attempt to achieve in ordered fashion results—even if minor for the time being—by persuasion and consent, lest failing them, refuge be sought in regimentation as the only possible prospect. Hence, also, the emphasis on the idea of the welfare state, the government making itself responsible for the taking of measures necessary to give at least some degree of welfare to the people. The role of government is extended and its power increased by these activities but "Governments exist to do that for their peoples which the peoples cannot do, or cannot do as well, for themselves."

The task of the Indian public servant has thus two aspects. There is the work he is normally appointed to do, whether it be the keeping of records, the maintenance of law and order, the conduct of irrigation, the prevention of disease, the improvement of agriculture, the administration of a railway system, the management of a state-owned industrial enterprise, or any other. There is the second aspect, to be kept firmly before his mind both in the doing of his work and at other times: the need and urgency of social and economic progress and justice. At a particular moment he may not be able to concern himself intensely about this aspect, but if it forms part of his essential thought, he may well be able to serve Indian democracy better than he would otherwise have done.

In India, systematic administration through well organized public services preceded by many decades democratic constitution making. The political leaders, on coming to power, thus found the machinery of government in working order. They could have shattered it to bits and built it anew according to their hearts' desire. They decided to continue it almost untouched. To the wisdom of that decision the history of the last nine years bears testimony. The dangers overcome, the tasks accomplished, the further tasks planned—none of these would have been possible had radical reshaping of administrative machinery with replacement of personnel been considered the primary necessity.

The national leaders had on occasion reviled the public services bitterly. They had seen little good in them. They had often called upon their countrymen serving in them, especially in the higher ranks, to withdraw. Yet, on assumption of power, not only did they leave the public services undisturbed and begin to use them forthwith as the instruments for their immediate purposes, but they proceeded as a matter of deliberate policy to go on with them, accepting their main features as the pattern for the future, a future that in their view had to be very different from the past as regards both a good deal of the work to be done and the spirit in which it was to be approached. Especially interesting were the decisions to safeguard the existing rights of serving members of the key public services and to continue those services themselves as all-India services, making only a slight change in the name of one, and bringing scales of pay for the new entrants in line with Indian conditions.

The considerations that led them to these conclusions have not, so far as recollection goes, been set out at length in any document or speech. It may not perhaps be altogether without profit to conjecture on what they may have been. Was it the inability of busy men immersed in day-to-day details of novel duties to think out and plan a new system and look for new men that was responsible very largely for acquiescence in what had been inherited? Was it the effect of custom, of being habituated through long years of struggle to regard this part of what they fought as something permanent, something that could not lightly be changed? Was it the feeling that the system, reaching back in some of its essentials to the Maurya and the Moghul, was suited in some special way to the nature of the people? Was it the realization that any new scheme was hardly likely to produce what had been one of the principal justifications of the old, namely quite a number of devoted public servants of all ranks with very high standards of integrity and efficiency? Was it confidence in the discipline and morale that the service idea inculcated and the sure knowledge that obedience not merely to the letter but to the spirit of what government desired would be readily forthcoming? Was it confidence in their own ability to manage men whom, whatever their complaints in the past, they had found from experience in the interim year of office to be able, nonpartisan, and as devoted to the country's interests as themselves? These may have been some of the reasons. The practical statesmanship of Sardar Patel had undoubtedly a great deal to do with the decisions, and he rarely needed or gave elaborate explanation for what his sound common sense approved.

The conception of public services involves not a man for a job, but a group of men specially chosen because of their qualifications for a class of jobs, this group generally not being recruited all at the same time, but being formed by continuing recruitment at a certain age over a period of years. In it accordingly arise hierarchy, training, accumulation of knowledge, expertness in technique, shared ideas, common ways of thought, and often an identity of feeling that mark it off from other citizens. Such a group, exercising power under an authoritarian government, is apt to become a bureaucracy which looks more to its own interest than to that of the people, and to attempt so to maneuver public affairs as always to safeguard itself and enhance its power, unless it is redeemed by exceptional characters willing to consider problems anew and to practice—no less with regard to themselves and their colleagues than with regard to others—the ancient official virtues of impartiality and independent thinking. Nor does the fact of a democratic government's being in power necessarily end all such danger.

Accordingly it was natural that the new political governments, although they had accepted the services pattern and decided on its future use, should be somewhat suspicious of the behavior and dealings of the services generally and of some individuals in particular. Differences in ways of living, in belief about the right ways of living, in educational and intellectual background also added to the suspicion so far as the higher public services were concerned. The impatience in the earlier years about the great deal to be done, and the little achieved, caused even some of the more considerate politicians to voice this suspicion. Their own intentions were so good, yet very little was happening. Somebody must be to blame. They could not be, of course. Why, it must be the services. They were being obstructive, dragging their feet. In fact, at one time responsible politicians in several areas came very near to declaring that the services were to blame, not because policy was not being implemented, but because the politicians had not decided on any policy. Fortunately, with the functioning of the Planning Commission, policy became fairly clear in economic matters. Yet the general tendency to suspicion remains, and from time to time it flares up, sometimes in quite unexpected quarters. Despite occasional tributes by ministers during debates in Parliament and state legislative bodies, the public services can never be sure that they are in reality esteemed by the men to whom they are responsible, much less by the men to whom these ministers are responsible, the legislators.

"Suspicion in itself is never healthful either in the private or in the public mind. Trust is strength in all relations of life," and the suspicion of the public services entertained by the politicians arouses in the mind of the services undesirable reactions. The frankness of speech, the free expression of independent opinion in note and minute—the practice when high officials regarded those above them as senior colleagues who could be counted upon, however much they disagreed, not to suspect their *bona fides*—have become very largely a thing of the past. There are probably still a few imperturbable spirits whose conception of duty includes the statement of honest opinion, however unpalatable, but the general rule becomes more and more to say what it is known will please. This naturally reduces the effectiveness of the public servant. It also, to any man of sensitivity, reduces the joy in doing a difficult job well, which after all is the principal reward of the good public servant.

Another unfortunate effect on the public servant is that it decreases his willingness to take responsibility. In the circumstances, he feels compelled to plan for safety. Heaven knows which way the cat will eventually jump. Why not insure one's position by not deciding oneself, or at least by getting the man above to express his agreement with one's views. Now, one of the principal merits of the Indian system was that it taught a man to take responsibility. That which was his job, he did. Those above watched him doing it, but left him to do it, only volunteering advice occasionally and hardly ever issuing instructions unless he was going very wrong. The young probationer for the administrative, police, and other services still receives the same training, but worldly wisdom, alas, soon teaches all but the exceptional to tread the modern path of discretion.

Woodrow Wilson, in his celebrated essay on "The Study of Public Administration," desired for the United States an administration "at all points sensitive to public opinion. . . . a civil service cultured and self-sufficient enough to act with sense and vigor, and yet so intimately connected with the popular thought, by means of elections and constant public counsel, as to find arbitrariness or class spirit quite out of the question."[1]

How do the Indian public services measure against these criteria? One of the difficulties of an answer is, of course, to arrive at a definition of "public opinion." Is it the opinion of the government formed by the party that came into power at the last election? Is it the opinion of the most important pressure group that supported the party and contributed largely to campaign funds? Is it the opinion expressed by the majority of the members of Parliament during a debate on any one occasion? Is it the view of the majority of the newspapers on any administrative matter? Is it the view expressed by the majority in a sample poll of the whole country? Be that as it may, there is no doubt that the public services of India are responsive to the opinions of the government under which they serve, even in fields which would seem to have little to do with government, such as the mode of personal dress. The ability to act with sense and vigor, too, is generally present, by reason of education, general character, and training, though of course there are exceptions due to personal failure or corruption either at the public servant level or higher up. An arbitrariness can scarcely be regarded as out of the question, though it would not be wrong to say that in the higher ranks instances of such arbitrariness occur rarely and are often traceable more to members of government than to public servants, while the same is generally true of class or caste spirit. Arbitrariness in the lower ranks is often an excuse for corruption. In all these matters, however, whichever the country concerned, the dictum applies: Where rests the power, there lies the responsibility. Governments have the power to control the conduct of public servants, and when the governments are determined to do this, appropriate conduct follows.

The Indian situation and the feeling about democracy described earlier in this essay give ample scope for leadership to the Indian public servant. By virtue of being a public servant, he has a certain amount of authority

[1] *Political Science Quarterly,* II, June 1887, p. 222.

both over subordinates and in the view of the general public. If, then, he has the qualities that inspire confidence in those with whom he comes in contact, so that they are prepared to follow his advice and act according to his directions, and further, if he is not deterred by some of the considerations discussed above, he can be a true leader in the creative sense. This leadership may be within the field of his official work, or outside of it, or both. The followers will differ according as it is one or the other, though on occasion some may be common to both. A senior official, very truly the chief of his department, furnishing it not only with ideas but also with guidance as to how they can be successfully worked out, full of encouragement and consideration for those under him, though capable of coming down like a ton of bricks on those who shirk or otherwise refuse to pull their full weight, is equally effective as the leader of an educational movement and as the head of a sports organization, both, though unofficial, quite as much in the interests of the country as is the public service as such. Some of his followers in the unofficial activities may also be members of his official staff. Again, a schoolmaster in a small village is, by reason of the backing his character gives his position, a leader not only in his school and in the adult literacy campaign he is waging in the village, but also in the cooperative society of the larger village nearby and in the cooperative processing concern set up by the local agriculturalists. The jealousy aroused in the breast of the local legislator by the success of this multiple leadership, and the reprimands from senior officials that come his way on account of that multiplicity of interests, are the penalties he has to bear for his efficiency. Both he and the other public servants have, of course, to sacrifice a great deal of their time and, in fact, seem to their friends to have hardly any private life.

Despite the fact that such leadership requires an unusual toughness of fiber and often brings on the head of its possessor much tribulation, the flame burns continuously, and not only in a very few individuals, in the Indian public services. Sometimes the circumstances that evoke its exercise bring it strikingly to notice. Some of the occasions since Independence when this has happened are the disturbances following Partition, especially in Delhi, the integration of the states, cooperative activities in certain districts, the two general elections, and the nationalization of the Imperial Bank and of life insurance.

The presence of leadership in the public services of the country is a matter for congratulation. It is equally a matter for congratulation that the glaring light of publicity does not as a rule rest upon such official leaders. Anonymity befits the public services. The work they undertake benefits therefrom. And since for one to whom popular attention is drawn there are quite a number who remain unnoticed, there is more than an element of unfairness about such publicity. A typical public servant of the old India dealt thus with this point in the preface to a book describing one of the finest feats of administration of at least the last hundred years: "Where so many strove so arduously, to mention only some would be invidious; accordingly, I omit all names."

DISTRICT ADMINISTRATION
AND LOCAL SELF-GOVERNMENT

RICHARD L. PARK

*T*wo of the more neglected aspects in the study of government and politics in India are local government and district administration.[1] It is in the district towns and villages, nevertheless, that the consequences, if not the initiatives, of Indian politics are to be found. The fact that the Government of India has determined a course of action favorable to a "socialist pattern of society" increases the significance of local administrative and political responses to central and state direction. This paper is addressed to the proposition that the success or failure of India's five year plans, and indeed of more general political aspirations as stated in her constitution, may well depend upon the adequacy of needed reforms in the governmental processes at village, town, and district levels.

Students of local affairs have been concerned in recent years by what may be called the "grass roots" approach to politics and administration. It is assumed in grass roots thinking that the clients of governmental policies, namely the citizenry, should be consulted regularly and, indeed, be encouraged to suggest lines of action that should be enacted by the higher organs of government to meet locally felt needs. In the Community Projects Administration's terminology this is known as the principle of "felt needs." Politicians and responsible administrators refer

RICHARD L. PARK is in the Department of Political Science and is Chairman of the Center for South Asia Studies at the University of California at Berkeley.

[1] The best review of the development of local government in India will be found in Hugh Tinker, *The Foundations of Local Self-Government in India, Pakistan, and Burma*, London, University of London, The Athlone Press, 1954. For more detailed studies on India, the *Quarterly Journal of the Local Self-Government Institute* (Bombay) should be consulted. (Dr. M. P. Sharma's "The Evolution of Rural Local Self-Government and Administration in U.P.," recently serialized in this Quarterly, is of special interest. These articles were published in book form by the Local Self-Government Institute in 1957.) The *Calcutta Municipal Gazette* contains valuable material on the Calcutta Corporation. In 1956 a new journal of the Bombay Corporation was inaugurated.

Few recent studies of district administration are available. However, the Research Programmes Committee of the Planning Commission has sponsored a research project on district administration in Bombay (Surat District) by N. B. Desai that has been published as the *Report on the Administrative Survey of the Surat District* by the Indian Society of Agricultural Economics, Bombay, 1958.

to this phenomenon as "consultation with the people," or "being aware of trends in public opinion." So far so good. The difficulty is that the principle of local consultation often is interpreted in odd and curious ways, to include the following: sentimentalists and naïve democrats appear to believe that a free society consists largely in a balancing of locally felt needs, with the sectional variants of opinion being channeled upwards primarily because of the necessity of balancing local interests on the scales of higher authority; or, administrators in particular, but no mean number of politicians also, manipulate the many voices of local opinion to suit their own views set a priori.

The manipulatory thesis of point two is such a common situation hovering in the interstices of all politics that little more need be said about that. Point one, however, is of special importance as regards India where the logical, theoretical—and very real—conflicts between central and state direction and local initiative and responsibility have not been squarely met as yet.

This conflict finds its nexus in the district. On the one hand, the central government in fact, if not always in accordance with federal distributions of authority, sets much of the policy and a good share of the detailed operating procedure to be carried out through the states' governmental machinery. As agents of state governments, but with national status and an all-India outlook, district officers have the job of translating the vast bulk of governmental decisions into effective action. The mission of the district officer, particularly on matters concerned with economic development, is to see that upper policies get lower acceptance, and on schedule. District magistrates (collectors) and their chief subordinates come mostly from the old Indian Civil Service or the new Indian Administrative Service; they are nearly as well prepared in 1956 as in 1926 to see that governmental decisions are effectively administered with the due avoidance of interference from politicians or local interest groups.

The other party at nexus is the local authority, such as the district board or union board in Bengal, the municipal committee (or, in large cities, the semi-autonomous corporation), and the authorized village panchayat.[2] Here one finds groups with highly circumscribed powers, who represent in one fashion or another the local citizenry. Yet it ap-

---

[2] A. V. Raman Rao's *Structure and Working of Village Panchayats*, Gokhale Institute of Politics and Economics, Publication No. 28, Poona, 1954, is valuable for its great detail. The various state governments have published "panchayat raj" acts and a great many commentaries have been published on these acts.

DISTRICT ADMINISTRATION AND LOCAL GOVERNMENT

pears that in the battle between local *self*-government and local administration the tradition-bound authority of the Collectorate, as a system of control, holds the upper hand on almost every significant issue at stake. It is not "felt need" that is encouraged in such a scheme, but rather "induced felt need," with the chief district administrator's induction coils freely distributed by those subordinate officers who must report results on plans to higher administrative authority.

It must be admitted that there now appears to be little demand in India for substantially increasing the real powers of local government, except perhaps in the cases of municipalities and the great city corporations. Respect for the relative impartiality and efficiency of the collectors of India remains high. Close observers of district administration seldom report local people pleading for an increase in local responsibility for local affairs. On the contrary, the bulk of opinion favors the retention of strong Collectorates as protection against predatory incursions against the purse and powers of local affairs by local politicians. How much of this negative attitude stems from a realistic appraisal of the shortcomings —inexperience, corruption, nepotism—of local authorities, and how much from an experienced understanding of collectors' *hukum* (power), is hard to say. That it is hard to say highlights the fact that we know little about the administration-versus-local authority aspects of Indian politics. But we can be sure that as long as administrative patterns of effective power and local government with limited authority persist, it will be to the collector, rather than to the district board chairman or the *pradhans* (headmen of villages) to whom one should go for authoritative judgments on affairs in the district.

One explanation of the failure of local government to flourish, politically, since Lord Ripon's famous resolution on local self-government in 1882 may be found in the purposes set forth on behalf of the resolution. Lord Ripon was concerned with the need for increasing participation in face-to-face problems of government. Ripon's was an early appeal to "grass roots" psychology. In addition to acquainting more people with the facts of government on home grounds, Ripon hoped to encourage the development of Indian leaders for Indian affairs. The formula was meant to encourage leadership education in the context of face-to-face local problems, eventually leading ever more responsibly to education in the abstract and complex problems at higher levels. This was an early statement of the kind of political education that Montagu spoke of as "gradual development towards self-government."

To a degree the formula worked. A number of Indian nationalist leaders found their early political experience on district or union boards, and particularly on municipal committees and in the corporations of Bombay and Calcutta. But the formula was unrealistic. Government operates within an ideological framework, and depends for its effectiveness on a decision-making apparatus that is concerned with the ultimates of political power. For nationalist leaders, or potential leaders, it was the substance and not the form of politics that was desired. Local administrative and advisory experience thus became only steppingstones to the politics of the nationalist movement where political power, not training, was the goal.

For a variety of reasons, local government in India appears to have low drawing power for any but persons with modest ambitions in politics or administration. As in the trade unions, in student organizations and, of course, in all-India politics, it is very often the least well equipped persons who aspire to represent the localities. As long as this situation exists, the district officers may remain secure in their domains. As and when one or more political parties decide to bring organized politics to the districts, the situation may change rapidly.

It has been the assumption, sedulously encouraged earlier by the British, and continued by the Congress Party, that local affairs should be basically non-political. It was said, though incorrectly, that the great strength of British local self-government rested upon the impartiality of local authorities. As most who have examined the facts know, whether for Great Britain, India, or the United States, local affairs are among the most difficult to carry on impartially. Intimate acquaintance with the facts seems best calculated to bring out contentious debate and to lead to factionalism, if not to organized, partisan, political action. As distance increases and issues become more abstract, compromise may well be easier to reach. In any event, we know that local government provides one of the most complex problem situations of group relations in conflict.

There were times during the nationalist movement when the Congress chose to use organs of local government either to strengthen Congress Party power by providing effective local government, or to capture local governmental bodies in an attempt to hinder the effectiveness of government from higher levels of British rule. Localities were the happy hunting grounds for instruments useful in nationalist politics. A similar pattern seems to be emerging today in the tactics of contemporary political opposition groups. Both the Socialists and more particularly the Communists have been showing an uncommon interest in capturing local governmental positions of authority. A network of control over local bodies might well be the best available means for such opposition parties to use in battering against entrenched Congress control in upper-level Indian politics.

From the evidence available it does not appear that concerted efforts have been made by opposition or Congress groups to enter the tangled web of panchayat politics, however. Village people, at least up to the present, seem to have withstood relatively well the full impact of independent India's politics as they withstood much of the organized force of the Moghul and British regimes before. Which is not to say that villages have been free of factionalism or political conflict. The record reveals just the opposite. At least until a very recent date, leadership at the village level has been more closely related to local kinship and economic status ties than to patterns of national politics. During the general elections of 1951-1952 the parties did make inroads on village India, particularly in certain critical areas. The Congress and Communist Parties, particularly the former, have made attempts to appoint party workers resident in major village areas. But with the exception of dramatic cases such as Telengana and parts of Andhra, the local party people have not been effective in contesting localized patterns of personal leadership. Where indigenous inclinations of localized leadership happen to coincide with a party's program and leadership, there may appear to be strong, party-involved support at village levels. The Congress, as the *sarkar* (the government in power), is much more likely to capture such unstructured support than any opposition. The major case indicating the possibility of encouraging an anti-*sarkar* campaign, of course, was Telengana.

To reach the social and economic goals being laid out in the five year plans and in complementary legislation, at least four programs of political and administrative development are being prompted by the Government of India.

1. First, the basic administrative unit of India, the Collectorate at the district level, is being continued as the long control and development arm of the central and state governments. In addition to his functions as the chief officer for law and order and revenue collection in the district, the collector (aided by his senior subordinates) has become the chief economic development officer too. In collaboration with some technical officers of the state government, and ruling over the rest in his district, the collector is the key figure in almost every line of endeavor within his district's boundaries. As development activities increase in complex-

ity, it is probable that the Collectorate will be less and less concerned with traditional law and order and revenue functions, and more concerned with development. Such an eventuality might open grounds for a greater sharing of the traditional powers with local authorities, But, for the foreseeable future, the collectors bid to remain the key leadership figures throughout district-level India, local self-government to the contrary, notwithstanding.

2. Secondly, there is reason to believe that the great city corporations and municipal committees in the larger municipalities will be granted increasingly greater powers. The cities and many towns of India have become so large—and they are growing daily—that attempts made by state governments to limit the corporations' and municipal committees' powers will justifiably be strongly resisted. There is every reason to believe that more capable young men will get training and experience in administration and politics at the city and town levels, thus providing the Government of India and the political parties with recruits for other (not necessarily higher) levels of public service. It is in the towns and cities that opposition parties, in all probability, will make their most significant strides in building an opposition to the Congress government.[3]

3. District and union boards may gain greater financial and thus policy autonomy if the states decide to risk lowering the prestige and power of district officers. As matters stand, these boards have few other than innocuous powers, and in an informal manner the district officer tends to dominate the boards' decisions even where particular powers rest with the board. If district board elections and operating procedures were to be rendered more political, and if the parties decide to organize their district or union board campaigns more vigorously and expect party discipline to rule at the district level, then one can expect to find the district officer under much greater attack than he is at present. Recent developments in Bengal, Andhra, Kerala, and Pondicherry indicate that this process may be under way.

4. At the village level, even more than at the district level, it is difficult to generalize on local governmental developments. On the whole, however, panchayat legislation has given only very modest powers to village organs of government. Elections of authorized panchayats are conducted (in every instance so far examined) by a show of hands.[4] This

[3] For a statement on the Communist Party of India's interest in capturing power at local levels, see *Times of India* (Bombay), March 17, 1956.
[4] For a statement in defense of *gram panchayat* voting by show of hands, see the *Bharat Jyoti* of February 26, 1956.

procedure is calculated to encourage the election of the leaders of the most powerful factions in the village. In Uttar Pradesh, at least, the *pradhan*, although the elected headman, seems to have little authority. In effect, the *pradhan* is an "elected" administrator who takes his orders through the panchayat inspector and the Ministry of Local Self-Government, and takes further orders from the collector of the district. On the other hand, in Bombay an experiment is being made in a controlled number of villages to see if panchayats are capable of taking on the revenue-collecting functions in their areas.[5]

In a welfare-bound state, a tremendous number of local leaders are needed to carry out the plans so carefully set out at state and central levels.[6] One of the major bottlenecks in the five year plans is the failure of the villages to produce a sufficient number of men capable of bringing planning philosophy and technical competence to the tasks at hand. These difficulties of personnel recruitment would seem to suggest that top planning be geared to the rate of recruitment of competent village workers. It is probable that greater priority given to the extent of local governmental powers of initiative, and greater attention given to the importance of local sentiments—seriously considered when put forth by elected panchayats—would help to create the atmosphere necessary to encourage the best of village men to seek employment in development activities.

One of the paradoxes of rapid economic development is the probability that more vocal discontent rather than a feeling of well-being will be the index of the success of development efforts. As opportunities increase, and as the apathetic environment of subsistence living is dispelled, one may anticipate ever increasing demands for more and more material advance. Also, one may anticipate a greater sensitivity to an understanding of political power as improvements in social and economic opportunity are presented. It is not unusual, following this line of thought, that the Communist Party of India only belatedly joined in support of rural development efforts. Relative success drew them into the fold.

As of 1956, administration rather than politically oriented local gov-

---

[5] A criticism of the working of village panchayats in Surat District will be found in the *Indian Express* (Bombay) of February 27, 1956. For a recent survey of local government in India, see *Report of the Team for the Study of Community Projects and National Extension Service*, New Delhi, Committee on Plan Projects, 1957, I, esp. pp. 1-23.
[6] The Swedish Minister to India, the distinguished sociologist, Mrs. Ava Myrdal, compares local democracy in Sweden and India in the *Statesman* (New Delhi) of May 12, 1956.

ernment is dominant at the district level. Aspirations for employment remain on the administrative front. By 1966 or so, local government may be expected to come into its own. The result in a country as immense as India is beyond prediction. If the importance of local government is given serious consideration now, and if Lord Ripon's plea for education in face-to-face problems of government is taken as meaning more than a sop to local administration-minded representatives of the villages, responsible—if more chaotic—government in rural India may be the result. In any event, it seems probable that the district officer will find himself under greater political attack as his official reports show more impressive successes in development endeavors.

7. RURAL DEVELOPMENT AND ADMINISTRATION

THE key to Indian planning is the village. Sushil K. Dey, former Development Commissioner for West Bengal, reviews the initial scheme for community development in Bengal and comments upon the changes made in procedure and aims as a result of experience gained. Baij Nath Singh presents a case study of the problem of finding and encouraging village leadership in the course of community development.

Despite these encouraging reports by members of the community development program, Evelyn Wood, from long association with rural development in India, cautions against the easy assumption of western-oriented administrators and economists that their present knowledge of village India is sufficient for use as a basis in development plans. He urges further study of village patterns of influence by social scientists, preferably working with development teams.

COMMUNITY PROJECTS IN ACTION IN INDIA

SUSHIL K. DEY

*T*HE purpose of this paper is to present an analysis of the impact of community development projects on different aspects of organized public activities in India. Reference is made not only to changes which have already occurred, but also to those which may be claimed to have been set in motion by the new forces released by these projects.

The most obvious of these changes is in the field of administration, where the demands of planning and implementing the projects have had to be met with new cadres of functionaries, requiring in turn the establishment of new relations between these and the old organs of government, the modification of previous methods of conducting business, and the addition of arrangements for training in the new practices. But these changes in the organization of public offices and procedures of work are accompanied by changes in many other fields which, while less immediately perceptible, are not less significant for that reason. Also, the changes in these different fields are not unrelated, but act and react upon one another. Consequently, some note is taken of trends and occurrences in other and wider areas of experience. The most important of these is voluntary action by individuals and groups, often starting on an *ad hoc* basis for performance of specific tasks, but continuing for the pursuit of long-range objectives through stable organizational forms.

These manifestations constitute the outward reflections of a new awareness, and new motivations and attitudes on the part of the government and the people. The projects were initiated because of a new understanding of the nature of the problem they were intended to solve. Subsequent development of the projects was made possible as this understanding and its attendant urges, at first fitful and confined to a few, became sharper and more widespread. No account of the process can be complete without reference to these psychological factors.

It is necessary to begin by recounting the essential features of India's community projects. The first of these is in their objective: to improve the quality of living of the people who are involved. The second is in their method. The major reliance for effecting this improvement is upon

SUSHIL K. DEY, *former Development Commissioner for West Bengal, and formerly a member of the United Nations Secretariat, is now on the staff of the Food and Agriculture Organization in Rome.*

the effort of these people themselves. These are the two cardinal features from which all other characteristics can be deduced. The point needs elaboration. A project for community development does not aim at higher productivity in agriculture and industry, better roads and houses, more schools and clinics. None of these constitutes an end which the project pursues. For a community project, there is not a multiplicity of ends, but only one, and this single and indivisible goal is better living.

This end or goal is the product of many factors. Many of these factors are perfectly tangible. The yields from farms and workshops are such, so are the amenities like roads, sanitation, and housing, concrete facilities for health, schooling, and recreation. But there are others, equally essential, which can be neither measured nor touched. These are powers of appreciation and assimilation, the inner human capacities which can turn the factors of the outer environment to the creative end-use of richer and fuller living.

Because each of these factors enters into the final product, a community project in reaching for this product has to take account of every one of them and cannot neglect any. For this reason its program of action has a comprehensive coverage. Its concern is with agriculture, industry, health, housing, and education—indeed, with all conceivable activities in the fields of wealth and welfare, and it wants to promote them all. But its concern with any of these is not as ends in themselves, but as means to an end. This end is human growth. Therefore the nature of the concern in respect of each item of the composite program is to see how best it serves this purpose. To borrow a concept from the field of industrial economics, the focus of interest is in "the factor mix," not in factors as such.

In other words, the central question in devising a program for community development is: what are the proportions and the order in which the elements of the program must be combined in order to produce the best result? There are two broad aspects of this question, one of them economic and the other psychological. The economic problem is that of distribution of resources among various demands of production and consumption, so that development can proceed in an even manner on all fronts. Progress in agriculture has to be matched by progress in industry, and gains for the economy have to sustain and be sustained by advances in education, health, housing, and other amenities. The problem is economic because the issue it raises is of allocation and use of material resources for competing needs, although some of these needs may be noneconomic in character. The question is of establishing an optimum pattern of investments in all fields.

But a deeper, psychological or human problem is also involved. The increase in material assets cannot proceed too far ahead of the maturing of human faculties, of the growth in people's power to understand and control the process through a strengthening of their mind, will, and character. There has to be a basic parity between material and moral advance, failing which the development of human qualities will be either overwhelmed through an excess of material accumulation or starved through its inordinate lack. In either case, the objective of human growth will be frustrated.

The emphasis on self-help in a community project is derived from this principle. Self-help ensures that the project will be geared to the capacity of the people all the time and that, from a modest beginning which is suited to the meagerness of this capacity at the start, it will keep expanding in scale and growing in complexity only with the increase in the human capacity itself.

Many of the practical injunctions follow from this rule. It determines the role which outside aid can play in a community development program. That role can only be marginal in character and its object can only be to stimulate self-help, not to supplant it. It indicates the nature of the advice, equipment, and supplies through which this aid is to be provided at each stage and the pace at which improvement of technology is to be applied. Finally, it highlights the crucial importance of developing the responsibility of the people for the planning and execution of the program for their own betterment.

These truths about community projects were not and could not be clear at the outset. That was in October 1952. A major economic concern at that time was to increase the production of food grains, of which chronic shortfalls were being met by imports at the cost of foreign exchange required for capital equipment. A campaign for growing more food had continued for a number of years without appreciable effect. This campaign had been conducted through demonstrations and other attempts at extension of improved agricultural practices. Responsible opinion was assailed by doubts about the efficacy of this approach. The main obstacle was the lack of interest and incentive on the part of the cultivators. They produced largely for subsistence, had very little surplus for exchange, and lived in conditions of extreme destitution. They suffered damaging privations of the body and the mind, had little resistance to disease and little hope for the future.

There were earnest heart-searchings. It was realized that the problem demanded an attack on a wider front. The cultivator's attention could be held and his spirit roused only with the promise of relief from his many immediate pressures. Besides facilities for better cultivation, he had crying needs for medical aid, potable water and drainage, roads, housing, and mental stimulation. There could not be a meaningful program without incorporating all these elements. The first series of 55 projects was drawn up to give effect to such a program. They were started in 165 blocks of 100 contiguous villages each, on the average. The Five Year Plan did not contemplate these projects at its commencement in April 1951; provision was made for them later.

The provision was small. It amounted to less than twenty million dollars to be spent over a period of three years. But it proved difficult to make prompt use of even these limited resources. Neither the administration nor the people were fully ready to take up the challenge. The attempt to work the projects brought to light weaknesses which had remained hidden, unsuspected, or only vaguely sensed. Many pretensions and incongruities were stripped bare. It was through facing up to this reality that the wider implications of the community projects began to emerge into view. There was an increasing compulsion to think them through.

The program had to combine different measures from many separate fields of specialization such as agriculture, health, road building, education, and the like. It was not enough to string them together. They had to be joined in their proper relation, one to another, and made to develop as an organic whole. There were two aspects of this enterprise: an understanding of the properties of the materials which were to be assembled from many sources, and an understanding of what would make the completed product recognizably meaningful to the cultivators in the village. It was necessary to get people who appreciated the dual nature of the program to undertake the responsibility for the projects.

The public administration in each of the constituent states of the federal Republic of India was already engaged in what were designated as nation-building activities. These activities were organized in separate departments according to the subject matters with which they dealt. Most of these departments had functionaries working in the field. This was particularly true of the revenue, agriculture, cooperative, education, and health departments. These were the administrative agents who were closest to the people who had to be reached by the program. They were consequently entrusted with its burden. The largest use was made of the extension staff in agriculture, partly because the new program bore heavy traces of its origin from the previous campaign for growing more food.

The staff drafted in this way for the projects were shorn of their specialized labels and were designated as workers at the level of the village. But a change in title was obviously not enough. They had all been used to working within their exclusive subject matter fields. They had now to be given some understanding of the problems in other fields and of how these were related to the problems in their own. They had to develop an insight into the close interdependence of problems in all the fields which together made up the compound problem of stagnation and decadence of rural living.

The essence of their task was to impart this understanding and insight to the cultivators in the village so that these people themselves would be impelled to take action. But this could not be accomplished by teaching and preaching of theory. The knowledge could be vividly and securely gained only through direct involvement in purposeful action. The village workers were needed to take the lead in such action. This action had to be so simple that it could be carried out with immediately available resources. It had to bear so directly on the pressing needs in many fields that there could be no mistake about its purpose. The village workers were to design such programs of action and demonstrate their practice. Only then could they evoke the interest of the villagers and draw them into the orbit of the program, first as participants in its execution, and gradually in its further planning and expansion.

Arrangements were hastily devised for training the workers in the requisite skills. These skills necessarily pertained to many different disciplines, although the technical performance in each was called for at an elementary level. Experts were brought together from various specialized fields to draw up the syllabus, organize the course, and impart the training. There were many controversies about the qualifications to be prescribed for admission of the trainees to the course, the length of the course itself, the subjects to be taught, the level of proficiency in each to be aimed at, and the proportion of attention to be devoted to practical application as distinguished from theory. But time was pressing and the work was started on a provisional basis before all such questions could be fully resolved. There have been repeated changes in curricula and methods since then, and it is now clear that these will never be final.

The training institutions set up for village level workers provide an excellent vantage point from which to survey the impact of the community projects both on the administration and on the patterns of action of the people. One of the earliest discoveries was the importance of training the trainers. They were hardly in a position to impart an integral understanding of the rural problem to the trainees until they had a full realization of this themselves. This brought up the need for a team approach on the part of the different disciplines and departments of government which provided the experts on the training staff. This problem of interdepartmental coordination came acutely to the front when the program went into operation in the project areas. The new cadre of village workers represented the point of convergence of the lines of action reaching down to the people from all departments. These workers could not function if the activities of the separate authorities were not synchronized at the higher levels. This could not be accomplished unless there were concerted planning for a common objective.

This called for modification in the administrative structure. It could not happen overnight. But the commitment of the Five Year Plan had already started the process. The community projects accelerated it. A continuous line of authority was established from the Planning Commission at the Center through the planning and development departments in each state and the development officers at the district, project, and block levels, to the worker functioning in the village. These became the successive coordinating points for the specialized activities in different fields carried out by the separate departments of agriculture, education, health, and the like. The development authority at each of these points was provided with staff advisers who were experts in their respective subjects and who were seconded by the specialized departments in charge of those subject matters. An attempt was also made to orient this structure to the objective, principles, and methods of the work by organizing study camps, seminars, and joint tours of the project areas for the staff at all levels.

These principles and methods had begun to undergo changes in the meantime. Deficiencies were becoming apparent in the scope and content of the program. It was found that agricultural improvement, which had been the main plank of the economic program, could not continue to make headway without opening out new opportunities for productive employment in other directions. The shortage of capital for building up industries on a large scale with modern equipment implied that these opportunities had to be created through expansion of craft production and other forms of rural enterprise which made the minimum demand on new investment. An industrial complement had to be found for the program to meet this need. The artisan and other classes in the rural areas were thus brought within its scope. One of these classes was the increasing number of cultivators who possessed no land of their own. The majority of them could only be reached through measures for redistribution of the land which, already initiated, received added impetus for this reason. One of the most significant developments was in respect to work among women. Women were added to the staffs at all levels and home economics became an important subject for training.

It is now necessary to turn from an account of measures, machinery, and methods which the administration has adopted to a consideration of their effects on the lives of the people. Has the impact of community development made their lives better and fuller? There can be no way of direct measurement of such a purely abstract and subjective experience. But there are material ingredients and objective conditions which are acknowledged to be essential to human growth, even if these are not sufficient by themselves to assure such growth. These are susceptible to concrete assessment. It is known, for instance, that there is widespread use of improved farming practices in community project areas and that scarcities of staple foods have been relieved. Kitchen gardening, dairying, poultry breeding, fruit growing, and fish farming are being practiced on a wider scale and are making for a more varied diet and better nutrition. The supply of drinking water is better protected and has become more ample. Villagers have better and more roads. Sanitation has improved and malaria has been largely controlled. Medical aid and education have become more accessible. The needs of women receive more attention and care. There is a revival of festivals and fairs, of performances of folk art, and of sporting events.

These improvements are general all over India, but they have reached a higher level and are more visible in the project areas. They are also relative, and are appreciable only when compared with what existed before planned efforts got under way. They still fall woefully short of standards which prevail in wealthier countries and may only excite consternation when measured against optimal requirements laid down by experts. They do not satisfy any one and are not expected to. They only whet the appetite for more and act as a spur to further effort.

For this reason, it is important to look for indications of change in attitudes and behavior, in patterns of group action, and in institutional forms, which the people are evolving for themselves. It is in these, rather than in the achievement of physical and measurable targets, that the promise of sustained future advance is contained. Some of the responses have proved embarrassing to the administration. Such was the insistent demand for a more rapid expansion of the projects than could be adequately met with the available resources of trained personnel and supplies. Yet it was considered inexpedient to disappoint expectations completely, and a compromise was struck through devising a pattern of less intensively worked projects of national extension. It was decided that this national extension program would precede the full-scale community development activities in all blocks to be taken up in the future. A proportion of these would be converted to community development blocks every year and would revert to the national extension pattern after an interim intensive phase. Nearly a quarter of the total number of India's villages would be covered by national extension or community development projects by 1956, and the entire number would be so covered by 1961.

Even the national extension program did not prove sufficient, and measures of rural improvement soon had to be stretched further. This third category of measures consisted of specific works of local development like roads, schools, libraries, health clinics, and playgrounds; the cost of these works was shared equally between the government and the local people, while the responsibility of construction and maintenance was assumed by the people themselves. There were misgivings in some quarters about a too wide dispersal of resources in sporadic improvements instead of through the systematic and integrated program of normal community development. But they apparently failed to notice the quickening of life which was taking place all over the country, well beyond the range of the original projects, through the radiating effects of the projects themselves. The consequence was that even a slight spark of outside aid was proving sufficient to set off a process of self-improvement.

An important evidence of the enthusiasm evoked by the community projects was the increasing contribution of cash, material, and labor which was offered by the people in project areas to help to finance their projects. A matching contribution had been prescribed as a condition precedent for undertaking certain improvement measures. This was to be an indication of the genuine interest and participation of the people in the program of the project. But the minimum proportions laid down were exceeded many times over in a number of areas. The people were poor and not many of them had cash to spare. But they came forward to offer free labor and there were some who offered pieces of their land for opening a new road or erecting a school or club house. Buildings and other properties were also donated. Such contributions have now become a dependable source of expanding revenue for expenditure on works of local benefit, and the state of West Bengal has proposed to take them into account in its financial estimates for the Second Five Year Plan.

There is a perceptible change of climate in India's villages. Despair and resignation are beginning to give way to a new alertness. The progress is uneven over a period of time. It is also uneven in different areas. But the over-all trend is unmistakably hopeful. Where the community projects have operated for some time under the care of devoted and sensitive workers, the urge to move forward and the willingness to take over responsibility are reflected in the faces, voices, and movements of the people. Barriers between castes and factions are breaking down as new opportunities for creative effort bring people together for making roads, excavating ponds, digging irrigation channels, and erecting community centers. These and other expanding activities have also served as an excellent testing ground for traditional leaders of the village community. Many of them are losing their positions because of opposition or indifference to these calls for action when the majority have wished to rally to them. On the other hand, the program became a natural proving ground for new leaders who emerged from relative obscurity by a display of unsuspected capacities for understanding, persuasion, and energy.

The projects have set in motion deep-seated shifts in the interests and values surviving from the past and, along with them, in the symbols, insignia, and criteria of prestige and prominence. That this shift is taking place so rapidly shows that the roots of the old code of deference and conduct had already rotted, like much else, and had been lingering only because no other alternative had appeared to take its place. The project administration has played and continues to play a critical role in this process of transference. It may be assumed that it was not conscious of this fact in the beginning. But those who were sensitive could not fail to sense this very soon. At the outset it was the project staff which had to give the lead to the program. But, well drilled in the formula of people's participation, they sought local allies at once, village representatives to whom they could shift the burden of leadership as quickly as possible. It was in making this selection that the workers could give a chance to new blood.

The temptation was to try the easy way of leaning on the acknowledged spokesmen. More often than not, these were the guardians of the old order who had vested interests to protect; they survived tenaciously by exploiting dissensions in a world of narrowing opportunities, playing village politics and currying favor with visiting dignitaries whom they offered garlands and fulsome praise, and importuned for public assistance which could be turned to their private gain. Such men had obviously to be shunned if the entire program and its objectives were not to be put into serious jeopardy. Yet there was no alternative local support in the beginning and it might be dangerous to alienate men who wielded influence before first making sure of other friends.

A set of special instructions was devised to deal with this situation. The workers were advised not to ignore men of influence and position in the village consultations which they held, but to refrain from giving them formal recognition and authority until their *bona fides* was clear. It might be preferable for this reason to delay the organization of village councils and committees for local development. The best course would be to initiate a series of specific measures of obvious local benefit which could be undertaken by groups of people mobilized on an *ad hoc* basis for the detailed planning and execution of each such measure. These would serve as tests for genuine leadership. It would be possible to spot those who consistently showed the greatest zeal and earnestness. Such people were often quiet and reticent and anxious to avoid the limelight. They could be encouraged to express their views in village discussions. Their neighbours would awaken to a recognition of their merits through this process. The time would come when groups could be safely constituted on a more stable and formal basis. There would then be a withering away of the tainted leadership.

There have been some surprising results. There is record of one village, Sukna, in West Bengal, where an aboriginal woman of middle age emerged to leadership when she kept the men on a job of restoring a derelict pond by threatening a strike of all housewives if they left it for other attractions. She has been wise and prominent in village councils since then. An obscure blacksmith in another village in the same area gained a wide reputation by sponsoring a new scheme for expanding craft production. There have been many others all over the country about whom there has been no time to make a record. One lesson has been learned. The most important instrument in discovering and promoting true leadership is an effective program of action which challenges and brings out the best of which people are capable.

There are many signs that the renascent vitality which gives rise to new leadership in the villages, creates new institutions, and invigorates the old in village life will not cease to flow at the boundary of the village or of the project area, but will have ever widening repercussions. It is creating new wealth and increasing the surplus which can be offered in exchange for goods and services outside the village. This acts as a stimulant to production and employment in the urban economy. It also makes clear that reciprocal interest which holds all parts of the economy together, sets new tasks in planning, and calls for an appropriate framework of institutions for their performance. It changes the calculations in politics by bringing into view new locations of power and an altered perspective, by thrusting forward new types of personalities professing rugged and rustic values, and by demanding a fresh approach in the organization of election campaigning. Above all, the challenge is of education—of a wider and deeper understanding at all levels, especially on the part of those who are in positions of authority and direction, so that wise anticipation may take care of timely adjustments in all spheres. These adjustments have been long overdue. Not the least of the virtues of community development is to force a clearer recognition of their character.

THE IMPACT OF THE COMMUNITY DEVELOPMENT PROGRAM ON RURAL LEADERSHIP

BAIJ NATH SINGH

*C*OMMUNITY development has been defined as: "A movement designed to promote better living for the whole community, with the active participation and, if possible, on the initiative of the community, but if this initiative is not forthcoming spontaneously, by the use of techniques for arousing and stimulating it in order to secure its active and enthusiastic response to the movement."[1] It is a democratic process to build a self-reliant and prosperous community through a planned development of the local human and material resources, with necessary assistance from the government or from other agencies in the shape of technical advice, financial aid, and social services.

One of the chief objectives of the rural community development program, therefore, is to arouse the self-confidence of the village people through their local leaders, who must form the nucleus of a program planning and execution organization for the locality. Local leaders thus occupy a central place in the community development movement.

Leadership is a group process through which individuals initiate activities for achieving the common objectives of the community by working together, stimulating each other, supplementing abilities and resources, and evolving an effective organizational or hierarchical pattern. Rural leadership, however, tends to operate in informal situations also, because of the primary and intimate nature of its social interaction. We assume that leadership is always relative to the situation, and to group tasks and goals, group structure or organization, and to the population characteristics of the group including their culture.

A participant-observer study of the leadership pattern of Newari

BAIJ NATH SINGH has been an officer of the Uttar Pradesh Government concerned with village development, both in the Etawah Pilot Project and in the Community Development Project. Since 1956 he has been undertaking advanced studies of rural sociology at Cornell University.

[1] From the 1948 Cambridge Conference on the "Encouragement of Initiative in African Society," as quoted by Team No. I in their *Report on Community Development Programs in India, Pakistan and the Philippines,* Washington, D.C., International Cooperation Administration, 1955, p. 8.

Kalan in pilot project Etawah, Uttar Pradesh, is presented to illustrate these principles. This pilot project, the precursor of the community development program in India, was started in 1948 by the Uttar Pradesh state government with a team of Indian workers, and Albert Mayer of New York as the planning and development adviser. The writer happened to be associated with it as a village participation officer in the first five years of the project.

The Village

Newari Kalan (the big Newari) is an important village in the Bharthana subdivision, Etawah District. It is six miles from Mahewa, the headquarters of the pilot project. Newari is a big village with a total population of about 2500, if the six hamlets which surround the big central village are also included. This paper will deal with the big village only, as it forms one community. The population of this community is about 1500, and the number of families about 235. The total area cultivated by the families residing in this community is approximately 2750 acres.

Newari Distributory Canal with its minor channels flows through this village and irrigates about 80 per cent of the land. Wheat, barley, peas, maize, millets, and sugar cane are grown on the irrigated land. Chick-peas and mustard are grown in unirrigated fields. Some paddy is also grown to the north of the village in an area which has recently come under irrigation. Most of the people live on the land as farmers or farm laborers. Some educated young men are engaged in teaching or other services outside the village. Handicrafts have languished, and today there are no other artisans except the carpenters who manufacture and repair bullock carts and other agricultural implements. Weavers no more weave the homespun yarn; difficulties of getting mill-made yarn during the war and after ruined this craft and the weavers took to agricultural labor.

A caste-wise distribution of the population is given to indicate the social organization of the village. It may be mentioned that the castes are no longer the impenetrable social barriers that they are sometimes made out to be. The social, economic, and political changes of the last three decades have taken the sting from the caste system, and it is neither the symbol of exploitation nor of severe stratification that it used to be. Nevertheless the caste system is indicative of different shades of economic and social organization and it may be interesting to note this class composition. The population of Newari Kalan is roughly distributed in the following manner:

Name of the Caste	Number of Families or Households
Brahman (Highest caste)	60
Rajput (Martial caste)	4
Bania (Vaisya) (Trader)	5
Bhurji (Vaisya) (Trader)	2
Kachhi (Vegetable grower)	15
Lodhe (Farmer)	12
Mohammadan (Muslim)	13
Nai (Barber)	7
Julaha (Weaver)	12
Dhobi (Washerman)	5
Barhai (Carpenter)	6
Luhar (Blacksmith)	4
Bahelia (Hunter)	35
Harijan (Scheduled caste)	55

Even the present occupational and social patterns indicate a certain amount of division of labor, but it is not rigid. For example, the Rajputs of this village are warlike people, but are no more engaged in any warlike profession. A large number of Brahmans are educated and are engaged in teaching and other social services, but their occupation is no longer confined to teaching or learning. Brahmans and Rajputs own most of the land and are engaged in agriculture. After the abolition of zamindari some land has gone to occupancy tenants. The so-called upper castes continue to have an advantageous position because they have relatively more land and influence than others. Education and social status have helped them to gain a place of leadership in the community.

Efforts to Approach the Leaders of the Village

The pilot project was started with eight village level workers covering sixty-four villages. There were thus eight subcenters where these workers lived and from which they carried on their Extension work in about eight villages each. Newari Kalan was selected as the subcenter for its area, but no village level workers lived there because no accommodation was available. The people of the village were not very keen to have a village level worker in their village because they thought he would cause unnecessary disturbances in their peaceful and relatively prosperous life.

The village level worker for this village reported that the people were not willing to accept the improved seeds or fertilizers being distributed through the project. He requested that the subject matter specialists visit the village and help him with his program.

There was a gentleman from this village who was a professor of Sanskrit in Allahabad which is about 150 miles from Etawah. He had come home for Dashahra[2] vacations and met the officials of the project. He invited them to concentrate on this big village which was so progressive as to have twenty-five graduate and postgraduate scholars, including a lady graduate. The rural life analyst and the deputy development officer for village participation took this opportunity to accompany the gentleman to Newari Kalan in order to study the situation on the spot and render necessary help and advice to the village level worker.

It was hoped that the professor would arrange a meeting of the educated people of the village and that they would be enthusiastic and interested in the development program. The two officers of the project stayed there for seven or eight hours. Only two or three educated young men came to meet them. Instead of showing any interest in the rural development plan they talked about the next examination they were going to take and a possible increase in their salary. None of the other villagers came, nor did the professor arrange any meeting.

It was realized that the graduates were neither influential in the village nor even interested. The professor was an older man and was sincere; but he did not know his village and the people did not care for his concern with village improvement. The number of highly educated people serving outside and coming to the village to live with their joint families during vacations was no index of the progressive preparedness of the village to accept a program of social change.

When asked about the names of influential individuals in the village the people replied, "Each one is the master of his own house." This was a difficult situation. It was found, however, that Chowdhary B. S. was the richest landlord and was most influential. Chowdhary R. N. was also very influential, being the second biggest landlord.

The occasion for the second approach was the spread of rinderpest (a fatal epidemic disease of cattle). The cattle were dying, but people did not accept the advice of the village level worker who urged them to inoculate their cattle against the epidemic. The village level worker again requested the help of the subject matter specialist. This time all

[2] A Hindu festival celebrated in September or October according to the lunar calendar.

the officers of the project went to the village, thinking that the presence of the whole group might help acceptance. They approached the second biggest zamindar (landlord) and tried to use his influence to get cattle for inoculation, but people drove away their cattle from the village and only forty-seven cattle were inoculated.

Another approach for the sanitation drive brought the same answer. The district development officer was making a round of the village. The lanes were stinking with knee-deep disposal water and filth. When it was pointed out that the lanes should be cleaned and soakage pits made, many people answered, "Nobody can do anything here. Each one is the master of his own family in this village." This meant that there was no leadership in the village. People were complacent and did not feel the need of any development program.

Social Disorganization

On a closer study of the situation further clues to the utter social disorganization of the village were found. Leadership could be divided into the following four groups: the group led by Chowdhary B. S., R. N.'s group, L. Mishra's group, and G. S.'s group. In fact the two richest persons no longer commanded the prestige and influence as they had before. Their power and prestige had been based on exploitation and repression. The people were now exposed to the renascent democratic spirit led by a new educated middle class. During the period when abolition of landlordism was in sight and the Panchayat Raj Act was to come into force, the two rich landlords had lost their influence.

The old professor represented the educated middle class. His group was led by an uneducated but practical businessman, P. D., who had established himself as a rising businessman and as one genuinely interested in the middle class. G. S. was comparatively young.

Rajputs had no position of leadership because three members of the four families were involved in a murder case and were serving life imprisonment. This murder was an incident of clash of leadership when a Bhurji had challenged the influence of one of the leading members of the Rajput clan which resulted in the Rajput's being murdered. The Rajputs retaliated by arranging for the murder of the Bhurji leader and thus were involved in the criminal case along with two or three Brahmans. During the investigations and the prosecution of the case repression had gone on so that no enthusiasm for leadership was left in the village. Old landlord families crumbled unless they found an alternative business because their tenants had stopped paying them most of the traditional favors in anticipation of the abolition of landlordism. The standard of living of these families was high, but sources of income were shrinking. The loyalty of the people who had supported and retained them as leaders was also in abeyance and they could no longer hold positions of leadership.

Contrary to a general notion, younger men in this community were rising as leaders. The older and richer leaders had become unpopular because of the deeds which kept them in power in earlier years—intimidation and exploitation. This trend was recognized by the rural life analyst and became clear in the village elections.

These elections to the Village Panchayat were held in March 1949, and Shri G. S., thirty years old, was elected the *pradhan* (president) of the village executive. D. N., K. C., S. D., and P. D. were the other prominent members. Most of these leaders were in the age group 25 to 35. They were enthusiastic and sincere and had aspirations for achieving some measure of community welfare.

The deputy development officer immediately seized the opportunity of these elections and held a meeting in the village. The new *pradhan* collected 34 out of 35 members. Members actively participated in a discussion on the rights and duties of the various subcommittees of the Village Panchayat and resolved to work out a good program for the village.

The Impact of New Activities on Leadership

In the meantime the intensive community development program had caught up. By April 1949 the outstanding wheat crop of Punjab 591, grown with fertilizer (ammonium sulphate), was applauded everywhere. Only six or seven farmers had accepted the improved seed in this village. Their rejoicing gave a keener edge to others' appetite for sowing improved varieties of seeds next season. The difference in the yield and the superiority of the grain and the chaff was so apparent that some farmers were even displeased with the village level worker who had not pleaded with them strongly enough. When they had refused, the worker had distributed the improved seed to the members of another village.

Another occurrence had made the villagers more conscious. Rinderpest took a toll of about 200 cattle between December 1948 and February 1949 in this village. The officials of the project had tried hard, but had been able to inoculate only 47 cattle. Two Barbers, one Rajput, two

Brahmans, and five or six Harijans who had their cattle inoculated had no losses of cattle. Others repented for their refusal to accept the inoculation program.

Now the people of this village seized every opportunity of introducing technical innovation or general education. A few of these activities which had a cumulative effect on the leadership structure of the village are mentioned in this connection. The project workers wanted to start literacy classes in some selected villages. Shri G. S., the *pradhan*, insisted that his village must be one. He suggested the name of a young man who had conducted classes for adult illiterates for three or four months.

There was a proposal to organize consumers' stores in some of the key villages, particularly for kerosene oil which was a scarce commodity. Newari Kalan people insisted that they must have it in their village. This shop was managed by the adult teacher. Later on it was taken up by another leader and managed on behalf of the Mahewa Cooperative Union for about a year.

The next technological program introduced was green manuring by turning under sannhemp, a legume generally used for its fiber. This program was accepted, but by only a few persons. Though the general attitude toward the program had changed, people had yet to see the success of specific items in their own conditions. The *pradhan* and a few others used green manure in their wheat fields. A number of agricultural implements such as cultivators and light soil-turning ploughs had been accepted by middle class farmers.

During the next winter crop (rabi) season, however, they procured from the project about 160 maunds (220 bushels) of the wheat seed which had already succeeded. They also applied fertilizers. Most of the farmer families were now involved in the agricultural program. Almost 99 per cent of the people had their cattle inoculated against hemorrhagic septicemia and rinderpest, the two most disastrous cattle diseases of the area.

The *pradhan* procured a medicine chest for common ailments from the project on a 50 per cent subsidy basis. The panchayat paid Rs. 25 as its share. The chest contained a number of standard indigenous medicines and some first aid materials. The *pradhan* learned to use these medicines and was able to establish closer contact with the people through the distribution of medical aid.

In January 1950 six selected village *panches* were invited to a village leaders' training camp organized by the workers of the project. Shri G. S., the *pradhan*, Shri L. P., the doubting member, Shri P. D., Shri S. D.,

Shri L. S., and M. L. joined the camp. They discussed various aspects of the rural development program such as agriculture, animal husbandry, public health, communications, and village organization—i.e., cooperatives and panchayats, recreation and social education. They went on a sight-seeing trip to Allahabad which is also a place of pilgrimage. They saw the Agricultural Institute at Allahabad, an excellent center of agricultural education. They were very much impressed with this program. They became confirmed village allies to project workers, and good leaders in Extension and general matters relative to the interests of the people of the village. Shri L. P. was even more enthusiastic than others. Next year he followed all the recommended methods in growing wheat and obtained 48 maunds or 65 bushels per acre.[3] He enthused other members of the community with the same zest with which he had opposed the program of technological development prior to his joining the village leaders' camp.

After their return from the camp these village leaders renewed their request for widening the village lanes and building soakage pits. But this time the request was different. In the first year they had requested that the workers of the project come with their spades and baskets and remove the obstructions from the lanes and build them wide. Now they informed the project that they had passed a resolution for widening their lanes and were going to carry out the program on such and such dates and would like the village participation officer to help them if there were disputes or technical difficulties.

The program continued for four or five days. Lanes throughout the village were widened. There came points of great difficulty for some people were unwilling to remove their encroaching verandas. But the village leaders, whose number grew through this movement, tackled all the problems peacefully. One recalcitrant gentleman allowed them to widen the lane only after a negotiation lasting three hours, and later on stopped the work and also filed a law suit against the *pradhan*. The whole panchayat supported the *pradhan* and arranged for funds to fight out the suit. There was a virtual replanning of the village. Thereafter the people built excellent soakage pits and gave a new shape to their village.

Towards the end of February 1950 they had a big wrestling match in which wrestlers from the neighboring areas participated. They invited the workers of the project to participate in this function. The

---

[3] The average yield of wheat per acre before the introduction of this program was 10 maunds or 14 bushels in this area.

workers came and assisted in the organization. It was a big event. About three thousand people witnessed it, and Newari Kalan village earned a new prestige in the area.

The developments mentioned above created a new craving in the village leaders and the village people to take up new programs and to see that their village became a center for all activities. They had grown new varieties of improved wheat and sold their extra produce to their project. Some of them needed seed again the following year, but did not like to travel six miles to procure seed. Others thought that the project workers would get improved peas next year and would distribute them to the villagers near Mahewa (the headquarters of the entire project), and the people in this village would not get as much seed and with as much convenience as they would if they had a seed store in their own village.

Others had got good yields and wanted to invest their extra income in building brick houses. Bricks were not available locally and transport cost from the nearest town was heavy. They wanted a brickkiln in their village. But starting a brickkiln needed a capital of Rs. 15,000 (about $3,200). The local leaders had a new challenge. A larger number of enthusiastic and interested people took the lead in raising share money and advance deposits. The brickkiln was started.

During this period project workers were building six cooperative union buildings so that their project area of 100 villages would be suitably covered. The Newari area was to have a cooperative union building. But the project officers had only Rs. 6,000 ($1,350) and a building cost Rs. 12,000 ($2,700). They were therefore planning to build on an old indigo factory site where they would get free land and a structure already raised about four feet above the ground and in excellent condition. Three to four thousand rupees ($700-$850) could be saved in this manner and with village participation the building was constructed. The factory site was in Newari Khurd village (the small Newari), about two miles from the central village. The members of this cooperative union were holding a meeting at Newari Kalan when the participation officer arrived. The members asked, "Why are you going to build the cooperative union building in Newari Khurd where people do not take interest, and why are you against our village?"

The participation officer stated that in building the cooperative union in Newari Kalan they would have to incur an additional expenditure of three to four thousand rupees. One of the village leaders said, "We shall pay you Rs. 3,000 at once." The village leaders collected Rs. 2,000 in cash and promised Rs. 1,000 within a week. They did deposit the amount in due course. They also donated some bricks from their kiln which had now started working. Thus the village had a building for their cooperative union and for the Village Panchayat.

New Leadership Structure

These activities demanded extra work. The major load of the increased activity fell on the village people themselves. The brickkiln required two or three intelligent workers most of the time, besides a full time clerk-salesman. Since the cooperative union through its brickkiln activity was handling thousands of rupees, a treasurer was needed. The treasurer must be a rich man so that he may stand security for large sums and may be trusted. R. B., the son of Chowdhary B. S., was elected.

The brickkiln and the cooperative program needed an active secretary. Shri K. C., a high school graduate and an enthusiastic young man who was also good as a speaker and canvasser, was elected secretary. He belonged to the rich family of R. N. Sri S., a retired army man of the neighboring village, was elected president.

It was interesting that the young members of both the rival families were elected to the cooperative union. Their presence was needed in the beginning because they contributed money and devoted time to the work; but they could not pull together, and the members of the cooperative union elected two other members as the secretary and the treasurer.

The *pradhan* of the Village Panchayat, P. D., the middle-class village leader, and the professor who had now come down to the area from Allahabad and was the principal of a local intercollege, continued to take interest in the affairs of the village. The professor could not hold any position in these organizations because he could not devote sufficient time to the village. He did command some respect, however, because he did show genuine interest.

The clerk-salesman, the accountant, two *kamdars* (workers), and a few part time workers were drawn from the village. They could not be called leaders, but they had some influence, and the members of their families also took interest.

A few new activities were added. A program for paving the lanes and constructing masonry drains had failed in the first year of the union, because people had paid for the building of the cooperative union. The next year they took up the program of paving the lanes. The *pradhan* alone could not organize the whole program. His colleagues on the council participated in raising funds from the house owners in their respective lanes and organizing the actual construction of lanes. With widened lanes already completed this program was facilitated.

Now the village people wanted their village to be seen by people from other villages and other areas and they also desired better communication for themselves. A good road was built connecting Newari Kalan to the canal bank, up to which point vehicles could come easily along the canal road.

The effect of these activities was to widen the base of leadership in the village. The two or three families which had led the village previously were mostly inactive at the time the project work started. Now about ten to twelve persons took leading roles in various situations and continued interest in others. Leadership of the village achieved a dynamic equilibrium. The leadership pattern that arose out of these numerous activities was functional, and people with various qualities and inclinations came up to fulfill these new roles in the community.

Within three years after the establishment of the cooperative union the local temple was repaired and a junior high school started. Self-initiated and self-generated activities of the school, the paved lane, the market, the repaired temple showed that a new optimism, new aspirations and desires, new values and beliefs had penetrated into a dormant village life and had become a part of the village culture. A new leadership structure had arisen to nurture these new values and aspirations. The village was no longer a place where "everyone was the master of his own house," but where new community ideals were being developed through their new institutions—the panchayat, the cooperative society, the grammar school, and the temple.

The leadership pattern thus evolved had certain characteristic features. The new village leaders were in the middle and younger age groups, contrary to the general belief that only village elders and headmen could lead rural communities. These leaders came from the upper-middle or middle income groups. The richest families that had wielded influence in the past could no longer be counted upon for two reasons: they could not go far enough in community welfare programs and frequently withdrew the moment their self interest was even remotely threatened; and various legislative and political changes had a dampening effect on their enthusiasm and also on their acceptance as leaders by the villagers.

Leadership was now open even to small cultivators, livestock keepers, or artisans if they showed qualities of leadership and initiative in productive activities. From those who had wielded authority and power, leadership now passed to those who devoted some time to the service of the community. Instead of being autocratic or authoritarian, leadership became democratic and had the strength to do away with warring individuals by a vote of no confidence.

It may be mentioned that the framework for the new rural leadership structure was provided by the enforcement of the Panchayat Raj Act, but it took a dynamic form through the various activities under the community development program. It cannot be claimed that the mere introduction of the program or the Panchayat Act created a new leadership in every situation. It can be asserted, however, that latent talents got an opportunity for self-expression through the community development program, and the community recognized their leadership as the new leaders helped fulfill some of the felt needs of the community.

Leadership development in many other villages of the pilot project, and later on in the community projects, had certain uniform features in spite of the uniqueness of each particular situation. These were the growing awareness, interest, and willingness of many members of the community to take leadership roles and to devote time to community activities. When the pilot project was started in 1948 people felt that no community activity was possible because some strong, selfish, and violent individuals would smash the effort. The fear was common that some opponents would attack the participants in a road program with sticks, or file a law suit, or that no one would participate. The community development program showed that community activities were possible and would be popular, and that there would generally be no violence.

People who had been accustomed to the paternal administration of colonial rule and who thought that government alone could build their schools or roads, and that these projects were beyond the reach of the people, now changed as they saw school buildings completed, roads constructed, or lanes paved with nominal or no financial assistance from the government. Whereas these activities built up the confidence of the people in general, they also provided a challenge to more dynamic individuals to take up leadership roles and build organization patterns to make the new leadership an integral part of the democratic process.

In the past some villages, awakened by the needs of the new community activities, realized that they had dropped out some individuals of exceptional ability and community spirit. In community projects in

Uttar Pradesh such people were coopted as members of specific subcommittees (on public health, education, agriculture, security, and so on) for which provision existed in the bylaws of the Panchayat Raj Act. If they showed interest and insight they had a further chance of being elected to the formal organization. This system has, however, to be developed and expanded on a much wider scale.

Village factions, apparently very acute in the years immediately after Independence, were the symptoms of a new social situation seeking readjustment. The community development program offered a channel for the ascendant and aggressive tendencies of some of the members of the community, and it was found that many of the faction-torn villages became leaders in the new program. Villages with no leadership struggled to find a leader. Those with an individual leader found a group leadership. Conflict-torn villages also readjusted to a group leadership situation. The community development program motivated the members of the community to arrive at this essential organizational arrangement to solve new problems facing the community. This process has started the necessary counterbalance to social disorganization and the breakup of the joint Hindu family in the wake of technological change. No observation, however, is rigidly universal and there are flaws and pitfalls in the expected social adjustment. It is hoped that a widely recognized and functionally organized leadership will gradually emerge as the community development program enters into the life habits of the coming generation.

Apart from the village level, the community development programs provided another leadership opportunity through their block or project advisory committees to which each *gaon sabha* (village assembly) sends one representative who participates in formulation of plans and programs and approval of subsidies. Apart from the prestige value, it provides a practical training ground for rural leadership. The expanded cooperative program of covering all the villages of the National Extension Service or Community Project area with the cooperative societies also helps the growth of leadership.

In the period of the First Five Year Plan the government officers and the local leaders were both cautious in their approach, and the democratic process was rather slow. Government officials were afraid of placing funds at the disposal of local leaders, and local leaders were not sure that the promised help or proposed program would come up in time. These four or five years have dispelled doubt and have proved that there is no short-cut to training people to take responsibility without actually giving responsibility to them. The state has realized the magnitude of the problem of nation building and it is believed that the community development program must be taken up by the people themselves. People on the other hand have shown beyond doubt their capacity to shoulder responsibility. The community development program has thus introduced changes in the people and in their local leadership. The program itself has also undergone a dynamic change in the process. It was initiated as a government program with people's participation and now it is being developed as a people's program with government participation.

PATTERNS OF INFLUENCE
WITHIN RURAL INDIA

EVELYN WOOD

*T*HE National Extension Service (NES) should not be restricted to routine agency work for the agricultural and other sciences. The Community Development Projects, which operated the first form of extension service in India through the Community Projects Administration (CPA), carried principles of social change along with them. But these principles were preconceptual and not founded on any knowledge gathered by sociological or anthropological disciplines. The NES, now including the Community projects, must itself become much more of a scientific vehicle of social and political development, and less of a transmitter of the village problems and the physical sciences' solutions. In fact, it does not appear as if the NES as now constituted can operate the village-to-city or inward channel of communications towards the scientific bodies which must consider village problems. To gather village problems in which the social and psychological components are inextricably mixed with the physical, and to assess village people's demands, needs, and reactions to changes proposed, seem to be impossible tasks, at least without some methodology borrowed from the social sciences. There is a need for more profound, more widespread, and better-linked studies in India.

The Programme Evaluation Organization (PEO) of the Planning Commission does employ many of the concepts and methods of social science in examining, constructively, the progress of the NES. There is, however, a certain danger that reliance on the PEO may tend to narrow the village-to-city channel of communications which should flow through the NES, so that Extension carries only outward communications from

EVELYN WOOD has lived in India's villages and cities for over thirty years. His special interest lies in the field of systematizing two-way communication with village people. Originally qualified in Great Britain as a mechanical and hydraulic engineer, he spent his first thirteen years in India working for a large East India merchant's business. This work took him to villages in every part of India except Orissa. During the following twelve years, four and one-quarter of which were spent in incomeless personal experiment with residence in several different villages, some attempts were made to promote or assist changes in the lives of village neighbors. The writer's last six years have been spent as a consultant in rural development through the techniques of Extension methods and through the use, by fieldworkers, of materials appropriate to teaching adults, particularly illiterates.

the cities to the villages. (In this context "cities" denotes also scientific institutions and other planners in the modern manner, wherever they may be situated.)

It would be of the greatest value for development through Extension (not only in the rural field) if it were possible to use leadership structures as two-way channels of communication, and hence of adult education. But to use leadership structures for this nonpolitical purpose, it is essential that they be sharply defined. Definition of this order will require intensive studies by social scientists. It would appear to this writer as if the social scientists in question must use interdisciplinary techniques; it may be that operation in teams of at least two members would be necessary.

Working for the PEO, Lewis, Dhillon, and others have produced studies of village situations relevant to developments through Extension which touch on leadership.[1] These are but a beginning. Besides leadership, many other factors in the social and culture patterns of villages in India need analysis before plans for development will work smoothly with villagers and prove durable in their changing situations.

A hypothesis which might be worth exploring is the likelihood that the "mass" of village people in some areas will be found to be "leader-prone," much as some factory workers are found to be accident-prone. The leadership involved in this possible proneness of village majorities would appear to be that of persuasive, sympathetic, and well-educated nonvillagers who come to stay with them for short periods. The success of the Communist Party of India in certain regions such as Telengana would appear to be largely explainable by such "leader-proneness."

The Assumptions of Planners

There seems to be no doubt that the survival of traditional cultures is

---

[1] Oscar Lewis, *Group Dynamics in a North Indian Village*, PEO Publication No. 1, Delhi, Planning Commission, Programme Evaluation Organization, 1954. A fuller version appeared in the *Economic Weekly* (Bombay) in the four issues, April 10, 17, 24, May 1, 1954. Harwant Singh Dhillon, *et al.*, *Leadership and Groups in a South Indian Village*, PEO Publication No. 9, Delhi, Planning Commission, Programme Evaluation Organization, 1955. Other useful studies of village life in India include: M. N. Srinivas, *et al.*, *India's Villages*, [Alipore], Development Department, West Bengal Government, 1955 (originally published as a series of articles in the *Economic Weekly*). Adrian C. Mayer, "Change in a Malwa Village," *Economic Weekly*, September 24, 1955, pp. 1147-49. McKim Marriott, ed., *Village India*, Chicago, University of Chicago Press, 1955. P. Alston Waring, "Reflections on Some of the Problems in Rural Development," Philadelphia, American Friends Service Committee, December 1953 (mimeo.). Albert Mayer, "Question of Leadership in Villages and of our Associations," Extension Project, Allahabad Agricultural Institute, April 1954 (mimeo.).

more nearly entire in India's villages than in her towns. The larger cities exhibit patterns of social organization and culture which have to a large extent absorbed western motives, habits of thought and social forms. This transitional stage of Indian social and cultural patterns shows its more western aspects in the higher-income urban groups. These are the groups who either have the political power or serve those who do have it. Such groups initiate planning and control its execution. Most members of these powerful groups now incline outwardly toward supposedly traditional patterns. At the same time, few of them are disposed to recognize that their knowledge of the traditional forms of culture and social organization as practiced in the villages is inadequate.

There is, for example, a persistent tendency among educated, urbanized Indians to generalize their own forms of thinking, motivation, and behavior as "Indian." It seems elementary to sociologists or anthropologists that patterns of society and culture differ radically in villages as between, say, Punjab and Travancore; yet this is not accepted by a large number—it seems an overwhelming majority—of Indians at the top planning levels. In this context, planning must cause social and culture conflicts when it comes to execution at the village level. The least danger from this anticipated clash is that village people will accept plans as made for them ostensibly with their assent; but that the improvements made by those plans will not, in fact, seem to be improvements to the minds of the villagers. If this be their unspoken value-judgment, the improvements will not endure in the actions of village people after the pressure of the nonvillagers has been relaxed. Improvements in village life and work can only prove durable if they are geared to the social mores practiced by the village folk of each particular area and if they are also in harmony with the motives or inhibitions which rise from the local culture pattern.

To be sure, the cultures will change with the improvements, and the social practices will adapt themselves to these changes. But changes of nonvillage initiation which are at first taken by village people to be improvement will have to offer them more than immediate economic advantage if they are to strike roots and put forth fresh fruits of new change with successive generations. Without some background knowledge and continuing control by social scientists, it does not seem that any rural development can easily become a self-generating process. At least, say, forty rather profound socio-anthropological studies, with a fair amount of contribution from psychologists, will be needed in different regions of India in order to secure an adequate base of knowledge on which to plan improvements in the villages.

It is generally acknowledged that India has large numbers of economists, but is short of professionals in the fields of the other social sciences. Indian economists are largely trained in concepts and methods developed in western countries. It is only very recently that the other social sciences which are taught in India have begun to develop approaches to these disciplines which have some regional, not to say national, characteristics. Rural field work in sociology, anthropology, and social psychology is not frequent or profound. The development of India, proceeding now under its Second Five Year Plan, is the product of ideologies which are mainly western in origin, though colored by regional adaptations, toward which the Gandhian philosophy is generally considered to be the dominant modifier. The techniques of planning are, however, entirely of western origin. The mechanisms of communication by the planners with those for whom the plans are made are also largely western. The execution of the plans, after they have been made, is entrusted mainly to a hierarchy of officials which is organized on western lines and which was developed principally during the British regime.

It is at the village level that this structure of planning and execution is seen at its weakest. Insofar as the village level worker (lowest in the official hierarchy) is either imbued with the western social concepts and methods implied in planning, or superficially adopts them for the sake of peace in his job, this field agent of government nearly always experiences some culture conflict with the village people.

In theory, the village folk participate in planning, but it is doubtful if there are more than microscopic areas in which they do more than assent to the plans made for them by nonvillagers. In this sense, the village level worker's dependence on his job for a living tends to rank him as a nonvillager.

In the execution of plans for rural areas, the collaboration of village people is readily forthcoming; but this may frequently be because they dare not refuse to act in response to the wishes of the government in power, and its representatives in the Extension Service. In fact, this pliability of village people to the designs made for them by others extends to unofficial workers, such as Christian missionaries, because the villager is accustomed to anticipate that the nonofficial who asks to carry out some supposed improvement is well connected with government officials and can therefore influence the favorable or unfavorable action of government towards village people.

⇨§ "There were brave men before Agamemnon...."

Rural development through Extension methods long preceded the independence of India, though the term "Extension" was not then used. Both western and traditional Indian approaches and methods were used to spread more knowledge and thus to influence change for the better in small groups of villages. The major characteristics of the western approach was its conviction that the villagers did not know what was good for them. The Indian approach sometimes took the opposite view that only the villagers could have the means of valuing improvement. In this sense "Gandhian" constructive workers of the Congress Party were westernized.

Among the western projects, Brayne of Gurgaon, near Delhi, offered one classical example.[2] Another was the Martandam project in South Travancore. One was semi-official, the other quasi-missionary. Neither probed deeply into villagers' sources of values. Little has remained of the supposed improvements which these two projects initiated.

A classical example of the Indian traditional approach is afforded by the former Aundh State, about one hundred miles south of Poona. In this early "Gandhian" experiment to improve village life and work, no violence was done to local conservatisms. The nonvillage promoters of changes (the present writer was one of two foreigners to the local culture pattern connected with this project) worked by persuasion. But we had to find the villagers' tempo and reduce our own speed almost to the fastest of theirs. We were perfectly aware, too, of the differences in mental orbit between ourselves and the most advanced of the more rooted peasants. Among ourselves, the initiators of the small, local plans, there was none who was not at least touched by western analytical thought. We soon found that such categorization had no meaning for our village counterparts in planning.

Our persuasion had no official sanctions whatever to back it. Though members of the ruling family were among the nonvillagers in planning, no hope for their favor or fear of their disfavor influenced the village people with whom we worked. As persons, the ruling caste was respected, but the villagers knew that there were no substantial favors to be got out of them.

Exploration of the rather differing values of people in the same village formed a major part of planning discussions. It proved necessary to proceed by trial and error, verbally at first, and then by the action of

---

[2] See F. L. Brayne, *Village ABC*, 456 *Hints on Rural Reconstruction*, Bombay, Oxford University Press, 1950.

field tests and the like. No side issues could be dismissed as irrelevant and no prejudices could be brushed aside—at first. Later on, the more progressive villagers themselves blew continuing conservatives out of the framework of discussion or action; in all cases the diehards begged to come back. [Habitual formulae which substituted for fresh thinking were very slowly replaced by reasoning.]

The changes which were accepted in Aundh State projects have proved durable through a second generation and are today thought of by those village people who resisted them as nothing more than a base for further improvement. This remains a fact of new thinking in those villages, though the state was dissolved over ten years ago and its people have since been rather ostentatiously disregarded by the government into whose administration they passed.

The experiences outlined above suggest that the procedures of the social sciences in India will have to be adapted to fit local conditions, perhaps to a greater extent than elsewhere. It would appear that the body-social in Indian villages is unusually sensitive to the introduction of the exploring instrument. This may be because that same body is now acutely conscious of long sickness and a need for healthy change. Whether it be an anthropologist pursuing his studies of village people's habits and motives, their ideas of cosmology and religion, or a sociologist charting the structure of human relationships within the village, and its activities, the very action of making inquiry seems at first to induce artificial, if not evasive or concealing, responses from villagers.

The fieldworkers of the National Extension Service could be in an optimum position to shorten this period of acute sensitivity and to render village people more apt to such inquiry, by helping them to understand its purposes. Social science studies in collaboration with NES cadres in the villages could proceed faster than studies not so based, with one proviso: that the governmental functions of the NES such as revenue collection and regulation of supplies, loans, and grants be subordinated to its educational and other communication functions. This is a possible future for the NES, but not a probable one. It may well be, therefore, that the distinct corps of social education organizers attached to the NES, but relatively free of governmental functions, could more readily serve as a base for social scientists.

It seems apparent that one or the other form of working within the NES by social scientists would help toward making the scientific findings influential in rural development. Another strong reason for this associative proposal is the grave need for NES field workers, including social education organizers, to have some insight into the concepts and methods of the social sciences.[3] While gaining such insight, the better village level workers and social education organizers might very well assist social scientists to form their necessary adaptations of method to fit the Indian village field; they could also be a help with their fluency in local dialects.

There has already been a trend toward broad economic studies in India, the conclusions of which have colored the attitude of planners. The economic aspects of village improvement thus tend to dominate the choice and priority of the improvements to be promoted. Such choices do not necessarily accord with village scales of values. Other social sciences are needed to explore the scales of values which are recognized and to keep track of the changes in values which occur as new practices became established in the villages.

Leadership and Change in Village India

Something has already been said about the tendency for village people at first to accede to the suggestions of educated persons toward improvements in village life and work. To some extent this is direct or indirect "playing it safe" with an eye on government favor or disfavor. Other factors are also involved. The educated person may personally be regarded as a provider of good for individual villagers or groups, if not for the village as a whole. Besides the possibility of his having powerful friends in government circles, from which good or evil may fall on the villagers, he may also be thought to have rich friends who could provide largesse to "us poor people" in some way or the other. And no educated person can live in a village which has, for example, no medical service without being compelled to operate a crude sort of first-aid clinic; this is the least of the benefits that a well-placed stranger is expected to dispense, by virtue of his superior education.

There is no question of such demands being made only on foreigners, or only on Indians who are obviously westernized and of a much higher living standard than the villagers. Any highly educated person of any national or racial origin is equally likely to be taxed by his village neighbors for information and skill on any difficult subject. It is useless to hold out against villagers' claims on one's nonexistent knowledge or skill. Their judgment that the educated person's mind is more orderly and his actions better coordinated to unfamiliar skills, if he will but try, is

---

[3] See Carl C. Taylor, *A Critical Analysis of India's Community Development Programme*, C.P.A. Publication No. 1-1, Community Projects Administration, 1956.

undeniably sound. Therefore to refuse their requests for aid when it is right outside one's own field is to court their corresponding refusal of information or other collaboration later on. The only likely inhibitor to such appeals acts where the educated stranger is an Indian of known caste. Then, if his caste be such as to disqualify him, in the villagers' estimation, for offering knowledge or demonstrating skill in the particular subject on which aid is sought, he will not be asked to help.

Any person starting for the first time to promote some new or changed practice in an Indian village would naturally look for distinguished persons whose livings were connected with the practice. If the improvement were something of apparent benefit to the whole village, like a protected water supply for domestic use, the promoter would perhaps make his first contact with the village panchayat, starting with the *sarpanch* or the panchayat secretary.

In any case, the newly arrived worker in the village would do well to get on good terms with the panchayat, whatever his objectives might be. So much is common procedure, but the approaches made could be of deceptive value if there happened to be a statutory panchayat, whether nominated by government or duly elected under law, provided that panchayat were not wholly satisfactory to a large or powerful number of the villagers. In such circumstances, it is often possible for the traditional panchayat, which is usually hereditary in composition, to coexist unofficially with the statutory body. The village worker would then be well advised to make himself and his objectives known to all members of both bodies. Frequently in such cases, there is some overlapping membership.

The error arises when the nonvillager supposes either panchayat to be composed of individuals who will necessarily lead while the rest of the village people follow, or at any rate obey the panchayat's orders. This may be the case; individuals or groups may even put on a show of such conformity with the panchayat's expressed wishes because it is safer to make such a demonstration for an educated visitor from the world of political and economic power outside the village.

Leadership does not seem to inhere for all purposes in any individual within any but exceptional villages; nor to inhere in groups of village worthies even when these are associated either in traditional or statutory panchayats. Leadership may accrue to such individuals or groups, but it is occasional, and usually the result of an *ad hoc* mandate given by the supposed "mass" of "followers" which has already been amply consulted on that particular issue. Majorities—at any rate those of the fifty-one per cent order—are not popular mechanisms in village India; something very close to unanimity is required on a matter of mutual interest, whether it be between a few families or the whole village as a group. The larger the group, the harder it is for any individual committee to get powers of decision and the ordering of action assigned. Where the action requires that a person or a small group be invested with powers of command over intervillage squads, the process of obtaining authority is still more difficult and protracted. Again, a show of obedience to a "democratic" body approved by government may be made as a matter of "safety first" policy.

Therefore, if present efforts at community development and change are to be permanent, social scientists must learn to distinguish between acquiescence to authority through deference or "safety first," and real interest and cooperation. It becomes essential to understand the kinds of social influence which operate on decisions, choices, and actions toward changed or new practices in the village. These mechanisms of influence differ markedly from the patterns of leadership more common in the West.

Oscar Lewis' study, *Group Dynamics in a North-Indian Village*, points out that patterns of influence, or at any rate of communication, within extended family groups (*kunba*) reach out to several villages. This pattern holds more firmly and operates at greater distances in North India than in the South. Dhillon's *Leadership and Groups in a South Indian Village* discusses rural leadership at some length, but does not quite define it, because he seems to recognize its protean forms and its unreliability as a mechanism for Extension work.[4]

It is quite possible that an Indian village or group of villages linked by largely family communications can get along very well without leadership in any of the meanings of that word which are common in the modern world of the West. There are, of course, tested mechanisms for taking group decisions and promoting action either by groups or by a large number of individuals within large groups. This mechanism, working at the level of the whole village group or even at that of the caste group within a village where important matters have to be decided, seems to work on the principle of the agora in the city states of ancient Greece. Sometimes the traditional panchayat thus works *coram populo*. In such public deliberation there is very seldom any suggestion of the *forum Romanum* in the sense that few of the speakers and pleaders at such a general assembly seem to have the popular power of tribunes.

[4] See Lewis, *op.cit.*, and Dhillon, *op.cit.*, respectively.

Elective processes are only now beginning to take root, though delegation of restricted powers to individuals by popular acclaim has been common, alongside the commoner pattern of hereditary spokesmanship.

Two major types of local leader in western societies are rare in rural India. The chairman type, who obtains from other persons a synthesis of promotive and regulatory decisions and who sometimes casts them into popular form, as he sees it, does occasionally occur. He is less rare than the *Führer* type. It is possible that the rare occurrence of both these types of leader is the result of social regress in the villages over some hundreds of years. Village people in India have been increasingly subjected to bureaucratic domination, and a natural reaction would tend to reject the *Führer* type of leader within the village. An equally inevitable distrust of the chairman type probably springs from the general experience of village people that such smooth characters usually arrange things with outside authority nicely for themselves; if they make arrangements in the public interest, it is because it also happens to fit the chairman's personal interest.

Within the several traditional forms of societies and cultures in the villages, but *not* in the acculturated urban form of Indian society, one common factor is noticeable. Conformity by individuals is approved and originality is disapproved, even as evidence of a strong and interesting personality. The individual with the latter characteristic will be tolerated and may even be popular. The popularity will come more easily if he is rich and not poor. But he cannot be a leader in any sense of having authority. Exceptions to this rule arise, of course, but usually well outside the confines of a rural situation. Shri Naicker, the Dravida Kazhagam leader, is an example.

An attempt must now be made to list the types of persons who are apparent in Indian culture patterns, through whom influence flows, however limited be the social power of the type considered. Almost certainly for rural India and probably for India as a whole, it will be necessary for social scientists to explore leadership structures by looking for processes rather than for persons. But a list of the types of persons who are immediately apparent will present a convenient condensation for some of the primary problems of definition and classification. Inevitably, some of the leader types tabulated below would not warrant as much consideration in western social structures as they do in India, more especially in the eyes of villagers.

Before any such schematic listing, however, the ground must be cleared as to the aims of social and political leadership which may have to be considered, and the capacities of the types of persons listed to serve either social or political change, or both. This can best be done by first setting up the two extremes of the human material available for high-level leadership.

The chairman type leans towards the idea of "pure" representation of the combined views and decisions of some group, of which he is himself a member. This group may be a general assembly of a whole community (traditional village panchayat meeting on some grave issue) or a meeting of selected and supposedly influential persons in the community. Note that these need not have even minor authority; they may be no more than channels of influence, or even of unstressed communication, not having any personal responsibility beyond that of accurate reportage, from and to their constituents. Or they may simply be casual groups of interested persons in the community. Most chairmen add their own individual color to summaries of discussion, resolutions, decisions, and even action programs. In the latter, it is common in village India for the chairman type to be the symbolical and initiative exemplar.

The ruler type may range from the rare *Führer*, or forceful seizer of political power, through the oligarch and the bureaucrat, to the autocrat, such as were many of the princes of India. It cannot be said that the present Prime Minister of India is free of this princely tendency to make *ex parte* and personal decisions on public matters. The Sanskrit word *neta* connotes a leader who has followers disciplined sufficiently to obey him, rather in the nature of the commander of a military formation. The type represented by this term is probably the nearest Indian concept to the German *Führer*. While the *Führer* type is rare in rural India, the aristocratic type of autocrat is common, for example, in Rajput-dominated villages; and original forms of oligarchy, sometimes systematized into bureaucracy, still flourish in the diminishing areas where Brahmans still hold local political power, as in parts of rural Mysore.

Those persons who either act as channels of influence, or who form decisions and promote action in rural areas, may be viewed as composing a spectrogram of grouped types ranging from, let us say, the violet of the purely representational and adaptive chairman to the red of the despotic ruler (now in abeyance, at any rate in his princely form). Some tentative groupings of the successive bands of this spectrogram may now be tabulated, noting the side-characteristics which are important to each group, and the possibilities of its social influence.

In this classification will be included those types who serve as channels of relatively unstressed communication, but whose personal reportage must rank as exerting some influence, however slight. Such types will not lay claim to any personal power. Yet the words and actions of several members of these carrier types are often crucial factors both in the formation of decisions and in the adoption of changes of practice or of new practices in the villages. Since it would appear that hierarchical patterns of society have always prevailed in India until this present day and age, the violet (desired future) end of the spectrogram of social influence will be placed last in this tabulation, and the red (immediate past) end will appear first.

THE ARISTOCRAT AND HIS SUBSTITUTES

Undeniably, the two upper castes, Brahmans and Kshatriyas, represent the oldest rule of hereditary groups and persons. There are parts of rural India where members of either or both these castes are still accepted as authorities, whose often arbitrary orders have to be obeyed. The possession of comparatively great riches can locally qualify a Vaishya as a similar authority; it has done so in Gujarat.

The impression for rural India as a whole is that mock-Brahmans and mock-Kshatriyas are more generally influential today. The teacher is traditionally a Brahman. But other castes have adopted the teaching profession. Though a teacher in a village primary school today may be a known Harijan, he gets at least part of the reverence and obedience formerly shown to the Brahmans. Adults, too, pay him some deference. The same ready acceptance of a teacher's social authority is also partly accorded to village level workers at least in their aspect as Extension teachers. As was pointed out previously, any well-educated person tends to be treated as a superior.

Bureaucratic types, such as a government's district officers and their subordinates in the field—even well-educated casual visitors and commercial representatives—can, by acting "boss," easily overawe most village people into treating them as if they were the Kshatriyas of a still-ruling caste. This reaction of village people, again, "plays it safe," since the educated visitor may be friendly with government or other outside organizations and persons having power over the villagers. To the extent to which the village level worker is the arm of government authority bearing gifts (as grants and the like appear to most villagers), he is further invested by village people with something of the bureaucrat's nimbus of worshipful power.

Lineage as a source of leadership is drying up. The village people's attitude to better educated persons who do *not* live in a village for any length of time is still inclined to be defensive, even if it does not play for safety. This attitude should not be mistaken for pliability to an imposed leadership, especially one from outside the village.

Very important persons in the new Indian political hierarchy, of whatever caste, will usually be treated with excessive deference. This super-respect does not appear to carry the love and loyalty which was felt for a prince of the region. Such a person is doubtless the prince's surrogate, but there is no longer the near-guarantee that the new ruler's exhortations will be accepted by the village folk, as would be the case if this person were really accepted as a social leader.

RELIGIOUS PROFESSIONALS

Although the organizations of Hinduism and Islam in India do not compare with Christian church systems, individuals are much influenced by their religion, and to some extent by those whom they recognize as sound practitioners and hence guides in religion. Albeit decreasingly, no action whatever is considered as separable from a religious context by the simple Hindus and Muslims in the villages.

Officially, India is a secular state in which religion has no social or political powers; yet this principle is blankly opposed to most village thinking. Not even those young village persons who do not trouble to practice their religion will accept the new principle of its separation from the rest of village life. If this is correct, those religious professionals who are really respected may at any time assume a more powerful influence in society.

The religious professionals may be divided into two types. The overtly socio-religious authorities include members of *devasthans* (temple trusts); *pujaris* (mainly priests of temples); *mahants* (custodians of shrines); and *purohits*, who are the locally accepted performers of ceremonies and, as Brahmans, authorities on Hindu legal principles.

On the other hand, there are those men who are exemplars of personal religion, the *gnyanis* (sages) and others who have attained a repute for spiritual eminence, sometimes by verbal skill in philosophy and scholarship in the Hindu scriptures; *sannyasis* (those who have renounced social ties); and *sadhus* (more or less *sannyasis* with a social mission, often having roots in their rich organizations, such as the northern *Akharas*).

All these and the analogous professionals of other religions are frequently consulted by village people, and their advice has special weight, especially where a religious tradition and a new practice seem to conflict.

THE OLIGARCH

Persons of high intellect and energy or—more rarely in recent decades—those with strong military talents have sometimes cut through the custom of aristocratic dominion to establish rule by individual uninherited power. The present Congress Party may best be described as an oligarchic group. It is, however, noteworthy that the Congress Party consists at policy-making levels very largely of Vaishyas even though the party holds to the dogma of repudiating caste, and that the voters' emotional support of the party seems to be drawn by its high-caste members. Examples of these latter are the Prime Minister, a Kashmiri Brahman despite himself, and Govind Ballabh Pant, a Maharashtrian Brahman, settled in Uttar Pradesh. The Congress Party seems mostly to have excluded—probably not deliberately—members of the Kshatriya caste from positions of policy making.

None of this political thinking can be apparent to any but an infinitesimal fraction of villagers. Where the Prime Minister is known by them personally, he is worshipped on three counts: as a member of a once-dominant Brahman family; on account of his successful accession to political power; for his considerable personal sacrifice. These qualifications make him a charismatic ruler who can be as absolute as he pleases and who is also certain to be obeyed, even when his orders are arbitrary.

It is likely that this type of new oligarchy will be the most important single factor in leadership structures of the future India, urban as well as rural.

THE BUREAUCRAT

The flower of this type is the ICS official, a British legacy to India. Yet the village level worker of the National Extension Service, earning less than Rs. 100 a month, is a new bureaucrat whether he likes it or not. It would seem that rural India is long conditioned to bureaucrats; the Muslims first, and then the British more effectively, took the hereditary social offices of record and decision forming in the villages and gave them some legal status. Governments in India today have carried this development a stage further in some areas: the statutory panchayat sometimes elected, sometimes nominated (and even in the latter case frequently consisting of hereditary members), has new legal, administrative, and political powers. Internally, however, the statutory panchayat seems to have lost some of the leadership which was exercised by the traditional form of this body. The new panchayats have acquired the undesirable robes of bureaucracy.

Most village people are still afraid of bureaucrats; they distrust officials, but dare not gainsay them. The better informed and hence more political villager pursues the available bureaucrats directly with flattery and demands in order either to benefit himself or to be exalted by his fellow villagers for having obtained government aid for the village. Leadership vested in bureaucrats or their sycophants seems unlikely to strike deep roots in rural India; it may not even be tolerated after one or two more generations.

The bureaucrats' impersonal "chain of command"—which is really a triangular network with a minister at the apex—is a growing force in India today. It seems to be thoroughly accepted by a majority of the persons so commanded.

Rural India of the nineteenth and previous centuries experienced this rule by "chain of command" in more acceptable forms. In areas under direct British rule, the chief English "kshatriya" bureaucrat of the district constantly toured his "kingdom"; he was personally available to discuss village problems and to hear the complaints and petitions of even unimportant village people. Occasionally immediate redress of complaints or granting of petitions was possible; it was then ascribed to the bounty of the known high official, as a person. In areas under the better Indian princes either the prince himself was personally accessible to any of his subjects or he had touring officers of high rank who were so available.

These twin aspects of modified bureaucratic or aristocratic rule seemed to offer exactly the social and political world of face-to-face negotiation which the rural people, as subjects, then desired. It would not now be possible to return to such a system of personally modified bureaucracy. It might, however, be both possible and desirable to enliven the present impersonal bureaucracy, which is wholly disliked by village folk, with something of the face-to-face techniques of rule which can humanize the political, social, and economic relations of villagers with the rest of India. It is no minor point that village folk believe "the rest of India" to be wealthier, better respected, and more powerful than themselves. Their cultures' tradition calls for condescension on the part of all such superior persons as rulers. Such a rehumanizing of bureaucracy seems a prerequisite to the desired establishment of a free choice, equal opportunity, and free speech democracy in rural India. The National

Extension Service could and should be the major organ of such rehumanizing activity on the part of an elected government.

THE FAMILY (OR FACTION) AUTOCRAT

Leadership of the most authoritarian kind, by the head of a household, is unquestionable where the undivided joint family persists; but that institution is breaking up. Over major areas of rural India the husband and father continues to be the leader of his divided household. Other hierarchical patterns within families, even when divided from the joint household, are still very strong in most of rural India. Where extended family systems such as *kunba* or *pirka* are still operative, leadership accrues to one or the other (often the richest) of the allied household heads in each of the villages to which the extended family spreads. It is often a nice question for these family heads mutually to decide which of them shall be recognized as the chief in a matter affecting the whole *kunba* group throughout several villages.

The landowner with tenants, and still more the landowner with laborers working for him on a farm for the cultivation of which he is directly responsible, are both analogous types of autocrats, who may also assume a wider, though *ad hoc*, leadership among neighboring farmers. The relationship is felt rather similarly to that in a family situation.

The caste head is also of the family-autocrat type, but he is today rather more driven to representation of the families comprising his caste in the village of his title. He will usually be an *ad hoc* leader, and will likewise have to consult his caste before making decisions or agreeing to promote action for which there is no clear precedent.

INTERMEDIARY CHANNELS OF INFLUENCE

The village servants, such as the *chowkidar* (watchman, guardian of community property); the professional serviceman such as the *nai* (barber), who was once upon a time the marriage broker in some rural areas, or the *dhobie* (laundryman), still a carrier of gossip from one family to another; and certain persons recognised as jokers, who frequently belong to the *nai* caste, all contribute to the flow of influence which is exerted in neighborhood or caste groups. A person who aims at obtaining political power in a village will often deliberately use such channels. This situation is paralleled, for example, in rural France. The conscious cultivation of public opinion is still strong within Indian villages, a fact which suggests that leadership of any internal kind is aware of the limitations of its powers. By ridiculing those who will not accept a new practice in, say, agriculture or sanitation, the *nai* makes a very definite and considerable contribution towards the establishment of the practice.

Professional performers who travel from village to village are also carriers of influential communications. Examples are the *charans* or heroic bards of the Rajputs, and the Rajputs' *putli-nataks*, or puppet-masters; the *ottam thullal* (topical miming plays) performers of Malabar, and the shadow-play producers of Andhra. The *kolatis* of Maharashtra serve similar functions; and, in a vicious sense of influence, the *hijra* sect of obscene and epicene jesters in Gujarat can be locally very powerful, though theirs is usually a negative pressure applied to a rich family who can afford to buy off their attentions.

Village housewives fall, at present, mainly within this category of persons *through* whom influence can be exerted. Their gossip at the well or out in the fields for the early morning latrine-visit can be a moderate factor in promoting or inhibiting changes in the village. There is evidence to show, however, that women only have to realize their strength as a decisive group in order to become the major rural power in community improvements. The master key to enduring improvements in village life and work may well lie in sympathetic Extension work among women. But this will need far profounder knowledge of the cultures and the social structures with which the Extension fieldworkers are involved.

In Northern India, women of richer families were confined to the zenana, and their poorer sisters observed purdah. This social form is dying, rather slowly in some areas. But zenana ladies exerted an enormous influence over their husbands and children; they had all the time in the world to plot and intrigue to this end, especially as cross-visiting between different zenanas was frequent. The working class *purdahnashin* (who got around the village, heavily veiled) had less time to work on her husband; but her interest in public affairs seems to have been no less sharpened by the fact of her seclusion. The women of Southern India, strangely enough, seem to have used their relative freedom to bury themselves more deeply in household duties. It is harder to work up a group resolution among women in parts of rural India where zenana and purdah have never existed, yet it can be done.

The commercial element in village India, brokers, *arhatiyas* (commission agents), and money lenders, is in the process of being pulverized by the controls of a socialist state. The capacities of such persons for influencing future changes are therefore not worth exploring, unless some toleration of their function be shown by a change in government policy. However, there are other forms of intermediary negotiators in villages whose commercial aspects do not incur the displeasure of a socialist bureaucracy. One example may be offered.

Chaudhuris, in some parts of North India, were persons of the upper castes who were sometimes recognized as headmen, for one purpose or another; and sometimes as high-level negotiators for others. They could perform both functions simultaneously. The *chaudhuri* thus acted as a superior broker; it might be to and from the moneylender; or in matters of marriage or land transfers; and where delicate negotiations had to be carried on between one village and another. Often the *chaudhuri* of a third village would act as a mediator between two villages in community conflict. The services of the *chaudhuri* were available, however, only to the more prosperous village groups who could pay his fees or commission (usually in kind). The principle is not yet dead; and it offers opportunity for development towards the establishment of a good chairman type of leader.

KSHATRIYAS AS DEMOCRATS

No one seems to have projected the possibility of using the dispossessed princelings, thakurs, and perhaps other zamindars of the traditional landowning and ruling castes, or strong characters from the "martial races," as leaders in the desired democratic and welfare society of the future India. It is common talk that some of these minor aristocrats, dispossessed of their lands and authority, have occasionally turned to bootlegging and dacoity. Others, on clearer evidence, have taken to various forms of business, not always of the most scrupulous order. It seems a pity that so many hereditary, and hence natural, leaders should be jettisoned in the formation of a new society. Generations of training fit them for the task of modifying bureaucracy with the personal touch of authoritative humanity which is so much valued by village people.

Conclusion

A more detailed analysis by social scientists of these various types of leader and of the influence that they wield would make it far simpler to promote a genuine self-development in village India. It is hoped, therefore, that this sketch of the patterns of influence in rural India will encourage the exploration of this field, preferably by teams representing different disciplines.

Whatever be the leadership structures which are found to operate in different rural areas of India, one factor is probably common to the whole countryside. A would-be or putative leader who offers counsel, or who gives orders calling for a new practice or a changed practice on the part of his fellow villagers, will not be taken seriously for long unless he himself and his family follow consistently the changes required. Verbalization is a pastime in the villages; it is there, at any rate, honestly recognized as such. He who talks but does not act is regarded with indulgence, but he cannot be accepted as a leader in that particular matter. Moreover, his capacity for leadership in other matters will be diminished insofar as he pursues his habit of talking without taking corresponding action.

8. LEADERSHIP AND CHANGE IN THE VILLAGES

PATTERNS of leadership vary in each of India's 558,000 villages. The most accepted generalization concerning the Indian village is that each one is different from all others. Yet in the six studies presented here certain similarities are evident. While the size and geographic location of the sampled villages vary, and their distribution is random, all of the villages are in a process of change. However, at the time they were studied, none of them, except Khalapur, was included within a community development project area. Therefore, the observation of change in most of the sampled villages is of particular importance; so often the Indian village is characterized as a relatively static social system.

Precisely because of the momentous change occurring in the villages due to direct and indirect ramifications of urbanization and widespread modernization of outlook the leadership in most of the villages is diffuse. Perhaps it is only as traditional leadership is undermined that new leadership can arise to unite the village. This would seem to be the conclusion reached in John T. Hitchcock's study. Here is a large village which has for some time presented a problem to administrative authorities because of its lack of cohesive leadership favorable to government policies. Located near Delhi, it has been subjected to the effects of modernization and urbanization for several generations. Only recently has any strong village leadership appeared. A second village, that of Gaon, near Poona, studied by Henry Orenstein, seems equally confused as to leadership. Bewilderment at the disintegration of caste, brought about by the introduction of irrigation canals and the consequent influx of new settlers with new and modern ideas, appears to dominate this village.

It may be the size of these villages that prevents the emergence of significant village-wide factions. The studies by Alan Beals and William C. McCormack show that factions in their villages are centered on the immediate interests of the personnel involved and that leaders and followers shift continuously. Probably in large villages the difficulty of organizing a large segment of the population around one issue prevents factions from assuming the proportions that they do in Namhalli and Morsralli. Padu, the Deccan village observed by Richard Bachenheimer (which is larger than either of the faction-rent villages of Namhalli and Morsralli) is relatively free from factionalism. But this may be due to the outward-looking orientation of several village leaders rather than to the size of the population. In the absence of challenge, traditional leadership continues to function in Padu, but passively. The only village in this group in which traditional sanctions continue to uphold the power of traditional leaders is Totagadde, the Kannarese village in which Edward B. and Louise G. Harper lived.

While in all of these villages the traditional caste panchayats continue to meet and to carry weight, in none of them does the government or judicial Panchayat have prestige. The long identification of government officials with an alien or unsympathetic government has apparently not been disturbed by the events of Independence. Police remain as outsiders whose presence in the village is to be avoided. Government officials are to be manipulated or by-passed. Hereditary officials are in some cases the village leaders, but such situations are apparently coincidental. Thus, in some villages, the village leaders of recognized stature have consented to assume offices in the government Panchayat. But such membership is not the source of their leadership. The implications of these facts for Congress and national policy are clear.

The difficulties of observing and defining leadership at the village level are apparent in these six studies. Hitchcock has chosen to illustrate the change in leader attributes necessary for village-wide recognition in Khalapur. He has presented case histories of two leaders, one contemporary and the other living a decade ago, comparing the men, the followers, and the social situation. A descriptive approach is favored by Bachenheimer who identifies and characterizes the various village leaders operating in Padu during his stay. Beals, McCormack, and Orenstein have divided the leaders of their villages into two categories, *formal* and *informal*, but even these categories vary in each case. Also the source of the strength of the leaders in these villages came from such different attributes as sheer economic power or brute force or ascetic detachment. The Harpers have analyzed the Brahman elite in Totagadde and have shown how it functions within both the formal and informal political institutions in the village.

Yet for all the disparate approaches, and for the variety of types of leaders, certain patterns and similarities do emerge. Indeed, it is almost possible to follow the steps involved in the disintegration of the traditional political organization of the villages by studying the Harpers' paper first, then reading the four shorter case studies of villages without united leadership, and finishing with the study of the modern leadership which is emerging in Hitchcock's village.

All of the villages have been given pseudonyms, as is traditional, but all, of course, are real villages. Several of the studies were abstracted from more detailed papers on the villages concerned in order to show the variety of approaches to the study of village leadership and to indicate the variations from village to village and area to area.

LEADERSHIP IN A NORTH INDIAN VILLAGE: TWO CASE STUDIES

JOHN T. HITCHCOCK

*T*his paper concerns two recent leaders who have been highly valued not only by the inhabitants of the village in which they lived, but also by those who have been responsible for, or concerned with, the administration of the area in which the village lies. In most social units there is a "web of government." In the North Indian village of Khalapur,[1] one finds many semi-autonomous units, such as joint families and caste groups, each of which has a varying number of individuals who in one context or another function as leaders.[2] This paper focuses upon two leaders who have functioned at an all-village level. Their use of power and their means of securing it will be examined and compared, and then a selection of common factors most useful in explaining their achievement will be made.

THE VILLAGE

Khalapur is a large village with a population of slightly over 5,000. But in spite of its size, when judged by its economic base and social structure it does not vary significantly from the majority of villages in North India. There are thirty-two caste groups in the village, the most numerous being the Rajput landholders with a population of 2,272 (including 95 Muslim Rajputs). After the Rajputs the most numerous are the Chamars (620), an Untouchable caste. These have given up their traditional caste occupation of leatherworking and for the most part

JOHN T. HITCHCOCK is in the Department of Anthropology, University of California at Berkeley. He has done ethnographic fieldwork in Utah among the Ute Indians, and in Uttar Pradesh, India. While in India he was Director of a Cornell University India Program Station.

[1] This village, like all others mentioned in this book, is given a pseudonymous name.
[2] Fieldwork in Khalapur, from October 1953, to July 1955, was supported by the Ford Foundation Board of Overseas Training and Research. The research in Khalapur was undertaken as part of a Cornell University India Program study of culture change. The writing of this article was made possible by the Cornell University India Program and the Cornell Social Science Research Center. The author is grateful to Professor Morris E. Opler and Dr. Rudra Datt Singh for their comments. The author is especially indebted to Shyam Narain Singh, whose knowledge of the language and practical understanding of the culture was of immense value in collecting information and establishing friendly relations with the people of Khalapur.

are agricultural laborers. Brahmans (282) are the next most numerous; most of them are agriculturalists and only a few are literate. The fourth-largest group consists of Bhangis (212), an Untouchable sweeper caste.

Castes having between 150 and 200 members include those of blacksmiths and carpenters, herders, water carriers, and merchant-traders. Other less numerous groups include grain parchers, washermen, leather workers, potters, barbers, goldsmiths, tailors, oil pressers, cloth dyers, and weavers.

During the early decades of the sixteenth century Khalapur was settled by a Rajput and his sons, who displaced those formerly in possession. With almost no exceptions all the males in the Rajput caste in the village today trace their descent from these men. Since the time of their occupation, the Rajputs have owned almost all of the land, and as a result have always held a position of economic ascendancy. This fact, plus culturally supported beliefs about their innate capacity for ruling and their right to do so, together with their high status in the caste hierarchy and their strongly held conviction that the village is theirs by right of conquest and ancient possession, have made them the ultimate seat of authority in most village affairs. Although the Brahmans of the village have a higher caste status than the Rajputs, the Brahmans are in a much weaker position politically and economically. Even in religious and ceremonial matters they have suffered some diminution of authority as a result of the strong influence of the Arya Samaj movement.[3]

The Rajputs of Khalapur have had a tradition of marauding outside the village and of intracaste strife and feuding within the village. When describing the group of Rajput villages to which Khalapur belongs, a British official wrote in 1921 that the Rajputs of these villages "are a strong and proud race, who in earlier days bore a reputation as marauders to which even the Gujars could not attain. . . . They are still addicted to cattle thieving, and frequently harbor Sansias and other professional thieves."[4]

An elderly Rajput made the following comment about what the village was like when he was a young man: "The village was full of thieves

---

[3] This was a movement of religious reform within Hinduism, affecting the village most intensely during the second and third decades of the twentieth century. It held that the Vedas were the first and final revelation; that priests and elaborate ritual apparatus were not necessary for worship; that castes were occupational groups to which individuals should belong by reason of achievement rather than ascription; and that individuals should follow the Vedic way of life, i.e., *Arya dharma*.

[4] H. R. Neville, *Saharanpur, A Gazetteer*, Lucknow, 1921, p. 103.

and robbers at that time.... It was a time when might was right." The majority of Rajput lineages or sub-lineages either have an elderly man who himself participated in various kinds of depredation outside of the village or remembers incidents of such activity involving his immediate forebears. And it is only recently, within the memory of middle-aged men, that vegetable sellers, cloth sellers, and other itinerant merchants could come to the village without being in danger of losing their wares.

A contemporary district police official spoke of Khalapur as a "criminal" village and he said the reason there was so much theft, especially cattle lifting, was that the village lay close to the borders of three different districts. A thief could escape the police of one district by crossing the border into another before they could apprehend him. The size of the village, too, has undoubtedly been a factor, as it precluded any fear of retaliation from other villages.

Rajput intracaste relations within the village have been marked by quarrels which quite often have led to violence and bloodshed. The memory of such quarrels is long-lived and even though descendants of the contending parties may not exhibit overt hostility, for a number of generations they usually continue to regard one another as potentially hostile—a situation which leads to anxiety and suspicion and to rifts in the social fabric that are difficult to bridge.

But if Khalapur has a tradition of Rajput marauding and intracaste strife and feuding, it now has a countertradition also—a tradition stemming from a period of about fifteen years under the leadership of a single unusual man. Then, the villagers say, "the cart was being driven nicely," and Khalapur was "still." It was also a period of cooperative endeavor, when projects and reforms were carried out to which the village now looks with pride. As a result of these fifteen years, from about 1915 to 1930, the village as a whole, and the Rajput caste in particular, have a different conception of themselves and their potentialities.

The Mukhia

The Rajputs stress the personal qualities of the leader responsible for this heritage. They recall his honesty, impartiality, insight into human nature, gifts of negotiation and arbitration, dignity, and habits of personal asceticism. These qualities played an important part. But what he accomplished is also a result of the social and cultural context within which he brought these personal attributes to bear.

He assumed a position of prominence when divisive tendencies within the Rajput caste had reached a particularly acute stage. Quarrelling over the allotment of the jointly-held village lands had led to their partition. Families who were more skilled in the use of the legal process and families who were able to lend money or grain were increasing their holdings at the expense of their neighbors. This led to animosity and an unwearying search to "pull them down." Authority for the management of village affairs was being dispersed. Government policies had led to an increase in the number of *lambardars* and at the same time to a curtailment of their responsibilities.[5] Cosharers, if they wished, could pay directly to the government, and many disputes which previously would have come before the *lambardars* now went to the courts. In addition, by about the turn of the century, the responsibility of the *lambardars* for cooperation with the police and the maintenance of order had been assumed by the *mukhia*.[6] Although there were a number of powerful *lambardars* during the latter part of the nineteenth century and the early years of the twentieth who could divide the village into opposing camps, there was no one individual, nor any group, especially remembered for minimizing contention and bringing the village an enhanced sense of unity.

There are a number of reasons why this leader was able to bring Khalapur an era of comparative harmony and accomplishment. By virtue of family status alone he could have played a prominent part in village politics. The Rajput family to which he belonged had one of the largest holdings in the village, and one of the largest in the district. A man from such a family not only had power but also had leisure, a necessity if he were to be active politically in a village of this size.

With this inherited advantage, plus personal qualities and other factors of great importance to be considered later, he was able to solve the problem of the dispersal of authority by himself assuming all available important village offices. By 1920, when he was about thirty years old, besides being one of the many *lambardars*, and one with considerable

[5] For purposes of revenue administration the village was divided into revenue units which after 1873 were called *mahals*. There was a *lambardar* to collect revenue from the cosharers in each *mahal*. Nominated by the cosharers and appointed by the government, he held office for life unless objection was made, and the office tended to become hereditary. During much of the nineteenth century the number of *lambardars* was small, and they received strong government support. They represented the village and were responsible for maintaining order and adjudicating disputes.
[6] The *mukhia* was expected to work closely with the police to maintain order. The incumbent was nominated by the landholders if there was consensus, otherwise he was elected. The *mukhia* was appointed by the sub-divisional magistrate and the district superintendent of police.

prestige because of the size of his *mahal*, he had become *mukhia*, and in addition held the two newly created offices of *sarpanch* and assessor.[7]

His assumption of offices which might otherwise have formed separate and competing nuclei of power showed that he had the strong support of most of his caste. What was it that made this possible, especially for such a young man? One important part of the explanation is that he very successfully took the role of mediator between the village and outside government officials. Any man who aspires to a position of highest authority among the Rajputs must be able to represent them in a fitting way before officials who come to the village. This means that a man must come from a family which has wealth enough to provide such symbols of status as a substantial men's house,[8] and generous hospitality. It means that he himself must have the manner and bearing, the leisure, and even the clothes deemed proper in a host. The *mukhia* belonged to the family of a former *lambardar*. By family tradition and personal ability he was adept at providing the necessary amenities.

The man who aspires to village-wide influence must also be regarded as an appropriate ambassador of the caste and the village. He must be a man who knows his way about in tahsil,[9] and district headquarters. He must be a man, as one villager put it, to whom the tahsildar would offer a chair. All of the attributes which make a man a good representative of the caste in the village are important, but of special importance to the ambassadorial function is the ability to read and write. This leader had learned to read and write Urdu. Literacy, then a rare attainment, placed those who possessed it in a position to be of great assistance to the uneducated in what were often to them mysterious, if not dreaded, contacts with officialdom.

Another very important aspect of the mediating role is that of village protector. This leader fulfilled such a role and was greatly aided in playing it well because he held the office of *mukhia*. As much as anything

---

[7] As *sarpanch* he was head of a village panchayat created by the government in an attempt to revitalize local administration and confine petty litigation to the village. This panchayat was empowered to try minor civil and criminal cases, and was encouraged to carry out programs of village development. The assessors, who were selected from among the most prominent men in the district, sat with the judges of the district sessions court when cases of a serious criminal nature were being tried. They acted in an advisory capacity. The office was not of much functional importance at the village level, but it did carry much prestige. Of these offices, that of *mukhia* was the most important, because the activities of the dominant caste involved much contact with the police.

[8] Rajput wives observe purdah restrictions and the Rajput dwelling unit consists of a women's house and a men's house.

[9] The tahsil is an administrative, revenue, and judicial subdivision of a district; the head revenue officer is a tahsildar.

else about him the villagers remember that during his leadership the police almost never came to the village. An especially deep-seated aversion to these officials had risen when a detachment during the closing years of the nineteenth century had been stationed in the village in order to prevent female infanticide among the Rajputs. In the pursuance of their duties the constables necessarily had to violate Rajput purdah restrictions. In addition, police contacts with the village, from the villagers' point of view, more often involved bribery and extortion than prompt retribution for wrongdoing. The police cooperated with this leader because he had been able to bring a degree of external and internal order to the village that it had not known before.

This man's work became so well known that a story was written about him by a local author.[10] The following excerpt reports an incident in which he figured as a protective figure.

> He was the High Court of his own village and easily settled countless quarrels. He was always deciding cases. Before he became *mukhia*, criminal acts were common in Khalapur. But his influence, love of justice and incessant though silent propaganda greatly minimized the amount of crime in the village.
>
> In 1924-25 a number of dacoities were committed in Northern India and a train was looted. The police went from village to village arresting all persons about whom there was the slightest suspicion. They came to Khalapur and asked the *mukhia* to give them a list of the *badmash*.[11] The village was frightened but the *mukhia* was not disturbed. He replied, "There are no *badmash* in my village."
>
> It was surprising to hear that Khalapur had no *badmash*. The police officer asked for the list a second time.
>
> "There is only one *badmash* in this village," said the *mukhia*. "I am the only *badmash*. If you want to, handcuff me."
>
> The police officer grew very angry. He said it was impossible that Khalapur had no *badmash*.
>
> "I am not joking. It is a fact. There are no *badmash* in Khalapur. If you don't believe me consult your register and you'll see that for the last three years no one from Khalapur has appeared there."
>
> The police officer had to go back without arresting anyone. . . .
>
> When the author one day was praising the *mukhia* for the courage shown in this incident, the *mukhia* answered, "In which Sastra does it say that a man is brave because he refrains from calling a good man bad?"

[10] Kanhaiyalal Misra, "Mukhia S - - - S - - -," in *Forgotten Faces*, Saharanpur, U.P., Wikas Limited, 1947. The book, written in Hindi, was brought to the attention of the author through the kindness of Dr. Leela Dube. The incident which appears here is an adaptation of her translation of the Hindi.

[11] The concept includes those who are engaged in criminal activities, and those who are regarded as sources of conflict in the village.

As a protector of the village this man sometimes went so far that he is said to have suffered pangs of conscience on his death bed. He was a reformer, as we shall see; but he was also a shrewd and realistic politician. He needed and obtained the support of a number of powerful Rajputs, some of whom committed offenses including murder, which he as *mukhia* should have reported to the police. He did not do so because it would have been the end of his regime and of all he hoped to accomplish in the village, including the reform of these men.

The protective role also included attempts to diminish litigation. When two parties were about to go to court he would get them both together and elaborate on their possible losses in time and money, and was often successful in convincing them that neither had anything to gain. He himself avoided participation in any cases other than those in which the village as a whole was concerned.

But his success in mediating between the village and the government would have meant little if he had not also utilized traditional methods of decision making. He seldom made decisions unless in council with the most powerful of the Rajput elders. Though he was the head judge of the formal village court, he settled a very small number of cases in this capacity. He preferred to consider them while sitting as a member of a traditional council. It is also of importance that he did not limit his contacts to a single stratum of power and leadership in the village. He sat as often with the *badmash* as he did with the *achha admi*.[12]

It should be noted that this leader on occasion could use force in order to bring a wrongdoer into line. He is said to have been a "very hard man" when anyone went against his wishes. He once had a police official who had come to Khalapur and beaten a man in order to obtain money from him waylaid on the way back to headquarters and served in the same coin; he is also said to have threatened less powerful Rajputs and the members of other castes with beatings if they did not give up practices to which he objected. He could rely on his more martial Rajput supporters for such work.

Finally, and perhaps most important of all, he was able to convince his caste that he was working for the good of the village and not for the good of his own family or himself. He was married (in itself of importance, as there is no evidence that an unmarried man was ever a prominent leader in this village), but he had no children. He would

---

[12] The "good men," or as it is often expressed, using the English word (though with a slightly different connotation), the "gentlemen." These men have a reputation for being conciliatory and just, and for not relying on chicanery and force in their dealings with others.

point this out and say that he regarded the villagers as his children, thus giving added support to a claim of impartiality and lack of kin group bias. By very many in Khalapur he seems to have been looked upon as a benevolent and patriarchal father figure.

The methods he used in dealing with his caste and the importance of his role as mediator between the village and officialdom help to explain the backing he was given. But these things do not provide what seems to be the most weighty reason why so young a man could come to occupy the position he did and could come to be regarded as a father figure by shrewd and ambitious Rajputs who were, some of them, more than twice as old as he was. This puzzling phenomenon is to be attributed to another kind of mediating role he assumed. He became imbued with ideas of village improvement and reform. He acted as mediator between the village and ideological currents of the time, currents which not only molded him but molded those among whom he worked and prepared them to accept his programs.

It is significant that while he was in school, the district board assigned a topic for a prize essay entitled: *What I Would Like to Do for My Village*. He won the first prize in the district and the district inspector of schools came to the village to make the award. Thus his personal orientation toward village affairs was partially formed at an early age by influences stemming from his formal education.

But the ideological current of greatest importance, and one without which he probably would never have become more than one of a number of politically able and powerful men on the village scene, was one of socio-religious reform. The period of his youth and leadership was a period of socio-religious concern, stimulated primarily by Arya Samaj activity in the district. Early in his career he began inviting Arya Samaj preachers to come to the village. Meetings were organized and great interest was aroused, especially among the Rajputs. The *mukhia* held long discussions with the Arya Samaj preachers and among other things was very much impressed by what he learned from them about the role of village leader in the tradition of Vedic culture (*vaidik pradhan*). But although he became very enthusiastic about Arya Samaj doctrines, he never took a rigid doctrinal position. He also invited orthodox preachers to come to the village and provided them with opportunities to present their arguments. One result of all this discussion about the appropriate Hindu way of life (dharma) was that motives to personal and village reform were engendered, motives which the *mukhia* was able to encourage and direct.

The Gandhian movement also played a part, but it was Gandhi's personal asceticism and concern for the Untouchables which had the greatest effect on the *mukhia*. Nationalist and anti-British feelings, though present in the village at this time, were not then and never became as strong as they did elsewhere. When a Congress worker attempted to elicit this leader's support, the *mukhia* said that he was in sympathy but would become active only when he was joined by the whole village.

The *mukhia* adopted the simple and ascetic way of life encouraged by the Arya Samaj and by Gandhi; when meetings were held in which Arya Samaj and other religious teachers spoke or read from the traditional religious writings, he would go about, after the meetings, alone or in the company of the preachers, trying to persuade his caste to give up drinking, eating meat and opium, and even smoking the hookah. He would ask, "How can you and I continue to sit together when we are so different?" He was able to persuade many men to give up these practices, and to give up thieving. He also mitigated the Rajput tendency to settle differences by resorting to force. There are elderly men in the village today who speak of him with deep respect, saying that he changed their lives and taught them "the difference between right and wrong." Thus he was a religious leader as well as a secular one. It is the assumption of these dual roles which is of utmost importance in accounting for the power he wielded.

Aside from using this power to bring a greater degree of unity to the members of his caste and to some extent changing their way of life, what are the other accomplishments for which he is especially remembered and in which the village takes the most pride? Khalapur is located in an area which has long been the center of Muslim influence. At the time of the *mukhia* the only prominent religious structure in the village was the large shrine of a Muslim saint. When one of the village Brahmans pointed out how anomalous it was that a Muslim shrine should be the only prominent religious structure in a predominantly Hindu village, the *mukhia* was able to get his own caste and others in the village to sense the anomaly and to give land and money for the construction of a Hindu temple. Since the Arya Samaj did not believe in temple building, this step was an indication of his flexibility in matters of doctrine.

On the occasion of the spring festival of Holi there were drinking bouts among the Rajputs, and prostitutes were brought into the various subdivisions of the village. There was frequent brawling and drunken Rajput groups went from shopkeeper to shopkeeper making a customary exaction of money and sugar, the sugar to be used for making liquor.

Whether the shopkeeper showed resistance or not, this often meant that his goods were damaged (water was thrown on them) or that he himself and sometimes his women were given rough treatment. After one especially riotous Holi celebration, the *mukhia* held a panchayat in which he requested reform, threatening to resign and leave the village to become a religious mendicant unless his requests were granted. He asked and was able to get consent for the following changes: no more prostitutes were to be brought to the village; the liquor shop was to be closed on Holi; a religious ceremony at the new temple was to take the place of the drinking bouts; and, finally, the exactions from the shopkeepers, instead of being taken as formerly, were to be taken in the form of money to be paid to him personally once a year and used to maintain the temple and its attendant.

An allotment of land which had fallen to the joint proprietary body as the result of a court case was the cause of much quarrelling. The *mukhia* was able to obtain consent to have the land used for the support of a *pathshala*.[13] A tank and the main building were largely constructed by voluntary labor, work in which he himself took the lead. It is often mentioned in the village that this is an early example of the kind of voluntary work program (*shramdan*) which is now an important aspect of the national development policy.

Former partition of the jointly held village lands had deprived non-landholding castes of a place to graze their cattle. The *mukhia* gave some land and was able to persuade others to contribute, so that a number of acres could be set aside as a common village grazing ground.

His reforms were directed primarily at his own caste, and although he was concerned to see that the lower castes were justly treated, one does not find as much enthusiasm for his regime among them as one does among the Rajputs. Some members of the lower castes, for example, have claimed that their labor on the tank of the *pathshala* was not voluntary. He spoke of "lifting up" the lower castes and thought of it as a gradual process to be obtained through education. The *pathshala*, however, never has been attended by members of castes other than the three highest. He appears never to have pressed strongly for changes in the structure of intercaste relations, with the exception that during one of Gandhi's refusals to eat unless Untouchables were admitted to Hindu temples he was able to obtain agreement that the Untouchables of Khalapur should be allowed to enter the new village temple.

---

[13] A school in which the students must live a simple, rigorous life and in which the teaching of Sanskrit and religion is emphasized.

Inevitably the *mukhia* made enemies. Orthodox Brahmans were not in sympathy with his religious preferences and many were embittered when he attempted to persuade his caste to change the marriage ceremony in accordance with Arya Samaj principles. Opposition consolidated within his own caste when he held a large panchayat to request bringing back into hookah relations the small Muslim Rajput community and two Rajput families who had been outcasted some generations previously because of cross-caste marriages. In the panchayat it was agreed to accept the Hindu Rajputs, though not the Muslims. There actually was also much opposition to the change regarding the Hindus, though it was not evident in the panchayat. Most of the people in three subdivisions of the village—the group which was also least sympathetic to Arya Samaj doctrines—continued to regard these people as outcaste.

The *mukhia's* downfall came about as a result of this opposition, plus his shame at a violation of a strongly held social norm. A man who aspires to a position of power and respect must first and always be able to control the members of his own family. A younger member of this leader's lineage had begun keeping a Muslim prostitute at his men's house. The *mukhia* and many others in the village objected to this open violation of a recently agreed upon reform. But although the *mukhia* made repeated attempts, he was unable to get his relative to give up the girl. When some of those who opposed the *mukhia* openly said in his presence that it was only a man who was the true head of his own family who could rightly claim to be the father of the whole village, he resigned all his offices and retired from public life. He died shortly thereafter.

Upon the death of this leader some of his reforms fell into abeyance. It is said that several of his closest associates were drunk soon after his cremation. Untouchables no longer entered the temple and, although Holi is no longer celebrated with the same turbulence and gusto as before his reforms, there has been a great decline of interest in the religious ceremony he hoped would become the central observance on the occasion. Interest in the *pathshala* has been mostly replaced by interest in the new intercollege,[14] and only a few students now attend. But the village, nevertheless, is different. This leader is remembered and he has would-be emulators, especially among younger Rajputs.[15] Most important is the

---

[14] A school which is between the primary school and the college or university. It roughly corresponds to a high school.

[15] In 1956 one of these men, a member of the *mukhia's* family and still in his early twenties, was made the head of the second and most recent of the post-Independence village courts.

belief he created among many that the village is capable, under the right leadership, of achieving greater unity and of carrying out programs of benefit to the whole population.

During the two decades between the death of the *mukhia* and the rise of a new leader of comparable stature, village affairs tended to resume the old pattern, though there was now less Rajput marauding, theft, and intracaste violence. This change is to be related to a number of factors, including the influence of the *mukhia*, increased education, preference for the courts as means of pursuing village rivalries, and improved economic conditions. The construction of two sugar mills in the area greatly increased the prosperity of the landholding caste.

In 1937 Khalapur, whose large population made it a political asset, gave strong support to a man who had won a seat in the U.P. Provincial Assembly. Following Independence this man became an important state official. The support of Khalapur had been so important in helping him win his electioneering campaigns that in January 1949 he was instrumental in getting the chief minister of U.P. to go to the village and lend his support to the founding of the new intercollege. In his speech the chief minister explained the functioning and powers of the new democratically based administrative organs which were to be set up in the village. These bodies were called the gaon panchayat and the adalati panchayat.[16]

It was at the time of the election of members to the gaon panchayat and adalati panchayat that the first real threat was made to the centuries-old Rajput domination of the village. When the non-Rajput castes learned about the new elective system, they immediately realized that in combination they might elect one of their own members to the office of *pradhan*. Guided by a number of Brahman, Vaishya and Untouchable caste leaders, they began to make plans. The Rajputs, who were unable to agree among themselves on a single candidate for this office, became uneasy. Determination among the non-Rajput castes was so strong and

[16] Under the Uttar Pradesh Panchayat Raj Act of 1947, gaon sabhas were created consisting of all the adult residents of a village. The gaon sabha elected a gaon panchayat which is the legislative and executive body of the gaon sabha. The head of the gaon panchayat was elected by the gaon sabha and is called the *pradhan*. Gaon sabhas also elected five *panches* to sit on the village court, called the adalati panchayat. Three to five gaon sabhas were included within the jurisdiction of each adalati panchayat. The five *panches* of each gaon sabha together elected the head judge, or *sarpanch*. The essential difference between the old form of village government and the new was, first, that the gaon panchayat and the adalati panchayat had greatly increased powers and were therefore potentially able to govern much more effectively; and second, that the bodies were to be elected by all adults in the village. The number of Untouchable seats was fixed by the government in proportion to population.

their hopes had been raised so high by Congress agitation, Independence, and the speech of the chief minister that the Rajputs realized their only recourse was to avoid an election and to reach a compromise agreement on candidates. By making a strong appeal in the name of village unity, which most villagers agreed was in danger of being seriously disrupted by the use of force if an actual election were held, the Rajputs were able to bring about agreement on candidates, by means of a large panchayat attended by them and the non-Rajput coalition. The result was a compromise on a Brahman for the office of *pradhan*. This man was acceptable to many of the non-Rajputs, and was supported by a powerful Rajput group in his own subdivision, a group which had reason to believe it could control him. Three Rajputs, a Vaishya and a Chamar were made *panches* on the adalati panchayat, and the *panches* from the five *gaon sabhas* composing the *adalati* circle later elected a Khalapur Rajput from the family of the former *mukhia* to the office of *sarpanch*.

The history of the gaon panchayat may be summarized by saying that it gradually ceased to function as an effective representative body. Toward the end of 1952 power over some of the land in the village fell to it as a result of zamindari abolition.[17] Subsequently some of this land was illegally allotted in the interests of the faction which controlled the *pradhan* and thereafter meetings were held much less frequently. The *pradhan* was said to have been reluctant to face the opposition. Whether this was the case or not, it is certain that the irregular land allotments made it impossible for the *pradhan* to obtain the cooperation of the village as a whole in drawing up and executing plans for village development. After the first few years most lower-caste representatives had ceased to attend meetings of the gaon panchayat; and later, as a rule, they were not informed when meetings were held.[18]

The adalati panchayat, too, lost the respect of most villagers. It was not attended at all after some years by *panches* from outside Khalapur. The *sarpanch*, a man of remarkable abilities, was unable to overcome his alcoholism, and all knew that decisions could be swayed by meeting his needs. The gaon panchayat was the instrument of a faction; the adalati more nearly became the instrument of a single man.

[17] The U.P. Zamindari Abolition and Land Reforms Act was passed in 1951 and was held to be valid by the Supreme Court in 1952. Most of the redistributed land in Khalapur went to Rajputs.
[18] Although the first Khalapur gaon panchayat by some standards could not be called a success, the experience in trying to operate a new type of government did teach the villagers how much authority was vested in the panchayat, and what its potentialities were.

The Principal

In 1953 there were many villagers who expressed the belief that Khalapur could improve itself only under the guidance of a single powerful individual. As one man put it, "It takes a strong hand to wash soiled clothing clean." He was thinking not only of the past, but of the present; for there was at the time an outstanding leader of this type in Khalapur, though he had come from outside the village. This was the principal of the new intercollege.

This young man, still in his twenties and an active member of the Indian National Congress, had come to the village first in 1949 as a result of a chain of events which had begun the previous year. The same politician who had been interested in Khalapur since 1937 believed that the creation of a large modern intercollege would help to improve conditions in the village and would also act as a center for the dissemination of ameliorating influences in the surrounding area. He approached an elderly and respected Rajput district official and told him of his idea. This man then went to Khalapur. Assisted by the wave of enthusiasm for reform which followed Independence, he was able to get a substantial contribution from the Khalapur Rajputs. Arrangements were made to present this money to the chief minister of the state, who visited Khalapur to receive the money in the form of a purse and then turned the money back to the village with the request that it be used to construct an intercollege. A school committee was formed and began looking for a principal. Through relatives by marriage, the committee heard of a prominent Rajput family in another district, two of whose sons had had a university education. The youngest son, who had just begun to practice law with his father-in-law, was persuaded to give up his law career and come to Khalapur to start the school. This man's elder brother was so distressed at what he learned about Khalapur's reputation that he told his younger brother he would "ruin his life" if he stayed there. He had already persuaded him to leave when a delegation of Rajputs came to the younger man and begged him to try them for a year. They also urged him to stay "for the sake of the country." He finally agreed and the school was begun in July of 1949.

It had been the idea of the officials and the school committee to locate the new intercollege in the old *pathshala*, but it was immediately apparent that this would be difficult. Accommodation was provided but the head of the *pathshala* began creating opposition among the villagers by telling them that "the new English kind of education" would be a bad thing for their sons and the village. Matters reached a head when some religious books were taken from the *pathshala* and partially burned. The head of the *pathshala* accused the new principal of this act. Later when speaking of this incident the principal said:

> Even my closest friends now began to have suspicions about me and the school. They were all angry with me. I again told them that time would prove my innocence. I was very careful to establish close contact with the people and to make them understand that I had no intention of harming the *pathshala*. I never said anything against the swami [head of the *pathshala*]. At this time I worked very hard in the village. I worked harder than I have ever worked. I went to see all the leaders of the village. Then people began to be impressed by my mission and my sincerity.

He succeeded so well that when the *pathshala* students and teachers forcibly evicted him and his school from the room they occupied, the Rajput leaders of the village came to his support and he was allowed to return.

But this situation, of course, was unsatisfactory and the principal began to make attempts to raise funds for a new building. The prominent state official came to the village and requested support from a gathering which consisted of the prominent men of Khalapur and other nearby villages. But although he talked with them for about four hours, he was unable to get agreement. In the words of the principal:

> He was very embarrassed. He went away and when he left he said he was leaving everything to me.... For fifteen days I went around from men's house to men's house, trying to see all the people and trying to change their minds. After fifteen days I called a meeting and didn't invite any officials. The resolution was passed.

The money was collected and a large and impressive plant was built, much of it by voluntary labor. The buildings were located on the opposite side of the village from the *pathshala*, on the side closest to and most directly communicating with the headquarters town of the tahsil. The separation from the *pathshala* and the closer communication with the tahsil town, in which the bus stop and railroad station also were located, were symbolic. Khalapur had started on a new course and from now on it was to have much closer connections with the state and the nation. In 1955 the President himself visited the village to see the new school and encourage its further growth.

Once the initial difficulties had been overcome the school was very successful. Though the student population of about 300 is predominantly Rajput, the school draws students of all castes, from Khalapur as well as from other surrounding villages. It is a source of pride, and visitors to the village are always taken to see it.

During the course of its inception and construction the principal himself gradually began to fill the vacuum created by the weakness of the gaon panchayat and the adatali panchayat, and to become the focus of village affairs. Outside officials began to speak of him as the "King of Khalapur" and the "Jewel of Khalapur."

The principal's support was solidly based upon the support of the dominant caste. Though an outsider and a member of a different subdivision within the caste, he was a Rajput and came from a high-status family. He had university degrees in both commerce and law, but he had a village background and knew village ways. Guided by a member of the school committee who was an astute village politician, he soon became well acquainted with the intricacies of Khalapur politics. He knew what men in each subdivision of the village had to be approached and convinced if a program were to be carried through. He knew in what cases a favor to one man had to be balanced by a favor to another if divisive jealousies were to be prevented.

Like the older village leader, he tended to by-pass the formal village administrative organization. He did most of his planning in consultation with the Rajput elders in informal conclave. He knew and respected Rajput values. Though he personally supported many changes, such as loosening of purdah restrictions and raising the age of marriage, he moved cautiously in these sensitive areas and did not push his views. He did not attempt to force the issue when objections were made to inter-caste dining at the intercollege. Members of the Untouchable castes had to cook and eat separately, though no overt discrimination was allowed in the classrooms or in recreational activities. He shared some of the Rajput stereotypes about the innate abilities of members of the lower castes, but believed that all castes should have an opportunity to get an education. He was a man of ascetic habits and tried to get individual Rajputs to give up drink and opium, though he was careful not to allow his reforming impulses to move him into positions extreme enough to weaken his support. Privately he could express impatience at having to permit practices of which he disapproved and he looked forward to the day when the school would become self-sufficient.

> As soon as I become self-sufficient, I will crack down on these people. There won't be any more drinking, or any more opium. If they object I will run them right out of the village. I have the support of the government from the top to the bottom and these people know it.

The basic reason for his success, the principal often said, was that he came from outside the village. He said he never could have had the same success in his own village because of the old animosities and suspicions he would have had to contend with as a member of a village family. As an outsider he said that it was much easier for him to claim impartiality.

His reputation for impartiality, as well as the knowledge that he had the support of high officials, made him the chosen arbitrator of a large number of disputes. Almost daily, from early morning until late at night, groups from this village and other villages came to him at his village house or at the school seeking solutions for their difficulties. He worked hard to maintain his reputation for fairness. When a member of the school committee with whom he had always been on terms of intimacy became entangled in a village factional dispute and began to use his connection with the principal to forward his own interests, the principal asked him to resign his post in favor of a man who had a more neutral position in village politics.

Also of crucial importance to his success was the principal's status as an educated man. Respect for the learned is deeply ingrained, and the principal's university degrees undoubtedly helped him to secure a following in spite of his extreme youth. In addition to this the Rajputs were beginning to value education for themselves much more highly. Traditionally they were not much interested in education, saying it was for those of lower status who had no land or who had such a small amount of land that it was necessary to augment the family income by some means other than farming. But this attitude had been changing gradually and the change was reflected in the much higher dowry an educated boy could claim. The principal was welcomed as a person who could satisfy the increased desire for education.

The principal became the chief mediator between the village and the outside. He assumed the protective role. When one of his close supporters began bringing the police to the village and realizing benefits thereby, he told him that he must stop or forfeit his friendship. As his authority increased, the police stopped coming to the village at all without first making contact with him and getting his permission. He helped a village official extricate himself from difficulties into which he had fallen due to mismanagement of his office, and he saw that a petty government official was transferred from the area for making illegal exactions.

Though not the sole representative of the village, he became the chief one, as he also became its chief ambassador. High-caste guests and visiting officials who came to the village were always taken to see him. When intercession regarding important matters was to be made—for example, when some of the landowners wished to undertake consolidation of their holdings, or wished a more favorable price for their sugar cane—he was asked to speak for them in the appropriate government circles.

Finally, and this is probably the most important reason for the acceptance of his programs, the principal was a member of the Congress Party, an active worker in the organization, and a follower of the ascetic and service-oriented pattern of life espoused by its most prominent leaders. He also had the personal backing of a highly placed Congress official. The villagers realized this and they regarded his staying in the village as something of a personal sacrifice, as he might easily have attained government preferment.

⊷§ Contrasts

There are a number of differences between the *mukhia* and the principal. The old leader had to win a reputation for impartiality within the village context. He faced the difficult task of convincing Rajput neighbors that he had lifted himself above the claims of kin and was motivated by concern for the welfare of the caste and, within certain limits, of the village as a whole. It is significant that his downfall was related to an inability completely to dissociate himself from his own family.

The principal, as an outsider, did not face this problem. But as an outsider he had to win support on the basis of claims which were new to the villagers. The old leader became the focus of village affairs because he was given all the important administrative offices in the village. The principal, on the other hand, represented something quite different. His work was based upon authority stemming from none of the village offices. He had to win acceptance for himself in a new role—that of creator of an intercollege. In the beginning the principal was aided to some extent by the known interest of the government. But at this stage it was interest and not the support which it later became. He had to rely mainly on being able to mobilize the increased desire for education and the reforming impulses stimulated by Congress and Independence.

Once the principal had won acceptance and was actually able to forward plans for a large, well-staffed and well-housed intercollege, he gradually drew the strong personal support of the prominent state official who had thought of creating the school; and it was this support which became in many respects the equivalent of powers the old leader held when he was *lambardar, mukhia, sarpanch,* and assessor. This, in turn, made possible the successful assumption of other roles the older leader had taken. Indeed, he was able to assume them more successfully because his connection placed him on a footing either of equality or, in many cases, superiority over most district officials. There was never a question of his being given a chair when he visited any district or tahsil office.

Although both leaders were negative in their attitudes toward the police, the two leaders exhibit a very different orientation to other aspects of government. The old leader did not look to the government to supply nearly as much stimulation for village reform. On the whole, government in the *mukhia's* time wanted revenue and order and its concerns other than this, though present, were vestigial. The old leader's reforms were stimulated for the most part by a socio-religious movement and it was primarily through the Arya Samaj that Khalapur was related to the broader national scene. The principal, in contrast, could depend upon the government for much encouragement as well as for financial assistance. It was primarily the stimuli which came from Congress, the political party in power, that enabled him to carry out his programs, and he envisioned his work as part of a nation-wide socio-political effort. Most of the officials who came to the village in the time of the *mukhia* did so in order to realize revenue and to see that disturbances of the peace were kept at a minimum. Now many government officials, some of them from the highest levels, come to praise what has been done and to encourage and plan for further effort.

The *mukhia*, finally, was occupationally immobile. His work began and ended in Khalapur. The principal's work began in Khalapur, but it seems quite probable that it will not end there, for his ambitions are not limited to this village and will probably carry him into the state government. Compared to the old leader he has much greater scope for the exercise of his talents.

Similarities

The common factors which have characterized the leadership of these two men may be summarized as follows. Negatively, both men show that advanced age is not necessary for leadership of their kind, providing other qualifications are present. Positively, both men were Rajputs and this ascriptive quality was an important qualification for the role of high-level leader. The importance of this qualification is a reflection of Khalapur's social structure and its basic political and economic equation. It seems doubtful whether members of other castes could have accomplished as much in this village. In their relations with the Rajput caste itself, both followed traditional patterns of decision making. But in each case as they became better liked, and inspired more trust and respect, the relationship between them and other prominent men in the caste tended to move from one which was nonhierarchical to one in which they assumed a role which was much more authoritarian. Both men derived power from their affiliation with government, and played important roles as mediators between the village and the district and state administration. Conversely, it may also be said that they obtained status in the eyes of officialdom, and were able to act successfully as representatives, ambassadors, and protectors because of the following they had in the village. Both men also were mediators between the village and the most prestigeful ideological movements of their time—the Arya Samaj and the Congress. These movements molded them and created a following for them. Furthermore, these movements provided both men with a status group outside the village to which they could refer their actions and from which they could draw psychological support. The status group of lesser leaders in the village is the family, lineage, and clique, and this makes it more difficult for them to act with the impartiality shown by both these men. Both the *mukhia* and the principal were associated with certain central values of the culture, all of them related to the value of personal renunciation. First, both men followed an ascetic way of life and, as is evident from the examples of such men as Gandhi, Bhave, and Jayaprakash Narayan, this in itself had a strong appeal. Like these national leaders, both men stressed peaceful dealings, though it should not be overlooked that on occasion both could be authoritarian and resort to coercive measures in the name of the right as they understood it. Second, both men were working to forward projects (notably in the areas of religion and education) which were associated with public benefit rather than personal or family aggrandizement. Third, in the pursuit of these ends, they indicated that they were willing to make personal sacrifices. The *mukhia*, for example, threatened to resign his offices and become a religious mendicant; the principal was perceived as a person who had given up a lucrative career and a chance for a high government position in order to work for the good of the village.

LEADERSHIP AND CASTE
IN A BOMBAY VILLAGE

HENRY ORENSTEIN

THE village of Gaon is situated in the Deccan region of Maharashtra, in Poona District, about one mile from the market town which is called Mot.[1] Its population is about 1500. As compared with many other villages in India, Gaon is well off, for the introduction of irrigation about sixty years ago gave its inhabitants sufficient water to raise sugar cane in large quantities. The cash return from raising sugar cane is relatively high, sometimes as much as Rs. 1500 per acre. The other crops grown in the village, such as millet, sorghum, wheat, and rice, are primarily for home consumption.

The majority of the people practice agriculture as their main occupation, but many have other occupations in addition: rope making, pottery, and basketry, for example. Most of the nonagricultural occupations are part of a traditional economic system (*baluta*). This system involves fixed relationships between individuals or groups by which goods or services are regularly exchanged for agricultural products. However, the village is far from independent economically. Several aspects of a market economy exist in Gaon: labor either from Gaon itself or from outside is often procured on a contract basis; raw sugar and other farm products are sold at market-determined prices; and a large number of items for home use or for use on farms are purchased in Mot.

The proximity of Mot exposes Gaon to outside influences rendering the latter highly susceptible to change, although this relationship is not alone sufficient to cause changes of any magnitude. One important factor which set off a series of changes in the village was the introduction of irrigation in 1894. When irrigation was extensively employed, money crops became a dominant feature in economic life and economic ties to Mot became close. The traditional system of economic exchange was attenuated. Newcomers came in to buy up the more valuable land, and many villagers left the main cluster of houses to build new homes near their fields.

HENRY ORENSTEIN is an Assistant Professor in the Department of Sociology and Anthropology at Tulane Univeristy.

[1] Research for this study was undertaken in 1954-1955 by means of a Fulbright grant, with additional assistance from the Department of Anthropology, University of California, Berkeley.

LEADERSHIP AND CHANGE IN THE VILLAGES

Other impulses to change, intensified by the closeness of Mot, are the economic and social objectives of the Government of India since Independence. Villagers often visit Mot and are exposed to new ideas; local government officials sometimes visit Gaon to make speeches. Villagers now know that there are alternatives to their old beliefs. Beliefs about the causes of disease, about methods of making a living, about marriage customs, about caste practices—all have been challenged by new ideas.

One result of these changes has been an increase in social disorganization. The newcomers to Gaon, from all parts of the Deccan region of Maharashtra, often choose to go their own way without regard for village custom or village leadership. The movement of people out to their fields reduced the frequency of face-to-face contacts and thus the rigor of village social control. This tendency toward individuation is further accentuated by the flood of new ideas which has swept through the village since Independence. People must choose between the new and the old ideas; we find that people often make different choices and that confusion reigns in the minds of many. Thus, the village is not very well integrated; extensive cooperation is unusual in Gaon.

Caste

The emergence of new economic conditions and new ideas, and the concomitant social disorganization, have left their mark on relations among castes in Gaon. There are a total of twenty-three castes in the village, not including Muslims. A number of these, however, are not very important, for some are represented only by newcomers to the scene and others have a very small representation in the community. Among the most important castes are the Marathas, who are the largest numerically, and the Rajputs,[2] from whom the village headmen are drawn. Both of these castes say that their traditional occupation is that of farmer and warrior. Other important castes are the Brahmans, the Gold Workers, and the Temple Priests. There are also Potters, Barbers, Basket Makers, and other caste groups. The most important Untouchable castes are the Scavengers, who are also traditional messengers, the Rope Makers, and the Leather Workers.

In the remembered past, there was never rigorous avoidance between most of the higher castes. For instance, Brahmans of Gaon will permit anyone to enter their kitchens other than Untouchables and a few other

[2] For convenience a shortened form of this caste name is used. The group adopted this name only within the last twenty years and therefore exhibits few of the traits normally associated with Rajputs.

low castes; this has been the case as far back as can be recollected. However, avoidance of Harijans about thirty years ago was very stringent. To non-Harijans, the touch of a Harijan was defiling. Transactions were made at a distance. When an Untouchable passed someone on the road, he stepped aside; and when he walked by a group of leaders in the village, he stopped, removed his shoes, and saluted before going on.

The idea of personal defilement is still present to some extent. Most women still maintain literal untouchability, and very few men have as yet brought themselves to take food from Untouchables. However, restrictions on caste interaction are now much less rigid, and Harijans no longer defer to others so much as in the past. Very few men consider Harijans literally untouchable. Many will enter Harijans' homes, and many—but by no means all—will permit Harijans to enter their homes. About one man out of ten will take water from the hands of a Harijan. Little or no attention is paid to caste in the schools of Gaon; children are not segregated. The tea houses and restaurants of Mot are now open to all, and a Harijan might be seated beside a Brahman in any of them.

The attitudes of the villagers toward the weakening of caste taboos are mixed. A few of them appear to be completely convinced of the relatively egalitarian ideas spread by the Congress Party; and there are some who overtly complain about the attenuation of caste customs. But in many cases people are confused. Some hold both kinds of belief simultaneously. It gives prestige to be strict in matters of caste. At the same time people feel that they are more important, that they stand higher in others' estimations when they identify themselves with the government and its programs.

In this period of transition and bewilderment the role of leadership in the community is of considerable significance; for though local leadership has been weakened in recent times, it is still an effective force in the conservation or alteration of custom. Leadership is found both in formal governmental positions and in informal achieved statuses. As we shall later show, informal leadership is more significant in village life. Formal leadership, however, is also of some importance. It is manifested in the village council and in the offices of the village headmen. In addition, the government position of *talathi* (record keeper and tax collector) wields a strong influence in the community.

Formal Leadership

The formal leadership in Gaon which is vested in the recently formed government Village Panchayat has clearly defined and strictly limited rights and duties. This panchayat is composed of thirteen members, elected for a period of three years. Elections are by secret ballot, and there has been fairly vigorous campaigning for office. All adults may vote, and any voter can be elected to the council. There are two committees of the council, the school committee and the judicial committee; both are elected by council members.

The duties of the panchayat have to do with repair and care of roads in the village, care of the cattle pound, lighting of lanterns on village streets, and similar matters. The village school committee supervises schools in the community and discusses problems with the district school board. Its powers are only advisory. The judicial committee has the power to try civil and criminal cases involving small sums of money and minor infractions of the law.

Most of the superficial obligations of the council are carried out. The council has hired people to sweep the streets and to keep the village lighted; but aside from this, it does very little. It rarely meets. Legally it is supposed to convene once a month; but during the year I spent in the village, it met only once. The judicial committee is not used by the people. Most civil suits involving small sums are settled by arbitration, without the use of official bodies. If legal proceedings are started, the courts in Mot are used. Since its inception only one case has come before it, and this case has never been decided.

Despite its ineffectiveness as an official body, most of the members of the council are people of status and power in the community. Most council members exercise considerable influence on village affairs and on the activities of individual members of Gaon. However, they do this in their capacity as informal village leaders and not as council members. The strict definitions of rights and obligations involved in the activities of the council are formulated far away from Gaon—far away in mode of thought as well as in terms of space. Since problems in the village are solved by reference to a sliding scale of values, one in which all people are not considered equal, the defined powers of the panchayat do not fit in with the way in which difficulties are customarily settled in the community.

It may seem peculiar that the *de facto* leaders of Gaon seek and hold positions on such an ineffective village council. They do so because membership in the council shows cooperation with the Congress Party, indicates "patriotism," and gives to the leaders an additional rationalization for the informal power they exercise. Furthermore, membership in a clearly defined governing body gives additional prestige, which in turn makes power more secure. Thus although the actions of the council are not important in themselves, membership in it does serve some purpose: the enhancement of the social and political positions of the informal village leaders.

The Village Headmen

There are supposed to be two headmen in the village: the revenue headman and the police headman. At the present time the positions are supposedly held by two brothers, but one performs the duties of both while the other tends to the family's lands. Both of the positions are hereditary in some households of the Rajput caste. The hereditary rights to the office of headman have been legalized by the government.

The responsibility of the police headman is to try to prevent violence and crime in the village and to make written reports to the local police in Mot if they occur. The revenue headman looks after tax collection, the recording of crops grown by farmers, and similar matters. The *talathi* is legally the assistant of the revenue headman, but he is actually more powerful, for the headman is never as competent in these matters as the *talathi*. He often merely mechanically signs the papers which the *talathi* gives him.

The police headman, on the other hand, does have an active role in village affairs, but his activities are not always those which the law prescribes. His first duty is to try to settle disputes in the community before they result in violence. His ability to do so is dependent not only on his status as headman, but also on his personality and his socio-economic status in the village. For example, the present headman is rather young, about thirty; therefore in many cases where the disputants are older than he, he tries to have the difficulties cleared up by referring them to one of the informal leaders of the village.

Much of his power can be attributed to his right to make reports to the police in Mot. In such matters, however, he is responsive to the informal leaders of the village and he often acts as a link between them and the government authorities. To quote the present headman:

In my job, I act according to what others think. If someone from the family line of headmen or some other important man in the village does something wrong, I may not report it if advised not to do so. But sometimes I am told to make a report. Then I do. When I make a report, it is a good one, and something is done about it.

He frequently tries to solve interpersonal problems in the village, criminal or otherwise, in accordance with the principles of justice prevalent in the community and without recourse to the police. Sometimes crimes are not reported because the acts are defined as criminal only in government law and do not violate the mores of the society. For example, in Bombay State it is illegal to marry children at a very young age; but among the villagers child marriages are still customary. When a marriage was held between a couple, both of whom were below the legal age, the headman did not report it. He protected himself by attending another marriage in another part of the village while the illegal one was taking place.

The headman may take steps to prevent government action where it would harm an important man in the village. On one occasion an informal village leader got drunk and misbehaved in public while a member of the police force from Mot was in the village, despite the fact that prohibition exists in Bombay State. The policeman wanted to arrest him, but the headman explained that the offender was an important man and requested that no action be taken. His request was granted.

On the other hand, where people of low status or ill repute are involved, the headman is known to have refrained from taking action to help them, though it was clearly his right—possibly his duty—to do so. Justice in Gaon does not mean that all are equal. It is not the justice embodied in the laws of Bombay State.

❧§ Talathi

The *talathi* is a government-appointed official, an employee of the revenue department. He is never a member of the community in which he serves and is generally not allowed to serve in any one village for very long, being rotated from village to village. As a result, any effect of the *talathi* on village life will vary with the attitudes and beliefs of the officeholder. However, the office is important since potentialities for leadership clearly reside in it and are sometimes manifested.

As we have observed, the *talathi* is technically subordinate to the revenue headman, but is in fact the more powerful. He collects taxes and keeps various types of land records for the village. All villagers have the legal right to call upon him for copies of any of the records in his possession, for which they are required to pay a nominal fee (less than one anna). Copies of some records are frequently required by villagers in order to get loans, to secure irrigation water, and for similar purposes.

It is the *talathi's* knowledge of details relating to land and allied matters that gives him power, particularly in view of the ignorance of the villagers with regard to their legal rights. He is often feared for his knowledge and because he is an agent of the government. As a result, he usually manages to extract extra money from the villagers whenever they require records copied. Sometimes sizeable sums—up to two rupees—may be extorted from individuals who are far from well off; yet it is a sign of his power that villagers are very unlikely to take steps to remedy this situation.

There are, of course, limitations on what the *talathi* may do. If he offends most of the village leaders his position is likely to be jeopardized. One record keeper in Gaon was transferred "by request of the villagers." He was a Harijan and this in itself probably irritated many of the people of higher caste. Furthermore, he attempted to better the position of his fellow Untouchables at the expense of the other villagers. He tried to encourage solidarity among Harijans by starting a public celebration of the birthday of the late Dr. B. R. Ambedkar (the all-India leader of Harijans), a celebration held yearly in Mot. He first persuaded the Harijans to prepare for the celebration; then, using his status as *talathi*, he went around to others in the village and "suggested" that they make financial contributions toward the event. They did so and the ceremony was held. After the celebration some villagers went to the *talathi's* superiors and successfully petitioned to have him transferred. Despite his transfer his efforts had some effect, for the event is now celebrated every year.

Informal Leadership

Informal leadership is of greater consequence in the community affairs of Gaon than formal leadership. Such leadership may be classified under two main headings: sanctioned and unsanctioned. Sanctioned leadership may be further subdivided into two types based on the sources of their effectiveness. Some are leaders primarily by virtue of the respect they inspire in others. Their advice is sought and their actions are imitated, but they generally do not attempt to compel obedience. This type of leadership may be called passive. Others are leaders because of the power they exercise over people. They instigate or prohibit activities and their right to do so is sanctioned by the majority, though their decisions may be contrary to the desires of many. This may be termed active leadership.

~§ Sanctioned Leadership: Passive

One of the oldest methods of resolving interpersonal conflicts in Goan is by seeking the advice of some individual who is highly respected. At present there are two men, both Brahmans, whose advice is often sought. They are the passive leaders. They make no effort to interfere in the actions of others; but they are always available to give advice or act as mediators in quarrels, and their opinions and behavior are often copied by others.

Necessary characteristics of this kind of leadership are high caste standing, a good economic position, and an age that may receive respect. People such as this are not in the struggle for status. They are not ostentatious about their wealth although they are generous with it. One of these leaders is known to "lend" seed to poorer people at planting time and then quietly to refuse repayment at the time of harvest.

The most important characteristic of this type of leader is that they must be men of strict morality and discretion. They must never defame other people or repeat to others what is told to them in private. The morality of these men goes beyond the moral norms of ordinary "good" men in the village. Their behavior approaches the ideal ethical code of the community.

Passive leaders tend to have a negative attitude toward change in intercaste relations; to the extent that their behavior and beliefs are imitated, they retard change. One of the two leaders believes that change in caste is inevitable, but appears to prefer that it were not so. He insists that change must be slow and offers justifications for the caste system. The other leader is even more conservative. He is highly religious and as such he maintains literal untouchability. His presence can act as a constraint on more liberal villagers; individuals who ordinarily pay relatively little attention to caste taboos may become strict on such matters when he is present.

~§ Sanctioned Leadership: Active

There are eight men in the village who are leaders in the sense that they have power over the fortunes of others and that they organize village affairs; these are the active leaders. They grade into the passive type, for some of them share the latter's qualities. But the most marked feature of their position is that they are men who can get things done their way despite the contrary wishes of other less powerful people, and that others recognize the propriety—perhaps inevitability would be a better word—of their doing so. They are men of power, and the fact that they have power is accepted as in the scheme of things.

Like passive leaders, their caste position is always fairly high—all are either Marathas or Rajputs—and like the passive leaders, they are always fairly wealthy. Unlike them, however, they need not live up to the ideal moral standards of the community. Many drink heavily, attend bawdy shows, and keep women of lower caste. Furthermore, they are all involved in an intense fight for status and all are given to ostentatious display. When their children marry, the ceremonies are always notable; during processions there is likely to be a fierce struggle among them to achieve a place of honor.

Active leaders often use their power simply to gratify their whims. They may command the services of many less powerful people. They can tell other villagers to run errands for them or to prepare tea for them, and they will be obeyed. A public well was once proposed for the village and it was decided to build it on the periphery of the village, adjacent to the house of one of the most important leaders of the village, rather than in some central spot accessible to everyone. When such men take loans from the government-sponsored Cooperative Credit Society, which is run by the villagers, it can be very difficult to get them to repay if they choose not to do so. The society was once closed for some time by the central bank in Bombay for this reason.

The influence of these leaders on the fate of particular people is usually felt through the village headman who is likely to find out their opinions on a case before he makes a decision. Most important, these men are the ones who organize activities which are sponsored by the village as a whole. They arrange matters for the annual fair. They decide what is to be done at the fair and see to it that sufficient money is collected. They decide whether or not the all-village ceremony in honor of the goddess Mariai is to be held, and they decide on the extent of the expenditure for the ceremony.

Like the passive leaders, the active leaders are conservative as regards changes in caste. In their day-to-day behavior they tend to maintain caste taboos. They insist that Harijans "know their place," and they will employ their power, where possible, to see to it that the Harijans stay there. Thus, when some Rope Makers wished to take legal action against a man of high caste, it was some of the active leaders who "persuaded" them, by means of threats, to drop their charges.

However, the attitudes of the active leaders toward caste sometimes place them in embarrassing positions, for most of them wish to be identified with the Congress Party. As a result, they will participate in ceremonies symbolizing the equality of Harijans when these are sponsored by the party. But when such ceremonies are held in the village and they are called upon to make speeches, they avoid references to Untouchables. They speak instead of such matters as Indian independence and the leaders of the independence movement.

Unsanctioned Leadership

The leaders thus far discussed have some qualities which are considered by the bulk of the villagers to justify their power of influence. But there are men in the village who have the power to get things done their way, yet who have few if any of these qualities. From the perspective of the majority of the villagers, this kind of leadership is based directly on force. They are unsanctioned leaders.

There are three men who wield this threat of force, all Rajputs. Fundamentally, their power is derived from an ability to manipulate the patterns of their culture and the people of their community for personal ends. It is gained, in large measure, by giving assistance to two castes of Harijans whenever difficulties arise between the Harijans and others in the village. By these means, the unsanctioned leaders have gained the allegiance of a goodly number of Harijans; and, more importantly, they have formed a small nucleus of Harijans who stand ready to assist them in any physical combat which may arise.

It is difficult to ascertain the motivations behind the behavior of these men. In part, it is probably a simple desire for power as such which prompts them to act as they do. In part, too, their manipulations are probably for economic gain; for by using physical force and threats, they extort money from some of their relations with whom they have had long-standing feuds. It is also said that some Harijans give them money in return for their help; but this could not be very much.

One thing is certain: at the present time, the unsanctioned leaders do not exercise their power in order to attain prestige. Bal, the most powerful of these leaders, avoids central positions in village affairs and never vies for an important position in village ceremonial processions. He seems neither to want nor to expect any of the symbols of prestige and leadership for which the active sanctioned leaders so often fight.

The unsanctioned leaders are the only ones who give support to the Harijans. They do not make speeches advocating better treatment for Untouchables, for they do not make any speeches. Nor are they obvious at public ceremonies symbolizing the new status of Harijans, for they are not obvious on any symbolic occasions. But they are effective. If they gain some power from supporting Harijans, they use their power in assisting Harijans. Thus in large measure, the exercise of their power sustains itself.

One event well illustrates their activities. It occurred on Independence Day, a year or two after the assassination of Gandhi. The young men of the village, from all castes including Untouchables, had been dancing in the ceremony in honor of the day. A pause was called because of the heat, and it was suggested that the dancers go to their homes for water. At this point, the son of one of the passive leaders invited Bal into his courtyard to take water from his well. It should be remembered that the passive leader is a Brahman, and Bal is a Rajput; so the invitation was not extraordinary. Bal then invited all the dancers, Harijans included, to follow him into the courtyard for water. They did so, while the son of the owner of the well stood by without objecting. The group soon dispersed, leaving behind a member of the Scavenger caste. One of the active leaders of the village came by and scolded the Harijan for taking the water. The Harijan defended his actions; and the leader departed, grumbling to himself. Nothing more was done about the affair.

In inviting the dancers into the courtyard for water, Bal was taking advantage of peculiar conditions. It was an occasion on which everyone was supposed to be treated equally, when overt discrimination against Harijans would have been unseemly. This was probably why the active leader waited until all but one man had left the courtyard before administering a reprimand. It was probably also what gave the Harijan courage to respond to the leader.

The Brahman might have avoided the predicament by employing some pretext, such as that the use of his well by a large number of people was objectionable. However, his position was particularly difficult, for it was a time when feelings against Brahmans were strong because of the recent assassination of Gandhi by a Brahman. If he had protested, he might have jeopardized his place in the community.

Thus, Bal used a special occasion for his advantage. He used it openly to declare his sentiments with regard to untouchability, and by those means to establish more securely his position as a "friend" of Harijans.

Summary

On the whole, formal leadership is of little importance in Gaon. The village council is ineffective in either hastening or hampering changes in caste; for this type of leadership is strictly limited by regulations which are foreign to the community and to the manner in which power and influence normally act in the community. So long as the informal active leaders dominate the council, it will probably remain weak; for these men are not likely to change their methods of exercising power. The village headman, another formal leader, acts as a link between the outside government and informal active leadership, and serves to reflect the desires of the latter. The *talathi* is more independent of these informal leaders, though he is still limited by them. Because the individual who holds this office is frequently changed, the effects of the office are not predictable.

Informal leadership is a more potent force in village life. Sanctioned leaders are all conservative with regard to alterations in the conditions of caste. Harijans have been heard to complain of these leaders, particularly the active type: "They want to keep us down so the work of the village will continue to get done." There may be some truth in this. The positions of the sanctioned leaders are defined in terms of the *status quo*; hence they have an interest in maintaining it.

The existence and effectiveness of the unsanctioned leaders is explicable mainly in terms of the rapidly changing and disorganized conditions in Gaon. The absence of strong social cohesion permits them to continue their activities without fear of effective cooperation aimed at obstructing them. The state of transformation of caste gives them an opportunity to use oppressed groups to their advantage; and the Congress Party program gives them a justification for their support of Harijans, support which would likely have been considered unjustifiable in the past.

LEADERSHIP IN A MYSORE VILLAGE

ALAN BEALS

*N*AMHALLI is a village of average size with a population of 615, located approximately fifteen miles from Bangalore City in Mysore State.[1] Namhalli was selected for study because of its proximity to Bangalore and the rapid cultural change which it had undergone between 1917 and 1952. Although the village might be described as an urbanized village, it is not actually urban in the sense of being part of the city. It is basically an agricultural village and is in no sense a suburb or "dormitory village."

The discussion of leadership in Namhalli will be restricted as much as possible to political leadership. By this is meant the kind of leadership which determines what individuals will occupy particular leadership positions in the village and the kind of leadership which is concerned with settling quarrels and generally running the affairs of the village. As 1952 and 1953 were not election years, it will not be possible to present much evidence concerning Namhalli's participation in the national political arena. It would appear that the average citizen of Namhalli has a rather vague idea of what goes on in an election. Decisions concerning voting appear to be made on a group basis. Generally, Namhalli's relationships with the government of Mysore are mediated through civil servants rather than through elective officials, and comparatively little importance is attached to political parties or to elections. The focus of political interest in Namhalli is the selection and behavior of local village leaders.

In the area around Bangalore, villages differ greatly in their economic and social organization. For this reason, it is not possible to generalize from the leadership situation in one village to the leadership situation in other villages. Villages which have been equally subjected to urban influences differ greatly in the way they are run. For example, one village located close to Namhalli is specialized in the raising of silk worms. It is dominated by a single large family whose members, although they are well educated and highly urbanized, have found the economic value of a large familial organization too great to permit the subdivision of the

ALAN BEALS is an Assistant Professor of Anthropology at Stanford University.

[1] This paper is based upon field work carried out between April 1952 and August 1953, while in India on a Social Science Research Council fellowship.

family. In this case, the village retains an essentially traditional pattern of leadership despite the pressure of urban influences. Another neighboring village is specialized in paddy cultivation. It is dominated by a single wealthy landlord who controls the land and the people on it. Here again, a traditional form of village leadership has survived extensive urban influence.

The traditional pattern of leadership in Namhalli has not survived under the impact of urbanization. One of the reasons that it has not survived is probably that Namhalli's economic and social organization has always differed from that of such villages as the two mentioned above which still retain their traditional leadership. The economic basis of production in Namhalli is not a single crop or a single industry. Instead the sources of agricultural wealth are highly diversified, with the principal source being the raising of millet on unirrigated land. This is a kind of activity which can be handled by independent small farmers with little capital to invest. The fact that Namhalli contains neither large families nor wealthy landlords could well be connected with the kind of agriculture practiced there.

It is possible to sort out three fairly well differentiated economic groups in Namhalli. There are five or six relatively wealthy families, fifty or sixty families of landowning farmers, and twenty or thirty families of poor people and agricultural laborers. These figures are stated in general terms because there is a considerable overlap between the three economic classes, and it is difficult to compute the actual wealth of any single family.

Another factor which may account for differences in the leadership patterns of equally urbanized villages is the kind of caste organization possessed by a particular village. There are villages containing individuals belonging to only one caste; there are villages containing one dominant caste and a number of subordinate castes; and, finally, there are villages like Namhalli which contain a number of roughly equivalent castes. Members of seventeen different castes live in Namhalli. Of these, nine castes can be considered important to the social organization of the village. The other eight castes are represented by temporary residents in the village or are numerically insignificant. Of the nine important castes, only one can be considered to be low ranking. That is the Madiga caste. The Madiga are neither Untouchables nor aboriginal Dravidians, but they are often described that way.

It is unthinkable that any Madiga could ever be a popular overt leader of the village, but it is not unthinkable that a Madiga could play an important role in village affairs. The Madiga are essential to the performance of village ceremonials and are economically important as laborers, watchmen, and scavengers. Some of the Madiga are comparatively well off economically, but most are poor. The leader of the Madiga caste represents one sixth of the village population and perhaps ten per cent of its wealth. When he speaks, other villagers are likely to listen although he must demonstrate that he knows "his place." It is not necessary to consider the role of the Madiga in the overt leadership of the village, but it should not be forgotten that the Madiga and other disadvantaged classes, just as women and younger brothers, may play an important role as advisors or as "powers behind the throne."

The remaining eight important castes in Namhalli include more than four sixths of the village population. As castes, there are no important differences in their political or economic status. All are large castes; all are well represented in Mysore State. While there are some social barriers between the members of these different castes in the village, leaders of the village could be drawn from any one of them. In the past, all have contributed wealthy, influential men to the leadership of the village. Taking into account, then, the caste system and the distribution of wealth in Namhalli, it is possible to draw a rather democratic picture of the social structure of the village. There are 122 married couples in Namhalli who make up approximately 98 individual economic familial units. If it is assumed that leaders of the village would for the most part be drawn from the heads of families in the eight more or less equal middle-class castes, there would be approximately fifty individuals in Namhalli who might qualify for leadership positions in the village.

Formal Leadership

The overt, formally acknowledged leadership positions which are available in Namhalli are of two kinds, one derived from the government and one derived from the traditional social organization of the village. From the point of view of the government, a village contains a headman, an accountant and an elected government Panchayat with a chairman. In theory, from the governmental viewpoint, these men are the leaders of the village. The headman and the accountant obtain their appointments by means of heredity, mitigated by the whims of local government officials. The *amildar*, the government official in charge of a group of approximately 300 villages, has the *de facto* power to remove or punish the headman and the accountant almost at will. The supposedly elected government Panchayat was actually nominated by the headman.

This does not appear to bother anyone in the village because the only function of the government Panchayat and of the headman and accountant, too, appears to be to do what the *amildar* and the government tell them to do. In western society the roles most closely approximating those of headman and accountant would appear to be those of factory foreman or of a boy left in charge of the class while teacher is away. The boy left in charge of the class may be a real leader or may have real influence in the class, but the fact that the teacher has put him in charge need not have anything to do with this. In the same way, a headman may or may not be a leader of his village. The fact that the government calls him headman does not mean that the village will call him headman.

The government Panchayat is evidently something left behind by one of those periodic legislative attempts to revive village democracy. A law was passed stating that every village should have a panchayat, but the legislators appear to have shied away from the question of giving the newly created panchayat any authority over anything. Hence, the government Panchayat has virtually no existence except on paper. Basically, the headman, accountant, and government Panchayat exist at the convenience of the government in order to fulfill certain very limited administrative tasks such as the collection of taxes and the keeping of village records. They have almost no real authority.

The other kind of leadership position in Namhalli is that sanctioned by traditional practices. The first of these is membership in the village panchayat, not the government Panchayat, but the real panchayat. Theoretically, in terms of traditional belief, the village panchayat consists of representatives from each of the important castes in the village. Decisions affecting the village as a whole can be made only with the unanimous consent of all members of the panchayat. Underlying the concept of village panchayat is that of caste headman. Traditionally, each caste had a single leader and it was this leader who belonged to the panchayat. In Namhalli during the last few years, several of the castes have been split up by internal dissension with the result that there are more individuals who claim the right to sit on the village panchayat than there were before. In practice, the panchayat includes every man of importance in the village.

It is perhaps a mistake to attempt to describe the village panchayat as a formally constituted group of individuals performing certain leadership functions; rather, it is a legal and administrative concept which involves the idea that whenever there is any trouble a group of concerned individuals can get together and discuss the problem and reach a conclusion. Thus, any man who is frequently called upon to settle quarrels or to discuss village problems may be referred to as a member of the panchayat. He achieves this designation by becoming a "big man"; that is, by having an ability to get things done, by being able to borrow and lend money, by being the representative of a noteworthy group of people, or by being possessed of exceptional wisdom and fair-mindedness. If a panchayat member agrees to a particular course of action, it is known that his followers will agree to it. His followers will follow him because they trust him, because he owes them money or because they owe him money, because he is a relative or a member of the same caste, because they went to school together, or because they all share the same enemy.

There are a number of important functions which the villager expects the panchayat to perform. The first of these is the preservation of the village from external threats to its welfare. In some ways, this function is not as important as it used to be. It has been a long time since Mahratha bandits swept down from the north looting villages. At the same time, proximity to Bangalore has produced serious threats to the village and its way of life. The existence of a complex body of urban law and law enforcement agencies poses a constant threat to the traditional way of doing things in the village. If things in the village are to be run the way villagers want them to be run, the panchayat must keep policemen and other government officials out of the village (unless, of course, they come bearing gifts) and must keep village matters within the village. Another external threat is that provided by wealthy landlords from Madras who, having fled from their enraged tenants, would like to establish themselves near Bangalore by buying up one or two villages. In this case, the obligation of the village leaders is to see to it that money is borrowed within the village and that exchanges of land take place within the village.

Inside the village boundary the panchayat is expected to settle quarrels and administer justice. Here it should be noted that the law courts in Bangalore rarely settle a legal matter to the satisfaction of the villagers. The law courts are compelled to struggle through vastly complicated legal disputes with nothing more than the aid of perjured witnesses, while the panchayat members know exactly what has taken place in any given dispute. The more positive functions which the panchayat is expected to perform within the village include the collection of money for public functions and village improvements. The panchayat is expected to maintain roads, wells, and irrigation works. When possible, the panchayat is expected to work through the village headman and other government officials to obtain assistance for such things as well and road construction.

All of the functions described as being functions which villagers expect the panchayat to perform are functions which the panchayat has performed in the past. All of these functions are things which need to be done in the village and they are mentioned here in order to demonstrate that urbanization has not removed the need for a village government which fulfills the functions expected of the panchayat. On the other hand, urbanization appears to have markedly affected the extent to which the panchayat can carry out its functions. One of the ways this has been accomplished is through the removal of many legislative and judicial functions from the village to the city. For example, the panchayat no longer has the power to tax, the power to punish by fines or excommunication, or the power to settle questions of inheritance, land ownership, indebtedness or family division. Suppose, for example, the panchayat meets and agrees to collect ten rupees from every house for the purpose of repairing a drinking water well. Several individuals refuse to contribute. The panchayat threatens to punish these individuals. The noncontributors tell the panchayat member that they will sue them in court in Bangalore if the panchayat punishes them. Lacking the ability to apply sanctions, it is difficult for the panchayat to give effective leadership to the village.

In short, while Namhalli has both a governmentally sponsored and a traditionally sponsored set of institutions which might serve to provide village-wide leadership, neither of the existing sets of institutions is capable of operating under present conditions. The most obvious reason for the failure of these institutions is the fact that they lack authority and have no means of enforcing their decisions. Underlying this, and perhaps even more basic, is the fact that Namhalli's leaders have not been successful in obtaining any kind of consensus from their followers. If there were consensus in the village, it would presumably be possible for village leaders to perform a wide variety of functions simply because everyone in the village agreed that they should be performed.

The absence of consensus in Namhalli can be considered to be partly due to population pressure which has forced the farmers of Namhalli into desperate competition for land. An even more important contributing factor would appear to be the introduction of conflicting sets of values into the village as a result of urbanization. From the point of view of the leader, this means that any decision can be justified in terms of several sets of conflicting norms. If, for example, a leader is engaged in arbitrating a dispute concerning the ownership of land, he has the choice of acting in terms of urban legal norms, in terms of traditional practices, or in terms of the way urban people actually handle such a dispute. In the meantime, the various parties to the land dispute will have selected for their own use the particular norms which are most favorable to their case. Under such conditions, the leader has no hope of pleasing both parties. Both parties consider themselves to be in the right and both are supported by considerable segments of village opinion. No matter what decision the leader reaches in adjudicating the quarrel, someone is bound to insist that he has been robbed. He can usually make a very good case for himself. Thus, instead of saying "All right, I was wrong this time," he says, "I was robbed by a gang of conniving scoundrels." Forthwith, he begins laying plans and enlisting support for his cause. What started as a dispute over land ownership becomes a snowballing conflict which may ultimately involve the whole village.

Factions and Cliques

As a result of disputes of this nature, Namhalli has developed a schismatic pattern of social relationships which has divided the village into a number of opposed groups. For want of a better term, these schismatic groups will be referred to as factions. The basis of the faction cannot be established by reference to previously existing traditional groupings. The faction need not represent opposed castes, a conflict between progressives and conservatives, or a conflict between economic groups. Generally, an individual belongs to a particular faction because his enemies belong to the other faction. Brothers, for example, frequently belong to opposed factions because of hatred generated in the course of the division of family property. Depending upon the situation at any particular time, Namhalli has between two and three such factions. As the ties which hold a particular faction together are extremely loose, it could be said that a faction exists for a particular dispute and that its membership changes as the dispute changes.

Underlying the factional structure of social relationships in the village are a series of more stable familial and clique groups. These groupings, which I will refer to here as cliques, are formed in several different ways. The commonest type is a family with its "in-laws" and servants. Another common type is that exemplified by some of the smaller castes in the village. Thus, the Muslim caste and the Jangama caste are highly organized and tend to participate in village affairs as a unit. In addition to these basically traditional kinds of clique groupings, there are groupings which consist of persons from several different castes. The basis of these groupings appears to be a common bond of friendship developed when the leaders of the groups went to school together. In nearly every case, cliques include relatives, friends, and persons bound together by economic ties, such as employee-employer or borrower-lender relationships.

A description of the origin of one such clique group and its relationship to factional disputes will serve to bring out some of the dynamic aspects of the interaction of clique and faction. Following is an account of the origin of a familial clique group as told to me by one of its members: the story begins about the time of World War I. At that time, the four brothers who head the family at the present time were living with their father and their uncle in an undivided joint family. Their uncle was a leader of the village who was constantly performing charitable acts and constantly engaged in the borrowing and lending of money. When the father and the uncle died in the influenza epidemic following World War I, the four brothers inherited the property. They found that their uncle had borrowed large sums of money for which he had signed promissory notes. In lending money, the uncle had not accepted promissory notes as he preferred to do business in the traditional manner with a "tree as his witness." The brothers were compelled to pay their debts by selling land, but they could not recover the money due to them because there was no written record of the transactions. The brothers were caught in a typical conflict between urban and rural values and impoverished because of it. The brothers felt they had been seriously wronged and decided that they were justified in using any means at their disposal to recover their wealth. Between 1920 and 1952 the brothers, acting with great shrewdness and taking advantage of every conceivable loophole in both urban and traditional law, managed to recover their "stolen" wealth and possibly a good deal more. The result of all this has been a running, unresolved conflict between the brothers and a large proportion of the other villagers which has lasted more than thirty years. The relationship between the brothers and those from whom they have "recovered" their wealth is one of fear, distrust, and burning hatred. Because there is no "right" on either side, or rather because both sides feel themselves to be in the right, there are no prospects for the resolution of the conflict. Further, whenever there is a dispute in the village, the brothers can be expected to take one side while their enemies support the other side.

Because they are leaders of one of the larger clique groups in the village, an examination of the leadership behavior of the four brothers should give an indication of what followers expect from a leader or, at any rate, what the ties are that bind leader and follower together. A methodological problem encountered early in my attempts to understand the leadership behavior of the brothers was that of determining how the brothers divided leadership roles among themselves. In referring to the clique headed by the brothers, villagers described it simply as "Doddanna's Party." The natural temptation here is to assume that Doddanna, the elder brother, is the leader of the clique. Further, in responding to a questionnaire which involved naming some of the leaders of the village, villagers mentioned Doddanna as a leader without mentioning any of his brothers.

It appeared that the best source of information about the operation of the clique would be Doddanna. At first, interviews with Doddanna revealed comparatively little information. It was assumed that Doddanna's reticence was the result of suspicion concerning the motives of the interviewer and that this suspicion would eventually wither away. After a number of inconclusive interviews, it was decided to attempt to obtain some information from Doddanna's younger brother, Chikkanna. Almost from the first Chikkanna was informative and seemed to have a better grasp of village affairs than did his brother. Further, he seemed much more intelligent than his elder brother, whose chief interest appeared to be in his bullocks and his crops. It appeared then that the planner whose chicanery had enabled his family to become wealthy at the expense of other villagers was not the elder brother whom the villagers nominated as the leader of the family, but his younger brother, Chikkanna.

Part of the confusion as to who was the leader of Doddanna's family can be traced to the linguistic habits of the villagers, who frequently refer to a family or to a member of a family by the name of the titular head of the family or the oldest person in it. It also appears likely that out of courtesy to his elder brother Chikkanna deliberately kept himself in the background. Doddanna, then, played the public role of leader while Chikkanna told him privately what to do. Covert leadership of this type would appear to be a comparatively widespread phenomenon in Namhalli, and quite a few of the village leaders are said to be dominated by their wives or by younger brothers.

Villagers consider Doddanna to be a successful leader largely because of his capacity for successful action. One of the reasons that people belong to Doddanna's clique is that they know that they will be protected and that they will probably be on the winning side in the long run. For the most part, the ties that unite Doddanna's clique are economic ties.

Being wealthy, Doddanna hires a large number of laborers. He pays slightly higher wages than do other villagers and he is quite charitable to his friends. He has lent money to a number of poor families and they are grateful to him despite the fact that other villagers warn them that Doddanna will take away their property. Doddanna's relationship with the members of his clique is basically a patron-client relationship in which economic protection is offered in exchange for political support.

There are two other large cliques in the village which contribute leadership to factional disputes. One of these, the headman's clique, is primarily composed of members of the Jangama caste plus a few members of Doddanna's caste of Lingayat agriculturalists. It is characterized somewhat less by patron-client relationships and its unified character would appear to derive from the close relationship ties inherent in a small, highly inbred caste. The other clique is rather amorphous and might be considered to be united more on a friendship basis than on a patron-client or a kinship basis. Its leaders include the village blacksmith, a factory laborer (the only one in the village), an oil merchant, a Muslim schoolteacher, and perhaps one or two others. All are the heads of small families; they are of approximately the same age; they are economically middle-class although one is considered wealthy; and they all have the equivalent of a junior high school education.

These three cliques—Doddanna's clique, the headman's clique, and the amorphous clique—are what might be called the politically dominant cliques in the village. Leadership in factional disputes tends to be provided by one or the other of these cliques. In 1952, there was a complicated three-way dispute between these three cliques which was replaced by an equally complicated two-way dispute between Doddanna's clique and the headman's clique on one side and the clique composed of the blacksmith and others on the other side. For the greater part of 1952 and 1953, the village was split into these two factions. The relationships between the two factions consisted of boycotting each other and of trying to create incidents which would cause some or all of the members of the other faction to lose money or property. For example, a Madiga who was associated with one faction happened to let his bullock graze on some land belonging to a member of the headman's faction. Members of that faction seized the Madiga and tried him before a panchayat. When he refused to pay a fine, they confiscated his cart. Members of the opposed faction immediately met and announced that the cart had never belonged to the Madiga in the first place. Hence it could not be confiscated. This is the sort of mutual harassment and obstructionism which characterizes the relationship between the two factions in Namhalli. Essentially the two factions are separated by a wall of distrust originating in interpersonal antagonisms covering a period of years. Any action of the opposed faction is to be regarded with the greatest suspicion, and reconciliation is virtually impossible.

The implication of this for village-wide leadership is, briefly, that there can be no village-wide leadership. To be sure, the village panchayat continues to meet occasionally, but it merely forms a platform for the airing of mutual grievances. In Namhalli urbanization appears to have prevented or at least postponed further urbanization because of its demoralizing effects upon the leadership of the village. If the village possessed political unity such things as improved wells, electric irrigation pumps, and improved agricultural methods could easily be introduced. Lacking political unity, the investment capital and much of the energy of the village is dissipated in factional disputes. The solution to this problem would appear to be the development of a system of local self-government which had police powers and the power to collect taxes, yet it may be too late for this because the enmity between the different factions is too great to permit a peaceful settlement.

FACTIONALISM IN A MYSORE VILLAGE

WILLIAM MC CORMACK

*T*HE village of Morsralli in Kankanhalli Taluk of Bangalore District approaches the modal size for Mysore villages, having a population of 504 (in October 1953).[1] The eight castes represented in Morsralli present neither an unusually wide nor an especially restricted caste composition for a village of its size. They include castes of cultivators, cowherds, shepherds, washermen, goldsmiths, barbers, beggars, and traders; but three fourths of the village's members are Okkaliga, the main cultivator caste of Mysore. It is usual for the Okkaligas to dominate the members of minority castes in villages of eastern Mysore, as they do in Morsralli, by means of their numerical and economic superiority.[2] The basis of the village economy of most villages in this area is dry-land *ragi* millet farming.

The shift in the effective leadership of Morsralli which has been occurring since 1900 is reflected in the two major types of leaders which can now be identified in this village. These two types of leaders are the hereditary leaders of the whole village group and the wealthy leaders of the village factions who have no traditional or hereditary claim to leadership. The village ceremonial chief (*gauda*), the four members of the village council of elders (panchayat), the cultivator caste headman, and the patel (who combines police and revenue duties in the village) claim leadership on the hereditary principle. These leaders are all patrilineal descendants of the individuals who held the same offices in Morsralli before 1850. The principal role of these traditional leaders in the village is the arbitration of disputes and the organization of cooperation for village festivals, marriages, and work parties for harvesting and road repair. Factional leaders, on the other hand, are nonhereditary and do not openly organize village cooperation for festivals and the like. The overt leadership role of factional leaders consists of pressing charges

---

WILLIAM MCCORMACK received the Ph.D. in anthropology from the University of Chicago. He has since undertaken field research in India studying the Kannada language, and social changes among the Lingayats.

[1] This paper is based on study of the village in which my wife and I lived for seven months in 1953-1954. The study was completed during our stay of fifteen months in Mysore, which was financed by the Ford Foundation.

[2] M. N. Srinivas, "The Social System of a Mysore Village," in M. Marriott, ed., *Village India*, Chicago, University of Chicago Press, 1955, p. 18.

that personal rivals have damaged the interests of the whole village group and therefore deserve to be boycotted.

The factors which are related to the declining effectiveness of traditional leaders include secularization of the villagers' outlook, the questioning of the neutrality and "good character" of certain impoverished members of the council of village elders, and a waning interest on the part of the village chief and patel in their traditional role of arbitrator of village disputes. The growing land shortage in the village has speeded the process of secularization in the village, in the main because some of the young men who leave the village for outside employment return and propagate a more secularized outlook. The land shortage also accounts for the impoverishment of the two village elders whose neutrality in arbitrating disputes is commonly doubted in the village.

Faction leaders in Morsralli have exerted a sharply increasing influence over village affairs between the years 1943 and 1954. These factions are revealed to be interest-holding groups which are formed through the working of personal opportunism. The goals of the village's three factions may be described, but the frequent occurrence of dual factional allegiance and the rapidly shifting composition of faction members belies the importance of these goals to the formation of factional groups.

Village Factions

The most fractious of Morsralli's three groups we may call the antigovernment faction. This faction principally argues that government officers are interested only in bribes. The overt goals of this group are to fine members of the government faction for cooperating with government officers or for alleged giving of bribes to them. Covertly, this group, which is headed by a cultivator moneylender, J M, engaged in a program of driving land holding minority castemen out of the village. The planner of the party's strategy is the village goldsmith who is himself landless.

An opposing group, which we may term the government faction, recommends that the village group follow the leadership of the patel in all matters. They argue that the antigovernment faction is only a gang for stealing land and that the government officers should "put down" the land grabbers. If the leadership of the patel were established in this fashion, the village group would presumably become dependent on the government party's ability to manipulate their officer friends. The nucleus of the government faction is the family of H, whose relative K was a friend and tenant of the patel. K's younger brother works as the patel's servant, thus further strengthening K's relationship with the village officer.

The third or "neutral" faction opposes both the village chief and elders and the other two village factions. The leader of this faction, the official government panchayat chairman, argued that all village funds should be handed over to him by the chief and elders. The pivot of the chairman's argument for his program was that the panchayat was the only governing body in the village recognized by government fiat. The chief and elders argued that the chairman, who was only twenty-nine when he was appointed by the patel and *sheekdar* (township officer) in 1947, was too young to assume responsibility. In spite of his youth, the village group cooperated with the chairman in road repair, which was one of the functions expressly delegated to him by government authority.

Three features are noteworthy when the personnel of factional groups in Morsralli are examined. These features are secrecy of factional membership, frequent shifts of allegiance from one party to another, and dual allegiance to opposed parties at the same time. These features were independently noted by Professor M. N. Srinivas in his study of Kodagahalli (Rampura) village in Mysore District. Professor Srinivas commented as follows on the factions in the village he described: "Only the hard core of a patron's following is willing to declare its allegiance to one patron, while many clients have a marginal affiliation to more than one patron. Marginal clients shift their allegiance from one [patron] to another over a period of time."[3]

A significant contrast exists between the traditional village social system in which castes constituted the major groups within the village and only a single allegiance was possible, and the present faction system where dual allegiance to interest-sharing groups is not only possible but common. Under the traditional system there was little scope for personal opportunism in the matter of caste formation. But under the faction system there may be no single large group with which an individual's interests are exclusively identified in the village. It so happens then that individuals may play off one faction against another in bidding for their support on a particular issue, or villagers may attempt to further the cause of two opposed parties at the same time in the hope of profiting from either party's loss.

Open allegiance in Morsralli's factions is notably limited to heads of households which are economically independent from the village group

[3] *ibid.*, p. 31.

as a whole, and where the heads of such families do not fear physical assault from members of opposed factions. Secrecy of membership in the factional groups is maintained because of fear of such physical assault and of economic retribution, and because cooperation with factional leaders is considered morally reprehensible. Each of the three factional leaders has been boycotted or publicly reprimanded by the village group in recent times, and partly as a result of this public censure they are often said by villagers to display "bad character."

Origin of Factions

The working of factional leadership in Morsralli is revealed in the incidents of a ten-year history of village-wide conflicts which can be related to the present major factional splits in the village. These incidents appear to have been generated from personal disputes and rivalries of factional leaders, which were then magnified into village-wide issues through the importance and persistence of the original disputants.

The present phase of factionalism began with an outright challenge by J M to the traditional authority of the chief. In 1943 the chief's brother, O, who was considered to be "really a good fellow" as he had given lenient loans to the poor people in the village, won a case against the moneylender, J M. The dispute overtly concerned the purchasing of cattle, but covertly the dispute may have been an attempt of J M or O to eliminate competition in giving loans, since J M and O were the leading village moneylenders at the time. J M refused to bow to the "partial" judgment of the village chief and elders in the case, and as a consequence of his defiance he was boycotted by the village group for a period of two years. The boycott did not trouble J M as he had sufficient debtors from outside the village to help him in his agricultural work and the need to arrange marriage within his family with the cooperation of the village group was not pressing him. In January of 1945, J M paraded his bullocks during the *sankranti* festival in defiance of the boycott of the village group. Later in 1945 he gave loans to the fourth son, M B, of the chief's elder brother (not O) for M B's forthcoming marriage celebration. J M also gave a considerable loan to an elder belonging to the shepherd caste. These two debtors urged a rehearing of the case between J M and O. This hearing was held at the beginning of the marriage season in April 1945. Since the new settlement favored J M, the chief's brother, O, refused to cooperate in his elder brother's son's wedding, which was subsequently held.

J M was at first able to ignore the villagers' boycott of him and subsequently to have it repealed by the village panchayat because he was economically independent of the village. He had achieved this position during the food rationing period of 1943-1953. At that time surplus grain producers were able to sell their crop at black market prices to the local traders and to their neighbors who had insufficient land to maintain their families. The cash accumulated from the sale of grain had allowed the hiring of laborers on an extensive scale, and, in the case of J M and the cowherd elder, the giving of loans to persons who guaranteed their free labor until the loan was repaid. Under the cash farming system existing in 1953, fifty of the village's harvest laborers were recruited from a nearby town and from three neighboring villages. Ten of these outside laborers were persons to whom money had been advanced by the faction leader, J M. Morsralli had been self-sufficient in free exchange labor force under the subsistence farming system of the nineteenth century.

Another circumstance which favored the recent shift to hired labor among the wealthier families in Morsralli was the adoption of a new variety of the staple millet. The new, higher-yielding *ragi* variety replaced the former variety during the period of food rationing. Although the new variety was previously known in the area, it had not been cultivated in Morsralli because its grain spikes were shed easily in rains. Rains of the northeast monsoon regularly occur at harvest time in the area, and they can destroy the crop in a field of the high-yielding type. Thus the new variety necessitates greater control over laborers at harvest time than cultivators regularly command over cooperative exchange labor.

J M's independence of his village was further illustrated in 1947 and in 1948 when he was again involved in village-wide disputes, each time with different supporters. The village chief and J M united against the washermen; later the government faction leader, H, and J M united against the shepherds with whom J M had previously been identified. This latter group then united against a village elder of the cowherd caste. The complaint against the elder was that his land was needed for the site of a prayer house, but indeed it was also a maneuver by J M to reduce the influence of a rival moneylender.

But the government faction leader, H, and J M split over an unrelated issue—a dispute concerning drainage in contiguous land that they owned. When further instigated by the cowherd, H built a house on the site in the cowherd's lands that had been proposed for the prayer house. J M's group insisted that H bribed the patel in order to build and refused to participate in village festivals until H was fined for bribery. After nearly a year of shifting power alliances and various incidents H was fined Rs. 25 by the village elders.

The village's patel was angered by the fining of H and the implication of this for his own reputation. His opportunity for revenge came when J M's sister's son assaulted the eldest son of H in May 1954. The patel reported this incident in his official capacity to the police subinspector, and further indicated that a "gang" was present in Morsralli which was causing local difficulties. The patel and the police visited Morsralli one evening during which, they had been informed, a meeting of the "gang" would occur. They entered the goldsmith's house and the police beat the assembled persons severely with leather belts. After the raid no one came forward to set the date for the 1954 spring festival of the village goddess. This festival had almost been stopped completely in 1953 by factional conflicts.

The patel temporarily gained from the police raid he led, since mobilization of village opinion against him by the antigovernment party could have resulted in boycott of him. The fining of the government party leader H was a strong indication that the antigovernment party had successfully mobilized the village group. The goldsmith, as strategist for the antigovernment party, had indicated on February 17 before the raid that a boycott of the patel was his next project. This boycott, if successful, could have resulted in the removal of the patel by causing trouble to his superior officers in the collection of taxes. Moreover, it was well known that the antigovernment faction had picked a successor to the patel!

The present role of the patel and the government faction in Morsralli suggests that the exercise of government authority in village affairs is productive of factional conflicts. The villagers often based their thinking about factions on the assumption that government officers intend to "make factions" in order to profit from selling their support to one of the leaders. It is also well known to villagers that in many places village revenue officers are themselves exercising a role of factional leadership.

Yet Morsralli is generally known in the vicinity as a village with little factionalism. One reason for this reputation is perhaps that officers' interference in Morsralli's internal disputes was less common than in many neighboring villages. Morsralli also differs from several of the neighboring villages which are locally famous as "faction villages" in lacking a government school. The presence of village schools is one index of government intervention in village affairs, since government is

443

required to initiate and maintain these schools in the face of prevailing attitudes among agriculturalists against education.

Conclusions

Two general changes have increasingly affected Morsralli in the twentieth century and appear to be related to the growing importance of factional leadership in the village. One of these changes is the shift from a village economy based on subsistence farming and depending on free village group exchange labor among families to an economy in which cash farming with hired labor and outside employment are important. This transformation in village economic organization has freed the wealthier individuals from dependence on the free cooperative labor of the village, and hence from the economic effects of the village boycott. Factional leaders have been encouraged by their freedom from the economic effects of the boycott sanction, which is the principal support of traditional leaders' decisions, to refuse to accept decisions of Morsralli's traditional leaders in the settlement of disputes. Secondly, the growth of factionalism in Morsralli appears to be related to increases in the extent of direct government interference in village affairs. This decrease in village autonomy has favored greater independence from village social control for those individuals who can use the threat of government intervention to delay applications of the boycott. It is also a fact that real or alleged official support can be used in Morsralli to strengthen the position of one side in the village factional power contests.

ELEMENTS OF LEADERSHIP IN AN ANDHRA VILLAGE

R. BACHENHEIMER

*P*ADU is a community of about 800 people situated on the dry, flat plain of the central Deccan in western Andhra.[1] The main food crops are a millet and a sorghum, but over a dozen subsidiary edibles are also grown. Cotton, however, occupies a large percentage of the land and provides the major income to both agricultural laborers and landowners. Cropping patterns are complex and demand not only a great expenditure of energy most of the year but also careful planning. Rain is the only source of water for the crops; falling at the proper times in the proper amounts, twenty inches of rain is sufficient to bring forth excellent crops. Unfortunately such an occurrence is rare and the region is known for its famines rather than for its bumper harvests.

Padu is made up of 156 households belonging to eighteen different castes. Five is the average number of persons in a household, while the range is from one to eleven, with two very large households of nineteen and twenty. Of the eighteen castes, ten are represented by three or fewer households; four have five to eight households each; the remaining four castes together total almost sixty per cent of the village.

A threefold division of the caste hierarchy will be examined here. First, there are the nine vegetarian castes, numerically one fourth of the village, including the goldsmith, the blacksmith, and the barber. The most important of this group, however, are the Reddys and the Jangamas. If the absence of the sacred thread is the mark of a Sudra then the Reddys are Sudras; others may wish to rank them as Vaishyas because they are cultivators and landowners. However that may be, the important point is that they adhere to many high-caste practices including strict vegetarianism, and they are considered high caste. Their mother tongue is Telugu and they are politically and economically important in Andhra. In Padu eight of the twenty Reddy families control over seventy-five per cent of village lands. Although they are not considered

RICHARD BACHENHEIMER is a Teaching Associate in the new unified social sciences program at the University of California, Berkeley.

[1] Research for this study was undertaken in India from 1953 to 1955 under a Fulbright grant and with aid from the Department of Anthropology, University of California, Berkeley.

members of the Lingayat sect, they associate themselves in religious matters not with Brahmans but with the Jangamas, the priestly caste of the Lingayats. There are few Brahmans in the area and though most of them are large landowners and educated to the point of speaking fluent English, as Brahmans they play a relatively small role in village life. This is due not only to their small numbers but to the great importance in this region of the Lingayat sect which, in principle, does not recognize the supremacy of the Brahmans. Without going into the doctrine, history, and organization of Lingayatism, attention is called to the status and importance of the Jangamas. They play a role among Lingayats similar to that of the Brahmans among other Hindu sects.

The second major caste division is comprised of six castes of meat eaters. The Pinjaris and the Naiks belong to this group and together they include one third of the village population. Both are castes of agricultural laborers. The Pinjaris are Muslims and Kannada speakers, while the Naiks are Hindu and Telugu is their mother tongue. Yet their common occupation and similar socio-economic status seem to bring them together in relation to other castes although they may fight between themselves.

The third group is that of the Harijans. Two Telugu speaking castes of thirteen families live by themselves off to one side of the village. The largest single caste in Padu is the Adi Andhras whose forty-one households take up one whole side of the village proper. They are Kannada speakers, as are all other castes whose mother tongue is not here specifically mentioned. The Harijans' primary occupation is also agricultural field work.

Other differentiations could be enumerated, but they are not of great consequence for a discussion of leadership in Padu. The gross structuring of the social organization splits the populace into three groups with accompanying social and economic disadvantages increasing from top to bottom. Economic power and technical skill, in addition to ritual purity and proficiency, are concentrated in the upper third, the lower two thirds providing the necessary labor force. The landowners are not inactive, however; most of them partake fully in the rigors of physical labor, working side by side in the fields with their laborers.

Village Leaders

There are eight men in Padu who may be considered leaders of the village. It is they who make decisions affecting the entire village. This does not mean that they have an equal say in village matters or that they agree on everything. But it is these men who are the active decision makers, the advice givers, the protectors, the threateners, the representers, and the communicators. Of the eight, five are Reddys. The most important among them, and in the village as a whole, is a strong, healthy man of thirty who is literate and well traveled in India. He manages the family lands of his two older brothers, as well as his own, because they have left the village to live in a nearby town. This family owns over one third of the village acreage, an equally large share of village houses, more than thirty head of cattle, and a steam cotton gin in the next village. Lands are owned in other villages, too, and the two brothers manage the family's two-vehicle bus company, a cotton brokerage, and their urban moneylending business. In addition, the eldest brother is an important local official of the Congress Party. The youngest brother is the biggest moneylender and the biggest employer in the village. Everything he does he does well. He works hard and is a good family man to his wife and three sons. Observance of minor caste practices is unimportant to him personally, yet he supports and participates in the ceremonial affairs expected of an important high-caste man. He encourages some traditional village activities such as the village drama and group dancing and singing on festival days. Nevertheless he is an innovator in agriculture, introducing new crops and new techniques into Padu, and he brought the first tractor into the area. Padu is only part of a revenue unit and all the government officers live in the other village of the unit. This No. 1 Reddy leader therefore holds no official position or responsibilities, but he is informally recognized as Padu's head man.

The second most important man in Padu plays a less direct part in village affairs. In his early forties, he is literate, well traveled, and capable. If anything, he is more energetic than the No. 1 leader. He is also a big landowner, a big moneylender, a man with sons (four), and an innovator. But he spends most of his time out of the village attending to his many business ventures, including the providing of contract labor for government construction projects. He is uninterested in village doings as long as they do not endanger his interests and he remains generally aloof. Nevertheless, as a moneylender and employer he controls the economic welfare of a large number of villagers. Furthermore, there is bad feeling between him and No. 1 because of a land controversy some years ago, and he is the potential leader of any faction that might flare up in opposition to No. 1. Padu is free of factional alignments in any rigid sense; rather there is a steady tug of forces in three or four directions below the surface with the general effect being that of balance. With No. 2 preferring to expand outside the village rather than fighting for power within it, no coalition is possible that would be powerful enough to challenge No. 1 openly. There is competition and conflict in Padu, but not so much that it drains village resources unduly.

The No. 3 man of note operates between No. 1 and No. 2 in village politics. He is an overt friend to all while attempting to improve his own position. He shares ownership in a large part of the best village lands, lends money and operates as a labor contractor, all on a much smaller scale than No. 2. Some of his early years he spent traveling with a guru and he continues to be interested in religious matters, though more in the literature and philosophy than in the ritual. At forty-eight he has no children, although he has been married twice. He dislikes physical labor and has rarely held the handle of a plow, but he does frequently direct the work of his field laborers.

No. 4 is a short, chubby, jolly man of sixty-five. He owns more land than No. 3 and he also lends money. He is literate and he has sons, but he does not engage in intrigue as much as No. 3. He is tradition-oriented and a sponsor of ritual. He married into a Padu family at a time when that family was the most powerful in the village, and that lingering heritage plus the personal popularity of the old man combine to maintain his status as a leader.

The last of the Reddy leaders derives his status in part from his close relationship to No. 1. He is his good friend and the father-in-law of No. 1's next older brother. His family was once much more important in the village, and he still owns sixty acres of land. Fifty-one, literate, a moneylender, he no longer is very active in the fields, but he does participate vigorously in village affairs. He, too, is traditional in outlook and something of a defender of the public morals. He has two wives and the second gave him the son that the first did not.

The three non-Reddy leaders of Padu are a Jangama, a Brahman, and a blacksmith. The Jangama owns twenty acres of land. The heads of the only other Jangama families owning more than ten acres are both widows, while two other Jangamas live only by begging. Because of this advantage and because of personality factors, this Jangama is the social leader of the caste in Padu and holds a place among the leaders of the village as a whole. He is meticulous in his observance of ritual requirements and fair and forthright in his relations with others. A close associate for many years of the important Reddy families, and blessed with a good mind and memory despite his sixty years, his advice and memory are often sought by the younger Reddy leaders of the community.

The only Brahman in Padu was sent there by the government sixteen years ago as a school teacher. At one time he spoke some English but now can only partially understand it. He is the only one of the village leaders who has ever studied English. He has attached himself to No. 1 as his advisor, confidant, and agent. His loyalty is repaid by support from No. 1 and the village recognizes him as No. 1's alter ego. He does teach school and this in itself is a high-prestige position, especially as government teachers are rare in the immediate vicinity. Apparently he also happens to be a good teacher and his former pupils continue to respect him.

The blacksmith-carpenter is the most remarkable person in Padu. He is sixty-six and still dynamically active. He is a rapid, accurate worker in iron and wood, as well as a capable artist. Recently he took on the task of building a large temple car, complete with carvings, in a village twelve miles away, a two-year job. He still walks the nine miles to the market town in two hours and returns the same way. With his son, who does poorer and slower work than he does, he supplies and maintains almost all the tools, including carts, needed to cultivate over 800 acres of village lands. He is a superb storyteller, the *pujari* to the temple of the village goddess, and a man of great strength and courage. In the light of these accomplishments it is understandable that he is also somewhat egotistical and opinionated. Finally, he is the owner and cultivator of forty acres of land. His workshop is a spacious natural gathering place for villagers in search of a discussion and it serves as a fit setting for his discourses.

These then are the leaders of the upper castes and of the village. There are others who might be leaders but are not: the goldsmith, for example. He plies a respected trade and is talented enough to draw his clientele from larger villages in the vicinity. He is literate and a devoted participant in all ritual. But he sticks to his work and is rarely seen chatting with the other men. There is also the uncle of No. 2; only a few years older, he is reticent and shy, concerning himself primarily with active work on the family's large holdings. He is literate, a moneylender in a small way, and a capable farmer. A close friend of the blacksmith and well thought of by all, his words are listened to when he speaks but he chooses to remain silent and passive. Already he has passed on active management of family affairs to his twenty-eight year old son. Another Reddy who owns over one hundred acres in and around Padu is not so retiring but is the active head of the largest family in the village. In his sixties, he continues in direct management of his lands and household, which includes his six adult sons and the families of four of them. He himself is the oldest of three brothers who split up the family property many years ago. He is the only one, however, to have enhanced his holdings. He and his sons are well educated, capable, friendly, properly pious, and well liked. Nevertheless, none of them demonstrates much desire for active participation in the affairs of the village. On the other hand, one of his younger brothers tries to aggrandize his status, but his relative lack of economic strength and the absence of any outstandingly positive physical, spiritual, or personality traits keep him from becoming more than a secondary leader.

Three other men must be considered as leaders of importance in the village though they represent only a part of the community. Two are low-caste meat eaters and the third is a Harijan. The former are Pinjaris and brothers. The oldest still owns some land, though the exact amount is difficult to ascertain, and he is one of the very few of the middle group who do. He is forty-eight, has seven children including three young sons, and a permanently attached laborer who has been with the family for twenty-five years. He is illiterate but able. Unfortunately ethnographic data about this man are more meager than usual, which may be a tribute to his unassuming manner. Nevertheless, it is definitely known that he is the respected leader of the Pinjari-Naik community in Padu. He acts as arbitrator between the two castes, helps arrange marriages, and is spokesman and representative of these castes in concerted dealings with the high-caste leaders. In turn, he is used by them as a communicator of information moving in the other direction.

His brother has not lived with him for many years and has lost the few acres he once owned. He continues to lease some land and works as a field laborer when he can. He is the bully of the village. He chafes under the restrictions of his low status and is constantly trying to emulate and associate with high-caste men. This is resented, and various sanctions are applied to chasten him. He has been known to strike back by burning his enemy's haystack, a common and crippling manner of revenge. It is probable that his position as a leader is based initially on fear of the man physically and then on identification with him as the great challenger of the powers that be. For the lower caste people do harbor resentment against the well off and, though usually dormant, this resentment is growing. Therefore they take pleasure in the tiltings of the bully against the system and help to cover up for him and protect him when he really gets into trouble, as he has done several times.

There are three Muslim families who are not Pinjaris, and the head of one of them is a mullah. He is the only one who can, under Muslim law, kill any animal that is to be eaten. He is fifty-eight, literate, speaker of the local variety of Hindi, and owner of eighteen acres of land. He came to Padu from the next village north because his three sons died within a short time in the same house. He believed it was cursed and left. By virtue of his economic and religious status he ought to be the leader of the Padu Muslim community which includes the Pinjaris. But he has tried in many little ways to attach himself to Reddys and may often be seen drinking coffee with No. 2 on the latter's verandah. Maneuvering in this fashion he puts himself neither here nor there and ends up by being intimidated from above and laughed at from below.

The Adi Andhra leader is an intelligent, able man of thirty-eight. He himself is uneducated but both his sons are literate. Among the Harijans he is the only one owning land, but again the acreage is difficult to determine. It is sufficient to maintain him and his family and to allow some surplus as he is known to lend money to other Adi Andhras. He, too, acts as the representative and communicator of his caste and he is suffered in that position by the Reddys because it is useful for them to have a real leader of such a large part of the populace with whom to deal, because "he knows his place" (he and the bully are compared on that score) and because he does not drink and is not insulting or dangerous to high-caste women. The Reddys say that they have campaigned and contrived to get the lands of the Pinjaris, Naiks, and Adi Andhras away from them because the men of these castes drank and were uncouth, and, especially the Pinjaris and Naiks, were insulting and threatening to their Reddy women. The Adi Andhra leader does not drink and is never seen in the upper-caste part of the village. The Adi Andhras take no part in any of the village religious festivals as they have been converted to Christianity and have their own holy places and ceremonials. Their leader is a notable moral force in this context.

Conclusion

In Padu it would seem that economic strength is the most important single attribute of leadership within each caste, and that wealth plus high caste tend to determine village leadership. Piety, while looked upon with favor, plays little active role in characterizing leaders. Further, it is the outward-looking families with party and economic interests beyond the village that wield the greatest power. This wider orientation also tends to provide greater opportunities for fluidity among the lower castes, particularly with regard to occupation. Yet none of the important leaders was born outside the village.

Language, which bifurcates the village, is also an important element in leadership in Padu, despite the fact that most individuals in the village are bilingual. Education is a valued asset for village leadership.

Lower-caste leaders are clearly allowed to exist only at the pleasure of the upper castes; a premium is placed upon staying in one's place. Yet such leaders are essential to provide a channel of communication between village leaders and lower castes. In Padu the Adi Andhra leader is careful to remain in this limited role and has not attempted to interfere politically with the village leaders.

Despite the outward-looking groups in Padu, leadership follows a fairly traditional pattern. The absence of government officials may help to explain the absence of disrupting factions. Change, resulting from the impact of a river valley project, is only beginning to affect patterns of leadership in Padu.

Among the changes that are sure to take place in the future are an increase in political awareness and the growth of political activity. As the literacy rate rises, as the general level of education improves, and as the media of communication increasingly affect the villager's sensitivity to external events, he will become aware that political acts and decisions may directly affect him. Thus the villager will become more prone to ally himself with, and even participate in, some political organization. The existing leaders of Padu would be natural local foci of a political organization, with the secondary, non-Reddy leaders (such as the bully) being the obvious choice of any protest party. As long as no factional conflict develops among the Reddys, it seems reasonable to conclude that all the Reddys would support the party that represents them as Telugu-speaking landowners. However, it is possible that a conflict of issues would divide the landless villagers along caste lines, the Adi Andhras on the one side and the Pinjari-Naik combine on the other. Then the Reddys might act as a third force: they might back the Adi Andhras because of traditional patron-servant ties; or might perhaps oppose them as being Kannada-speakers or Christian converts, or both. On the other hand, the Reddys might split to provide high-caste leadership for both groups. The possibilities are numerous. But no matter what party alignment develops in the Padu of the future, for greater understanding of the political affairs of the village and of the state, it behooves the would-be student to find out who the nonpolitical leaders of Padu are, and why.

POLITICAL ORGANIZATION AND LEADERSHIP IN A KARNATAKA VILLAGE

EDWARD B. AND LOUISE G. HARPER

*T*OTAGADDE, a village in the Western Ghats of Mysore State, is a multi-caste village composed of six dispersed hamlets.[1] The nearly five hundred inhabitants of the village are related to each other in a strong and functioning caste system, which, although eight castes are represented, can conveniently be divided into a three-class system for the purposes of this analysis.

At the top of this class system are the Havik Brahmans, a single caste group which is numerically the largest in the village. They command positions of control and leadership in the political and economic aspects of village life and provide its moral and religious leaders as well. The economic basis of this group, the raising of arecanuts, allows many Havik Brahmans a fairly high standard of living and a good deal of leisure time. Next is a group of six Sudra castes who are either artisans or paddy-growing agriculturalists. Some of the latter own their lands but many lease from a nearby temple or from local Havik Brahmans. At the bottom of the economic and social scale are the Untouchables who are traditionally and usually the servants for Havik families and who may be landless laborers.

Positions of Leadership

A paper concerned with village leadership in Totagadde is of necessity primarily concerned with the dominant caste,[2] the Havik Brahmans.

EDWARD HARPER has been a member of the Department of Anthropology at the University of California at Berkeley. He is at present in the Departments of Sociology and Anthropology at Bryn Mawr and Haverford. Louise Harper received her M.A. in anthropology in 1954 from Cornell University.

[1] The census figures for people living in Totagadde in 1955 are: Havik Brahmans, 27 families, 191 people; Lingayat, 2 families, 13 people; Okkaliga, 5 families, 28 people; Divaru, 21 families, 140 people; Kumbara, 5 families, 24 people; Hasaluru, 10 families, 40 people; Hajjama, 1 family, 4 people; Adikarnataka, 13 families, 39 people. Caste names used are those most commonly heard but not necessarily the ones preferred by caste members. The castes are listed in the ranking usually given by Brahman informants.

[2] For a discussion of the concept of "dominant caste" see M. N. Srinivas, "The Social System of a Mysore Village" in McKim Marriott, ed., *Village India*, Chicago, University of Chicago Press, 1955, pp. 17-19.

The greatest all-village social prestige, economic wealth, religious leadership, and political power are concentrated in this one caste. All other castes regard the Haviks as the village leaders and any decision involving the village as a whole is made by them. This applies as much to the programs of change introduced by the government as to the all-village religious festivals. The position of the Haviks is reinforced by many economic controls as they are the dispensers of many necessary favors and commodities.

As a group the Havik Brahmans form the village elite.[3] All but one Havik man in Totagadde are literate while few Sudras and no Untouchables are. Some Haviks even know a little Sanskrit and most have read some classical literature; many take part in elaborate dramatic portrayals of the classic epic myths. Lower castes within the village treat the Haviks with respect and deference in a manner defined by a highly patterned mode of interaction. Much of a Havik's daily life is ceremonial; activities such as eating and bathing are overlaid with ritual and formality. Others in the village regard the Havik Brahmans as moral leaders and are afraid of their ridicule and judgment. When there are breaches of morality Haviks may be asked, or may take it upon themselves, to pass censure.

But there is another aspect to the Havik's life. When he leaves the village and goes to town, he leaves his superordinate position and assumes the position and behavior of a subordinate. He feels less well educated than the city person who in all probability has had more Kannada and certainly more English education. The Havik Brahman must wait outside government offices until the whim or the crowded schedule of the official permits him to enter. When he sells his arecanuts he must accept the price given by the merchant. When he eats in town there is no time or place nor are there facilities for ritual cleansing and purification. What is usual behavior between castes in the village may not hold true in the city. First of all, if a village Brahman treats a low-caste person according to village caste standards there is a noncaste-oriented law to punish him. In addition the "superior" village Havik is often the debtor of the arecanut merchant who is frequently a member of one of the Vaishya castes, or the petitioner of the government official who may

---

The Havik Brahmans in Totagadde are viewed, in this paper, in their context of being a dominant caste. Therefore, in order to avoid confusion with the more general term Brahman and its religious connotations, the term "Havik" is used either by itself or in conjunction with Brahman.

[3] See Gideon Sjoberg, "Folk and Feudal Societies," *American Journal of Sociology*, LVIII, 1952, pp. 233-235.

be of any caste,[4] or the briber of the clerk who holds his position more by virtue of education than of caste. In fact, the Havik of the village elite becomes the country hick who may be teased and thwarted by the more sophisticated city person.

Perhaps the dual role of the Brahman is a reflection of what is produced when stratification in a culture is combined with peasant and urban societies. Not only is there a status difference between the city person and the villager; but also, owing to rigid social and economic stratification, there are differences within the village itself. It is the top group, the Havik Brahman caste, that forms the connection between the city and the village. Government officials and government orders affecting the village come to the Haviks; the Haviks, as all-village representatives, go to governmental offices for permits and licenses. The western gadget culture comes to the more wealthy Haviks as only they and not the Sudras have a cash crop that they sell to the town.[5]

In another sense, the Havik Brahmans, in their capacity of being Brahmans, are leaders for all castes in the village. They are the preservers of both the "little" and the "great" traditions.[6] Frequently when non-Brahmans were asked questions about village history, or legends regarding local spirits, the reply would be to ask either "the Brahmans" or a specific Brahman. Similarly, when non-Brahmans were asked about the Hindu epics the most characteristic reply was in the vein of "the Brahmans can give you the answer to that." In many ways the Brahman is the carrier of the classic culture within the village. He knows a little about dance, drama, art, epic literature, Hindu philosophy, ritual, history, and music—although he is a novice in all.

Thus both from within the village and from without, the Havik Brahmans, the dominant caste, are viewed as the village leaders, the village elite. In the conception of both the villager and the city person, the village does not form a homogeneous unit but is a social group having an elite that forms the main link between the rest of the village population and the professional, business, and official classes in the town.

[4] Several years ago the *amildar*, the highest government official in the area, was a man from one of the Untouchable castes. Villagers knew this and yet he was treated with the respect and courtesy accorded to his government position, not his caste affiliation.

[5] For a comparison, see Robert Redfield, *Peasant Society and Culture: An Anthropological Approach to Civilization*, Chicago, University of Chicago Press, 1956, pp. 62-64, for his summary of J. A. Pitt-Rivers, *The People of the Sierra*, London, Weidenfeld and Nicolson, 1954.

[6] See Robert Redfield, "The Social Organization of Tradition," *Far Eastern Quarterly*, XV, 1955, pp. 13-21.

LEADERSHIP AND CHANGE IN THE VILLAGES

Within the Havik caste there are positions of individual leadership. One such role is that of the political leaders, the persons whom the government officials seek out when dealing with the village, who schedule and decide the course of all-village undertakings, and who collect the necessary funds for them. These nonhereditary village leaders obtain and maintain their positions—within the village as well as with outside groups—by struggle in the village political setting.

Certain characteristics of political leaders in Totagadde set them apart from other Haviks. In the area of religion, these men are fairly orthodox but are without religious fervor; they observe the many taboos but without fanaticism. They cooperate with and give support to religious leaders, and although they organize large religious functions and often participate with the purely religious leaders in the pujas, they always show deference and respect to their more learned compatriots.

Another characteristic of political leaders is that they tend to have the least number of primarily friendly contacts with members of other castes; their contacts are formal and their behavior regulated by strict caste rules. The households of the three outstanding elder Havik political leaders observe the greatest caste distance, but these men tend to be more just and fair in their dealings with lower castes than those who are not leaders. The three most deviant Haviks in Totagadde have the most informal contacts with lower castes, participating in cockfights, gambling, drinking, friendships, and sexual relations. Two of these three are regarded by many Sudras and Untouchables as very unreliable, whereas the three political leaders, who exhibit strong support for the traditional caste system, are respected and trusted by many members of the lower castes.

Men who are leaders must have free time for their role of leadership. This means they must have a certain degree of wealth. Also wealth is important as leaders constantly reinforce their position as other people come to them to ask for free arecanuts or plantain leaves, or to borrow tools or small amounts of money. It is almost incumbent upon such men to give. From this standpoint it might be said that leadership is partly based on obligation—the dispenser of favors can expect favors in return. Also, if a Havik is really poor he has to do most of his own work, such as cleaning his own cattle shed and bringing firewood from the forest, or he must take up a supplementary occupation, such as carpentry or cooking. A poor man has much less time to devote to community activities and has fewer inter- and intracaste contacts that create respect for or obligation to him.

Although decisions involving the whole village are always made by the Havik Brahmans, and in particular by the individuals classed as political leaders, other castes also play a part. As Brahmans discuss village plans among themselves so do non-Brahmans, and the two meet to talk together informally. The non-Brahman leaders are consulted by the Havik leaders and their opinions are given weight. Each caste has one or several representatives, men who have acquired or earned their reputations, who act as spokesmen for their caste in dealing with the Haviks. In some senses it may be said that these non-Brahman leaders are chosen by the leaders of the dominant caste. For example, when a government representative came to the village to discuss the digging of a well in a Sudra hamlet, he went to one of the most active elder Havik leaders who in turn sent for the Sudra man of his choice to come and discuss the matter. This non-Brahman returned to his own caste hamlet with knowledge about the program and thus enhanced his own position among his peers.

This informal influence that the Haviks have over leadership positions in the other castes of the village was formalized when, for the first time, non-Brahmans were elected to the Village Panchayat, a government-sponsored body. There were nine posts to be filled and the government ruling prescribed that there should be an all-village election if there were more than nine candidates. Three days before this election the Havik leaders met and decided who the members were to be. Non-Brahman leaders who were recognized by the Haviks were the ones that were chosen to represent their castes. When the official came for the election, Haviks and Sudras met with him in the school building. The Haviks passed among themselves the book containing nine names of the people to be nominated. These names had previously been agreed upon by a small group of Haviks. As each man received the book he read off the name of a candidate. After each name was read a Sudra, sitting on the other side of the room, seconded it. Nine names were read and the "election" was complete. The formal sanctioning of an informally made decision is a common pattern.

Haviks, then, can create, strengthen, or weaken the position of a non-Brahman leader. Interestingly, non-Brahman leaders chosen by the Havik Brahmans appear to have certain traits in common. They represent the most socially striving element within their own caste and they have, to a larger extent than their caste fellows, internalized Brahmanical values. They are what Srinivas calls the most highly Sanskritized.[7] This fact helps to minimize conflict between leaders of different groups who must work together, as the leaders of both groups come closer to using the same values in arriving at decisions. In addition, the non-Brahman leaders are more strongly motivated to cooperate with the Haviks since they owe their position of power in their own castes at least in part to their standing with the Havik leaders.

There are, however, other informal non-Brahman leaders who tend to assume authority in situations involving only their own castes. In an all-Sudra festival, for instance, it was the more conservative, least Sanskritized Sudra men who took over management. This group of informal leaders has a value system quite different from the ideal Brahman value system.

In addition, there are several formal, hereditary, and ascribed positions of leadership in all non-Brahman castes. The main one of these is the *hiria*, who is the official spokesman for his caste. His chief function is to enforce caste rules and to try cases of their infringement. It is theoretically possible for him to be deposed, but in practice this is not done; even if he is incompetent in his role he tends to be supported and guided by the men in positions of acquired leadership rather than deprived of his position.

The Haviks have no hereditary caste leader in the village such as the one just described. There is, however, one position, the *uru ejmanru* or village head, informally chosen by the Havik leaders from among themselves. He is usually a wealthy man belonging to one of two lineages among the eleven Havik lineages in the village. During a transitional period it is quite possible for the village to be without an *uru ejmanru*.

One of the main functions of the *uru ejmanru* is to organize and conduct an elaborate five-day festival for Mariamma, the village disease goddess, which takes place every three or five years. Also at any Havik life-crisis ceremony when arecanuts and leaves are distributed to various people having certain kin or status positions, the *uru ejmanru*, if he is present, will accept as the village representative the offering intended to honor the village of Totagadde. He does not, however, have such clear-cut duties and powers in other activities, although he is a person of great influence and his power of veto is strong. He is assumed to be a figure of power in the village and is expected to be capable of uniting

---

[7] See M. N. Srinivas, "A Note on Sanskritization and Westernization," *Far Eastern Quarterly*, XV, 1956, pp. 481-496.

others on the most important issues that confront the village. Further, he is the man of last resort in deciding difficult panchayat cases. But his role of leadership is based only upon his personal status, for the position of *uru ejmanru* does not carry the right to use legal sanctions to enforce decisions.

One of the most important divisions in the competition for Havik leadership in Totagadde is based upon age. A few years ago the *uru ejmanru* began to withdraw and retire from active village politics, and this fact was the main cause for a recent change in the power structure initiated by the young men of the village. As long as the *uru ejmanru* was active, he was strong enough to enlist cooperation of feuding individuals and faction groups and the affairs of the village could go ahead. As he began to participate less and less, however, new undertakings began to fail. In this situation the younger people banded together and blamed their elders for inefficiency and a "do-nothing" platform. Reflecting a belief in "progress" and in the utility of a structured organization, the young men took over a nongovernmental village organization, the Grama Samiti, through which they tried to initiate their programs. The power vacuum created by the withdrawal of the *uru ejmanru* has not been easy to fill owing to the ill-defined and loosely structured nature of the position, and the young people are finding it difficult to obtain the needed cooperation from the various divisions in the elder group. It appears, however, that in time the past *uru ejmanru*'s paternal nephew, who is now only chairing the Grama Samiti and accepting the offering of arecanuts and leaves at ceremonies, may eventually have the age, status, and power to fill completely the vacant position of leadership.

There are several kinds of religious leaders in the village. Though the *uru ejmanru* is the religious leader for the great worship of Mariamma, there is a hereditary priest for this temple and another priest for the other Brahman temple in the village. While both these men do weekly puja and act as priests for special ceremonies held in these temples, one of them is wealthy and respected whereas the other is generally regarded as a rascal. Although each holds a hereditary ascribed position of potential prestige, it is quite clear that personality traits of the status holder are most important in determining the amount of respect accorded the individual.

A *purohit*, another type of village religious leader, has a hereditary right to act as priest for certain specific Havik families whenever ceremonies are held in the household. Three families in the village hold this hereditary position, but only one is actively engaged in this priestly activity. While according to tradition Brahmans are priests and religious leaders, all Totagadde Brahmans own arecanut gardens, and the tending of these is their main occupation. Only five out of forty-one adult male Brahmans occupy active positions of priestly leadership.

Any Brahman may dispense religious knowledge to Sudras, such as information about auspicious hours. Also there are two Brahmans who have assumed a position of religious leadership within their own caste because of their special knowledge of the Shastras. Their advice is sometimes sought on moral questions, since the Shastras are regarded as containing the "ideal culture" upon which present standards of morality should be based.

Political Dynamics

In order to understand the context in which the Havik Brahmans operate in their capacity of both collective and individual leadership, it is necessary to examine briefly elements of the political structure. Some of these are patterns of friendship, feuds, factions, and "parties."

The Haviks in Totagadde tend to be highly sociable and gregarious. While this is true of other castes as well, Haviks have more leisure time to express this disposition. Extreme gregariousness, however, does not necessarily imply many deep and intimate friendships. A Havik is likely to have very close relations with one or two other Haviks, and hostile relations with perhaps one or two. In dealing with most others, he tends to follow a pattern of behavior that is formal, marked by infrequent contacts and accompanied by a rigidly defined hospitality. Close friends may or may not be kin. Friendship patterns are characterized by frequent and intense interaction; friends attend each other's small family ceremonies, and no corner or possession in the house is barred. The relationship of friendship is supportive as there is constant exchange of compliments and public praise. But friendships do not necessarily involve all members of the households concerned; for example, wives may be friends even though their husbands are not.

Among themselves Haviks are divided into several types of antagonistic groupings. A great deal of emphasis is placed on individuality and Haviks are reputed, both by themselves and by people of other castes, to be petty, mean, jealous, and quarrelsome. This cultural stereotype, however, appears to be a good deal blacker than the fact. On the other hand, Havik enmities are frequent and long, whereas non-Brahmans have fewer and more momentary hostilities in which aggression is more freely, openly, and physically expressed.[8]

The feud is one type of antagonistic relationship that exists within the Havik Brahman society. This is a relationship of strong hostility between two individuals which may be associated with attempts to harm each other economically, or to slander or humiliate each other. Feuds between Haviks tend to run deep and there are few moral limits to the tactics employed. Often government assistance is enlisted by one or the other antagonist's reporting of real or mythical infringements of the law. Sorcery may be resorted to, but physical violence is rare. In spite of the strong feelings involved, if they are thrown together in a public situation, people who are feuding may work together and show respect to each other and appear friendly to the outsider.

An interesting feature of feuds is that they tend to take place between men of similar status. For example, in the village's most overt and active Havik feud each of the parties is poor, each has a reputation for unorthodoxy, each supplements his income by cooking for large ceremonies, each is an actor in local dramas, and each prescribes herb medicines. The principals in other Havik feuds are two young shopkeepers (and there are only two shops in the village), two elder political leaders both of whom deal with government officials and direct village affairs, and the two experts on Hindu epic literature.

Friendships and feuds tend to remain within caste boundaries. Relationships between castes in this South Indian setting are governed by such highly ritualized concepts of status and pollution that the more informal interaction is almost precluded. Only among the more nearly equated "middle" castes is one likely to find expressions of friendship cutting across endogamous caste lines. Castes live either in separate and distinct hamlets or in groupings within a hamlet, and intense interactions, whether friendship or feud, are most likely to be within this setting. If a quarrel arises between men of different castes, it is often minimized by members of both castes and immediate steps are taken to resolve it.

---

[8] There is much more economic cooperation among Sudras than among Haviks. There also appear to be somewhat fewer Sudra factions, feuds, and "parties." It may be that greater Sudra unity is in part due to the focusing of their hostilities toward the Haviks. Following this line of reasoning, it would appear that one factor influencing Brahman individualism is that there is no superordinate group against which to unify. If caste organization were taken as another criterion, the theory that the unity of a group is related to its position in the social scale would gain additional support. The formal caste organization—both intravillage and intervillage—of the Untouchables, who are repressed by all other castes, is more tightly knit than that of the Sudras, while the latter's is more highly structured than that of the Havik Brahmans.

But if a feud starts within a caste, and this is particularly true of the dominant caste, other members of the caste often encourage and aggravate it.

Faction is a much more difficult term to define and identify than is feud. Faction groups are not obvious in the village. There are no hookah groups since hookahs are not smoked, and the sharing of an arecanut tray is an expression of caste solidarity rather than a pattern of friendship (inclusion) with its concomitant concept of faction (exclusion). Informants consistently denied awareness of a faction-type grouping within the village in the sense of cohesive groups pitted against one another, although they readily acknowledged feuds between persons—a fact which reinforces the concept of individuality among Havik Brahmans. However, in Totagadde there is a type of elaborated feud that consists of two leaders, each of whom has a few persons actively supporting him. Such a social group in this analysis is labelled a faction.

The members within a faction may have cordial relations with one another, but this is not necessary. As we have indicated, these factions are not tightly knit antithetical groups but consist of leaders, each with a following. Moreover, members of a faction may not have any feelings of animosity against members of another faction, but may support only their own leader in his actions and decisions. If a man who is not a leader has a feud, he may have the help of only one other person, or of no one. If he has the help of one this could be termed a faction. When two nonleaders have a feud, however, others tend not to become involved; they may minimize the quarrel and say both sides are wrong.

In the village today there are two Havik factions, one closely related by kinship, the other with almost no kinship ties. But the majority of Havik families are not aligned with either group, and even within these two factions not all the friends of the leaders are included. For example, one very close friend of one of the leaders, whom the leader often visits and praises enthusiastically, gives him no visible support in the controversy.

Feud relationships are much more important than factions in village dynamics. Overtly the feuders are civil to each other, but actually they may be employing against each other legal weapons in the form of court suits, or social weapons such as the spreading of malicious rumors about the other. Although there is no form of social organization in Totagadde that corresponds exactly to *dharra*, or faction, as described for Rampur by Oscar Lewis,[9] it is apparent that a Havik "feud" parallels it more closely than does a "faction."

Methods of Social Control: "Party" and Panchayat

A "party" is both an element in the political dynamics of the village and a method for controlling deviants. The English word is used in the village to mean an individual or household that is placed in economic and social isolation with respect to the rest of the village. A "party" is usually created when one man has pressures put on him by others about matters in which he feels he should have autonomous decision, or when a decision has been made against him that he feels is unjust and therefore refuses to accept. To declare a man a "party" is the severest sanction employed by Sudras, but Brahmans and Untouchables have the additional coercive measure of declaring a person outcaste. Declaring a man a "party" is much more frequently utilized by the Haviks than by other castes.

In Totagadde there have been at least six "parties" in the last twenty years. Examples of "party" situations should help to clarify the term. A married Havik girl returned to her parental home saying that her husband had mistreated her. Later, her husband came for her and an informal panchayat decreed that she should return with him. Her father refused to send her, and consequently was declared a "party." Another example of a "party" as a measure of social control concerns a Sudra who felt that the Havik panchayat's arbitration of his quarrel was unjust and did not obey the rulings; his caste fellows, with the support of the Haviks, declared him to be a "party." In this case the underlying motivation was a long series of quarrels between this man and others in his caste. In addition to its use as a means of social control, a "party" may also be a mechanism of political and social dynamics in which an individual may express his contempt for and dissatisfaction with the controlling elements of the village. One young headstrong Havik boy felt this way and refused to pay his share of a road repair scheme or to contribute to a mass feeding on the occasion of the guru's visit to the village. In effect, he seceded from the village and was declared a "party."

A man is never passively allowed to remain a "party." Instead, *kattu* (literally, building a fence around) is declared against him. If he is a

[9] Oscar Lewis, *Group Dynamics in a North Indian Village*, Delhi, Planning Commission, Programme Evaluation Organization, 1954.

Havik, coolies are not allowed to work for him, priests cannot perform ceremonies in his house, no one in the village will visit him, and often he suffers petty thefts. If anger in the community mounts high enough he may have arecanuts stolen from his trees or have his pepper vines cut. If he is a non-Brahman neither will he be employed by anyone in the village nor will he be loaned money. If he were to be employed, all other members of his caste, and probably of other castes as well, would refuse to work for his employer. Other people in the village cannot visit him. This relationship is often expressed among Sudras by saying "no one will even lend him fire."

A man is usually a "party" only in the village in which he resides. Others of his own caste from different villages may invite him to ceremonies, visit him, take food in his house, or help him to maintain his status as a "party" or as a man excommunicated from his own village. He may find employment in another village. Even so a man is usually forced eventually to give in to group pressure and ask to be taken back into the village on the other villagers' terms.

The English term "party" is occasionally used in its more conventional sense—as one united group opposed to another. It was used in this sense when individuals from a number of villages in the area took sides on an issue involving a decision about a large local temple, but this usage of the term is less common.

There are a number of institutions that a person may turn to if he wishes to have a conflict adjudicated. He may go to the government courts or to the large temples, or he may call a village panchayat.

Sometimes disputes go to the legal courts in town, but this method of adjudication is expensive and is regarded by many as ineffectual—ineffectual because it does not solve the main problem. Courts are frequently used as a tool in a feud; a man will take a case to court in the belief that he can win a point over his opponent, fearing that if the case is tried by a local panchayat the background of the dispute and the personalities of the disputants, rather than the purely legal arguments, will influence the decision.

Whether a case goes to court or not depends largely upon the caste of the contenders. Ten years ago the first Sudra family had recourse to the courts and no Untouchable has yet gone, but Brahmans have used the court system longer than anyone can remember. There are several reasons for this difference. One is economic. Most Brahmans can afford lawyer and court fees more easily than most Sudras, and almost no Untouchables have more than a precarious day-to-day income. But more important is the fact that Brahmans are more litigious-minded than members of other castes and that feuding is quantitatively and qualitatively more elaborated by them; the courts are used as but one weapon in their feuds.

Another recourse for the solution of disputes, especially land disputes, is the large Dharmasthala temple about a hundred miles south of Totagadde. A weak and poor man who has lost his last piece of land by foreclosure by a wealthy and powerful man many appeal his case to Dharmasthala. If support is given him by the temple, he can exert great moral pressure as well as the threat of supernatural punishment against his opponent.

Besides these two permanently constituted bodies, there are transitory village panchayats called to adjudicate certain controversies. This institution is frequently used in the village today. The issues the informal panchayats deal with may involve problems of caste rules and morality or may stem from personal quarrels.

Punishment for infringement of caste rules such as the ones prohibiting eating with or having sexual relations with members of a lower caste or forbidding widows to remarry, is meted out by the hereditary formal leaders of the caste. For such cases the panchayats are composed only of members of the particular caste concerned. When a Havik widow gave birth to a child it was Havik men from the village who took the case to the caste guru who lives some fifty miles from the village and who enforced the guru's judgment that she be outcaste. When a Sudra widow became pregnant, the village *hiria* and the men of the village formed a panchayat and fined the woman. Then the *hiria* found her a husband, after assuring the *hiria* in the groom's village that the woman's illicit relations had been with a member of her own caste.

Serving on a panchayat is an important function of a Havik leader and status is gained by being frequently called to serve. When a fight occurs in a non-Brahman caste, a panchayat of members of that caste may first be called, and if no solution is found or if the decisions are not abided by, recourse may then be had to a Havik panchayat. Many times such cases are taken directly to a Havik panchayat. When a quarrel occurs among Haviks, either Havik leaders in Totagadde or men from other villages well known for their fairness and abilities as panchayat members will be asked to adjudicate the matter. The only type of panchayat that is likely to contain both Havik Brahman and non-Brahman members is one concerning the partition of property of a non-Brahman joint family.

Panchayats are loosely structured. There are a variety of procedures for selecting the members, as either or both of the disputants may choose the men. Generally the injured individual, or the one who believes he has the better case, calls the panchayat. In most castes panchayat members are chosen from a group of men who have a reputation for justness and impartiality, but a panchayat composed of Sudras nearly always contains the formal caste leaders. In theory, panchayat members should not serve unless asked by one or both of the parties, although there are cases of a man's "appointing" himself.

Once the men have gathered there are few rules governing the process of making decisions. Panchayat members may energetically participate until the case is solved or they may lose interest and even leave. The panchayat does not sit together, formally hear testimony, vote and then pass judgment. Instead, the men on the panchayat, the disputants, and the onlookers may wander in and out. At some point one or two panchayat members may give suggestions that have a sense of finality about them and if others do not disagree these stand as the solution.

In some, but not all, instances the disputants promise to abide by the decision of the panchayat. If one or both contenders disregard the solution, there are several modes of action that can follow. The case may be dropped; it may be taken to another panchayat; it may be referred to the courts or to a temple.

Panchayat members have several sources of power to enforce their decisions. One of the most effective is the threat of not coming to another panchayat called by an individual who refuses to accept the original decision. Another and perhaps the most powerful threat is that of making *kattu* against a disobedient individual—of declaring him to be a "party."

The fact that a very wide variety of situations are called panchayats can best be illustrated by presenting several cases.

A fist fight occurred between two non-Brahman schoolboys of different castes. An adult of one of the castes brought the boys to the first Havik he saw sitting outside his doorway and asked the Havik to reprimand the aggressor, which he did.

Another case involved a man from a neighboring village who farmed paddy land in Totagadde. This man quarreled over water rights with a Totagadde resident of his own caste and was beaten slightly. He then ran from one house to another showing his wounds, complaining vociferously, and threatening to go to court. Later he asked three Haviks from Totagadde to act as a panchayat for him. Twice they did, but both times his opponent sent excuses, and the case was finally dropped when the

Haviks, motivated by their unwillingness to punish a son of a Sudra leader in their own village, counseled the injured outsider to drop the matter.

There is a well-known case in Totagadde of a fight between a man and a woman both of a low Sudra caste. Her children defecated in his yard. He complained, tempers flared, she cursed him, and he beat her with sandals—the greatest of insults. She herself went to some Havik Brahmans to ask that he be punished. There followed a fairly elaborate panchayat of six members. A great deal of testimony was presented; a decision was given, and both were fined for their actions. The money went to a Brahman temple-repair fund.

These cases range from a schoolboys' fight to disputes between adults. Disagreements between members of different castes and even different villages were arbitrated by Havik Brahmans. The number of adjudicators varied. The single man was casually chosen whereas the panchayat of six was selected with great care. In all these situations, ranging from extreme informality to formality, the term "panchayat" was used by informants.

There is another kind of case that should be illustrated. The *uru ejmanru* became involved in a long and bitter quarrel with a young neighbor over the boundary between their houses. The issue became a point of pride for both men. The case was tried by several village panchayats before it finally went to court. It passed through three progressively higher courts and each time the decision was against the elder leader. Still the quarrel continued until a panchayat composed of men from other villages with an intervillage reputation for their ability to solve difficult cases and with stature greater than that of the *uru ejmanru* recommended that the younger man sell the disputed property to the elder man, which was done.

There is no evidence to suggest that panchayats in Totagadde have ever significantly differed from the way that they are now organized, or that the institution has disintegrated, except for the fact that the court system acts as a supplementary means of arbitration. The functions of the panchayat and of the courts only partially overlap. In the first place, only the wealthier higher-caste people have ever been involved in court cases. Also decisions in the courts and in panchayats are decided on different grounds. Evidence is often used in a panchayat that a court of law would consider inadmissible or irrelevant. Courts determine who is legally right on the basis of written law and then give a verdict in that person's behalf. Panchayats usually look for a solution to the problem and are more likely to give a compromise decision rather than a verdict of guilty or not guilty.

Conclusion

In Totagadde there are two constituted village organizations in which most leaders participate and through which their decisions can be effected. One of these, the Village Panchayat, is a government-sponsored organization; the other, the Grama Samiti, was established by the villagers. A discussion of these two bodies is perhaps the most succinct way to summarize both the various aspects of village leadership that have been outlined, and the dynamics of feud, faction and "party."

The chairman of the Village Panchayat is the patel, the government-appointed, hereditary, official head of the village. When the government put pressure on the recalcitrant Village Panchayat to undertake some road repairs, the patel himself had to finance the project. Later the patel's request for village reimbursement was denied as his opponent in a feud, who was also a Village Panchayat member, was influential enough to effect a refusal. The patel stood a financial loss as well as a loss of face.

The patel's defeat on this issue was but one incident in a long feud. In addition each man had several others who supported him, thus enlarging the feud into factions. After this last round three Brahmans, all friends of the patel's opponent, took various cases to court against the patel. The patel's action after this defeat and humiliation was to assert his independence and to refuse to cooperate with or contribute to any village project undertaken by his opponent. He thus was declared to be a "party."

Following the road repairs incident the Village Panchayat did not meet again until the election described in this paper was held. Village affairs were all conducted in the Grama Samiti. The chairman of this body was the *uru ejmanru*, but when he began to go into retirement this organization also became defunct. Subsequently the active younger men in the village demanded that the elder men release their positions on the Grama Samiti. About six months before this study was started the younger men took control and at that time included the Sudras of their choice in the representation. It was another year or more before full control of the purse strings was obtained.

When the *uru ejmanru* handed over the books, he lost one of his last remaining tools of power. His retirement was complete when he organized the elaborate festival for Mariamma in conjunction with his paternal nephew and then announced to all, including the goddess, that this was the last time he would take part. He asked the goddess to show her satisfaction with the way in which this feast had been run as well as with his retirement by not visiting any catastrophes upon the village of Totagadde.

Thus it may be seen how on the whole the village of Totagadde retains its traditional forms of leadership, decision making and censure. Major leadership roles are filled by the Havik Brahmans and the political dynamics of feud, friendship, faction, and "party" play an important part in determining which individuals will attain these positions. Serving as arbitrators on informal panchayats is an important expression of leadership for both Haviks and non-Brahmans. Panchayats still function as a method of social control in this more traditional village, and the village political organization is still preserved in a time of change and reorganization in India.

INDEX

Acharya, C. M., on language problem, 161
Acton, Lord, on great men, 297
adalati panchayat, defined, 406—*footnote* 16
Adhikari, G., personality of, 240
Adi Andhras (caste), 446, 451, 452
administrative processes:
  changes in, 347, 349, 352; Collectorate, role of, 339; conflict in, 338-339, 343; and development planning, *314-327*, 337, 341-343, 350-351; development bodies (listed), *317*; and district administration, 341-343; and government leadership, 323-324; and local self-government, *337-343*; and research, 318-321. See also, Community Development Program, district administration, District Officer, Five Year Plans, public administration, public services
Advaita, Bhave on, 288
Agarwal, S. N., on language problem, 159
Agrarian Program, 181-182
ahimsa [non-injury], 11
Aitareya Brahmana, 6
Akali Dal Party, 33; parliamentary strength, 124
Ali, Aruna Asaf, 198, 200
Ali, Maulana Mohamed, 51
All India Congress Committee (AICC), 94, 180f.
All India Federation of Backward Classes, 112
All India Manufacturers Organization, 256
All India Organization of Industrial Employers, 256
amildar, defined, 429
Almond, Gabriel, on political cultures, 37
Anand (Swami), and Bardoli campaign, 91
"Andhra Letter," 230
Andhra State, village study in Padu, 445-452
Anjaria, J. J., 307
anti-Brahmanism, 22
Anushilan Samiti, 177
aristocrat: as leader, 383-384, 389; in politics, 118, 119—*footnote* 6, 126
Arthasastra, 6, 9
Arya Samaj, 16, 212, 281, 402-403; caste and, 213; ideology of, 396—*footnote* 3; social change and, 413, 414
ashram [retreat], 116
Aundh State, Gandhian approach to development in, 376, 377

Aurobindo (Shri), 70; Aurobindite movement, 287-288; Yoga and mysticism, 74
authoritarian leadership, authoritarianism, 23-24; classical concepts, 5-10; in Communist Party, 227-228; Marxist-Hegelian concepts, 13-15; in Parliament, 29-30, 135; Patel and, 97; in RSS, 216; rural, 382, 387, 414; in socialist parties, 192-193, 201, 206
Axis, the, Indian attitudes to, 84-85, 86
Azad, Maulana Abul Kalam, 80, 97, 112

Bajaj, Jamnalal, 258
Bajpai, Sir Girja Shankar, 151
baluta system, defined, 415
Bangalore area: village studies (Morsralli), 438-444; village studies (Namhalli), 427-437
Bardoli campaign, 90-92; effect on the Congress, 92; organization and technique, 90-92
Batlivala, S. H., on role of industrialists, 265
begar, defined, 147
Bengal, partition (1905) of, 176-177
Bengalis: characteristics, 66-67, 71; and linguistic particularism, 155
bhadralog [gentlemen], 175
Bhave, Vinoba, 5, 17, 31; on Communism, 15f.; government views on, 292; as nonconventional leader, 279, 284-292, 294-296; views on government, 294-295, 296
bhoodan movement, 285-295; and Aurobindo, 287-288; defined, 285ff.; goals, 288-289, 291, 294-295; and J. P. Narayan, 292; origin, 285; and satyagraha, 288-289, 295; and religion, 289. See also, Bhave, Vinoba; *sarvodaya* movement
Birla, G. D.: business family, 252ff., 256; on labor relations, 278; and socialism, 262-263
Biswas, C. C., 111
Bombay Mill Owners' Association, 255
Bombay Plan, 259
Bombay State, village study in Gaon, 415-426
Bombay textile unions, 271ff.
Bombay Trade Disputes Conciliation Act, 273
Borsad campaign, 89
Bose, Sarat Chandra, 72

INDEX

Bose, Subhas Chandra, 40, *66-86*; appraisals of, 84-85; and Aurobindo, 70; and the Axis, 80-86; and British, 73, 79-80; and Congress, 75-77, 84, 97, 183, 290—*footnote* 19; and Congress Socialist Party, 85, 188-191, **193**, 194; and Deshbandhu C. R. Das, 74; Gandhi on, 83, 84; and Gandhism, 72-77, 80; ideology, 78-79, 85-86; and Indian National Army, 81, 83-84; Indian views on, 80, 83, 84; and language problem, 163-164; Nehru on, 73; and Nehru, 78; and USSR, 82; and Vithalbhai Patel, 76, 97; and Vivekananda, 68
Bose, Suresh, 82
brahmachari, 217
brahmacharya vow [celibacy, chastity], 217
Brahmanas, and origins of kingship, 6
Brahmanic leadership concepts, 6ff., 10, 12
Brahmans, 15, 21, 360, 396, 448; anti-Brahmanism, 22; authority of, 9, 382, 383, 454-455; and Congress Party, 385; in Council of Ministers, 110, 114; and extremism, 176; and government, 9; non-Brahman conflict, 93; and non-Brahman leaders, 457-458; Rajput relations, 395ff.; as village elite, 453-462. *See also*, Havik Brahmans, Hindu communal groups, traditional leadership concepts
Brahmo Samaj, 212, 213, 281
British language policy in India, 151
Buddhist leadership concepts, 8, 10
bureaucracy and rural leadership, 385-386, 420-421
business, *251-267*; and development, 257, 259, 260, 261-265; Gandhian views on, 259; and government, 260-264; control of, 261-262; Indian views on, 257f.; and nationalism, 177, 258-259; and nationalization, 261, 265
  organizational structure: "communities," 254-255; families (listed), 252-253, 263; role of families, 252-253, 255; managing agency firms, 251-253; trade associations, 255
  in Parliament, 256f.; and the press, 256; and public service, 265, 267; small business, 263-264; and society, 256-260, 264; and "socialist" pattern, 260, 262-265, 267

Cabinet: functions of, 104-105; list of members (1956), 105
cash farming system, 442, 444

caste: and clique, 435-436; and Code of Manu, 5; and Community Development, 355, 392; in Congress Party, 384; distribution in Cabinet, 109-110; and extremism, 176; and government courts, 464; and Hindu communal groups, 213; and individual rights, 6, 9, 13; and kingship, 9; and national leadership, 22; rules, infringement of, 465; and rural leadership, 383f., *415-426*, 428-429, 451-452, 454ff.; as source of influence, 379, 457; -system, changes in, 359-360; and traditional panchayat, 141ff., 430, 465-466; and Village Panchayat, 141-145, 146, 150, 432, 457; and "westernization," 21, 22. *See also* Brahmans, factionalism (rural), Hindu communal groups, intercaste relations, intracaste relations, panchayat, rural leadership; articles on language problem
caste interaction, *see* intracaste relations
caste leaders, 429-431, 438, 450-451; functions, 458
caste panchayat, 465-466; in rural election, 149
Chakravarti, Renu, 126; personality, 246
Champaran campaign, 179
charismatic leadership, 10, 93; attributes of, 286, 291; defined, 27; and Gandhi, 280-283; and Gowalkar, 217; and nationalist movement, 186; and politics, 28; Sidney Hook on, 64; and unity, 32; Weberian concepts of, 280—*footnote* 2, 286, 291
Chatterjee, N. C., 31, 224
Chatterji, S. K., on language problem, 165
chaudhuri, defined, 389
child marriage, 420
Choudhary, Nabhas, 200
civil service, and language problem, 157-162, 212. *See also*, language problem, public services
cliques: bases of, 433-435; and caste, 436; and factionalism, 436
Code of Manu, and caste system, 5
Collectorate, 339, 341f.
Committee on Government Assurances, 122
Committee on Medium of Instruction, on language policy, 153f., 155f., 157
communalism, defined, 211. *See also*, Hindu communal groups, Hindu communalism
Communism: Bose on, 78; Indian views, 15-16, 17; Nehru on, 78; and Patel, 92, 98; theory of classes, 225, 245f.
Communist Party of India, *225-248*; communications system, 231-234; "democratic centralism," 225-229; dissent and

472

INDEX

factionalism, 227, 229-231, 234, 242-243; finances, 237ff.; "fractions," 244-247; geographic representation, 241; leadership, 228-230, 239-241, 246-247; and local self-government, 340, 341; and nationalist movement, 188—*footnote* 2; origin, 242; PHQ unit, 233-234; in Parliament, 123, 124, 246-247; party schools, 235-236; and rural development, 343; structure and organization, 225-228, 230, 240, 247; "technical apparatus," 232

communists: and Congress, 123; and Congress Socialist Party, 189-190, 193, 194, 195; in Parliament, 126; and socialists, 200; and unions, 272, 273

communities: in business, 254-257, 263; in the Cabinet, 109; conflict among, 212; defined, 211, 254

Community Development Program, *347-371*; administrative bodies (listed), 317; administrative structure, 352; background and development, 349-350, 352, 376; and Congress, 187; defined, 358; and Five Year Plans, 350-355; goals and methods, 19, 347-349, 350-351, 352, 355-356, 358

impact on:
administrative process, 347ff.; caste, 355, 392; culture patterns, 374, 377; politics, 357; rural leadership, 355-356, 363-371, 373; social change, 353-357, 413; traditional values, 355, 368; village, 347-357, 363-367, 397

psychological aspects, 349; and rural patterns of influence, 372-389; scope, 348, 350; and village level worker, 351-352; village participation, 349, 354, 375; and westernized elites, 18ff. *See also*, administrative processes, development planning, economic development, Five Year Plans, modernization, National Extension Service, public administration

Community Projects, *see* Community Development Program

Community Projects Administration, 19, 319, 323, 337, 372

Company Law, 261

"composite leadership" theory, 191, 193

Congress Party, *169-187*; bifurcations in, 178, 181, 183, 184; Bombay session, 57; and Bose, 84, 97, 183, 290—*footnote* 19; and caste taboos, 417, 424, 426; committees, 177, 180; and communists, 127; conflict in, 28, 95-96, 181-184, 186; and Congress Parliamentary Party, 129-134; and Congress Socialist Party, 182-183, 189-191, 197-198, 204, 209; decision making, 129ff.; development of, 93, 95, 170-172, 180, 186; and extremism, 174-177; and Gandhi, 61; goals, 169, 183; and government, 326-327; and Hindu communal groups, 223ff.; and Hindu revivalism, 175; Indore session, 130; and Khare controversy, 96; and labor force, 274; and language problem, 28, 159; and legislature, 103; and local government, 340-341; and local politics, 185, 340; "Moderate" period, 170-175; and Muslims, 178, 180; Nagpur Constitution, 180; and nationalism, 176f., 183; as oligarchy, 385; organizational problems, 180-182; and Parliament, 123, 124, 128; strength in Parliament, 103; Patna session, 54; and peasants, 179, 183; as political party, 186f.; problems of leadership, 187; role of caste in, 385; and Sardar Vallabhbhai Patel, 92-94, 96, 98-99, 199; and social change, 182, 187, 412f.; and socialism, 55, 196, 204; and socialists, 188-210; as source of influence, 412, 414, 418, 424; and special interest groups, 181, 184; structure, 94, 180-181, 185; and trade unionism, 273, 274. *See also*, "Moderates"; articles on Bose, Gandhi, Nehru, Patel

Congress Parliamentary Party, *129-134*; structure and functions, 131-132

Congress Socialist Party, *188-195*; authoritarianism in, 192-193, 201, 206; and Bose, 85, 190-191, 193, 194; and Communists, 189-192, 194, 195; and Congress, 182-183, 189-191, 194, 198, 204, 209; factions, 193; formation, 54, 182, 188; and Gandhi, 55, 56; goals and assumptions, 190-192, 195; indiscipline in, 193-194, 201, 206-207; and Kisan Sabhas, 183; leadership, 189-194, 199; and Marxism, 189, 191, 192, 194, 195; opposition to, 197; organization and structure, 192-193, 194, 195

Congress Working Committee: formation of, 180; functions, 134; and language problem, 28, 30, 154, 161—*footnote* 31; membership data, 257; Parliamentary board, 129, 182; Parliamentary subcommittee, 94-95; role of, 30, 94; and Sardar Vallabhbhai Patel, 87, 94; and socialism, 54-55; and states reorganization, 130

Constituent Assembly, composition of, 103

Constitution, 29, 103

473

INDEX

Council of Ministers, *103-114*; and British Cabinet, comparison, 108—*footnote* 9, 112, 113; and Congress Parliamentary Party, 132; geographic representation, 107-108, 114; functions, 103, 104 members: analysis of, 105-114; listed, 105
Council of States, *see* Rajya Sabha
CPI, *see* Communist Party of India
creative leadership, 9, 17
crore [ten million]

dacoit [bandit], dacoity, 89, 389
dan, defined, 285
dan movements, *see bhoodan* movement
danda, defined, 6, 9
Dange, S. A., 230
Das, Deshbandhu C. R., Subhas Chandra Bose and, 74, 77
Daudpur-Senapur, village studies in, 137-150
decision making: in development planning, 323-324; in Parliament, *115-136*, especially 133-136; village patterns of, 401, 414, 430
Delhi Pact, 221
democracy: attitudes to, 16, 17, 116-117, 329-330; and administrative process, 338-339; and caste, 26; and Community Development, 358, 368, 371; and former ruling classes, 389; and Hindu-minded, 37; and nonconventional leadership, 297
    and parliamentary institutions: eastern and western compared, 37; handicaps of, 117, 136
    and public services, *329-336*; and social change, 329-331
    traditions of, 7, 117; religious, 12
    See also, authoritarianism, local self-government, rural leadership, traditional leadership concepts
"democratic centralism," 225-229
Democratic Nationalist Party, composition of, 124-125
"democratic socialism," goals, 200-201
Deo, Shankarrao, 296
Desai, Morarji, 30
Deshmukh, C. D., 133; background of, 308; and Planning Commission, 307-309; resignation of, 129, 305—*footnote* 5
Deshpande, V. G., 224
Deva, Acharya Narendra, 97; and Socialist Party, 189, 196, 198
development planning, *301-313*, 314-328; approaches to, 377; assumptions of, 373-375; background, 314; and business enterprise, 260-262; economists, role, 310-313; government leaders, role, 323-324; limitations of, 310, 375; and local self-government, 337-339; need for, 372-374; and political dynamics, 326-328; public participation, 138, 302-305, 316, 322, 324-325, 328, 343, 375-377; public servant, role, 330-331
    research: need for, 26, 27, 38, 243, 312-313, 315, 372-374, 377; organizations, 315, 318-321
    specialized planning units, 322, 323; wealthy, role, 374
dharma: defined, 5, 7—*footnote* 8, 15, 402; king and, 8-9, 10-11, 14; leader and, 15; and village reform, 402
dharra, defined, 462
Dhebar, U. N.: on Bhave, 292; on rural leadership, 294
Dhillon, Harwant Singh, quoted, 380
Directive Principles of State Policy, 19
disputes, solution of, 464-467. *See also*, panchayat
district administration, *337-344*; and central government, 338, 342; Collectorate, role of, 339; and Community Development, 337, 341-342; and local authority, 338-339. *See also*, administrative processes, District Officer (especially) local self-government, public administration, public services
District Collector, *see* District Officer
District Officer: and development, 325-326, 338, 339, 341-342; role, 338, 341, 344; and rural factionalism, 443
Draft Plan Frame, 262, 309
Draft Outline, Five Year Plan, 319

economic development: attitudes to, 25, 259 western and Indian contrasted, 376
    and business, 259-265; demand for, 24, 34, 314, 315, 328, 329, 330, 343, 354; and labor relations, 275-277; and local participation, 326, 349-350, 375, 376; and political dynamics, 23-24, 326-328; public servant, role, 331; and westernized elite, 18-19, 374; and states, 325-326, 328. *See also*, Community Development Program
economic research, 310-313, 378; need for, 312-313, 315; organizations, 315, 318-319, 323-324; and planning, 302, 315; and public administration, 321-322. *See also*, social science research
education: and national leadership, 110, 240; and rural leadership, 142, 362f.

474

INDEX

Employers Federation, 255
English language: in education, 152-157; in civil service, 157-158, 160-162, 212; Gandhi on, 152; and governing process, 163, 165; Mehta, Asoka, on, 165; and national leadership, 151-153, 157, 162-163, 165; Nehru on, 163; Tagore on, 152. *See also*, language problem
Etawah Project, 358-371
extended family, and rural leadership, 380, 387
Extension work, program, *see* National Extension Service
extremism, extremists: and Hindu communal movements, 212ff.; and Hindu revivalism, 174-177; middle class and, 179; 1905 campaign, 176-177; Tilak and, 176. *See also*, nationalist movement, RSS

factionalism: and Communist Party, 242ff.; and Congress Party, 28; and socialist parties, 193, 201, 204-206. *See also*, Congress Party (conflict in), opposition parties, rural factionalism, socialist parties
families, business, 252-253, 263; named, 252-253, 263; in Parliament, 257; socio-economic importance, 253. *See also*, business
family: and political dynamics, 145-146; role in business, 251-253, 255, 263; role in rural leadership, 146, 380, 387, 398
fascism: Bose on, 78-79; Nehru on, 78
Federation of Indian Chambers of Commerce and Industry, 256, 263; and development planning, 304
female infanticide, 400
feud, in village dynamics, 461-462
Fitzgerald, C. P., quoted, 14
Five Year Plans: administrative relations, 324-328, 337ff.; and business, 259-265; development of, 301-302, 314-316; and district administration, 341-342; expenditures, 316, 324; goals, 310; and government-Congress relations, 328-329; and government-village relations, 370; limitations of, 310-312, 318, 343, 375f.; and local government, 326, 337; and local leadership, 343; and Nehru, 306, 323; and politics, 306; public participation, 138, 302-305, 316, 322, 324-328, 343, 375-377; research projects, 318-321; river valley projects, 317; and states, 325-326; and states reorganization, 327—*footnote* 38; and trade unions, 276-277. *See also*, administrative

processes, Community Development Program, development planning, Indian Administrative Service, National Extension Service, Planning Commission
Ford Foundation, 319
formal leadership (rural), 397-406, 417-421, 425, 429-433, 458. *See also*, rural leadership
Forward Bloc: analyzed, 77-78; formation of, 77, 184; parliamentary strength, 124
"fractions," 244-247
fragmentation in politics, 25, 31-32, 37, 93, 116-117, 125-127, 173-175; in Congress, 181, 187. *See also*, language problem, linguistic particularism, Hindu communal parties, "westernization"

Gadgil, N. V.; quoted, 123; on states reorganization, 129
Gandhi (Mahatma), Mohandas K., 5, 6, 41, 279-298; ambivalent role of, 28-30; assassination of, 220; and Bose, 76-77; on Bose, 80, 83-85; as charismatic leader, 27, 45; and Congress, 57—*footnote* 18, 61, 289-290; and Congress Socialist Party, 55, 56; on English language, 152; goals, 53, 284, 289; and Hinduism, 179; Indian views on, 280; on Kheda campaign, 89; and labor relations (Ahmedabad), 278; Narayan on, 292-293; as nationalist leader, 93, 178-180; and Nehru, 42ff., 51ff., 62-63; Nehru on, 63, 289; as nonconventional leader, 279-283, 289—*footnote* 19; and Patel, Vallabhbhai, 92-93; personality, 179, 184, 281; philosophy of, 48-53, 282-284; political concepts, 11; on power, 296; socialism, 54, 55; and socialists, 195, 196. *See also*, *bhoodan* movement, Gandhism, Hindu communal groups
Gandhism, 48, 61, 74-75, 184, 296; and Aurobindites (contrasted), 287-288; Bose on, 81; and business, 259; and development, 259, 375-376; leadership pattern, 279ff.; and modernization, 25, 375; and Narayan, 293-294; Nehru and, 49, 52-53; opposition to, 73-77, 84; and political attitudes, 116-117, 282 approach, 282-284
and rural self-government, 138; and social change, 25, 287-289; and untouchables, 403; in the village, 403ff. *See also*, *bhoodan* movement, Gandhi, Hindu communal groups, nonconventional leadership, satyagraha
Ganguli, B., quoted, 313
gaon panchayat, defined, 406—*footnote* 16

INDEX

gaon sabha, defined, 406—*footnote* 16
Gaon (Maharastra, Bombay State), village study in, 392, *415-426*; caste, 416-417, 425; economy, 415
formal leadership:
headmen, 419ff.; Village Panchayat, 417ff.
informal leadership, sanctioned: active, 422-423; passive, 422
informal leadership, unsanctioned, 424-425
gauda, defined, 438
Gautam, Mohanlal, 200
Ghosh, A. K., 230, 240; personality, 241, 244
Ghose, Aurobindo, *see* Aurobindo (Shri)
Giri, V. V., on industrial relations, 277
Goebbels, Joseph, on Bose, 79
Gokhale, G. K., 213
Gokhale Institute of Politics and Economics, 315
Gopalan, A. K., 126; personality, 246
Gopaldas, Darbar, 91, 92
Gorwala, A. D., 316, 321
government: and business, 260-267; growing impact, 34-36; and language policy, 159, 163, 212; and local self-government, 337-344; and party organization, 327-328; and political parties, 23-24; and social change, 36; and trade unions, 273-276. *See also,* administrative processes, Community Development Program, Council of Ministers, development planning, local self-government, Lok Sabha, panchayat system
government, Indian views on: and Gandhian politics, 116-117; modern theories, 5, 10-12, 13-17
and Marxism, 13-14
rural attitudes, 386, 393, 413
traditional concepts:
Brahmanic, 8-12; cyclical, 8, 15
See also, dharma, rajadharma
Government Panchayat, *see* Village Panchayat
Gowalkar, (Guru) Madhav Rao, 31, 217, 218, 220
gram sevak, defined, 326
Grama Samiti, 459, 468-469
gramdan [village-gift], 286, 295. *See also, bhoodan* movement
"grass roots" approach, 172, 337-339; limitations of, 339
Gujarat Provincial Congress Committee, 88, 89
Gujarat Sabha, 88

Gujaratis, 92; and Congress, 93; social organization of, 93
guru [religious teacher], 217
Guru Purnima, 217

handicrafts program, 259, 261-262
Harijans, 417-426, 446, 450. *See also,* Untouchables
hartal [closing of shops and suspension of work], 176
Hartog, Sir Philip, on language problem, 152, 156
Havik Brahmans, 453-468; intercaste relations, 456, 460-464
feud, 461-462; "party," 463-464, 466, 468
and intracaste conflict, 467; leadership role, 454-457; religious leader, role of, 458-460; temporary panchayats, 465-467
Hedgewar, Keshav, 217, 218
"High Command," Congress, 96, 181f. *See also,* Congress Working Committee
Hindi: in civil service, 158ff.
opposition to, 160, 163
in education, 155; as federal language, 158, 161, 162; Rajagopalachari on, 160
Hindu Code Bill, 19; Mahasabha and, 221
Hindu communal groups, parties, 37, *211-224,* 251, 281; and Gandhi, 220; goals, 21-23, 25, 212-219; handicaps of, 21, 224; Kalidas Nag group, 223; and Muslim relations, 212-215, 218, 224; and nationalist movement, 213; and Parliament, 125ff., 222-224; role of, 219-224; and social change, 21-23, 25, 213, 225; and traditionalism, 21; and untouchability, 213, 219. *See also,* Hindu communalism, Hindu Mahasabha, Jan Sangh, Ram Rayja Parishad, Rashtriya Swayamasevak Sangh
Hindu communalism: and democracy, 37; and Gandhism distinguished, 25; and linguistic particularism, 22. *See also,* extremism, Hindu communal groups, Hinduism, religious revivalism, "westernization"
Hindu Mahasabha, 37, 214, 218; attitudes to untouchability, 21; and Congress, 184, 220; and Hindu Code Bill, 221; and linguistic particularism, 224; Mookerjee, S. P., and, 222; parliamentary strength, 124, 222, 223; and states reorganization, 221
Hindu Marriages Act, 223
Hindu militarism, 177. *See also,* Rashtriya Swayamasevak Sangh

INDEX

Hindu-Muslim relations, 212-220, 403
Hindu Rashtra Dal, 215
Hindu revivalism, *see* extremism, religious revivalism, Hindu communal groups, Hinduism
Hinduism, 212; and extremism, 213, 215; and Gandhi, 178; and Moderates, 171; and nationalist movement, 175-176, 177, 212-213; and western influence, 174-175, 212. *See also*, Hindu communal groups, religious revivalism
Hindustan National Guard, 215, 218
hiria, defined, 458; functions of, 465
Holi, defined, 403
Hook, Sidney, on the hero, 64

Independent Group (Jaipal Singh), 126
Indian Administrative Service, 159, 324-325, 338
Indian Civil Service, 266, 385
Indian Council of Ministers, *see* Council of Ministers
Indian National Army, 83-84, 219; formation, 81
Indian Statistical Institute, 308, 309; role in development planning, 319, 322
individual rights: Constitutional provisions for, 29; and orthodox Indian theory, 9, 17
individualism, the individual: caste and, 13; Indian concepts of, 6, 280, 460, 461; and rural leadership, 381
Industrial Policy Statement, 264
Industries Development and Regulation Act, 261
Industry Policy Resolution, 264
informal leadership (rural), 408-415, 421-425, 456-458
intercaste relations, 426, 435-436, 459; Havik Brahman, 460-468; sudra, 461—*footnote* 8; in village election, 141-144. *See also*, caste, factionalism, social control
intracaste relations, 21, 405-407, 417, 422, 425, 429, 446, 450-451, 455-457, 461; change in, 355, 359-360, 365, 417; conflict, 143-144, 362, 395-397, 406, 414ff., 467; and social change, 416; in village elections, 141-144, 146, 406-410. *See also*, factionalism, Hindu-Muslim relations

jagirdar [landowner], 126, 222
Jallianwala Bagh massacre, 47
Jan Sangh, 37; and Communists, 38; formation of, 31, 222; in Parliament, 123, 124, 223, 224; and untouchability, 21

janashakti, defined, 291, 295
Jangamas (caste), Andhra village, 445ff.
Jaya Hind ["Victory to India"], 81, 83
Jayaswal, K. P., quoted on Indian democratic tradition, 7—*footnote* 7
joint family system, 395, 427; in business organizations, 251-253; defined, 251—*footnote* 1
Joshi, P. C., 230, 231, 236, 243; personality, 240

Kamath, H. V., and socialists, 205
Kanpur Compromise, 197
Karachi Resolution, 55
Karapatri, Swami, 31
karma marga, 11
karma yoga, defined, 281
karma yogi, defined, 85
Karmarkar, D. P., posts held, 111
Karnataka, village study in Totagadde, 453-469
Karve report, 323
Katju, K. N., 128
kattu, defined, 463-464
Kaul, M. N., 121
Kaur, Rajkumari Amrit, 112, 113
Kayasthas (caste), and extremism, 176
Keer, Dhananjay, quoted on Hindu-Muslim relations, 214
Keskar, B. V., posts held, 111, 113
Khaira campaign, 179
Khalapur (North India), village study in, 392, 395-414; attitude to government, 413; caste distribution, 395-396; election in, 406-407; ideological influences, 402-403, 413-414; intracaste relations, 396-397, 405-407; the Mukhia, 397-406; the Principal, 408-414; Rajputs, 396-397
Khan, Syed Ahmed, 213
Khare, N. B., 31; and Gandhi's murder, 220, 224; "Khare" episode, 96, 218
Kheda campaign (satyagraha), 89
Kher, B. G., 95
Khilafat movement, 51, 214
kingship: concepts, 8-12; legends, 5-7
Kisan Mazdoor Praja Party: -Socialist merger, 125, 202-203; parliamentary strength, 124
Kisan Sabha, and Congress, 183
KMPP, *see* Kisan Mazdoor Praja Party
Kosa, Muchaki, tragic case of, 120, 126
Kripalani, (Acharya) J. B., 97, 98, 126; and language problem, 206; and Socialist Party, 203
Kripalani, Mrs. Sucheta, 122, 126

INDEX

Krishnamachari, T. T., 305—*footnote* 5, 385
Krishnamachari, V. T., 305; background, 307
Kshatriya (caste), 6, 15, 77; Bhave on, 287; characteristics, 66; and Congress Party, 385; as democrats, 389; and rural leadership, 383, 385, 389
kunba, 380, 387

labor relations, *see* trade unions
lakh [100,000]
lambardar, defined, 398
language problem, *151-165*; Bose and, 163-164; in civil service, 157-162, 164; and Communist Party, 234, 235; and democracy, 163-164; in education, 152-159; and leadership, 151, 152, 157, 158, 162-163; Mehta, Asoka, on, 165; and national unity, 153, 162-165; in Parliament, 119-120, 164; Sinha on, 165; and socialists, 205-206; Tagore on, 152. *See also*, English language, linguistic particularism, regional languages
lathi [staff, quarterstaff, club, stick] drill, 216
leader roles: ambivalence in, 30-31, 70, 75; "father figure," 63, 236, 401-402, 405, 411; guide, 294, 296-297; mediator, 179, 399-401, 411-413, 414, 419, 420, 422, 431, 438, 450, 459, 469; outsider, 411-412; reformer, 403-404, 410; religious leader, 31, 403-404
leadership: ambivalence in, 30-31, 70-75; in Congress, 169-188
and Congress role, 187
criteria of, 283; defined, 3, 358, 427; factors in, 239-241, 279-280, 283
age, 112-113, 118; asceticism, 217, 412, 414; education, 110, 240; language, 151ff.; moral force, 296; "orthodoxy," 240; wealth, 93, 114, 139, 142, 171, 451
and language, 151-152, 157, 158, 162-163, 164; modern Indian theories, 5, 10-12, 13-17, 116
and Marxism, 5, 13-14
Nehru on, 64; nonconventional, *279-298*; and Parliament, 134, 136; public servant, role of, 330, 334-335; requisites, attributes, 4, 85, 98, 239-241, 246
change in, 209
in socialist parties, 189-194, 198-199; traditional concepts, 6-12, 15, 16
attitudes, 386
western theories, 4, 12-15, 16, 115

communist, 245f.; and Indian compared, 13-17; Marxist, 225
left-wing nationalists, 178; and Congress Socialist Party, 189-191, 193, 194. *See also*, article on Bose
Lewis, Oscar, quoted, 380, 463
liberalism, *see* "Moderates"
linguistic particularism: in Bombay, 155, 159, 186—*footnote* 24; Bose and, 163-164; linguistic pressure groups, 30; Maharashtra-Gujarat controversy, 129; and Mahasabha, 224; and national unity, 28, 153, 163-165; Nehru and, 28; and Sikhs, 33; socialists and, 205-206; and "unsuccessful" western-minded, 22. *See also*, language problem, regional languages
local self-government, *337-344*; and Community Development Programs, 369; and Congress, 340; development and, 343-344; and government, conflict with, 338-339; lack of demand for, 339-340; and nationalist movement, 340-341; and party politics, 340-342; and social change, 137ff., 343; and village factionalism, 437. *See also*, democracy, panchayat
Local Self-Government Institute, 315
Lohia, Rammanohar, 189, 198, 200, 204, 207
Lok Sabha, *117-136*; committees listed, 121-122; communalist parties in, 222-223; Congress and, 103, 129f.; and Council of Ministers, 104; and language problem, 119-120; membership analyzed, 118-120; opposition parties, groups, 124-129; parliamentary parties listed, 124; procedures, 121-123. *See also*, Congress Parliamentary Party, Congress Party, Parliament
Lok Sevak Sangh, 196, 199
Lucknow Pact, 214

MLA [Member of the Legislative Assembly], 238
Macaulay, Thomas B., on Bengalis, 66
Madiga (caste), village role, 428-429
Mahabharata, 5
mahal, defined, 398—*footnote* 5
Mahalanobis, P. C., 30, 302, 305; background of, 308f.; role in planning, 308-309, 319
Maharaj, Ravishankar, 91, 92
Maharashtra, village study in Gaon, 415-426
Mahasabha, *see* Hindu Mahasabha
Mahtab, Harekrushna, 197

478

INDEX

managing agency firms, role of, 251-253
Manu, 10, 15; Code of, 5
Manusamhita, 6
Mao Tse-tung, 14
Marathas (caste), 416f., 423
Marathi, in education, 155, 160
Marathi Sahitya Sammelan, 160
Mariama, worship of, 458, 459, 469
Marxism: and Congress Socialist Party, 189-191; doctrines, 13, 14, 15; and Indian leadership concepts, 5, 13, 14; Indian views on, 13-14; leadership theories, 13-14, 15, 17, 225, 245ff.
Marxist parties, listed, 127
Masani, Minoo R., 55, 189
Mascarene, Annie, 125
Mashruwala, K. G., on Nehru, 49
mass campaigns: Bardoli, 90-92; Borsad, 89; Champaran, 179; and Congress, 93; Khaira, 179; Kheda, 89; Nagpur Flag, 90; Salt, 51. See also, satyagraha
Mass Contacts Program, 185
Mavalankar, G. V.: quoted on British Parliament, 115; quoted on Sardar Vallabhbhai Patel, 88
Mayer, Albert, 359
Meherally, Yusuf, on Patel, 97
Mehta, Asoka, 126, 129
  and language problem, 206
  quoted on, 159, 165
  and socialists, 189, 198, 200, 204, 205
Menon, V. K. Krishna, 30, 110; posts held, 111, 112, 113
Menon, V. K. N., 321—*footnote 16*
Merriam, Charles E., on leadership attributes, 4
Mitchison, Naomi, on leadership, 297
mixed economy, 260. See also, "socialist pattern," "socialistic pattern"
"Moderates," *170-175*; and Bengal agitation, 176; early leadership, 170-172; and extremism, 177; and mass movements, 172; and social reform, 171; withdrawal from Congress, 177
modernization: and authoritarianism, 24, 29, 30; conflict re, 19-26, 32, 37ff., 41, 116, 165; Indian attitudes to, 20-26; and westernization distinguished, 19—*footnote 3*. See also, Community Development Program, Five Year Plans, fragmentation, National Extension Service, political dynamics, western influence, "westernization"
Mookerjee, Hiren, 126
Mookerjee, Shyama Prasad, 31, 123; and Democratic Nationalist Party, 124-126;

and Jan Sangh, 222, 223; and Mahasabha, 218, 220
Moonje, B. S., 214
Morris-Jones, W. H.: on Indian political patterns, 116; on Lok Sabha, 118, 119, 122, 134
Morsralli (Mysore State), village study in, 392, *438-444*; caste distribution, 438; factionalism, 439-444
  role of government authority in, 443, 444
  traditional leaders, 438
Mosca, Gaetano, on ruling elite, 4, 16
Mukerji, K. P., 246; political theories, 16, 17
mukhia: defined, 397ff.; as formal leader, 397-405; functions of, 398, 399
municipal corporations, 338, 342
Munshi, K. M., quoted, 95
Muslims: -Hindu relations, 212-220; communalism, 212; concept of government, 8, 21; and Congress, 178, 180; in Council of Ministers, 109; and nationalist movement, 178; village relations, 403, 433, 451
Mysore State, village studies in: Morsralli, 438-444; Namhalli, 427-437; Totagadde, 453-469

Nag, Kalidas, 223
Nagpur campaign (Flag Satyagraha), 90
Nagpur Constitution, 180
Nagpur University, and language problem, 155
Namboodiripad, E. M. S., 238
Namhalli (Mysore State), village study in, 392, *427-437*; factionalism, 433-437; formal leadership:
  traditional panchayat, 430-432, 437; Village Panchayat, 430
  impact of urbanization, 428-437; intra-caste relations, 429
Nanda, Gulzarilal, 197, 265, 305; background, 307-309
Narayan, Jayaprakash, 30; and Congress Socialist Party, 184, 189, 192, 196-197, 198, 200, 209; 14-point program, 204, 205; and language problem, 206; as nonconventional leader, 292ff. (*bhoodan*)
Nariman, K. F., controversy, 95-96
National Development Council, 322, 323
National Education Conference, report quoted, 153ff.
National Extension Service, 354, *372-378*, 387; background, 376; functions, 372, 377; impact on rural leadership, 360-

INDEX

371, 385, 386; and research, 377. *See also*, village level worker
National Planning Commission, *see* Planning Commission
National Sample Survey, 308, 309; limitations, 310—*footnote* 9
nationalist movement: and Bengali nationalists, 282; and business, 177, 258-259; and Congress, *169-180*; and Congress Socialist Party, 188; and extremism, 174ff.; and Gandhi, 178-180; and Hindu militarism (RSS), 212ff., 219 revivalism, 175-179
and local governing bodies, 340; and Muslims, 178; and Narayan, 293; and peasant movements, 179; pre-Independence goals, 169; Swadeshi movement, 176, 177; and Tilak, 10; and vernacular press, 186; and western influence, 173-175. *See also*, extremism, "Moderates," Rashtriya Swayamasevak Sangh
nationalization, 261; and business, 265
Nehru, Jawarharlal, 28, 30, *41-65*; and Bose, 78; on Bose, 73; as charismatic leader, 27, 28, 43, 44, 64, 385; on Communism, 78; and Congress, 51-56, 60, 75; and development planning, 305-306, 311—*footnote* 11, 323; Gandhi on, 49; and Gandhi, Gandhism, 42-57, 62-63; on Gandhi, 289; and Indian National Army, 83; Indian views on, 41, 43, 60; on language problem, 163; on leadership, 64, 280; opposition to Bose, 84-85; on Patel, 98; personality, 41-64, 306; political concepts, 11, 23, 49, 63; as Prime Minister, 61-63; self-appraisal, 43-45, 50, 59; and socialism, 53-54; and socialists, 41, 54f., 188-190, 196; youth, 45-47
Nehru, Kamala, 56, 58-59
Nehru, Motilal, 56; and Gandhi, Gandhism, 45, 47, 74; personality, 45, 46; and Swaraj Party, 74, 77
Neogy, K. C., 222, 311
NES, *see* National Extension Service
Netaji (Subhas Chandra Bose), defined, 81
Neville, H. R., on Rajputs, 396
Newari Kalan (Uttar Pradesh), village study in, *358-371*; caste, social organization, 359-360; community development program, 360-370; disorganization, 361-362
non-Brahman leaders, 457-458
nonconventional leadership, *279-298*; Aurobindò, 287-288; Bhave, 285-291, 296 and *bhoodan*, 285ff.
Gandhian, 280-285; government attitude to, 291-292; Narayan, 292-294; potentials of, 296-298
North India, village study in Khalapur, 395-414

Okkaliga (caste), 438ff.
opposition parties in Parliament, 124-129, 192ff.
organized interest groups, 33; in the Communist Party, 244; in the Congress, 181, 184; importance of, 34ff.; and social change, 35. *See also*, Hindu communal groups

Padu (Andhra State), village study in, 392, *445-452*; caste, 445-446; economy, 445; intracaste relations, 450-451; leader attributes, 447, 451-452; patterns of leadership, 446-452
panchayat, panchayat system: caste-, 141ff., 465-466; and Community Development, 343; and democratic tradition, 8, 16; Dhebar on, 294; elections for, 136-150, 406-407; legislation, 342, 430; limitations, 432, 437; and national politics, 340-341; role, 379f., 385, 393, 406-407, 438, 464; structure and functions, 406—*footnote* 16, 430-432; temporary, 465-467. *See also*, Village Panchayat
Panchayat Raj Act, 369f., 406—*footnote* 16
panches [members of a village panchayat or council], defined, 406—*footnote* 16
pandal [temporary pavilion], 221
Pandya, Mohanlal, 91, 92
Panel of Economists, 311, 312, 319, 323
Pant, (Pandit) Govind B., 27; and language problem, 161; and Socialists, 197, 385
Parliament: and British Parliament, compared, 115, 120; coalitions, 126; committees, 121-122; and Congress Party, 129-131; decision making, 29-30, 133-136; handicaps, 135-136; opposition groups, 124-129; parliamentary parties (listed), 123-124; political environment, 115-117, 136; structure and functions, 29, 104; Chief Whip, functions, 133. *See also*, Congress Parliamentary Party, Congress Party, Lok Sabha, Rajya Sabha
parliamentary institutions, eastern and western, compared, 37
parliamentary parties: coalitions, 126; listed, 123-124; opposition groups, 125-128. *See also*, Congress Parliamentary Party, Congress Party

480

INDEX

Partition, 220; effects of, 219, 221, 223, 317
"passive" leaders, 422
patel, defined, 438
Patel, Jhaverbhai, 87
Patel, (Sardar) Vallabhbhai J., 30, 40, 87-99; achievements, 98-99; background, 87-88; and Bose, 97; and business, 263; as charismatic leader, 27; and Communism, 92, 98; and Congress, 92ff., 199; and Gandhi, 92-94; ideology, 92; and Khare, N. B., 96; mass campaigns, 89-93; Nariman, K. F., controversy with, 95; personality, 93, 98; and public service, 332; and Telengana revolt, 98; and socialists, 197, 199
Patel, Vithalbhai, 87; -Bose statement on Gandhi, 76; and Swaraj Party, 77
Pater, Walter, quoted by Nehru, 45
pathshala, defined, 404—*footnote* 13
Patil, S. K., and socialists, 197
Patwardhan, Achyut, 189
patwari, defined, 326
People's Party, formation of, 142
People's Publishing House, publications of, 231
Plan Frame, *see* Draft Plan Frame
planning, *see* development planning, Planning Commission
Planning Commission, 61, 301ff.; and Nehru, 305-306; role in development, 301-305, 316, 317-318, 322-324, 328, 352; structure and personnel, 305-309
Planning and Development Department, 316
Planning Research and Action Institute, functions of, 320
Poleman, Horace I., on language problem, 157
police, and village relations, 413, 431, 443
police headman, 419-420
Politburo (Indian), 226ff., 247
political action, patterns of: "amalgamate," 27; Bardoli campaign, 90-92; development, role of, 306, 310-311, 327; "fractions" (Communist), 244ff.; Gandhian approach, 282-283; and Gandhism, 116-117; government-party relations, 326-327; and language, 163; Nehru's, 63; in Parliament, 132-134; religious revivalism in, 175-177; rural, 137-150; and social change, 25-38; in the states, 327; trade unions and, 272-276, 268; violence, 33-34, 177. *See also, bhoodan* movement, Hindu communal groups, mass campaigns, nationalist movement, political action (rural patterns), political dynamics, Rashtriya Swayamasevak Sangh, religious revivalism, satyagraha
political action, rural patterns of, 92-93, 98, 137ff., 460-469; and caste, 141ff.; and family, 145; and social change, 427, 452; in village elections, 137-150, 406-407; and women, 145-146. *See also,* factionalism
political concepts, East and West contrasted, 14, 15
"political cultures," conflict between, 37, 116
political dynamics, *26-38*, 460-469; absence of consensus, 31-32; charisma in, 27-28, 32; and education, 173; and government, 34-36 administration, 326-328 and Indian environment, 115-116, 186; party cohesion, 327-328; "real" versus "ideal," 29-31; religious element, 116-117; and social change, 35-36; and special interest groups, 32; unions and, 268-269; in a village election, 137-150, 406-407; western influence and, 18-38. *See also, bhoodan* movement, factionalism, Hindu communal groups, language problem, nonconventional leadership, opposition parties, political action (patterns of), political system, religious revivalism
political environment, 115-116; contrasted with West, 186
political parties, social and integrative functions of, 35, 216, 236-237
political system, conflicts in, 19-37, 116-117, 187, 224, 230, 243-244. *See also,* factionalism, fragmentation, Hindu communal groups, modernization, "westernization"
pradesh [state], 129
pradhan, defined, 339, 406—*footnote* 16
Praja Socialist Party, *205-208*; Allahabad thesis, 204; and Communists, 204, 205, 209; counter trends, 207-208; formation, 125, 126, 203, 207; Gaya thesis, 205, 207; goals and ideology, 203-207, 209; indiscipline and conflict, 193, 201, 204-206; leadership, 189-207; in Parliament, 123, 124, 203-205, 208; parliamentary strength, 208
Prajapati, 6, 12
Prasad, Beni, quoted on Indian democratic traditions, 7—*footnote* 7
Prasad, Rajendra, 97; and charisma, 27; and language problem, 161; and socialists, 197
President, office and functions of, 103-104

INDEX

Preventive Detention Act, 23; debate on, 128
Prime Minister, office and functions of, 104, 107, 109
princes, in Lok Sabha, 118, 119—*footnote* 6, 126
Program Evaluation Organization, 319, 323, 372
proletarian rule, acceptance of, 15
provincial development programs, *see* Five Year Plans
Provisional Government of Free India, 81
public administration, *314-328*; change in, 347ff.; development of, 331, 352; versus local self-government, 338-339, 343; and political dynamics, 326-328; research in, 319-322; and states, 324-326; and Five Year Plans, 315-326. *See also*, administrative processes, district administration, government, Planning Commission, public services
public services, 324-325, *329-336*; background and development, 331-332; and business leaders, 266-267; and economic development, 329-330, 333; recruitment, 324; role of, 332, 334; role in leadership, 336; rural bureaucrat, role of, 385-386, 420-421; and social change, 329-331. *See also*, public administration
pujari, defined, 384, 449
purohit, defined, 459

"Quit India": movement, 80, 83; Resolution, 196

Radhakrishnan, Sarvepalli, 5, 8; quoted on Bose, 84; political concepts of (concepts of democracy), 11-12
Rai, Lala Lajpat, 77
rajadharma: defined, 8; concept, 8, 9, 11
Rajagopalachari, Chakravarti, 27; quoted on language problem, 160; on role of business, 264, 266
Rajputs (caste), 360, 396ff.; -Brahman relations, 395ff.; intracaste relations, 396-397; and unsanctioned leadership, 424f.; and village leadership, 405, 406, 410, 413, 416, 419, 434
Rajya Sabha, 117, 118
Ram Rajya Parishad, 21, 22, 31, 37, 127, 224; parliamentary strength, 124, 222, 223
Ramakrishna, 67ff., 281
Ramakrishna Mission, 212, 281; and caste, 213
Ranadive, B. T., 229, 230, 231, 240
Rao, P. Kodanda, on political parties, 23

Rao, Rajeshwar, 240, 241
Rashtriya Swayamasevak Sangh, 23, 37, *213-221*; ban on, 219, 221; formation, 214, 215; and Gandhi's assassination, 220; and Jan Sangh, 222; leadership pattern, 217; organization and goals, 215-216; "Organizers," the, 216, 217
Reddy, K. C., posts held, 111
regional languages: and civil service, 157-162; and education, 152-156; and national leadership, 152; and national unity, 163; in politics, 161, 164-165, 176. *See also*, language problem
religion: and politics, 70, 75, 116, 176, 281, 287; role of, 384. *See also*, *bhoodan* movement, nonconventional leadership, religious leaders, religious revivalism
religious leaders, 384, 459-460; in politics, 224
religious revivalism, 25; and Bose, 70; and extremism, 174-176, 177. *See also*, Aurobindo, *bhoodan* movement, Hindu communal groups, Vivekananda
Research Programs Committee, 311, 313, 318-319
revenue headman, duties of, 419
Rig-Veda, concepts of leadership, 6
Ripon, Lord, on local self-government, 339, 344
river valley projects, *see* Five Year Plans
Rockefeller Foundation, 320—*footnote* 13
Rowlatt Bills, 47
Rowlatt Committee, 67—*footnote* 2
Roy, Dilip Kumar, quoted on Bose, 71, 85
Roy, M. N., 193, 242
Roy, Ram Mohan, 212
Royists, 77, 190
RSS, *see* Rashtriya Swayamasevak Sangh
"rule of Rama" (*Ramrajya*), 12
rural factionalism, 392, 406-407, 433-437, 438-444, 459, 462, 468; caste and, 141ff.; development and, 370; and government authority, 443, 444; in a rural election, 140-149. *See also*, cliques, feud, *kattu*
rural influence:
channels of, 381ff.
chaudhuris, 389; entertainers, 388; National Extension Service and, 372-375; panchayat, 379; women, 388
sources of, *374-382*
the aristocrat, 383; the bureaucrat, 383, 385-386; caste, 383, 410; Congress, 184; covert, 429; the family, 387; language, 159; panchayat, 138,

482

INDEX

393, 418; public servant, 335; religious professionals, 384
See also, District Officer, rural leadership (factors in)
rural leadership, *415-437*; attributes and requisites, 146-147, 149, 378, 397-405, 410-414, 421, 422, 447, 451-452, 456-458; caste and, 141-145, 383, 410, 413-414, 428-429, 454ff.
  and caste relations, 406-407
  and change, 137-150, 378-383, 438ff., 444; and Community Development, 363-371; dynamics of, 141-149, 377-390, 392-393, 397ff., 417-426, 441ff., 446-452, 460f.
  factors in:
    age, 148, 413, 422, 459; asceticism, 403, 410, 412, 414, 422; caste, 141-145, 399, 401, 405, 410, 413, 415ff., 422-423, 451; attitudes toward caste, 426, 456; Congress affiliation, 412, 418; education, 142, 411, 452; family, 145, 146, 387, 398; government affiliation, 413, 414, 417; panchayat affiliation, 139, 418, 430; wealth, 142, 327-328, 399, 422, 427-428, 436, 438, 447, 451, 454, 456, 458
  force, role of, 424, 450, 452; new, 149, 367-371, 408-414
  patterns of:
    change in, 294, 355-357, 408-414, 446-452; formal, 343, 395-406, 417-421, 425, 429-432, 458; informal, 408-415, 456-458; patterns sanctioned, 422; patterns unsanctioned, 424-425; mechanisms of influence, 380-381; new (the principal), 408-412; traditional (the *mukhia*), 397-407
  problems of (Dhebar on), 294; role of educated, 142-143, 378-379, 399, 411; and social change, 417, 422, 426; traditional, 141-145, 395-408, 412-414, 454-462
    hereditary, 383, 419, 438-439
  types of leader, 446-449
    bureaucrat, 385-386; "active," 423-424; chairman, 382; clique, 435ff.; faction, 431ff.; headmen, 419ff.; *hiria*, 458; "passive," 422; *patel*, 438, 468; *pradhan*, 343; religious, 384, 459-460; ruler, 382; *talathi*, 420
See also, factionalism, leader roles, panchayat system, rural influence, village offices
rural patterns of political action, *see* political action, rural patterns of
Rustow, Dankwart, quoted, 26, 34

Salt satyagraha, 51
sanctioned leadership (rural), 421-424; active, 422-424; passive, 422
sannyasi, defined, 384
Sanskritization, 21, 458
Saraswati, Dayanand, 281
Sarkar, Benoy Kumar, on *dharma*, 5-6
sarpanch, defined, 146, 379, 399, 406— footnote 16
Sarva Seva Sangh, 290-291
Savarkar, V. D., 213, 221, 222
sarvodaya, defined, 284
sarvodaya movement, 250, *292-296*; goals, 284, 286, 293, 295; and *bhoodan*, 287-295; and Narayan, 292-294. *See also*, *bhoodan* movement
Sarvodaya Samaj, 290
satyagraha, 51, 75, 89; Bardoli campaign, 90-92; and *bhoodan* movement, 289, 295; Bose on, 81; defined, 283; Patel and, 89-92; and politics, 23; techniques of, 75, 89-92, 283-284, 289, 293. *See also*, Gandhism
Scheduled Castes, 109, 144; in Parliament, 127
Schmidt, Richard, on concepts of leadership, 3, 4, 9
Second Five Year Plan, *see* Community Development Program, Five Year Plans
Secondary Education Commission, report quoted, 153
Sedition Committee, on religious revivalism, 176
self-government, *see* local self-government
self-help and Community Development, 349, 355
Sen, Indra, on humanism, 288
Senapur-Daudpur, village studies in, 137-150
Servants of India Society, 23; and Nehru, 47
Seva Dal, 218
sevak, defined, 284
Shakti, 66, 68, 77
Sharma, M. P., quoted, 109
Shakti Sangha, 218
Shastras, 460
Shastri, Hariharnath, 200
sheekdar, defined, 440
Shivaji, 10, 85, 213
shramdan [labor-gift], 318, 404
Sikhs, 32, 218; and linguistic issue, 33
Singer, Milton, on Community Development, 27
Singh, Jaipal, 124, 125; and Independent Group, 126
Singh, Tarlok, 304

483

INDEX

Sinha, K. K., on language problem, 165
Sinha, Satya Narayan, on party whips, 133
Sitaramayya, Pattabhi: on Bose, 84, 97; on language, 152; quoted, 75, 76
Smith, Vincent, on Indian democratic tradition, 7—*footnote* 7
social change: and Aurobindite approach, 287-289; and *bhoodan* movement, 288-289; and business, 258—*footnote* 8, 260, 262-263, 267; and Congress, 182, 187, 412, 413; and Community Development, 353-357, 375; and economic influences, 415f.; and Gandhian groups, 25; government, as instrument of, 36; and Hindu communalist groups, 21-23, 25, 213; and Hindu-minded, 38; and "Moderates," 171; and party membership, 35; public service, role in, 330-331
in the village:
    and caste, 355, 416; and factionalism, 444; informal leader and, 421-423; political dynamics and, 139-150, 417ff.; rural leadership, role of, 417; and traditional leadership, 439; unsanctioned leadership and, 426
    western influence and, 174-175, 374; and westernized elite, 19. *See also*, Gaon study, modernization, urbanization
social control, rural, methods of: boycott, 441, 444; disputes, 464-467; *kattu*, 463; the *mukhia* and, 401, 403; "party," 463-464
social disorganization (rural), 361-362; and intracaste relations, 416, 426; and unsanctioned leadership, 426; urbanization and, 431, 437. *See also*, rural factionalism
social organization (rural), 93, 359-360, 416ff., 428-429, 438, 445-446, 453
social science research, 251, 375-378; need for, 26, 27, 38, 243, 373, 377; -organizations, 318-321, 328; role in the village, 372-373, 377-378
socialism: business views, 263; and Congress, 55, 204; Indian views, 258—*footnote* 8, 259; and Nehru, 53-54. *See also*, *bhoodan* movement, socialist parties, "socialist pattern," "socialistic pattern"
socialist parties, *see* Congress Socialist Party, Kisan Mazdoor Praja Party, Praja Socialist Party, Socialist Party of India
Socialist Party of India, 188, 195-202; and Congress, 197-199; formation, 195, 207; goals, 199; organization, 200-201
"socialist pattern," 205; defined, 260; and industry, 267; and local administration, 337-338; and private enterprise, 260, 262-265
"socialistic pattern," defined, 260
socialists: and nationalist movement, 198—*footnote* 12; in Parliament, 125, *188-209*; and trade unionism, 273. *See also*, socialist parties
society, traditional view of, 258, 280
socio-economic reform, and Community Development, 347-350, 353-357
socio-religious reform, 402, 412-414. *See also*, Arya Samaj, social change
special interest groups, 32-34; in CPI, 242; and CPI "fractions," 244ff.; in the Congress, 181; and social change, 35. *See also*, Hindu communal groups
Srinivas, M. N., on village factions, 440
Srinivasan, N., on Committee on Government Assurances, 122
States Reorganization Bill, 29, 30; -Commission, on language, 164; debate on, 128-129, 130
states' reorganization movement, 22, 33, 223
Statutory Panchayat, *see* Village Panchayat
Stevenson, Adlai, quoted, 151
Sudras (caste): and cyclic rule, 15; intercaste relations, 461—*footnote* 8; and village leadership, 445ff.
Sundaram, Lanka, quoted, 127, 133
Swadeshi [belonging to or made in one's own country], 176
Swadeshi movement, 176, 177
swaraj, defined, 284
Swaraj Party, formation of, 74, 77

Tagore, Rabindranath: on language, 152; and Mahalanobis, P. C., 308—*footnote* 8; and Nehru, 45
tahsil, defined, 399—*footnote* 9
tahsildar, defined, 326, 399—*footnote* 9
Taitiriya Upanisad, 6
talathi, defined, 417, 419ff.
taluk [administrative subdivison of a District], 94, 180
Tandon, (Babu) Purshottamdas, and Nehru, 98, 133, 186
Tata family, 251ff.
Telengana revolt, 98, 341
Textile Labor Association, 92
Theosophists, 212; and caste, 213
Tilak, Bal Gangadhar, 5; concepts of leadership, 10, 11, 92; and religious revivalism, 176—*footnote* 11, 177, 312; and untouchability, 213, 282
Totagadde (Karnataka, Mysore State), village study in, 392, *453-469*; caste dis-

484

INDEX

tribution and organization, 453; disputes, resolution of, 464-467; Havik Brahmans, 454-462:
    intercaste relations, 460, 468; factionalism, 462, 468, 469; feud, 461, 462, 468; "party," 463-464, 466, 468; religious leaders, 459-460; role of, 454-457
    panchayats, 465-468
Trade Associations, 255ff.
trade unions, 268-278; Bombay textile unions, growth of, 271-274; and collective bargaining, 274-275; and development, 275-276; as disciplinary force, 268-271, 275-276; and Gandhism, 278; "Giri" approach, 277; and government, 273-276; and political parties, 272-274, 276; and Communists, 272-273
traditional leadership concepts, 2, 5-17, 224, 267, 280; Brahmanic, 6-12; karma-yoga, 85, 281; Kshatriya, 2, 66, 77; and Marxism, 5; Nehru on, 280; personality and, 279-280; Shivaji, 77, 149, 213, 286; Vaishya, 77
traditional patterns: authority, breakdown of, 35, 355-356; culture, rural and urban, 374
    change in, 355
    political organization, breakdown in, 393; values, 149
        breakdown of, 37
Tricumdas, Purshottam, 206

unions, *see* trade unions
unity, national: challenges to, 25, 31-32; and language problem, 153, 163; problems of, 28, 136. *See also*, fragmentation in politics, language problem, "westernization", panchayat
universities, language problem in, 152, 154-156, 158, 162
University Education Commission, on language problem, 154, 157-158, 164
unsanctioned leadership (rural), 421, 424-426, 450-452; and intercaste conflict, 424; role of force, 424; and social change, 426
untouchability: and change, 417; and communal groups, 213; Congress and, 417, 424, 426; Ram Rajya Parishad and, 21. *See also*, caste, Hindu communal groups, intracaste relations, social change
Untouchables, 395, 403, 416, 453; caste organization, 461—*footnote* 8; Harijans, 417-426, 446, 450; in Khalapur, 405, 410; in panchayat, 406—*footnote* 16; in politics, 144

urbanization: and caste, 428-429, 455; and leadership, 437; rural impact, 392, 428-434
uru ejmanru, defined, 458
USSR, and Bose, 82
Uttar Pradesh, village studies in: Newari Kalan (Etawah Project), 358-371; Senapur-Daudpur, 137-150

vaidik pradhan, defined, 402
Vaishyas (caste), 77; role in policy making, 385
"Vedette," on Preventive Detention, 128
vernacular press, role in nationalist movement, 186
village conflict: methods of resolving, 464-465; role of panchayat, 464
Village Constructive Program, 185
village economy, 349, 359, 415, 427, 445
village headman, 343, 419ff., 426, 429ff.
village level worker, 351-352, 360ff., 375, 383, 385; suggested procedures for, 379
village offices: *amildar*, 429; caste-headman, 428, 430f., 450f., 458; *patel*, 438; police headman, 419; *pradhan*, 343; revenue headman, 419; *sarpanch*, 146, 399, 406—*footnote* 16, 407; *talathi*, 420-421, 426; village headmen, 343, 419, 420, 426, 429. *See also*, District Officer
Village Panchayat, 141, 363, 430, 468; and caste, 141-145, 146, 150, 432, 457; elections for, 137-150, 342, 406-407, 457; and government, 138, 338ff.; limitations, 393, 419, 425, 430; and local self-government, 342, 407; role, 138, 385, 393, 397—*footnote* 7; structure and functions, 138, 377, 418ff., 431, 439. *See also*, panchayat
Village Studies: Gaon (Bombay State), 415-426; Khalapur (North India), 395-414; Morsralli (Mysore State), 438-444; Namhalli (Mysore State), 427-437; Newari Kalan (Etawah Project, Uttar Pradesh), 358-371; Padu (Andhra State), 445-452; Senapur-Daudpur (Uttar Pradesh), 137-150; Totagadde (Mysore State), 453-469
Vinoba, *see* Bhave, Vinoba
Vir Dal, 218
Vivekananda, 281; Bose and, 66ff.; cyclic theory, 15

wealth and rural leadership, 139, 142, 149, 399, 422, 427-428, 436, 438, 447, 451, 454, 456, 458

485

INDEX

welfare state: attitudes to, 16; demand for, 258—*footnote* 8, 329, 330; and labor unions, 274

western influence: and Congress leadership, 171; development of, 18, 36, 174-175; and Hindu Communal movements, 212, 281; on Indian society, 18, 21, 31, 171; and leadership concepts, 2, 9, 17, 18-38; and nationalism, 169, 173-175; opposition to, 20-23, 25, 37, 175; and Parliament, 115; and traditional religious groups, 168, 174; in the village, 375-376; on village and city, compared, 374. *See also*, language problem, modernization, "westernization"

"westernization": opposition to, 19-23, 25, 37, 171-175, 187, 212; problems of, 187. *See also*, modernization

westernized elite: and Gandhi, 179; goals of, 18-19, 23-24, 35, 36-37; and linguistic particularism, 22, 151; problems of, 165; and rural development, 170, 374. *See also*, language problem

western-minded, 22ff.; -oriented, 23, 24; versus traditional-minded, 187; "unsuccessful," 22, 173, 175

Wilson, Woodrow, quoted, 334

women: in Communist Party, 126, 200; and Community Development, 353, 356; as covert leaders, 435; and Indian Independence Army, 81; influence of, 388; as leaders, 112, 113, 122, 126, 198, 200, 246; in Lok Sabha, 119, 122; and rural voting, 145-146

Working Committee, *see* Congress Working Committee

Zamindari Abolition and Land Reforms Act, 407—*footnote* 17; effects of, 139, 143, 360, 406, 431

The Library of Congress has cataloged this book as follows:

Seminar on Leadership and Political Institutions in India, *University of California, Berkeley, 1956*. Leadership and political institutions in India, edited by Richard L. Park and Irene Tinker. [Princeton, N.J., 1959] 469 p. 22 cm. "The papers . . . are a selected group, edited and revised, of those originally presented at the seminar . . . August 12 to 17, 1956."

Bibliographical footnotes. 1. India—Pol. & govt.—1947- 2. Leadership. I. Park, Richard Leonard, ed. II. Title. JQ215 1956c.S4 (342.5403) 59-5601 Library of Congress

DATE DUE

DEC 1 6 1968

JAN 8 6 9

JUL 5 1969

Paid

DEC 5 1968

MAY 01 77

JUL 1 6 1978

JAN 0 2 87

JUN 2 2 1991

Vincent A. Smith.

3 3311 00312 9030